THE ROCK YEARBOOK

VOLUME VI

EDITED BY
IAN CRANNA

Virgin

VIRGIN BOOKS
LONDON

In-house Editor
JANE CHARTERIS

Picture Researcher
DILL ANSTEY

Interior designed by
THE FISH FAMILY

Cover by
SUE WALLIKER

First published in Great Britain in 1985 by
Virgin Books, 328 Kensal Road, London W10 5XJ

ISBN 0 86369 089 0

Printed in Great Britain by The Thetford Press, Thetford

Bound by D R Skinner & Co, Cambridge

Typeset by Capital Setters, London W1

Distributed by Arrow Books

THE ROCK YEARBOOK CONTRIBUTORS

THE EDITOR

IAN CRANNA is a man of many parts, most of them working. After writing for the *NME* from Edinburgh, 'Jocky' pioneered the pop sensation *Smash Hits* before graduating to Nick Drake sleevenotes. When not managing the Virgin Prunes, the world's No.1 Blue Nile fan likes nothing more than to press wild flowers, leaf idly through cheekily romantic novels and engage in a lively correspondence with other subscribers to *Lawnmower Enthusiast*. Is now setting up a rest home for ageing OMD, XTC and Undertones fans.

Lloyd Bradley is a freelance writer currently working for *Look-In Magazine* and the occasional grown-up publication. Having successfully reached the age of 30 with few noticeable malfunctions, his hobbies include waiting for the next series of *Grange Hill*, feeding his cats and dreaming up ways of getting money out of Channel 4.

Geoff Brown, a former editor of *Black Music & Jazz Review* and music editor of *Time Out*, has written books on Diana Ross and Michael Jackson (the latter a *Sunday Times* bestseller). He is currently sports editor of *Time Out* and has contributed to other publications from *Company* to the *Times Literary Supplement*.

Simon Buckland, became a staff writer for *Echoes* in the summer of '84. He's still unsure quite how he got the job – "could have been the references as window cleaner and welder that most impressed them" – but is happy to spend his time trying to quench his insatiable vinyl thirst.

Julie Burchill ran away from home at the age of fifteen and worked as a shopgirl. She was taken back home to Bristol, but at sixteen returned to London to work for the *NME*, which was recruiting young untried writers. She has since graduated to *New Society*, the *Literary Review*, *Time Out*, *The Face* and the *Sunday Times*, and become a much-loved/much-loathed essayist.

Steve Bush has had an eventful trip down rock's lost highway. After spells as art editor of *Smash Hits* and *The Face*, he helped launch *Just Seventeen* before taking up his present role as editor of *Smash Hits*. An enigmatic figure perpetually clad in black, his pastimes include spinning Marc Almond "waxings", exploring London's seedier corners and generally being dead arty.

Pete Clark, a freelance rock scribbler, has appeared in heavy metal cabaret in Rotheram and currently runs the Mums 'n' Dads disco in a holiday camp on the Isle of Wight. He awaits *Johnny Quest* repeats impassively.

Mark Coleman is the deputy editor of *Star Hits* and a frequent contributor to the *Village Voice*. He lives in New York City, watches television on a 12-inch black-and-white screen and his favourite member of Duran Duran is Nick Rhodes.

Richard Cook has consumed most of the eighties as a commentator on music and films. He disdains the term "pop writer" and prefers to be seen as a critical analyst. After a distinguished career as *NME*'s most prolific critic, he has returned to his first love by becoming editor of the jazz-based publication *The Wire*. He lives noisily in a quiet London suburb.

Peter Culshaw is a freelance researcher and has written for *Echoes*, *The Face*, *NME*, *Tomorrow* and *Anti-Apartheid News* among others. His favourite fruits are water-melons and plums and he has only once ever been on Japanese TV.

Fred Dellar has been a regular contributor to *NME* and *Hi-Fi News* for several years. Books he has authored or co-authored include *The Illustrated Encyclopedia of Country Music*, *The Essential Guide to Rock Records*, *The NME Guide to Rock Cinema* and *The Country Music Book of Lists*.

Malcolm Dome, who has a degree in in biochemistry from London University(!), has contributed to a number of music publications and now works for *Kerrang!*. He has also written two books on the subject of heavy metal, viz *Encyclopedia Metallica* (with Brian Harrigan) and *AC/DC*. He has also appeared on a number of rock radio programmes.

Mark Ellen: The former editor of *Smash Hits*, he was talked into early retirement the day he broke down and confessed to knowing the lyrics to all of Hazell Dean's records. Known as 'Mr Music' to viewers of BBC2's *Whistle Test* (whose hearts he won with a series of truly disgusting shirts), his hobbies include playing the mouth organ and taking a sideways look at today's rock scene and beyond.

Helen Fitzgerald is a Dubliner and writes for *Melody Maker*.

Pete Frame lives in remotest Buckinghamshire, isolated from reality. There he continues to convince himself that the world of rock is still exciting enough to write about and is *still* bashing together a third volume of *Rock Family Trees*.

Dessa Fox is video editor of *NME* and contributes to *Time Out*.

Simon Frith teaches sociology at Warwick University when not being a rock critic for the *Sunday Times* and a columnist for *Village Voice*.

Nelson George is a cynical, heartless young man who learned all he knows about ill moods from covering the American record industry. Currently the black music editor of *Billboard*, George is the author of *The Michael Jackson Story*, and co-author of *Fresh, Hip Hop Don't Stop*, and *Where Did Our Love Go?: The Rise and Fall of the Motown Sound* due in 1986. He is now writing a book titled *The Death of Rhythm and Blues*.

John Gill has been music editor of *Time Out* for two years, having been disgracefully abandoned by Geoff Brown who had shared the burden for the previous two years. Earlier he had spent five years as *Sounds*' captive pseud, and has written for publications as diverse as *The Times* and *Smash Hits*.

CONTRIBUTORS

Fred Goodman is a New York-based writer and editor for *Billboard* magazine. His work has also appeared in numerous publications including the *New York Post*, the *Village Voice*, *Musician*, the *Record* and *Cash Box*. He also contributed to the *Rolling Stone Jazz Record Guide*.

Brian Harrigan has helped to kill off several music publications but *Melody Maker*, *Record Mirror*, *Time Out*, *Smash Hits* and *Video Business* – where he is currently deputy editor – have managed to survive his "assistance" thus far. He has written three rock books – *Rush*, *Encyclopedia Metallica* (with Malcolm Dome) and *The HM A-Z* whose main selling point was a life-size cardboard guitar.

Mary Harron is a Canadian who has written for the *Guardian*, the *New Statesman*, the *Sunday Times* and other papers. She now works for the *South Bank Show*.

Michael Heatley recently retired to suburban Surrey with his wife, child and two cats after occupying the editorial hotseat at the *History of Rock* and *Soundcheck*. He confidently expects to emerge from the spare room in early 1986 with most of the rock entries for the upcoming *Penguin Encyclopedia of Popular Music*.

David Hepworth: Formerly editor of *Smash Hits* and *Just Seventeen*, he is now involved in launching new titles for EMAP. He divides his spare time – what's left of it – between practising "that really difficult bit" on Bruce Springsteen's 'Darkness On The Edge Of Town' on a rather cheap acoustic guitar, making snidey comments about internationally acclaimed pop stars on BBC TV's *Whistle Test*, and being kind to children and animals.

Tom Hibbert (of *Smash Hits*) is a phenomenon of the pen – the man of whom it's been said: "Sky Saxon! Richard Basehart! Vanilla Fudge! *Et al!*" So who better to toast the name of Skippy Peanut Butter before the American TV viewing millions than Ms Annette Funicello, the *woman* of whom it's been said: "Never mind, we'll all be dead soon."? Step forward Mr Paul Morley!!!!!!!!!

Bev Hillier hails from London's Docklands where she resides with two young Norwegian sailors (whom she uses as bookends) and her complete set of saucy seaside postcards. After her humble beginning as *Smash Hits* lone disco correspondent, she is currently working in *Just Seventeen*'s features department and is the only female journalist known to have survived interviewing Spandau Ballet's Steve Norman in the back of his yellow Capri – furry dice and all.

Colin Irwin, former sports reporter, marathon runner and proud owner of two pussycats, is assistant editor of *Melody Maker*. He co-presents a weekly folk music programme for BFBS and when not out on the town indulging an unreasonable taste for champagne, he lives quietly in Long Ditton with his dear, long-suffering wife and family.

Alan Jones has penned *Record Mirror*'s 'Chartfile' column since 1979, and is also a regular contributor to *Music Week*, *T.S. Beat* and *American Top Forty*. He became a journalist by accident, and is equally passionate about cricket, football, natural history and Ireland. Last year he joined chart compilers Gallup as Deputy Charts Manager, and his ambition is to unite his record collection under one roof.

David A Keeps was born and raised in Detroit, Michigan and attended the University of Michigan. He is currently editor-in-chief of *Star Hits*, America's premier pop monthly for today's troubled, trendy teens. He also contributes regularly to *Esquire*, *Sportswear International*, *Smash Hits*, *Creem* and anyone else who'll pay. He is currently working on a book about the history of swimwear.

Kimberley Leston: Until recently designer, writer and in-house sex kitten for *Smash Hits*, 'Miss Posh' (as she is known to her many admirers) was formerly a designer with *Radio Times* and *Men Only*. She has now taken up editing the v. swanky 'Intro' section of *The Face*. At weekends she attends gymkhanas with the rich and famous (John Taylor).

Ray Lowry has drawn cartoons for most of the regular humorous magazines – *Punch*, *Private Eye*, etc. – and has drawn and written occasionally for the *NME* for a number of years. He wrote and illustrated for *The Face* for its first three years and is currently planning a retrospective collection of drawings.

Vici MacDonald is a prime example of that growing menace to journalists – designers with ideas. Give 'em a set of crayons and they think they can write. Since marching into *Smash Hits* from the Royal College of Art, she's become equally ruthless whether writing or "trimming" all features over fifty words. Her hobbies include embarrassing her colleagues by buying junk in street markets to use as background artwork.

Phil McNeill, a graduate of the *NME* School of Editorship, launched *No.1* in 1983 and *The Hit* in 1985. Earliest musical memory: 'Cathy's Clown' by the Everly Brothers. Most memorable childhood experience: the Jimi Hendrix Experience at Billy Walker's Upper Cut Club, Forest Gate. Favourite single: 'Give Me Tonight' by Shannon. Favourite music feature: *The Liver Lads – Frankie Goes To Hollywood At Home*, by Max Bell, *The No.1 Book 1985*. Favourite group: Wham!

Cath Murphy earns her crust as *Just Seventeen*'s D.I.Y. fashion expert. Never happier than when converting a couple of washing-up liquid bottles and a bit of sticky-backed plastic into a Yashi Yamamoto original, this stylist extraordinaire – 'Cheap Tricks' to her friends – spends the rest of her time crying at the opera, collecting tin toys and trying to make her car work properly.

Tony Parsons has published five books, sold more than 300,000 copies world-wide, written a screenplay for rich people in Hollywood, has lived, laughed and cried, has travelled each and every highway – but more than this, he is exactly the same height and weight as Richard Gere, though lacking a moustache.

Dave Rimmer has written for *Smash Hits*, *The Face*, the *Sunday Times Magazine*, *Harpers & Queen*, *City Limits*, *Company*, *The Listener*, *Honey* and several other publications he'd sooner forget. His first book, *Like Punk Never Happened*, was published in October '85.

Jon Savage spends his time in Maida Vale reading books. He makes frequent trips to Soho and plans to clog up the media still further with a televisual polemic about the History of the Music Video and an account of his life with those radical spunkers, the Sex Pistols. His favourite colours are red and black.

Charles Shaar Murray is a contributing editor to *NME*, the co-author of an excellent book about David Bowie, a citizen in good standing of the People's Republic of Islington and a collector of eccentric shirts. His journalism has also appeared in *Vogue*, *Rolling Stone* and *The Face*, and he is currently occupied on assorted book projects and independent record production.

Mark Sinker is a freelance journalist who contributes to the *NME* and *The Wire*. He makes a living teaching Maths as a Foreign Language, and is currently finishing *Tansi Stark's GLORIA*, his first and best novel. He also writes short stories and screenplays: 'Real Life Drama', a video-short co-written with Phil Hughes, was filmed earlier this year, and *Powers*, a film based on his short story *The Sacred Family*, is currently in production.

Tim Sommer is twenty-three and lives and works in the New York City area. His main source of income is from journalism, but he also plays bass with the Glenn Branca Ensemble and has his own group, Hugo Largo.

Phil Sutcliffe writes for *Just Seventeen*, sub-edits for *Time Out*, believes Springsteen is The World's Greatest Living Artist and wishes someone would pay him to expound on this theme but they never do. Knocking on a bit nowadays.

Adam Sweeting of *Melody Maker* has devoted a considerable amount of time and energy to his 50-word autobiography for this year's Virgin Rock Yearbook. Though a firm believer in the "first draft" theory, he has regrettably found himself throwing away several attempts to define himself adequately. "To hell with it," he says.

Neil Tennant, erstwhile editor of Marvel Comics and *The Diary Book of Home Management*, recently quit his day job as assistant editor of *Smash Hits*. He is now one of the Pet Shop Boys.

John Tobler managed to escape from a life sentence in the music business by finding a real job. His mother is pleased by this, but will retain her vast library of rock books written by her son, as he keeps giving away his own last copies.

Paul Vernon has contributed to assorted small specialist publications over the years and appeared on radio shows in UK and US as guest speaker. Currently co-editing *Blues & Rhythm – The Gospel Truth* magazine with Maureen Quinlan, he is interested in many forms of music, and lists Sir Edward Elgar and Terry Allen as heroes alongside Robert Cray and Muddy Waters.

Don Watson is a music and film writer for the *NME*. He is also President of the British Fan Club for Buster Keaton and is looking for recruits.

Guru Weirdbrain surfs the cosmic airwaves to the soundtrack of a generation for whom peace, love, being hip and lookin' good are where it's at. When in the Northern Hemisphere he shares head-space with Dublin's Hotwire label ring-leader, the thinnest man in Europe, Eamon Carr.

Bob Woffinden was Associate Editor of *New Musical Express* a long time ago. However, his association with rock music has declined sharply since the birth of his two children. The albums he is now most familiar with are the *Fraggle Rock* soundtrack and *40 Favourite Nursery Rhymes*. He warmly recommends *Fraggle Rock*. His book on the UK's criminal justice system will be published in 1986.

CONTENTS

THE YEAR 7
A diary of events

THE YEAR IN MUSIC 13
Rock, Soul, Reggae, Hip Hop, Electronic, Jazz, Heavy Metal, Blues & Gospel, Folk

EVENT OF THE YEAR 36
Live Aid remembered

SINGLES 38
A look at fourteen months of 45s!

THE YEAR'S ALBUMS 42
Reviews of a selection of good, bad and indifferent releases

ACTS OF THE YEAR 63
Prince, Wham!, Madonna, U2, Sade, Billy Idol, Cyndi Lauper, Nik Kershaw

FEATURES 80
Band Aid; updates on European, American and African music; the roles of God, politics, personal politics, and advertising in pop; the crossover of black music to white audiences; and how it's still possible to make it to the charts from your bedroom

QUOTES OF THE YEAR 102

BEST AND WORST ALBUM COVERS 113

THEY ALSO SERVED 119
A cameo selection of those who brightened up the year

THE MEDIA 121
Assessments of music on radio, TV and in the music press

BOOK REVIEWS 130

THE YEAR IN VIDEO 138
Plus the making of *Labour of Love*; the influence of video on record success; reviews; music on film; and the decline of the pop promo

BEST AND WORST VIDEOS 156

THE YEAR IN FASHION 158
What the fans were sporting, while the stars were conforming

THE BOY GEORGE WELCOMING COMMITTEE 162
A moment of lightheartedness recalled

IN MEMORIAM 164

THE BUSINESS YEAR 168
UK and US overviews

THE YEAR'S AWARDS 174
The BPI and RIAA gold and platinum awards

CHART ROUND-UP 182

THE YEAR'S CHARTS 183
UK and US singles and albums, week by week

ROCK REFERENCE 210
US and UK record companies, distributors, recording studios, publications, music publishers and music associations

ACKNOWLEDGEMENTS

Hey! We made it! In which case it must be that time of the year (for such is the rhythm of life) when humble postures are adopted and thanks offered to the various individuals and organizations who turned this publication from the theoretical into the possible . . .

That this not-so-slim volume appeared at all is almost entirely due to the heroic Jane Charteris at Virgin Books, who not only subbed tirelessly, chased fearlessly and read the proofs but also came up with several irritatingly good ideas into the bargain. (If only the same could be said of her Editor.) Respect and gratitude in equally generous measures therefore go to this apparently inexhaustible woman. Identical dues must be paid to Iris, Angela, Tracey and Jenny at Capital Setters, whose endless patience and good-humour saw us through the worst; and of course to Mark and Neil of The Fish Family, without whom . . .

Mentions in despatches are also due to: Simon Buckland, Dessa Fox, Don Watson and especially Malcolm Dome and Mark Ellen who provided emergency services at embarrassingly short notice; to *Just Seventeen* magazine for the use of their copyright photographs; to Rob Partridge at Island Records (and photographer Richard Croft) for the special photo session with Phil Fearon; to the Virgin Megastore for allowing Steve Bush to play shoplifter for a day; and finally to Phil Sutcliffe who, by donating his fee to Band Aid, gave us his considerable services for free.

As ever, there would be an awful lot of creative white space were it not for the record companies, book publishers, video and film companies who supplied us with material and photographs, and for the editors of the various music publications for permission to reproduce extracts from their papers. The helpful individuals are far too numerous to list but *they* know who they are: to them all, many thanks.

The following foolishly sentimental persons also allowed their arms to be twisted on our behalf and should not go unrecognized: Linda Gamble, Tessa Watts, Terri Anderson at the BPI and Ferida Suarez at the RIAA, Bob Killbourn at *Blues and Soul*, Debbie Geller, Elisa Wright, Tim Sommer, Mark Coleman, Rick Lander at Diverse Records, and Evie at *Black Beat International*. The BBC, Channel 4 and MTV also gave generously.

We would also like to thank the following photographers: Brian Aris, Joe Bangay, John Beecher, Fritz Brinckmann, Andy Catlin, Donato Cinicolo, Paul Cox, Eric Crichton, Chalkie Davis, Robert Ellis, Francis Fashesin, Caroline Forbes, Guido Harari, Pierre W. Henry Photography, J.S.P. Records, Denis W. Lewis, Dragan Lobojevic, London Features International, Peter Mountain, Rowan Main, Sylvia Pitcher Photography, Dave Peabody, Pictorial Press, Steve Rapport, Paul Rider, Joseph Stevens, Brian Smith, Syndication International, Justin Thomas, Val Wilmer, Nick White.

This book is dedicated to Tom Rapp, wherever he may be.

Thank you and goodnight,
I.C.

THE YEAR

AUGUST 1984

5 Film star and actor Richard Burton dies, aged 58.

13 During a microphone test, President Reagan jokes that he "will begin bombing Russia in five minutes". After tape recordings are made public, the Kremlin issues a statement deploring his sense of humour.

14 West Indies beat England's cricket team in the fifth Test Match, winning the series 5–0.

16 John De Lorean, still facing bankruptcy proceedings in connection with his car firm in which the British government invested £77 million, is cleared of all eight charges of possessing and distributing cocaine.

18 'Careless Whisper' by Wham! man George Michael replaces 'Two Tribes' by Frankie Goes To Hollywood at the top of the British singles chart. 'Two Tribes', after nine weeks, becomes UK's longest reigning chart topper since Slim Whitman's 'Rose Marie' in 1955 ... however, despite weeks of heavy airplay, it fails to make any impression in America.

22 Violence at pit heads and in pit villages escalates as paramilitary style gangs build burning barricades, loot shops, wreck mining equipment and property, and attack police with missiles. Both police and pickets claim to be innocent of provoking violence.

22 In South African elections, blacks, who form more than 70 per cent of the population, are still excluded from voting or participating in government. Black dissatisfaction and unrest increases over the weeks to follow.

25 The *Mont Louis*, a French cargo ship, collides with a German ferry and sinks in the English Channel. Thirty 15-ton containers of radioactive, toxic gas are retrieved after an extensive salvage operation. Questions of nuclear waste disposal are raised by concerned bodies.

• FRANKIE GOES TO HOLLYWOOD

25 American novelist Truman Capote, 59, is found dead at his Los Angeles home.

● Captain Sensible leaves the Damned, which he helped to form in summer 1976.

● Virgin boss Richard Branson announces plans to close the Venue, which had become one of London's most prestigious gigs during his two-year ownership.

SEPTEMBER 1984

1 After a 25-year recording career, 46-year-old Tina Turner has the number one American single, 'What's Love Got To Do With It?' – by far her biggest hit.

3 Norman Willis is elected to succeed Len Murray as General Secretary of the Trades Union Congress.

3 After several people are killed by South African riot police, citizens of black townships near Johannesburg go on the rampage, looting shops and setting fire to property.

7 Striking dockers vote overwhelmingly to return to work after resolving a dispute over unloading imported coal.

13 Six South African activists take refuge in the British Consulate in Durban after security police track them down.

15 A second son, to be known as Prince Harry, is born to the Prince and Princess of Wales.

15 After 43 weeks, Frankie Goes To Hollywood's 'Relax' becomes the longest running chart hit since 'Release Me' kept Engelbert Humperdinck buoyant for 56 weeks in 1967/8. It has also become the fourth best selling single of all time ... behind 'Mull Of Kintyre' by Wings, 'Rivers Of Babylon' by Boney M, and 'You're The One That I Want' by John Travolta and Olivia Newton-John.

20 More than 20 are killed when an Islamic suicide driver rams a car containing explosives into the US Embassy in East Beirut.

28 The pit deputies union, NACODS, votes to strike in support of the NUM's opposition to colliery closures – but after negotiating with the NCB and ACAS, they decide to keep working.

29 Police seize an Irish trawler carrying a massive haul of weapons and ammunition to the IRA from American sympathizers.

• TINA TURNER

30 The music division of Thorn EMI, once said to be the greatest recording organization in the world, reports a world-wide loss of almost $5 million during the last six months.

● Helen Terry leaves Culture Club after 18 months' continuous work with the group

● Following a police raid and the confiscation of 17 offending titles from a local record shop, magistrates in Northwich, Cheshire, rule that albums by Crass, Crucifixion, Agent Orange and various others are obscene.

OCTOBER 1984

1 NUM President Arthur Scargill is served with a writ for contempt relating to a High Court judgement that the 30-week-old miners' strike is unlawful. He is subsequently fined £1000 and the Union £200,000.

4 Unemployment in Britain reaches a record total of 3,280,000 – representing 13,6 per cent of the workforce.

4 Six million Ethiopians are reported to be in desperate straits after a prolonged drought, which has decimated grain production ... but the western world is slow to react.

12 An IRA bomb explodes at the Grand Hotel, Brighton, where the Prime Minister and many colleagues are staying during the annual Conservative Party conference. Four people are killed and 32 injured.

● BIG COUNTRY

12 In their biggest clampdown yet, the Home Office authorizes raids on seven London-based pirate radio stations, seizing equipment and closing their operations.

14 Bruce Kent announces the decision to give up his post as General Secretary of the CND, which he has held for five years.

17 Alberta Hunter, described by many as America's foremost female blues singer, dies at Roosevelt Island, New York, aged 89.

18 Anita Brookner's Hotel Du Lac wins the Booker McConnell prize for fiction.

23 Television pictures revealing the severity of the famine in Ethiopia prick the conscience of richer countries, who begin sending food supplies and medical aid.

30 Indira Gandhi, India's Prime Minister, is shot dead by two of her personal guards – both Sikhs. Her son, Rajiv Gandhi, succeeds her as hundreds of Sikhs die in Hindu revenge reaction.

30 Polish authorities announce the discovery of the body of Solidarity supporter, priest Jerzy Popieluszko, whose kidnapping had reunited the union and the people of Poland in demonstrations of defiance against the Communist regime.

● American boffins predict that Compact Discs will have rendered vinyl production totally obsolete within seven years.

● This month sees the deaths of jazz drummer Shelley Manne, aged 64, and bluegrass picker Don Reno – originator of 'Duelling Banjos' – aged 58.

● American critics slam Paul McCartney's feature film *Give My Regards To Broad Street*. Variety describes it as "characterless, bloodless and pointless".

● Pete Townshend, Big Country, Style Council, the Specials, Madness and Tom Robinson are among rock stars endorsing a nationwide anti-heroin campaign.

NOVEMBER 1984

4 Britain begins a grain airlift to Ethiopia.

4 Gerry Adams, Sinn Fein President and MP for West Belfast, describes the Brighton bombing as "a blow for democracy".

6 After pleading no contest to a reduced charge of voluntary manslaughter, Marvin Gaye Sr receives five years probation for shooting his son, who is ruled to have "tragically provoked" the incident. The singer's mother, Alberta, sole witness to the shooting, has since filed for divorce against Gaye.

6 Ronald Reagan carries 49 states to sweep to victory in the US Presidential election. His comprehensive defeat of Democrat Walter Mondale was never in doubt: 525 to 13 electoral votes ensured a second term in the White House.

8 Fela Kuti, one of Africa's most militant and internationally acclaimed musicians, is convicted of currency smuggling charges in Nigeria and sentenced to five years in prison.

10 After establishing a new record for advance orders – 1,099,500 copies, representing over £5 million of business – Frankie Goes To Hollywood's debut album *Welcome To The Pleasuredome* smashes into the UK chart at number one – as expected!

● A Federal Court judge dismisses rock pioneer Little Richard's $50 million suit for back record and songwriting royalties. The singer's action sought to rescind an agreement that he had signed in 1959, by which he received a lump sum of $11,000 and waived all claims to royalties.

12 After 38 weeks on strike, some 2000 miners return to work, lured by the Coal Board's high financial inducements for the Christmas period. The drift back continues during the days that follow, though the majority of strikers are resolute in their determination to win. Forty-five arrests are made in the worst violence yet seen at pit heads.

12 Pinnacle, one of Britain's leading independent distributors, is put in the hands of the Official Receiver after mounting financial problems. Independent labels face deeper gloom a week later when another distributor, IDS, finds itself in a similar predicament.

14 38-year-old Jamaican reggae star Keith Hudson dies in New York, where he had been undergoing treatment for lung cancer.

22 Common Market officials meet to discuss the possibility of imposing a 100 per cent levy on blank audio and video cassettes to compensate copyright owners whose products are pirated by "home tapers". Any decision is postponed until further research has been carried out.

23 During Neil Kinnock's visit to Moscow, President Chernenko stated that if Labour came to power, any nuclear arms reduction they instigated would be matched by Russia, where missiles aimed at Britain would be dismantled.

25 A host of stars, led by Bob Geldof and Midge Ure, join forces to record 'Do They Know It's Christmas?' – all proceeds from which will go towards famine relief in Ethiopia.

DECEMBER 1984

2 The Hope & Anchor, one of London's longest-standing "pub circuit" venues, closes after insurmountable financial difficulty.

The rush for British Telecom shares results in the issue being four times oversubscribed.

2 Nick Heyward, Feargal Sharkey and Alvin Stardust are among those participating in a Benefit for Ethiopia at London's Royal Albert Hall – one of many concerts organized for the same purpose.

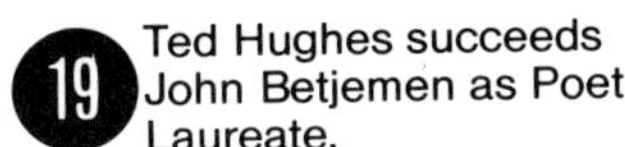

19 Ted Hughes succeeds John Betjemen as Poet Laureate.

20 The Court of Appeal bars any doctor from prescribing contraceptives to girls under 16 without parental consent.

21 Following the visit of Russian diplomat Mikhail Gorbachev, Mrs Thatcher visits Washington to urge President Reagan to consider an early ban on space weapons.

25 Among those spending Christmas in British jails are American film star Stacey Keach, on drugs charges, and footballer George Best, convicted of drunken driving.

● FEARGAL SHARKEY

8 'The Power Of Love' gives Frankie Goes To Hollywood their third UK number one – the first group since Gerry and the Pacemakers in 1963 to achieve the pole position with their first three releases.

8 One time Coasters' manager Patrick Cavanaugh is convicted of first degree murder in the slaying of group member Buster Wilson, whose dismembered body was discovered near Modesto, California, in May 1980.

27 Movie director Sam Peckinpah dies in Los Angeles, aged 59.

LA groups the Dream Syndicate and Gun Club split up.

ZZ Top bassist Dusty Hill accidentally shoots himself in the abdomen with a .38 Derringer he keeps in his boot! After surgery and intensive care, he recovers.

JANUARY 1985

2 A Soviet Cruise missile crashes in Finland after being fired from a submarine in the Barents Sea. Russian apologies are accepted after they explain that it was only a target which went astray.

7 Prince still holds the number one album position – as he has since August, making *Purple Rain* the biggest seller since Michael Jackson's *Thriller*. In Britain, Sade's *Diamond Life* has spent 23 weeks (its entire chart life) in the Top Ten, becoming the best selling UK album of 1984.

8 Baby Cotton, born of a British surrogate mother whose pregnancy was arranged by an agency on behalf of a childless American couple, is made a ward of court. She is subsequently handed over to her natural father.

9 In the coldest winter for 50 years, temperatures drop to record depths. Even Texas and the South of France are obliterated by snow and blizzards.

11 A Brazilian rock festival, held in Rio, is claimed to be the biggest ever staged. Among the stars are Queen, Rod Stewart, Yes, Iron Maiden, Whitesnake and AC/DC.

14 Band Aid's 'Do They Know It's Christmas?' becomes the best selling British single of all time – outstripping 'Mull Of Kintyre' by Wings.

20 President Reagan is inaugurated for his second term at the White House.

29 Miffed by government cuts in education budgets, Oxford dons veto the award of an honorary degree to Margaret Thatcher.

29 Forty-six artists – America's version of Band Aid – record 'We Are The World' to raise funds for famine relief in Ethiopia.

31 President Botha of South Africa offers to release Nelson Mandela, the jailed leader of the outlawed African National Congress, if he agrees to certain demands. Mandela rejects the offer, refusing to give any assurances while he and his people are denied freedom.

Bluesman Willie Dixon files a Federal Court complaint charging that Led Zeppelin's giant 1969 hit 'Whole Lotta Love' was substantially plagiarised from his copyrighted composition 'You Need Love' – first recorded by Muddy Waters in 1962.

● ROD STEWART

● FRANK ZAPPA

Three former Mothers Of Invention, Don Preston, Bunk Gardner and Jimmy Carl Black, sue Frank Zappa, alleging breach of contract and fraud.

FEBRUARY 1985

4 Wide cuts in domestic programmes and heavy increases in defence spending are the main features of President Reagan's budget submission to Congress.

5 In a nocturnal swoop, troops reclaim RAF Molesworth in Cambridgeshire from anti-nuclear protesters demonstrating against its scheduled use as a cruise missile store.

11 Ministry of Defence secretary Clive Ponting is acquitted of breaching the Official Secrets Act by leaking information about the sinking of the General Belgrano to a Labour MP.

19 During a visit to Washington, Margaret Thatcher expresses her support for the Star Wars programme, but appeals to Americans not to finance IRA operations.

25 Jerry Dammers and a host of colleagues record a benefit single, proceeds of which go towards famine relief. The song, 'Starvation', was originally recorded by the Pioneers, who are among those contributing to the new version.

26 In a ceremony at the Shrine Auditorium in Los Angeles, the American record industry announces this year's Grammy winners. Tina Turner's 'What's Love Got To Do With It?' is Record Of The Year, Lionel Richie's *Can't Slow Down* is Best Album, and Cyndi Lauper is Best New Artist.

● In Britain and America, record and cassette sales show a 14 per cent leap as the industry begins to pull out of the recent slump.

● JERRY DAMMERS

● Paul Weller, Madness, Alison Moyet and Frankie Goes To Hollywood are rock acts supporting a movement to stop the Government axing supplementary benefit for jobless school leavers who do not participate in the Youth Training Scheme.

● Stevie Wonder is among 47 arrested during an anti-apartheid demonstration outside the South African embassy in Washington.

● Spandau Ballet serve Chrysalis with a writ alleging mismanagement of their affairs and requiring their recording contract to be terminated forthwith.

MARCH 1985

3 The National Union of Mineworkers vote to abandon their strike after almost a year. The dispute is estimated to have cost over £3 billion.

10 President Konstantin Chernenko of the Soviet Union dies after only 15 months in office. 54-year-old Mikhail Gorbachev succeeds him.

13 Forty-seven are injured and 31 arrested during riots by football fans at a game between Luton and Millwall. £45,000 of damage to a train is just one item in a heavy bill. Concern grows over the behaviour of soccer hooligans.

21 On the twenty-fifth anniversary of the Sharpeville massacre, South African police open fire on a black funeral procession at the township of Uitenhage, killing at least 20.

29 Thompson Twin Tom Bailey is discovered on the floor of his hotel room suffering from exhaustion. After being flown to Paris to see his private doctor, he is ordered to take a total break from work.

Paul Simon spends two weeks in South Africa recording local music with prominent Soweto bands. He is said to have doubled the salaries of black musicians employed on the sessions. Meanwhile, the South African Broadcasting Corporation drops records by Stevie Wonder from its playlists after the singer accepts his Academy Award for Best Original Song ('I Just Called To Say I Love You') "in the name of Nelson Mandela" – a reference little understood by the Hollywood audience at the time.

● POWER STATION

26 A High Court judge awards singer Ray Jackson £25,000 damages and £50,000 costs after deciding that EMI failed to honour a contract agreed in 1976. (One can only hope this precedent opens an interesting can of worms!)

28 The road outside Madame Tussaud's is blocked by fans anxious to glimpse Michael Jackson as he arrives to witness the unveiling of his wax effigy.

● While Stewart Copeland confirms that Police "have broken up in the same way that school breaks up every summer", he releases a solo single. Meanwhile, Sting, backed by prominent jazz musicians, makes his solo concert debut in New York.

● Robert Palmer launches Power Station, a part-time outfit comleted by Andy and John Taylor from Duran Duran, and Tony Thompson of Chic/Bowie fame.

APRIL 1985

5 The number of unemployed in Britain falls to 3,267,592 – though the underlying trend is still upwards.

7 Wham! play a concert in Peking – the first appearance ever by a Western rock group in the People's Republic of China.

13 USA For Africa's Ethiopian famine relief single, 'We Are The World', featuring 21 different solo vocalists and lasting almost six and a half minutes, is the new top seller in America.

19 60-year-old Chicago R&B pioneer Willie Mabon, famed for his Chess recordings in the early fifties, dies in Paris, France, after a long illness.

● MEATLOAF

7 After a show at the Orange Bowl in Miami, Florida, Prince declares that he is retiring from live performances. Most people take the statement with a pinch of salt!

8 Over 20,000 anti-nuclear protesters spend Easter surrounding Britain's second Cruise missile base at RAF Molesworth in Cambridgeshire.

27 The USA For Africa album, *We Are The World*, rises to the top of the American chart.

Meat Loaf's *Bat Out Of Hell* drops out of the UK album chart for the first time in six years!

The BPI starts a new wide-reaching investigation into chart-rigging after Gallup reports irregularities in some of the retail outlets they monitor.

MAY 1985

1 President Regan bans all US trade with Nicaragua on the grounds of the Sandinista government's strengthening military ties with the Soviet bloc.

6 The National Coal Board announces that targets for a cutback in jobs and production have been achieved and that many more miners than necessary had applied for early redundancy.

7 Only half of Ethiopia's million famine victims are receiving food because a transport shortage is causing a huge grain backlog.

8 As the world celebrates the fortieth anniversary of VE Day, President Reagan and Mr Gorbachev trade insults: Reagan condemns Soviet expansionism in Africa, Afghanistan and Nicaragua, while the Russian leader describes America as "the only country which waxed fabulously rich on the war".

11 Over 50 are killed when a football stand catches fire during a match at the Bradford City ground.

12 While teachers and nurses struggle for realistic wages, Prince Andrew opens the new £400 million airport in the Falklands.

15 Bruce Springsteen marries Julianne Phillips in Lake Oswego, Oregon.

20 Harlem's Apollo Theatre, for decades a showplace for leading black American entertainers, reopens for business.

21 A bipartisan group of influential Washington wives known as PMRC (Parents' Music Resource Centre) asks the music industry to launch a rating system warning consumers of records containing violent or sexually explicit lyrics. "Young girls who listen to Madonna are learning at a very young age how to be a porn queen in heat," claims their organizer.

29 At least 38 football fans die during riots between Juventus and Liverpool supporters before the start of the European Cup Final in Brussels. The FA subsequently announces a twelve-month ban on English clubs taking part in European competitions, but the international body UEFA, aghast at the behaviour of English fans generally and Liverpool fans specifically, imposes a ban "for an indefinite period of time".

● BRUCE SPRINGSTEEN

The Go Gos split up. Three original members of the Jefferson Airplane regroup under a new, undecided name. Meanwhile, the Jefferson Starship, a seventies modification of the Airplane, lose a court battle to retain their "Jefferson" prefix.

Bill Wyman and Charlie Watts launch Willie & the Poor Boys, an ad-hoc group which records and gigs to raise money for Ronnie Lane's ARMS (multiple sclerosis) charity.

JUNE 1985

1 Hundreds of police in full riot gear arrest 84 members of a 140 vehicle hippie "Peace" convoy bound for their annual festival at Stongehenge. Authorities ban the festival and Stonehenge is closed to the public during the summer solstice.

4 Elton John begins a High Court battle with Dick James Music, seeking the rights to early songs and recordings, plus damages estimated at more than £30 million.

6 In his speech at the International Music Industry Conference in Munich, RCA President Robert Summer warns that the home taping of records has reached such proportions that it threatens "the viability of the music business as we know it".

9 The NME agrees to pay Cliff Richard "appropriate damages" and legal costs after a High Court action over defamatory imputations contained in a concert review. Cliff donates the money to charity.

13 Reclusive millionaire Paul Getty Jr becomes Britain's biggest individual patron of the arts by promising the National Gallery £50 million.

15 National Springsteen fever sees all seven of his albums on the UK chart – but Bryan Ferry's latest, *Boys And Girls*, jumps in at number one. Twenty-two years after topping the singles chart with the same song, Gerry (then leading the Pacemakers, but now fronting the Crowd) repeats the performance with 'You'll Never Walk Alone' – a fund-raiser for the Bradford fire victims.

21 Channel 4 begins a series of *Ready Steady Go!* episodes – the first time they've been screened since the sixties.

24 After 15 arrests in Glasgow and London, police uncover an IRA plot to plant bombs in twelve British holiday resorts during the summer.

30 John Lennon's Rolls Royce, psychedelicized to his specifications during the days of Flower Power, fetches over $2 million at a New York auction.

● Pete Cetera, lead singer with Chicago, leaves to pursue a solo career; Hanoi Rocks split up; Jimmy Somerville settles on a name for his new band – the Communards; Motorhead celebrate their tenth anniversary.

● MOTÖRHEAD

● His label president, Jean Karakos, leads an international effort to secure the release of Fela Kuti, currently serving an unappealable five year prison sentence. The politically outspoken musician is said to have been arrested nearly 200 times in his native Nigeria.

● With almost six and a half million copies sold, Bruce Springsteen's *Born In The USA* is certified as Columbia's biggest success of all time – surpassing Journey's *Escape* and Billy Joel's *The Stranger*.

JULY 1985

4 The Liberal SDP Alliance candidate beats Labour into second place in the Brecon and Radnor by-election, wiping out the previous 9000-vote Conservative majority.

7 Seventeen-year-old West German Boris Becker becomes the first unseeded player to win the Men's Singles final at Wimbledon.

● BOB GELDOF

9 Police shoot dead at least ten blacks during demonstrations at the funeral of four youths in a township near Johannesburg.

10 The Greenpeace flagship Rainbow Warrior is sunk by saboteurs in Auckland Harbour, New Zealand, where it was being prepared to lead a protest flotilla opposing French nuclear tests in the Pacific.

13 Organized by Bob Geldof, Live Aid is the most prestigious, star-studded and praiseworthy rock concert ever mounted. A satellite link-up connects shows in Wembley and Philadelphia, providing a 16-hour spectacular attracting a global television audience of over one and a half billion. Donations totalling some £50 million pour into a fund set up to aid the starving in Africa.

13 President Reagan's White House schedule is interrupted for only one week when he undergoes an operation to remove a cancerous growth from his colon.

18 Top civil servants are awarded pay increases of up to 46 per cent while teachers are being offered 6 per cent and nurses 9 per cent.

20 In South Africa, escalating black protest against discrimination results not in reform but in more repression as a state of emergency is declared, extending police powers to arrest and imprisonment without trial or explanation. As the UN calls for world-wide sanctions, the number of "suspects" in custody totals over a thousand.

● Despite constant anxiety about home taping, the number of albums certified platinum (over one million units sold) in the States shows a 46 per cent rise over last year.

THE YEAR IN ROCK

SPANDAU BALLET

BRYAN ADAMS

KATRINA AND THE WAVES

There's a girl I've known for about six years now who knows what's going on in music. She wouldn't waste time on the theory but she's always displayed an instinct for locating the action that's little short of spooky. Every time anything of consequence has come to pass in the way of pop – by that I mean things that really count beyond the boys' own world of rock critics – she's been there and she's been there first.

When Disco ruled she was regular at the Zero 6. Two-tone: she was in the front row. Spandau Ballet: I distinctly recall a frilly shirt. Culture Club: she toyed with hair extensions. Wham!: she damn nearly developed a tan.

She's taken exactly what she wanted and no more from every bright, brittle and bankable trend that modern pop has thought fit to throw up and I can't recall her going for anyone who didn't pan out to be Big Potatoes. And when there's nothing happening of any interest she goes off and does something more amusing.

The most significant single factor governing music in the eighties is the way its direction has been dictated by young women like my friend rather than rockist recidivists like me. Or, I wouldn't mind betting, you. This decade has not produced one really major star whose popularity hasn't been substantially founded amongst females.

Anyway, the point of all this is that one evening in 1985 my friend did something that really surprised me. She went to see Bryan Adams.

The evening involved a certain amount of air-punching and much hymning of the virtues of something called "rock 'n' roll", a term as arcane to a young woman of her generation as sweet rationing. This is not to imply that 1985 was a year dominated by Men-Bearing-Guitars-With-Intent-To-Boogie but there was precious little else you could call a trend and meat was back on the menu in a big way – albeit mainly in the form of rump steak.

It was certainly a long time since Londoners had been able to go out more or less any night of the week and immerse themselves in the kind of racket that shakes floorboards and causes patrons to twist and shout. Now most of it may not have been exactly profound, but British groups like the Screaming Blue Messiahs, visiting Americans like the Long Ryders and transatlantic crossbreeds like Katrina and the Waves restored to audiences the precious and long-withheld right to *enjoy* themselves. And if pop music isn't entertainment first then it'll never be anything else second.

Pub rock, huffed unbelievers. Well, so it was, but there are worse things than pub rock. Ask Elvis Costello or Mark Knopfler or Sting or Paul Weller or any musician who got the precious chance to practise their moves and make their mistakes within concussion distance of the Hope and Anchor's low ceiling.

This renaissance of live music came along a few months too late to save the Hope which closed its doors for the final time in the face of video pubs, cocktail bars and a thousand groups who couldn't have performed live even if they'd wanted to. Round about the same time the *nouveau riche* kids who'd vaulted over the gig listings and gone straight to video heaven were celebrating Christmas at London's grandest and biggest indoor venue, Wembley Arena. Spandau Ballet, the Thompson Twins and Wham! each in their turn took to that stage and tried to emulate the Hollywood production values of the advertising films that had put them in pole position. The reviews all returned to the same grudging points; the quality of the lighting, the perfectly drilled choreography, the sparkling costumes, the props, the ranks of extra musicians drafted in to disguise the fact that the music was deeply, deeply boring.

Groups like these can never be as good as celluloid cracks them up to be for the same reason that "E.T." could not be presented live. Those who live by the artificial heightening of expectation that video involves should stay indoors lest they die by the disappointment that comes about when client confronts product at point of sale. Ask any marketing man. Those who live by publicity shall perish by over-exposure. Ask Boy George.

Culture Club's fall from grace was a cautionary tale that should echo down the annals of beat music for a long time to come. One bad LP, *Waking Up With The House On Fire*, and down they went, faster than shares in De Lorean. Not one ounce of residual loyalty put the brake on that slide or made it any more bearable for a group who had in some senses started at the very top.

One of the advantages of being a regular old-fashioned boys' rock group is that you can make poor records and people will still buy them. Led Zeppelin got away with it for years. U2 could probably do the same right now. But George was constructed of different stuff. As a star there was nobody who did it better. As a loser he was embarrassing to have around.

Frankie Goes To Hollywood, who employed every marketing ruse known to modern science (covered with a light frosting of sub-literary twaddle), took the Culture Club approach even further.

Here's a group who generated as much revenue from T-shirt sales as they did from records; here's a group who have managed to keep the lid on their no-doubt burning urge to create for a full calendar year; here's a group who have chosen instead to travel the world's skyways milking the success of 'Relax' and 'Two Tribes' for all they're worth and a good deal more; here's a group who increasingly resemble a bunch of pro footballers who feel the joints stiffening and see their long-term future in menswear.

All groups are in the business of sales promotion and marketing. Nobody knows it like Frankie. Frankie say: coin it while you can.

One colleague of mine accompanies them to an Italian song festival where they appeared alongside Duran Duran, Spandau Ballet and various other young millionaires. He came back enthusing over how accomplished they all were – at miming. When it comes to the finer points of the lip-synch and the quality of their backing tapes there's nobody to touch your eighties pop star. Small wonder: it's the main professional skill demanded of them.

Record industry accountants are starting to ask awkward questions about the Frankies of this world, the foremost being why don't they sell the quantities of LPs their massive fame seems to suggest they should?

Indeed the word was that Frankie's *Welcome To The Pleasuredome* shipped gold and returned platinum, which isn't exactly brilliant even for a record that was made up of three previously released singles, an uncalled-for version of 'Born To Run', two sides of meandering nonsense and an overpriced mail order clothing catalogue (merchandise, thy name is Frankie).

Look a little closer and you'll find that Frankie fans had started to act like the obedient consumers the campaign had been posited on. They *wanted* 'Relax'. They wanted it so much they bought five different 12″ versions. They needed it so bad they even bought the T-shirt that advertised it. What they didn't want, thank you very much, was a bunch of songs they'd never betrayed the slightest interest in.

The 12″ single has had a profound effect on buying habits, particularly amongst teenage boys. Why shell out for an LP containing two hits, two good tracks and a bunch of filler drafted in to boost the product to a completely arbitrary 40-minute running time when you can have one version of your favourite track that goes on and on for hours (nearly)?

Even with mass unemployment and enforced leisure and all that, life is still far too short for any sane person to devote forty minutes to listening to an LP by Duran Duran. Nobody listens to Duran Duran LPs, not even Duran Duran. Listening to a record like *Rio* I am irresistibly reminded of old favourites like *A Session With The Dave Clark Five*; exactly the same creative and commercial forces are at work.

Today's biggest-selling LPs are, for want of a better word, *useful*. They're purchased like Nike shoes or woks or Volkswagen Golf's; because they seem appropriate products to have about the place and, with a bit of luck, they say something about their owner.

Look no further than Sade's *Diamond Life*, as profoundly uneventful an LP as ever found its way into that crucial little pile of records next to the music centre in so many homes. Carole King's *Tapestry* is some kind of precedent but that at least had the odd memorable song. No, the promised jazz revival may have been delayed indefinitely but there was quite enough advance ballyhoo to ensure that Sade's Billie Holliday backless look and carefully tilted cigarette triggered off all the right associations.

And then there was Alison Moyet, a gifted singer unaccountably sidetracked and only sporadically able to dramatize the emotions her songs describe. Every time the British entertainment industry gathered to hand out awards SadeandAlf were bracketed together near the top of the tree, like some sort of convenient shorthand for that most irrelevant of pop virtues, Quality.

You could blame Michael Jackson for this stultifying obsession with the How rather than the Why of pop. He did nothing all year except have his image cast in wax for Madame Tussaud's and it's a measure of how far he's strayed from the path of sanity that that particular puerile accolade was the only thing that could get him across the Atlantic all year. The Jacksons couldn't tour Europe, we were told, because the stage they used was too big to import. You won't find a better illustration of how wrongheaded people can be than that little explanation.

In his absence the crossover crown was delivered unto Prince, a man just as talented but no more sensible. The one event of 1985 I dearly wish I'd been a witness to took place on the day that Prince delivered the tapes of his follow-up to *Purple Rain* to Warner Bros. In he came to their offices accompanied by fawning retinue and platoons of minders. On the floor he sat doodling with a flower (*a flower!*) while the big wheels sagely listened to the fruits of his labours. What they heard must have chilled them to the marrow. Here he was, the hottest act in America, the man who had sold millions to both black and white, and what had he produced? *Around The World In A Day*, a record that made *Their Satanic Majesties Request* sound like quite a good idea.

The sharp clip round the ear may not be the most efficacious method of artist liaison in the long run but it's a sight better than constantly telling them they're wonderful, omniscient and perfect in every way. Particularly when the artist you're dealing with is Prince, a man with a lot of musical talent and the intellectual grasp of a gnat.

The more successful pop stars become, the more they fall into behaving like

● *FRANKIE GOES TO HOLLYWOOD*

● *GEORGE MICHAEL*

● *ALISON MOYET*

● *THE STYLE COUNCIL*

● PRINCE

children or medieval potentates. If you don't believe me you obviously haven't heard about George Michael cancelling an entire day's filming in China because his hair wasn't quite as he would have wished. If you *still* don't believe me then you've definitely not seen a copy of Nick Rhodes' book of Polaroids.

It took Bob Geldof and Band Aid to prove that things don't really have to be that way. What was truly impressive about that Sunday morning at Sarm Studios was the complete lack of fuss, the way all those people turned up without minders or managers, engaged in civilized conversation with each other, sang their parts and went home.

By the time the idea had travelled to Hollywood and become 'We Are The World' it was a question of closed circuit TV, champagne and caviar and somebody suggesting they sing the thing in Swahili; nevertheless the idea survived and the money found its way into the right hands.

Undeniably Geldof and his American counterparts had mastered the crucial trick of persuading people that they were very privileged to have been invited to take part, but whether people's motives were entirely altruistic or not is secondary to the importance of the gesture itself. Band Aid is one thing the music industry needn't be ashamed of.

It's ironic that the very same people who were earning sums of money that their sixties predecessors could only dream of were simultaneously lending their support to causes in a way their more overtly radical ancestors had shrunk from doing. It was no surprise to find the Style Council playing benefits for striking miners but it shouldn't be forgotten that Wham! and Sade did the same. The very people whose music seemed to promote the most rabid consumerism (few who saw the video for 'Last Christmas' could ever forget it) did more in financial terms for beleaguered working-class communities than, for instance, the Clash had ever managed.

Bruce Springsteen, whose year-long world tour is reckoned to have grossed £37,000,000, the kind of money that would induce a twinge of guilt in anyone, embarked on a policy of making donations to local food banks, shelters for the homeless and strikers' support groups in cities where he played.

Whether gestures like these are directly responsible for raising anyone's consciousness is anybody's guess, but this year saw more explicitly political hit records in Britain than any earlier era. It must be puzzling for someone like Paul Weller that records like Paul Hardcastle's '19', Billy Bragg's 'Between The Wars', Bronski Beat's 'Smalltown Boy' and his own 'Walls Come Tumbling Down' can get hours of exposure on the very choicest national media without bringing about some perceptible shift in the distribution of wealth.

What it really proves is that pop has never been more popular and it's never seemed less important to the majority of people. It's become a truism that the more that groups aspire to cultural weight, the more fatuous they become. Witness the Redskins, who announced that they wanted to walk like the Clash and sing like the Supremes, which is as good as a solid promise that they're not going to do either. In this case the Redskins were impeded by the fact that they couldn't sing, play or write songs. I mean they *really* couldn't.

If evolution continues on its current course, groups like the Redskins and the equally preposterous Jesus and Mary Chain will eventually stop making records and devote their time to giving interviews to the music press about how they would change the world if they could only sort out their problems with this music stuff.

Faced with the kind of dreary racket purveyed by the Redskins *et al*, many British people started to look towards the former colonies for sustenance and this year America was not found wanting. The West Coast, long assumed to have drifted off towards Japan, produced excellent acts like the Bangles, Lone Justice, the Beat Farmers, Los Lobos and True West, groups who were many times more encouraging than anybody the British business unearthed all year. As a group their tendency to don buckskin jackets and quote old Flying Burritos Brothers songs could be worrying but that was outweighed by the fact that they all operated on a human scale. Better Green On Red's Neil Young impressions than the Roaring Boys doing Bryan Ferry via David Sylvian. That way madness lies.

At the same time as the new Los Angeles acts were being snapped up on the old bulk-buying principle by the major record companies, something stirred on a nearby mountain top. After ten years of inactivity and litigation John Fogerty was emerging in order to give the effortless lie to just about every piece of received wisdom upon which the record business operates, with particular reference to the clause about comebacks never working. *Centerfield* was an American number one LP.

If Fogerty was the most dramatic case of an old stager showing everybody else the ropes, he was by no means the only one. Don Henley, voice of the Eagles, reappeared with *Building The Perfect Beast*, an acute piece of work that almost made up for the fact that Donald Fagen had not got around to following up *The Nightfly*.

Anybody who spends as much of his time attached to a mixing desk as Phil Collins is bound to come up with a success every now and then, but 1985 saw him in finer form than ever with hits from his third solo LP, one from the soundtrack of *Against All Odds* and another with Philip Bailey, whose *Chinese Wall* he produced.

Nor could you find a better example of the rewards that persistence brings than Tina Turner's *Private Dancer*, which probably had more good songs on it than anything else all year, thanks to the employment of everyone from Mark Knopfler to Heaven 17. But everybody's favourite comeback boys seemed to be ZZ Top, who demonstrated that at the very height of pretty boy pop it was still possible for three middle-aged Texans (bearded ones at that) with a stock of pithy riffs and some gravelly vocals to go platinum purely because they had the smarts to realize that a successful video is both funny and sexy.

Of course there were many of pensionable age who had a pretty miserable 1985, so it's not a simple question of old foxes versus young bloods. Paul McCartney's *Give My Regards To Broad Street* was a cinematic disaster on the scale of *Magical Mystery Tour*. Mick Jagger's *She's The Boss* must have had a few fellow Stones sniggering to themselves as it manifestly failed to make a major impression and Bob Dylan's *Empire Burlesque* shuttled between fair and dismal.

No, what separated the winners from the losers in 1985 was a simple matter of attitude. What neither McCartney nor Duran Duran, Jagger nor Spandau Ballet, Dylan nor Culture Club had were standards, self-imposed or otherwise. You got the feeling that if their music was below par they would genuinely be the last ones to realize. This was a year when the work ethic reasserted itself as a major force in pop.

We had to get to this eventually. Springsteen's 150-date tour wasn't just the result of a desire to make fabulous amounts of cash and promote *Born In The USA*. It was born of his almost unbalanced view that music matters, fans matter and they are owed nothing less than the best shot an artist can give. It's that belief that drives him to put the most practised band in the world through five-hour rehearsals in the middle of a tour, it's that that causes him to introduce entirely new songs at a day's notice, it's that that fills 100,000-capacity venues and sends everybody home feeling glad they came, it's that that makes most other acts look as if they just aren't trying.

It's not genius or inspiration or even a great deal of talent. It's the result of bloody hard work and a dogmatic belief that it matters an awful lot whether the guitar solo goes here or over there.

Springsteen's British dates were posted at the same time as Jimmy Somerville announced he was leaving Bronski Beat. Why? Because he couldn't take the pressure of being a famous pop star. Expecting some unemployed teenager in the North of England to sympathize with you because too many people want you to appear on TV seems to me like the kind of surpassing arrogance no pop star should be allowed to indulge in.

Nobody would deny that it's tough at the top but it's a hell of a sight tougher at the bottom and if your career's out of control then you've only got yourself to blame and you've no business going whingeing to the general public. Just think. Some day they might buy your book of Polaroids.

David Hepworth

● *THE JESUS & MARY CHAIN*

● *MICK JAGGER*

● *BRONSKI BEAT*

● *ZZ TOP*

THE YEAR IN SOUL

At the blockbuster end of the black American music market, each of the past three years has been dominated by one man. First it was Michael Jackson, whose *Thriller* became a blue-print for pop-soul records in the subsequent eighteen months. Then came Lionel Richie, cutting himself loose from the Commodores and breaking into the mass white pop market in a platinum way. It's hard to imagine that the third and latest dominant character will be as much of a musical trendsetter in the market from which he sprang. What the selling and selling and selling of Prince in 1985 should unquestionably do is make black artists demand better, more varied and more imaginative marketing from their recording companies, as well as greater artistic freedom.

For the traditionalist, neither of Prince's big LPs, *Purple Rain* and *Around The World In A Day*, bear comparison (or much stylistic similarity) to his earlier, superior albums. Good tracks on both, but they're more interesting for what they're attempting, the directions suggested, styles dabbled in, than for their content. He has become a Jimi Hendrix for the eighties.

The two stars he succeeded as Person Of The Year have fared variably. Richie kept his counsel, counted his money, collected many awards and prepared for another assault, but it was good to see his old band, the Commodores (who'd lost another member, Thomas McClary), release easily their best track since Richie's departure – 'Nightshift', a touching tribute to the late Marvin Gaye and Jackie Wilson.

Michael Jackson, meanwhile, reminded us that he was still a member of the Jacksons when they released the stupefyingly ordinary *Victory* album, comfortably the group's worst LP, and later set off on a nation-wide tour of the vastest stadia that the USA can offer. The tour followed interminable managerial squabbles, much hiring and firing, PR ballyhoo and complaints about the price of tickets which allowed the holder entry to a massive barn, therein to observe the brothers like so many fireflies on the distant horizon. In every respect, a Pyrrhic Victory.

The recent successes of the above three artists have led many to follow in their direction and this has prompted the first serious debate in the American trade press on the vexed question, "Whither Soul?". And believe me, brothers and sisters, if the largely pusillaminous US trades become the stage for a polite row then there are assuredly questions that need answering. The debate has two main themes. The black radio stations are moaning because the artists whom they support and nurture in their early days chase the white pop-rock market, "deny their roots" when they get a sniff of the big greenbacks and produce records almost solely for the white stations. Their singing becomes less infused with powerful emotional commitment, the arrangements are laced with ugly heavy metal guitar riffs, and the songs tailored for an accompanying video to be aired on white-aimed MTV, access to which is possible via the aforementioned vulgar axe solo. The artists, not without reason, complain that this is a form of censorship, that they should be able to make whatever music they please in order to appeal to as many people as possible and, later, for culture and tradition. The smart ones, of course, can have their cake and eat it.

Take the former Earth, Wind & Fire singer Philip Bailey (I say former because EWF seem to have ceased operations). He cut an enormously commercial pop-rock LP with Phil Collins – the eminently forgettable *Chinese Wall* with its number one pop hit, 'Easy Lover'. Yet he's also able to satisfy those who prefer less production-line music with the infinitely preferable gospel album *The Wonders Of His Love*, a fine collection of self-produced pop-soul gospel tracks rather in EWF mould.

In fact, it's in gospel that a good fifty per cent of the year's best "soul" singing has been heard. Considering the proportion of gospel to soul records released, this is a high percentage. Remarkably, gospel records (lyrics aside) are, like Bailey's, almost indistinguishable from secular pop-soul recordings. Al Green continues to produce splendidly sung records, but perhaps the biggest ear-opener was an LP by the New Jersey Community Gospel Choir, a mighty host with a handful of outstanding solo singers and an ear for very commercial pop songs with a religious burr – 'Time After Time', 'Someday We'll All Be Free', 'Shine A Light', 'Yah Mo Be There'.

The growing interest in gospel – even among heathens – has also meant increased availability of essential archive recordings. Excellent, rousing compilations such as

● *AL GREEN*

● *PHILIP BAILEY*

ALEXANDER O'NEAL

Charly's *Jesus Is The Answer* and MCA's double LP *Black Gospel*, vinyl companion to Viv Broughton's fascinating and well-illustrated book on the subject, plus two or three TV documentaries formed the basis of an unexpected abundance of material now available on this magnificently expressive type of singing.

Although Prince remains the figurehead of the large group of distinctive and gifted musicians and singers to emerge (in his wake) from the city of Minneapolis, two writers and producers have unequivocably done as much for the city's musical reputation. Jimmy Jam and Terry Lewis were, respectively, keyboard-player and bassist with Flyte Tyme, a local band that Prince moulded, with personnel changes, into Time. When it became clear that they'd have little opportunity to write or produce for their own band, Jam/Lewis quit and began writing and producing what now amounts to one of the most impressive bodies of work, in their market, in the past three years. Change, the S.O.S. Band, Thelma Houston and, most recently, Alexander O'Neal have all benefited from Jam/Lewis's complete understanding of the ballad and from their sensitive awareness of the possibilities offered by modern studio technology and the latest instrumentation. In their use of synthesizers and synthetic drum machines, Jam and Lewis have few peers today. They also excel at annoying neighbours – their bass lines do not stop at rattling the odd window pane but actually loosen floorboards, dislodge plaster and cause bricks to crumble.

JENNY BURTON

O'Neal was one of two hugely promising men singers to emerge this past year. A former singer with Jam/Lewis's Flyte Tyme (he was removed to make way for Prince protégé Morris Day in Time), O'Neal has a rich, caressing vocal tone which has been compared to an imposing array of soul singers at the light tenor end of the range. The year's other major find, whose voice is more "standard" in soul terms, is Glenn Jones. His *Finesse* is a wonderfully consistent set of catchy and commercial tunes and in the next three or four years he'll develop into a singer of considerable class.

FREDDIE JACKSON

JOANNA GARDNER

Much the same is also expected of Freddie Jackson whose *Rock Me Tonight* was a heavily promoted album. He, again, is obviously a singer of great ability, but the material he is given is not top quality and he shows a certain lack of restraint – several of the vocal performances seem to be crying "Look how clever I am" instead of just concentrating on getting the song's message across. Maybe he feels he has something to prove after several years as a background singer for others.

There weren't too many women singers who made a first-time-out impression but Jenny Burton sounds to have potential, and Philly World, one of the most consistent labels of the period, launched Joanne Gardner, a good vocalist.

GLEN JONES

Each year produces artists near the "veteran" end of the soul spectrum who make unexpected and welcome comebacks. High on that list is Thelma Houston whose *Qualifying Heat* re-established her after a long fallow spell. It seems almost superfluous to add that the first side of the LP was written by the ubiquitous Jam/Lewis and by Monte Moir, another old Timer and former Flyte Tyme player. It's rare that a singer or group can recut a classic pop-soul tune and convince the listener that it hasn't been a totally wasted exercise but the Manhattans, another long-time-no-see act, turned up with a very fine reading of Sam Cooke's 'You Send Me', a highlight of their *Too Hot To Stop It* LP.

In an era when synthetic instrumentation of all types proliferate, it's always good to be reminded that the most perfect instrument ever evolved is the human voice. This the classic close-harmony quartets and quintets such as the Manhattans, the Temptations and the Four Tops frequently do, and even more so the acapella group the Persuasions. Their theme tune, 'Still Ain't Got No Band', was featured on their Rounder album *No Frills*, picked up for the UK by Demon. That label also released, through the same deal, an extraordinary

THELMA HOUSTON

double live album by Solomon Burke recorded back in 1981 at a club in Washington. It exhibits the R&B, soul, gospel, ballad and preachin' strands of the singing of one of the genre's genuises.

We had for some while been waiting for Luther Vandross, perhaps the greatest find of the eighties to top his 1981 debut *Never Too Much*. With 1985's *The Night I Fell In Love* he did it. A great and lasting achievement, it's a collection at once possessing the sophisticated gloss of contemporary production values, the deeper, darker sensuality of another era's ballad singing and exuberant pop singing.

Bobby Womack, after two Beverly Glenn LPs, attempted to extricate himself from the label amid the not entirely unexpected confetti of writs. The label also dashed out what sounds like an album of tracks he considered not quite good enough for *Poet* and *Poet II*, though *Someday We'll All Be Free* does have some good moments. Bobby also guested on Crusader Wilton Felder's *Secrets* album, his vocal on '(No Matter How High I Get) I'll Still Be Lookin' Up To You' being one of the very few memorable moments on a singularly dull record.

● *BOBBY WOMACK*

● *THE MANHATTANS*

Speaking of out-takes, the residue of Marvin Gaye's vinyl estate has been too long in appearing. The CBS set *Dream Of A Lifetime* was culled half from work in progress at the time of his death and half from tracks which had been gathering dust at Motown for many years. His latest work – especially the edited single 'Sanctified Lady' plus 'Savage In The Sack' and 'Masochistic Beauty' – revealed his determination to pursue the physical and sexual side of his writing which stretches back through *Sexual Healing* to *Let's Get It On*. But now he was taking it to even more controversial, er, lengths, if you'll pardon an innuendo of which Gaye would surely have approved, judging by the last songs he wrote. For purer evidence of his greatness as a singer, however, we must wait for the album of standards said to be scheduled for release.

● *LUTHER VANDROSS*

On stage, Chaka Khan's London show – after the success of her *I Feel For You* album – was an unmitigated disaster, her throat so painfully shredded she seemed scarcely able to speak let alone sing. Tina Turner, also suffering from flu, overcame her illness triumphantly in a typically vigorous performance. Both women, incidentally, now sport backing bands that owe far more to American AOR acts in terms of sound and presentation than they do to Rufus or the Ike & Tina Turner Revue.

Despite several important changes in personnel, Maze featuring Frankie Beverly were again an unqualified gas on stage. Superb ensemble playing (perhaps the only fault being gaps left by the loss of keyboard player Philip Woo), Beverly's honeyed high tenor and the marvellous rapport he's created with his following made his shows just about the best of the year – and not for the first time.

Woo, in fact, turned up as part of the classy backing band put together by Ashford & Simpson, celebrating 'Solid', their biggest hit. A kind of rousing slogan of a song (almost the pop-soul equivalent of a Slade chant sung with great gusto), it's a far less subtle piece of work than their best writing – 'Send It', 'Is It Still Good To Ya?' – but forms an entirely appropriate salute to their marital and musical successes.

● *THE TEMPTATIONS*

And, finally, what of the UK scene? Well, the apparent inability of any black British artist to build a consistent, developing career only reinforces the oft-repeated criticism that British recording companies are either totally disinterested in the continuous well-being of black acts (normally signed for only one or two singles) or genuinely don't know how to develop these careers. Junior and David Grant have justly been very vocal about this subject at every opportunity. And *they're* the luckier ones, being both articulate and not untalented.

● *DAVID GRANT*

● *THE PERSUASIONS*

On the British scene perhaps the most effective, useful and enjoyable aspect of the past twelve months has been the continuance, despite harrassment by police and licensing agencies, of the specialist pirate radio stations such as JFM, Horizon and Solar, which have all been on my dial far more frequently than Radio 1 or Capital. The DJs may have some of that wordy conceit associated with national or 'pro' jocks, but at least they sound as though they truly like the records.

Geoff Brown

■ THE YEAR IN REGGAE

This past year saw few startling changes on the reggae scene. Electronics – hinted at in the early seventies – were responsible for the biggest single difference in sound, but many producers, Jamaican and English, merely used them to add another dimension to the same old rhythms that have been the staple diet of reggae fanciers since time immemorial.

The single biggest electro reggae record was Wayne Smith's 'Under Me Sleng Teng', an original produced by Prince Jammy in Jamaica, using only synthesizers. This one rhythm led to a spate of versions, starting in February/March and continuing unabated even as I write. Prince Jammy alone now reckons to have around a hundred cuts.

Veteran Jamaican producer Bunny Lee turned up in the UK in late '84, quickly latched onto the electronics craze and is currently turning out tunes at an alarming rate using just a trio of studio staff, none of whom have been involved in reggae before. Bunny's even had old stars working in the new format while they've been in the country – Dennis Brown, Leroy Smart, Dave Barker, Horace Andy and Sugar Minott are a handful that spring to mind. This year has also seen him reissuing large chunks of his back catalogue, and compilations have been forthcoming from the likes of Johnny Clarke, Jackie Edwards, Delroy Wilson and others.

Another old time Jamaican producer, Phil Pratt, also settled in the UK for the time being, releasing new material with local bands backing both established and new artists, and of course, reissuing past glories. The biggest part, naturally, belongs to mainman Clement 'Coxsone' Dodd, whose Studio One outlet produced what must rank as the largest and most consistently satisfying collection of music ever, from the fifties up to the present day. The resurgence in popularity of his productions and rhythms has meant that even more of his classic singles have been reissued. He's also released unforgettable albums of material that should have seen the light of day years ago – an Alton Ellis *Showcase*, a "new" Wailing Souls set, *Soul And Power*, and *Presenting Larry Marshall*, gems each one. People are still willing to pay out for original pressings of his work, because of the sheer quality and originality, even though many are terribly pressed and virtually unplayable. Heartbeat Records, an established company in the US, has been responsible for the collation and issue of two murderous Studio One compilations albums that *are* up to today's audiophile standards.

Originality is still not, unfortunately, the byword for reggae. Filching lyrics and rhythms has been going on for years in the reggae scene, but this year, with "dance hall" music supposedly "carrying the swing", has been worse than many others. The "dance hall" craze has spurred an ever-growing glut of new format singers, and few do more than just go in and chant over a rhythm with off-the-cuff lyrics. Producers, particularly in Jamaica, are content to continue in this way because it's so much cheaper than hiring musicians and studio time to lay down new music. George Phang, for example, who took over the Powerhouse outlet from the riddim twins Sly and Robbie, has had just about every vocalist – from relative newcomers such as Michael Palmer, Frankie Paul *et al*, to established artists like Sugar Minott and Barrington Levy – jumping on the same set of tracks, but the exciting buzz he generated at his outset peaked around Christmas. Michael Palmer's 'Lick Shot', which took Jamaica by storm in the summer of '84, and Barrington Levy's *Money Move* LP, epitomize the finer aspects of Phang's craft.

The long-established Sugar Minott had a massive run of material on the market, due in some part to the producers' habit of hanging onto recordings until the artist is hot, but also down to the fact that Sugar works so rapidly. Once Sugarmania was on, there was no stopping it, and although much of the material was merely in the dance hall vein, he still lent the genre an air of quality, and sometimes humour. What did one of the more versatile performers think of dance hall and his part in it? "Modern music – dance hall style – you don't want to hear that next year. Some of the songs that I've done, I know they'll only last, say, five months, but there are others that *will* sell for a long time." He knows that it's instant music, but there's some music you do for love, and some for money. Dance hall spells immediate returns. Strange that his Wackie's-produced 'International Herb' did little, but when recut in a dance hall style, over a Sly 'n' Robbie electroid cut of a well known rhythm, 'Heavenless', did well as 'Herbman Hustling' . . .

That pair, Jamaica's rhythmic heroes, don't look like stopping for anything. Sly and Robbie, now in demand all over the world – they've even played with Dylan! – still manage to keep up the session work in Jamaica, appearing on a sizeable quantity

● *WAILING SOULS*

● *FRANKIE PAUL*

● *SLY AND ROBBIE*

of releases. Their pet project Black Uhuru – of whom they'd taken the unprecedented step of calling themselves members – split just before Christmas and failed to play the Superjam festival in Jamaica. Michael Rose had apparently gone his own way, and the guessing game was on for a replacement. The name of former Uhuru-ite Don Carlos was mentioned, but in March it was announced that Junior Reid – ex-vocalist with Voice Of Progress and a massive dance hall star in his own right thanks to a succession of popular releases – was the new man. June '85 brought recorded evidence of the revamped group, 'Fit You Haffe Fit', dance hall style, with a touch of class and plenty of clout!

The second album of Sly 'n' Robbie's other protégé, Ini Kamoze, didn't quite live up to the expectations of the first and failed to ignite the reggae world. It shows the continuing musical policy of Island to cut down on the "minority" aspect of the music, to concentrate only on material that is guaranteed to be accepted by the mass record-buying public. That invariably means it must be stamped in the Sly 'n' Robbie mould, and usually remixed in a fashionably splendid manner by Island's inhouse man Paul 'Groucho' Smykle.

On the subject of Island records (the original outlet for Caribbean music), Lee Perry – the producer responsible for exciting new music in the sixties and seventies, and now much of a collector's area – came to the UK in the autumn of '84 with a new album, *History, Mystery And Prophecy*, and immediately caused a rumpus in the press by making libellous accusations against Island supremo Chris Blackwell. Could it have had anything to do with Island's refusal to release the album in this country? The passing of time saw Perry recording – at the Mad Professor's Ariwa studio – and releasing a vicious personal jab at Blackwell, 'Judgement In A Babylon', which was available only for a short time before being withdrawn. No reasons were given, but you may draw your own conclusions.

Another event which caused a furore was Jimmy Cliff's return to the UK for a benefit show at London's Crystal Palace Bowl to help raise money for Nelson Mandela and other political prisoners of South Africa. Cliff almost didn't get to go onstage because there were objections to him having played SA. He had to make a statement, onstage, explaining his actions to a hushed audience before he was permitted to perform for the cause.

There were benefits, too, of a different order. Once the blinkered public were fully awakened to the fact that an entire nation was dying, things started getting done. Bob Geldof's Band Aid project made millions for the starving, and not long afterwards came the reggae benefit records and shows. In Jamaica, a group of artists came together – various members of Third World, Steel Pulse, Rass Brass, I-Threes, Freddie McGregor, Triston Palma, Edi Fitzroy, Gregory Isaacs, Mutabaruka, Brinsley from Aswad, and others – under the collective blanket of Music Is Life to record 'Land Of Africa', which topped London's Capital Radio's phone-in, Hitline, after only one play!

The UK followed suit, with over two hundred musicians and singers coming together under the umbrella of British Reggae Artists Famine Appeal (BRAFA) to record the stirring 'Let's Make Africa Green Again', organized, written and co-ordinated by veteran vocalist Gene Rondo, and the UK's longest-reigning harmony group, the Blackstones. Though the song was recorded in one day in February, with everybody giving their services free, it was not until two months later that the record, after overdubs and final mixing, hit the streets, and by then it was up against the USA For Africa's 'We Are The World' effort. A shame, because with similar promotion it could have been a massive seller.

Various former 2-Tone stars also came together with the Pioneers to re-record an old hit of theirs, 'Starvation', with the good cause in mind. It's heartening to see so many selfless musical artists. Popular music seems to be the only art form willing to donate its services in this way.

On the DJ front, after the success of Phillip 'Papa' Levi's 'Mi Go Mi King', UK MCs (as they are now known) took the country by storm – although Levi failed to come up with anything nearly as strong. Smiley Culture, who had caused minor ripples in the national charts with his 'Cockney Translation', made it right to the top with his side-splitting follow up, 'Police Officer', accompanied, as records are obliged to be, by a video – albeit one put together on a shoestring budget. Fashion, the South London label that produced the Smiley goods, went from strength to strength with their distinctive sound and good business sense, specializing in the new breed of MC.

Greensleeves, the UK's largest independent reggae label, also took the plunge and launched a label specifically for UK MC's, UK Bubblers. First signings were Tippa Irie, Daddy Colonel, and Rusty from Saxon Studio International sound system – currently considered to be the hottest sound around and who, incidentally, made their first trip to the States, for a successful short tour, earlier in '85.

One of the UK's longest-established sound systems, Sir Coxsone Outernational, also became heavily involved in the production of music, with some highly essential items released through their own S.C.O.M. outlet.

For the Jamaican DJs – always considered a cut above the English b'woys because *they* were the originators – things didn't look so good. Although Jamaican DJs were still popular at home and in the States, and on "yard" tapes, everyone wanted to hear and buy all these new styles that were from

● *BLACK UHURU*

● *GREGORY ISAACS*

● *JIMMY CLIFF*

Britain's own backyard. Albino DJ Yellowman, who sold out on his first UK trip, must have been very disappointed with the turnout on his return – he was definitely last year's flavour, if not the year before's. Jamaican DJs that have managed to pull through the sticky patch are the ones with strong lyrics – Early B, Charlie Chaplin and General Trees are three of the choicest and are currently doing well.

Frankie Paul – very much in the Dennis Brown vocal mould and voted most promising newcomer of '84 by the *Jamaican Rockers* magazine – finally released his excellent debut album, *Strange Feelings*, after a wait of months and months; then we were suddenly swamped on all sides by Frankie Paul product. That other promising youth, Michael Palmer, suffered a similar case of over-exposure, though his natural talents will hopefully help him ride such patches.

Frankie's first visit to the UK was very successful, due to the promotion that the organizers, Capital Radio, put behind it and his show's live broadcast, but his second trip in April '85, after being 'Americanized' by new American tour managers, ended in an anti-climax at Brixton's Academy. The teenybopper image of the two dancing and singing girls flanking Frankie Paul plainly didn't match up to the rootsy picture most had of him.

English reggae in general developed faster than Jamaican produced material, because this is the one place where risks *are* still willing to be taken; there is so much more fusion of varying musical styles. Most of the established UK bands, such as Black Roots, Jah Warriors, Misty In Roots, and the Natural Ites and Realistics, are still delivering original material, and small independent producers and labels do often try to come up with new music, but it's usually quickly smothered or forgotten.

The Mad Professor, best known for his bizarre dub albums that get progressively more histrionic and electronic, even moved into the dance hall arena in '85, but is now utilizing artists in his recording stable to cover others' hits. 'Country Living' – formerly by the Stylistics – from Sandra Cross is a good example of the Professor's latter-day work (if indeed anything of his can be considered typical enough to be an example!)

Soul/funk is having a great deal of influence on reggae, and more and more artists and producers have been turning to that format for local hits. The Investigators' 'Woman I Need Your Loving' just missed scoring nationally last summer, and One Blood's 'Get In Touch' actually hit the lower end. Shinehead, a new name, appeared with one rocking yard style cut of Michael Jackson's 'Billie Jean' – that didn't quite make it, but long-time local success Trevor Walters *did*, with his interpretation of Lionel Richie's 'Stuck On You'. He failed with a national follow up – he's now signed to Polydor – and seems stuck in limbo between being an "ethnic" artist and a nationwide star. Winston Reedy, former Cimaron, made a big splash with the crisp 'Baby Love' – under the auspices of keyboard ace Jackie Mittoo – but the involvement of UB40's DEP Records didn't give it the necessary impetus to push it that bit further. Mikey Dread, one time dread folk hero, also released with DEP, but the reggae market didn't want to know – he's changed his style – and the others just weren't interested. As always.

Mid '84 brought the first rumblings of a great original singer and band, Maxi Priest and Caution, who, a mere year later, were to wow UK Sunsplash '85 with their high energy. From the same London origins as Phillip Levi, working on Saxon sound, Maxi Priest is an individual singer in this world of plagiarism, and after four progressively improving hits on the reggae market – 'Hey Little Girl', 'Sensi', 'Throw Me Corn', and the culminating 'Should I' – he was signed to Virgin's 10 Records. The first album, *You're Safe*, looks poised for world-wide success; live, Maxi and Caution are invincible.

Aswad – always with the distinction of being the English Lions of reggae – released a remarkably thin version of Toots and the Maytals classic, '54-46 Was My Number', followed by a patch album, *Rebel Souls*, which found them looking ever more to a widening rock-orientated audience. As sessioners, though, they are second to *none*. Stateside, Aswad were taken to the people's hearts, as Steel Pulse continue to be. What kind of situation is it that forces groups like these to go to the US, and virtually live there?

Still Stateside . . . producer Jah Life – who does most of his work at Long Island's HC&F Studio when he's not running backwards and forwards to Jamaica and England – has been one of the main single forces from America, judging by sheer number of releases. The most interesting sound coming from the US has to be Wackie's. Based in the Bronx, their unique mixes have been used to brain-curdling effect in the past, and with many dedicated and hard working people, their name is slowly spreading. They are now established in the UK, and though releases have been few and far between this last year has seen some high quality material become available, commencing with the release of Sugar Minott's *Wicked Ago Feel It*.

RAS Records, based in Washington, managed to get their product into major record retailers, and are becoming more and more potent with a strong duty roster of artists led by Freddie McGregor, Michigan & Smiley, and the Studio One Band. Japan and Central America are just two of the areas they've won over with their crack squad.

Alton Ellis – a classic singer through Coxsone Dodd and Duke Reid days – celebrated his Silver Jubilee in true style with some magnificent shows in the US and UK, and a pair of albums issued to mark the occasion. Alton, alongside the likes of

• *MAXI PRIEST*

• *YELLOWMAN*

• *ASWAD*

other seasoned singers John Holt and Pat Kelly, still earns the respect of the younger ones for keeping the flag flying over the years.

Of the other established artists, Dennis Brown has been making hits aimed specifically for the "roots" market this year, with little acknowledgement to the soul/funk crossover set at which his A&M material is directed. He teamed up in early '85 with Gregory Isaacs to record the duet 'Let Off Sup'm', which showed Gregory in a firmer mood than much of his recent material. The self-styled Cool Ruler has also had localized success with the kind of material the ladies love him for. The occasion of his formal release from custody prompted the very strong *GP* – detailing the indignities of prison life – but by mid '85, rumours of his incarceration abounded once more, again on drugs-related charges. He was out, though, in time for Sunsplash '85, when he performed to an expectant and receptive crowd.

Barrington Levy, long on the lips of those who like their music hot, broke loose to acquaint himself with a larger audience. After a good return year on the local scene – he's now living in the UK – his 'Under Me Sensi' for producer Jah Screw became almost an underground anthem, and the follow-up 'Here I Come' shot him through those local airwaves to land squarely in the national Top Hundred. London Records signed him up in January after weeks at the top of the reggae chart, but nothing much has happened since. The single went no higher, and the subsequent 'Give Me Your Love' – very jerky and unlikely to get the national toes tapping – was relegated to the flip of a recut of an earlier success for George Phang, 'Money Move'. Such is life! We wait on the album.

Jah Screw, one-time operator for the late Ray Symbolic Jamaican sound system, did particularly well production-wise. After just a few releases on his own Time label of which 'Under Me Sensi' became a biggie, he went on to produce some other scorchers with the likes of Frankie Paul, Dennis Brown and, just at the close of this musical year, came up with a fabulous cover of Teddy Pendergrass' 'Turn Off The Lights', with Leroy Smart vocalizing.

The biggest musical event of '85 should have been the GLC's Easter Reggae Festival at London's South Bank – with stars of the calibre of Jennifer Lara, Edi Fitzroy, Earl 16, Sassafras and a host of others – but due to bad organization and promotion, it only served to reinforce the reasons for reggae's lack of national potency. Eventually, the title "event" went to UK Sunsplash '85, where good music filled the air for eight hours. So successful are the Sunsplash ventures that a yearly European tour seems most likely.

But unfortunately, everything comes back to airplay – records cannot sell without people hearing them first. Pirate radio stations, particularly in London, have played an important part in getting the music to the people. The original Dread Broadcasting Corporation seemed to disappear altogether, unable to keep up with Home Office raids, but Miss P was recruited from their ranks to run the BBC's first national reggae show! Tucked away late Sunday night, and only for an hour, it's at least a start. Solar, Horizon, JFM, LWR and other pirates played cat and mouse with officialdom but too often were caught and had everything confiscated. Unlike DBC, some of them have been and still are back on the air intermittently, because they run commercials and can so afford to lose a certain amount. For how much longer, though?

Community radio stations have now been given Government go-ahead, but quite what form they are to take and how it will affect the airing of reggae is not yet known. On the official airwaves, David Rodigan from Capital Radio was once again acknowledged top dog, but after continuing harassment and threats from producers, artists and their friends for not playing their records, he decided to stem the tide of pressure and abuse. He said on air that he would no longer be pressured into playing "rubbish" that wasn't fit to be heard . . . a difficult situation.

So, while reggae is watered down to form the basis for TV commercials and pale, imitative pop hits, the "minority" market carries on as usual, with the occasional glimpse of nationwide status for artists lucky enough to get the right promotion and exposure. Every year people prophesy that next year is going to be the year when reggae breaks international, because this year was so close. Every year . . .

Simon Buckland

● *TIPPA IRIE AND DADDY COLONEL*

● *SMILEY CULTURE*

● *INI KAMOZE*

● *BRITISH REGGAE ARTISTS FAMINE APPEAL*

THE YEAR IN

HIP-HOP

Forget, for a moment, all the clubs and DJs and rappers and producers and crucial import 12″ singles. To spot what was happening in hip hop this year, all you had to do was watch the ads. With inane regularity, every time a commercial break came rolling round, there they were: cartoon skinheads breakdancing their way out of breakfast cereal packets; old men blithely backflipping in the street after a shot of the beer which refreshes the parts others don't reach; robot-dancers jerking excitedly around high-tech hi-fi systems; garishly-hued computer-generated figures body-popping the praises of some brand of blue jeans; lithe young bodies smurfing to show off a collection of designer sportswear; nice young women feeling so damn liberated after an invigorating squirt of deodorant that they just had to get up there and then and start spinning on their foreheads.

For all the folk at Saatchis and elsewhere, breakdance fever is much like the jogging craze of a few years back: a convenient symbol for youth, vitality and energy. But I catalogue all this not simply as an example of the advertising industry getting things, as usual, subtly but completely wrong. Only two or three years after it began to move out of the Bronx, hip hop has emerged as the only clearly identifiable international youth style of the eighties.

After a host of videos and last year's batch of "breaksploitation" movies, hip hop is now everywhere. This year I've seen white Geordie kids breaking in Newcastle (one of the only major English cities without an Afro-Caribbean community to speak of), Turkish kids breaking in Berlin, Filipino kids breaking in Hong Kong. There were break teams doing half-time displays at football matches where once there were army bands and performing police dogs. There was Prince Charles attempting to smurf on the *Six O'Clock News*. There was, in short, no getting away from it.

Techniques of cutting,scratching, sampling and remixing – all largely imported, however indirectly, from hip hop – continued to be used to spice up scores of pop singles. At times it seemed like no record was complete without it coming in at least three different versions, containing a handful of those overused (but still somehow exciting) orchestral *whoomph* noises and juddering along with a lot of those bi-bi-bi-bi-bits that go like thi-thi-thi-thi-this. Nor, over the Pond, were the stalwarts of American rock above sprinkling a little hip hop fairy dust over their compositions. Even Springsteen, Patron Saint of Rock and the New Authenticity, called in Arthur Baker to furnish the 12″ mix of 'Dancing In The Dark'.

● *RUN D.M.C. AND JAM MASTER JAY*

● *CHAKA KHAN*

● *AFRIKA BAMBAATAA AND THE SOUL SONIC FORCE*

All of which goes to show that we have now indeed arrived at a point where it's almost fatuous to talk about "white" and "black" music at all. One of the main trends in hip hop this year was the drift towards heavy rock. On one side there was Run DMC, a black rap combo who take the stance of "Kings of Rock". On the other side was the Beastie Boys, a trio of white rap punks with an even harder brand of heavy metal hip hop.

Well, children, what does it all mean?

In the technologically wired-up eighties, the sound sampling capabilities of the now nearly ubiquitous Emulators and Fairlights have extended the possibility of cultural plunder to an almost microscopic level – a drum sound here, a guitar part there. The growth in video and communications technology allows new sounds and styles to be beamed ever more rapidly about the globe. Elaborate exercises in crossover logic, like Chaka Khan's pop-soul-disco-hip-hop 'I Feel For You', are used to scurry after bigger and bigger slices of a shrinking world record market. With Wham! in China, Rod Stewart and Queen in Brazil and a white East Ender, Paul Hardcastle, at number one with a home-produced hip hop epic based around a theme from *Tubular Bells* and a cut-up of a documentary about Vietnam, only one thing seems clear: in 1985 there are no longer any absolute boundaries between races, music and styles. Nowhere is this clearer than with hip hop.

In 1982, with Afrika Bambaataa and the Soul Sonic Force's pioneering 'Planet Rock', hip hop began fusing an extensive Afro-American tradition that stretches right back to the griots of West Africa with Japanese video game culture and a tradition of European electronics that can be traced back to the Italian Futurists. The constituency for that record, and the thousands of beat box epics that followed in its wake, was as much white, Italian and Hispanic as it was black. "Demographics" and the complexities thereof were the favourite talking point of the people behind labels like Tommy Boy and it was clear that the melting-pot was being given a refreshingly vigorous stir.

After 'Planet Rock', what had been called "rap" was dubbed instead "electro". But though things steadied for a while, the fusion didn't stop there. So much else is now being picked up, pottered about with and pasted irreverently into the hip hop scrapbook that "electro" has now become a wholly inadequate description. What sense does it make of Afrika Bambaataa collaborating with John Lydon on Time Zone's exceedingly heavy 'World Destruction'? Or Run DMC getting together with Yellowman for a bout of 'Roots Rap Reggae'? Precious little.

The main tendency of the year was to leave European electronics behind and lurch instead into full-tilt heavy rock. The result was that, three years after it moved into the Manhattan mainstream, hip hop often ended up sounding more basic, brutal and joyously crass than ever. Stars at this game were Run DMC, but there were others. Some of the year's best records came from the austere-looking but crazed Def Jam label. Based largely around the work of producer Rick Rubin and featuring artists like the Beastie Boys, Jazzy Jay and MCA and Burzootie, Def Jam recordings are daft, dense, resolutely uncommercial and heavy enough to make Van Halen sound like Simon and Garfunkel. There were also some fine manic moments on the Pop Art label with NYC Cutter's 'D.J. Cuttin', a mad, murky mix of Roxanne Shanté and various heavy metal riffs, standing out.

"Roxanne" was very definitely the fad of the year. A tough young lady who first appeared on UTFO's 'Roxanne Roxanne', she soon began turning up all over the place. Roxanne Shanté came up with 'Roxanne's Revenge'. Roxanne (With UTFO) hit back with 'The Real Roxanne'. Soon the import racks filled up with replies and accusations from Roxanne's Sister, Roxanne's Brother, Roxanne's Parents, Roxanne's Doctor and even Roxanne's Granny, all bashing out the same beat, orchestral stab and clipped stacatto rap.

Runner-up in the fad stakes was the proliferation of human beat boxes, all of whom, of course, claimed to be the original one. Whether the first was in fact Dougé Fresh, or his near-namesake Dougy Fresh, or Darren Robinson from the Fat Boys, I have no idea, but the sound and spectacle of any of them impersonating a DMX was unflaggingly funny and often frighteningly sharp.

The hippest record to have was a bootleg copy of Double D and Steinski's 'Payoff Mix' of G.L.O.B.E. and Whiz Kid's 'Play That Beat Mr DJ'. Winner some time back of a Tommy Boy Mastermix contest, it was a thrilling cut-up of everything from James Brown and the Supremes to Culture Club and Humphrey Bogart, but was never released because of copyright wrangles. This year copies began changing hands at around £40 a time. Whizz Kid, meanwhile, sought fame and fortune with the rather poor pop hip hop of 'He's Got The Beat'.

Commercial success was, however, left largely to Melle Mel who, having rapped the intro to 'I Feel For You' and watched 'White Lines' hang about in the charts for a year or so, went on to have hit after hit. But

● *THE FAT BOYS*

● *GRANDMASTER MELLE MEL*

● *CHUCK BROWN AND THE SOUL SEARCHERS*

● *KURTIS BLOW*

● *REDDS OF REDDS AND THE BOYS*

the best pop hip hop was that provided by producer Ron Dean Miller and his Nuance Featuring Vikki Love outfit. Their two singles, 'Love Ride' and 'Take A Chance' were damn near perfect: hard, exciting, commercial and not entirely without an element of camp, taking up somewhere after Sharon Redd left off. Some of the credit for Nuance must go to the Latin Rascals, Tony Moran and Albert Cabrera – two 19-year-old Puerto Ricans who, for their work with Miller, the Def Jam stable, the Force MDs and others, have to be remixers of the year.

And then there was go-go.

Which was nothing at all to do with hip hop really, being a live hard funk dance craze from Washington DC apparently based almost entirely on a riff from Chuck Brown and the Soul Searchers' '78 classic, 'Bustin' Loose'. Despite some fine cuts from Chuck Brown ('We Need Some Money'), Trouble Funk ('Drop The Bomb'), Redds and the Boys ('Moovin' And Groovin' ') and, the one overlap with hip hop, Kurtis Blow ('Party Time'), all of which were plugged into the hard and extremely danceable beat that is go-go's main distinguishing mark, it was difficult at times to see what all the fuss was about. In Britain it was Authenticists who made the most noise about it: here was *real* black music, none of this juvenile beat box rubbish. Indeed, it is all their guff about go-go "taking the place" of hip hop that leads to it being included here.

Really, the comparison does neither justice. Go-go is a live, functional, jam-length call and response dance music based around certain clubs in Washington DC and is only just beginning to find its feet in the big wide world outside. Hip hop is a whole complex of musics and styles and techniques that is now fully international in aspect and effect and which embraces live performance only as a small part of the whole. While go-go develops into whatever it will, hip hop continues to ask questions: questions about the role of the DJ and the musician, about the relationship between live and recorded music, about the boundaries between white and black musics. It replaces the virtuoso of the instrument with the virtuoso of the turntable or mixing desk. And it treats everything it touches, every text it cuts up with a joyous irreverence that is as funny as the beat is compulsive.

In a way, it's been a thin year for the genre: fewer great records and less exciting moments than the last. To an extent, its absorption into the crasser end of the mass media is killing it off. But as long as people continue to equate political commitment with musical authenticity, to invoke a flagging spirit of rock 'n' roll, to refuse to see that banality is what pop music is all about – and there's been altogether too much of that kind of twaddle this year – then we should continue to treasure hip hop if only because even in it's most politicized moments (and there have been precious few of those this year) it is still so unashamedly, resolutely, and hearteningly trivial. **Dave Rimmer**

THE YEAR IN

ELECTRO

● PHILIP GLASS

● MAN JUMPING

● LAURIE ANDERSON

It was a serious temptation simply to submit the words: STILL NO KRAFTWERK ALBUM, but then the cheats went and re-released the 11-year-old album *Autobahn* mere days before deadline. I wonder if we should bother about them any more; four years after *Computer World*, the *Techno Pop* album is as elusive as ever. So far, spies have only been able to ascertain that, whatever the reasons for the delay, *Techno Pop* has only four, long tracks. A snitch in Dusseldorf did pass on an amusing anecdote, though. The head of their American label, Elektra, flew personally to Dusseldorf to collect a master mix from Kling Klang Studios. Back in New York, he took the sealed package to a meeting of department heads, all eager to hear the album at last: the package was empty. They must have gone out and had a few beers on that one.

After last year's note that you could then buy electronic music in Bejams, it's my bemused duty to report that they have now discontinued the line. The revival of the Guitar has, with a few notable exceptions, sent synthpop packing and left the scene split in two. On one side we have that perennial horde of ninnies who nod gamely along to gimmicky wallpaper merchants (Kitaro, Vangelis, Jarre, most Germans with long hair and/or granny glasses). On the other hand we have the mutants, maniacs and eccentrics who, while hardly comprising polite company, give the genre its impetus. In the middle, of course, there are always the Residents, but this year all they released was the soundtrack from the film *The Census Taker*, a rather cheeky reappraisal of certain themes from the *March Of The Moles* trilogy.

And there was always Laurie Anderson, who released not only a five-album box set of *United States* but a twenty-dollar book of the show, and proved that, after all, there *will* be room for vaudeville on Space Station Number 9. In *United States* she fires off a neat squib about how she went to her record company, Warners, and told them she saw herself in the grand sweep of American humour, Daffy Duck, Roadrunner *et al*, but they replied they were hoping for something a bit more, well, *adult*. Hey, she says, I can adapt! Despite her games with philosophy, linguistics and paranoia, and her quite unalloyed musical experiments, this may be closer to the truth than either she or we realize.

Event of the electronic year – even though this is being written days before it takes the stage, inviting the likelihood that cast and orchestra might be whisked off to the planet Tralfamadore before curtain call – had to be "systems music" composer Philip Glass finally bringing one of his massive operas to Britain. Even though there is only one synthesizer in the orchestra, and that relegated to well down in the "mix", systems music has had such an impact, from the German "school" through the English punk innovators to NY funk and scratch, that a few acoustic instruments shouldn't be allowed to get in our way. From a tape of its American production and a pre-performance run-through, *Akhnaten* is Glass's most sombre work. It is, however, as powerful as either *Einstein On The Beach* or *Satyagraha*, and should see Glass finally, belatedly, established in Britain, which has been alone in the West for the last ten years in resisting the many charms of the man's music.

Glass's influence broke through in what was one of the most exciting arrivals of the year, Man Jumping. Mentioned in their embryonic form last year, they released their first album, *Jump Cut*, on Bill Nelson's Cocteau label, to unanimous acclaim. Spinning off from the late lamented systems orchestra Lost Jockey, they find an almost perfect balance between the exacting structures of systems with the relaxed swing of funk, jazz and ethnic musics. At times it may seem to be too much about "ideas" and less about music, but *Jump Cut* was the healthiest musical pointer of the year.

While there are many contenders for the title, the most interesting label of the year was London's independent Illuminated Records. While the quality of output varied, it chose to position itself at that most dangerous vantage point, on the rim of the dancefloor and at the maw of the avant-garde. The excellent 400 Blows (who fiercely deny having "borrowed" the name from Truffaut), 23 Skidoo, Dormannu, Portion Control and I suppose we'll have to mention Andi Sex Gang, all put out powerful variations on the cocktail of aggressive electronics, gloomy gothic punk and dancefloor carve-up. The label neatly, if rather repetitiously, stated its case with the *Heavy Duty Breaks* album, an album-long scratch/cut-up mix of tracks from the abovementioned and others.

This, if there was a trend or if we have to

invent one, was the only notable motion during the year. For all his polysyllabic sins, if ZTT's Paul Morley left us anything it was proof that Art can be Fun, and vice versa. Look no further than *Stella*, the fourth album from Switzerland's stupendous Yello. They have come a long way from the eccentricities they committed for the Residents' Ralph Records label. Like its predecessor, *You Gotta Say Yes To Another Excess*, *Stella* mixes dizzying dance music – some of it propelled by a thumping Glitterbeat – with some of the most innovative electronics around. Some have called it a sell-out, but the whingers, like the poor, are always with us.

Similarly Cabaret Voltaire, whose *Micro-Phonies* (possibly a pun on Stockhausen's *Mikrophonie*) was a tighter, meaner progression from *Crackdown*. They even named a track after James Brown. In their own radical, subversive way, they have become an institution, but don't tell them I said that.

The desire to dance was noticeable elsewhere. After the blistering *Jam Science*, Shriekback followed it with another, equally blazing album of menacing avant-garde funk, *Oil & Gold*. New Order, on *Low Life*, would have appeared to have gained entry to God's very own blues party (in their lyrics, noticeably the Siegfried Sassoonish wartime love song, 'Love Vigilantes', they also put things straight about their philosophies). Bands as diverse as Australia's excellent Severed Heads (*City Slab Horror*), Sheffield's stunning Hula, Jah Wobble's *Neon Moon* and various exotic European imports all offered up swiping electronic detours from the black American beat. Given that the bulk of it was programmed on Fairlights and their like at the Power Plant NY, Scritti Politti's *Cupid & Psyche 85* – already a serious contender for my album of the year – could be seen as the zenith of this trend.

As for ZTT, they spent the whole year pointing and giggling at us all – business-people, media and punters. While never less than entertaining, Frankie, Propaganda, Art Of Noise, one-time Lost Jockey Andrew Poppy, all seemed founded on a base of cynicism. Propaganda say nothing new of either genre or Germany. Art Of Noise lack the vulnerable heart of their most obvious influence, the Residents, and ultimately are revealed in their bald attempts at playing lego with the innovations of others. Although his first live performances were disastrous, I still hold hopes for Andrew Poppy's debut this autumn.

Much preferable were the small noises made on the sidelines by, to spill a jamboree bag of names, Band of Holy Joy, 1000 Mexicans, Go Fundamental – back and signed to Arista after a few years silence – The Flowerpot Men (whose 'Jo's So Mean' chased the hardest of DAF tracks out of the playground), Non, Fontana Mix (who even named themselves after a Cage piece) and, my personal infatuation of the moment, Startled Insects. This (largely unemployed) Bristol six-piece are a collective of musicians, technicians and film/video workers, who produce the most startling videos on shoestring budgets, and whose music darts between the hot sultry swing of the late Machito's salsa orchestra, the drum sex of Africa and the East and the electronic soundscapes of, again, the Residents. Further recommendation? I've lost count of how many copies of their records (LP: *Startled Insects*; 12", 'Underworld'; both Antenna Records via the Cartel) people have stolen from me.

While thin on the ground, the harbingers of doom and gloom were also still with us. The riotous Einsturzende Neubauten contented themselves with just one 12", 'Yu-Gung', more of which elsewhere. While earlier in the year London's Test Dept. had released their debut *Beating The Retreat* box set, they spent most of the year throwing themselves whole-heartedly into working to support the miners' strike. The vision of a group of young South Londoners stripped to the waist in preparation for work at their musical foundry finding any sort of welcome in the coalfields raised a cynical smile in more than one observer. Yet they did it, touring northern and southern coalfields and playing benefits for what must have been thousands of bemused but grateful miners and families. The project produced a collaboration between Test Dept and the South Wales Striking Miners Choir, the album *Shoulder To Shoulder*, which alternated TD's apocalyptic metal-bashing with the choir's own repertoire and featured a duet between both sides. They avoided elitist London audiences, returning only to play the "Convention of Hysteria", where avant-garde American banshee Diamanda Galas curdled the blood while TD's usual battery of hammers, drums, coils and metal sheets was augmented by a massive industrial water tank, suspended from the ceiling of the Albany Empire like a giant metal whale and beaten with hammers until the whole building shook. Extraordinary.

If grim has become passé, it's because few people listen to their cries of "wolf" any more, much like those quaint religious sects who rush up the nearest hillside once or twice a year to avoid the flood. Foetus, in all his incantations (On Your Breath/On The Wheel/Over Frisco), kept a scabrously high profile, and the reclusive Biting Tongues provided a splendidly eerie soundtrack (and album) to the film, *Feverhouse*. The real saving grace from the charnel house, however, was Coil.

● *THE RESIDENTS*

A duet of performance artist John Balance (aka Geoff Rushton, editor of the seminal grimzine, *Stabmental*) and Peter 'Sleazy' Christopherson, late of Throbbing Gristle and Psychic TV, their debut album, *Scatology*, on Force & Form/K.422, reduced all earlier manifestos from TG/PTV and their spin-offs to mute silence. On paper their manifesto might seem just another ride on the old Heart Of Darkness routine – but on vinyl it was something altogether different: high technology used to produce anything from violent metallic funk to quicksands of electronic noise to Persian-sounding skirls and medieval fanfares. Disturbing, certainly, but I have not heard so successful an experimental album in some time.

And finally, Song from a Soapbox. The year saw the first visit to Britain from American composer Conlon Nancarrow, Nancarrow has spent the bulk of his career writing for the player-piano. His pieces, averaging five minutes in duration and taking a year to stamp on to piano rolls, shame systems music, free electronics, improvised jazz and scratch trickery in their maverick invention. Conlon Nancarrow is *seventy-three* . . .

John Gill

■ THE YEAR IN JAZZ

Jazz? There's really no such thing, not now. Ask any jazz musician.

But because nothing suitable's come along to replace it – to reflect with any accuracy the mutations undergone by what was once played by Oliver, Armstrong, Parker and Coltrane – we still call all these musics "jazz". So for jazz, it was a good and a bad time, like it always is. A very few musicians found huge exposure, some did comfortably, most scuffled, and most listeners couldn't decide what to listen to. The jazz fan is always spoilt for choice: you have to seek it out to start with, and once you've gone that far you can go anywhere.

In the summer of '84 it was still (as it had been the previous year) two trumpet players scrapping for a king's throne. The old guvnor, Miles Davis, was playing his best music for years, fronting a touring band that seemed to revive most of his interest in creating; the young no-pretender, Wynton Marsalis, released a flabby LP with strings but continued to electrify the world jazz audience and make inroads into the larger crowd outside through brazen coolness of style (those Italian suits!) and statement. Just as Miles himself once did.

The most striking alteration in jazz, wrought by its ceaseless and confusing change, is the loss of titular leadership. Fans love to zero in on heroes, but jazz heroes have been hard to find for twenty years: hence the rush to chair Marsalis. On and off the stand, he is obviously a brilliant young man, interested as much in European classical music as in his own jazz tradition. Yet his criticisms of figures like Davis and Herbie Hancock over their commercial attitudes are at once refreshing and faintly irritating. Because, if anything, Marsalis' music is less than a giant step forward. He insists that he plays "no be-bob licks", but the timbre of his music is conservative beside that of Edward Wilkerson, Roscoe Mitchell and Leo Smith – players whose public profiles lag far behind the importance of their music.

Nevertheless, Marsalis held centre stage throughout '84 and the first half of '85. Musicians were working, but there was a paucity not only of new stars but of new music altogether. As pop grew ever more shabbily cosmetic, a whiff of wider recognition made its periodic stopover in the house of jazz. And record companies began looking in their vaults again: the chief

● *WYNTON MARSALIS*

feature of this year was the rash of jazz reissues. Well, it's cheaper than paying for new records.

The major showing came with the relaunch of Blue Note, the coolest and most distinguished of jazz labels, bossed now by Bruce Lundvall and masterminded by Michael Cuscuna. Original sleeves and high quality pressings maintained the integrity of the first batch of reissues in the spring of '85, although the initial "new" issues suggested that Lundvall is still looking at a jazz easy-listening market.

A couple of Lundvall's signings are particularly instructive in the struggle between jazz and commerce. Stanley Jordan, a young guitarist, is an intensely gifted player with an armful of new, revolutionary techniques: his *Magic Touch* debut brims with technically dazzling music that sounds like the work of three or four players instead of one. Yet the material, including 'Eleanor Rigby' and vaporously pretty themes like 'The Lady In My Life', cashes this fine musician's meal ticket in the *Songs For Horizontal Lovers* account.

Blue Note has also picked up Charles Lloyd, the saxophonist who nearly broke as a superstar in the Summer Of Love and found himself disastrously beached a season later. There's something approaching pathos in the attempts to rehabilitate Lloyd: he is the Donovan of his field. On strictly musical terms there are many saxophonists who more fully deserve his exposure; but Lloyd's one sniff at success lingers in company minds.

● *MILES DAVIS*

Blue Note's reissues, though, were just part of a bonanza. From RCA came records drawn from Prestige, Riverside, Fantasy, New Jazz, Debut and Jazz Workshop; and now the entire Contemporary catalogue, a pristine archive of West Coast music, is due to reapperar. EMI sifted through their oldest classics, Armstrong, Ellington and Bix Beiderbecke. *The Cotton Club* provoked a flash of interest in Harlem dance music. One requires a very deep wallet to keep pace with the flood.

The unfortunate side of this activity is its neglect of contemporary music. America and Europe alike are full of powerful jazz voices that have to settle for deals with small independent labels. Those few musicians who had garnered a major label deal felt a sudden chill: guitarist James Blood Ulmer was dismissed by CBS, the company which has made the great saxophonist Arthur Blythe resort to making a mundane funk record. If old jazz is cool again, the modern beast is still considered dangerously unprofitable.

Live music – and jazz has always been a live music at heart – has found itself bound up in a similar dilemma. Dissatisfied with the small returns from a hard core of faithful followers, promoters throughout Europe bring visiting stars in bundles to wow crowds with their weight in reputation (gee! All those guys on *one bill*?). Predictably, the music tends towards routine, prepackaged excitement. The festival has displaced the club setting: in Britain, the venerable Ronnie Scott Club survives mainly on a tourist audience. On reflection, it's an inevitable course. With the content of popular music retreating before its visual elements, everyone wants to make jazz more "attractive".

NLEY JORDAN

NNY ROLLINS

In Britain, at least, something nearly happened as a reaction. Clubgoers were regaled with hard bop and Cannonball Adderley's soul-jazz by DJs like Paul Murphy and Gilles Peterson. People were *dancing* to jazz again.

It was even more amazing that these people were young. Every London pirate radio station had its jazz hour; Murphy and Dean Hulme managed to start a jazz-based record label, Paladin; and rock groups like Working Week, Sade and Everything But The Girl flaunted with pride jazz associations like saxophones and rimshots. It was unfortunate that the movement quickly took on the connotations of elitism (which was the charge that, naturally, got levelled at any doubtful voices in the rush back to "real jazz"). Jazz dancing soon became as enclosed as the highest techniques of hip hop, and by this summer the music was taking on the form of a soundtrack – something vaguely cool, and something to enthuse about without ever thinking why. Working Week struck success when they made their LP a soul record; Sade's huge success has come through smart tunes and a languorously pretty voice, not "jazz".

● *LEE MORGAN*

● *BIX BEIDERBECKE*

If some people have genuinely picked up on it, then the cult is justified. But talk of a real revival may have been as premature as it was with Rip Rig And Panic in 1982. As of June, it was hard to see it as much more than an unusually sturdy London club phenomenon. And, in those already immortal words, where does that leave Albert Ayler? Or jazz record sales, which have scarcely been commensurate with media interest? We still wait to see Sonny Rollins in the Top Forty.

Rollins, the saxophonist who's one of the last great heroes of the jazz tradition, visited London this June. His marvellous display of playing stood as a beacon, still, of what jazz is about. This is the key to any fresh interest in the music; and, thankfully, the movement back to jazz does seem to be based on its inherent qualities rather than any nebulous facets of style or sartorial kudos. In hard times, people frequently turn to the music of the dispossessed, and that thread of discontent with the norm is the constancy that spreads through all the avenues of jazz.

Alas, that is also one reason why it stubbornly resists any breakthrough to a wider popularity. If the year was marked by Marsalis, Miles and Murphy, Blue Note and Beiderbecke, it was also tarnished by a British National Jazz Centre that failed to open and a communal tightening of belts on an already thin-waisted family of free music players. The esteemed improvising guitarist Derek Bailey took to playing at London's Bethnal Green library every Saturday; in Connecticut, world music genius Anthony Braxton couldn't even pay his phone bill. It's a global problem. From Russia, the Ganelin Trio visited the West and played out their own thoughts on jazz under heavy manners.

The romantic view that the music needs this kind of sufferation to flourish would be greeted with disgust by the people who actually play it. Jazz will always find things to kick against; and it will always need all the supporters it can get. As a note of optimism, let's run through a few moments from this past year that speak of the living music: Chico Freeman playing the most authoritative, impassioned tenor sax since Rollins' greatest days, followed by the old master doing it for himself; Braxton appearing in London to play a lengthy saxophone piece, forgetting the score and playing the damn thing anyway; teenagers walking into a record shop and asking for something by Hank Mobley; Art Blakey, ageless grandmaster of the drums, spurring his latest Jazz Messengers through their paces; neglected giants like Paul Bley ('Tears') and Don Pullen ('Evidence Of Things Unseen') releasing magnificent records; Sun Ra continuing to implore the world to leave the age of darkness . . .

And how did the year end? With Branford Marsalis, brother of Wynton, appearing on Sting's solo record. Maybe this jazz might catch on, after all. **Richard Cook**

THE YEAR IN HEAVY METAL

Aside from the oft-repeated pub cry of "it's your round", undoubtedly the music industry's fave cliché is: Heavy Metal is dead! If I had a mere £1 for every occasion when this phrase has been mistakenly uttered by *hoi polloi* across showbiz, then . . . well, I'd have retired to the misty haze of the California sunshine/beaches/women eons ago. As it is, I'm here standing in the rain proud an' ready to proclaim that HM is alive an' well, kicking hefty sand dunes into the faces of those trendy, haircut-besotted grandees who would have buried it many mayhemic moons back.

August 1984 stands as that day which firmly cemented just how popular this most dynamic, larger-than-life form of bottled music still remains. On the eighteenth day of that fateful month, Castle Donington played host for the fifth time to the Monsters of Rock Festival. Headlined by the everblue AC/DC (Aussies with a touch of vice and a snatch of steam), the bill also featured the revitalised Van Halen, mega-guitar hero Gary Moore, the indefatigable Ozzy Osbourne, San Francisco quartet Y&T, Germanic gargantuawatt gladiators Accept and that torrential tornado from Los Angeles, Mötley Crüe. Seventy thousand fanatical 'eadbangers firmly entrenched themselves in the Derbyshire mud to celebrate the clash of riffs and the smell of bodily odour from comic-strip inspired guitar duels.

Indeed, 1984 was a good year for the HM hordes, arguably the best since the halcyon days of the late seventies when the world danced to the bullet-rife tune of the New Wave of British HM. However, last year belonged firmly to the LA metal batallions, in particular Mötley Crüe (whose second album, *Shout At The Devil*, was certified double platinum – ie sales in excess of two million –Stateside), Ratt (a quintet fronted by giant blond guitarist Robbin 'King' Crosby and star-studded vocalist Stephen Pearcy, whose first full album on the Atlantic label, *Out Of The Cellar*, hit the same US sales mark) and W.A.S.P. (second generation Poe-esque siblings of Alice Cooper). It was these outfits who led the way from the likes of Twisted Sister (who first broke through in the UK and now have a firmly based platinum history in America), Iron Maiden (consistent sellers in all parts of the world), Sammy Hagar, Krokus and the astonishingly back-from-the-dead Kiss.

The success of these acts was inevitably spurred on in the States by considerable radio/MTV horseplay. The HM bandwagon rolled incessantly on and seemed to throw an almost incredible number of metal/hard rock acts towards the firmament. However, as with every type of so-called "trend", the brake was soon applied. In the case of HM, the spark that led to the ignition of the backlash was the discovery by various radio programmers that despite the high listenership afforded most rock radio shows, nonetheless advertisers, on whom American media outlets primarily rely, were not reaching their primary consumer audience – ie professional females in the 25-35-year-old age bracket who spend fortunes on advertised products. Thus recent months have seen a dramatic move away from hard rock towards softer options. Yet, bands like the Crüe, Ratt, San Francisco quintet Night Ranger and tough German five-piece the Scorpions still continue to sell vast quantities of records in the US.

And, just to keep matters afloat, along came the reformation of the classic early seventies hard-core metal act – Deep Purple. After twelve years of continual conjecture, Ritchie Blackmore (lead guitar), Ian Gillan (lead vocals), Roger Glover (bass), Jon Lord (keyboards) and Ian Paice (drums) joined forces once more to re-enact the glories of Deep Purple Mk II. An album *(Perfect Strangers)* sold well across the globe, whilst the resulting world tour has grossed millions of dollars.

Yet by fleshing out this legend, there's little room for argument that DP have permanently tarnished the fantasy so long associated with that name. They have been demoted to mere mortals. Certainly, the comparatively disappointing attendance at the Knebworth Fayre on 22 June (Purple headlined a bill also featuring the Scorpions, Meat Loaf, UFO, Blackfoot, Mountain plus Mama's Boys and Alaska) suggested that UK HM fans in the mid-eighties do not want to see the past summarily resurrected. Moreover, it also underlined the fact that the following in Britain for traditional/hardcore metal is quantitively stagnant. The likes of Ossy Osbourne, Dio, Kiss, Judas Priest, Iron Maiden plus "newer" heroes such as

● *MÖTLEY CRÜE*

● *RATT*

● *GUIFFRIA*

● *IRON MAIDEN*

Metallica, Venom, Accept, Keel and Grim Reaper will always have a firm 'n' vitally central place in HM, but it's those acts who have learnt to combine age-old values such as powerchord effects trickery with contemporary commercial considerations who have succeeded in "crossing over" to a far wider audience.

The recent British chart impact of Foreigner (a number one single in 'I Want To Know What Love Is', plus a chart-topping album, *Agent Provocateur*) was followed by a tour that sold out such venues as Wembley Arena for three nights. ZZ Top (*Eliminator* has now sold in excess of 500,000 copies in the UK) are the bill-topping act at the 1985 Castle Donington Rock Festival. Bryan Adams (he hit the Top Ten with the single 'Run To You' and followed this with the successful *Reckless* LP) proceeded to establish such a strong live base by touring with Tina Turner that he leapt straight off that tour and on to three SRO nights at London's Hammersmith Odeon. Pat Benatar had hits with 'We Belong' and the re-issued 'Love Is A Battlefield'. Marillion's 'Kayleigh' hit the number two spot and provided enough momentum to put *Misplaced Childhood* straight onto the LP charts in pole position. Former Thin Lizzy cohorts Gary Moore and Phil Lynott joined forces to record the single 'Out In The Fields' – a Top Five earner.

All of the above broke out from established metal-associated roots. Perhaps the band most responsible for opening the majority of eyes world-wide to the way the style, swagger and energy of metal could be combined with modern electronic/synthesized touches was Def Leppard. Their painstakingly constructed '83 LP *Pyromania* showed the way forward; sadly, the band's attempts to provide the waiting world with a suitable follow-up have yet to come to fruition. Indeed misfortune struck last New Year's Eve when drummer Rick Allen lost his left arm in a car crash whilst on his way to Sheffield. Surgical efforts to re-connect the arm failed and, at the time of writing, it's unclear whether he'll ever perform again.

This tragedy was only surpassed by the death (again in a car crash) on 8 December at Redondo Beach, California, of Hanoi Rocks drummer Razzle, a fatality that led in early June to the dissolution of *la* Rocks (a band many thought capable of great things). The driver of the fateful vehicle, Mötley Crüe vocalist Vince Neil, is still living under the haunting spectre of a hefty jail sentence.

Back on the musical path, there's clearly no question that metal is spreading its wings. Even *Kerrang!*, once renowned as "the bible of HM", has evolved/matured in recent months, taking a far more diverse stance in response to the general pattern discernible within the music. The likes of Billy Idol, Tom Petty, Robin George, Billy Squier, Rick Springfield, Lindsey Buckingham and Don Henley have shown in their various manners the way in which a guitar-oriented approach can be dragged into the contemporary arena, a process likely to continue throughout the coming years.

Indeed, the majority of upcoming acts in this sphere all have one thread in common – a respect for melody interwoven with an awareness of modern production techniques. So, just who will be the stars of '85/'86? For a start there's Tarazara (a London-based quintet now managed by the CMO organization, also responsible for Phil Lynott). In their wake will come the likes of Fiona Flanagan (a New Jersey-born vocalist set to usurp Pat Benatar's crown), Rogue Male (a quartet from London very much in the mould of Motörhead), Joe Lynn Turner (former Rainbow vocalist, now a solo artist), Giuffria (formed by ex-Angel keyboardsman Gregg Giuffria), Bon Jovi (a New York-based act who toured the UK with Kiss last year, establishing a sufficient base to return early in '85 as a headlining band), John Parr (Nottingham-born, US-based and of high pedigree) and FM (a London-based quintet). More hardcore fans, meantime, will doubtless soon be swooning to the frenetically furious sounds of Keel, Slayer, Malice, Armored Saint and Warrior – all from the US – plus UK gargantuawatt gansters Savage, Warfare, Waysted, Persian Risk, Tormé and Chariot.

There's no question that HM is entering its most uncertain (and consequently most exciting) phase. The revival of Led Zeppelin and the reformation of the original Black Sabbath for the Live Aid extravaganza were readily watchable *one-off* novelties, but the comparative failure of the Firm (put together in December '84 by ex-Zeppelin guitarist Jimmy Page and former Bad Company/Free vocalist Paul Rodgers) has shown that today's metal fan isn't prepared any more to accept meekly a diet of rehashed past glories. He/she (yes, there are more and more women both playing and enjoying HM music) expects, nay demands, that hard rock conforms to modern attitudes and parameters. This is a lesson that hopefully will be taken to heart by the reunited ELP (featuring keyboards wizard Keith Emerson, bassist/vocalist Greg Lake, plus nomadic drummer Cozy Powell).

Today's heroes *will* inevitably become tomorrow's history lesson. There's always someone to fill a void. The emergence of Ratt and Mötley Crüe has already breached the gap caused by the (apparent) split of Van Halen (as David Lee Roth turns his panoramic personality from vocally fronting VH to the movie world) and the unmasked Kiss respectively. Iron Maiden have long since taken Black Sabbath's "band of the people" crown and even Led Zeppelin have found worthy successors in . . . U2.

Heavy Metal, though, remains the one form of music capable of exaggerating life to the point of ballooning, clowning mirth and of finding a way of combining Chuck Berry, Beethoven, Wagner and Laurel & Hardy. It has no pretensions to change the political map or halt rising poverty, nuclear threats etc. It long ago accepted a raging role as entertainment. Perhaps no act has given more in this laudable pursuit, raising a few smiles and banging a few heads in the process, than the evergreen Motörhead, who recently celebrated ten years of music-hall-associated mayhem. Bassist/vocalist Lemmy is still leading his troops (now boasting Pete Gill on drums plus twin guitarists Phil Campbell and Wurzel) from atop the most torrential hillside in music. And it's when you hear this band pounding into sharp-nail classics like 'Motörhead', 'Bomber', 'Ace Of Spades' *et al* that you realise HM still possesses an extra dimension that is indefinable, inescapable and inestimable. Ah well, *plus ça change, plus c'est la même chose!* **Malcolm Dome**

● *W.A.S.P.*

● *FIONA*

■ THE YEAR IN BLUES & GOSPEL

If I had to trot out a cliché, polish it up and present it as a motif for the events of the past twelve months, I suppose it would be that old favourite, "The Blues Reflect Life". This past year has carried old friends and heroes away, introduced fresh blood, witnessed a landslide of recorded material, a rash of live gigs, a growing awareness of the genre by the media, and the continuing reassessment of the music. In short, a year of lively activity, some of which I welcomed, some of which I could have cheerfully done without.

Any music which exists purely on record can be pronounced dead without too much fear of contradiction, so it's good to report that blues, R&B, soul and gospel are still

● EDDIE C. CAMPBELL

being played in concert halls, clubs, bars and festivals around the world, and that a fair chunk is worthy of attention. From my own vantage point in London, I've witnessed enjoyable performances by Lowell Fulson, Johnny Copeland, Eddie C Campbell (the latter now resident in the UK) and, most especially the Robert Cray Band. If there were a half-dozen artists of Cray's calibre currently working, then the modern blues guitar would be in ridiculously good shape, but he appears to be an original. Two live shows in London and a splendid album helped to inject a freshness into the music that is necessary if we are still to view it as relevant.

While the Guitarist as Hero is the most readily accepted image in contemporary blues, the last few years have seen a steady growth of interest in some previously overlooked areas and therefore it was both a joy and a revelation to see the likes of Big Jay McNeely, Katie Webster, Little Willie Littlefield and Queen Ida receiving attention from critics and fans alike. Gospel music too has broadened its appeal across the world, with the Clark Sisters, Al Green, the Barrett Sisters and, soon, Reverend

● ROBERT CRAY

James Cleveland carrying the message out of the spirit world and on to the concert stage. A good live gospel performance can often produce more energy and emotion than many find comfortable, but the power of the music is undeniable and remains undiminished; as it gains more of a foothold in public consciousness, so it becomes more apparent to a large number of people that black gospel is, in many ways, the *real* roots of contemporary soul and R&B.

Elsewhere, too, the music flourishes. Across the European continent during the last twelve months there have been major festivals, minor gigs, one-day events and tours featuring a wide selection of diverse styles and a liberal cross-section of musicians, the majority of whom have been enthusiastically received. A cynic might tell you too enthusiastically; not *every* performance is that mind-expanding, but often a festival audience will behave as if it were.

Continuing correspondence with *aficionados* in Los Àngeles, New Orleans, Chicago and the East Coast indicates that working musicians are still often doing more than justice to their art. In short, live music is probably much as it always has been, a good number of worthwhile performers, probably an equal helping of the average, and just a few for whom anyone with half an ear should cancel all previous appointments to catch at every opportunity.

One area that reflects a rude vigour is the record industry. New releases appear with almost mind-numbing regularity, and a great deal of material, both vintage and

● LOWELL FULSON

contemporary, is seeing the light of day under the auspices of people who understand the medium they operate in. The continued rise of the independent record company, both in the US and all over Europe, has meant that much previously unobtainable music in a wide variety of styles has become readily available. Here again, there are efforts to applaud, and others to raise a quizzical eyebrow at.

Without wishing to seem overtly patriotic, British record companies have been especially industrious in placing a large and varied menu at the disposal of the public. Between them, Ace, Charly, Demon/Edsel, The Interstate Group and Red Lightnin' have consistently made available a large and interesting body of music from the twenties to the present day. Interstate's twenty-first and final volume in its mammoth Piano Blues Series (issued during September 1984) completes the most comprehensive survey ever undertaken of blues and boogie piano styles up to 1945. This energetic company has also been responsible for ground-breaking albums of post-war gospel obscurities, unissued blues and R&B from the immediate post-war period, and previously unavailable field recordings by long lost blues legends. While Joe and Flo Public might look askance at albums by folk like Junior Wells, the Heavenly Gospel Singers, Tarheel Slim & Little Ann or Ann Cole, the enthusiast and collector must surely be very grateful.

In terms of marketing, presentation and sheer volume though, the year has found Charly and Demon/Edsel running neck and neck, with major licensing deals being undertaken at every turn. Between them, they have leased material from Atlantic, Stax, Vee-Jay, Hightone, Sun, Goldband, ACC, Capitol, Rounder, Okeh and others; moreover, they've largely done it extremely well. Thoughtfully programmed records, well mastered and attractively presented, coupled with effective distribution, have meant that a large selection of vintage and contemporary music has been readily available in accessible retail outlets. You really cannot ask for more.

Meanwhile, Ace Records has steered more or less the same course, leasing material mainly from West Coast labels like Modern and Speciality. Ace has also displayed impeccable judgement in having its releases mastered at CTS Studios, Wembley, probably the single best company ever to undertake the remastering of old material; the sound quality on, say, the Little Richard reissues – all that classic stuff you bopped around to thirty years ago – is truly remarkable. Red Lightnin' continues to plough its chosen field effectively, issuing mainly modern blues from sources one would not immediately think of. Their albums of film and TV soundtrack recordings by the likes of Buddy Guy, Billy Boy Arnold and Fred McDowell, for instance, have all proved interesting.

● *QUEEN IDA*

Activities on the European continent fall into two distinct groups. On the one hand, companies like Isabel, MCM and Black & Blue continue to record every blues artist who sets foot in France (with varying degrees of success), and on the other industrious Dutch, French and Austrian outfits document the history of the music in reissue programmes. A great deal of this is worthy, but some of it is frankly worrying. The policy of reissuing pre-war recordings in strict chronological order, artist by artist, is ultimately, I feel, self-defeating. Certainly it could be viewed as useful by those who enjoy filing things away and gleefully ticking off titles in discographies, but it makes for difficult listening, especially when worn originals are employed for mastering. The American Yazoo releases of venerable legends Blind Lemon Jefferson, Ma Rainey and Blind Blake in the past year have proved conclusively that if you programme an album well, use clean originals and master them with good equipment, then listening to pre-war music can be the engaging and enjoyable experience that it always ought to have been.

One European reissuer, however, who really has come across with the goods is Jonas Bernholm of Mr R&B Records. His stable of labels, which includes Route 66, Crown Prince and Jukebox Lil, has put out vintage compilations by the likes of Louis Jordan, Lucky Millinder and Jack McVea that are models of taste, which have rightly been received with enthusiasm.

● *JOHNNY TAYLOR*

In the US, too, the record scene continues to exude good health. As mentioned above, Yazoo keeps a flag flying in the vintage reissue field, while Malaco in the South, Hightone on the West Coast, and small indies all across the country regularly issue contemporary blues, soul-blues, R&B and gospel. Malaco in particular has proved itself industrious, recently signing Johnny Taylor to their roster to stand alongside Denise LaSalle, Little Milton and Latimore. Airplay for Malaco output has largely been effective, and Denise LaSalle especially has benefited from this welcome exposure.

On the literary front, the enthusiast's bookshelf will have filled out handsomely since the middle of last year. Biographies, discographies and histories have all been published which can only help to create a greater understanding of the genre. The Apollo Theatre has had two volumes celebrating its history; Little Richard has had one (with an accompanying hype the like of which I've seldom seen); the University of Texas has produced a book entitled *Living Texas Blues*, featuring some rare and unusual photographs; and small specialist discographical/research publications continue to proliferate. Paul Oliver, an acknowledged father of blues literature, published two books around Christmas, one a retrospective (*Blues Off The Record*), the other a ground-breaking research piece (*Songsters and Saints*), proving that it *is* possible to look both backwards and forwards at once without falling flat on your face. On the gospel front, Viv Broughton's highly readable and exceptionally well illustrated *Black Gospel* is the first serious attempt to document the rich history of this vastly important field, and is soundly recommended. Specialist magazines continue to be published monthly, quarterly and occasionally, all achieving their aim of covering the current scene at large. There are perhaps a dozen such publications worthy of attention in at least six languages, pointing to the global appreciation of this peculiarly American music.

Unfortunately, we've lost a lot of old friends and familiar faces this year, including Esther Phillips,, Bumps Blackwell, Alberta Hunter, Percy Mayfield, Reverend C L Franklin, Viola 'Miss Rhapsody' Wells, Lloyd Glenn, and Tuts Washington. Not by any means a complete list, but depressing enough nevertheless.

However, TV and film exposure has probably been greater this past year than at any time since the sixties. British TV's Channel Four mounted a major series entitled *Repercussions* which included absorbing portraits of gospel quartet singing in Alabama and rhythm 'n' blues in Los Angeles. The music turns up regularly on European TV stations, mainly featuring currently touring artists, and releases on video now include titles such as *Good Morning Blues*, *Chicago Blues* and *The Last Of The Blue Devils*, which make a refreshing change from sport and pornography.

● *DENISE LaSALLE*

It's been encouraging to see a widening of interest from enthusiasts, *aficionados* and the public at large, which must point to an overall maturing of the scene. It's been an interesting year that has given me hope for and faith in the music for the coming fifty-two weeks.

Paul Vernon

THE YEAR IN FOLK

It hasn't been easy being a folk fan these past few years. If it wasn't the jibes about Aran sweaters, it was grotesque impersonations of whiny singer-songwriters and/or fingers being violently thrust into eardrums. There was no real reason to suspect that the Pogues' amiably shoddy debut single, 'Dark Streets Of London', might begin to change all this.

The folk clubs were cursorily dismissive of the Pogues' irreverent primitiveness, while the Pogues themselves certainly wanted no truck with *them*. But gradually, reluctantly, almost imperceptibly, the two paths have begun to cross. For the Pogues, the Boothill Foot-Tappers, Billy Bragg, the Men They Couldn't Hang *et al*, the influence of long-standing, even *veteran* folk club artists has been both vital and visible . . . yet by far the bigger beneficiary has been the folk movement itself. For years the justifiable complaint has been that folk clubs are insular and – as a consequence – ageing and stagnating. That's only half the story and obscures the fact that many genuinely brilliant, often radical, musicians have been making their living playing in this environment, which has long desperately needed something cataclysmic to shock it into the lives of a new generation.

Musically, the Pogues have made enormous strides since their early defiantly brash emergence. Though he would doubtless deny it furiously, singer and main songwriter Shane McGowan appears to have studied and come to grips with the true misty-eyed nature of Irish bar-room music, recognizing the essential ingredients of romance, nostalgia and myth and fully reflecting them in two excellent singles, the poignant 'A Pair Of Brown Eyes' and the romping 'Sally Maclennane'. These songs reveal a depth and maturity in his songwriting that wasn't discernible in the amusing but limited frolics of their *Red Roses For Me* first album. It's absurd to imagine that an arresting ballad like 'A Pair Of Brown Eyes' owes nothing to the folk club revival – it clearly owes an awful lot, most notably to the Dubliners – but equally it's a song of superb qualities in its own right deserving to become a folk club standard in the manner of 'Black Velvet Band' and those other big ballads that have obviously inspired the Pogues.

Yet it's probably not the Pogues at all who've made the most crucial impact on changing attitudes and the social revolution in folk music. In the early part of 1985 Billy Bragg from Barking released an EP entitled 'Between The Wars', which so thoroughly absorbed the original ideals and lyrical approach of the folk club tradition that you might have assumed Bragg to have been absorbed in it all his life.

Bragg's researches have served him well. They have not merely given him the traditional vocabulary to construct songs with the bite and meaning of 'Between The Wars' or 'In Days Like These', but have led him to some of the more radical, criminally-neglected artists on the folk scene. Bragg shared the bill at a Labour Party concert in Manchester with Leon Rosselson and Roy Bailey and was knocked out by Rosselson's strident lyrics, particularly on 'The World Turned Upside Down', a rousing and impassioned account of a workers uprising in Weybridge in the nineteenth century. Not only did Bragg put his own angry version of the song on the 'Between The Wars' EP, he gave Rosselson's career the biggest push it has had for years – one of the most bizarre but gratifying sights of the year was Bragg, acting as a guest presenter on the rock TV programme *ORS*, introducing the two middle-aged folkies, Rosselson and Bailey.

Having established that you can put a couple of respectable-looking geezers in proper shirts with acoustic guitars on prime-time rock TV without clearing the building, it's a small step on to the other jewels in the crown. Dick Gaughan, *naturally*. Bragg discovered Gaughan early; Gaughan, as strident and proud as ever, discovered he had another new audience. There's plenty more discovering to be done on both sides – we are talking, after all, of *years* of neglected talent – but while there are people like Bragg recognizing its existence and its value and while there are artists like Gaughan, Christy Moore, the Oyster Band and Martin Carthy willing to embrace the outside world and its influences, then all concerned will continue to flourish.

The enormous folk festival circuit at least appears to have cottoned on to the exciting potential of this new wave of folk. The Boothill Foot-Tappers were the first of the genre to make a folk festival appearance, playing a celebrated set at the Farnham Folk Day alongside such diverse luminaries as Peter Rowan, Flaco Jimenez, Dick Gaughan and the Oyster Band. In July the Boothills were at it again, appearing at Bracknell Festival, while Billy Bragg made his folk festival debut deep in the folk credibility belt of Trowbridge; the Pogues took on the big one at Cambridge, joining their own particular heroes, the Clancy Brothers, alongside Tom Rush, Loudon Wainwright, John Martyn, Paul Brady and other more conventional names from the folk mainstream like Vin Garbutt, the Chieftans, Pyewackett and the Doonan Family.

The other young guns to make a big impact on both rock and folk circles and use positively the traditional influences at their disposal are the Men They Couldn't Hang. Following a similar path to the Pogues', the Men have a much broader range of ideas, from their send-ups of 'Rawhide' and 'Donald Where's Yer Troosers' to a considered lament like 'Scarlet Ribbons' to their emotive interpretation of Eric Bogle's 'Green Fields Of France', which has seen them in the upper echelons of the independent singles chart for well over a year. Most important, of all, however, was one of their own songs, 'Iron Masters', their second single, depicting the Chartists' struggle for unionisation in Wales and their subsequent violent destruction. With Elvis Costello taking them in hand and 'Iron Masters' clearly indicating their interest in the dramatic value inherent in traditional influences, the barnstorming emergence of the Men has possibly been the most exciting feature of the year.

Not that the idealistic merging of eras and cultures has been completely smooth. In May 1985 Richard Thompson's re-emergence as a hard-rocking guitarist and startling lyricist (a superb new album, *Across A Crowded Room*, on a major label)? was underlined by a big concert at the London Dominion Theatre. What better way to welcome the king back to the fold, some bright spark said, than to put him on with the new young guns of folk? And so it came to pass, Richard Thompson topped the bill supported by promising duo Terry and Gerry, the Boothill Foot-Tappers and the Pogues. And what happened? The Pogues fans invaded the stage and sang "Who the fuck is Richard Thompson?" and Thompson fans sat in stupefied silence watching all the primitive mayhem unfolding before them.

Thompson himself thought the Boothills

wonderful, but declared the Pogues a huge disappointment, making the point that their particular form of Irish boogie was straight out of the Clancy/Dubliners rather limited guide book to Irish bars and that the purpose of bands like the Chieftans, the Bothy Band and Planxty had been to extinguish this basic nonsense. For the record, the general verdict of the punk folk brigade on Thompson was that he was excruciatingly dull.

Ironically, Richard's return coincided almost exactly with the debut solo album of his former wife Linda Thompson. Linda returned to the fray spitting venom in her ex-husband's direction (he left her for another woman) and armed with an album devoted almost exclusively to the wrongs he'd committed against her. Out of the Muslim faith as well as the marriage, Linda was a changed person, charging around the stage like a demented punkette when she got to appear at Ronnie Scott's Club in London, although the relatively bland country-style of much of the music on the album scarcely matched up to the gripping lyrics.

Linda also joined a veritable *army* of folkies involved in a trilogy of plays titled *The Mysteries*, staged in London. A highly original and unusual interpretation of the Bible, *The Mysteries* provided the most dramatic and ambitious example yet of the mutual flirtation of folk and theatre. Based around the ever-burgeoning Home Service line-up, there seemed scarcely a folk singer in the country who wasn't enlisted in *The Mysteries* at some point on its run at London's National Theatre and The Lyceum. When Linda Thompson eventually dropped out, she was replaced by the ubiquitous Maggie Holland.

The most extraordinary occurrence on the club scene was the emergence – as virtually the most popular act – of the Kipper Family, an irreverent but hilarious duo from Norfolk who brilliantly (and affectionately) parodied traditional music in general and the Copper Family in particular.

It was also a good year for the excellent Oyster Band, underlining their status as the best and most innovative dance band in the country while broadening their horizons ever further with a new album, *Liberty Hall*, delving deep into their own song-writing talents. Coupled with some inspiring work from the likes of Blowzabella, Brass Monkey, Pyewackett, Mara and the Cock and Bull Band (back as a force in their own right, having extricated themselves from a not entirely satisfactory involvement with the Albion Band), instrumental virtuosity flourished.

And if the Oysters reaffirmed their right to be considered the best *English* band, then De Danann did much the same thing as kings of Celtic music. They've had their personnel problems along the way, particularly with girl singers, but on the immaculate *Anthem* album, issued half way through the year, they resolved their problems by featuring all three girl singers who have ever worked with them – Dolores Keane, Maura O'Connell and Mary Black. Without doubt these are the three finest singers in Ireland and all diamonds in their own right, helping to make *Anthem* a magical record.

If *Anthem* was the album of the year, the Easy Club debut wasn't far behind. Here again we have a group (from Scotland) thoroughly versed and immersed in the tradition, stepping outside their own immediate terms of reference to produce a stunning, completely refreshing work – in this case mixing Scottish traditional music with jazz swing, the ghosts of Django Rheinhardt flirting rewardingly with the Highlands.

● *THE POGUES* ● *MARTIN CARTHY* ● *LEON ROSSELSON* ● *CHRISTY MOORE* ● *LINDA THOMPSON* ● *VIN GARBUTT* ● *RICHARD THOMPSON* ● *THE BOOTHILL FOOT-TAPPERS*

I could mention more: Kathryn Tickell, Rory McLeod, the extraordinary R Cajun, Hokum Hotshots, Dead Sea Surfers, and the incomparable Jim Eldon, all of whom produced some magnificent and startling music, all stretching the outer limits of the folk umbrella. A robustly healthy year for folk music, then, both in and out (but mostly out) of folk clubs, reflected in Ian Anderson's bold decision to turn his quarterly magazine *Southern Rag* into a monthly with news-stand availability (along with a name change to *Folk Roots*). The Chieftans in China, Jim Lloyd put in charge of the EFDSS, and Billy Bragg in the charts: an admirable state of affairs.

Colin Irwin

■ EVENT OF THE YEAR: LIVE AID

● *DAVID BOWIE*

● *ADAM ANT*

At 12 noon on Saturday 13 July 1985, someone broke a record. He spoke to more people than had ever been addressed at one time in history. He wasn't a president, or a pope or an astronaut: he was a BBC presenter and his name was Richard Skinner. The words he'd scribbled just a few minutes previously reached the ears and eyes of an estimated one billion people across the planet and declared open an event in which records would be shattered with an almost tedious frequency; an event that would make previous global telecasts – like *Our World* in '67 (in which The Beatles played 'All You Need Is Love' to 400 million) or the Apollo Moonshot in '69 (685 million) – seem like examples of regional programming; an event that would play host to fifty-two acts performing 200 songs beamed off nine satellites onto 500 million TV sets in 100 countries, watched by an estimated 1.5 billion souls who were to dredge from their pockets the astonishing sum of £50 million to help relieve the starving people of Africa.

"Promoter Geldof Goes From Rat To Saint" ran a typical US headline, but how had he *done* it? How, in God's name, had this unshaven denim-clad 33-year-old Irish pop singer – hardly a model of tact and diplomacy – managed to generate such intense and universal compassion? Pop stars normally separated by continents, law suits or open animosity were to be found linking arms in tearful chorus. Others interrupted lucrative concert and recording commitments to give their services for free. Volunteers in their hundreds elected to man the phones, build the sets, lay the cables, anything at all, just to feel a part of what was being billed, unchallenged, as The Greatest Show On Earth.

Bob Geldof had done it simply by being Bob Geldof. He'd abandoned the usual luggage of sensitive negotiation and got straight to the point, winning few friends but a great deal of respect on the way. Faces fell in horror at an MTV press conference (arranged by the man himself to promote the event) when Bob announced the other participants were "boring me to death". He was equally abrupt with the artists. "He called up," claimed Pete Townshend, "and said one million people would die if we didn't perform." On the day, his outbursts became quite aggressively emotional as he thrust his collection plate at the viewing millions. His message was uncomfortably simple: to refuse to donate was to collude in the famine itself; it was, in effect, tantamount to murder.

This had the desired effect. £13 million was raised in the United Kingdom alone. Spontaneous whip-rounds were held at parties, pubs, offices (a regular donation was £25 per person, the price of a Wembley ticket). Someone rang the London club where the BBC was broadcasting and offered to auction their Bentley. The ruler of Dubai's son gave £1 million. The most generous were the Irish who forked out roughly £2 for every man, woman and child. One of the least generous was Japan – admittedly unused to the idea of charity donations – who could only muster £½ million from 60 million inhabitants, a source of great national shame, apparently, as the concert "broke all existing TV records".

As it did just about everywhere else. In the UK, Live Aid notched up a total of 30 million viewers and listeners in the BBC's "biggest ever simultaneous broadcast". It shattered ratings for the Cup Final, Wimbledon, the Olympics, even *Miss World* (a measly 20 million), and was edged into second place overall only by the Royal Wedding (which reached 38 million but was aired on three channels at once).

The stars of *that* particular show were to miss the most memorable moments at Wembley – "lunch with mother" was the given excuse. Nor was there any shortage of extraordinary spectacles to choose from: scores of pop stars standing in the wings, legs splayed, scrubbing invisible guitars, as Status Quo kicked the show into motion; the strict dressing-room rota – twenty minutes before you're on and twenty minutes after, then *out*; a chain-smoking David Bowie, desperately afraid of flying, shrieking "I *know* it's going to run out of petrol!" while being choppered into Wembley (he later cancelled a photo session to retreat, alone, to his dressing-room, moved to tears by the whole occasion); Cat Stevens wandering about in his usual robes and turban and no one having a clue who he was; Adam Ant's stupendous dancing; Bob Geldof rushing *le tout ensemble* backstage for a brisk finale rehearsal, and giving up when the electric guitar conked out; Queen cantering triumphantly through a set they'd worked on for weeks; the Who wobbling through one they'd rehearsed for thirty minutes; a sea of people swaying and singing to music being performed on another continent; and Elvis Costello's "Northern English folk song", 'All You Need Is Love', something of a substitute for the Beatles "reunion" *the Sun* had so confidently predicted.

American fans were being promised something else – "your Woodstock". And in many respects they got it – few problems, a truly stellar cast, two-hour queues for the loo, ninety-degree sunshine and an even higher degree of backstage chaos. The artists' enclosure was so swamped with the children of various heads of companies who'd made vast donations that Mick Jagger found his caravan besieged by autograph hunters. Bob Dylan's door remained firmly closed all day. Keith Richards' trailer, on the other hand, echoed long and loud with the sound of revelry (possibly explaining his performance). Madonna – unaccountably the only person with her name on *two* caravans – insisted the entire surrounding area be cleared before she'd use the toilet. No sign of Stevie Wonder – Geldof's habit of evading the manager and going direct to the star seemed not to have paid off in this case – and Michael Jackson's excuse that it was a "Jehovah's Witness Holiday" didn't quite ring true somehow.

● *COOLING THE CROWD IN PHILADELPHIA*

● *PHIL COLLINS IN PHILADELPHIA*

But, again, there were many remarkable moments: Phil Collins, aboard Concorde, thwacking at imaginary drums as he listened intently to Led Zeppelin tapes in preparation for his part in their drumstool; the dumbfounding sight of Crosby and Stills who must have been *winched* onstage with Nash to rejoin Young after eleven years; Young's own surprisingly sprightly solo stint; the portly but impeccable Beach Boys; Sheena Easton holding forth on the problems of diarrhoea in the Third World on MTV (pur-*lease*!); the electrifying Jagger/Tina Turner duet (rigorously rehearsed the day before); and the astounding lack of technical hitches – or what *the Washington Post* called *"concert interruptus"*. (The same organ, I might add, referred to the British Band Aid release as "a faminist ditty" – true!)

● *THE GRAND FINALE*

Back in London, in the heat of the moment, David Bowie declared that Live Aid should "become an annual event". Would that it could; it would surely be an impossible act to follow. Would a yearly Led Zeppelin, Black Sabbath, Who or Status Quo reunion have quite the same magic? Would musicians of sufficient stature still make cash-sapping sacrifices to be there on the day? Would the lure of self-promotion eventually override the true purpose of the event? Perhaps not.

What may have a more lasting effect is the way Geldof, together with BBC reporter Michael Buerk, managed to alter completely the public's perception of the African crisis. For as long as I can remember, one's image of the terrible famine was solely those forlorn adverts nudged apologetically into the pages of Sunday newspapers; a wafer-thin child clutching an empty bowl – an image so frequent and unchanging as to somehow bypass the conscience altogether, a human suffering to which one had almost become immune. Through its constant barrage of heart-rending newsreel and video, Live Aid seemed to breathe life back into that very image itself: the motionless waif suddenly became a real child, tottering on spindly limbs, in real pain and in desperate need of real money *right now*. That this prompted, in so many people, a completely unselfconscious urge to help is something no government, appeal or advertising campaign has ever – could ever? – achieve.

It was Geldof himself who said it: "Live Aid is the ultimate expression the pop industry can make."

Mark Ellen

SINGLES

■ Phil McNeill looks at fourteen months of 45s!

In terms of statistics, June 1984 – July 1985 broke records in all directions. Wham!, Frankie, Prince, Madonna, Phil Collins, Stevie Wonder, Tina Turner, Band Aid and USA For Africa all had a platinum-plated twelve months. But in artistic terms, George Michael stands alone.

Before June 1984, Wham! had never had a number one. At that moment, Duran Duran had just had their biggest hit ever with 'The Reflex' and Frankie Goes To Hollywood were firmly established as the hottest new group in year. Yet by Christmas there was no doubt who was Britain's top group.

'Wake Me Up Before You Go Go' was the start, as Wham! emerged from a year-long industrial dispute with gleaming grins, a fluorescent video to cement that summer's most pervasive fashion, and a sound of unadulterated bubblegum. Even to a lover of the Jackson Five and New Edition, listening to 'Wake Me Up' was like being force-fed candyfloss, but it was still an amazing record: probably the most unstoppable number one ever. Not surprisingly, it went on to become Wham!'s first American number one too.

It took 'Two Tribes' to drive 'Wake Me Up' away, and two months later Wham! and Frankie completed their dominance over the summer of '84 as 'Two Tribes' finally gave way to 'Careless Whisper'. Both sold millions –and both deserved to.

After 'Careless Whisper', 'Freedom' was a holding operation: a spare Motown pastiche which was irresistible for the first thirty seconds. But George wasn't yet finished with 1984. For a final flourish, and in a bid to be the first artist to score four number ones in a year since T.Rex, Wham! produced a Christmas single to rank alongside 'White Christmas' and 'I Wish It Could Be Christmas Every Day'. 'Last Christmas' was an exquisite confection which left audiences for the *Make It Big* tour walking on air as it provided the exhilarating climax to those brilliant shows.

Unfortunately, Wham! reckoned without Band Aid, but at least George had the satisfaction of singing on the top two singles in Christmas week. Immediately after Christmas, Wham! flipped their record to make the Isleyish 'Everything She Wants' the A-side. They still didn't beat out Band Aid, but 'Everything She Wants' went on to top the American charts in its own right.

Since then, Wham! have maintained vinyl silence in this country, but those four singles were so strong that even over six months later, Wham! remain Britian's undisputed number one pop group.

"Ladies and gentlemen, we present Frankie Goes To Hollywood. Possibly the most important thing this side of the world." Thus spake "Ronald Reagan" at the start of 'Two Tribes' – and amazingly, we believed him.

Looking back, it's hard to recall the epic scale of Frankie's success last summer.

"If your grandmother or any other member of the family should die while in the shelter, put them outside but remember to tag them first for identification purposes" . . . as the Cruise missiles rolled into Britain, that was the most repeated phrase on a record that went to number one within hours of release and stayed there for two solid months.

Remix followed remix, each fabulously different, like tanks parading across Red Square. Every household in the country had to have at least five different versions, plus three separate wonderful *Top of the Pops* recordings, plus of course a wardrobe full of designer *and* bootleg T-shirts. While this wonderful record took over top spot, 'Relax' crept back up to number two in July – five months after it had made number one and ten months after release!

Of course, it wasn't just Frankie's doing. Trevor Horn produced a record which equalled his own grandoise drama for ABC's 'Look Of Love', allied to the band's instinctive hard rock attack. ZTT propagandist Paul Morley supplied endless enigmatic remixes, perfectly packaged by London's leading image-makers XL Design.

Veteran artificers Godley and Creme dragged Frankies and a cast of dozens into a video studio to witness Reagan and Chernenko lookalikes slugging it out in a ham wrestling match, then aped the record's remixes with video scratching effects on Richard Nixon's nose. Horn spent endless hours in the studio with Art Of Noise remaking and remodelling Frankie's fury, going so far as to commission actor Patrick Allen to re-record the official nuclear warnings which he himself made for the government.

● FRANKIE GOES TO HOLLYWOOD

And through it all, Holly, Paul, Mark, Nasher, and Ped turned up every Thursday on *Top of the Pops* grinning evilly and looking wonderful. If you didn't give them your heart, you didn't have one to give.

Frankie themselves ended 1984 with something of a whimper. The overblown balled 'The Power Of Love' (Holly Johnson's favourite Frankie song) just managed to reach number one before Band Aid. Their only single of '85, the LP title track 'Welcome To The Pleasuredome', did surprisingly well to get to number two – so in the end Frankie couldn't quite beat Gerry and the Pacemakers' record of having their first three singles go to number one.

● MADONNA

At one time an overnight sensation *couldn't* happen in America. Major artists like Springsteen *paid their dues*. But that was before MTV. These days the US has its own pop sensibility, somewhere between the staid rock of old and Britain's candy culture, and the ideal US hit sounds great on the car stereo and looks even better on the TV screen. In '83/4, Michael Jackson was master; in '84/5, Madonna is mistress of all she surveys. She had two singles in the American Top Thirty almost every week this year.

Madonna's first LP, and hits like 'Holiday' and 'Lucky Star', had already established her as a white disco star, a downmarket Grace Jones. But Madonna wanted much more. So she enlisted Nile Rodgers to do for her what he'd done for Bowie with 'Let's Dance' and for Duran with 'The Reflex': kick her career into a new, higher gear. But rather than the hi-tech rock sound that he'd brought to Bowie and Duran, Rodgers gave Madonna a garish saccharine pop sound that defined her persona in the way 'Wake Me Up' defined Wham!.

If 'Like A Virgin' gave America its most unlikely Christmas number one ever (and it was still there in February), 'Material Girl' gave that country's youth its most telling role model for many years. While ZZ Top and David Lee Roth preached an entertaining reversion to girls 'n' cars for the boys, Madonna spread the gospel of female self-determination through self-love: McLaren's "golden youth" Bow Wow Wow prophecy made flesh.

On the face of it, Madonna was a traditional sex symbol, but that was turned totally on its head when she toured to adoring audiences of teenage Madonna clones. Also, on the face of it, she couldn't sing. Minnie Mouse was the derogatory comparison. But that too was shown up when the movie theme ballad 'Crazy For You' followed its pure pop predecessors to the top of the charts on both sides of the Atlantic.

In Britain, Prince never quite cracked it – though an outrageous TV appearance alongside minder Chick Huntsbury at the BPI Awards helped to push the two-year-old classics '1999'/'Little Red Corvette' to the top of the charts in January.

But the real meat of Prince's singles campaign was the *Purple Rain* movie soundtrack. First came 'When Does Cry' – the perfect way to introduce this mercurial man to mainstream Britain, through a veil of sucking synths and obscene sensuality. Despite some of the most intoxicating lyrics committed to music, it was one of the many records held off the number one spot by 'Two Tribes'.

If 'When Doves Cry' established Prince's sexual identity, the follow-up 'Purple Rain' set out explicitly to establish his musical links with James Brown and Jimi Hendrix – and, in its overwrought way, it succeeded brilliantly. Next off the production line was 'I Would Die 4 U', another superb single which got lost in the Xmas rush and was immediately withdrawn in favour of '1999'/'Little Red Corvette'.

By now there was no stopping His Royal Prolificness, and 'Let's Go Crazy'/'Take Me With U', Prince's third single in three months, showed the metal brigade the slick way to take guitar mayhem into the upper reaches of the charts.

We waited with bated breath for the following month's single, but the flow dried up. Were there no tracks left on *Purple Rain*? No . . . little did we realize, Prince had become a hippy, and hippies don't make singles.

That, at least, was the original intention when he issued *Around The World In A Day*. But with the LP stiffing badly, Warners reluctantly put out 'Paisley Park', a likeable effort not a million miles from the Small Faces' 'Itchycoo Park', but also not a patch on Prince's purple period when he seemed to soundtrack our lives.

And if it wasn't Prince, it was once of his much-maligned acolytes. OK; so *he* did all the work – but Sheila E ('The Glamorous Life', 'The Belle Of St Mark'), Apollonia 6 ('Blue Limousine') and Sheena Easton ('Sugar Walls') got their names on a body of tacky but not tawdry pop funk that rates alongside Nile Rodgers' Chic/Sledge/Devotion heyday.

These, then, were the four names that dominated the singles charts from June '84 to July '85: Wham!, Frankie, Madonna and Prince. Great pop stars all, with many traits in common – the strangest being their lack of resonance. They cast no shadow. They are not part of any musical trend; indeed they are all so isolated that they haven't even *inspired* any new music.

Prince and Madonna *were* however part of a business phenomenon: the American invasion. A couple of years ago, as Brit-pop went video, there was what was known as the second English invasion of America, led by such musical giants as the Fixx and A Flock Of Seagulls. Now the Yanks turned the tables, as their legions of smooth AOR rockers learned to use video themselves.

Gnarled old men who'd plugged on for years ignored by the great British public were suddenly all over the singles chart: ZZ Top taking 'Gimme All Your Loving' into the Top Five, Bruce Springsteen setting up his UK tour with a string of hits led by 'Dancing In The Dark', Foreigner striding ponderously to number one with 'I Want To Know What Love Is', Bryan Adams reducing hard rock to its banal basics with 'Run To You', 'Somebody' and 'Heaven'.

● SHEENA EASTON

● BRYAN ADAMS

● APOLLONIA 6

Most of these records were actually quite good. But the surprise leader in the AOR formula stakes was Kool and the Gang's superbly streamlined 'Misled'. It was going to take a great record to beat that, but it came along in February in the shape of ex-Eagle Don Henley's 'Boys Of Summer', which managed to combine exciting freshness with mature lyrics and song construction. Henley's laid-back Los Angeles masterpeice, displaying all the virtues of classic sixites pop, also made America's various "underground" attempts to revive psychedelia/pub-rock/etc look pretty sick.

The American invasion coincided with a revival in the fortunes of female singers. Foremost among these was the remarkable Tina Turner, who made her best single since 'River Deep Mountain High' in the form of 'What's Love Got To Do With It', and followed that with another four chart entries off the *Private Dancer* LP.

The Pointer Sisters also released their best single for eons with 'Automatic', followed by another five consecutive chart entries including the excitable 'I'm So Excited', AOR fake-rock at its gleaming best.

On top of that, Chaka Khan swept regally to number one in November with the rap/scratch/funk maelstrom of 'I Feel For You', and Sister Sledge breezed to number one in July with 'Frankie', produced by their old guru Nile Rodgers. (Ironically at the same time a Dutch trio called Mai Tai were in the Top Ten with a brilliant revival of the old Chic/Sledge sound, 'History'.)

Inevitably, the leading British female singer was Alison Moyet, who launched her solo career with three good pop singles produced by Jolley/Swain – 'Love Resurrection', 'All Cried Out' and 'Invisible' – then topped them with a startlingly successful version of 'That Ole Devil Called Love'. None of them, however, had the personal element that made her best work with Yazoo so gripping.

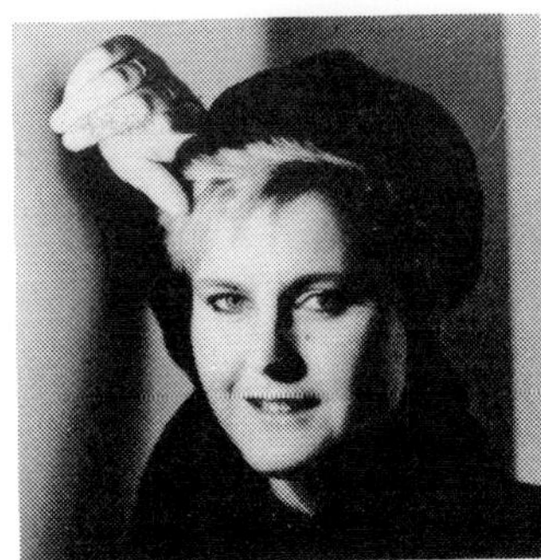

● ALISON MOYET

● BILLY OCEAN

● RIC OCASEK

● PAUL YOUNG

However, in going solo Alison Moyet joined the hallowed ranks of British AOR, a platinum-plated set which also includes Bryan Ferry, Sting, Phil Collins, Queen, Sade, Paul Young and, if he can sustain his past year's efforts, Billy Ocean.

Ocean was perhaps the most unlikely chart resident of the year. A forgotten name from the early seventies when Brit-pop was at its lowest ebb and most inward-looking, Billy returned with a riff taken from 'Billie Jean' and a single which seemed to change its title for each country it was released in. Yet 'Caribbean Queen' launched him to unexpected success both in the UK and US. 'Loverboy' and 'Suddenly' showed it was no fluke.

Paul Young returned from a long absence due to voice and confidence problems to regain his rightful place on the charts with the electrifying 'Tear Your Playhouse Down'. On tour, too, Young showed himself to be thoroughly revitalised, but his subsequent hits threatened to lapse into MOR formularization.

When it came to formularization, however, no one could match Queen and Freddie Mercury, who between them managed no less than six hit singles between June '84 and July '85.

But the undisputed king of MOR has to be Phil Collins. After hitting number one last year with the slushy movie theme 'Against All Odds', he found himself in the embarrassing position this year of having records queuing to follow each other into the Top Ten. His solo efforts 'Sussudio' (February funk) and 'One More Night' (April angst) sandwiched his triumphant number one duet with Earth, Wind & Fire singer Philip Bailey 'Easy Lover' – yet more hi-tech AOR.

An interesting side-effect of the AOR boom was the number of ballads, ranging from the magnificent ('Careless Whisper', 'Drive' by the Cars) through the magnificently mawkish ('Hello' by Lionel Richie, 'I Just Called To Say I Love You' by Stevie Wonder, 'One More Night' by Phil Collins, 'Everytime You Go Away' by Paul Young, 'No More Lonely Nights' by Paul McCartney, 'Suddenly' by Billy Ocean, 'I Want To Know What Love Is' by Foreigner), to the plain mawkish ('I Should Have Known Better' by Jim Diamond and 'I Know Him So Well' by Elaine Page and Barbara Dickson, both of which went to number one).

The AOR boom was also deeply entwined with another new development: movie themes. In the era of John Carpenter and Walter Hill, you'd expect movies and music to inspire one another to new heights of creativity. Sadly, that's all too rare. Most "youth" movie soundtracks consist of compilations of predictable AOR rock such as the Pointer Sisters' 'Neutron Dance' and Glenn Frey's 'The Heat Is On', both from *Beverly Hills Cop*.

● ELAINE PAGE & BARBARA DICKSON

Still, there were a few gems. BB King made an astounding single for *Into The Night*, Simple Minds made a deserved American number one with 'Don't You (Forget About Me)' for *The Breakfast Club*, Duran Duran surpassed themselves with the 'Rio'-meets-'Goldfinger' theme for *A View To A Kill*, and Ray Parker Jnr provided the most insistent single of the year for *Ghostbusters*.

In the face of this transatlantic MOR onslaught, most British pop acts crumbled into confusion. But a few showed that it was still possible to make imaginative, individual pop records. Tears For Fears emerged with both new-found integrity and superstar status with 'Shout' and 'Everybody Wants To Rule The World'. Depeche Mode made a series of superb, simple, mature singles: the sweetly sleazy 'Master And Servant', the quaintly controversial 'Blasphemous Rumours', and finally a brilliant song of obsessive love, 'Shake The Disease'.

● PAUL HARDCASTLE

● DEPECHE MODE

● THE DAMNED

Scritti Politti released most of an LP before the album itself, in the form of the Jacksonoid 'Absolute', the hiccupping, imperfect pop of 'Hypnotize', and the sweetly clipped reggae of 'The Word Girl'. China Crisis also retained a certain integrity in the face of beckoning pop stardom.

But the most bizarre example of an established group finding new ways into the pop chart was the Damned, with their Dickensian 'Grimly Fiendish' and Doorsian 'Shadow Of Love' – and they looked better than ever as well.

Only one major new British group emerged in the last half of 1984: Bronski Beat, who hit upon an exhilarating variation on the Yazoo formula of synth and soul. Jimmy Somerville's remarkable voice powered 'Smalltown Boy' to number two and 'Why?' to number six. When the Bronskis tried to break out of their gay disco straitjacket with 'Ain't Necessarily So', it was a commercial flop and an artistic disaster.

Finally, Bronski Beat got together with Marc Almond to record a version

● GO WEST

● FINE YOUNG CANNIBALS

of Donna Summer's 'I Feel Love'. It seemed inspired, but the end result was pretty sloppy. Nevertheless, as the Bronskis disintegrated under a welter of personal pressures, it shot to number two in April. In ten months, Bronski Beat had gone through more acclaim and criticism, success and depression, than most groups experience in ten years.

If the back end of '84 was dominated by established artists, the absence of so many superstars in the first part of '85 opened the way for a motley collection of new boys and girls.

Groups who'd plugged away for years and now grabbed their chance included King ('Love And Pride'), Strawberry Switchblade ('Since Yesterday') and Dead Or Alive ('You Spin Me Round'). Already, they're all struggling again, but Pete Burns at least deserves his success for flamboyance beyond the call of duty.

Total unknowns established themselves almost literally overnight. Stephen Tin Tin Duffy put out an outrageously arty 12" package of 'Kiss Me' and rocketed into the Top Five. His beautifully constructed follow-up, 'Icing On The Cake', showed him to be more interesting than his initial image led you to believe.

Paul Hardcastle's '19' similarly shot from nowhere to the Top Five in the space of a week. The cut-up of a Vietnam documentary over an insipid funk backing earned Hardcastle a reputation as a remixer; novelty artist might have been more appropriate.

Also stuck somewhere on the border between novelty and new wave were Art Of Noise, the ZTT house band, who quit ZTT after the unexpected success of 'Close (To The Edit)' and may never be heard from again.

Two new artists who certainly *will* be heard from again are Go West and Fine Young Cannibals. Got West appeared in February with a macho video to match the muscular attack of 'We Close Our Eyes', positioning them somewhere between Wham! and Paul Young. Unfortunately they couldn't match that with the innocuous follow-up 'Call Me', but Peter Cox and Richard Drummie have the accomplishment and acumen to build.

Fine Young Cannibals, formed by Beat guitarists Dave Steel and Dave Cox, excited great interest with 'Johnny Come Home', which managed to establish a strong visual and musical identity for the band in just three minutes.

Another new group, Jesus and Mary Chain, established an interesting musical identity in three seconds with 'Never Understand'. Hopefully their feedback fetish won't be a complete dead end.

Mainstream black music, sad to say, was pretty anonymous in '84/5. Outside of Prince, there was just one soul hit of sheer genius: the Dazz Band's 'Let It All Blow', funk with a hint of scratch and a twinkle in its eye that brought to mind the Gap Band and Ohio Players.

● THE COMMODORES

Honourable mentions however, go to James Ingram's mellifluous 'Yah Mo B There', Eddy Grant's ignored 'Romancing The Stone', Loose Ends' sneaky 'Hangin' On A String', The Commodores' heartfelt 'Nightshift', Phyllis Nelson's ultra-smooth number one 'Move Closer', Steve Arrington's summer special 'Feel So Real', Kool's 'Fresh' and 'Cherish' (the titles speak for themselves), David Grant and Jaki Graham's revitalised 'Could It Be I'm Falling In Love', Denise LaSalle's rather rude 'My Toot Toot', Ashford and Simpson's one-liner 'Solid', DeBarge's delightful 'Rhythm Of The Night'.

Two dance fads grazed the charts: Washington's go-go came and went, leaving behind Chuck Brown's classic 'Bustin' Loose' and Little Benny and the Masters' itchy 'Who Comes To Boogie'. More substantially, British hi-energy produced two quite brilliant singles in Evelyn Thomas's 'High Energy' and Hazell Dean's 'Whatever I Do Wherever I Go', as well as such oddities as Divine's 'You Think You're A Man'.

But in the end, one record overshadowed all. 'Do They Know It's Christmas?' by Band Aid, written by Bob Geldof and Midge Ure, went to number one for Christmas, sold more than any single ever in the UK, inspired the American reaction 'We Are The World' by USA For Africa plus dozens of other Ethiopia records, and led to hundreds of offshoot activities, from School Aid to the world's most extraordinary rock concert, Live Aid.

● ASHFORD & SIMPSON

● PHYLLIS NELSON

● THE DAZZ BAND

Band Aid was followed by a rash of charity records, most of them worthy in cause if not in quality. The best of the rest was 'Soul Deep' by the Council Collective, a fierce pro-miners benefit by Paul Weller and a cast including Junior and Jimmy Ruffin. The worst singles in a good cause were Marti Webb's gruesome 'Ben' and the Crowd's cheesy 'You'll Never Walk Alone', both big hits.

So, an eventful year. 1984/5: the year of Frankie and Wham!, of Brit-pop on the run and America AOR on the march, the year of Prince and Madonna, the year of ballads and movie themes.

1984/5: the year of Band Aid. In more ways than one, maybe, the year that rock grew up.

ALBUMS

AC/DC

Fly On The Wall (ATLANTIC)

... a whole feast of goodies. Ten tracks to dynamite your ears in the nicest possible way.
RECORD MIRROR

Yeah, get down and boogie baby, this is a grade 'A' DC album.
SOUNDS

... what you get is ten tracks – give or take – of discordant, squalling mess, albeit a LOUD mess.
MELODY MAKER

... another cretinous slab of outdated guitar "mayhem" and frenzied screaming ...
SMASH HITS

BRYAN ADAMS

Reckless (A&M)

... God he writes some boring songs, especially when he rattles on about kids and breaking down barriers.
RECORD MIRROR

You wonder how many hours of MTV and AOR radio monitoring went into the creation of this.
MELODY MAKER

... a helluva record to beat.
SOUNDS

KING SUNNY ADE AND HIS AFRICAN BEATS

Aura (ISLAND)

... a work of enormous pleasures ...
MELODY MAKER

... makes for great background music but if you concentrate too hard it tends to get on your nerves.
SMASH HITS

... yet another slice of jolly juju ...
NME

MARC ALMOND AND THE WILLING SINNERS

Vermin In Ermine (SOME BIZARRE)

Marc might be some way short of his avowed intention of declaring germ warfare on pop.
NME

... POLISHED grime.
MELODY MAKER

... Almond's most balanced and consistently good album so far.
SMASH HITS

... a REAL MAN, who doesn't eat shit but probably would if it would wind you up.
SOUNDS

LAURIE ANDERSON

United States Live
(WARNER BROS)

Anderson has a wit and vision that is all too rare in pop ... Let's hope this recording is just a momentary four-hour aberration.
NME

FELA ANIKULAPO KUTI AND EGYPT 80

Army Arrangement (CELLULOID)

... a textural tinderbox afire with musical insurrection.
SOUNDS

... Laswell has given Kuti what he needed after all these years, a new angle, a fresh sound.
NME

JOAN ARMATRADING

Secret Secrets (A&M)

... anonymous retreads of previous works.
RECORD MIRROR

A predictably consummate, sensitive offering ...
SOUNDS

... the singer's equivalent of a coffee-table glossy book ...
NME

... three moderately interesting numbers, and a lot of standard pop wallpaper.
MELODY MAKER

STEVE ARRINGTON

Dancin' In The Key Of Life
(ATLANTIC)

... a little cranky, a little rambling ...
RECORD MIRROR

... pulsing dance music that crackles and pops with chart potential and – most important of all – fully fledged soul.
SOUNDS

ART OF NOISE

Who's Afraid Of The Art of Noise? (ZTT)

... concocting mixes and shades of exhilaration hitherto unheard by human ears.
NME

... brilliant – without it you will be incomplete.
MELODY MAKER

... what am I doing listening to this shit when I could be doing something like taking drugs ...
SOUNDS

ASHFORD & SIMPSON

Solid (CAPITOL)

...it's nice to see two old pros upstaging the upstarts.
RECORD MIRROR

Solid? Anything but, chum.
NME

THE ASSOCIATES

Perhaps (WEA)

...perhaps 'Perhaps' is perfect.
NME

... a definite treasure.
MELODY MAKER

... disappointing ...
RECORD MIRROR

ASWAD

Rebel Souls (ISLAND)

Precision's no good without any songs.
MELODY MAKER

I can't register anything but profound disappointment ...
NME

... heavier next time please.
SOUNDS

AZTEC CAMERA
Knife (WEA)

. . . a pity that Roddy seems content to rest on his laurels . . .
SMASH HITS

. . . a veering towards airless achievement.
SOUNDS

. . . I'd encourage anyone to balance the narcissistic maunderings of the modish with its tender, tenacious alchemies of the soul.
NME

BANGLES
All Over The Place (COLUMBIA)

. . . the Bangles uphold the best traditions of the classic girl groups, without the spector of a Spector or the shadow of a Morton hanging over them.
NME

. . . does EVERYTHING have to sound like a Journey album, for crying out loud?
SOUNDS

. . . any of you guys out there who aren't smitten . . . have my deepest sympathies.
CREEM

. . . as much clout as a two-day-old kitten.
RECORD MIRROR

. . . great pop, CLASSIC pop . . . as good as anything you'll ever hear . . .
MELODY MAKER

THE BEAT FARMERS
Tales Of The New West (DEMON)

. . . should complement every copy of 'How Will The WOLF Survive' thus far sold.
SOUNDS

. . . a delirious switchback ride through the badlands of American music . . .
MELODY MAKER

. . . kings of the bop, fiery cross-breeders of rock'n'roll sentiments.
NME

GEORGE BENSON
20/20 (WARNER BROS)

. . . a predictable snooze.
SOUNDS

. . . faceless tunes for millionaires.
RECORD MIRROR

. . . 20/20 doesn't contain a single moment of engaging or obtrusive music . . . nothing dirty or exciting leaves the confines of the studio . . .
NME

. . . whiter-than-white black pop
MELODY MAKER

MATT BIANCO
Whose Side Are You On? (WEA)

. . . like all the most plausible salesmen, Matt Bianco can rip you off and still leave you smiling.
MELODY MAKER

You'll probably hear it down your local supermarket soon.
SMASH HITS

. . . an album of polished proficiency, without ever feeling the need to venture into the field of exploration.
SOUNDS

BIG COUNTRY
Steeltown (MERCURY)

What a pity we're not allowed to say "it's only rock 'n' roll" anymore . . .
SOUNDS

. . . music for rebels without causes to march aimlessly around to . . .
SMASH HITS

. . . a bloody good night out at the local Palais but . . . not making the greatest records of a generation.
RECORD MIRROR

. . . some records live forever. STEELTOWN is one of them.
MELODY MAKER

DAVID BOWIE
Tonight (EMI AMERICA)

. . . a fine album . . .
CREEM

. . . an uneasy, bumper-to-bumper mixture of styles . . .
SMASH HITS

. . . as he approaches 40 Bowie is relaxing into music that seems to possess a personal skin.
NME

. . . by Bowie's standards, it stinks.
RECORD MIRROR

BILLY BRAGG
Brewing Up (GO! DISCS)

. . . the bard of Barking has managed to follow last year's most talked about indie album with another better.
NME

. . . about as far removed from an ELO album as you can possibly get.
SMASH HITS

. . . an unmitigated success – and STILL no sign of bass and drums!
SOUNDS

BRONSKI BEAT
The Age Of Consent (LONDON)

It may scream too long and too hard but give me that any day in place of the vacuum that lies at the core of pop circa '84.
MELODY MAKER

Bronski Beat have seriously overestimated the public interest in either their welfare or their practices.
NME

Sex, sax and schmuck. What more could a girl want?
SOUNDS

CABARET VOLTAIRE
Micro-phonies (SOME BIZARRE/VIRGIN)

The Cabs are at their best when they're dead weird. Here they're just mildly eccentric.
RECORD MIRROR

Nobody takes the pulse better.
NME

. . . the avant garde is deserted for a dance sensibility that, largely, fails to motivate.
MELODY MAKER

THE CARS
Heartbeat City (ELEKTRA)

. . . mechanically sound but woefully frigid . . . This seamless AOR is a sprawling plague, finding easy prey.
MELODY MAKER

DAVID CASSIDY
Romance (ARISTA)

. . do young girls want this sort of thing today? Do they hell, they want Wham! songs about ski holidays and shagging. Bad luck, David, too old to be George Michael, too young to be Julio Iglesias.
NME

. . a pleasant and palatable collection.
SMASH HITS

David sings like an actor.
RECORD MIRROR

NICK CAVE AND THE BAD SEEDS

The First Born Is Dead (MUTE)

Fraud beyond DISBELIEF, which is why it works so well.
SOUNDS

It's sordid, it's predictable, it's sickening, and it's quite indispensable!
MELODY MAKER

... there is a yawning distance between what Nick Cave aims for and what he actually achieves.
NME

Probably not one for most of you pop kids out there but that's your loss.
RECORD MIRROR

SHEILA CHANDRA

Quiet! (INDIPOP)

... trying to redefine the boundaries of Indian music ...
SOUNDS

... a specialist record for specialist tastes.
MELODY MAKER

It's taken a long time for Indian music to recover from George Harrison's "helping hand". It's been worth the wait.
NME

CHANGE

Turn On Your Radio (COOL TEMPO)

A definite change for the worse.
SMASH HITS

... the apotheosis of eighties dancefloor chic.
NME

... nothing to get excited about ...
MELODY MAKER

ALEX CHILTON

Feudalist Tarts (NEW ROSE)

... I still reamin unmoved.
SOUNDS

... a revitalised post-alcoholic Chilton.
MELODY MAKER

CHINA CRISIS

Flaunt The Imperfection (VIRGIN)

... a whimpering heap of slush ...
SOUNDS

Hardly your typical Mersey sound.
RECORD MIRROR

Apt title ...
MELODY MAKER

Silky but soporific.
NME

COCTEAU TWINS

Treasure (4AD)

... the best thing the Cocteau Twins have ever done – a selection of very beautiful music indeed.
RECORD MIRROR

For all its enchanted garden Laura Ashley-ness, there's something which haunts – something more than most music does now.
NME

... too important for comparisons ...
MELODY MAKER

LLOYD COLE AND THE COMMOTIONS

Rattlesnakes (POLYDOR)

... the most refreshing, uncontrived, GORGEOUS lump of gold to be mined from Scotland in ages ...
SOUNDS

A record collection without this LP will be like a kitchen without tea.
NME

... a superb exercise in dexterity and musical punning, the sort of record Elvis Costello might have made if he'd ever been young and fun.
MELODY MAKER

PHIL COLLINS

No Jacket Required (VIRGIN)

... an album to suit all tastes.
RECORD MIRROR

Collins is a generally sound sort of bloke who makes fairly ordinary records for very ordinary people to play at their desperately ordinary parties.
MELODY MAKER

... a model for a little hits factory.
NME

THE COLOURFIELD

Virgins And Philistines (CHRYSALIS)

... one gets the feeling he's only dabbling.
SMASH HITS

... unrelenting and humourless.
SOUNDS

... a cocoa and slippers set ...
RECORD MIRROR

.. close, but not the stuff of champions.
NME

.. an incurably cynical album of articulate anti-pop.
MELODY MAKER

THE COMMODORES

Nightshift (MOTOWN)

... rather dull.
SMASH HITS

... a really remarkable renaissance.
RECORD MIRROR

... proves old dogs will learn new tricks and still deliver.
NME

JULIAN COPE

Fried (MERCURY)

... in playing the fruitcake, Cope's become our foremost free spirit.
MELODY MAKER

... may be a bit too idiosyncratic for some ...
RECORD MIRROR

... a record that only a real fan could love.
NME

Moments of genius; moments of imperfection; moments of energy; moments of inadequacy. FRIED, probably, is as definitive as any Cope album ever could be.
SOUNDS

STEWART COPELAND

The Rhythmatist (A&M)

... considerably more than a superstar's indulgence.
NME

... meanders its way through the murky heartland of discarded Bow Wow Wow audition tapes.
MELODY MAKER

... this album don't 'arf go on.
RECORD MIRROR

Hey Stew, forget it.
SOUNDS

ROBERT CRAY BAND

Bad Influence (DEMON)

... some of the tightest, earthiest soul music of the eighties ... essential.
NME

THE CULT

Dreamtime (BEGGARS BANQUET)

Wonderful.
RECORD MIRROR

Something MAGNIFICENT glows within these songs.
MELODY MAKER

... the ramblings of your average tinpot dictator ... this record is pure artifice ...
SOUNDS

Dropping the 'Blue Oyster' prefix has certainly made a world of difference to their looks.
NME

CULTURE CLUB

Waking Up With The House On Fire (VIRGIN)

... a clever pop confection – as clever as that ...
NME

... another LP of gold star quality ...
RECORD MIRROR

... .it's difficult to sit through a whole side without making a cup of tea, delousing the cat, going for a walk ... ANYTHING.
MELODY MAKER

... there is a track called 'Mistake No 3' which is as good a description as any.
SOUNDS

... a disaster of mediocrity ...
SMASH HITS

THE CURE

Concert And Curiosity (FICTION)

... a fresh perspective on a band captured at its creative peak ...
MELODY MAKER

One of the grooviest existentialist albums of the year.
SOUNDS

... no more than an average live album backed with another, tattier one.
NME

MILES DAVIS

You're Under Arrest (CBS)

Miles does something he hasn't done for 20 years: he applies his most burnished, caressing tones to a few modern ballads ...
NME

... certainly Davis' most accessible album ...
RECORD MIRROR

THE DAZZ BAND

Jukebox (MOTOWN)

... a slick, hip and well-drilled bunch. Washing machines will love 'em.
NME

... dangerously ho-hum.
RECORD MIRROR

DEAD OR ALIVE

Youthquake (EPIC)

... the usual soundtrack-to-the-laser-show Hi-Energy stomp.
NME

Pete Burns deserves wild success. Unfortunately, this music doesn't.
SOUNDS

... a bloody good laugh and a perfect drunken party record ... disco drosso all the way ...
RECORD MIRROR

... there could be a genuinely inspiring rock band somewhere in that dull mix trying to get out.
MELODY MAKER

DEBARGE

Rhythm Of The Night (GORDY)

... five anorexic American coffee-coloured clones.
MELODY MIRROR

... a higher ratio of unexpected melodies and interesting lyrics than in most other black outfits.
RECORD MIRROR

... generic dance fluff.
NME

THE DAMNED

Phantasmagoria (MCA)

... nine piles of parrotpoop ... sub-Hazel O'Connor "mood music" ...
NME

... a fine rock band have come of age. After eight years, the Damned have at last produced their meisterwerk.
MELODY MAKER

GEORGE DARKO

Highlife Time (OVAL)

... infectious enough to set whole continents dancing.
MELODY MAKER

... George has deliberately slowed down the tumultuous pace of Ghanaian syncopation for the benefit of indifferent dancers.
SOUNDS

... a must for those in need of that rare commodity – dance music that you can also sit back and listen to ...
NME

DEEP PURPLE

Perfect Strangers (POLYDOR)

... full of all the boring old rock shapes and manoeuvres ... a somewhat offensive reflection on the assumed average intelligence of today's record-buying public.
MELODY MAKER

... a real fine record – genuinely good.
CREEM

THE DEL FUEGOS

The Longest Day (ROUGH TRADE)

I honestly can't think of a better start to 1985.
MELODY MAKER

... the first great trad-rock album of '85 ...
NME

... a sublime record of raw rock and fragile power.
SOUNDS

DEPECHE MODE

Some Great Reward (MUTE)

... a carefully assorted, daintily arranged symphony ... one that carries emotion, devotion and yet never gives way to feebleness or predictability.
SOUNDS

Depeche Mode can be one of the few acts worthy of the name "pop group". It's just that they should be so much better.
NME

Depeche Mode make your spine tingle and your foot tap, and they'll probably cure your acne too.
RECORD MIRROR

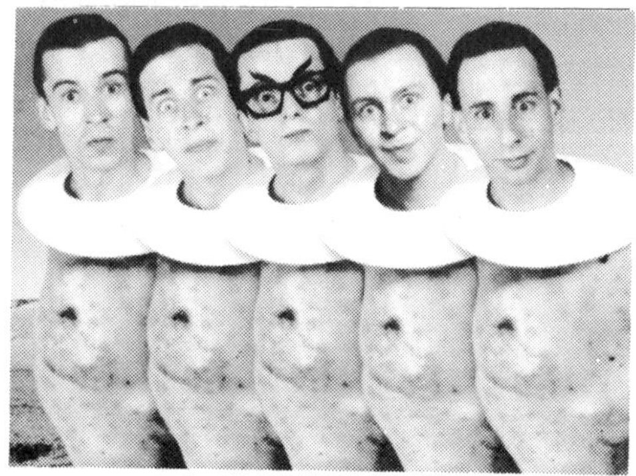

DEVO

Shout (WARNER BROS)

... they seemed like genuine wackos but they've grown up sadly normal.
SMASH HITS

Ten devoted token meagre bites of symbolism add up to a sub-tract, some sort of grope identity ... The joke's worn thin.
NME

DIFFORD & TILBROOK

Difford & Tilbrook (A&M)

... a work of frequently quite staggering maturity and insight, whose songs breathe fresh compassion and ingenuity into pop's tired frame.
MELODY MAKER

... white soul bluster ...
NME

DIRE STRAITS

Brothers In Arms (VERTIGO)

... proves conclusively that punk never EVER happened.
SMASH HITS

I HATE this stuff.
RECORD MIRROR

... it all sounds just a bit too like the last Dire Straits album ...
MELODY MAKER

Slotting into the same yuppy wallpaper bracket as the Police, Tina Turner, Phil Collins and Sade ...
NME

NICK DRAKE

Heaven In A Wild Flower (ISLAND)

... a punt ride to a poisoned paradise.
SOUNDS

... the choices are well made, though you could pick any 14 Drake tracks and still have a breathtaking set.
NME

STEPHEN 'TIN TIN' DUFFY

The Ups And Downs (10 RECORDS)

... far better than anyone had a right to expect.
MELODY MAKER

... sounds like Marc Almond singing with a clothes peg on his nose ...
SMASH HITS

It's genius.
RECORD MIRROR

Insubstantial joy.
SOUNDS

... an album of pap and purity, sense and nonsense ...
NME

DURAN DURAN

Arena (EMI)

At very least ARENA spares us the spectacle of Le Bon's idiot-dancing but at very worst it's smothered with his grunts and whoops, clumsy, studied stabs at spontaneity ...
MELODY MAKER

It is not, one suspects, terribly live, this round-the-world-in-80-limos live album ... I had imagined the lads might be able to play their instruments by now, but one can't demand everything ... Even Nile Rodgers cannot disguise their apparent lack of feel for this art form ...
NME

If it's critical approbation they're seeking, it won't happen this way.
RECORD MIRROR

E

SHEENA EASTON

A Private Heaven (EMI)

... just another vocal mannequin, pursing those sickening strawberry jam lips, babbling the worthless sentiments of worthless songwriters ...
RECORD MIRROR

EURYTHMICS

1984 (VIRGIN)

... an addictive blend of the poignant and the ominous.
SMASH HITS

Definitely worthy of a wallow, even for those of you who have concluded that George Orwell is a giant pain in the posterior.
RECORD MIRROR

... doubleplusgood? Not exactly.
NME

Collectors only ...
MELODY MAKER

Be Yourself Tonight (RCA)

... the converted wil not be disappointed.
NME

There's no rawness, no anger, no hunger – not surprising since they're now successful and happy.
RECORD MIRROR

EVERYTHING BUT THE GIRL

Eden (BLANCO Y NEGRO)

I'd like to have seen a little of that frost and fire. All I saw in EDEN was drizzle.
NME

Love Not Money (BLANCO Y NEGRO)

... just a bit too delicate, fragile, transparent ... Some snap next time please.
RECORD MIRROR

Don't expect Thorn and Watt to light up your world.
SOUNDS

Why so world-weary?
NME

... never really loses its lingering smell of narrow self-righteousness ...
MELODY MAKER

THE FALL

The Wonderful And Frightening World Of . . .
(BEGGARS BANQUET)

The Fall are an acquired taste but that's no excuse for ignorance.
MELODY MAKER

With a little patience you too will be entranced by the MAGIC of the Fall . . .
SOUNDS

GOD BLESS THE FALL
NME

Hip Priest And Kamerads
(BEGGARS BANQUET)

Musically, lyrically and atmospherically, this is nothing short of mesmerising.
SOUNDS

. . . an excellent introduction.
SMASH HITS

It could be some time before the Smiths get to be as demanding and creative as this.
MELODY MIRROR

FAT BOYS

Fat Boys (WEA)

. . . repetitive and boring in a big way.
SOUNDS

Big is beautiful and they won't let you forget it.
MELODY MAKER

. . . the boys do spread themselves just a little thinly.
NME

PHIL FEARON AND GALAXY

Phil Fearon and Galaxy (EPIC)

As unashamed commercial pop music it boasts a consistency and natural fizz few competitors could match in this field.
MELODY MAKER

. . . it's the complete ABSENCE of ANY personality that makes his smooth, jaunty silage so popular.
SOUNDS

. . . Fearon has bugger-all to say . . .
NME

BRYAN FERRY

Boys And Girls (EG)

. . . well produced banalities drifting aimlessly amongst the empty gestures of a sanatised, soulless backdrop. This is his epitaph.
RECORD MIRROR

He is already like an old man with his memories.
NME

Brushed and scrubbed to within an inch of their lives, these performances actually have very little to say.
MELODY MAKER

FLOY JOY

Into The Hot (VIRGIN)

. . . very bright, in all senses of the word.
RECORD MIRROR

After two spins this collection had knocked the cobwebs from the prize-winning end of the Clap-O-Meter.
NME

JOHN FOGERTY

Centrefield (WARNER BROS)

This downhome DIY triumph – every instrument played by JCF – fights for simple American glories as staunchly and lovingly as BORN IN THE USA.
NME

. . . the John Ford of rock 'n' roll: a traditionalist, certainly; sentimental, yes: but rebellious, too; the last of the independents, if you like . . .
MELODY MAKER

CENTREFIELD hits nine home runs in a row!
SOUNDS

FRANK CHICKENS

We Are Frank Chickens
(KAZ RECORDS)

. . . certainly the most visual and most humorous attraction doing the rounds at the moment, recommended without reservation.
SOUNDS

Hard to tell whether they're making fun of themselves or of us . . .
SMASH HITS

. . . no long-playing record can really impart the full force of their colourful Oriental magnetism.
NME

FRANKIE GOES TO HOLLYWOOD

Welcome To The Pleasuredome (ZTT)

A pretty thin package at times, but it still seems a real ADVENTURE.
SMASH HITS

MM say: Frankie singles yes, double albums no!
MELODY MAKER

It's rather good modern pop . . . but too much here is simply not up to the standards the band and the label have set themselves.
RECORD MIRROR

It's the kind of extravaganza one needs a ticket to know and then. By next week I'll be tired of it, but today this "play" is funny, sharp, gorgeous.
NME

It's a put-on and a con, a flim-flam scam of a sham, a hip hype calculated solely to separate as much money as possible from as many people as possible as fast as possible before all the young rubes wake up and realize they've been fleeced . . . a shuck worthy of Sgt Bilko at his best.
CREEM

ARETHA FRANKLIN

Who's Zoomin' Who? (ARISTA)

. . . just a bit TOO full of all those ultra-slick studio dance moves . . .
RECORD MIRROR

Despite unsuitable songs and bombastic production jobs, there still remains that nagging residue of voluptuousness in the voice . . .
MELODY MAKER

MARVIN GAYE

Dream Of A Lifetime (CBS)

. . . an audacious, heart-rending, last wave from a troubled genius . . .
NME

. . . compelling – morbidly so . . .
MELODY MAKER

It's difficult to regard this as more than a hotchpotch. . .
RECORD MIRROR

How could a man be so sensitive and yet so gross?
SOUNDS

GENERAL PUBLIC

All The Rage (VIRGIN)

. . . sounds like a new group trying too hard to be contemporary and "with-it".
NME

. . . a colourless, punchless no-man's-land of flat production . . . bland instead of brave . . .
SMASH HITS

Wakeling and Co have ignored the red flags of past mistakes and General Public drown.
MELODY MAKER

THE GO-BETWEENS

Spring Hill Fair (SIRE)

... over-flowing with fresh uncluttered pop music.
SMASH HITS

... plenty of sustenance here ...
NME

GO WEST

Go West (CHRYSALIS)

... you'd have to go a long way to find an album as weak, wimpy, soulless, and soggy.
SOUNDS

Britain's answer to Hall & Oates
MELODY MAKER

... exciting, exhilarating pop-rock with a dance slant ...
RECORD MIRROR

... the aural equivalent of senile dementia.
NME

GRANDMASTER FLASH

They Said It Couldn't Be Done (ELEKTRA)

... sounds as though all life and ideas have deserted him ... a safe, no-motion, parade of gestures.
SMASH HITS

The ceaseless outpouring of fatuous boasts has the hollow resonance of middle-aged men who have lost what it takes to get up or get down.
MELODY MAKER

GRANDMASTER MELLE MEL AND THE FURIOUS FIVE

Work Party (SUGARHILL)

... they sound like nothing so much as second-rate Lionel Richie
RECORD MIRROR

Buy it now and you've got more money than sense.
NME

DAVID GRANT

Hopes And Dreams (CHRYSALIS)

... a new haircut (VERY Michael Jackson) and another batch of standard disco-soul songs.
SMASH HITS

... a succession of numbingly banal lyrics and soulless arrangements.
RECORD MIRROR

... bland brooding of the turgid kind.
SOUNDS

... the product of talented people on a high budget with not a lot to say.
NME

AL GREEN

Trust In God (DEMON)

... the more than competent artistry of a happy, content man.
SOUNDS

What I want from the Rev, I suppose, is rougher and livlier. Most of the arrangements would do for any old popular balladeer.
MELODY MAKER

GREEN ON RED

Gas Food Lodging (ZIPPO)

The intensity and the unexpected plain-speaking in these songs are remarkable ...
MELODY MAKER

... has the feel of a finely bound book of illustrated short stories, some of which could become classics.
SOUNDS

... sweaty, unshaven denim melancholy ain't smelled so sweet in years.
NME

Green On Red (ZIPPO)

... a heartfelt scooping up and dusting down of American rock classicerama ...
NME

THE GUN CLUB

Two Sides Of The Beast (DOJO)

... why is this nonsense so attractive to so many?
SOUNDS

... shows the extremes of excellence and appalling dross The Gun Club WERE capable of creating.
MELODY MAKER

... a bit of a tired old party act.
RECORD MIRROR

... like some Club 18-30 holiday in Majorca.
SOUNDS

All very jolly and quite acceptable ...
NME

"In Praise Of Men With Giant Egos" might be a more accurate title.
MELODY MAKER

... four sides of uninspired indulgence ...
RECORD MIRROR

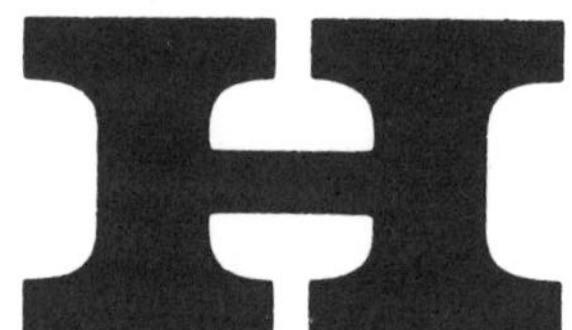

SAMMY HAGGAR

V.O.A. (GEFFEN)

What other LP sleeve has ever featured a "rock star" in front of the White House with absolutely no irony?
CREEM

Who does this wally think he is? I have never heard so much pretentious, facistic garbage in my life.
MELODY MAKER

HALL & OATES

Big Bam Boom (RCA)

... sounds like a messy collision between Michael Jackson and the Eagles.
MELODY MAKER

... top-class adult bop fodder ... music to iron your plaid shirt to.
NME

... the loudest and proudest album of their long career.
RECORD MIRROR

HEAVEN 17

How Men Are (VIRGIN)

I doubt anyone but Glenn, Martyn and Ian really know what they're on about.
SMASH HITS

Yet another bunch of minor talents whose rhetoric far outstrips their substance.
NME

DON HENLEY

Building The Perfect Beast (GEFFEN)

... the fact that he's not only survived but is also still capable of coherent thought is a minor marvel.
MELODY MAKER

... full of Californian lyrics about sunglasses, combed back hair and convertible cars.
SMASH HITS

... quite enjoyable, mindless AOR piffle ...
SOUNDS

This is a supremely clever record. But for all that, it should carry a government health warning.
NME

ROBYN HITCHCOCK

I Often Dream Of Trains (MIDNIGHT MUSIC)

... songs about the fixations of the lonesome eccentric, this album all but commits suicide in its suffocating self-obsessions.
NME

ROBYN HITCHCOCK AND THE EGYPTIANS

Fegmania (MIDNIGHT MUSIC)

The Soft Boys were unlistenable YEARS before it was fashionable . . .
SOUNDS

Syd Barrett and Lou Reed attempting the Monkees' catalogue . . .
NME

. . . re-establishes Hichcock's bewildering vision of psychedelic pop with great vengeance and dexterity.
MELODY MAKER

BILLY IDOL

Vital Idol (CHRYSALIS)

. . . makes Frankie's PLEASUREDOME sound like a Nick Lowe slapdown – it's dead made live, old made new, mouldy made modern.
MELODY MAKER

One day, he'll be properly appreciated as a talent instead of a porridge-brained pin-up.
SOUNDS

. . . showed kids everywhere that the tiniest amount of talent was needed to get a record deal with Chrysalis.
NME

I-LEVEL

Shake (VIRGIN)

The synthesis of contemporary black music and white pop . . . is remarkably seamless.
MELODY MAKER

. . . hinting at an ambiguous night-clubbing aura somewhere between London Bridge and ancient Egypt . . .
SOUNDS

. . . a sense of adventure is missing . . . Not one to put the cats amongst the pigeons.
NME

IRON MAIDEN

Powerslave (EMI)

. . . major bludgeoning music but with pretensions . . . to subtlety and intellect.
SMASH HITS

. . . they've learned to play properly as well as write good songs.
MELODY MAKER

Awesome is an over-used epithet, but nothing else seems to properly convey the overpowering bollocks of this thermonuclear package.
SOUNDS

IMMACULATE FOOLS

Hearts Of Fortune (A&M)

Best thing would be to bury all copies in a time-capsule for the enlightenment of future generations.
NME

What is distressing is that a group so young can be content merely to rehash elements of their own influences like one of those TOP OF THE POPS cover version albums.
MELODY MAKER

. . . already a contender for album of the year in my book . . . a real gem that in years to come will be recognized as a classic.
SOUNDS

GREGORY ISAACS

At The Academy Brixton (ROUGH TRADE)

Simply sad.
SOUNDS

. . . it does no one any favours – neither the star nor his paying public.
NME

. . . a fine collection which manages to capture the magic of a Gregory Isaacs live show.
MELODY MAKER

Easy (TADS)

. . . cold porridge . . .
SOUNDS

. . . devoid of colour, devoid of conviction, devoid of WORK.
NME

JACKSONS

Victory (EPIC)

. . . no direction, no fire, no sense of excitement . . .
SMASH HITS

VICTORY isn't bad, it's just a record which any Wet-Look Hollywood supertroupe could have made.
NME

FREDDIE JACKSON

Rock Me Tonight (CAPITOL)

. . . one of the finest new voices to appear for ages.
RECORD MIRROR

The search continues for Marvin's replacement and a commercial race is on for the new voice of midnight love . . . this year's most outstanding debut album.
NME

MICK JAGGER

She's The Boss (CBS)

. . . a good deal sharper and more 1985-sounding than the Rolling Stones look capable of . . .
SMASH HITS

. . . it's SO predictable, so dated.
RECORD MIRROR

. . . a jam session of Grammy Award winners.
SOUNDS

. . . a sardonic atonement from the man who wrote 'Under My Thumb'.
NME

. . . stands up by itself as a record every bit as vital and contemporary as anything the latest crop of teenagers may be shifting in the indie stores.
MELODY MAKER

RICK JAMES

Glow (MOTOWN)

. . . he scores effortlessly . . . and without ever mentioning the word "freak".
NME

James may consider himself a sexual aesthete, but in reality he's as predictable as a weekend bash with a pack of three.
MELODY MAKER

. . . possibly James's best dancer ever . . .
RECORD MIRROR

JAPAN

Exorcising Ghosts (VIRGIN)

Their music remains like the spectral shape of a heat sensitive photograph.
NME

The creeps who wouldn't give Sylvian and co the time of day two or three years ago are crawling out of the woodwork saying how crucial they were.
RECORD MIRROR

... bears testament to one of the eighties' most precious talents, a rare band that defied gravity and grew and got better ...
MELODY MAKER

... the most evocative deep soul music ever made by white boys.
SOUNDS

AL JARREAU

High Crime (WARNER BROS)

... hardly adequate as a testament to the man's abundant talent.
MELODY MAKER

Excellent softcore funk in a glittering shell of sophosticat values.
NME

JASON AND THE SCORCHERS

Lost And Found (EMI AMERICA)

... proof that Jason and the boys are THE hardcore punks of country music ...
SOUNDS

... perhaps the finest trad-rock album in years. A stone killer.
NME

... hasty and incomplete ... A disappointment.
MELODY MAKER

JELLYBEAN

Wotupski!?! (EMI)

... exposes his essential mediocrity.
MELODY MAKER

... very meek stuff – heartless, artless and smartless.
RECORD MIRROR

At least Frank Zappa might have cracked a joke or two.
NME

BROTHERS JOHNSON

Stomp (A&M)

... a disastrous collage of lost direction.
RECORD MIRROR

Out Of Control (A&M)

They've sold their soulful to the land of the bland for the rustle of green notes.
SOUNDS

All round, their best in ten years.
RECORD MIRROR

HOWARD JONES

Dream Into Action (WEA)

The philosopher of nouveau vulnerability ...
NME

... seems in such a hurry here to cover all his options that he never really shines.
SMASH HITS

Jones is fast maturing into an artist of imagination, style, vision and credibility ... It's time the rock snobs opened their eyes.
SOUNDS

... no SPARK, nothing we didn't already know about him.
RECORD MIRROR

In his way Howard Jones is more subversive than any overtly radical tub-thumpers because of his determination to resuscitate a repellent category epitomical of waste and decadence.
MELODY MAKER

RICKIE LEE JONES

The Magazine (WARNER BROS)

She has never been as JUBILANTLY passionate.
NME

Newman and Waits are much better on this turf, as is Joni Mitchell.
MELODY MAKER

JONZUN CREW FEATURING MICHAEL JONZUN

Down To Earth (TOMMY BOY)

... more dated than a 1975 calendar.
SOUNDS

... fairly undistinguished clutch of state-of-the-art soul and dance tracks ...
MELODY MAKER

JOOLZ

Never Never Land ... (ABSTRACT)

... the best album of the year ... Forget the Style Council, Smiths and other would-be social realists – THIS is how it's done.
SMASH HITS

... Joolz throws a harsh, chilling light on modern life ... an outrageously funny woman ...
SOUNDS

THE KANE GANG

The Bad And Lowdown World Of The Kane Gang
(KITCHENWARE)

... there is a distinct lack of gel here ...
RECORD MIRROR

... The KG brand of earthy truth 'n' justice testifying – honest and worthy as it may be – does become dull and repetitive when stretched over an album.
NME

... an evocative tribute to an intoxicating period of soul ...
SOUNDS

There's no fun here, no joy, no spontaneity, a sheen but no sparkle. All invention, no intuition.
MELODY MAKER

KATRINA AND THE WAVES

Katrina And The Waves
(CAPITOL)

Fresh faced, natural charm, economic guitar pop 'n' spark and an independent strongheaded female front person ... she may be the finest white girl since Dusty Springfield.
NME

They're young, bright, unpretentious, energetic, enthusiastic, optimistic, ridiculously naive – and damn good fun.
SOUNDS

... a sparkling diamond-hard collection of pert pop ...
RECORD MIRROR

Why do all these songs sound like rejects from Status Quo's MA KELLY'S GREASY SPOON?
SMASH HITS

NIK KERSHAW

The Riddle (MCA)

A commendable offering from the thinking person's Limahl ...
SMASH HITS

Like the magpie he is, he's collected lots of shiny bits and welded them into a fair concoction.
RECORD MIRROR

The basic problem with Nik is that he refuses to be seen and heard just as a piece of teenage fluff ...
MELODY MAKER

... you could listen to it over and over again for three or four days and not even notice.
SOUNDS

CHAKA KHAN

I Feel For You (WARNER BROS)

... is a one-dimensional tinny album ...
SOUNDS

Nice 'n' modern, nice 'n' safe ...
RECORD MIRROR

No more sleazy romps with Rufus.
NME

With 57 varieties of New York soul on offer you can't really fail to find something here to set feet in motion.
MELODY MAKER

KID CREOLE

In Praise of Older Women ... And Other Crimes (SIRE)

Darnell has been making records exactly like this for five or six years now ...
SMASH HITS

KING

Steps In Time (CBS)

King may have Soul on their boots, but there's little enough in their hearts.
MELODY MAKER

All they really need is a hit single.
SMASH HITS

... they smell distinctly fishy to me ...
RECORD MIRROR

In fairness, King are primarily a live band ...
SOUNDS

KOOL AND THE GANG

Emergency (PHONOGRAM)

Once wicked, they've plumped for the security of a very successful formula ...
NME

They always have three hits lurking within their dreadful sleeves.
RECORD MIRROR

... the fact is you CANNOT get down to Kool and the Gang.
SOUNDS

This record is a lie. It means nothing.
MELODY MAKER

LINTON KWESI JOHNSON

Reggae Greats (ISLAND)

. . . a worthy representation of his powers.
SOUNDS

The intelligent choice of tracks here does him a service.
NME

LASH LARIAT AND THE LONG RIDERS

Bitter Tears (BIG BEAT)

. . . a third-rate copy of the fast stuff John Denver borrowed from some airbrushed Nashville star selling a fourth-hand vision of thirties hick hoedown sentimentality.
NME

We're talking something purty fine here, folks, yes indeedee!
SOUNDS

. . . becomes a bit tedious here and there but t'aint half bad for starters.
MELODY MAKER

THE LAST POETS

The Last Poets (CELLULOID)

. . . the Poets are the precursors of everything currently black, musical and militant.
MELODY MAKER

. . . as rap becomes more and more the stuff of street "romanticism", I'd advise any young pretender to look this way.
RECORD MIRROR

. . . we should be more grateful than ever for this dark and brooding anger.
NME

It's simplistic in its rhetoric but contains grains of truth the size of mountains.
SOUNDS

Oh My People (CELLULOID)

One fine day these wise men will put the world to rights again. Meanwhile dig (out) the old classics.
SOUNDS

Rinsed, wrapped and recuperated, the Last Poets are part of the revolutionary furniture.
NME

. . . their message is still poignant, determined, and relevant.
MELODY MAKER

JULIAN LENNON

Valotte (CHARISMA)

. . . he never once infuses this record with the wit or compassion that highlighted his Dad's best work.
RECORD MIRROR

. . . it's difficult not to be impressed by a first album as accomplished and confident . . .
NME

LET'S ACTIVE

Cypress (IRS)

. . . a miniature masterpiece . . .
CREEM

. . . some of the most exciting and, yes, SPIRITUALLY resonant rock 'n' roll in many a marquee moon.
NME

It's just the best LP I've heard all year and proves that not ALL American twangsters have been driven stupid by MTV.
SMASH HITS

. . . another chunk of evidence pointing to an American renaissance quietly gathering strength.
MELODY MAKER

LEVEL 42

True Colours (POLYDOR)

. . . mild, milky, moderately intelligent, unadventurous and synthy smooth but about as welcome this autumn as Alka Seltzer to a goldfish.
NME

They still get bogged down in limp rhythms and turgid melodies . . .
MELODY MAKER

. . . an album of variety and taste, thoroughly recommended for any latent patent-leather soul boy.
SOUNDS

A Physical Presence (POLYDOR)

I prefer the studio band, stripped of solos and audience participation/desecration. The involvement of the Amalgamated Union of Referee's Whistle-Blowers and Chorus-Chanters soon becomes irksome.
SOUNDS

. . . strictly for the fan.
MELODY MAKER

LONE JUSTICE

Lone Justice (GEFFEN)

. . . a disappointingly safe debut, soaked in the sanitised rifferama of American rock.
NME

Disappointing but not unexpected, Lone Justice have yet to prove they're not the vanguard for The Pub Rock Revival.
MELODY MAKER

Barefaced Chic, I call it . . .
RECORD MIRROR

. . . stands out above the dross . . .
SOUNDS

THE LONG RYDERS

Native Sons (ZIPPO)

. . . the pizazz of the Beatles playing the Byrds.
RECORD MIRROR

A song like 'Ivory Tower' is reason enough for buying this record on its day of release . . .
SOUNDS

. . . An album I'd unhesitatingly describe as an American classic.
NME

LOOSE ENDS

So Where Are You? (VIRGIN)

. . . the new age of soul/jazz, welcome in any wine bar.
SOUNDS

. . . on the whole impressive.
NME

. . . a modern "soul" record without a heavy metal guitar solo in it anywhere.
MELODY MAKER

Not quite the earthshaker we dared to hope for . . .
RECORD MIRROR

LOS LOBOS

How Will The Wolf Survive? (LONDON/SLASH)

It's the values, morals and infatuations of their home community which perforates through the R&B, Tex-Mex hot licks of Los Lobos and makes them special.
SOUNDS

. . . a purity and honesty of feeling that recalls America's all-time finest, the Band.
NME

MALCOLM McLAREN

Fans (CHARISMA)

... this is not the revolutionary blend of cultures Malcolm would have us believe it is ... but you CAN dance to it and it IS hugely entertaining. Who could ask for anything more?
MELODY MAKER

It will either drive you completely bonkers or you won't be able to stop playing it.
SMASH HITS

It's hybrid, bastard stuff of course, but it's full of the wicked turns and naughty tricks that can make pop so wonderful.
RECORD MIRROR

Claiming disinterest and boredom in the recording process ... hardly covers for the important fact that TACKIE MACKIE is NOT VERY GOOD at anything anymore. He can't sing, he can't write ...
NME

MADONNA

Like A Virgin (SIRE)

... like opening a box of chocolates only to find it's full of sawdust.
RECORD MIRROR

... the whole project has a curiously weightless, vacuous feel about it.
MELODY MAKER

No wonder the poor darling has to drop her nylons to shift units ...
SOUNDS

MAI TAI

History (VIRGIN)

An unexpected pleasure.
SMASH HITS

... they get the old style Sister Sledge thrills down with textbook accuracy and some subliminal fire.
SOUNDS

MAN JUMPING

Jumpcut (COCTEAU)

... this is the most exhilarating debut album to have come out of Britain in the last six months.
MELODY MAKER

... a terrifying debut from a band Eno has called "the most important in the world". A slight exaggeration? Maybe not.
SOUNDS

MARILLION

Real To Reel (EMI)

... it would be cheaper to sit at home and listen to 'Trick Of The Tail' than to buy REAL TO REEL.
MELODY MAKER

... it beats me why people want to buy music to get depressed to.
SOUNDS

Misplaced Childhood (EMI)

... in the seventies the album charts were full of "progressive" rock groups like Genesis, Yes and Gentle Giant who made very boring "concept" LPs full of endless guitar solos and daft mystical lyrics. Marillion are the eighties version.
SMASH HITS

It's not exactly hip to like Marillion, but always remember they've sold more records than Working Week.
RECORD MIRROR

... the overriding sense of blood, sweat and tears manages to triumph over the in-built mock heroics and occasional delusions of grandeur, thus ensuring that Marillion can now enjoy their finest hour to date.
MELODY MAKER

... at least they're getting better at it!
SOUNDS

MARILYN

Despite Straight Lines (MERCURY)

Somewhere in the yawning gap between Vanity and Authenticity, Marilyn stands alone, with an album in his hands. Poor boy.
NME

All that production, the girl back-ups and arty cover cannot disguise the monotony of the record.
RECORD MIRROR

... too indigestible for even the most retentive colon.
SOUNDS

JOHN MARTYN

Sapphire (ISLAND)

... elegant and in places ravishing ...
MELODY MAKER

... his return to Island has dropped him back into the liquid, gear-slipping mould of the old, magical Martyn.
NME

MARY JANE GIRLS

Only For You (GORDY)

... like the girlfriend who invites you back for coffee and just gives you the coffee. Plenty of hints but no action.
RECORD MIRROR

... the cover says it all. The girls posing in their cheapo fetish gear looking sad, cheap and most telling of all ... bored as hell.
MELODY MAKER

... doesn't merit serious discussion.
NME

... a large slice of musical stroke-mag.
SOUNDS

MAXI PRIEST AND CAUTION

You're Safe (10 RECORDS)

...Maxi's reggae is a studied reorganization of already received (and adored) sounds ... the sweetest British pop record of 1985.
NME

... sunshine in a grey world.
MELODY MAKER

MAZE FEATURING FRANKIE BEVERLY

Can't Stop The Love (CAPITOL)

... trite tripe ...
SOUNDS

... rates with Maze's best ...
RECORD MIRROR

... too easily succumbs to the clammy hand of the soft-sell MOR market.
MELODY MAKER

Don't give up your day job Frankie.
NME

MEAT LOAF

Bad Attitude (ARISTA)

Perfect for mindlessly enjoyable escapism.
SOUNDS

Fast and furious but curiously unmoving.
SMASH HITS

... we are talking about somebody who, with a little push, could quite easily turn out to be a sort of Bruce Springsteen with beef.
MELODY MAKER

THE MEN THEY COULDN'T HANG

Night Of A Thousand Candles (IMP)

... the most pert and pertinent set of songs to be released on a debut album in a year of wet Sundays.
SOUNDS

... dances wildly over the grave of MOR garbage ...
MELODY MAKER

... consumate craftmanship, an attention to detail that is rare indeed.
NME

FREDDIE MERCURY

Mr Bad Guy (CBS)

Freddie's dedicated the record to his cat; I'm not saying it's bad, but someone should report him to the RSPCA.
SMASH HITS

... a real epic ...
RECORD MIRROR

Obviously this man has got a personality problem. Must stem from not having a personality.
SOUNDS

... a diverse album filled with dextrous tunes that are infinitely more pleasurable than the past 17 Queen albums.

VAN MORRISON

A Sense Of Wonder (MERCURY)

... here is an album of celestial celebration, as well as of sheer enjoyment.
SOUNDS

... drawing on all the best aspects of Van's glittering past, delivered in a voice that's still just second to none.
MELODY MAKER

... on the back he stands in a pose of awkward insouciance and wearing a significant, faintly ridiculous air. His music too has these qualities.
NME

MOTORHEAD

No Remorse (BRONZE)

... strangely enough it's actually not bad.
RECORD MIRROR

... as this album proves, Motorhead are just about the finest exponents of cranked-up rock 'n' roll rioting known to man.
SOUNDS

After Motorhead, nothing sounds quite right, including silence.
NME

ALISON MOYET

Alf (CBS)

... it sounds like too many record company questions and marketing suggestions have shaken her idea of herself.
NME

... a disappointing first solo LP.
SMASH HITS

... there's nothing that really leaps out and grabs you ...
RECORD MIRROR

ALF is that undistinguished, I'd offer a hanky if I had one.
SOUNDS

... a rare undercurrent of passion rumbling beneath the surface is sufficient to lift this album well above the pack ... ALF is an outstanding talent – no question about that.
MELODY MAKER

BILL NELSON

Trial By Intimacy (The Book Of Splendours) (COCTEAU)

... where four LPs of instrumental music (83 tracks lasting nearly three hours) doesn't mean a struggle.
SOUNDS

The pleasure's low-key, maybe, but it's there.
NME

NEW MODEL ARMY

No Rest For The Wicked (EMI)

... a re-hash of a punk-thrash sound which is now gloriously out-of-date.
SMASH HITS

Very impressive.
RECORD MIRROR

... mightily pungent and magnificently potent ...
SOUNDS

... their ideals are a cut above the average, but their execution falls below the mark.
MELODY MAKER

... a well-meaning but disturbingly unexciting, uncharitable record.
NME

NEW ORDER

Low-life (FACTORY)

... not just doomy electronic workouts but memorable melodies with a sense of humour lurking in the words.
SMASH HITS

I can't think of anything I can't do with this record – it informs and illuminates so many emotions.
MELODY MAKER

A slab of American pie among mushy peas, and the direction suits New Order as naturally as a baggy suit.
SOUNDS

New Order have gone commercial with class ... a brilliant album. Worth the wait – three times over.
RECORD MIRROR

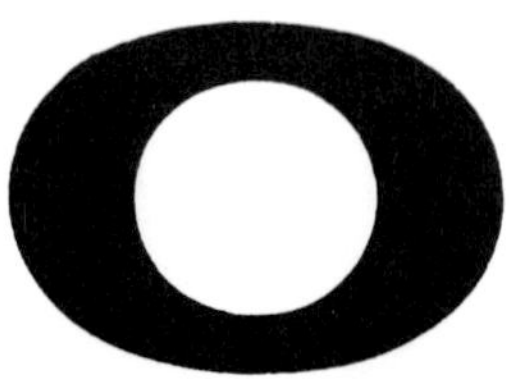

BILLY OCEAN

Suddenly (JIVE RECORDS)

... one long streak of paralysed piss ...
SOUNDS

... tepid ...
RECORD MIRROR

... welcome ...
MELODY MAKER

1000 MEXICANS
Dance Like Ammunition (FIRE)

Gone is any spirit of adventure.
NME

... it's a toe-tapper's delight.
SOUNDS

ORANGE JUICE
The Orange Juice (POLYDOR)

Can I be the only person left in the world who takes one swig of Orange Juice and longs instead for a shot of the hard stuff?
SOUNDS

... already my favourite white soul album EVER.
MELODY MAKER

... fairly unmemorable.
RECORD MIRROR

... his best and most consistent set for years.
SMASH HITS

... the heavy-lidded drawl has already become a parody of itself ...
NME

ORCHESTRAL MANOEUVRES IN THE DARK
Crush (VIRGIN)

...it's the welcome return of the thinking person's dance music, and isn't it good to hear real drums again!
SMASH HITS

... OMD show that they now have little to flex in the imagination department.
NME

They'd really like to do Something Bold again (as in DAZZLE SHIPS) but their accountant thinks that one risk is one too many.
SOUNDS

... the finest OMD long player to date.
MELODY MAKER

THE PALE FOUNTAINS
From Across The Kitchen Table (VIRGIN)

... they sound like every guitar band that's come out of Britain in the last four years.
RECORD MIRROR

... not unlike passionless sex; good while it lasts, to be valued and tried again certainly, but – no, the earth doesn't really move.
NME

... the first great album of 1985.
MELODY MAKER

FRANKIE PAUL
Pass The Tu-Sheng Peng (GREENSLEEVES)

... an album of brooding beauty.
SOUNDS

The discovery that the title track is about, wait for it, smoking ganja and eating fried chicken ... is mildly disappointing.
MELODY MAKER

TEDDY PENDERGRASS
Love Language (ASYLUM)

... straight away it's obvious that his voice has suffered, reduced by about a third of its original potency.
NME

... how all those ladies who used to throw their knickers at the man on stage will react is something of a poser.
MELODY MAKER

... Teddy struggles and fails to regain the cool control that was once his trademark.
SOUNDS

TOM PETTY AND THE HEARTBREAKERS
Southern Accents (MCA)

... the sound of the modern world, aware and alive.
MELODY MAKER

... great in places, downright dull in others ...
NME

JEFFREY LEE PIERCE
Wildweed (STATIK)

... a major detour, a brilliantly executed surprise and Pierce's most resonant body of work.
MELODY MAKER

A grower in every sense of the word.
SOUNDS

It's flawed but by no means the fall from grace reports of his live free-for-alls suggested.
NME

ROBERT PLANT
Shaken 'n' Stirred (ES PARANZA)

... should be force-fed to Morrissey at least ten times a day.
RECORD MIRROR

Glamorous Fossil Makes Half-way Decent LP.
NME

... a scrappy addition to a solo career which started off promisingly enough but soon got bitten by indulgence.
MELODY MAKER

... a series of the low-key vocal gymnastic exercises ...
SOUNDS

THE POGUES
Red Roses For Me (STIFF)

The needle on the Intox-O-Meter races into the red, and stays there.
RECORD MIRROR

... totally irresistible collection of lasting resentment, rebellious roars, watery-eyed romance and uproarious jigs.
SOUNDS

Respectable folkies will be appalled, pop people will be obliterated. It makes me feel dizzy and I love it.
MELODY MAKER

POINTER SISTERS
Contact (RCA)

... will not be the smash that its predecessor became ...
RECORD MIRROR

THE POWER STATION
The Power Station (EMI)

The album which proves that John 'Duran' Taylor is every micrometre the *noveau riche*, styleless, vain young shitball he always hinted at.
NME

... the sheer muscle of sound does hold a sort of forcible fascination.
SMASH HITS

The Power Station have fused nothing with nothing, and produced something less than something.
MELODY MAKER

... for all the talent present, the record sounds remarkably unoriginal.
CIRCUS

PREFAB SPROUT
Steve McQueen (KITCHENWARE)

... terrifically good.
SMASH HITS

Eventually the tension snaps and they begin to sound limp and wishy-washy ... For all that, Steve McQueen has no need to turn in his grave.
MELODY MAKER

... without a shadow of a doubt the finest album you will hear this year.
RECORD MIRROR

... a very fine record – by the standards of most contemporary pop, exemplary.
NME

PRINCE AND THE REVOLUTION

Around The World In A Day (WARNER BROS)

. . . a thing of madness.
SMASH HITS

. . . dippy surreal psychedelia.
RECORD MIRROR

His dip into period mysticism corresponds with a drop in libidinous punch, even as it ties in with his conversion to God.
NME

. . . by the look in his eyes of late he appears to be suffering from a bad case of the Howard Hughes syndrome.
MELODY MAKER

PROPAGANDA

The Secret Wish (ZTT)

I don't know how they do it – none of them can really sing, but it's fab.
RECORD MIRROR

It is the Abba factor that makes Propaganda so promising as a major pop happening.
NME

. . . four technocrats in love with imagination.
MELODY MAKER

. . . like any good concerned evolutionist, I love it because Claudia Suzanna Ralf and Michael do not come from Sydenham.
SOUNDS

PSYCHIC TV

New York Scum Haters (TEMPLE RECORDS)

At times it's like overhearing a badly tuned short wave radio which wavers between the Velvets in acidic flow and the Jesus and Mary Chain without melody.
SOUNDS

. . . the popstasy of PTV's faith in their ability to play the record industry at its own game. They lost. All their subsequent self-disgust with failure, coupled with their contempt for the industry, comes through here.
NME

PUBLIC IMAGE LIMITED/KEITH LEVENE

Commercial Zone (ROUGH TRADE)

. . . a collection of original PiL ephemera which puts the tin lid on Levene's involvement . . .
SOUNDS

. . . it's difficult to see why this scrapbook should be opened at all.
MELODY MAKER

RAIN PARADE

Emergency Third Rail Power Trip (ZIPPO)

. . . the grit and power of their ethereal vision is definitely of the eighties.
RECORD MIRROR

The first time I played it, I thought I had a visitation from God . . . a staggering debut.
MELODY MAKER

. . . some very pretty, gently unhinged pop songs – nothing dramatically hallucinatory.
NME

Explosions In The Palace (ZIPPO)

Either TRP are destined to be megabuck Floyd mk two or they're aspiring set of lysergic losers. Hot stuff, either way.
SOUNDS

The Rain Parade's dreamy drizzle of psychedelia at its most erratic.
NME

THE RAMONES

Too Tough To Die (BEGGARS BANQUET)

. . . living proof that America . . . doesn't know its pimpled ass from its elbow when it comes to the important things in life. How can they lap up all that AOR slush when they've had one of the best bands in the universe vandalizing their backyard for a whole decade?
MELODY MAKER

. . . has all the ingredients of any of the previous nine Ramones gross outs.
SOUNDS

. . . classic . . .
NME

RANK AND FILE

Long Gone Dead (LONDON)

. . . edges further than its predecessor into the realms of pure country music . . .
SMASH HITS

. . . as much as the objective listener in me hears invigorating music, my subjective self remains untouched, just out of reach.
NME

RED GUITARS

Slow To Fade (SELF DRIVE)

. . . a good brew of modern rock . . . intelligent entertainment.
NME

. . . a rock record with a brain by a group who have a point of view worth hearing.
MELODY MAKER

No demanding concepts, no immature egotists, just great songs.
SOUNDS

R.E.M.

Fables Of The Reconstruction (IRS)

. . . will creep up on you rather than wallop you over the head . . .
RECORD MIRROR

If the Smiths are hailed as England's primary "lyric" band . . . then R.E.M. are America's equivalent.
MELODY MAKER

. . . there's something glum and curiously passionless about what appears to be another quest to thrust enigma into rock melody.
NME

Highly recommended for those who listen to records with their ears rather than their feet.
SMASH HITS

THE REPLACEMENTS

Let It Be (ZIPPO)

. . . a supreme and wildly intoxicating slice of pure pop infection . . .
SOUNDS

R.E.M. meet the Smiths . . .
NME

. . . one of the brightest hopes on an American gar(b)age scene which has existed solely in the fevered imaginations of PEBBLES compilers for far too long.
MELODY MAKER

JONATHAN RICHMAN AND THE MODERN LOVERS

Rockin' And Romance (ROUGH TRADE)

. . . sheer unadulterated honesty . . .
RECORD MIRROR

So obvious, so natural, so brilliant!
SOUNDS

This LP, one of his finest, should be melting every heart.
MELODY MAKER

More songs about Boston, baseball, beaches, Bermuda, jeans, UFOs, famous dead painters and faded chewing-gum wrappers. It'd be churlish to ask for more.
NME

SMOKEY ROBINSON

Essar (MOTOWN)

. . . an utterly classic recording . . . his writing is full of life again.
RECORD MIRROR

. . . he drifts into a vapid amalgam of contemporary dance clichés . . .
MELODY MAKER

Who would've thought the tears of a clown would turn into the dribblings of a middle-aged, glycerine-faced, one-dimensional, cloying creep?
SOUNDS

NILE RODGERS

B-Movie Matinee (WARNER BROS)

. . . Rodgers, having done more good things in the real world than anyone has a right to do, cannot make decent records under his own name.
SOUNDS

. . . I can't hear anything here that will achieve the classic status of earlier work.
NME

ROMEO VOID

Instincts (CBS)

Romeo Void sing about sex; pure, emotionless sex. They could be the most honest band you've ever heard.
MELODY MAKER

The noise herein may almost make the grade as instinctual, but the words are excruciating (SOAP OPERA) rubbish.
NME

DIANA ROSS

Swept Away (CAPITOL)

Play to your mum while you bop to Madonna.
SMASH HITS

A female Rod Stewart album.
RECORD MIRROR

Diana Ross – once the epitome of heartbreaking innocence with the Supremes – stultifies.
NME

Five stars for little Diana . . . When Sade is pulling pints in the Rover's Return, STYLE will still be making grown men and women aspire to higher mountains.
SOUNDS

DAVID LEE ROTH

Crazy From The Heat (WARNER BROS)

. . . throbs with the infectious fun of playing around with nostalgia whilst still remaining incorrigibly Dave. I like it.
NME

RUN DMC

King Of Rock (PROFILE)

. . . intelligent, danceable culturally accurate document that explains why "other rappers can't stand us but give us respect".
SOUNDS

. . . a superb synthesis of funk and HM . . . Hip hop is not dead.
NME

S

MATHILDE SANTING

Water Under The Bridge (WEA)

. . . if you've the slightest capacity for dreaming then give the delicacy and strength of Ms Santing a try.
MELODY MAKER

If this is to be the age of the torch, Mathilde Santing makes the others pale to insignificance.
NME

SCRITTI POLITTI

Cupid & Psyche 85 (VIRGIN)

He does go on a bit actually, and each song sounds much like the last.
SMASH HITS

What Mel Gibson is to leather, Scritti are to sophisticated pop sounds. Heaven.
RECORD MIRROR

. . . the most flimsily gorgeous white lovers' rock since the Police walked on the moon and George asked us if we really wanted to hurt him.
MELODY MAKER

. . . the effusions of Bo Diddley, Howlin' Wolf and Captain Beefheart seem more honest, trustworthy representations of male sexuality than Green's horrid Violet Elizabeth Bott vocalizings . . .
NME

SHRIEKBACK

Jam Science (ARISTA)

. . . almost letting you forget the irritatingly obtrusive fact that they don't half reckon they're a bunch of clever bastards.
NME

Those clatterings noises aren't the latest sound effects – it's just the clash of instinct meeting with intellect.
MELODY MAKER

. . . clever lyrics and definite manic depressive tendencies.
SMASH HITS

Oil And Gold (ARISTA)

The contrived vocal style of Carl Marsh gets on one's tits pretty quick . . .

There's certainly fun to be had from the company of these boys, but whether I'd actually invite them to one of my parties is debatable.
MELODY MAKER

SISTER SLEDGE

When The Boys Meet The Girls (WEA)

A case of producer Nile Rodgers rescuing some rather weak material.
SMASH HITS

. . . I can't hear anything here that will achieve the classic status of their earlier work.
NME

. . . has some forgettable moments . . .
MELODY MAKER

SISTERS OF MERCY

First And Last And Always (MERCIFUL RELEASE)

Currently riding high in the LP charts and thus proving a long-held demographic truth . . . this being the inordinately high propensity of angst-ridden teen people to consume dark-laden albums rather than commit suicide.
RECORD MIRROR

. . . ten repetitive tunes . . .
SMASH HITS

. . . this stuff is about as angry as Roland Rat.
SOUNDS

. . . until they stop taking themselves seriously . . . the Sisters Of Mercy will be just another Shake The Funky Moisture Off Your Hands dance band.
NME

. . . packed with glistening gems . . . a startling array of timeless jewels.
MELODY MAKER

THE SKATALITES

Scattered Lights (TOP DECK RECORDS)

. . . native Jamaican improvisational brilliance . . .
SOUNDS

. . . the record's dated pleasantry subsides too easily into dullness.
NME

THE SMITHS

Hatful Of Hollow (ROUGH TRADE)

Seeking splendour in simplicity and bringing magnificence out of misery, these charming Smiths are vivid and in their prime.
NME

. . . I urge even the most ardent Smiths non-supporter to delve into this mixture . . .
RECORD MIRROR

. . . should find a place in every collection . . .
SOUNDS

Perhaps Morrissey should be read and not heard.
MELODY MAKER

Meat Is Murder (ROUGH TRADE)

. . . their music is well beyond the trivial novelty we've come to know as pop.
MELODY MAKER

The Smiths' artistic achievement is genuinely beyond doubt . . .
NME

. . . he'll never convince me that one man's nut loaf isn't another man's baked nosepickings . . .
SOUNDS

THE SOS BAND

Just The Way You Like It (TABU)

. . . this music can rival the feeling of silk on bare skin . . .
MELODY MAKER

These guys aren't sending the SOS, they're the ones answering it.
RECORD MIRROR

The same chords, the same synth signatures. It's not the way I like it.
NME

. . . escapist music of great depth, sureness and soulful inner spirit.
SOUNDS

RICK SPRINGFIELD

Tao (RCA)

. . . no worse than Bryan Adams.
SMASH HITS

. . .you CAN pine for the days when the scope of a teen star's ambition encompassed only a desire to find his summerlove sensation.
MELODY MAKER

STING

The Dream Of The Blue Turtles (A&M)

. . . Sting has finally come of age.
SOUNDS

This isn't a terribly interesting set of songs.
NME

Sting is a one-trick pony.
MELODY MAKER

THE STRANGLERS

Aural Sculpture (EPIC)

. . . great listening . . . Henry Moore would be proud.
SOUNDS

. . . the most accessible music the Stranglers have produced in their ten years of play . . .
RECORD MIRROR

. . . Celebrating their hundredth year in showbiz is no excuse; this is shocking.
MELODY MAKER

. . . descends from mellow to miserable . . . to just plain depressing.
SMASH HITS

. . . aural torture . . . unmitigated shite . . .
NME

STRAWBERRY SWITCHBLADE

Strawberry Switchblade (KOROVA)

. . . wimp-out muzak.
SOUNDS

. . . woeful lack of diversity . . .
MELODY MAKER

. . . great name, rotten group.
NME

. . . desperately lightweight and quite relentlessly tedious . . .
RECORD MIRROR

THE STYLE COUNCIL

Our Favourite Shop (POLYDOR)

. . . it's all rather heavy going.
SMASH HITS

. . . not the noise of revolution . . .
SOUNDS

He's made politics the first item on the agenda . . .
NME

Laid-back, easy-listening sounds accompanied by hard-hitting words and messages.
RECORD MIRROR

. . . slicker and more confident than ever.
MELODY MAKER

SYLVESTER

M1015 (CHRYSALIS)

. . . it's alarmingly clear that the Bronskis have a long way to go before they're vaguely close to catching up . . .
MELODY MAKER

. . . rests too easily on surface style and seldom cuts deeper.
NME

. . . a globby stodge of pie-in-the-sky hi-energy and eclectic electro.
SOUNDS

THE SYSTEM

X-Periment (ATLANTIC)

. . . a replicant pop-funk.
CREEM

The originality and variety of the electronics is a delight . . . we're talking truly modern soul.
NME

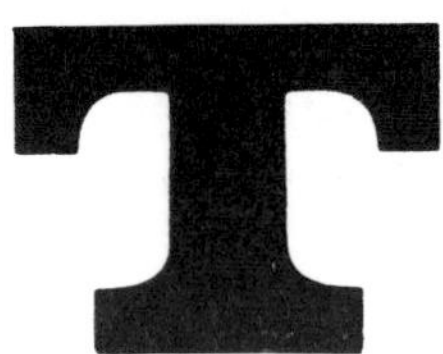

TALKING HEADS

Stop Making Sense (EMI)

Without the benefit of its visual counterpart, it may be presumptuous to pass a fatal judgement but the material IS surprisingly OBVIOUS.
MELODY MAKER

... the Heads have crumbled into a shadowy parody of themselves.
SOUNDS

... is, truly, the American pseudo-intellectual equivalent of a Prize Wally.
NME

... a very fine record.
RECORD MIRROR

Little Creatures (EMI)

I still don't know what they're burbling about most of the time ...
RECORD MIRROR

Talking Heads have started to make sense ...
MELODY MAKER

Not since this particular band's second album have more songs about houses, factories, windows, babies' pee-pee and kitchens sounded so good.
NME

TEARS FOR FEARS

Songs From The Big Chair (MERCURY)

... they build rhythmic catchphrases and wonderful melodies upon sturdy song structures and sing with compelling conviction.
SMASH HITS

... a calculated and brilliant peak, a quintessence of their polished pop putty ... a marvellous, seamless, vindicating triumph.
NME

... fully justifies the rather sneering, told-you-so looks adopted by Curt Smith and Roland Orzabal on the sleeve.
MELODY MAKER

... glorious pop – as fiercely convincing as Magazine, as playful as Wire, but with the dream gloss of the hit parade!
SOUNDS

TEENA MARIE

Starchild (EPIC)

... comes across like a clumsy female model of Prince.
SMASH HITS

... don't you think it's about time you forgot Madonna and discovered the real woman?
SOUNDS

I want her to be Aretha Franklin and she wants to be Elizabeth Barrett Browning.
RECORD MIRROR

... an intoxicating relief from the endless beige pretenders.
NME

... knocks all other non-black pretenders into a cocked hat.
MELODY MAKER

THE TEMPTATIONS

Truly For You (MOTOWN)

... most of the album is an uncomfortable attempt to recall past glories while juxtaposing them with the – uh – contemporary sound.
NME

10,000 MANIACS

Secrets Of The I Ching (CHRISTIAN BURIAL)

... should be towed in for repairs or sunk with gunfire.
NME

TEST DEPARTMENT

Beating The Retreat (SOME BIZARRE)

Using anything from lumps of old scrap metal and plastic to cellos and harps, they beat out huge chunks of fiercely tribal rhythms and create a variety of dark menacing moods.
SMASH HITS

... such a momentous, magnificent NOISE, that I beg you to pay attention.
MELODY MAKER

Test Department attack stagnation and society's programming with ferocious emotion and peculiar adventure.
SOUNDS

It's actually sonorous, frequently foot-tapping.
NME

LINDA THOMPSON

One Clear Moment (WARNER BROS)

... a collection of exquisitely crafted songs from a voice that has endured unobtrusively over the years ...
SOUNDS

Up there alongside BRIGHT LIGHTS, Richard's HUMAN FLY and the first two Sandy Denny albums ... It's THAT good.
MELODY MAKER

RICHARD THOMPSON

Across A Crowded Room (POLYDOR)

I'd like to think I'll be able to claim ultimate hipness for sticking with Richard Thompson through thick and thin.
SOUNDS

... further evidence of a current malaise afflicting rock's quota of elder statesmen – good guys gone to seed.
NME

... the most powerful, singleminded rock album he's ever made ... this is pretty damn perfect.
MELODY MAKER

THE TIME

Ice Cream Castles
(WARNER BROS)

. . . continues to sound like Prince's opening act . . .
CREEM

. . . leaves you with the feeling that you walked in halfway through somebody's jam session . . .
SOUNDS

Their smut-funk fetishism loses its initial wit with repeated plays . . .
NME

TOYAH

Minx (PORTRAIT)

. . . some of the most bland and faceless music ever cut.
RECORD MIRROR

. . . a more flat version of today's post-Horn SONIC pop I've yet to hear.
MELODY MAKER

Sad second stream Roxy-isms clash unceremoniously on Gal Numan meets the Nolans out-takes.
SOUNDS

THE TRIFFIDS

Raining Pleasure (ROUGH TRADE)

. . . deservedly earmarked as the Band Most Likely To in 1985.
MELODY MAKER

. . . where did I put that "Bomb Australia" badge?
NME

Treeless Plains (ROUGH TRADE)

. . . a disappointment.
MELODY MAKER

It is beginning to seem as if Australia houses more Jim Morrison fans than any other country in the world.
NME

UB40

Geffrey Morgan
(DEP INTERNATIONAL)

The best thing that can be said about this album is that it's another UB40 record.
MELODY MAKER

. . . wider ambitions have got the better of them on this LP and they haven't been able to meet their requirements.
NME

. . . UB40 get more EXCITING as they grow older.
SMASH HITS

. . . it's all pretty fab, despite my inherent loathing of reggae as a genre.
RECORD MIRROR

The UB40 File (GRADUATE/VIRGIN)

. . . this collection of their early work is heavy going . . . they skank like champs and their politics are impeccable, but they work best in small doses . . .
NME

Delicious stuff . . .
RECORD MIRROR

. . . a lousy rip-off . . . A complete waste of time and money.
MELODY MAKER

U2

The Unforgettable Fire (ISLAND)

. . . one of the few groups still worth bothering with.
SMASH HITS

. . . this dramatic new tack is brave and welcome.
MELODY MAKER

. . . music worth spending some months getting to know.
NME

U2 have become disturbingly average.
SOUNDS

THE UNTOUCHABLES

Wild Child (STIFF)

. . . a hasty messy blend with a production mix Kenwood would laugh at.
SOUNDS

All the tracks here conjure up an image of men dancing badly but enthusiastically, people trying to revive something already over-revived . . .
NME

. . . sheer sixties stamping soul . . .
SMASH HITS

All in all, not just another dodgy guitar band from LA.
MELODY MAKER

USA FOR AFRICA

We Are The World (CBS)

Regardless of your politics or musical preference, a worthwhile record.
CIRCUS

. . . far more worthy than it is interesting.
SMASH HITS

All previously unreleased stuff on what is, surprisingly, not a dog of an LP.
NME

. . . a pity so much vinyl had to be wasted along the way.
SOUNDS

LUTHER VANDROSS

The Night I Fell In Love (EPIC)

Beautiful stuff . . . a sleek black panther of a record, shimmering and simmering with guile and style and subtle tender soul.
SOUNDS

. . . a notable and welcome exception to the norm in the peacock park world of the male soul singer.
MELODY MAKER

Vegas beckons if Luth doesn't try something new here.
NME

SUZANNE VEGA

Suzanne Vega (A&M)

. . . very Al Stewart, very bedsitter-rooted.
SOUNDS

. . . as Voltaire remarked, that which is too silly to be said is instead sung.
NME

THE VELVET UNDERGROUND

V.U. (POLYDOR)

. . . cuts through most of the moment's crap like a razor with its blade on fire.
MELODY MAKER

. . . generally five-star grist . . .
SOUNDS

. . . belongs right up there between the third album and LOADED – a masterpiece.
NME

TOM VERLAINE

Cover (VIRGIN)

. . . Verlaine has triumphantly rediscovered and redefined the inspiration that fuelled so much of his early work.
MELODY MAKER

VIOLENT FEMMES

Hallowed Ground (LONDON)

. . . about as entertaining as an evening in the mortuary.
SMASH HITS

. . . a medicine show of hellfire preachers, shysters, hucksters, lonesome killers, bluegrass pickers, jazz honkers, gospel wailers and other picturesque types.
NME

. . . not so much an album as a kind of sermon . . .
MELODY MAKER

VIRGIN PRUNES

Over The Rainbow (BABY/NEW ROSE)

. . . rare and hitherto unreleased material 1981-3.
SOUNDS

. . . one of the few truly independent bands of the last ten years.
NME

. . . Only Dublin could have spawned their intricacies, their perverse and outrageous humour, only England could have failed to see their brilliance.
MELODY MAKER

VISAGE

Beat Boy (POLYDOR)

. . . all I seem to hear are the distant cries of an act well past its prime and all the make-up in the world isn't going to cover up the cracks.
RECORD MIRROR

Steve and co may have missed the boat . . .
SOUNDS

Pack it in, chaps.
SMASH HITS

. . . to be welcomed as an attempt at public education.
NME

WAH!

The Way We Wah! (WEA)

A wonderful album . . .
RECORD MIRROR

. . . a welcome opportunity to check out Wah!'s chequered past . . .
MELODY MAKER

. . . proving that when you scratch a soapbox pop star you find someone who wanted to be one of the lads but couldn't quite make it.
NME

THE WAILERS

Reggae Greats (ISLAND)

. . . the days when the drums sounded like a clatter of dustbin lids and the bass was just a warm rumble.
SMASH HITS

You won't find a modern reggae record that sounds as good, that's for sure.
MELODY MAKER

. . . more a showcase for a promise about to be fulfilled than an outright classic in itself.
SOUNDS

WHAM!

Make It Big (EPIC)

It even had me humming along, that's how insidiously clever it is.
MELODY MAKER

George Michael certainly has an ear for a tune – and it's usually someone else's.
SMASH HITS

It is too synthetic and transparent. It rings hollow, without invention or mystery . . . They should have called it "The Art Of Pandering".
NME

. . . one is tempted to conclude that Mr Ridgeley had a bit of time to kill after the soft-focus sessions were complete.
RECORD MIRROR

THE WHO

Who's Last (MCA)

A 16-track live double album of well-varied and well-recorded material from the only sixties band I rate and relate to.
SOUNDS

. . . any band who say they come from Shepherds Bush and fail to mention QPR in any of their songs are decidedly dodgy. Like this particular package.
NME

WHODINI

Escape (JIVE)

. . . the kind of record FACE readers pretend to own, but nobody actually hears outside the playground.
MELODY MAKER

. . . this electro percussion jogs, wiggles and never gets out of breath . . . Keep your tracksuit on.
RECORD MIRROR

. . . rapping brilliantly over seas of sensuous electronic sound.
NME

KIM WILDE

Teases And Dares (MCA)

Mills and Boon has nothing on this.
NME

Somewhere beneath all the WOMAN'S OWN rubbish, Kim has a talent to match her looks. Whether it will ever fully emerge I wouldn't like to say.
SOUNDS

There is an irreproachable honesty behind all this mendacity, an effect perhaps more truthful than bands like the Fall, who suppose they have a grasp on reality.
MELODY MAKER

WOMACK AND WOMACK

Radio M.U.S.I.C. Man (ELEKTRA)

... a bit of a let-down.
SMASH HITS

... Womack and Womack are God.
SOUNDS

... accomplished but not triumphant ...
RECORD MIRROR

... has already staked out my stereo until Christmas ...
NME

... isn't likely to inspire that same thrill ...
MELODY MAKER

STEVIE WONDER

The Woman In Red (MOTOWN)

Only half an LP really, but much better than most "complete" ones.
RECORD MIRROR

... there's nothing here to suggest that anyone will remember this album ten years hence.
NME

Stevie seems to have got pretty sloppy of late, with none of that taut lyricism that made his early seventies albums such a joy to hear.
MELODY MAKER

WORKING WEEK

Working Nights (VIRGIN RECORDS)

... it'll go down a storm with the bedsit student brigade ...
SOUNDS

... an achievement worth applauding. From the ashes of Weekend has risen a band of dreams and sophistication.
MELODY MAKER

If at times it's more an LP of moments than songs, then some of the things within are actually worth waiting for.
NME

XTC

The Big Express (VIRGIN)

Partridge and Moulding are writing classic songs again ...
SOUNDS

Gee, it's unfashionable. But this is the best XTC record.
NME

No doubt the large audience XTC entertained at the turn of the decade has mostly lost sight of them ...
MELODY MAKER

XTC make records for themselves these days ... THE BIG EXPRESS will be remembered more for its circular sleeve than its somewhat square contents. This ain't pop!
SMASH HITS

YELLO

Stella (ELEKTRA)

... meanders through sophisticated disco in a silky, mesmeric fashion to the land where hardcore electro meets Vangelis ...
SMASH HITS

... oozes sex appeal ...
RECORD MIRROR

Each haunting episode reeks of a sublime suspense with a liberal coating of electric eccentricity.
SOUNDS

Welcome to the pleasure dome.
MELODY MAKER

PAUL YOUNG

The Secret Of Association (CBS)

... uncomfortable, irritating and just a little disappointing.
SMASH HITS

... a terrible album from a wonderful singer ...
RECORD MIRROR

He never strikes as being a major performer, but hard work has made him a very capable one.
NME

... far beyond the cosy, adult conservatism that Young and his admirers might be assumed to occupy.
MELODY MAKER

FRANK ZAPPA

Thing-Fish (EMI)

As ever, Zappa's over-the-top enthusiasm is inspired tongue in cheek and, in the main, successful.
SOUNDS

... satire of the most heavy-handed kind ... contains no decent tunes, some very ordinary playing, and too much narration. Where does he get his money from?
NME

... an album for people who haven't outgrown flares.
MELODY MAKER

ZERRA

Zerra 1 (MERCURY)

... most of this first album is neither passionate, spirited nor inspiring ...
SMASH HITS

... sounds like Neil Diamond with balls ... could establish Zerra 1 as a major band.
SOUNDS

... reminding me once again what U2 could have sounded like, if only they hadn't stopped playing Ramones cover versions.
MELODY MAKER

Zerra 1 are a bunch of rip-off merchants, and I say "Bugger off" to their Todd Rundgren production and their Robert Mapplethorpe sleeve photos.
NME

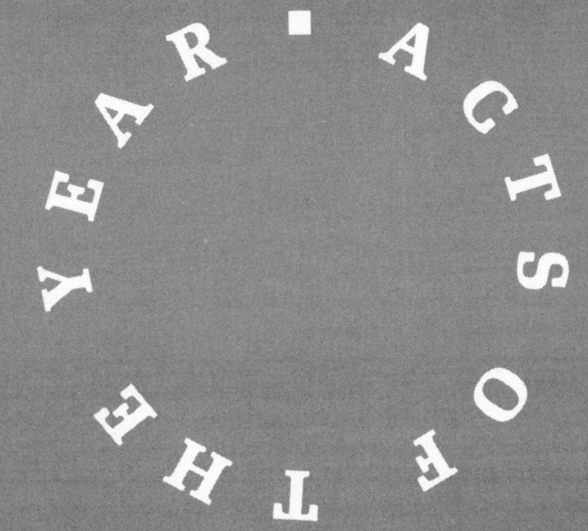

ACTS OF THE YEAR

ACTS OF THE YEAR •

PRINCE

"Prince is really hung up on God," remarked the actress who had been turned down for a part in *Purple Rain*. "I think he thinks he's *related* to God in some way . . ."

And, lo, it came to pass that God did appear during the recording of *Around The World In A Day*. And catching Prince in full saucy flow, God was angry — *"Oh sinner man!"* And verily Prince did whimper and repent — *"I'm sorry. I'll be good . . ."*

God as guest vocalist? *Most* peculiar — but then as everybody knew by now, Prince was a most peculiar soul . . .

Ever since the *Purple Rain* film and soundtrack LP had turned Prince Rogers Nelson into Rock's-Very-Hottest-Property-Including-Michael-Jackson in the autumn of 1984, the press had been probing the singer's eccentricities with glee and much sniggering. The sulky silence, the purple petulance, the mountainous minders, and the Thanks-Be-2-God-with-not-very-many-clothes-on syndrome had kept the world amused, sometimes amazed, for months.

It was the strength of Prince's music which had aided his ascent, but over the final slippery rungs it was his uncommon persona and contradictions — arrogance holding hands with vulnerability in the man; God frugging with Sex in the disco — which had intrigued the public enough to turn "His Royal Badness" into an everyday household phrase. Prince was a Mystery — Greta Garbo and Jimi Hendrix in one small but perfectly formed package. Prince was an Engima, toasting the Almighty and breathing heavily at the same time. Prince was a True Star and, if he was to be believed, it was all Thanks 2 God . . .

Prince had dedicated his very first album, in 1977, to God. But any resemblance to Cliff Richard, Pat Boone and other worthy Christian pop folk ended there. Far from being wholesome and saintly, *For You* was all about doing IT; 'Soft And Wet' was just one title. From such beginnings Prince would thrust forwards to establish himself as rock's leading lascivious impresario. His vibrant blend of black dance rhythms and white rock'n'roll — lusty funk with squealing guitars — was exciting enough in itself, but when it was topped with lashings of spicy porno celebrations, well . . .

"Sex-related fantasy is all my mind can see," Prince confessed in 'When We're Dancing Close and Slow' (from the second LP, *Prince*), and who could quarrel with this admission? On stage the man was swaggering about in black lace underwear, orgying with his geetar, getting over-friendly with backing vocalists Vanity 6 ('Nasty Girls'), and even bringing a bed into the proceedings for more realistic sexual simulation antics. The third album, *Dirty Mind*, contained celebrations of oral sex ('Head') and incest ('Sister'). The fourth, *Controversy*, featured compositions with such savoury titles as 'Jack U Off' and 'Do Me Baby'. "I write everything from experience," Prince remarked. Some swooned. Others called him a "faggot".

So where was God in all this? Well, He put in a brief appearance on *Controversy* when, during the title track, Prince chanted The Lord's Prayer, much to the disgust of the Moral Majority. But otherwise, as Prince didn't consider himself "a great poet or interpreter à la Moses", he generally confined himself to testifying "do whatever you want, wear lingerie to a restaurant" and similar pearls.

With 1982's startling *1999* album — a double LP that was to sell some five million copies — Prince became a commercial giant (five foot two and getting rich). The dirty stuff had done its work: he was *noticed*. It was now time to become a Legend . . .

How to become a Legend: Plan A — The Eccentric-Recluse-With-Closed-Lips-Method-As-Pioneered-By-Howard-Hughes-And-Little-Michael-Jackson. It might just work. God willing . . .

In 1982, whether as a deliberate attention-courting ruse or prompted by haughty delusions of grandeur *or* "paranoid vibrations", Prince let it be known that he would not be granting any more interviews. *Ever*. He might possibly be available for a photo session every once in a thousand years or so, but then again he might not; he was acutely sensitive and having his picture taken made him physically ill. Besides, he had a most demanding full-length feature film to create . . . Press persons rose to the bait: if his Royal Tetchiness wouldn't stoop to being interviewed, why then, they'd just have to make something up . . .

Shot in a hurry on a weedy budget with a cast of "newcomers", *Purple Rain* opened in 700 cinemas across America in August 1984. Response was warm. The *LA Herald Examiner* spluttered something about Prince dominating the screen "with all the allure, menace and vulnerability that made Marlon Brando so irrefutable in *The Wild One*". Other responsible journals used words like "juicy", "high-powered", "great" and *"Citizen Kane"* and within two weeks the film was topping the US box-office ratings ahead of that season's "sure-fire blockbusters" *Indiana Jones and the Temple of Doom* and *Ghostbusters*. It was all too much for the British tabloid soaraway *Sun* which gasped — in a sizzling scoop headlined "SEXY WEIRD WORLD OF POP'S PURPLE PRINCE: Girls Lose Out To God And Music" — "the film's huge success has left even the people who made it gaping with astonishment!!" . . . Yes! Prince hysteria had been invented . . .

In the sober light of day, *Purple Rain* seemed no less corn-filled than most other pop/youth movies: *Catch Us If You Can* met *Psych-Out* with pinches of sex (and sexism), meanness and streetwise-assery chucked in for the eighties. The script was soap and some of the acting was "reluctant" to say the least. Not that this mattered much in the case of Patty 'Apollonia' Kotero — recently "discovered" by Prince and thrown in at the deep end as leading lady — all she was called upon to do was slink around with her satin undergarments half falling off, get tossed into the odd trashcan and engage in prolonged bouts of soft-focus snogging. She was quite good at that.

But it wasn't *all* bad. Prince, with his obsessive pouting and wobbly charisma, had undeniable screen presence. The heavy hints that here was a work of autobiography helped to feed the Legend, and the music — well, that was quite superb. Prince and the Revolution embraced pop keenly, conjuring up such beaming creations as 'When Doves Cry', the jerky, exuberant 'Let's Go Crazy' and the tufty guitar-soaked title ballad (which went on forever — and why not?)

For some old Prince fans, the *Purple Rain* music was a betrayal; their sex hero had gone safe and mild. For Prince himself, however, the more mainstream approach turned out wonderfully; for every former devotee alienated, he had won fifty new admirers.

While the *Purple Rain* LP was outselling everything including Springsteen — Prince occupied himself pursuing a secondary career as producer/composer, groom and creator of female pop product. Around his girlfriend Vanity (later spurned for Apollonia), he had fashioned a so-called vocal trio, Vanity 6 (later Apollonia 6) and, like a new Hugh Hefner or a disciple of Kim Fowley, he set his girls to work as singing sex objects, writhing in lingerie. He also took percussion dervish Sheila Escovedo under his wing, co-masterminded the come-back of Chaka Khan with 'I Feel For You', and concocted the spicy 'Sugar Walls' for little Sheena Easton.

But with whom was Prince engaged in, ahem, "friendly discussions", *that's* what everyone wanted to know. "Our love will never die," gushed Apollonia. Poor deluded girl, smirked Sheila E. Persons "close to" his Majestic Platformbootedness dropped sly hints about Prince and Revolution guitarist Wendy Melvoin; others tipped Vanity to stage a romantic comeback while even — gasp! — Madonna was in the running. Then there were those who said that actually the only one for Prince (apart from Prince himself) was . . . God.

So where *was* God all this time? Well, He had had a *Purple Rain* song all of his own. 'God'. Plus, if you played the end of the LP's one overtly sexual number, 'Darling Nikki', backwards, you'd hear a tiny voice saying "Hello. How are you? I'm fine. Because I know the Lord is coming soon . . ."

"Detroit — my name is Prince and I've come to play with you." Confetti rained down, smoke bombs banged, feverish squealing filled Detroit's Joe Louis Arena. The massive Purple Rain tour — Prince's victory lap — was underway. And here was the new Prince, the not-so-dirty-as-before Prince, the mass-markety Prince, the Hollywood Star Prince who, according to alert press reports, demanded at every concert: sixty chrysanthemums, lavender roses, candles, a navy blue couch, a Queen Anne-style chair, a grand piano, a chocolate vending machine, popcorn, cough syrup, wine, potato chips, etc, to be placed in his dressing-room or thereabouts.

"Sex-related fantasy is all my mind can see . . ."

It could all have gone horribly wrong, this opening night. Prince was rattled, that much was clear from the first time he did a foxy little pirouette and fell over. Would his new showbiz/glamour formula work? Abandoned displays of an animal nature had been replaced by things far less suggestive: instead of making lurve to his geetar, he used it as a water pistol; instead of trenchcoats and bikini briefs he sported frilly shirts and that purple jacket; the bed was now a bathtub; the brutish slut of yesteryear was a fragile and delicate matinée idol . . .

It *did* work. The tour was a wild success. After a shaky start, Prince and the Revolution had become a dazzling live "experience". Tonkling the ivories on stage Prince would burble, "As you know, I'm not one for words" and the crowds would fall prey to his glistening charm.

Offstage, however, he was proving a rather less appealing character. At countless awards ceremonies during the early months of 1985, he was seen mincing up to podiums, dwarfed by burly minder Charles 'Big Chick' Huntsberry, to mumble inaudible acceptance "speeches". At the BPI Awards in London, Holly Johnson made a crack about having sex on the telephone with Prince and the drunken gathering laughed; Prince turned hoity-toity and peevish and stomped into the night complaining that Britain hadn't shown him enough respect. At the Grammys he tumbled over on his high heels (again) and whacked himself in the mouth with the microphone. Following the American Music Awards he flounced off, refusing to join in on USA For Africa's star-studded sing-along. Gradually the press sniggers turned into one long guffaw. Prince's prima donna behaviour — he even employed a foodtaster, haw haw — was becoming ridiculous. This was not a Legend. This was no Engima. Prince was a *buffoon.* The Mystique was crumbling . . .

So where was God now? Well, in March Prince let it be known that he was retiring from live performance and was going to "look for The Ladder". Many took this mystical mumbo-jumbo to mean *"My God, why hast thou forsaken me?"*

Around The World In A Day, released in April, had none of *Purple Rain's* tingling energy. A strange concoction of sub-psychedelic gumbo and addled funk — with just an occasional spark of magic — it suggested confusion, the sound of a man at some grim personal and creative crossroads. On the closing track 'Temptation' Prince panted in sensual frenzy — just like the old days. But just when things were hotting up, in stepped God wagging the finger . . . *"I'm sorry. I'll be good . . ."* pleaded Prince, *"Love is more important than sex. Now I understand . . ."*

"There is a real dichotomy between Prince's sexual hang-ups and his belief in God and the Bible," said the actress.

". . . I must go now. I don't know when I'll return . . ." said Prince.

"He saved all the money on shrinks and put it in the movie," said *Purple Rain* scriptwriter William Binns.

". . . Bye bye . . ." said Prince.

"This little man is very dangerous. Prince is a mentally disturbed young man," said his ex-friend and now arch-rival Rick James.

". . . Bye bye . . ."

Bye bye or adieu? Whatever his problems, there still lurked a huge talent within that minute frame. Prince *would* return. God would insist upon it . . . Wouldn't He?

Tom Hibbert

WHAM!

. . . youth, suntans, pleasure, money, endless holidays and endless sex.

It was indisputably Wham!'s year in pop. Boy George's time was up – killed by over-publicity, he looked strangely old and frumpish, like a pantomime Dame. Duran Duran kept on having hit records and creating teenage hysteria, but there's never been a *real* story there – just pretty boys in suits, which is not enough to engage a nation's heart and mind. By Christmas, in poll after poll, George Michael replaced Simon Le Bon as the teenager's main heart throb.

That George Michael was able to do this is a triumph of ambition over nature. It has taken a lot of hair gel and sun lamps and careful styling to make him what he is today and beneath the sheen you can still see the fat little Cypriot boy who hated the way he looked. Like Madonna, with whom Wham! have a lot in common, George Michael has *willed* himself to be a sex symbol. Striving is part of their appeal: both acts represent the eighties' reverence for success.

Wham!'s main rival was Frankie Goes To Hollywood, who certainly won out in terms of critical attention; no one devoted much newsprint to the cultural significance of Wham! And Frankie was fashionable, which Wham! haven't been since their first single. Frankie certainly created more drama, but they were really only interesting as long as they rode a wave of success. They were exciting because everyone was excited about them, but once that died down all the manifestos and slogans and theories about pop subversion seem as windy and overblown as their debut album. They were just too contrived. You can dismiss Wham! for many reasons – for *nouveaux riche* vulgarity, for shallowness, for plagiarism – but they weren't contrived. Their publicity was, of course, but Wham! made it because they really did strike a popular chord.

The true story of George Michael and Andrew Ridgeley is known only to themselves and perhaps their mothers and a few close friends. What we are concerned with here is the Wham! story as we know it through the press . . .

One day in 1975 Georgious Panayatiou, a fat little boy with glasses and bushy eyebrows arrives at Bushey Meads Secondary School. He sits next to Andrew Ridgeley, who is thin and dark and good-looking, the rebellious hero of the class. Mysteriously, Andrew seeks out the friendship of the unprepossessing new arrival. They become inseparable. In the early years Andrew is the boss and he leads George Michael away from flared trousers towards style. They decide they want to become pop stars, and spend their spare time with guitars and tape recorders in each others' bedrooms; it turns out that George Michael is the one who is really talented, who can sing and write songs. The friendship between them is so deep that George will continue to carry Andrew long after they have made it, when he contributes almost nothing but his style, barely playing guitar on stage. But Andrew made George what he is. Their loyalty to each other is the most appealing aspect of their story, and an essential part of their success.

Growing up in an affluent London suburb, they and their friends were indifferent to punk: they didn't see the sense in it. Instead in the late seventies they took part in the booming white soul scene. George and Andrew spent time in suburban discos, occasionally ventured to London, and were deeply affected by *Saturday Night Fever*.

This was southern England, and although they didn't find work when they left school they didn't try very hard and there

was still money at home. They did a few odd jobs, then signed on and determined to make it as pop stars. The result was 'Wham! Rap', their suburban funk anthem to the freedom of unemployment. Seventy per cent of the sales were in the north of England, and it was the first and last time they were considered politically sound.

George and Andrew had signed a disastrously bad deal with a little independent label set up by an old friend, Innervision, which signed them to CBS. From Innervision Wham! got an advance of £500 apiece and eight per cent royalties. The next single they released was to open everything up in a big way. 'Young Guns – Go For It' defined the Wham! image for the public: youth, suntans, pleasure, money, endless holidays and endless sex. It was Duran Duran, but with a new angle. Simon Napier-Bell saw them on *Top of the Pops* and said, "I just knew they were going to become the biggest band in the whole world." The new angle was the friendship between George and Andrew, which Napier-Bell described as Butch Cassidy and the Sundance Kid: "What I saw immediately was this fantastic image that has been the basis of the film industry right through this century. That is two guys – two straight guys – who care more about each other than they care about the girls, and at the end of the movie ride off together. That sort of macho, homo-erotic image has never been used in pop before . . . The thing that will continue to sell Wham! is the relationship between them. A public look at a private affair."

Napier-Bell was real Tin Pan Alley, via Swinging London: hustle, calculation, publicity stunts. And he had a history of turning beautiful boys – Marc Bolan, David Sylvian – into stars. He was as perfect a manager for eighties pop, with his sixties roots and his knowingness, as McLaren had been for punk. It is also very difficult to know when he is telling the truth, but the facts are that when he found them Wham! were fledgling stars and under his management they did indeed become the biggest band in the world.

In 1983 Wham! sold ten million records world-wide, but earned only £100,000; their legal bills came to £100,000 and they ended up with almost nothing. From October 1983 to March 1984 Simon Napier-Bell and Wham! fought a legal battle with Innervision, and although they had a hit album, *Fantastic*, and a hit single, 'Club Tropicana', they couldn't promote them. In March 1984 the dispute was resolved, they signed to Epic and the real money began. Curiously enough, the fact that Wham! have had the worst business experiences in contemporary pop has never tarnished their image of endless pleasure and success.

The spring of 1984 sees 'Wake Me Up Before You Go Go' hit number one, and proves that George Michael is really Elton John, or someone like him. The future looks radiant. Andrew has a nose job which causes much excitement in the press. The summer is marked by Frankie fever, and everyone despises Wham! because they also try wearing Katharine Hamnett T-shirts. They play a miners' benefit, but no one thinks they're sincere.

However, in late summer George Michael scores hugely with his first solo record, 'Careless Whisper'. The future looks even more radiant, at least for George. He could now be Barbra Streisand or Barry Manilow, and the way forward is clear: an eventual move to Hollywood, film soundtracks, duets with other stars. He's musical, he's prolific, people's mothers like him, he has mainstream appeal. He also has indulgences: George dumps the £70,000 video for 'Careless Whisper' because he doesn't like it, and does the same with the video for their next hit, 'Freedom'.

George Michael and Andrew spend the summer in the South of France recording their next album. But no one is sure what Andrew actually does, as George takes care of the producing and writing and singing. "My contribution is my being there" Andrew says, and on some level George still needs him. Lucky for Andrew that their manager agrees. The album, *Make It Big*, is what George calls a "black pop" LP as opposed to a "black disco LP". It is, of course, monstrously successful. He has found his forte. The papers and magazines are full of photos of George and Andrew nestling against each other, unnatural burnt-orange tans gleaming with sun oil, hair delicately streaked.

In January there are reports that George has bought Diana Dors' house. It has an indoor swimming-pool with rainbow lights, gold-plated doors, ankle-deep carpets and mirrored ceilings in the bedrooms. "I think it's just right for me," George says. Wham! tour Australia, accompanied by their parents, and are pelted with miniature kangaroos and koalas on stage. George Michael reveals he can't cope with the pressures of stardom.

In February Andrew's function is revealed. He is necessary to scotch the rumours about Wham! being gay. Two topless models argue over his love in the pages of the *Sun*; meanwhile he goes off and sleeps with a student who sells her story: "STOLEN NIGHT OF LOVE – My saucy antics with Andrew". The *Daily Express* reports that George and Andrew have just become millionaires. And on 5 March the papers revealed that Wham! would become the first Western pop group to play in Communist China: they had been invited by the All China Youth Federation and the Minister of Culture to play Peking's People's Gymnasium and a former opera house in Canton.

George continued to be depressed, buckling under the strain of too much success. "It's like living in a goldfish bowl," he explained, with that flair for a cliché that was part of Wham!'s charm. Andrew continued to get drunk and obnoxious in public. In a soap opera future, you would have George becoming lonely and paranoid in his millionaire's mansion while Andrew, abandoned by George, becomes ever drunker and less charming, causing scenes in night-clubs. But not now. They continue to look tanned and glamorous; they go to China and play before 15,000 bemused-looking Chinese.

As a publicity stunt they can never beat Peking, and in any case next year won't be theirs. All the signs are that "authenticity" is back and we'll have some new Springsteen, a new ethnic revival or some Los Angeles psychedelic re-vamp. Personally I will miss Wham!'s ascendancy. They were a perfect pop group – shameless and vulgar and catchy and gossip-worthy and fun. 'Wake Me Up Before You Go Go' was pop music at its most brilliantly inane.

Andrew's future looks quite worrying, but there can be no fears for George Michael who tells us: "Unless something dreadful happens to me or I get bored with the business, I'll still be writing derivative, catchy, huge-selling records in ten years time. My songwriting is getting better all the time." In March 1985 George Michael was given the Ivor Novello Songwriter of the Year Award. At the ceremony Elton John paid him a tribute which so moved George that he burst into tears. Nirvana – and what a future ahead.

Mary Harron

"Do you really think I'm a material girl? I'm not. Take it – I don't need money I need love."

The world, as Frankie Goes To Hollywood would say, is now Madonna Louise Ciccone's oyster. After the stunning success of her starring role in *Desperately Seeking Susan,* she can take her pick from a host of offers including projects developed by Ray Stark, Herb Ross and Barbra Streisand. In the USA alone, Madonna has sold well over seven million LPs, landed six consecutive singles in the Top Ten (two of them simultaneously!) and made a hit out of the soundtrack from the extremely naff film, *Visionquest*, in which she performs 'Crazy For You' (her second number one after 'Like A Virgin').

On her debut "Virgin" tour (geddit?) $20 T-shirts were reportedly selling at the rate of one every six seconds in San Francisco, and those who couldn't scrape up the up-to-$60 fee for scalpers' tickets or buy concert merchandise, could put together the Boy Toy look from a selection of clothing called Madonnawear. In New York City 18,000 tickets for three shows at Radio City Music Hall sold out in half an hour — putting Our Lady of the Sacred Charts in the boys club with Prince, Bruce and Michael.

Wherefore all this fuss? "Madonna's living out our fantasies," a 16-year-old fan told *People* magazine. "She's able to do something our parents would never let us get away with — that whole slut image. It's usually just the guys who get to do that." But she represents far more than the shakin', rattlin' role model for acquisitive, thrill-seeking Yankee teens. Madonna is the first disco artist to transcend the anonymity of recording studios and dancefloors, shrewdly combining athletic dance moves with glossy pop grooves and a fashion sensibility that's spawned a mini-industry in rubber bracelets, crucifixes and dayglo mesh fabrics.

As befits her religious name, Madonna is an icon for the eighties, using sexuality like a blunt instrument to get whatever she wants. Feminists are livid with a visual style that provokes male hormones and a vampy psyche that offers women a vicarious buzz, but in the same breath, Madonna's self-transformation, forthright determination and artistic control are wholly admirable. Madonna herself plays both ends against the middle: "I know the aspect of my personality, being the vixen, the heart-breaker and the incredibly provocative girl is a very marketable image — but it's not insincere," she told *People*. "You just can't take it seriously."

You must, however, take Madonna seriously. "I've been working my ass off for seven years," she'll tell anyone who dares to call her An Overnight Success. "I've worked for everything that I got and I worked long and hard so when I got it I thought I deserved it. I always knew that it would happen.

"I knew I was different when I was five," she recalls. "My father brought me up to be competitive. I was encouraged to aim for the top rung of the ladder."

Madonna Louise (named after her mother) was born into an Italian family on 16 August 1958 (or '59, depending on who you believe) in Detroit, Michigan.

"I had a very musical upbringing," she remembers. "I studied piano for a year, but my teacher made me quit because I used to hide in a ditch instead of going to lessons. When I was supposed to practise I turned the timer back so it looked like I only had fifteen minutes left. I convinced my father to let me take dance lessons instead. I watched Shirley Temple and used to try to copy her when I was a little girl. I used to give the girls in my neighbourhood dance lessons in the basement in my five-year-old manner. As I got older I gave lessons to boys.

"Eventually I decided I should try and get pro about this. At about twelve or thirteen I started going to the schools where they teach tap, jazz, baton twirling and gymnastics. It was just a place to send hyperactive girls, basically. When I was fourteen or fifteen I started taking ballet every day."

She graduated from Rochester Adams High School in 1976 and attended the University of Michigan on a full dance scholarship. Even then Madonna was attracting attention to herself by wearing ripped-up tights and leotards festooned with safety-pins, but not, surprisingly, because of her unconventional name. "I never remember feeling tormented for my name," she says. "But then I went to Catholic schools. It wasn't until I came to New York that I became aware that it was such an unusual name. People just assumed it was a stage name."

She moved to New York in 1978 at the urging of her ballet teacher and soon found herself training with Alvin Ailey and a former Martha Graham soloist named Pearl Lang. She describes her two years with Lang as "interesting work. The style is very archaic, angular and dramatic. Painful, dark and guilt-ridden: very Catholic." Modern dance, she surmised, "just wasn't

satisfying enough, 'cause there are so few good companies and so many dancers competing with each other, you just worked your ass off for nothing."

She started auditioning for musicals and that led to a spot in the Patrick Hernandez Revue, a Paris-based show centring around the huge disco hit 'Born To Be Alive'. Hernandez' producers took an exceptional interest in Madonna — to the point of writing a ditty for her called 'She's A Real Disco Queen' — but despite all the luxuries a Material Girl could crave, including limousines and a voice coach, Madonna quickly grew tired of being a showpiece and returned to New York.

"I play guitar and keyboards," Madonna reveals. "But the first instrument I learned was the drums. I was the drummer for a band called the Breakfast Club with Danny and Eddie Gilroy, two crazy brothers that lived in a synagogue in Queens. I was an excellent drummer, really strong because I had all this dance training so I had lots of energy. I used to practise for four hours a day. It drove everyone mad!"

Madonna stole the limelight by stepping to the microphone and singing a few numbers (to good response), then stepping in

front of the cameras to make an underground film called *A Certain Sacrifice* (for which she was paid $100) which has recently been released on videocassette. By 1980 she was on her own again, fronting a rock band called Emmy (her Breakfast Club nickname) with college chum Steve Bray (who co-wrote four tunes on *Like A Virgin*) playing drums. By 1981 Emmy had attracted a cult following and Madonna had signed to a management contract, but there was trouble ahead. Responding to the street culture of graffiti artists and breakdancing, Madonna wanted to explore a funkier musical turf and broke her management contract, leaving behind financial security and a tape with four never-released songs.

Madonna then hit the club circuit and made a key connection with Danceteria DJ Mark Kamins, who squired her round to Sire Records after hearing a demo of 'Everybody'. Legend has it that the record deal was negotiated and agreed to in principle within an hour. 'Everybody' was released in April 1982 and did so well in the clubs and on "urban contemporary" radio that the next single was budgeted immediately. Kamins was jettisoned in favour of producer Reggie Lucas, who made another smash with a double-sided 12" incorporating 'Burning Up' and a song he wrote especially for her called 'Physical Attraction'.

"After I put out two 12" disco records and they did fairly well," Madonna says, "I thought I must have a manager. So I thought 'Who's the most successful person in the music industry? I want Michael Jackson's manager.' He came out to New York and saw a show I did. I was so nervous because he'd just seen Prince and he thought he was terrible. But he liked my show."

Madonna, the debut LP, was released and lingered toward the bottom of the charts until 'Holiday' came out in June 1983 and climbed steadily to the top through the Christmas season. 'Borderline' and 'Lucky Star' carried the momentum and the album finally hit the Top Ten one year after its initial release. By 14 July 1984 she had finished a second LP and the video for the title track 'Like A Virgin'. It was shelved for four months while *Madonna* finished collecting multi-platinum awards but when released it went Top Ten in a scant four weeks. Meanwhile she also kept busy that summer by starring in Susan Seidelman's *Desperately Seeking Susan.*

"When I read the script I felt immediately that I could play the part," Madonna reveals. Seidelman obviously believed in her, badgering Orion Pictures to take a chance on this not-quite-that-famous singer. "Madonna is incredibly disciplined," Seidelman notes. "She's the kind of person that really does get up at five in the morning to go swimming. She wasn't at all prima donna-ish. She really wanted to be good and tried so hard, but she'd still goof around with the crew. She wasn't one of those people that want to be alone and sit in their trailer the whole time. I think she has much more of a sense of humour than people give her credit for. Too many people take that *femme fatale* stuff at face value."

Though she does indeed play a *femme fatale,* almost the cinematic embodiment of Madonna's persona, the actress doesn't feel all that close to her character. "Oh, I shared a lot with Susan. She's a free spirit and says and does what she wants. She's also an incredibly resourceful girl. She's one of those people who you don't know how she manages to look so good with so few pieces of clothing. But I have a focus and a direction. I don't think she has any of those qualities. I'm a disciplined person and I've got goals."

And that, according to the gospel of Madonna, doesn't make for an angst-free existence. "I worry about worrying too much," she confesses. "I worry too much about what other people think. I worry about hurting people and I do it a lot, though not intentionally. And I worry about living up to my own expectations. That's helped make me a very determined individual, but it's also made me too much of a manic about things and too hard on myself, too."

Madonna has already achieved her goal of "becoming a memorable figure in the history of entertainment in some sexual, tragi-comic way, like Marilyn Monroe." And just like Monroe, she shrugged off the publication of early nude photos in skin-mags and newspapers in the US and UK. (She was a figure model at New York's New School and some 2,000 prints are said to exist.) But in true Hollywood tradition, there's a hidden desire behind her superstar strut. "Do you really think I'm a Material Girl?" she asked Los Angeles concert-goers. "I'm not. Take it – I don't need money, I need love."

David Keeps

ACTS OF THE YEAR

U2

"A group like us need a good clip round the ear . . ."

Only U2 would have considered releasing an impressionistic piece of music like 'The Unforgettable Fire' as a single. Obviously it was an album track. Clearly it couldn't be chart fodder. So perhaps it was only U2 who could have made it a hit.

Before *The Unforgettable Fire* (the album) was released in the autumn of 1984, U2 were at a difficult stage. Their January '83 album *War* had brought them commercial success both in Britain and, more significantly, in America, but at a price. Hitherto sympathetic critics had detected in the record's strident rhythms and unequivocal messages a hardening of the arteries ("U2 Run Aground On Rock" semaphored an affronted *NME*). In place of the twilight mysteries of adolescence that *Boy* had etched so atmospherically, and of the wracked self-doubt exposed in *October*, *War* sounded bombastic and almost smug.

The live mini-LP *Under A Blood Red Sky* was released as a holding operation in the absence of new material, but it served its purpose more than admirably. It was a searing collection of performances, and a salutary reminder of what U2 were really capable of on a good night. But live albums are too often a money-spinner for artists at the end of their creative tether. And the *Blood Red Sky* video, dynamic though it was, showed Bono erecting a white flag onstage, a gesture whose lack of subtlety became infuriating when repeated on TV and again during U2's live shows.

We know now that U2 were merely experiencing some sort of mid-life crisis, but the change of tack signalled by *The Unforgettable Fire* was both radical and vital. Had U2 made *Return To War*, they might by now have become lobotomised stadium-rockers permanently on tour somewhere in America. But they didn't, and in March 1985 the front cover of *Rolling Stone* bore a portrait of the group, and alongside it the rather startling legend "Our Choice: Band Of The '80s". This was praise indeed, especially since the same magazine had been barely lukewarm about the album when it was released.

U2 had been honest enough to admit their own mistakes, and strong enough to face up to them. "That record *War* in a way has enabled us to make *this* record," guitarist Dave 'The Edge' Evans told me one sunny Parisian morning during U2's 1984 European trek. "If we hadn't made *War* and created the sort of economic freedom we now have, there is no way we could have made *Unforgettable Fire*, so I'm very glad we did . . . We will probably never make a record like *War* again — it's done us harm in some quarters but it's also done us an awful lot of good."

"I think a group like us need a good clip round the ear, a good kick in the pants," Bono commented. "Rock'n'roll groups need it."

He also admitted that U2's unwillingness to speak to the press had made them appear to be prima donnas, a group perhaps too wrapped up in their own self-righteousness to want to communicate with outsiders. "There was this band with this song 'Sunday Bloody Sunday' with a white flag. That's all people saw when they saw U2. Some saw and realised the potential of what we were doing, and others were just saying 'what *is* this . . . ?' So I meet people who have a picture painted of U2 without having ever listened to our music."

The Unforgettable Fire was the sort of record you had to listen to, often and attentively, if you were to derive anything from it at all. The album was preceded by the single 'Pride (In The Name Of Love)', Bono's hymn to Martin Luther King. 'Pride' marked a return to the original U2 virtues of clean, strong melody, a clear soaring vocal and the uplifting ring of The Edge's guitar. It reached the American Top Twenty, in the process becoming U2's most successful single to date. It was also probably the best, but the song's strongly drawn contours were in marked contrast to the blurry atmospherics of the rest of the album.

The Unforgettable Fire was a commercial success, though not of the same order as a Wham! or a Prince. More important to U2, though, was the fact that the album restored a great deal

of faith in the band. Critics, even when they weren't sure what U2 were after, were inclined to give them bonus points for trying. The group's audience, which has never been faddist or especially fashionable, might have been expected to view *Fire* with a certain amount of caution. But no — they took to it with zeal, perhaps recognizing in Brian Eno/Daniel Lanois' production an attempt to probe further into some of the creative recesses U2 had hinted at on early recordings such as *Boy* or the single '11 O'Clock Tick Tock'. Then, U2 had suggested a familiarity with the folk roots of their native Ireland, both in the modal structure of some of the music and in Bono's words and singing. Alone at the microphone, he sounded like a man in shadows, trying to summon spirits from a collective Celtic past.

Bono touched upon something of this spirit when he described how 'Pride' came to assume its finished form. "I wanted 'Pride' to be really poisonous at one point, and it was written in an hour. Not even an hour actually, half an hour, the whole thing — *'Pride, one man come in the name of love, one man come and go, one man come here to justify, one man to overthrow'*, and the pride then was the negative side. And it was only when the positive side was owned up to that the song was born.

"It was strange. It's an Irish tradition, y'know, that of twilight writing. You know, just when you're about to nod off kind of writing. I write a lot on the microphone, like 'October' and things, as I sing I write. On the microphone I find out things about myself I often don't know before I sing, and I have to own up to them later."

The Edge added: " 'Pride' was kind of thrilling for Bono because in a way it's probably the most concise lyric on the record, without being over-simplistic, because the actual sentiments involved are not particularly black-and-white. It was my instinct — I think Bono's as well — to leave the more simplistic political stances out of this record. *War* was a record we decided would have that kind of side to it, a very simple hard-edged side, almost as a reaction against what was happening around us at that stage. This record was definitely not that."

Yet at the same time, U2 had made a record which, in its diffuseness and diversity, somehow felt authentic. If it differed stylistically from much of the group's past output and didn't even feel finished within itself, it had a distinct mood. The results were not perfectly polished, but they defined an attitude of quest and a determination to push back boundaries.

Perhaps it was just coincidence that U2 had re-emerged in this particular form at that moment, but it so happened that their approach chimed fortuitously with the movement back to authenticity in music which was gaining ground, particularly in America. Bono is a firm fan of Georgia quartet R.E.M., who shared the bill at U2's Milton Keynes appearance in June '85, and U2 have also toured with Dream Syndicate and Lone Justice, two rather different representatives of the new tide of American groups. None of these sound like U2, but they share an urge to build a supercharged contemporary relevance from roots uncontaminated by disco pap and computer pop.

According to U2 bassist Adam Clayton, the rock star of the group, "Part of the attraction of the band is that there is an integrity there, an honesty that comes over, and I also think there is an understanding that U2 are inevitably going to strive for the best thing they can possibly do when they make a record. And it will never be the same as the last record they made, and if you don't like it first time round it's not your fault and it's not our fault, but they will not be turned off by that. I think our audience will listen to it, will give it a chance, and ultimately if they don't like it, well then we've failed. But I think the records are made essentially for us with the belief that the audience will enjoy them as much as we ultimately will."

The strength of the restored U2 lay in the four group members' ability to be their own men while recognizing the demands that had to be fulfilled to keep the group as a whole strong. Drummer Larry Mullen continued to turn down requests for interviews with polite firmness, but his steely beat lay at the core of the group's performances. While The Edge and Bono were the chief statesmen for the group, The Edge playing straight man to Bono's man-in-the-confessional, Adam Clayton adopted a floating role, commenting on any and every aspect of the group, even their own shortcomings.

"There is something in the group we've had to fight for, and it's there," said Bono. "It's a real love of each other and love of what we do, and it is a flame, y'know . . . There's times when it feels like it's nearly been blown out, but it's still there."

There had been a crisis in the band between *War* and *Unforgettable Fire*, which had been solved, according to Bono, by breaking up the band and reforming it with the same personnel. This was perhaps a way of indicating a severe bout of soul-searching, a reappraisal of the group's objectives and what sacrifices were worth making to attain them.

U2 had never been keen to discuss their religious faith openly, and when they began to open up to the press again in 1984 this was an area around which they continued to tread with the utmost caution. It was reasonable to assume that this spiritual side of the group had been a source of strength in difficult times. Meanwhile, when the group returned to America, they were brought face to face with the faith industry in its ugliest form.

"We've seen a lot of the falsehoods and rejected them," said The Edge. "I think we're probably more *temperate* than we were a while ago . . . seeing the Jerry Falwells and all those sort of guys on TV, you understand why people are suspicious and therefore you apply that to your own situation."

And as Bono put it to *Rolling Stone*: "Sadomasochism is not taboo in rock'n'roll. Spirituality is."

Obviously any group working in the rock industry and trying to maintain some kind of moral line is asking for trouble. By choosing to expose their doubts and dilemmas, U2 have gone some way towards bridging that credibility gap, though they will always be a prime target for the people who are fond of declaring that "rock music" is *per se* for dinosaurs and criminally unstylish people with a taste for pomposity. But not even Bruce Springsteen could claim to have a more loyal following than U2.

"I can't point the finger at anyone other than myself," said Bono. "I never have."

Adam Sweeting

SADE

. . . a world of grace, cool and sophistication as imagined by people who are young and broke.

How many records has Sade sold by now? The four million mark is probably ancient history: she was well over three million even before *Diamond Life* was released in the US, and since both the 'Smooth Operator' single and the album from which it was drawn have sailed into the Big Market's Top Ten, it seems fairly safe to state that large portions are the order of the day.

Sade's success is one of those pop phenomena which become eminently logical with the benefit of hindsight. Clearly, the entire Western pop world has been waiting for someone to come along and make music like this: music with a firm, understated pulse, simple arrangements meticulously played and recorded with tonal values that would not have been out of place on a mid-to-late-sixties Miles Davis Quintet album, simple and melodic songs sung coolly and carefully; music which operates within clearly stated parameters of both sound and emotion, music which positively bellows quiet good taste. *Diamond Life* is the hippest of hip MOR: it carries with it an aura of effortless sophistication which is eminently flattering to an audience weaned on rock and funk. It makes a youthful audience feel pleasantly grown-up; it allows an older listener to feel hip and snazzy without having to submit to any unpleasant jolts. *Diamond Life* was born to sell. Wasn't it?

Of course, pop-soul with a slightly jazzy ambience is by no means something invented recently by Sade and her producer Robin Millar. There are a handful of significant precedents: the outstanding and highly successful juxtapositions of the voice of Astrud Gilberto, the music of Antonio Carlos Jobim and the mellifluous tenor Stan Getz on bossa-nova pop hits from the early sixties like 'Girl From Ipanema' and 'Desafinado'; the Zombies' miraculously cool and tender 'She's Not There', with Colin Blunstone's aching vocals set against the backdrop of Rod Argent's electric piano; and a whole string of smart, witty Steely Dan singles from the seventies – the period of Sade's teens – including 'Do It Again' and 'Rikki Don't Lose That Number', which coincidentally (?) boasts an intro not significantly dissimilar to that of 'Smooth Operator'. It's music which has the clean simplicity of pop, its danceability and melodicism, but lacks all that embarrassing exuberance and vulgarity.

In other words, it's not particularly teenage.

Which is an essential part of its appeal. The notion of pop as teen property is one that dates back to the fifties and the birth of rock 'n' roll, when the unfettered energy and emotionalism of black music provided salvation for frustrated white teenagers like Jerry Lee Lewis and Elvis Presley. The resulting detonation reverberated through the sixties, when it coincided with unprecedented levels of Western affluence and widespread political unrest. Pop – and its noisiest and most prominent offshoot, rock – was thereby rendered easily identifiable as the music of the g-g-generation gap, the music of don't trust-anybody-over-thirty. This intense polarization between age-groups was less marked in black music, despite conflict between, say, parents who liked downhome blues and children who followed James Brown, because blues, jazz, soul and gospel were never specifically youth-oriented musics.

In the seventies, pop became far more pervasive while simultaneously retreating from its former radical associations, and by the eighties its institutionalization was more or less complete. This occurred against a background of economic recession and a political drift to the right, and these factors combined to loosen the teenager's grip on pop. Both in Britain and in the United States, being a teenager ain't what it used to be. Money is, as they say, too tight to mention, and youth unemployment in Thatcher Britain is long past the stage where the adjective "scandalous" would be adequate to describe it. Unemployed is simply another way of saying flat broke and in any highly industrialized (ho ho) society, flat broke itself means miserable. A lot of the glamour has gone out of being teenage; these days, too many people are alienated and poor for real for anybody to want to play about with the symbolism of being (out on the) street. Poor old John Lennon to the contrary, modern youth spends most of its time imagining having as many possessions as possible.

Which brings us back to Sade. Her music, her image and style depict a world of grace, cool and sophistication as it is imagined by people who are young and broke – as, indeed, Sade and her team of musicians were when they conceived, composed and recorded the music on *Diamond Life*. It is a vision of the lush life as it appears to people who have no reason to believe that they will ever be able to enjoy such a thing. The story of how Ms Adu wrote the words to 'When Am I Going To Make A Living' on the back of an envelope while walking home from the bus stop in the pouring rain may seem drenched in bathos by repetition, especially when viewed from the perspective of her humungous success, but it nevertheless strikes an authentic note. Everyone wants to make their presence felt, and nobody in their right mind identifies poverty with freedom. Hence, a craving for a music that celebrates style without glorifying consumerism, for a music which is subdued and tasteful without being baffling or smartass. In other words, for Sade.

Diamond Life thereby plugged a giant gap in the market that hadn't previously seemed to be there. It had been approached before by musicians from the same club scene from which Sade emerged, from all the talk about the Jazz Revival (a pink herring in this context: yes, there is one; no, Sade doesn't have a lot to do with it except in terms of presentation). However, it took someone with considerable taste and little experience or formal technique to create something along these lines which could seize the imagination of a mass audience: someone who knew what to leave out.

It has been suggested, with a fair degree of accuracy, that Sade's music has been carefully tailored to flatter her capabilities and avoid her weaknesses. The same could be stated of many artists: Miles Davis' style is built around the fact that in his earliest years his execution of rapid passages was sometimes faulty, while his command of the trumpet's highest registers was too shaky and faltering for him to attempt the kind of bravura flourishes beloved of Dizzy Gillespie. All artists work with what they can do while simultaneously working to extend their boundaries. Sade is good at singing medium-tempo songs in her rich, careful alto. Just as she shies away from what she dismisses as "wackiness" in her appearance – of which considerably more later – she avoids the flamboyant neo-gospelisms of the pop or rock singer raised on the exuberance of soul or blues.

There's a very good reason for this: basically, she can't sing like that. There is no way that Sade can sing like – to name another best-selling British female singer signed to CBS – Alison Moyet, though it can be argued that Sade has a far better sense of what constitutes an appropriate context for her voice than Alf has. Moyet is part of the great-god-mama school of vocalising: a Bessie Smith rather than a Billie Holliday, an Aretha Franklin rather than an Astrud Gilberto, a Janis Joplin rather than a Laura Nyro. Sade simply doesn't have the pipes or the improvisatory flair to essay that kind of pyrotechnic display, and since she has the kind of personality which shuns extravagant shows of emotion (or anything else) her singing is wholly appropriate.

However, it was noted during her winter '84 British tour that her singing was lacking in confidence and that her pitching was occasionally unreliable. How much more evidence could anyone want that Sade's immense success has caught the artist by surprise? What we are seeing is a London club act that has achieved what every London club act has ever sought – ie major international success – while being essentially unprepared for that success. Most people who sell four million records have been working towards that end for years. Sade is – as international mega-acts go – as raw as they come.

And – contrary to popular belief – being exceptionally good-looking only has so much to do with it. Sade is an astonishingly beautiful woman, and her huge eyes and mouth, high forehead and lean frame haven't hurt one little bit, but *Diamond Life* has been purchased by a huge number of people who haven't seen any photographs of her other than the ones on the album cover. The mini-media hype that launched her first performances in London might be thought – if you vastly over-estimate the influence of *The Face* – to be sufficient to account for a small success in the UK, but it is untenable as the justification for the European and American success that has followed. Sade is, by conventional standards, not that much of a media hound. She never shows up in Fleet Street gossip columns slagging off other artists or getting caught in night-clubs with notorious men.

You only see her when she's performing. Her photographs and stage demeanour are demure in the extreme. Even the famous backless dress constitutes elegance rather than provocation; there is no eagerness to please in her approach. She presents herself as being the way she is for her own sake and for her own reasons: she seems to beg no one's approval.

Sade represents, simply, the impact of soul stylings plus the qualities of fifties jazz instrumentation and visual symbolism upon contemporary pop. She is fundamentally a pop singer, and it is as such that she excels. It may be facile to remark that few comments on "the beigeing of pop" would be applied to her if she were not half-Nigerian, but her style is the result of soul and jazz affecting what is a basically English pop sensibility.

Despite her success, Sade Adu is in an unenviable position. She is a comparatively inexperienced and unsure performer attempting to follow up one of the most successful and individual debut albums for several years. Expectations are both extremely high and extremely specific, ie in order to maintain them she must exceed or at least match the achievements of *Diamond Life*. She must also move beyond that album's somewhat narrow musical and emotional range with as much assurance as she did within her previous boundaries. It is the ability to respond to situations like this that makes the difference between the kind of seasoned international stars who keep working for years, and the kind of pop star who manages to surf a rising moment and who then disappears into the attics of popular culture. Sade has put what is an essentially limited gift to some startlingly intelligent use, and it may well be the intelligence rather than the gift which ultimately pulls her through.

Charles Shaar Murray

ACTS OF THE YEAR •

BILLY IDOL

"Now I see people laughing at rock 'n' roll. But they will learn."

"Everyone expects the singer to be an idol, you know," the young Bromley punk declared in 1977, "always in the centre of the photo. I'm an idol — but I go home by bus." Eight years later the punk was still wearing ripped T-shirts and chains, still twisting his upper lip in imitation of Elvis Presley and still punching the air, but it had been some time since he had seen the inside of any form of public transport.

Billy Idol was born as William Broad in Stanmore, Middlesex, on 30 November 1955. Three years later his father ran into business problems and the Broad family emigrated to America. They stayed there for six years, returning to Britain as Beatlemania was breaking. Billy was fascinated: "I could see how they were using American culture and turning it around into something new and exciting." Meanwhile the boys at school laughed at his American accent and crew cut.

His mother's family were musical — his Irish grandmother could play fourteen different instruments — and when he was ten, his grandfather took him to Woolworth and bought him a guitar and a book to help him figure out the chords. He fell in love with rock'n'roll, grew his hair long and argued with his Dad who, he says, didn't talk to him for two years because of it. Mr Broad worried about Billy's education taking second place to rock music but his long-haired son still managed to acquire the necessary qualifications to be accepted by Sussex University to study English Literature.

"He was a nice chap then," one of his university contempories once told me. "He had black hair and he was in a band called the Rockettes." To this day he reads a lot and beneath his gruff, rock'n'roll star's growl, the polite educated tones of someone who has attended tutorials on Chaucer and read *The Wasteland* are still audible. His song 'Eyes Without A Face' had been inspired by Gogol's *Dead Souls,* he told a *Rolling Stone* reporter, going on to quote chunks of Emily Brontë at her.

He didn't finish the degree course, however, but returned to the family home in Bromley to play his New York Dolls and Velvet Underground albums too loud. He was twenty when the Sex Pistols materialized and he became one of the legendary Bromley contingent — which also included Susan 'Siouxsie' Ballion — which regularly ventured up to London to see the Pistols, hang round the Kings Road and form their own groups. Billy put an advert in the *Melody Maker* saying, "I want to form a group", and bass guitarist Tony James answered. Together with singer Gene October they formed a punk band called Chelsea. Two months later, Billy and Tony left and started Generation X.

Billy had a vision of punk which was a little at odds with the mainstream image: "I was never interested in those people who said that the Sex Pistols were the end of rock'n'roll. I got really pissed off with what punk rock was supposed to be and I got really excited about what punk rock *could* be."

Generation X, consequently, were more rock'n'roll, even more pop than most of their contemporaries. No one took them very seriously. They never seemed as authentically punk and radical as, say, the Clash or as wild as the Damned. They were too flash and glamorous and their singles didn't have the usual "blank" and bored references but were reminiscent of the Sweet with titles like 'King Rocker' and 'Ready Steady Go!', the latter a tribute to the sixties TV show. They looked great on *Top of the Pops.* They were pin-ups. They looked as though they wanted to be rock stars.

By 1980 Generation X had released three albums, seven hit singles, split up and reformed as Gen X, and gone through a legal battle with their manager which left them demoralized. Billy and Tony James wrote their best song, 'Dancing With Myself', but the accompaying album, *Kiss Me Deadly,* didn't sell well. It was time to move on. Billy wanted a fresh start, so he left London and went to New York.

"If I'd stayed in London, I'd always be 'Billy Idol of Generation X'. Like that geezer in Big Country, Stuart Adamson. It's always 'Stuart Adamson, formerly of the Skids'." He arrived in New York with less than a thousand dollars and slept on friends' floors "just like I did when I first came up to London with Generation X from Bromley". He still considered himself a punk — still does, actually — and decided that in America there was "a whole generation who are the same as the people who were in punk rock here — but they won't turn their backs on it in America as long as it survives for longer than one album."

He started to write songs with Phil Hawk of Suicide but the collaboration didn't work out. Then he met a spiky-haired guitarist called Steve Stevens and began to write songs with him. They hit it off perfectly. Through Steve he met Kiss's manager, Bill Aucoin, who agreed to take him on and then persuaded Chrysalis to go on funding Billy. One night in a club in the Village, Billy witnessed a packed floor dancing to 'Dancing With Myself' and realised he should be making punk rock you can dance to. He and Steve Stevens went to Los Angeles to record a cheap mini-album, *Don't Stop,* which included a version of the old Tommy James & the Shondells hit, 'Mony Mony'. Club DJs picked up on it, so Chrysalis released it as a single. But no radio stations would play it, they found, because of the punky picture of Billy on the sleeve.

"So we took my picture off the next single, 'Hot In The City'. They didn't know who it was so they played it and it went to number 24. That's when we learned that we were suffering from the same kind of prejudice everywhere."

America had never taken to punk rock in a big way. The Clash had had some degree of success — and been accused of selling out to an American audience in the process — but the nearest thing to a mass appeal punk band in America was Blondie and by 1982 they were on the slippery slope. The sight of a leather-clad Idol with his patent punk sneer was not a reassuring one for American rock radio programmers.

Then MTV started.

Along with Duran Duran and Adam Ant and all the other British groups with a backlog of flash videos for the new channel to draw upon was Billy Idol. The video for his new single, 'White Wedding', went into heavy rotation and his cartoon punkness didn't come over as threatening to MTV's new young audience — it seemed . . . cute. 'White Wedding' itself was a devilish blend of rock and disco and another club hit. Radio began to play it and it entered the pop charts. The video for his remake of 'Dancing With Myself' consolidated everything. Directed by Tobe 'TCM' Hooper, it presented Billy dancing by himself on top of a decrepit skyscraper in a post-apocalyptic city with hordes of ghoulish mutants trying to touch him and being kicked away. It was silly and over the top and somehow sexy.

By autumn '83 Billy had completed his second LP, *Rebel Yell,* with producer Keith Forsey. The Idol-Stevens songwriting team turned in a bunch of morbid, rock'n'roll songs with Hammer Horror titles like 'Flesh For Fantasy', 'Eyes Without A Face' and 'The Dead Next Door'. Middle-American kids had long had a fascination for creepy-crawly, sicko movies and bands and now they adopted Billy. By the middle of '85 the LP had sold nearly two million copies and spawned a string of hit singles. Billy and his band toured the US solidly for six months from the end of '83. They began by playing colleges and two to three thousand seater theatres and ended up playing to crowds of 20,000 and causing the occasional riot. Billy was hot.

Star Hits "the American version of *Smash Hits*" was launched in January '84 and has included a pin-up or feature about him in every single issue so far. After Duran Duran he has the biggest and most loyal following of fans in America. Even members of Duran Duran can be numbered amongst them and Madonna has expressed a desire to make a record with him because, like her, he's "white and plastic".

In September '84 Billy returned to England to promote 'Eyes Without A Face', his first British hit of the eighties. Coming home evidently unhinged him a little, although he had already adopted "rock'n'roll" standards of behaviour. He made a fool of himself on Radio One's *Roundtable* show, having to be led out of the studio midway through the live broadcast for swearing incoherently. He smashed up his rented flat in Mayfair. He went to visit the Frankie "lads" — Mark, Nasher and Ped — and reputedly helped them to smash up their flat as well. He ranted to me when I interviewed him about how he was going to see his father on his sixtieth birthday and "give him hell for the fact that he didn't believe me". He wanted a "certain level of respect", he said, and was pissed off by "the terrible pessimism which is killing music" in Britain. He'll never get the respect he wants in Britain and growling, as he did on *Top of the Pops*, about how he'd "come here to rock'n'roll" is not going to help. But talking about his obsession with punk and rock'n'roll he becomes quite eloquent.

Rock'n'roll, he has said, "is a type of music that goes beyond whether you can play a guitar or not. That goes beyond synthesizers. It's really a world that exists and it talks about love and beauty. It talks about realness. It talks about suffering, pain, dying, loving things. It's country-and-western music. It's to do with black people and white people. It's to do with a type of *soul* that England's totally rejected. You hear it in reggae music and I listen to reggae music a lot. You hear it in Jewish songwriters. You hear it in loads of different types of cultures which have been repressed. But I don't hear it in English music right now. It's about time that England opened its arms to music and believed."

And the resentment he still feels about not being taken seriously floats to the surface.

"All people did was laugh and I can remember that. I remember people laughing at rock'n'roll — even when punk was happening. Now I see people laughing at rock'n'roll. But they will learn."

They won't learn anything from him, of course, and in his heart he'll always remain the resentful punk. But it'll be a long time till he travels home by bus again.

Neil Tennant

ACTS OF THE YEAR

CYNDI LAUPER

"I wouldn't call it mainstream what I'm doing, though it's digestible for the masses."

Born in New York, Cyndi Lauper has been singing for as long as she can remember. She wrote her first songs aged eleven or thereabouts, singing them in the basement of the family home accompanied by her sister on guitar and a local girlfriend on snare drum. Extremely reticent to talk about ages and dates — "In my country they're fanatical about age and beauty and when you're sixty-five you may as well drop dead" — she eventually ran away to live on Long Island before taking off for Canada with her dog, Sparkle, for a spell of self-seeking among the pine forests.

"I stayed two weeks in the woods by myself, drawing. Tree studies, of course, pictures of Sparkle — Sparkle sleeping next to a rock, Sparkle sleeping next to a tree, Sparkle sleeping next to a bush, Sparkle chasing a frog . . . and lots of pine trees!"

Returning to New York, she teamed up with John Turi, a canny, rock'n'roll éminence grease, who played her a lot of early rock'n'roll records she hadn't heard. Between the two of them, they recruited the personnel of Cyndi's first group, the legendary Blue Angel. This wonderfully gifted outfit consisted of Arthur 'Rockin' A' Neilson on guitar, Lee Brovitz on bass, Johnny 'Bullet' Morelli on drums, with John and Cyndi handling keyboards/sax and vocals respectively. Guided by John Turi's rock'n'roll sensibilities and fuelled with Cyndi's explosive vocal propellant, Blue Angel cut a rumbustious swathe through the New York music scene of the late seventies long before the recent and spectacular blossoming of Cyndi Lauper's career as a solo singer.

This little-known history is important because it helps to explain the underground, semi-mystical, semi-hysterical reputation that Cyndi enjoyed as a great, white female hope when the group's blazing, raunchy, first, last and always sublime album sneaked out from the blaze of indifference and apathy that constituted Polydor Records' promotional efforts. *Blue Angel* escaped in 1970 and would seem to have wound up on the turntables of only a small number of embattled and embittered types looking for an honourable alternative to a pop world busy laying down the blueprints for today's feeble musical soup-kitchen scene.

The album presents a young, great looking five-strong group, seemingly cognizant with, and able to tap at will, the source of some of the very best, wildest moments of post-Presley American popular music. Further, it's blessed with a God-given production (by Roy Halee, actually) that polishes everything to pristine clarity while retaining maximum volume and managing to capture all the immediacy and spontaneity of the best "cut it while it's hot" school of record engineering. Above everything is this awesome female voice: swooping, rocketing and growling over and around the most irresistible tidal rush of definitive, guitar-driven, good time music.

The fact that they were totally unknown on this side of the Atlantic, coming out of a jaded and quiescent New York scene still looking to England for squeaky clean, post-punk pop inspiration, with a touch so sure, the record so magnificently uplifting and the whole endeavour so royally ignored in most quarters lent an air of the miraculous to the astonishing artefact and gave the unshakeable conviction of religious zealots to the scattered fanatics who latched on to the record and attempted to hype it through those distant days of the British youth riots and the rise of the cocktail set in the pop weeklies.

At the time of writing Cyndi hasn't bettered her singing on the *Blue Angel* collection. The occasional tendency to flighty excess in the upper ranges of her wild vocal range, so much in

evidence on her later solo work, is tempered and countered by breathtaking examples of superb control and thrilling vocal invention all through the album. Singing straight from the heart of a throbbing, torrid soundscape, Cyndi swoops and dives and rides those notes like she was born to stand at the eye of this musical hurricane and wail.

That the whole album is a group triumph, albeit one showcasing and starring one C. Lauper, is nowhere more evident than in the sound of the ramshackle, roaring geetar holocaust that underpins the very wonderful 'Cut Out' with its raspberrying, honking, geese-gone-berserk-style saxophone wailings. The lyric sheet prints the words of this one in their entirety as "*Wo wo, wo wo, wo wo, wo wo, Cut out, cut out, cut out, cut out!*" — a veritable blitzkreig of minimalism and I can't think of a better way to spend an hour or so than listening to this lunacy a couple of hundred times.

Above all, Blue Angel featuring Cyndi Lauper were a blazing, eighties rock'n'roll band: not a bunch of aged veterans or some clutch of callow revivalists, but the genuine contemporary pop thing. A glorious rush of exciting, emotional, life-enhancing music.

The *Blue Angel* album was some kind of aural near-masterpiece, but that was then and this is the age of video

music. Cyndi Lauper has fulfilled some part of her manifest destiny and the rest of the band are left losers in the dust of pop history. Management problems, lack of record company push and the ensuing disappointments and frictions within the group all contributed to the acrimonious demise of Blue Angel in 1982.

"The band didn't happen so it doesn't matter now. I stuck with it for two or three years after we made the album. That was through thick and thin. I started with John in '77/'78 and there was no chance of advancement, so what are you gonna do? And you know what really killed it? When we went on stage and the magic that we used to have was no longer there; when that goes, then it's over."

Involved in a lawsuit with the group's management that tied them up effectively for a long time, the group broke on the rock of public indifference and company neglect.

"The Polydor management was in transition and we were, like, the last regime's special project. It wasn't right, the management, the business end wasn't right and I'd have been stuck there with that forever if Blue Angel had took off."

Cyndi turned to David Wolff, a longtime friend, for help and advice and he eventually became her manager. "I found a manager that really has got a lot of energy. If you make sure that your management is strong, that what you're doing is right then all the energy that you put into it will break through. But if nothing is connected and you think you're gonna break through, then forget it — you sing to the woodworks!"

It worked for Cyndi, of course. After she secured a new contract with Epic she decided to make sure that the record was centred around her. "Because if you have musicians that you play with, and you do it live, what happens is that it's a tug and a compromise. It's always gonna get changed 'cause there's five or six elements and each person has their own personality, chemistry; it's a natural thing that happens but I didn't want that. I wanted to start with a very small core and build on that."

And so Cyndi hit the pop big time with *She's So Unusual* and the hit singles that it spawned. Slotting herself into the pop market place by pushing a fairly repellant, big-mouthed, squeaky flibbertigibbet image, she popped up regularly talking various kinds of nonsense on interview slots and, of course, joining America's finest on the USA For Africa record.

At the time of writing we have only the *She's So Unusual* collection with which to gauge her artistic progress from the Blue Angel days to her present state of total satisfaction with record company, management and her new sound. Given the benefit of hindsight and many playing hours, *She's So Unusual* is, perhaps inevitably, something of a disappointment, featuring as it does heavily discofied, synthesizer assisted slabs of backing music to many of the songs and suffering heavily by comparison with the human warmth of the hand-crafted Blue Angle instrumental and vocal surrounds. A single Lauper/Turi composition is included and Cyndi has a hand in a couple of others but the whole collection really doesn't stand comparison with the rampant musical bravura of the previous work. Stripped of the pallid, electronic ping-ponging sound and backed by a more gutsy guitar-driven thing, the album could have been a strong contender, particularly in view of the 1985 guitar renaissance and burgeoning success of groups like the Bangles and Blue Angel headbanger derivatives, Katrina and the Waves. Considering the fact that it sold in truckloads this line of reasoning is purely academic, of course, but I persist in the cause of musical magnificence.

She's So Unusual also displays an ominous tendency on Cyndi's part to leap to the higher and gloopier reaches of her vocal range instead of further perfecting the dazzling vocal balancing, bravura act that characterized the first album, rather as though the cutesy Minnie Mouse public persona had been allowed to influence her approach to a song. That said and reservations plainly signalled, there are fine moments elsewhere in this collection. 'Time After Time' is a lovely performance and the other US hit single 'All Through The Night', is a similarly yearning, controlled and compelling song. These songs share an elegiac feel and both burn with a quiet but intense fire.

Again, the first big hit 'Girls Just Want To Have Fun' and the album's opener 'Money Changes Everything' are strong performances that only needed a real group sound — less distance between Cyndi and the instrumental settings — to turn them into something much more special and aesthetically satisfying. The curse of the synthesizer once again. All in all a halfway decent album which is, I suppose, another way of saying a half unsatisfying one.

Half way through 1985 Cyndi Lauper looks set for bigger and better successes. Film parts are mooted and the advertising world has borrowed copiously from *She's So Unusual*. Anyone who fell heavily for the *Blue Angel* album can only rejoice that she managed to obtain some degree of artistic justice after the wilful neglect of her triumphant debut and that she has attained the public platform that she fought for.

"I'm a rocker I guess, I'm a rock'n'roller. I have my own form. I wouldn't call it mainstream what I'm doing, though it's digestible for the masses which is what I want. I WANT to communicate! I know what it's like not to. I feel I have something to say and I want to speak my piece." Despite the vindication of her talents, it's hard not to regret that certain something that seems to have been lost in the transition from lead singer with a remarkably talented bunch of New York rockers to *bona fide* international solo success.

Lauper-watchers will wait to see if she can ever recreate that first, fine frenzy or if the "deranged first lady of kooky-pop" persona is here to stay.

Ray Lowry

"I can have anything I want – whether it's heroin or hot and cold running women on tap – but I just don't want to know."

Elton John hailed him as one of the greatest songwriters of the decade, this diminutive ex-double-glazing salesman, ex-dole office clerk from Ipswich. Nik Kershaw has come a long way in a short time.

The first Kershaw single ('I Won't Let The Sun Go Down On Me') was released in September '83 and achieved a healthy Top Fifty rating. Not bad for an unknown signing's first single but not quite enough to ruffle any *serious* feathers. He'd never threaten the big league. Besides, Kershaw was all *wrong*. Small, foppish and awkward, he was almost embarrassing to watch. Dancing, he jiggled nervously like a schoolkid about to wet his pants. A total wimp and a muso to book – a hero for all the clumsy Nigels of this world. No threat to the established pop aristocracy from *this* corner.

But suddenly the Nigels rallied round. People *liked* that "this is the real me" attitude. They *liked* his straight and forthright viewpoint. Suddenly Kershaw was the underdog – one bright, untarnished soul taking on the music business. Clean, wholesome and cute, a Cliff Richard to our present day Rolling Stones.

Once his underdog status had been confirmed and the eyes and cheekbones had cast their spell over enough teenage pituitaries to send 'Wouldn't It Be Good' to number four in February '84, there was no turning back for Nik Kershaw. His features were hung on bedroom walls the length of Britain much in the same way as David Cassidy would once have adorned my own. *Every* little girl, you see, has got to have her fantasies. Sexually non-threatening and thoroughly unavailable, these characters are important emotional stepping-stones from childhood through puberty and probably constitute an acceptable alternative to the real thing. The boys you know when you're thirteen really aren't very nice at all. At that age girls like silly pop and silly fashion; boys crave to ape the rock 'n' roll strut. The stereotypes don't always apply but they're true enough to keep a lot of lousy bands on the road for most of the year.

The music papers then found out Nik had been in an Ipswich band called Half Pint Hog and as such had clambered onstage in flares and headband to belt out Black Sabbath and Deep Purple songs. His next venture was with a glorified cabaret band, Fusion, who would, for an agreed fee, perform "current hits" (including 'The Birdie Song') at private functions dressed in the full crushed velvet regalia.

Kershaw pledged allegiance to elements of pomp rock, his whole image screamed "pose" yet he pleaded absolute honesty. Here was a man with a good woman at his side to help him shoulder the heavy responsibility – small wonder he has been the target of more vicious castigation than most of his forebears. "The music press write in the mistaken belief that there's some finite truth about what's right or wrong in music," is his typically level-headed reply to such criticism.

There will always be a plentiful supply of thirteen-year-old girls and accommodating young (and not so young) men in pop to satisfy their needs. But Kershaw wants *more* than that, more than the obsessive attentions of these acolytes. He wants to "be taken seriously as a musician" (a curious disease that seems to afflict most acts just after their first gold record). Like Duran and a host of others, he wanted to be accredited with depth and skill beyond the call of duty. If you believe that pop music has more than a transient commercial value, that it holds emotions and memories, then yes, anyone who acheives a high level of recognition within it has the right to claim talent. But should a modicum of musical skill and a lyric shrouded in "mystery" be enough to buy your way into the history books? Is artistry Art? And does Art always have to be "alternative"? This is the pop industry conundrum.

But Kershaw is unorthodox even in his beginnings and the very anonymity of his previous existence (three years a dole-office clerk in Ipswich) would explain the plaintive desperation in his eyes in those early videos. If he put a foot wrong he knew exactly what he had to go back to. When Fusion breathed their last in '82, Nick (as he was then) borrowed a friend's Portastudio and gave himself six months to write songs or bust. "I go back to Ipswich now and see friends who are doing what I was doing ten years ago. They're just going to the office every day and dreaming of something better. It makes me feel guilty about my incredible success." Nik was clearly one of the few lucky ones.

When he had accumulated enough songs to hawk around the record companies, he compiled demo after demo but the rejections were across the board. Most of them didn't even bother to proffer any constructive advice. This was not a good time in the life of Nik Kershaw. So he placed an ad in *Melody Maker* looking for a manager and teamed up with Mickey Modern who had adequate experience of the business to secure Nik a deal with MCA.

In a few short months, Kershaw's debut album *Human Racing* was in the Top Ten. Its songs were a bizarre amalgamation of early seventies pomp rock tradition and eighties precipitation, all jazzed up by Peter Collins' fancy production. Reviews were mixed in the extreme but Kershaw was continuing to attract a wider audience. It wasn't just the little girls; their mums quite liked him as well. All round family entertainment, and such a *nice* looking young man he was too.

His first live concerts were awkward but enthusiastic and the new four-piece band, the Krew, allowed him to skip blithely out front and cavort for his public. Gradually his dances became a little less awkward though the rap with the audience between numbers was still thoroughly inane. But they *loved* it! The rousing 'I Won't Let The Sun Go Down On Me' chorus almost brought the roof down instead.

Elton John, a professed admirer of Nik's work, invited him to play as his special guest at the Summer Of '84 concert at Wembley Stadium. Elton's approval is to Nik Kershaw what the "By Appointment To Her Majesty" seal is to merchants everywhere. Playing that day to 72,000 people was for Nik an unprecedented success.

Further accolades were on their way. Your soaraway *Sun* voted him best newcomer of the year in a readers poll and 'Dancing Girls' reached the Top Twenty to be followed by the re-release of 'I Won't Let The Sun Go Down On Me' which peaked at number four. His second album *The Riddle* was recorded in only eight weeks. It went gold within a month of release and the title track was a Top Five Christmas single. In the space of only one year Nik Kershaw had bridged that vast divide between obscurity and guaranteed celebrity.

At the 1984 British Record Industry awards Nik was nominated for Best Album, Best Newcomer and Best British Male Artist, only to lose out to Sade, Frankie and Paul Young, much to the chagrin of his many fans. And Fleet Street was becoming more and more intrigued. "*Sun* special on pop's Mr Clean; he doesn't take drugs, get drunk or sleep with the groupies" ran the headline on 19 November. Nik seemed naively unaware of their barbarous intentions and picked up on his cue each time. "I'm at the stage where I can have anything I want whether it's heroin or hot and cold running women on tap – but I just don't want to know." He was so insistent on emphasizing the solidity and importance of his marriage to Sheri (four years his elder, the papers sniggered) that it seemed almost as though he was trying to convince *himself*. The reasons later unfolded. For some time after signing to MCA, he had been advised to pretend she didn't exist. Bad for the image, old chap, they said. Sheri herself is a musician and nobody's fool. "Eventually they just gave up trying to exclude her because we wouldn't let them," Nik said in an interview later.

Ask Nik Kershaw how he'd describe himself and the first thing he'll say is "level-headed". "I enjoy a few drinks the same as the next guy but never when I'm working." He's bought a three-bedroom farmhouse in Suffolk, nothing too ostentatious, mind you. "I don't blame the guys who do go berserk and grab everything that's going because you never know how long it will last. Success in the music business is often very temporary".

Kershaw has no intentions of being sucked down the plughole. He intends to dabble in the Thespian arts as well, and film roles have been discussed. Elton invited him to play on his new album which Nik sees as a way of abandoning the dreaded tenny idol image. Exactly from whom he's seeking credit is uncertain but this is the prevalent chip on those 5′ 3″ shoulders. "I take my music very seriously. I write all my songs and do the arrangements myself. Obviously I enjoy the fame that comes with being a Top Ten pop star; I would be lying if I said I didn't. But my music is more important. Being a pop star is a very short career. Being a musician is for life."

If there's one perennial interview question that he hates, it's the one asking him about comparisons with Howard Jones. The parallels between them are obvious. Both are older than the usual pop heroes (Howard is thirty), both had Emerson Lake and Palmer records in their collections, both aim at a very defined image, songs with messages, maximum fan contact and wholesome ideals. And both, of course, have been phenomenally successful. Nik won't really comment on this old chestnut but he'll go so far as to say that he's really tired of them both being lumped together "as total wimps".

The two men also have wives who actively participate in their careers. This defuses their sexuality, or potential sexual availability for their female fans, but transforms them into chummy boy-next-door types, as comfortable and familiar as a well-worn teddy bear, though Nik still attracts his fair allocation of the other as well. "It'd be nice if they treated me like a human being but you can't really expect it when all they know of you is what they've seen on TV and in newspapers. I get all these girls going crazy because I'm successful and in the public eye."

The artificial glamour of celebrity is one obstacle he'll never overcome but he's determined to remain as "ordinary" as possible. While still, of course, riding the "up" escalator.

Helen Fitzgerald

BAND AID

DOING IT: "I was never interested in talking things out – either you *do* or you don't." – BOB GELDOF

When Bob Geldof, lead singer of fading Irish pop group the Boomtown Rats, and Paula Yates, journalist and TV compère, sat at home on the evening of 23 October 1984, watching the BBC's *9 O'Clock News* and saw Michael Buerk's special report on the Ethiopian famine, they, along with millions of others, were deeply moved. They wondered what they could do and their immediate answer was the same grievous, frustrated shake of the head as everyone else's.

Then Paula said that at least they knew some pretty well-heeled people. She would go out and demand money from them. To commit herself, she wrote down her target figure on a piece of paper: £2,000. Geldof went on brooding about how they could come up with more, something much bigger. Music, of course, but what?

A month later, on the morning of Sunday, 25 November, Geldof stood in the middle of Sarm West Studio, London, with his Scottish partner Midge Ure of Ultravox, hoping everyone would turn up. After a couple of days on the song and a couple of weeks on the phone, he'd got all the hottest stars in British pop – and their royalties – promised, and a dozen or more businesses covering every single aspect of the recording, manufacture, distribution and sale of a record to give their work absolutely free. On every 7″ sold at £1.35 it was calculated that 96.03p would go to famine relief (including Geldof/Ure's writing royalty of 8.43p), the rest to costs of manufacture and the Government's 15 per cent Value Added Tax. Band Aid, the "plaster on the world's wounds", was going to happen. And Geldof had raised his financial sights: he wondered publicly whether they might possibly make a million.

Duran Duran, Wham!, Culture Club, Sting, Bowie and the rest came, sang, played; they were interviewed, filmed and splashed on the front page of the four-million circulation *Daily Mirror* next day; the session was shown on BBC2 TV's *Whistle Test* and featured in a half-hour documentary on Channel 4's *The Tube*; the single received saturation airplay on national and local radio. On the first day of its release – Monday, 3 December – 'Do They Know It's Christmas?' became the fastest selling single in the history of British pop. By the end of the week 600,000 copies had gone and another half million orders had been placed. This could make £3 million, said Geldof.

Geldof also coined his phrase about having made "compassion fashionable" and to prove it other Band Aid-type projects started springing up all over the place: British Reggae Artists Famine Appeal, Irish Show Biz, Welsh, German, Latin American, Classical, Australian . . . But by Christmas the big one, the US, still hadn't got involved. In early January Geldof went to America to publicize 'Do They Know It's Christmas?', but it was a hit already and he seemed more concerned to stir the enormous fund-raising potential of the American rock world. By then he'd visited Ethiopia and seen mass starvation at first hand. If persuasion didn't work he was quite ready to offend and shame people into action. At a press conference on 10 January he said he'd proposed the launch of a US Band Aid to Van Halen, Cyndi Lauper, Huey Lewis, Hall & Oates and they were all open to it. But, he added acidly, the managements of the great black stars, the most commercially crucial of them all – Michael Jackson and Prince – had given him the brush-off when he'd tried to talk Africa, famine relief and charity with them. With that he flew home to keep Band Aid rolling and play a Rats tour.

At first it looked as though nobody who mattered had been watching TV that night. No cries of outrage from the Jackson or Prince camps. But Harry Belafonte was hopping mad. The old showbizzy "folk" singer had been a black civil rights activist alongside Martin Luther King and a founder director of the internationalist Peace Corps in the sixties. He heard Geldof and was wounded on behalf of American black music. He picked up the phone and luckily his first contact, promoter Ron Delsener, directed him to Lionel Richie's manager, Ken Kragen. Executive suit, serious specs, early to bed, and carefully worded statements, Kragen bears no resemblance at all to loudmouth, unshaven shambler Geldof – except that he was similarly moved to turn over a piece of his life to raise money for Ethiopia.

With Kragen's organization on the case, USA For Africa's gestation was even quicker than Band Aid's. His name cut through the crap Geldof had been given. Richie was immediately inspired by the project and, oddly enough, next day his wife Brenda met Stevie Wonder in a shop and *he* was in. Kragen called Quincy Jones who leapt at the idea of producing and in turn spoke personally to Jackson who said he'd help write the song, an offer which was not unwelcome. While he and Richie started work together, Kragen threw himself (decorously) into what he does best. "It was all an organizational problem," he said with obvious relish. "It was a jigsaw puzzle, putting it all together, contacting the right people, setting up a goal for each day." He booked the recording for 28 January because that night many of the stars were due in LA anyway to attend the *American Music Awards* TV show.

Interestingly, for all the pulling power of the names gathered within the first 24 hours, there was one man he was after to "authenticate" the project: Bruce Springsteen. "He has tremendous credibility," said Kragen. "He's kept a pure image about what he's done. To some extent you are who you associate with, and people wanted to associate with someone like that." Springsteen was to finish a US tour in Syracuse, New York, on 27 January and agreed to catch a 5am plane in order to be in LA for the recording.

And it was all right on the night.

In March, with 'We Are The World' already one of the all-time greatest hits, *Rolling Stone* estimated that, with the album to come, ancillary video rights and so on, USA For Africa could eventually generate $250 million for famine relief. In Britain, with the Band Aid UK-US concert and other schemes afoot, Geldof was speculating that the international music community might put together half a billion. These guesses may prove wildly over-optimistic. As this book goes to press perhaps £100 million of that is actually in the bag. But then it's a handy advance on the £2,000 target that the Geldof household set itself when it first decided to *do*.

"'We Are The World' enters 'into the archives of humanity one bold paragraph against the suffering, the despair, the starvation plaguing Africa – and by the dawn's early light, the paragraph was near completion. A masterpiece crafted from the sweat and dedication of more than 50 artists and musicians. A classic of unity . . .'" – Yamaha advert in Billboard

"The whole thing serves a dual purpose – it can raise a lot of money and I'm really proud of it because it's a celebration of British pop music. I've always wished something like the Beatles' 'All You Need Is Love' could happen now." – John Taylor in Smash Hits

TRAINS AND BOATS AND PLANES

The first wave of Band Aid fund-raising – 'Do They Know It's Christmas?' and associated videos, computer games and merchandise – brought in about £8 million. The single sold more than 3,100,000 copies in the UK (a new record) and at least a further 4,000,000 around the world. By the end of April, accountant Phil Rusted's office had also received £100,000 in donations from the public – neat cheques and unwieldy "half-ton bags" of coins collected by school children. In addition, by placing the cash on special terms in the money market, Rusted garnered £1,000-£2,000 a day in interest for several months. Collecting had turned out to be no great problem. Spending was the real test.

Geldof and Ure had established Band Aid on the principle that all receipts should be used to buy what the Ethiopian people needed, to be transported to them direct with no organizational overheads and no other agencies involved. It was a tall order. Obviously it demanded professional expertise. So they got together a team of amateurs who'd never worked in a Third World aid project before. But they were all people in their thirties with wide-ranging experience and, for various reasons, time they could make available. Rusted and lawyer John Kennedy were drawn in through record company connections. They then formed the security net to vet the other volunteers – £8 million might attract a vulture or two, after all.

The warehouse, an old bus garage lent by the Greater London Council, was run by barrister Judy Anderson and former restaurant manager Valerie Blondeau. Anthropologist Penny Jenden also worked there full-time in charge of purchasing. Transport journalists Dee Flowers and Phil Hayes organised the Truckers For Band Aid network which shifted anything any item anywhere in the UK for nothing. Ken Martin, a shipping agent, took care of chartering ships and planes. Kevin Jenden, an architect and Penny's husband, became overall co-ordinator and linkman between the "shopfloor" and the weekly meeting of the trustees who decided policy. The trustees were Maurice Oberstein (UK chairman of CBS), Kennedy, Geldof, Ure, Chris Morrison (Ultravox's manager), Michael Grade (head of BBC1 TV) and, the biggest rock promoter in the UK, Harvey Goldsmith (who replaced Lord Harlech after his sudden death). They operated on a quorum of four. Geldof and Ure made a point of one of them always being there to represent the musicians who'd started it all.

While this group was assembling, Geldof took the first steps towards answering the most basic question for any aid programme: "What do they really need?". His January visit to Ethiopia (fare paid by a national paper) was very practical. He established key contacts, especially Brother Gus O'Keefe of the Christian Relief Development Agency who agreed to act as a clearing house to see that Band Aid supplies reached their intended recipients (they *did* run a security check on Bro Gus too!). All the volunteers have since gone to Ethiopia at least once to get an idea of what they're dealing with.

Then the haggling, and the spending, began. The first two flights were donated by the Nigerian Government and multi-millionaire Adnan Khashoggi (after a Geldof buttonholing), but since then they've been costing around £50,000 a time (to carry 40 tons), though Band Aid hoped to persuade an oil company to "sponsor" the fuel retrospectively. At first, expecting to pay commercial freight rates, they set aside £1,200,000 as the shipping budget. Then, when the persuasive Ken Martin came up with far more capacity than they could fill, they maintained the funding but offered a free freight service to other agencies – with the strict proviso that the money saved was ploughed back

"It was a space-age Woodstock . . . The idea of this global coalition of artists is the most exciting thing I've ever heard of. The idea that that can work – and it CAN work – is a dream. It's something I'd like to be involved in for the rest of my life." – Quincy Jones in Billboard

"It's difficult to know how much to send to Ethiopia when you're a millionaire." – Sting in the Daily Star

"If we take, say, six months and not spend any money on nuclear weapons, and just spend it on food, I think we could make a dent. Of course, that's just an old country boy's simple way of saying something." – Waylon Jennings in Billboard

into famine relief and development goods.

Penny Jenden probably had to go through the quickest hard-knocks training course. Her previous experience of bulk purchasing had been confined to Saturday in *Safeway's*. Now she was talking hundreds of thousands and life-or-death emergencies. Where do you buy 36 tons of reinforced plastic sheeting? In May, when the rains hit the refugee camps, she found out. The sheeting, plus attendant rope and gaffer tape, was on its way nine days after she received the telex request. Buying medicines presented particular problems. When Bro Gus passed on an urgent call for the antibiotic tetracycline, the British drugs suppliers' response was "Fine! Will three weeks do you?" She got what she wanted in Germany and booked a flight from Frankfurt.

Band Aid feels that one of the reasons for crucial delays and shortages is competition between the relief agencies, all seeking the same product at the same time. As Ure says, "It's very odd to find all these people trying to get better deals out of companies, Oxfam v the Red Cross or whatever". One thing Band Aid prides itself on is that, with the honeypot lure of that £8 million, it was able to draw all the British agencies together for what, it transpired, was their very first joint discussion of the African famine!

To everyone's credit, after the introductory niggles when Band Aid explained that they weren't giving any handouts, co-operation developed well and the amateurs can chalk up some good references from the professionals. Oxfam say of Band Aid "They've done excellently. They have gone to a lot of trouble to find out what other people are doing and avoid duplication. That's very valuable." And REST, Eritrea's own relief society, say "They're very interesting to work with because, as volunteers, they're a bit more flexible and sensitive to our needs than other agencies. Their shipping department is very well organized and the free freight service is particularly useful."

At the time of writing Band Aid still saw itself as a short-life project even though it was possible that new ventures, like the US-UK concert, the Fashion Aid show, and Rusted's pet scheme of a fancy Eurobond launch to tap the ultra-rich, could earn anything up to another £50 million by the end of 1985. The accountant favoured going out with a bang no matter what – some major development scheme perhaps like the well-drilling they were already involved in. Ure agreed they should get out before permanence could change the character of Band Aid, but he suspected the only way to stop it rolling might be to give all the cash they had left to the established agencies after all.

USA FOR AFRICA

The returns on 'We Are The World', the compilation album, and all the ancillaries plus donations hit $40 million in 16 weeks from the foundation of USA For Africa. They had supposed it would take them three years to reach that figure. Though their wealth was thus much greater, they still modelled themselves on Band Aid – with significant variations. These included their target area: they named twelve African countries (among them, interestingly enough, socialist Angola and Mozambique), while also setting aside ten per cent of US receipts for the "hungry and homeless" of America.

Their "trustee" board of directors consisted of Kragen, his clients Richie and Kenny Rogers, plus Jackson, Jones and Belafonte. From the outset they envisaged USA For Africa as a long-term venture, so, while welcoming the help of dozens of volunteers, they appointed a five-strong core of paid staff based in their LA office and headed by executive director Martin Rogol. But, pursuing the Band Aid "no overheads" principle, the board decided to cover all salaries out of their own pockets without drawing on funds given by the public.

Clearly they have even greater problems of transport and communication with Africa then do Band Aid, but they are trying to overcome them with the help of Operation California, an aid agency with several years' experience (including a small progamme in Nicaragua when the collaborated with Oxfam). USA For Africa's potential is enormous though their work has only just begun. Their first "air lift" of medicines, food and clothing flew out on 10 June.

Veteran social campaigner Belafonte has put his heart into it and hopes there'll be an annual artists' event for the project. But it's worth noting too his grizzled advice that those involved "should constantly temper their enthusiasm against reality".

BOB: A JOB

Bob Geldof has been the moving force behind the entire Band Aid/USA For Africa phenomenon. It's quite possible that without him *none* of it would have happened. He captured the moment by exactly appropriate action. But why Geldof?

It would be silly to contrive some tendentious explanation slotting Band Aid neatly into his development, but there were precedents in his earlier life. He was 33 when he created Band Aid. Since his teens he'd intermittently been a campaigner – his bounding, sometimes quixotic enthusiasms reined back by suspicion. He remembers speaking against America's war in Vietnam in a debate at his Dublin school and losing the vote 516-1. At 15 he was doing late-night soup runs to the city's down-and-outs as a volunteer for the Simon Community. He imported Mao's Red Book from Peking and *sold* it to his classmates! He was active in the anti-apartheid movement and the Campaign for Nuclear Disarmament. Later, when working as a journalist in Vancouver he became engrossed in the Save The Whale Campaign through a story he did on Greenpeace.

But, when he formed the Boomtown Rats in 1975 and came to England in the wake of the punk eruption, his notorious statement of policy was "I want to get rich, get famous and get laid". Back then, he talked to sell himself. But he talked too much and come the autumn of 1984, nobody was buying. The Rats' run of hits was over, their uncouth punk/R&B ousted by handsome young men with synthesizers, slick haircuts and very considered clothes. Geldof had become passé; that is, an embarrassment.

So it's no wonder that Geldof's upfront role in Band Aid attracted not only the instant esteem of millions who'd probably never heard of him even when he was famous but the venom of rockbiz's cynics. In his *Daily Mirror* column professional stirrer Jonathan King bitched: "I rather think publicity was the major factor behind the good deed". The implication was that Geldof was setting up the whole thing to resuscitate his own career.

Fortunately, Geldof wasn't shy about counter-attacking. "The [Band Aid] idea is so intrinsically decent," he said. "If by their carping they stop someone putting their hand in their pocket to give 5p that is, by extension, murder." The evidence supported his rhetoric. Mike Gardner of pop weekly *Record Mirror* pointed out that Geldof had, in effect, "deliberately sabotaged his own career" by holding back all publicity for the Rats' pre-Christmas LP *In The Long Grass* to avert cash-in accusations. The final irony for the band was when, in January, their single 'Dave' entered the chart at 100 – with Band Aid at number one – only for Gallup to disqualify it because the sleeve included a free concert ticket voucher.

Surely, when an interviewer asked him why he wasn't donating the proceeds of the Rats' tour to Band Aid, Geldof was entitled to the passion of his reply: "I work 20 hours a day on it. I've donated my life to it. What more do you want?"

He made those cynics, who after all pride themselves on their intellectual couture, look utter mugs, pathetic wallies. Unreservedly, he was accorded the people's trust. Geldof is a foul-mouthed roughneck, yet, as soon as Band Aid was launched, complete strangers started coming up to him in the street and thrusting money at him. On the Rats' tour they'd put Band Aid buckets at the edge of the stage and every night they'd be full. After the show, queues waited outside the dressing-room to shake Geldof's right hand while pressing cheques, notes or coins into his left. Journalists dubbed him "Saint Bob", with varying degrees of sarcasm. Sometimes Geldof himself could hardly bear it: "What do people *want*? I mean, they come up to me and they *cry*, they hold *on* to me . . . it's preposterous! What the fuck do they think is going on?"

Presumably the straightforward answer was "giving". Because Geldof wasn't offering any ideology to follow. His thinking, under extreme pressure, was often ambiguous and erratic – in a sense, he liked it that way. He couldn't be pinned down as "Conservative" or "Socialist". If he had any doctrine at all it seemed to be individualism (rugged as necessary). But perhaps his ultimate popular appeal came from the faith he admitted in one interview that his actions were "for right against wrong".

"It wasn't an ego bath; it was just spiritually uplifting. I'll tell you, there's nothing like peer recognition. It made up for every bad review I've ever had!" – Billy Joel in Billboard

Supreme naiveté, unimpeachable honesty.

Geldof was believed and believed in. It may also explain the excess self-assurance he sometimes spilt in unseemly splatterings of indiscretion. The best-known was his description of Hitler's concentration camp holocaust as a "tea-party" compared to the African famine. That came in a spontaneous speech at an award ceremony, but, in the less exposed setting of the London weekly *Time Out*, he permitted himself the remark that "so-called freedom fighters to me are nothing but murdering fascists". Yet the people of Tigray and Eritrea who are struggling for their independence from Ethiopia and receiving famine relief because of Geldof's efforts for Band Aid, would probably think of themselves as "freedom fighters". Geldof, naturally, had a phrase for these tongue-biting moments: he called them "verbal infelicities".

It was as well then that another Geldof quality was that he was easy to forgive. Partly, no doubt, it was sheer charisma. As Midge Ure says, fondly, "He's the guy you hate to walk into a room with! He's got such a presence you blend into obscurity." What's more, Geldof's outspokenness became a positive asset when he was giving stick to the mighty – Maggie Thatcher, the Ethiopian minister for famine relief, Prince, whoever. Clearly he knew no fear.

A special pleasure for insiders was overhearing his end of a phone conversation. One Phonogram office favourite was Geldof's roar of "No, I won't fuckin' talk to Colonel Gaddafi!" Midge Ure recalls Geldof phoning *Daily Mirror* proprietor Robert Maxwell from the studio on the night of the Band Aid recording, basically to thank him for the next day's promised front page. It went "Yes, thanks, great, thanks a lot, thanks," and then, alarmingly, "No! You fuckin' can't! Fuck off!" Slam! Apparently a disagreement arose about the amount of credit the newspaper could claim for the project; ie, in Geldof's view, none. Maxwell the magnate yielded. And next day Geldof was back on to him asking for more help and getting it. "Bob doesn't care," says Ure. "He's absolutely ruthless with people like that."

"For good against evil" as a practical proposition? Perhaps it was possible within the one-off Band Aid game. Geldof knew the score, the politics of his temporary magic: "I don't have to attract votes. I can say and do exactly what I like. I don't *mind* being the world's clown, if I'm allowed to do things that are effective." It was a special kind of freedom and he made the most of it. So what odds would you give against him being the first clown to receive the Nobel Peace Prize?

Phil Sutcliffe

WRANGLES AND ANGLES. Not quite everything was sweetness and light . . .

1 In December, Britain's Conservative Government refused to re-route the tax gathered from the sales of 'Do They Know It's Christmas?' into aid funds. Under fire, the minister responsible announced an extra £1m to go to Ethiopia through the UN. Opposition MPs pointed out it came from funds already earmarked for aid and was therefore not a counterbalance in real terms to the 'lost' VAT (which amounted to more than £500,000).

2 Although the major retail chains agreed to sell 'Do They Know It's Christmas?' at the cost price of £1.35 for the 7" version, some local shops were taking up to 60p per copy. One owner, exposed in the press, snarled "I'm not a charity!" No legal controls could be imposed on them and the same applied in America where it was estimated that dealers charging up to double the official price had creamed off $4 million.

3 When CBS presented the British retail chains with the deal they proposed for the release of 'We Are The World', Virgin and HMV were ready to accept the Band Aid-style no-profit arrangement, but WH Smith voiced the more general feeling that it couldn't be done again. After a day or two of tension, Maurice Oberstein, chairman of CBS (UK) and, ironically, one of the Band Aid trustees, placated them by announcing a ten per cent cut in the dealer price "designed to enable dealers to cover their costs and to ensure that the maximum amount of stores stock this record".

4 On the night when 'We Are The World' was recorded, it was widely reported that Prince was carousing a couple of miles away. Naturally Geldof, the only person involved who didn't feel that charity was a house of cards that would collapse with one rude word, was the man to publicly denounce his absence. Within hours his manager had pledged royalties from a B-side – possibly $250,000 – and an unreleased track for the USA For Africa album.

5 On 23 May, the spell of total press co-operation with Band Aid was broken by the previously helpful *Daily Star*. Unable to resist the smell of an exclusive, they blew many of the details of the planned 13 July UK-US concert and live satellite hook-up extravaganza. Band Aid had been waiting, in fairness, to release the story to all the media simultaneously; they expressed their feelings by remonstrating with the *Star* in private.

EUROPE:

HIGH NOTES FROM THE LOWLANDS

As the big guns fall silent, John Gill hears the best and most varied Continental sounds in unexpected places

The smart money – that is, money found lounging behind typewriters at magazines like *I-D* and *The Face*, propping up cocktail bars or ligging through album-release and après-gig parties – would have you believe that this year's European name is Propaganda, signed to ZTT and at least one of them married to at least one prime mover in the ZTT organization. Smart money is often safe money, relying on the assurances of budgets, promotion and media/broadcasting complicity. Propaganda's releases so far suggest they'll need all the help those three can give them, and their chart action so far suggests they can't even rely on that. Instead, out here bouncing wildly on the end of the gangplank, I'd tip or, more modestly, *suggest* Die Zwei.

Literally "The Two", Die Zwei are a young Berlin duo made up of the not-particularly-German-sounding Danny Wilde and Brett Sinclair. Signed to the highly-respected Zensor label, so far they have only produced one single, the 12″ 'Countryboy'. This, with its two-track flipside of 'Fairheaded Squaws' and the rather ungainly 'Western Union', was at first listen the only sound that could conceivably knock Bronski Beat for six. Classically trained singers, Die Zwei's exquisite choiring voices steal the show from Jimmy Somerville's untrained falsetto, and from what I've heard of Somerville's new band they would seem to have beaten him to that state of lavish pop camp by at least a year. When last heard of they were on the verge of signing to a British label.

Having attained a level of sophistication, not to mention *exposure*, the European new wave in all its glories and idiocies seemed to pan out in a way that suggested that either the continent was in rude, eclectic health, or something had gone the teensiest bit wrong somewhere.

After last year's comment to the same effect, the big names really *did* seem to close down. Tangerine Dream were "let go" by Virgin. Can, and most of their individual parts, were silent this year, as were Kraftwerk. The only upbeat note from Germany was that Gabi Delgado Lopez and Robert Gorl are working in the studio as DAF again. The same radio static came out of France – traditionally the only other continental country capable of penetrating the international market. Both Richard Pinhas and Bernard Szajner seemed to retire, injured, after coming up against insensitive British audiences, while the gloomy art-rock brigade were sneaking around on tiptoe, if they were around at all.

The most impressive album to come out of Europe this year was *Holy Wars*, by American immigrés (!) Tuxedomoon. Resident in Brussels since the late seventies, Tuxedomoon have had a more than bumpy half-decade, but *Holy Wars* is the pinnacle of a pile of solo albums by members Blaine Reininger, Steven Brown and Peter Principle released in the last year. Second only to their Ralph debut *Half-Mute*, *Holy Wars* (like those solo works, released on Crammed), is a powerful mixture of eerie chamber music, eccentric Weill-esque marches, melancholy atmospheres and bristling mutant electropop.

For my money, the Lowlands took the lead this year, with all manner of bands and styles appearing on labels like Les Disques du Crepuscule, Factory Benelux, Crammed and LAYLAH. Strangest, and not a thousand kilometres from the aforementioned Tuxes, was the "new career" Crepuscule 45 from one-time member Winston Tong, 'Theoretical China'. Like violinist/singer Blaine Reininger, Tong has now left the band. 'Theoretical China' is an exotic East-West funk dance track, produced by none other than ex-Associate Alan Rankine and Magazine contributor Dave Formula. Instrumental support came from these two, augmented by Jah Wobble, Steve Morris and Simon Topping. Not content with invading the dancefloor, Tong is soon to breach Harlem when he tours Europe with his "play-it-for-straight" tribute to the songs of Duke Ellington.

Even if they did only enumerate the sum of Tuxedomoon's separate parts, the solo albums from its members also took their seats in the first class section; Reininger, on *Night Air*, mixing American Cowboy Epic and film-noir to the accompaniment of a gypsy violin and drum machine; Brown, on *Sex & Sorrow*, leaning towards the conservatoire and, finally, Peter Principle, on *Sedimental Journey*, mixing scratch, cut-ups and funk with Tuxmoon's weird landscapes.

Belgium had further random exotica to offer, if not all its own work. Canada's vibey Skinny Puppy released an entertaining guerrilla synthpop 6-track on Play It Again, Sam!, echoing primitive Human League,

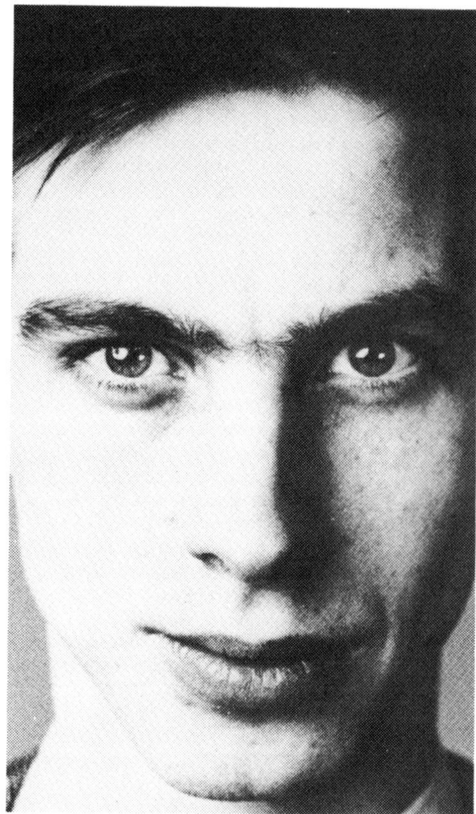

● *HOLGER HILLER*

● *EINSTURZENDE NEUBATEN*

Kanda Bongo Man is one who definitely has, but any nagging feeling that he owes at least some of his success to acting the perfect European imagined stereotype of an African pop star is dispelled in the presence of his bright gold guitar-pop.

The presence in London of large numbers of Ghanaian expatriates has created a natural market for West African Hi-Life music; records by A B Crentsil, Pat Thomas & Ebo Taylor, Jewel Ackah, Eric Agyemang, and the African Brothers have all sold well over the year. On the whole, the rural feel of this dry and subtle music seems likely to limit its crossover appeal and so far attempts to gloss it up have drained it of much of its character. Many of the local bands that keep African Pop alive in London clubs base their sets round Hi-Life, and these are the best places to hear it. Orchestra Jazira and Hi-Life International have been around longest and are perhaps getting a little stale. Lately, Abdul T-Jay's African Culture have begun to punch themselves a space, and the recent arrival of A K Yeboah from a respected career in Ghana augurs well.

● *FAN FAN OF SOMO SOMO*

African Pop has always suffered from the British press's need to pigeonhole: a huge continent bustling with diverse music tends to get crammed all into one corner. One musician well appraised of a need to jumble categories and crosswire is Manu Dibango, the Soul-Makossa Man. To prove Africa is a centre for hi-tech innovation, he contributed to the brooding, boggling sound of Bill Laswell's NY avantfunk project to startling effect, and a devastating London show in the autumn extended his reach — no music is safe! His own Cameroonian crown is a bit wobbly though, with the emergence of handsome young pretender Sam Fan Thomas whose LPs *African Typic Collection* and *Neng Makassi* have proved popular on the dancefloor.

Thomas Mapfumo built further on his reputation for peacetime excellence with a striking show and a third Earthworks LP, *Mabasa*. Another artist who's benefited from the youthful westerner's attraction to a rebel stance, he made his name in Zimbabwe singing songs in Shona for the Resistance, but since Independence has continued to develop and demonstrate that his importance wasn't entirely confrontational.

The political constrictions of the evil regimé at present on the rampage in Azania (South Africa as is) have been less kind to South African music. Although the raw township sound makes an impression on rock audiences, it seems fair to say that this music will never be able fully to explore itself until Africa is truly free. The moral complexities of the boycott were brought home by the bust-up between Rough Trade and Earthworks over payment of royalties through South African publishing firms. In the meantime, our introduction to Azanian culture must come through the mediation of such exiles as Hugh Masekela, Abdullah Ibrahim, Miriam Makeba, Julian Bahula, and the serried ranks of the London AfroJazz contingent. As long as oppression remains, however, all will be only a pale shadow of the actuality and potential of the life of the South.

Much of the thrill and threat of African music comes in its assault on things we take for granted in music. Rhythm and melody constantly attempt to usurp one another's position, styles shifting and stealing, no simple contentment with what is or what's been or what ought to be — the whole combining to undermine our reliance on words in songs. Not only are songs sung in Yoruba, Lingala, Wolof, Twi, Swahili and many other languages, but alongside them guitars chatter and drums talk . . .

. . . but voices still count for something. In the last year Samba Mapalanga, Youssou N'Dour and Salif Keita have all made records that reaffirm that; respectively, *Malako, Immigrés,* and *Mandjou* find ways of holding onto beauty in bad times. And the tangled kora music of the North West has become a recognizable sound of late, thanks to griots Foday Musa Suso and Mory Kante. Mory Kante was also responsible, with Manu Dibango, for setting up 'Tam-Tam Pour L'Ethiopie'. The response of a clutch of African musicians to the hideous drought in Africa that finally became News, it was released as the B-side of Jerry Dammers' 'Starvation' disc.

● *HI-LIFE INTERNATIONAL*

British promotion networks have yet to spread beyond London which is a pity, but in the capital Tsafrica and the Foundation for African Arts have arranged numerous festivals. Possibly *too* many, in fact: the idea is getting around that this everyday music needs some kind of kidglove treatment and can only flourish in hothouse conditions such as festivals; more one-offs would be welcome. Meanwhile small corners have been captured in those music papers and magazines prepared to take black music seriously, and two specialist magazines, Jon Harlow's *Africa Beat* and Nick Carnac's *Umoya* have appeared.

On the record label front, established names Sterns, Earthworks and Celluloid have continued to bring over new names (new to us that is!). Earthworks in particular deserve congratulation for its recent Miniworks series which handed on songs from Tony Allen, Dele Abiodun, and from Souzy K'Asseya a follow-up to last year's Paris hit 'Le Telephone Sonne'.

Just as important, a number of small independent labels are flourishing: Ben Mandelson's GlobeStyle (devoted to strange sounds world-wide), Kwabena Fosu Mensah's Afroboom (concentrating on music from Ghana), and Iain Scott's Triple Earth (looking at more traditional musics, though to be honest that distinction makes little sense in Africa, and is more the product of our own folk-embalming industry).

A K Yeboah and Tanzania's Fan Fan have also chosen to base their operations in London, and that Fan Fan's band Somo Somo have immediately provoked a favourable response is an indication that confidence in the continued strengthening of the music isn't misplaced. A certain strength in depth is also beginning to emerge locally: in addition to those already mentioned, such varied names as Dade Krama, African Dawn, Dudu Pukwana's Zila, District Six, Ekome and African Connexion are going to keep it all bubbling between visits from prestigious internationals. Until such time as it seems perfectly natural to go out and dance the night away to agbadza or kwela or mbalax or ziglibithy or mbaqanga . . .

BEING SEEN TO BE BELIEVING

Is God responsible for the current state of black music? Lloyd Bradley raises a questioning eyebrow.

"First of all, giving all praises and honour to God who makes this whole thing possible" . . . "But most of all thank you Jesus for the strength to make it through every vixen plague. God is the greatest and forever will be" . . . "All thanks 2 God – the light" . . . "God bless you all" . . . No, not quotes from an evangelist meeting but readings taken from the sleeve notes of a quartet of soul albums pulled at random from the box marked 1985.

Such tub-thumping does not stop at production credits. The last five or so years have seen a clutch of very public rebirths and conversions among American soul acts, a couple of famous faces beaming out from above clerical collars and James Brown telling a television interviewer how he saw himself as Moses.

If this were twenty years ago when the route from soul back to spiritual was an easy one to trace and a grounding in church singing was a must, then these conspicuous acts of piety might be easier to understand, but the wide-eyed innocence that made the likes of Tamla Motown universally palatable has long disappeared under the combination of seventies street funk and the Gaye/Hayes/Prendergrass school of advanced erotica.

Being beaten over the head with holy humbleness has in the past embarrassed practically everybody into ignoring it, but after Prince's ludicrous acceptance speech at the BPI Awards and Steve Arrington and James Ingram going Top Twenty with prayers set to soul music, religion has become a current focus of public attention. These occurrences are – at the moment anyway – an American phenomenom; Brit-funkers are more likely to credit whatever allnight burger bar is closest to their studio.

Objective discussion about someone else's faith is usually strictly taboo, but some of these characters are so bizarrely at odds with popular concepts of God and Jesus that all worries about causing offence simply vanish. We are not dealing here with recordings like 'What's Goin' On' or Curtis Mayfield's 'Sweet Exorcist' which were works of true spiritual inspiration, but with, for instance, the sheer nastiness that was the film *Purple Rain*. Even the least cynical would find it tough to equate *that* with anything found in the Bible. Besides, if the clothes, lyrics and videos of artists like Rick James and his Mary Jane Girls, the new Shalamar and Vanity, are so questionable, then so are their trite homilies.

But why are so many soul people party to this trend? Leaving aside the possibility of real reverence – which in so many cases seems laughable – it helps if it is looked at in three stages: sleeve note hallelujahs, rebirth and owning your own church.

The first is the most confusing. Why go to the trouble Frankie Beverly went to with his verse of humility on the inside cover of *Can't Stop The Love*, or infuriate your record company to the extent DeBarge do by putting your faith before your music in "interview situations"?

Money? Hardly. This is not the gospel/church music scene that dominates America's Sunday airwaves and works within its own healthy marketing plan, but a sphere where if you can't dance to it, forget it.

● *FRANKIE BEVERLY & MAZE*

● *THE BROTHERS JOHNSON*

● *AL GREEN*

Respectability? Maybe. A kind of street funk backlash – the heavy funk of five years ago was locally dubbed "Dust Music" for its associations with PCP. This theory is supported by the fact that today's rough-edge performers – the rappers, scratchers and go-goers – never go "Thanks be to God" until their second album, after the surprise hit that took them out of the neighbourhood and into the world at large. However, the respectability theory is heavily undermined when you know that Smokey Robinson and Ashford & Simpson only ever credit musicians, and who could be more respectable than them?

Future salvation? A novel idea, but I seriously doubt if thanking the Lord for your talent will, come the day of reckoning, mean He forgets how you used it to abuse women in your promo videos. Anyhow, if it is some kind of penance, then it is hardly appropriate for Lionel Richie to do the same as a girl who sings about dildoes.

No – this production credit piety must be examined alongside stage two: rebirths and conversions.

Someone I know once speculated that you could spot a born-again Christian by their expressions on their album covers: spacy, fey smiles and intensely shining eyes. I checked and my friend had a point – it is as if the light they have seen is still being reflected. The list of recent rebirths includes Michael Jackson, Al Green, Luis Johnson, George Benson, Donna Summer and Philip Bailey, and they all had two things in common at the time they got the call – they were (a) fantastically wealthy and (b) at the peak of their careers.

As these comings-out increased, so did the number of sleeve-note "All thanks be"s by soul music's lesser beings. The two must be connected – if I'd modelled my bass playing on Luis Johnson, or my dancing on Michael Jackson, and discovered my hero had got God, I'd be interested too.

Rebirth can bring in its wake some pretty strange behaviour. Already mentioned are the disco prayers, for which Steve Arrington wins bonus points for the biblical(ish) robes and sandals. Donna Summer caused a lot of raised eyebrows when she shucked her Bad Girl image to present herself on a cover dressed up like Little Bo Peep – and *meaning* it. These don't however, in the grand scheme of things, count for much and are really for the artists' own consciences rather than public benefit – just like those records that set a catalogue of urban deprivations to a hip hop rhythm. As Gil Scott-Heron said, "The kids are so busy hipping and hopping you could be saying 'Freddy the Frog' for all they care."

The wealth and success factors mentioned earlier do have important roles in rebirth. Not because you have to buy your way in, or pass some sort of test, but because of all that goes with fame and fortune. Picture the cliché of the kid from Hicksville who, a couple of years ago, was shining shoes but is now shovelling money round his Bel Air mansion. Add to that all the self-abuse – physical, chemical and mental – that goes into a coast-to-coast tour and album a year. Then imagine how many people are going to lose a meal ticket if the strain gets too much for the kid to handle. The need for a safety valve is plain to see.

I cite two encounters with Luis Johnson, a year apart and separated by his rebirth, BC and AD so to speak.

At the first he was breakfasting on packets of salted peanuts and Bloody Marys, and even allowing for jet lag and the previous night's show he looked a wreck. His disposition was so, to put it mildly, twitchy I felt sure he wouldn't last the year. Next time round, he's still a little jumpy, but at least eating meals. He tells me he's got God. Not with a flash, but *after long discussions with his wife and brother George*, during which time they had browsed through different religions and decided Christianity was the one for him. As Luis and his bass were what made the Bros Johnson special, and as his wife and brother had become used to a certain lifestyle, I leave you to your own conclusions.

There are too many occurrences of intense pressure at the time of these conversions for them all to be coincidental. It is also worth noting that, with the exception of Bailey, none of the aforementioned have recorded anything worth a hoot since their rebirths, and that, a little eerily, Bailey is the only one whose beliefs are credible. Rather than wear his faith on his (record) sleeve or in the press, in a recent round of interviews he had to be pushed hard to talk about it; he conducts himself with the dignity you would associate with true resolve. Bailey records gospel songs for a small, little publicized company, and commercial soul for CBS - he sees there must be a definite divide.

Perhaps – probably when cures for AIDS and herpes are discovered – much of this being seen to be believing will fade away in a couple of years. Like kung fu or skateboarding, it will be just another fad. For those who stick with it though, there are the rewards of the third stage: the first division – buying your own church and becoming the Rev Whoever.

Like practically everything else in the US, the Baptist church is operated on a very business-like level. While living in the black section of Inglewood, Los Angeles, I visited the local church a few times, and the preachers and their entourages (simply) oozed wealth from the moment they emerged from their Rollers (Royces, not holy). There was some serious money going into the collection plates, nothing jingly.

A friend of mine's father who is a London vicar, while on holiday in Chicago, was offered $500 to do a guest spot on a Sunday; a black English preacher would be guaranteed to swell the congregation. He declined on what he said were moral grounds.

Although the bucks are bigger than welfare, they cannot really compare to what world-wide record sales could bring –

● *LITTLE RICHARD*

what is more important is the performance factor. A Baptist preacher will put on a show. He will be a star in his church, holding open air rallies or "guesting" somewhere else. Hoardings outside the churches will announce the billings; headliners, special appearances and support acts. The better your show, the bigger your earnings and the greater your adulation.

At the church in Inglewood I would try to listen to the actual words (lyrics?) of the star-preachers' sermons, and taken coldly they didn't make much sense. What counted was the pitching and phrasing of the voice, each peak getting higher until the congregation was in raptures. Two that I saw left the pulpit and collapsed, to have coats put over their shoulders and then be led away – yes, you've seen James Brown do that, so now you know just how close we are to showbiz here.

When the Reverends Al Green and Little Richard appeared in television profiles earlier this year, what came across strongest – apart from their seemingly precarious mental states – was their desperate need to carry on performing to an audience.

Finally, here's a thought from the other side: in the early seventies Stevie Wonder recorded 'Have A Talk With Jesus', and a little while later Richard Pryor introduced a new story to his act. That too dealt with talking to Jesus and told of a chap who heard His call coming from a nearby alley. He pursued it to discover "that it was not the voice of the Lord I heard calling to me, but two or three niggers with a baseball bat!"

LIP-SYNCH SERVICE

Julie Burchill argues that what is considered commercial pap is often the best political pop

● *BOB DYLAN*

● *THE ROLLING STONES*

● *TOM ROBINSON*

In the winter of '84, you knew straight away just exactly *who* amongst your acquaintances would think that Band Aid was a Bad Thing – those same people who had been against the Falklands war. No matter that the end result had been to bring down a genocidal junta or go some way towards alleviating starvation in the far from cornucopian horn of Africa, the *motive* was the thing. What were Thatcher's motives for fighting the war? What were Geldof's motives for feeding the dying? If you had a grain of practical common sense, of course, the answer was *who cares*? If you were a terminally woolly-minded wallowing wallflower, the sort of person who buys the pop papers to read about Dionysius rather than Dion and the Belmonts, you paid minute attention to debating *detail* and *motive* while EFFECT – kicking the butchers out of Argentina, saving some lives in Ethiopia – went by the board. To these people who wore their integrity like aftershave, the nuance had become more important than the *action*, as Norman Mailer had said it would.

Face value and lip service counts an awful lot in pop, especially at the clever-clever end of it. People are judged on the way they pose rather than the actions they carry out. Scowl and you're a genius. Smile and you're a Thatcherite dupe agent of evil. Band Aid were disliked by certain people because they made formerly integrity-ridden heroes look suddenly silly and shoddy. All those songs people had written about how bad meat-eating and the monarchy, the Latin American death squads and the National Front were – AND KEPT THE MONEY THEY MADE FROM THE RECORDS. Band Aid flew the nest and blew the gaff. It demanded FEED THE WORLD – it was *of* the world, seeking to effect *change* in the world – far beyond the Pavlovian tantrum which had been coming from the playpen of pop for the past thirty years. It was the first protest record not to leave the world in the same sad state it found it in. Of course people hated it – because it showed that you *could* change the world if you passed on your royalties. What young hero needs information like that? There are *limits* to wanting to change the world . . .

Protest pop began not with a banjo but with a whimper as Jimmy Dean and the other Methodists in the church of Lee Strasberg began to pout their way to freedom. Films like *Rebel Without a Cause* (how true) and *The Wild One* showed that youth temper tantrums dressed up in pop psychology and scuffed leather were a marketable farce – sorry, *force*. The cinema was the first medium of mass culture to discover what till then had been the minority interest of a few mad, bad and deluded romantic poets. The protest song as practised by Bob Dylan and the subsequent band of weekend whingers was a travesty of the true protest songs of Mr Dylan's heroes, men like Woody Guthrie and Pete Seeger.

But their songs were not drama-documentaries for earnest college kids to consume at their leisure; they were songs rooted in the struggles and experiences of the American labour movement. Their songs were designed for action, not reflection; political activity, not consumption; rabble-rousing, not stereo relaxation. Their purpose was functional, to be sung at rallies and demonstrations to keep up the spirits of the working man as he faced danger from the bought brawn of management – Woody Guthrie was beaten up more than once for his work with the unions. The worst thing Bob Dylan ever had to face was the fury of betrayed folkies who heckled him the first time he plugged in his electric guitar – hardly spitting in the eye of the hurricane.

Nevertheless, young people came to expect more from their crooners – salvation for starters, tomorrow the world. By the end of the sixties the bands were getting nervous, and put out disclaimers – vinyl equivalents of "I made my excuses and left", such as the Beatles' 'Revolution' and the Rolling Stones' 'Street Fighting Man'. The latter became very popular with crooners due to the line *"What can a poor boy do but to sing for a rock 'n' roll band?"* – Bruce Springsteen currently does it as an encore. The answer was obvious: *you can put your money where your mouth is, and if the world's as rotten as your songs say then you can throw some of your massive earnings at the problem. Try it; it might work.* But of course the giant jobsworths of pop weren't having any of it; *it's more than my job's worth to try and change the world.*

The pop stars of the seventies were doomed to repeat the mistakes of their elders, and the cycle of anger, wealth and contentment continued. From punk to Two Tone, from Tom Robinson to Pauline Black, time and time again the prime movers proved that all they really wanted was A DECENT JOB IN ENTERTAINMENT. Please God, let me have one and I promise I'll never gob again. Uncle Tom Robinson, the foremost figure of the Rock Against Racism Class of '79, began writing the soundtrack to the gay feminist black revolution and ended up singing jingles for white male heterosexualist, leering DJ Mike Read . . . 'Rising Free' indeed.

This is not to say that all purposefully political crooners are two-faced swine. It's just that the bad ones outnumber the good ones. Almost impossibly so. The bad ones use the social ills they condemn to excite themselves and the listener into a state of extreme hysterical superiority, like the tabloid that titillates the reader under the guise of moral outrage. Hearing the Clash, the Alarm and the Redskins, you know they will make a drama out of a crisis rather than seek a remedy.

The patron saint of these people must be Barry McGuire, the New Christy Minstrel who protested all the way to the bank with the sixties hit 'Eve Of Destruction'. Most remarkable and give-away is Mr McGuire's vocal; the song begins with the "Western World" "exploding" and builds UP from there. As it catalogues every social injustice real and imagined, home and abroad, going from bad to worse, you can hear Mr McGuire getting more and more excited. Just a couple more tantalizing telegenic images of social wrongs and wham, bam, thank you Walter Cronkite.

It is this school of protest pop which is most objectionable and prevalent, and which has gotten the political song a bad name. Of course there are exceptions; Billy Bragg, though labelled (libelled?) a "youth spokesman", speaks to and for people from troubled adolescent to reluctantly "resting" working man. He does not wallow in the power and the gory of protest; he is not so conceited as to try to create a new England but does call for the preservation of the old one, the England of consensus and the Welfare State. (Punk, ever uninformed and glorying in its ignorance, saw the Welfare State as a pacifying evil akin to Mogadon.) It takes maturity and daring to write a line like *"Sweet moderation, heart of this nation"*, for it is not the stuff of pyrotechnic street protest. Billy Bragg writes songs, not slogans for the self-indulgent habituees of the teen ghetto. Addressing himself to the mainstream of history rather than the slipstream of hysteria, he has chosen plodding truth over instant celebrity – AJP over NME.

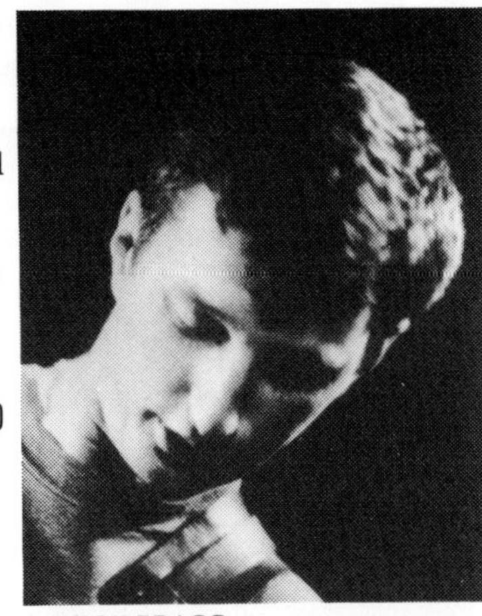

● *BILLY BRAGG*

But for the most part political crooners use current affairs as cologne pour l'homme; splash it all over and feel big man stage centre. Punk, naturally, produced the worst petty offenders: the Clash, whose records provided their audience with the drama and danger of political insurrection IN THE SAFETY OF THEIR OWN HOMES – revolutions per minute at the flick of a switch.

Like the Clash, the Alarm – which comparison they will cringe at *and* deserve – offer rebellion as a leisure option – just another – in the great teen theme park. *Wild in the Streets* meets *Westworld*. Alarm songs have that mock grandeur – crashing chords and square-bashing chants – that aim to take the listener out to a high noon shoot out with history. The young and the brave never die in these teen manifestos of muddled bravado; that's the *feeling*, anyway – the actual substance of their songs is a total mystery. Listening to the Alarm, you get the feeling that to them an uprising is ultimately something you do with your hair.

● *THE CLASH*

If the Alarm are the glossy magazine heirs to the Clash, the Redskins are the grotty Xerox right down to the public school background of the singer. They cannot see that protest pop is only valid and potent when it comes from a source which has proved itself commercially viable – otherwise it is not genuine protest but gripe-water. (Of course unsuccessful pop groups hate the way the world is run – namely, with them not at the top of it.) The irony is that rock rebels who believe that music maketh the new socialist man have exactly the same faith in the power of the plectrum that the smalltown preachers of the Bible Belt America had in the fifties; the devil's music, capable of turning decent WASP teenagers into Jewish Bolshevik Negro sex maniacs (some hope). THEY BOTH BELIEVE THAT POP MUSIC CAN CHANGE PEOPLE. Of course, this supernatural belief in the power of music is typical of primitives; yesterday's Red-baiters and today's Redskins are both yesteryear's Red Indians pounding on drums to make the rains come or bring harm to their enemies. Electric guitars are the twent cent's white man magic.

Philanthropy is one thing. Only good can come from the actions of such shimmering stars as Sade and Wham! who are nil lip service and all action – quite the reverse of the stance bands. In pop, money is the root of all virtue; a million songs about miners' rights don't help a fig, but a mime in time – see Wham! at the Miners Benefit – feeds families. Nothing can convince me, despite the copious digs at these exemplary young beauties, that it is more useful to shove your views down some small audience's throat than to shove a four-figure cheque into the hand of an NUM executive, as Wham! and Sade have done.

● *THE ALARM*

"Revolutionary entertainment" is another. It must be about as rare as revolutionary sport. Entertainment in its entirety, Junior League included, is probably the most conservative invention ever, ALWAYS a decoy and an admission of defeat. (Beam me up, Scottie. Divert me, Sting.) If rock 'n' roll had never been invented, and white Western youth had not been stuffed to bursting point with blue suede shoes and what have you, the world would be a very different place by now. Far from rock 'n' roll carrying within it the germs of the overthrow of capitalism, there is a very good case for claiming that Elvis Presley was a CIA-funded conspiracy against the true power of youth.

Philanthropy is one thing. Only good can come from the actions of such shimmering stars as Sade and Wham! who are nil lip service and all action – quite the reverse of the stance bands. In pop, money is the root of all virtue; a million songs about miners' rights don't help a fig, but a mime in time – see Wham! at the Miners Benefit – feeds families. Nothing can convince me, despite the copious digs at these exemplary young beauties, that it is more useful to shove your views down some small audience's throat than to shove a four-figure cheque into the hand of an NUM executive, as Wham! and Sade have done.

"Revolutionary entertainment" is another. It must be about as rare as revolutionary sport. Entertainment in its entirety, Junior League included, is probably the most conservative invention ever, ALWAYS a decoy and an admission of defeat. (Beam me up, Scottie. Divert me, Sting.) If rock 'n' roll had never been invented, and white Western youth had not been stuffed to bursting point with blue suede shoes and what have you, the world would be a very different place by now. Far from rock 'n' roll carrying within it the germs of the overthrow of capitalism, there is a very good case for claiming that Elvis Presley was a CIA-funded conspiracy against the true power of youth.

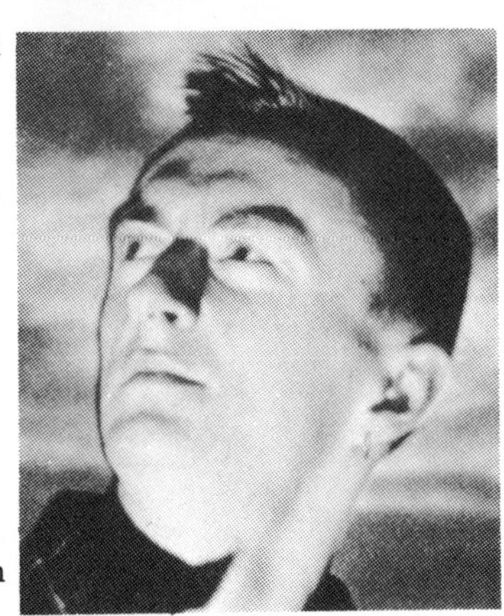

● *THE REDSKINS*

THE FIGHT AGAINST FROCKISM

Personal politics in pop are still only tolerated if they're dressed right, argues John Gill, and makes his stand against face values.

The day Bronski Beat singer Jimmy Somerville pleaded guilty to gross indecency with another man at London's Bow Street Magistrate's Court, he paid me a visit at my office in nearby Covent Garden. Accompanied by manager Anthony Kowalski and a friend, Somerville asked another gay colleague and me to guess where he had just been.

We obliged. Clap clinic. Jail. Police station. Public toilet. A rival magazine. I "won" the game when I trumped with "court".

A week or so earlier Somerville had been cruising a well known gay area of Hyde Park, late at night and out of sight of anyone who might have good reason to be there. In particular, he had been cruising what turned out to be one of a pair of "pretty policemen", police *agents provocateurs* indulging the illegal sport of entrapping homosexuals. While disinterested in Somerville's debatable charms, the jailbait were prompt in arresting him and another young man of his age when they were discovered having oral sex in a secluded part of the park. The initial cost of £100 – Somerville paid both his and his co-defendant's £50 fines – later rose to a somewhat more substantial, if less quantifiable amount.

The day of his court appearance Somerville was sheepishly joky: arraignment is a constant risk to homosexuals who pursue those avenues of their sexuality deemed criminal by a society which has it in for them anyway. He and manager Kowalski shrugged off fears that the conviction might endanger Somerville's future visits to the US – proven homosexuality and a criminal record being godsends to immigration officials wanting to keep undesirables out of their green and blessed.

A few months later, with singles and debut album rising on both sides of the Atlantic, that arrest caused the cancellation of an American tour which should have been the stamp on the Bronski's success there. American and Canadian immigration had read of the case on the transatlantic wire and began an investigation into Somerville's inopportune application for a visa renewal. While the investigation was never completed – or at least its results released to the public – it was enough to undermine that all-important first push in America and to start a souring process which eventually split the Bronskis.

In court Somerville had been contrite, probably as instructed. The day his lawyers informed the Bronskis' label, London Records, that he would no longer work with the band, Somerville was raging, swearing that but for company politics and the fears of his co-defendant he would have stood up and fought for his sexuality, his politics. He has a new working unit, Body Politic (named, ironically enough, after the Canadian gay liberation newspaper) which might win him similar success. But thus was another committed young hothead put through the mangle because of his personal politics.

More than Tom Robinson and Joe Strummer before him, Somerville's collision with the grubby realities of the music industry was spectacularly violent. From their earliest days playing half-empty night-clubs in Brixton, it was obvious that the voice and the sound were destined for something big. They thought so, too, but felt sure they could succeed without compromising their radicalism. We were beside ourselves with gay pride when the Bronskis sailed up the charts and on to the front pages, awash with pink triangles and rhetoric. It ended after fourteen months – only half of them happy times for the band – in gloating newspaper stories about their messy tangles with the promotion machine, a crossfire of recrimination and the Ortonesque farce of the arresting sergeant telling Somerville how much his ten-year-old daughter liked the Bronskis: this while he was entering Somerville's details on the arrest sheet.

In these baleful days, belief in anything but your tailor's standing is a liability. The atmosphere finds its perfect barometer in *The Face*, visually and journalistically a triumph of form over content with its spreads of unaffordable Montana couture and Memphis furniture and its assertion of brutish solipsism; Orwell's *petit bourgeoisie* discovering Wolfe's Me Generation in the bleak eighties. The likes of Somerville will be indulged their only too predictable fifteen minutes of topicality. Afterwards we are expected to join in the cruel sniping about their choice of frock. One wonders what Gandhi or Schweizer would have done if the success of their world relied on the benificence of *The Face*. Hire Paul Morley, maybe.

This is not to say that the likes of *Face* editor Nick Logan would not have recoiled at the images from Ethiopia, or indeed at the Vietnam war, against which he very probably demonstrated while wearing loon pants and wreathed in patchouli oil. It is simply that when personal politics enter the conveniently sanitised arena of "pop culture" (a phrase that promises adults that, therein, they'll find nothing more dangerous than a Shirelles love song), the frock is all. Thus Paul Weller, a talented poseur, is deemed to have year-round credibility, and Billy Bragg probably knew Lloyd George's father. Even Bob Geldof was let off after Band Aid, although the echoing media silence which greeted 'Starvation'/'Tam-Tam pour L'Ethiopie' serves to remind us that, after all, Bob the Mouth always did make brilliant copy. Otherwise, if one has made some crucial error in one's wardrobe, political belief in pop is rendered naff, saving the singers the bother of thinking, the writers the bother of asking and the listeners the bother of wondering in the first place.

Like many I feel betrayed by the childish, self-deluding antics of the original hippies, and despair of the similar fantasies of today's too-late punks, all glue and vegetarianism. During the mass take-over of Trafalgar Square the night Parliament voted Cruise into Britain, it wasn't Marxism, New Aquarianism or psilocybin that made me sit down in the road in front of a line of policemen, simply desperation and fear. Two quotes:

Joe Strummer in an interview with this writer in 1982;

"If it (nuclear war) happens, would you rather go having tried to do something or done nothing?"

And a German priest who, silent when the Nazis came for the Jews, then the homosexuals, then the communists, noted grimly that "there was no one left to speak up when they came for me."

Big words from a small typewriter, and indeed political comment can get through via anyone from Simple Minds to Holly Near to Poisongirls. But to succeed in the mainstream they will have to allow the media to pack and process their beliefs as though they were a new style in trousers, a hair-do or a fad-like androgyny.

A colleague – also a gay journalist – recently took me to task for what he saw as a streak of moralism, as though I required every three-minute slice of pop fun to contain a Searing Indictment. Like large Manhattans, I do have an affection for such statements, but not all the time, and can happily windmill along to the most air-headed pop. Simply, and especially in the case of gays in pop, the opportunity to present one's case is too important to be wasted on small talk or, worse, lying.

I have no personal desire to read about Morrissey's sex life, nor that of Boy George or Marilyn or Steve Strange. Quite the reverse (honest). But in these times of civil rights clawbacks, and the media manipulation of the AIDS epidemic – akin to handing a Klansman a noose and pointing out the "nigger" for him – basic humanity would demand one make some sort of commitment.

The beauty of Bronski Beat was that after years of image manipulation, lies and sheer tackiness – from Bowie's contrived shock tactics to Frankie's stylishly vacant naughty-but-nice act – three Joe Blow queens step out of the closet with a few nice tunes and, still dressed in their street clothes, get up on stage and sing it like it is. No sten guns in Knightsbridge or presumptuous little slogans about Central America. Just them, up there, talking about coming out in your teens, workaday oppression, falling in love, having fun. It could be us. It could be Cliff Richard in *Summer Holiday*. It could equally be a murdered homosexual in a Fassbinder movie. The Bronskis story, and Jimmy Somerville's crisis of conscience versus commerce, throw up only more and more contradictions.

On one hand, perhaps their success proved that we can now all come out without fear. After all, arresting officers tell us how much their ten-year-old daughters like us.

Perhaps their success proved that the entertainment industry can assimilate anything and render it harmless. Surely, the only taboos now left are paedophilia (I think Morrissey's working on that one), bestiality and necrophilia.

Perhaps their success proved that old adage about all marginals – that you only have to meet a nice one to realize they're not all monsters.

Perhaps their success proved that *other* old adage about marginals – that just because they like you it doesn't mean they won't beat up, sack, evict or imprison the next one they encounter.

Perhaps their success proved that the entertainment industry is so replete with badge liberalism it doesn't matter what you do (note the increasing fashionability of sado-masochism) as long as it can be denoted as nothing more than a trend or fashion accessory.

Perhaps their split proved the unspoken motto of *The Face*: The Frock Is All.

Creaky syllogising will get us nowhere, although irresponsible Frockism (now there's a new one for you) will get us there faster. But for all my criticisms of the sixties, there are two of its bumper stickers which the eighties would do well to note. The personal *is* the political, and if you aren't part of the solution you *are* part of the problem.

Politics, with a P or a p, are indivisible from the personal experience which gives us the ability to communicate. Jimmy Somerville's experience with queerbashers, or uncomprehending parents, are as much to do with pop as any of the millions of heterosexual love songs (and a sight more so than Ultravox's affection for *fin de siecle* Vienna). And if you're not doing anything – at home, at work, over the dinner table – about homophobia, racism, sexism or all the other "isms" sneered at by the press, then by default you are contributing to that problem.

Whatever success Somerville and the Bronskis achieve in the future, the story is ultimately a sad one. They started out with the classic "Hey, let's put on a show ourselves right here!" pop dream. Unfortunately, that dream was rooted in the eighties of unemployment, miners' strikes, squatting, racialism, discrimination and the rise of the New Right. Although, as has been pointed out, they were "allowed" to do as many benefits as they wanted to, the music industry ultimately proved itself unable to accommodate them. And this was no Ulrike Meinhof or Andreas Baader, just a dizzy Glaswegian queen barely over five feet high. Somerville ran head first into the perimeter fence, and the mere knowledge that this perimeter fence exists is both a cause for concern and – I have to say it – a searing indictment of Frockism. End of sermon.

HARD ROCK SELL

Tom Hibbert is unmoved by the snap crackle 'n' pop of TV shows and commercials.

● GO-GOS

● PAT BENATAR

● BILLY JOEL

Scene from a TV show (act one): The sun-kissed blonde in the denim cut-offs (who has just landed a job at the local television station) stares at the flickering screen and fiddles with the controls. Ping! Her monitor set sparks into living sound and colour with moving pictures of a long-haired youth and a midget in medieval court jester's garb prancing down a country lane singing a song. Yes, the sun-kissed-blonde-in-the-denim-cut-offs is watching a pop music video – Men Without Hats' 'Safety Dance' – and *we* are watching it over her shoulder.

Is this *Top of the Pops*? No, it's another thrilling episode of the US adventure series *Legmen*, and as soon as the video has come to an end the sun-kissed-blonde-in-the-denim-cut-offs will be finding herself whisked into Danger! Intrigue! Gosh! Will the hulky villain in the loud plaid jacket get to bump her off as he intends? Or will our two young, athletic, stupidly handsome, wise-cracking "heroes" save her in the nick of time? Of *course* they will – but not before they've spun a few rockin' Loverboy discs on their fancy hi-fis, cranked up Quiet Riot on their gleaming sports car radio during a couple of high-speed chases and paid a visit or two to the kind of niterie where young folk frug 'til dawn to Stevie Nicks. You never know, our macho buddies might even decide to hunt for clues in the TV studios where the whole thing started. And if they do, you can bet your life that the station's monitors will be playing the latest Rick Springfield "vid".

Now they haven't stuffed all this contemporary rock into the yawnsome crime caper simply to draw attention away from the flimsy plot, embarrassing script and terrible acting. There's more to it than that. TV programmers of the mid-eighties (along with film producers and assorted ad persons) have decided that nothing sells a product – cop show, young-lurve flick, gunk to put in the hair – to the young consumer like rockular music. The sales generators are talking "MTV Generation" and aiming their pitches at "kids" who, it is supposed, have become so accustomed to receiving images in short, sharp flashes with lashings of glaring music on the side that their attention spans have become severely abbreviated: these "kids" find even *Starsky and Hutch* too highbrow.

Poor old David Soul. All he ever wanted to do was make some groovy music but as TV police detective Hutch, he never got to strut his funky stuff. In frustration, Soul inflicted the ghastly 'Silver Lady' – a mega-hit due to freak accident – on the world; when last heard of, he was "guest-directing" an episode of *Miami Vice* whose hip cat protaganists, Crockett and Tubbs, make Starsky and Hutch seem like the unenlightened squares they always were.

Miami Vice is touted as a "new wave cop show music video" which means that when the cops pursue minority-group reprobates down dingy alleys, they're accompanied by hectic synthesizers rather than frenzied trumpets, and that when the only exit from the dingy alley turns out to be through a boxing stadium and past a "Big Fight" we are treated to snatches from Pat Benatar's 'Hit Me With Your Best Shot'. The show's tales of drug heists and banditry down in Florida are awesomely predictable, but no one's watching the show for crafty plotlines. They're watching for the glossy promo-video style, for the cameo appearances by pop celebs like ex-Eagle Glenn Frey (who has appeared as a drug smuggler), Iggy Pop (who is *due* to appear as a drug smuggler) and Phil Collins (who may be appearing as a particularly ugly drug smuggler), and for cool thrills'n'music from the Rolling Stones, Tina Turner or whoever's latest waxing is available (*Miami Vice* spends $50,000 on music each episode – eight and a half percent of the total budget). And they're watching for the classy charmless presence of Don Johnson (Sonny Crockett) and Philip Michael Thomas (Richard Tubbs), the most "tuned-in" law-enforcement team you could ever wish to meet. Why, their faces have graced the cover of *Rolling Stone* while their ability to stride around in expensively casual gear ("The Vice Look" – it's official) and simultaneously rap with the street-wise is breathtakingly impressive. *Newsweek* magazine has complained snootily that "roughly a third of all that slangy lingo whizzes by the ear before the mind can even attempt to decipher it". As if the *mind* had anything to do with it. Don't the guys at *Newsweek* watch their MTV? Don't they ever go to the movies and wonder why the American film industry is still churning out pop fodder features – movies whose only stars are on the soundtrack? Just how many films about jiggling breakdancers and/or teenagers having sex to the sound of the Go-Gos can the USA take? Rather a lot, it seems.

Scene from a TV show (act two): Dave Lee Travis, flanked by two glistening lovelies, is asking us to give a big *Top of the Pops* welcome to Belinda Purcell because it's her first appearance on *Top of the Pops*. Her record, 'Laughing And Dancing' has rocketed into the charts at 27 and here she is in the *Top of the Pops* studio woo-hoo clap clap clap. Only this isn't *Top of the Pops*, it's *Roll Over Beethoven* - a situation "comedy": dizzy Modern Ms gets tangled up in the wacky whirlwind world of pop while her stuffy old buffer of a father wonders what things are coming to. For example – spiv manager: "Mike Read is going to play our record." Cheeky assistant in the Frankie Goes To Hospital T-shirt: "Great (pause/comic timing) but it'd be better if he *banned* it!" (Cue canned laughter). *Top of the Pops* producer: "Right, Belinda, you come on after Motorhead." Spiv manager: "Could be worse, love (pause/comic timing), you could be on *with* Motorhead." (Canned laughter). Such is the thigh-slapping repartee of *Roll Over Beethoven. Terry and June* in Raybans. And guess what! When Belinda actually sings her dreadful song on *Top of the Pops*, her stuffy old buffer of a father loosens his tie and starts a-swingin' away on the dance floor – just like Cliff's father Robert Morley in *The Young Ones* a thousand years ago! Hurrah! How like life!

Meanwhile, over on Channel 4, the voice of "computerised" talking head, Max Headroom, is stammering away in gibberish. In Max's video half-hour, no distinction is made between pop promos and commercials: an ad for Dunlop running shoes butts into David Bowie's 'Loving The Alien' and it's hard to tell the difference. Jingle follows jingle in a comforting blur.

In the UK, the amount of screen time devoted to pop has increased twentyfold since 1982 when the new upstart Channel 4 was first aired. And that's not counting the advertisements. In his *Observer* TV column in June 1985, Julian Barnes commented: "Study any clutch of half a dozen advertisements, even at peak time, and four or five will be aimed at the sort of person who is clamped to a Sony Walkman but not yet out of nappies . . . Today they sell you even grown-up things like exhaust pipes (kwikly-fitted) by luring you into a milieu of jaunty pre-pubescence."

Daley Thompson sprints down the track in slow-motion and swigs Lucozade to the sound of Iron Maiden trading meaty riffs. Herbie Hancock's 'Rockit' blares away in aid of Polly Perkins undergarments. Cockney cartoon Weetabix men take to breakdancing to synth-drum backings. Midge Ure and Chris Cross from Ultravox create a well arty instrumental in support of Levis. Quatro – a fizzy green drink in a can, Falmers – a range of blue denim slacks, Kelly Girl – an employment agency for the Modern Miss, Glints – cosmetic goo to "make your natural hair colour a shade more daring" – all these and more are using squiggly ultra-modern beatbox sounds and images borrowed from smart rock promos – which nicked *their* style from classy aperitif and slimmers crisp-bread ads in the first place.

Then for those of the more advanced age and wage brackets – the nostalgic fogeys – there are Beatles songs flogging computers and Beach Boys tunes shifting power drill attachments, while Steppenwolf's 'Born To Be Wild' – which accompanied that fabled pair of droning hippie bikers across America in *Easy Rider* a thousand years ago – is now piping up on behalf of posh cars for thrusting executives. *"Like a true nature's child"*? Some mistake here, perhaps.

It could be worse: in Japan and the States, they don't just use lots of music, they even use the stars who *make* the music as "special guest" on-screen TV salesmen. Would you buy a motor scooter from a mumbling, wizened old rock'n'roll crone like Lou Reed? Honda evidently believes you would.

One man alone speaks out against the indignities of televisual racketeering. Step forward Mr Billy Joel: "My songs are *my* songs. I made them and they're like my children and *no* one's gonna use them to sell frying pans and junk." Strong words from the man who once played organ on a Bachman's pretzel commercial. Most other artistes are quite content to accept lucrative royalties from ad agencies. And why not? It's money for old rope. So next time you're passing through Atlanta airport, cock an ear to the gentle music filtering throughout the building. Instead of the orthodox muzakal renditions of 'God Didn't Make The Little Green Apples', *this* place (and, no doubt, many more) goes for a more modern ambience and thus pipes in bemusing instrumental versions of Duran Duran's 'The Reflex' and other chart-busting airs performed by zombies, robots and processed cheese triangles. Most disconcerting.

Scene from a TV show (act three): Our host sportif, David Vine, is in the snooker studio. "Just for a bit of fun," he smirks, "watch this. It's given us all here a laugh . . . " Into a zany film sequence – all the "lighter" moments of the tournament's "action", snooker celebs picking their noses and bumping into the ref, etc – with music. Frankie Goes To Hollywood's 'Relax', no less. Frankie the most "outrageous" group since the Sex Pistols, supposedly "banned" by the BBC, living in a world of sex and horror, are twanging away to a bit of snooker trivia. How fitting. Rockular music lost any lingering shreds of genuine shock value years ago when the "proper" world stumbled upon this simple wheeze: why *give* the kids what they want when you can *sell* it to them for lots and lots of money? Brilliant.

If one wanted to be gloomy about it, one *could* say that this was a glimpse of the imbecile future. But *actually* the imbecile future arrived in January 1981 when the eternal jaunty pre-pubescent Donnie Osmond serenaded Reagan at his inauguration with a hoop-la jive tune called 'Ronnie B. Goode'

CROSSING THE GREAT DIVIDE

Nelson George looks at the various and nefarious ways in which black artists have reached white audiences.

RAY PARKER JR

LIONEL RICHIE

The term "crossover" is a product of the incorporation of black pop music that occurred in the early-to-mid-seventies. It became a buzz-word conjured up in the corridors of CBS, Warner Bros and RCA for selling recordings by black artists that were popular in black America ("special markets" as it was known for a time at CBS) to white Americans (aka "the pop mainstream") by corporate marketeers. Before the seventies, those long years when the bulk of black pop music was produced, manufactured, and distributed by independent labels, this term did not exist. Black records, such as the creations of the Motown hit machine, that sold in large quantities to whites were not stigmatized by such jargon though they were quite explicitly aimed at pleasing *all* available customers.

What "crossover" did was put black music into a box, one which had a lot to do with corporate cash-flow and little to do with music and which defined black records that didn't reach white audiences as failures. No longer could black performers feel secure that they could sustain a recording career just by appealing to fans of black music. Corporate America bought into black music for the black *and* white sales that Motown had so often demonstrated were possible. The sales of Philadelphia International, fuelled by the creativity of Kenny Gamble and Leon Huff and the marketing power of CBS, set new standards for crossover sales consistency – standards black musicians have been striving to match ever since.

In the ten years since Philly International's peak of influence much has changed. Strings and horns have been replaced by a battery of computer chip paraphernalia; rock guitar chords are now nearly as ubquitious as hair grease in black music; and polyester suits are out, chordless mikes are in. The pressure to cross over, however, has never been more intense. In an era when black acts find it difficult to remain signed to major labels, the black entertainers – often with guile, sometimes in desperation – try to seduce the MTV hordes. The successful crossover efforts of Ray Parker Jr, Lionel Richie, Tina Turner, Run D.M.C., the Pointer Sisters and Kool and the Gang reflect the ways, both natural and nefarious, in which a wide range of performers has dealt with the desire for a bigger pay day.

The most natural crossover performer of the eighties is not Michael Jackson or Prince, but the genial Ray Parker Jr, the writer of cool, hooky and wonderfully well structured songs that recall Holland-Dozier-Holland and the other legendary tunesmiths of his native Detroit. By virtue of his music's quality Parker just simply charms the hell out of listeners. 'Ghostbusters' was his biggest hit because it was in a remarkably popular film. That doesn't obscure the fact that Parker's craftsmanship and droll sense of humour (few others could have sung "*I ain't afriad of no ghost!*" with the appropriate mock bravado) have served him well since he debuted with 'Jack & Jill'. Maybe it was his years as a Los Angeles session ace. Maybe it was his tenure in the first edition of Stevie Wonder's Wonderlove. Whatever sparked it, Parker has evolved into one of the few young black songwriters who maintain a pleasing balance between groove and melody. It should also be noted that Arista Records president Clive Davis, a fanatic for strong songs, saw his potential from the beginning and never hesitated in marketing Parker's handsome mug to the "mainstream".

● *THE POINTER SISTERS*

To mention the Pointer Sisters in a piece on crossover does and doesn't make sense. Yeah, they are a black vocal group who sell plenty plastic to pale faces. But for all their vocal brilliance it is Richard Perry's production that defines the Pointers. They are his heart. He is their head. A sonic chameleon who changes his sound with the trends yet maintains a unifying concern for intelligent arrangement, Perry has shrewdly relied on June and Anita's poppish chops instead of Ruth's deep, rootsy voice. As a result the Pointers' vocals have all the fresh scrubbed fervour of early Linda Ronstadt, but since the Pointers could sing South Africa's favourite vocalist right under a diamond mine, their records have a thrilling vitality. 'Jump' is a brilliant record. 'Automatic' wasn't bad either. In an era when pop radio finds it difficult to accept black female singers on a consistent basis (poor Irene Cara) the Pointers' flexibility allows them to masquerade their ethnicism.

More demeaning is the route taken by Tina Turner. Once an R&B queen and closet rock 'n' roller, Tina appeared on *Private Dancer* as the year's greatest phantom; a passionate soul (voice) disguised in trendy London garb. A fine hustle. Yet something smelled. In her ardour to seduce, Turner has forsaken her racial identity. She went to South Africa for the dollars. She turned down a part in Steven Speilberg and Quincy Jones' film of *The Colour Purple* because it was too black. She made ridiculous claims that the white singers on 'We Are The World' stole the record from its black composers. (Did Steve Perry really out sing Ray Charles?) In interview after interview she continued to stomp on her down-and-out husband in the most ungracious public flogging since *Mommy Dearest*. Tina's talent got her back in the ball game. Her legs burn holes in the groin of many a young buck. Yet does one detect an embarrassing rejection of the people who for so long nurtured her?

● *TINA TURNER*

Lionel Richie, like Ray Parker, is a celebrated songwriter, though at times you suspect he'd be more comfortable on Tin Pan Alley than the Brill Building. As a consequence Richie's major crossover in 1984-85 wasn't to whites. 'Still', 'Truly', 'Easy' and other similar songs with more words in their titles won the ex-Commodore a vast audience. Yet going into last year he was in real danger of totally alienating the black youth market until the perculating 'All Night Long' and 'Running With The Night' gave him dancefloor credibility. It opened him up to a generation of record buyers who know less than zero about 'Brick House', 'Too Hot Ta Trot', etc. No longer was he simply the sepia Kenny Rogers. If not hip, old Lionel was at least no longer a joke to dancers. If he hadn't doubled back and tapped black America again, Richie was in danger of becoming a complete Vegas act.

The most skilful crossover journey of recent years has been navigated by Kool and the Gang, a bunch who have succeeded Earth, Wind & Fire and the Commodores as the black band everbody loves. Like Styx and Journey or any of America's completely wholesome pop aggregations, Kool and the Gang have a way with the trite and melodic. Of course, these dudes can still throwdown. They just do it a lot more delicately then in the early seventies. Since 'Ladies Night' their 1979 comeback vehicle, Robert 'Kool' Bell and company have realized that their funk trademarks – live horns, raunchy lead vocals, rhythmic intensity – have to be played down today. The distance between 'Hollywood Swinging' and 'Joanna' is immense and testimony to the fact that serious pop crossover demands a rethinking of many black acts' songwriting concepts. In Kool and the Gang's case, lingering in the land of the good groove has given way to an emphasis on hummable melodies.

● *RUN D.M.C. & JAM MASTER JAY*

Run D.M.C.'s crossover story has nothing to do with mass marketing, but revolves around the uniting of two 'fringe' audiences. With the guitar-laden 12" 'Rock Box' and 'King of Rock', rappers Run D.M.C. attempted to hold onto their inner city rap crew while reaching for suburban heavy metal heads. Huh? On the surface they have nothing in common. Yet producer-manager Russell Simmons thought they did and damn if he wasn't right. Their self-titled debut album and *King Of Rock* both went gold, partly because Run D.M.C.'s black hatted, outlaw image looked great on MTV (in light rotation of course). The crowds at their gigs, b-boys in painters' caps worn sideways and hip white kids, is a far cry from the suburban malls that coalesce at Richie and Pointer Sister appearances. Yet it all represents the fruits of crossover thinking.

Is crossover good or bad? Hmmm . . . My best answer is that, like video screen radiation and Steven Spielberg movies, it is the price of progress.

HE DID IT HIS WAY

Ian Cranna finds out how fearless Phil Fearon DIY-ed his way into the charts

From the outside, the end house looks no different from the others in the terrace. A little neater perhaps, with its fresh paintwork and smartly kept front yard, but certainly nothing to suggest that here in a suburban backwater of London NW10 lies the home and heart of operations of Britain's biggest black artist.

Everything about 28-year-old multi-instrumentalist Phil Fearon of Galaxy has the air of barely contained energy. A self-confessed workaholic, even his well rehearsed explanations seem infused with an almost missionary fervour. When posing patiently for a photograph, a finger will be drumming to some unfinished music running through his head. He's also a thoroughly charming person, totally free of any affectation: someone who is happy to conduct you on a tour of the much-interfered with domicile and even show you his bedroom – still with his aged bunk bed enlarged with a sheet of wooden board – where he built the studio that proved them all wrong . . .

Arriving in Britain from Jamaica at the age of six, Fearon was a more than adequate pupil at school – two years at teacher training college give the lie to his protests otherwise – but from his early teens, making music was virtually his all-consuming interest. After a spell with Hott Wax (a US-funk inspired band), in 1976 he formed the more melodic Kandidate who eventually scored a British Top Twenty hit three years later with 'I Don't Wanna Lose You' and became one of the first British bands to challenge the American supremacy of funk. There was no happy ending, however; Fearon, realizing that Kandidate were going nowhere, decided on the last day of the seventies to see in the new decade by putting into action his own plans for breaking into the upper echelons of the music business.

"I began to realize," he recalls, "that the only way in was songwriting, so I stopped trying to be George Benson and really studied my songwriting. Then I couldn't get anyone to take my demos seriously, but I believed in them so I had to become the keyboard player, the guitarist, the bass man – I also had to become the producer. So I started producing my own records at 8-track studios – sometimes 24-track if I could sneak in late at night and give the engineer a few quid – and trying to get deals. Nothing was happening but I knew you're going to keep falling over before you pick up your strength, so we'd do a few jobs, get some more money, try another studio . . . It was really depressing."

The way out of this vicious circle, decided our practical hero, was to invest the money you'd have spent in other demo studios on building a home studio, where you could spend as much time as you liked getting your songs right because the overheads were so low. If nothing else, Fearon reasoned, it was a more efficient way of losing money. And if all else failed, the machinery was still there to be sold at the end of the day.

"I think my biggest single asset is that I'm a thinker," he says without a trace of big-headedness. "More than a musician, I'm an organizer. It all seemed to make perfect sense. I tried discussing it with the band (Kandidate), with other musicians, but nobody could see it. None of the musical integrity types – 'you can't make *serious* records in a bedroom' – you know? I had that from *so* many people – that and 'what are you doing working with third-rate musicians and amateurs?' I was told I was making a fool of myself, basically."

Undeterred, Fearon went ahead. Although completely broke, he, schoolfriend Gordon Jago, Steve Rowe and brother Paul Fearon – who saw the logic in Phil's ideas – formed FJR and set about raising funds as best they could (at one point this included running the "Juicy Jobs" employent agency from the Fearon family front room) and "taking out Access loans we couldn't afford" to buy the necessary basic hardware. And so, with two telephones on the floor and a filing cabinet in the corner – not to mention the support of his remarkably understanding parents – the HQ for FJR was set up in Phil Fearon's bedroom.

It takes a combination of several things to break into the music business – determination, talent, luck . . . Fearon and his partners already possessed the first, believed they had the second – what they had to do now was work at reducing the luck factor.

"We wanted musicians around us, so I got some friends who could play – my kid brother and his friends – who did it for fun, basically. The girls came in and sung for nothing. If I couldn't get a good bass player, I'd learn to play bass enough to make records with.

"Then, rather than pay out on a studio, we built our little cheap studio, so now we had everything and could make records at no cost. With a studio around us, producers available, instruments available, it was like if you didn't make it, you were *unlucky*."

Having got his basic tools together, Fearon could now set about breaking into the music business.

"There's a definite way into it. There's always a market for reggae and dance music – you just hit the ceiling of sales very soon, that's all. The next one up from that is dance music with an element of pop.

"With a pop record, if the boss at the big station doesn't like it, they won't play it. That's it, and there's nothing you can do about it, because you need airplay to get a pop record across. But with a dance record – no matter what anyone says – if you take it to a club, even on an acetate or a cassette, and it sounds good, they'll play it and so people hear it and you will definitely get in the dance charts."

Having set his sights on the George McCrae 'Rock Your Baby' style of club/pop records, the first product of Fearon's way of working was 'Pay Up' by Proton (a disguise for Fearon himself and brother Lenny) which was a club hit in 1981. Fearon was on his way. He was now working on a number of projects, one of which was Galaxy, and the following year a set of home-produced demos got him a deal with Ensign Records.

"When I got a deal and the company said 'now go and make it in a proper studio', we did that with one record. The second one, we said 'why don't you upgrade my demo studio?' They didn't like the idea at all. It was a bit of a fight actually but they gave us some money and I borrowed some more. I bought a 24 Sound Graph machine and a really cheapo-cheapo desk, and that's what I made 'Dancing Tight' on!"

'Dancing Tight' was of course a Top Five hit in Britain (and elsewhere) for Galaxy, at which point a lot of people decided that perhaps Fearon's bedroom studio wasn't quite so ludicrous after all. By invoicing the record company for studio time used, Fearon could now afford to upgrade his studio still further – a process which still continues. The commercial success of records like 'What Do I Do?' and 'Everybody's Laughing' – not to mention an LP which entered the British charts at number nine – has now enabled Fearon to purchase the neighbouring house and convert *that* into a new studio, thus allowing the original studio to be converted back into the Fearon family home. Not bad going for a bedroom studio and a bunch of third-rate amateurs.

"No other band's got this arrangement," enthuses Fearon of his moulded troops. "Everyone does everything. There's no hierarchy – everyone just gets down and *does* it. It's better than being in a band, because bands are aggro: everyone's a star. Being in a band isn't really where it's at – it feels good and you feel you're doing something, but you're going nowhere. You've either got to be a writer or a producer before you start doing anything.

"To do your own kind of personal music that satisfies you and your friend next door is good for that, but for selling records you've got to think commercial. Commercial isn't a dirty word. In fact, it's a very, very good word."

Of course Fearon's approach has its detractors, especially certain blacks who look askance on Fearon's calculated, conformist approach. This inverted snobbery drives him close to abandoning an otherwise thoroughly positive outlook.

"Being a black artist, all the soulboys say 'you gotta be hip, man' and that just makes me *mad*! There's people out there who like that sort of music and if you cater for that audience, there's nothing wrong with that. To me, if the amount you like a record depends on how much everybody else likes that record, then you've got no soul anyway."

Amen. Fearon also has little time for credibility – "garbage" he calls it – and reckons what he's doing is the most *honest* music in the business.

"It's not easy to write a pop song," he continues. "The funky grooves are the easy stuff – it's the carefully structured, planned pop song for the general public that's difficult."

Consequently, the jibes that he's been lucky – however wildly wide of the mark they are – do still irritate Fearon.

"In real terms it's been nothing but hard work that's got me there," he says earnestly. "It's taken years to try and build this thing up. It's total self-denial. I've never had any nice clothes – I didn't even have a wardrobe: everything, including my stage clothes, was hanging from the picture rail around the room. I've never had a car of my own – I'm just catching up now."

Nevertheless, it's typical of the man that he's not bitter about it at all. He's already nurturing young talent, and even dreams of eventually opening his own academy to blow away all the myths and ignorance that prevent more people from having a go at the music business.

"People are growing up in an environment where the way to make a record is to go into a big name 48-track studio. That's garbage. You can make a record in a toilet if you've got the right attitude. You don't *need* all the gear, even though it's nicer. Once you've got a good mike – the best you can get – once it goes onto tape, it doesn't matter about the Space Invaders next door or carpet on the walls. That doesn't make any different whatever.

"My approach to the business, the world, the universe, is like the studio – always 2 + 2 = 4, all the way along. And they think, yes, it looks good but it can't be that simple – it *can't* be. And I say it *is* that simple. Even when you are broke – if you sit down and structure things, it's quite amazing what you can come up with a careful plan.

"It's not easy, but the principle is very, very simple. I'm amazed more people don't do it."

QUOTES

None of us really like beer; we just drink it to get pissed.

William Reid, Jesus and Mary Chain

Sometimes when I come off stage, I feel like I've been having sex for a week! And, oh, I do like it!

Chaka Khan

Basically, I hate pop stars unless they're me or personal friends of mine.

Shane McGowan, The Pogues

I'll tell you something: there's not a band that'll actually go into print and slag us off, because we'll kick fuck out of them, quite honestly! Most bands are just gutless. If they slagged us off and then they met us in a club afterwards, we'd just kill 'em! **James King, The Lone Wolves.**

I think people listen to popular music, as made by popular groups, to tap their feet and be distracted. People listen to serious music in order to be moved in some way or other. You can't change anything through music, but you can reinforce ideals and ideas.

John Martyn

I have been called in my time a stupid northern prat, a slimy little creep, the Dorothy Squires of electropop, the new Judy Garland, a tuneless idiot, a little runt with taste, a middle-class boy with a bondage fixation, a stupid fucking queer, a misunderstood genius.

Marc Almond

As for you poor little cows who buy Duran Duran records, you need serious help because these people are conning you.

John Lydon

Doing this job is like being a housewife. Everyday, I get up and I've got lots of chores to do. Really, you know, it's not very spectacular. Freddie Mercury, Queen (speaking in his seafront hotel in Rio)

I had the haircut first. I think it's a great compliment that Carl tried it out, although I've noticed he's changed it since. Maybe he got too many comments.

Grace Jones (on Carl Lewis)

We don't agree with all this shit about painting your head, cutting your face with glass and shaving one eyebrow off. I just can't relate to someone who goes around spitting at people.

Danny Joe Brown, Molly Hatchet

I could work in transvestite bars all over Germany, be quite rich, and generally have an incredible life . . . but it just wouldn't be me. Jayne County

The thing about George is, he's always been a big-headed, arrogant bastard – so success hasn't really changed him!

Jon Moss, Culture Club (on Boy George)

We did our first single with John Cale as producer. He likes to work pretty fast, you know! He said there's no such thing as a bum note – just put another note on top and make it a discord. I think he's under the impression you can still walk in and do the Stooges album in one week! **James King, The Lone Wolves**

America was weird. I just couldn't believe that Reagan's biggest support is within the 18-25 age group. I find it worrying that people of that age are showing no significant signs of rebellion. In fact, they seem almost middle-aged in outlook; they want everything stable . . . preserve the status quo at all costs. **Howard Jones**

I'm just an ordinary member of the public that got lucky, just an ordinary working-class bloke . . . nice, humble, pleasant! I'm as ugly as sin, but I don't care – you won't find me having a nose job! **Captain Sensible**

In Japan, fans don't ask about your star sign, they ask about your blood group! They were astonished that we didn't know what ours were!

Gary Kemp, Spandau Ballet

My pet hate is the Smiths . . . they're so pathetic! What are they on about? I don't know!

Ozzy Osbourne

We're apart from everyone else, and we don't feel an affinity to anyone else or anything else. We get lumped in with 'rock' and I find that mildly offensive.

Robin Guthrie, Cocteau Twins

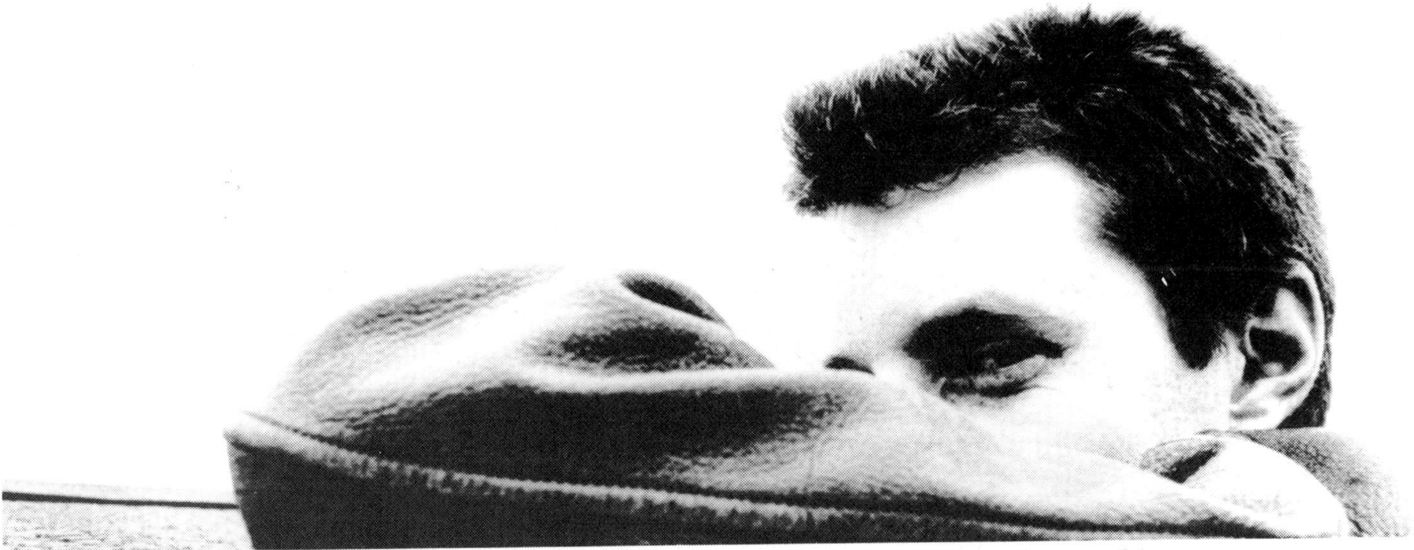

When a folk club artist goes out with his guitar, he might think he's James Taylor or Bob Dylan. When I go out, I still think I'm the Clash!

Billy Bragg

I think maybe the older you get, the more humorous you become . . . more flippant, in some ways.

David Sylvian

True entertainers don't ever grow old . . . their trousers just get a bit tighter. Gary Glitter

Sometimes, I've been away in the States or in Canada, and I've just wanted to wake up next to somebody – and sex becomes an obligatory part of it. You have to go through it. It's more than promiscuity, too . . . it's also very experimental – but you realise you become a guinea-pig yourself. I'd rather find THE lady and get married and have kids and stuff. **Fish, Marillion**

The pirate look and the warrior look were great, but I don't think the Prince Charming look did me any justice at all. It was based on a very dodgy Regency buck . . . I felt a bit of a prat in it. Adam Ant

We were playing loud, angry music – so smashing up guitars and wrecking hotel rooms was an extension of that. I cut a bed in two with a Bowie knife once, but we always paid for the damage. **John Entwistle, ex-The Who**

There's nothing more unattractive in an artist than a false sense of importance. Simon Le Bon, Duran Duran

We're fed up with getting exotic diseases in places like Sri Lanka. All that exotic stuff has got a bit passé now. Roger Taylor, Duran Duran

The social consciousness that was part of the sixties has become, like, old-fashioned or something. You go out, you get your job, you try to make as much money as you can, and have a good time on the weekend. And that's considered OK. **Bruce Springsteen**

The baby wore me out, with the breast-feeding and everything, but I'm never going to have a nervous breakdown . . . it's just not in my zodiac. **Chrissie Hynde, Pretenders**

Too much marijuana is a bad thing. I don't think people on marijuana realise how much it affects them. It's like taking their legs away or something. It's such an insidious drug because it claims to be harmless. **Joe Strummer, The Clash**

Because there are people getting killed in Central America doesn't mean people want to hear about it. When they come to the shows, they want to escape from that. **Mick Jones, Foreigner**

We tried to create an Egyptian feeling in the studio. We put up a stepladder to look like a pyramid. You can laugh, but if that stepladder wasn't there, we wouldn't sound half as good. It's the power of the pyramids, you see. **Bruce Dickinson, Iron Maiden**

I think if I shaved my head, no one would recognize me. Robert Smith, The Cure

Here I am, pop's answer to Wes Montgomery, and I prefer George Harrison! I'm a crazy mixed-up kid! Ben Watt, Everything But The Girl

I'd rather see an actor as President than a politician. At least Ronald Reagan has a sense of humour. When he said "we've launched the missiles at Russia", I cracked up! **Meat Loaf**

The type of fame that Elvis had, and that I think Michael Jackson has, the pressure of it, and the isolation that it seems to require, has gotta be really painful. I wasn't gonna let that happen to me. **Bruce Springsteen**

The biggest gift that your fans can give you is just treating you like a human being, because anything else dehumanizes you. That's one of the things that has shortened the lifespans, both physically and creatively, of some of the best rock 'n' roll musicians – that cruel isolation. If the price of fame is that you have to be isolated from the people you write for, then that's too fucking high a price to pay. **Bruce Springsteen**

I still talk about the dead guys. I'll always be paying my respects to Pete and Jim for starting the idea, creating this thing. It's important that the audience understand the role the dead guys played. **Chrissie Hynde, Pretenders**

I just like getting to see the world, I suppose. Sound like a beauty queen, don't I? I want to travel and meet people! Paul Rutherford, Frankie Goes To Hollywood

Kids are really sophisticated now. They don't need to be sheltered. Little girls wanna be fucked, teenagers, little boys, they wanna fuck. They do! Paul Rutherford, Frankie Goes To Hollywood

The last couple of years of the Clash, I was a miserable git. We all knew that we were just doing it for the money. We couldn't face each other. **Mick Jones**

The world dictates that heteros make love while gays have sex. **Boy George, Culture Club**

I think my six whippets are
the current music scene.

Adult Orientated Rock was
nation, but thankfully it fin
biting the dust. It was us w
those doors.

We seem to around the down.

The only reason I signed wit
paper that said 'National We
top and had lots of numbers

We had a great time trying to
record company when we were
them out to get us drugs, and t
about over there is coke. We a
panicked . . . they thought we
were all these secretaries runn
God, we don't know any pushe
Finally, one of them said "I know
Black Music department – they
drugs down there!"

I always think that a society that condones vaginal deodorant is a society in real trouble.

John Peel

I've actually tried every type of razor, including the electric one where they say they'll give you your money back if it doesn't shave as close as a blade. I got my money back! **Sal Solo**

There are only two bands in the whole world that are any good – us and Motorhead.
Dee Dee Ramone, The Ramones

We have a riot on tour. We've just got back from America and we just smashed places up, cruised around LA crashing into other people's cars . . . we're like four yobs abroad. **Billy Duffy, The Cult**

I don't think Echo & the Bunnymen will ever be forgotten. The fact is that we're the best.
Ian McCulloch, Echo & the Bunnymen

I've always thought it incredibly stupid that people in the music business have to lie about their age. I mean, I read a thing the other day about Wham! being 21-year-olds. That's a farce! I cannot believe that! I've seen those guys, and they look more debauched than I do! **Midge Ure, Ultravox**

We certainly want to be remembered for the quality of our music rather than the quality of our haircuts, or for being the flavour of a particular month.
Pat Gribben, The Adventures

I hate anything I hear by Culture Club. His voice really gets on my wick! A year ago, they were all saying he's a great white soul singer . . . now he's just an old sodding queen, mincing around like some sickening Danny La Rue. I don't mind a good mincer, but he's not even that. Bowie was good at mincing at one point, and Jagger's a good mincer, but Boy George doesn't even know what to do with his hands! Billy Idol's even worse! **Ian McCulloch, Echo & the Bunnymen**

It seems like rock 'n' roll has gotten more concerned with fashion and image lately. I miss the feeling of community that rock had in the sixties. **Neil Young**

Margaret Thatcher has achieved a lot. She's given us back our self-respect; nobody thinks they can piss all over Britain anymore and get away with it. Thatcher is the first great leader since Churchill. **Gary Numan**

The people who vote for Margaret Thatcher think they're going to join some exclusive club; they don't realize that they're being completely fucked up the arse. To vote Conservative you've just got to be a wanker. **Julian Cope**

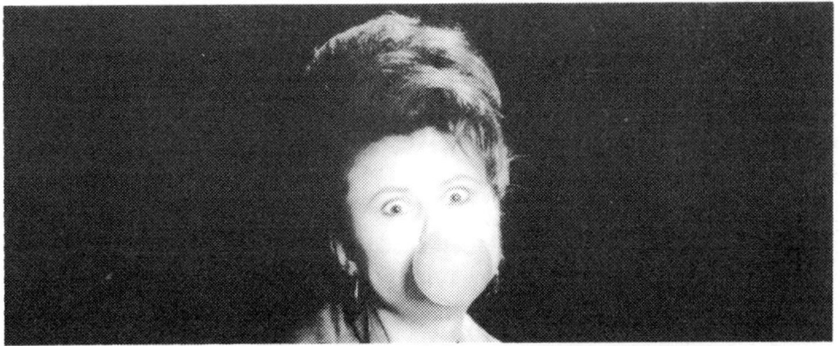

I think he (Arthur Scargill) should be called Shifting Mould or Creepy Wee Shitebag. He's just disgusting. His hair's so stupid. My husband and I adore Mick McGahey. He always looks pissed! The poor man is probably a teetotaller, but we think he's a real hysterical drunk! **Tracey Ullman**

I used to be in love with Donny Osmond. I used to have a poster of him on my wall, and my dad used to go off his head! He couldn't understand why I should have a picture of him on the wall.

Jimmy Somerville, Bronski Beat

I personal
things. I'r
stage, anc

Unfortunately, we're still i
loads and loads of people
doesn't understand. Two
and I told him to say I wa
not in, come back later". T
don't know what he thinks

Everyone thinks I'm fat,
quite skinny. I've been c
and 'Porky', but I've nev
about weight at all.

It would be
significan

The whole thing of materi
sickening after a while. Ha
that it doesn't bring you h

I wouldn't enjoy sitting at h
thumbs, watching the telly
It's not me – I'd be bored. I
house ... get out from und

I hope people will see th
laugh at myself occasion
David Byrne, T

We may have been away
some boxer struggling a

I get a worse sore throat
from singing.

Whatever I do is capable of being a classic. I could probably mumble anything and somebody would think "Great, that . . . passionate".
Ian McCulloch, Echo & the Bunnymen

People say, over and over again, "you're a sixties band". Are they talking about Pat Boone, or Petula Clark, or Arthur Lee, or what? **Vicki Peterson, The Bangles**

It's such a weird coincidence to wake up every morning as the same person . . . I'd quite like to wake up as the Isle of Wight ferry.
Robyn Hitchcock

In an abstract way, the audience weren't smashing up the hall, they were smashing up pop music. The Jesus and Mary Chain are putting excitement back into rock'n'roll and promoters will have to bear the consequences. This is truly art as terrorism.
Jesus And Mary Chain (explaining a riot at their gig)

After ten years of incredible lows, there has to be something special that we're hanging onto, something intangible. **Luis Perez, Los Lobos**

I'm not a rock star. I don't have any image to keep up, don't have anything to defend. I'm simply not playing their game. Van Morrison

I've always supported Liverpool, but the last time I went to the Kop, I was really disgusted. People were pissing all over the place and it really stunk. It's like an animal pen in there ... very uncivilized.
John Hawkins, This Island Earth

I've got a lot of time for pigs. They're intelligent creatures, and they make a good bacon sandwich.
Rat Scabies, The Damned

A lot of drinking and paranoia was all that kept us together. There was a lot of drugs, and all the typical garbage you associate with bands. It stemmed from the insecurity of it all. We were afraid to try anything new.
Pete Cetera, Chicago

Under the influence of hard work and drugs, anything can happen! J J Jeczalik, Art Of Noise

I'm doing just fine now. I'm not a raving lunatic.
Mick Fleetwood

I tend to sit naked when I'm in the house.
Paul King, King

Too many people are trying to dig up old music – like the rockabilly thing that happened recently. Everyone was a hillbilly for twenty minutes, and then it all disappeared because there was nothing interesting in it. You can't have cowboy singers from Camden – it doesn't make sense! **Midge Ure, Ultravox**

I really am not a fan of this synthesizer stuff at all. It doesn't even sink in. It's just this bland, whooshing noise going by. **John Fogerty**

All I can ever think when I see the First Lady is "imagine what a horror it must be to fuck her!"
Jeffrey Lee Pierce, Gun Club

I may be 43, but I have a mental age of 14.
John Cale

I always thought Napoleon had quite a neat image. He was small, so he and I have at least one thing in common . . . and I believe he was quite a charmer with the ladies. I go for that kind of lifestyle really.
Johnny Marr, The Smiths

The sixties was hashish and Hendrix, the seventies was cocaine and herpes, and the eighties are Perrier and push-ups. **Michael Des Barres, Chequered Past**

I wish we'd won the Eurovision Song Contest, but there's not much else I'd change. Mick Jagger

We're not slags, really. I won't sleep with anyone unless I've talked to them first. **Nick Linden, Terraplane**

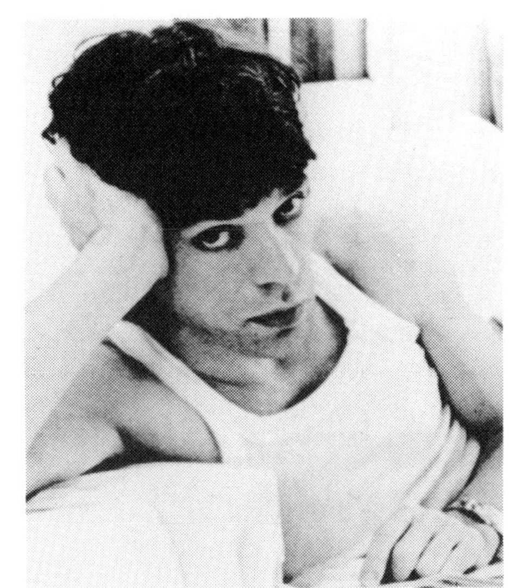

I have a sneaking suspicion that moist 14-year-old girls are our audience, and boys with big hard-ons that wanna rock! **Michael Des Barres, Chequered Past**

I could drop down dead tomorrow, and I could count the people who would care on one hand. **Marilyn**

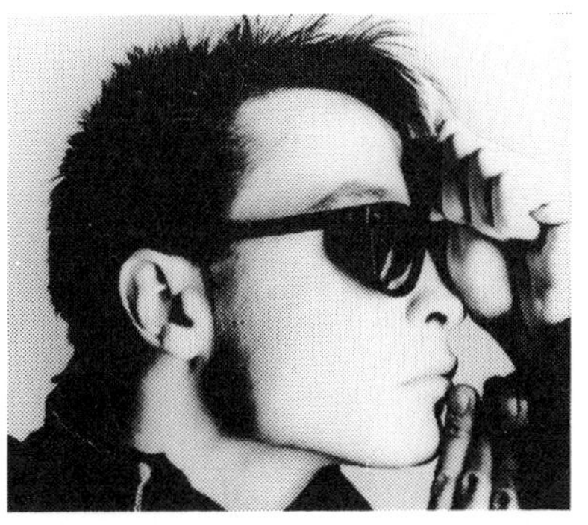

Anyone with long hair in 1985 is a mega-prat.
Green, Scritti Politti

There's too much shit around, too much fashion, and too many people who think they should be in a group because they've got the right clothes. That's not a good enough reason. **Terry Hall, Colourfield**

We're not into the clichéd rock'n'roll thing where you bring the 12-year-old boys backstage, have a coke party, and then have oral sex.
Vicki Peterson, The Bangles

I've been advised to take salt tablets before I go on stage. We all lose so much perspiration that it could be dangerous for our bodies if we didn't take the right precautions. The doctor estimated that I lose a gallon of sweat during a show. **Alex Cooper, Katrina and the Waves**

I'm brilliant at acting . . . I want to be a really special actor. I want people to notice me and say "he's good". So I'm always practising. Sometimes I even look at myself in the mirror and imagine I'm looking at myself on TV. Barrington Levy

Neil [Pat's husband] and I are two of the straightest people in rock. We got all the drinking and drugs out of our systems when we were younger. I don't want to sound like Mary Poppins, but we're really simple people who like simple things. **Pat Benatar**

We are hot news at the moment, but we are tomorrow's fish'n'chip paper. **Paul, The Roaring Boys**

Miles Copeland tried to insure me with Lloyds of London – but they wouldn't have me! Only ten per cent of my liver was working at one point.
Stiv Bators, Lords of the New Church

The Reverend Al Green is the only person who could get me into a church. Jimmy Nail

When I first met Bernard Edwards, he thought I was the weirdest guy in the world! I had green hair – a hippie, totally acid and Hendrix, the whole bit! **Nile Rodgers**

I saw *Paris Texas* and I thought it was rubbish, actually. It was like looking at a lot of postcards. Ry Cooder is a very fine guitarist, but the impression I got was that it [the soundtrack] took him ten minutes.
Mark Knopfler, Dire Straits

I really think autographs are daft. What do they want them for? What's the point? But you can't ask them that – they'd just think you were being snotty.
Bernie Sumner, New Order

I watch *Top of the Pops* every week – and then I throw up!

Maurice Oberstein, Chairman of the British Phonographic Industry

I made it through the seventies, alive and with my brain reasonably intact – it surprises a lot of people. We did our share of every substance known to man, but we all came through it in reasonably good shape. **Don Henley**

It takes the Stranglers about four minutes to write a three-minute song. Hugh Cornwell, The Stranglers

My doctor told me I'm only allowed one drink a day. I'm up to 13 May 1999 already! Ozzy Osbourne

I think drink increases reality; I always feel a hundred times more depressed once I've had a bottle of whisky. Alcohol is the path to awareness, I feel.

Shane MacGowan, The Pogues

People do seem to think that Dave Roth is in love with the mirror.

David Lee Roth, Van Halen

Most people in groups are fucking ignorant bastards, aren't they? They're all locked into their own little world and all they really give a fuck about is themselves and what they do. This business thrives on people being selfish. **Paul Weller, The Style Council**

I went potty on limos – I was really pining for them when we weren't working! We used to commandeer them for shopping sprees! I mean, how many normal people get to sit in a limo? You can be sick in it, shag in it . . . and they put up with it on the basis of "well, that's rock'n'roll!"

Pete Burns, Dead Or Alive

The album's about all those predatory, ball-breaking chicks who rate men on a scale of one to ten. I even fancied myself as one for a short time.

Marianne Faithfull

We're fundamentally opposed to someone like Howard Jones in every possible way, in every aspect. I think somebody like that epitomizes the entire music scene. The fact that someone is in that sort of position and does that sort of rubbish, that piffle. It perpetuates the mindlessness of the record-buying market, patronises young people. It's vile . . . inexcusable. Severe measures should be taken. **Jaz, Killing Joke**

I wouldn't mind being the Tommy Steele of the eighties.

Paul King, King

Tony Blackburn won't play my single because I'm a white artiste playing soul music – and he thinks that isn't right. Please put that in big . . . I want to make sure he reads it. Phil Collins

Why the fuck should we want to copy a band like Genesis who took ten years to break through? We have the musical capability to copy any band if we wanted to. We'd be better off copying Police or Spandau Ballet; we could do that, no bother . . . those lyrics are easy to write!

Fish, Marillion

We have this real fear of being asked on the Benny Hill Show! All of us running around, being chased by that little bald man!

Merrill Heatley, The Boothill Foot-Tappers

I can't think of one pop singer who's been knighted. And if they did start knighting them, I'm sure I'd be at the back of the queue – behind Paul McCartney and Cliff Richard, for instance. **Mick Jagger**

That really is our number one priority – to upset the critics! Ritchie Blackmore, Deep Purple

Sometimes I'm on stage and I'll feel like I'm in the Who! I've never felt more positive or strong. I could have been just another dead glitter star.

Michael Des Barres, Chequered Past

People don't like me because I'm so smart-assed. I probably wouldn't like myself if I didn't know myself better! Bob Geldof, Boomtown Rats

AND THUS SPAKE MORRISSEY....

I'm probably extraordinary.

To be quite honest, we are very angry. I mean, in very simple terms, we are very, very angry. We're angry about the music industry; we're very angry about pop music.

There's no point being incredibly enlightened and incredibly aware if nobody can actually hear you. You do have to break through – and I think the Smiths are the first group in musical history to do that.

Ultravox have become Total Industry; their big band glossiness seems like a shameful concession to all the wrong values. Will they ever revolt?

If somebody from the *Daily Mail* comes along and shoots me, that's the way it has to be. I'll die defending what I say.

Everything we produce is wonderful.

MORE MORRISSEY....

I've always believed that whatever I wear is fashionable and whatever somebody else wears is unfashionable.

I don't try and inflict the way I feel upon other people, because that's quite boring.

To me, the Smiths are great by definition. Once they stop being great, they'll cease to exist.

Age shouldn't affect you. It's just like the size of your shoes – they don't determine how you live your life. You're either marvellous or you're boring, regardless of your age . . . and I'm sure you know what we are.

Nothing in the past is important really. I was alive, that's all.

In all the accounts of Frankie Goes To Hollywood, you're more likely to read the names Paul Morley or Trevor Horn before you read the name Paul Rutherford or Holly Johnson. If that was the arrangement with the Smiths, I'd pack up and go home. I couldn't tolerate that. As individuals, they seem to have no interest or control. They've been peddled in much the same way as groups in the sixties were peddled. Their entire career has been orchestrated by unseen faces.

I think the Smiths are under a great deal of pressure – more pressure than any other group.

When the day arrives when I can't write, when I'm drained, I'll just step down – I won't go on. There's nothing worse than the writer, the singer, who's outlived his usefulness, who's drained his diary, as it were. When I've drained the resources, I will step down – much to the relief, I'm sure, of the British public.

A drunken goat could direct a Duran Duran video.

Without wishing to sound bloated, I always thought we were steering everything very precisely. We always felt that we couldn't possibly be stopped.

We'll never make a video as long as we live!

I think it's tuneless . . . I mean, it's one thing to want to save lives in Ethiopia, but it's another thing to inflict so much torture on the British public. It's quite easy to sit here and agree and feel very passionate about the cause – everybody does – but what about the record? Nobody's actually mentioned that foul disgusting thing!

(on the Band Aid single)

It's about to emerge [a track called 'Father and Son'], and I'm sure it will change your life.

There are indeed worse groups than Modern Romance, but can anybody seriously think of one?

The image the Smiths provoke is so strong. It does provoke absolute adoration or absolute murderous hatred. There are people out there who would like to disembowel me, just as there are people who would race towards me and smother me with kisses.

I've got a new policy: I'm not going to drag people down anymore. I've too many enemies – it's quite distressing . . . and it's a bit of a strain, because one is welcome almost nowhere.

I still have things to say.

THE BEST AND WORST

ALBUM COVERS

OF THE YEAR

Steve Bush finds choosing the former dishearteningly difficult and the latter all too easy.

I thought reviewing the past year's album sleeves would be easy. I was wrong. So few sleeves stuck out as being exceptionally well designed that I spent literally hours mooching sulkily around the enormous Virgin Megastore (under the suspicious gaze of tough-looking Virgin security men) trying desperately to complete my brief. In the end I had to make up the numbers with two 12″ singles sleeves.

Graphic designers whizz in and out of fashion even faster than pop stars. This year's fifteen minutes of fame went to XL, whose clients included Frankie Goes To Hollywood, Spelt Like This and OMD. Frankie's album sleeve was notable only for the illustration with all the willies in it, while for Spelt Like This XL produced a rather over-designed sleeve with an inner bag devoted entirely to two photos of the part of the body ever so slightly above the naughty bits.

The highly influential and much-copied Neville Brody produced only a handful of sleeves this year, concentrating instead on his award-winning work for *The Face*, while the very talented C-More Tone (is it a person or a company?) now seems to be getting the recognition he deserves. Another thumbs-up goes to 23 Envelope (Vaughn Oliver and Nigel Grierson) at record label 4AD for the consistently high standard of their work over the past two years or so.

It was far easier choosing the worst sleeves of the year because there were so many of them. I steered clear of the really dire ones where the designer obviously couldn't be bothered, and concentrated on the ones on which someone had spent a lot of time, money and effort and *still* managed to produce something that a first year graphics student would be deeply ashamed of.

Well done to all of you . . .

THE BEST

Cupid & Psyche 85 – Scritti Politti

Designed by KEITH BREEDEN

Glossy, expensive and special, this sleeve makes me want to buy the album and I don't even *like* Scritti Politti.

THE WORST

Now That's What I Call Music 4 – Various Artists

This looks like an advertising agency's desperate attempt to appeal to the mysterious "youth market". Winner of the much-coveted "Even-my-cat-could've-done-better" award.

THE BEST: RUNNER UP

Low-Life – New Order

Designed by PETER SAVILLE ASSOCIATES

From the photography to the labels to the printing, everything is just right. A perfect package.

Crucial Electro – Various Artists

Designed by RED RANCH FOR CARVER'S

Sharp, distinctive and with exactly the right feel for their market, this series of sleeves must have made an important contribution to Street Sounds' success.

THE WORST: RUNNER UP

Explorers – The Explorers

Surely these men have been in pop groups long enough to know better? No wonder the designer left his name off the credits.

Brothers In Arms – Dire Straits

The fact that Dire Straits don't have to do an awful lot to encourage people to buy their records is absolutely no excuse for this dull and boring effort.

THE BEST

Steps In Time – King

Designed by ASSORTED iMaGes

Even though this design incorporates four individual photos and lots of other graphic elements, it still stands out fantastically well among hundreds of other records in the racks.

90125 – Yes

Designed by GARRY MOUAT AT ASSORTED iMaGes

Good design is knowing exactly when to stop, and this designer got it precisely right. Clean, simple and attractive.

THE WORST

Berserker – Gary Numan

This would be a great sleeve if it weren't for the terrible photo and the awful lettering.

The Firm – The Firm

You don't need a trained graphic eye to tell you what's wrong here. What a stinker! Even a picture of Jimmy Page would have been better.

THE BEST

THE WORST

Master and Servant (Limited Edition) – Depeche Mode

Designed by TOWN & COUNTRY PLANNING UK

They probably agonized for hours over exactly where to place the "and" which is the only thing that spoils an otherwise very pleasing piece of work.

History Mix (Volume 1) – Godley & Creme

If a group like Duran Duran were to feature five self-portraits on the inner sleeve of one of their albums it would be fascinating, but here it looks ugly and would surely put off even a Godley & Creme fan. Yuk!

Jazz Club – Various Artists

Designed by PETER JONES AND J.B.

This sleeve manages to look both traditional and modern, and has exactly the right feel for the music.

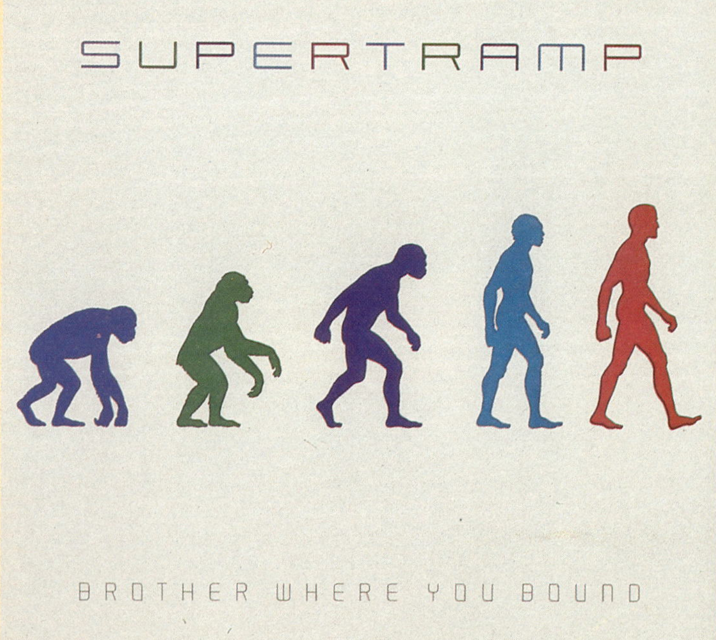

Brother Where You Bound – Supertramp

If this was the 1973 Virgin Yearbook, then this album may have scraped into the Best Sleeves section. But it's not. So there.

THE BEST

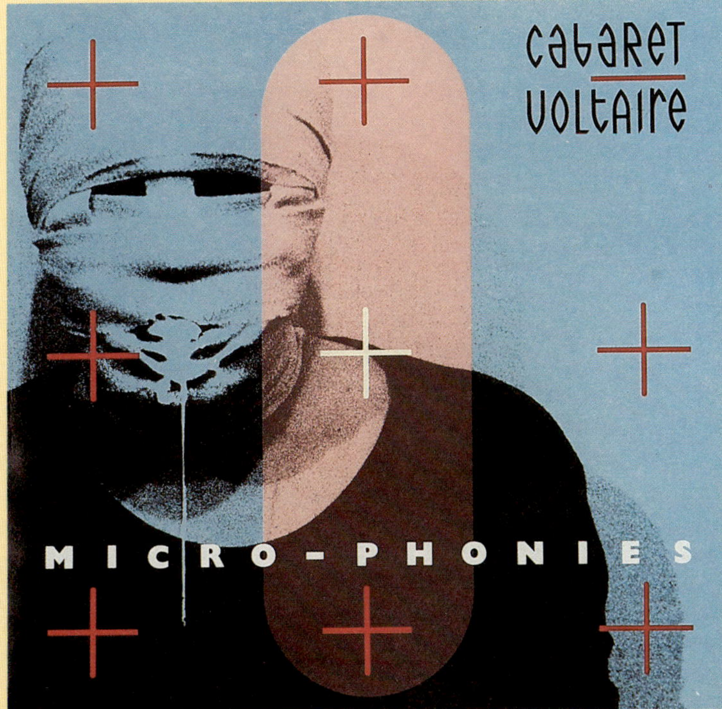

Micro-phonies – Cabaret Voltaire

Designed by NEVILLE BRODY

I'm not 100 per cent convinced about the Cabaret Voltaire logo, but it's still a nicely balanced, well thought out sleeve with some real ideas and good use of colour.

Say What You Mean Mean What You Say – Durutti Column

Designed by 8VO

With little panels, stickers and tiny reproductions of famous paintings, Durutti Column records always look intriguing – they make you want to find out what the music sounds like. That *must* be effective design.

THE WORST

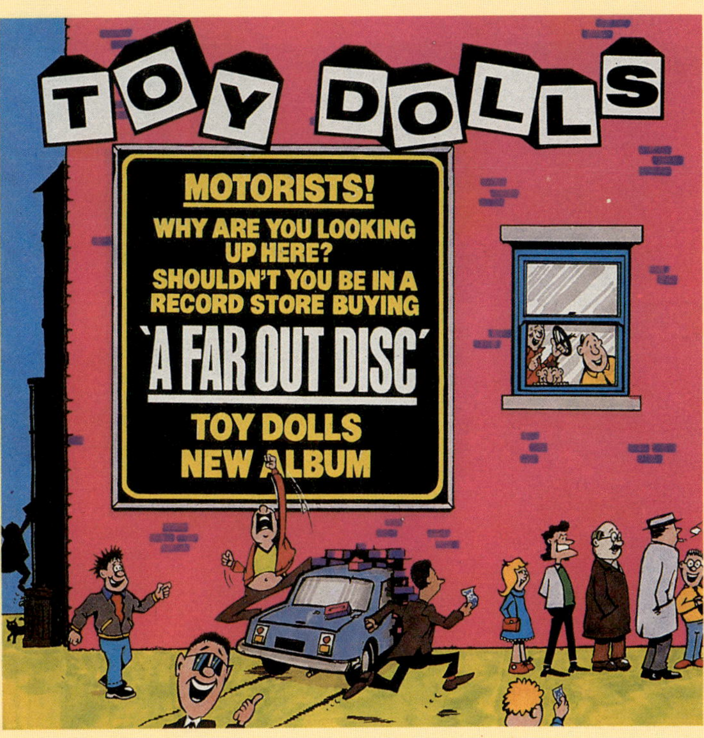

A Far Out Disc – The Toy Dolls

This has all the hallmarks of being designed by the drummer's sister's best friend's boyfriend. On a scale of 1-1000, it rates about 7.

Big Bam Boom – Daryl Hall and John Oates

Very dodgy American "new wave" graphics. This sleeve achieves nothing other than making Daryl Hall and John Oates look stupid.

THE BEST

Leder-Nacken – Various Artists

Designed by C-MORE TONE

Combining printing and hand-painting, this has all the charm of a home-made sleeve without looking cheap, twee or too gimmicky.

Neon Moon – Jah Wobble & Ollie Marland

Designed by BRETT WICKENS AT SPACE

If this had been a good year for sleeve design, this would have been too slick to scrape into the first eleven. But it wasn't, so it did.

THE WORST

Teases & Dares – Kim Wilde

Oh dear. This looks like the designer couldn't decide which photo to use so he copped out completely and stuck them both on. It's a shame he didn't put a third one on to hide that dreadful logo.

Around The World In A Day – Prince & The Revolution

Prince's dodgy mysticism (lots of ladders and doves) and the awful, self-consciously weird painting are very boring and deeply unattractive.

THEY ALSO SERVED ...

... to brighten up a year that was often less than inspiring. Ian Cranna makes a moderately subjective selection from some of the other talents on display.

GENERAL PUBLIC: Two of the nicest, best looking and most politically aware guys around – how can they fail? And the music's not bad either.

ORCHESTRAL MANOEUVRES IN THE DARK: Another good album in *Crush*, a welcome return to real drums, and a witty and intelligent band who aren't afraid to strive for great things.

PHIL COLLINS: Desperately unhip I know, but I quite like ol' Phil Collins. Not exactly trendy, but strong sound songs (we'll overlook 'One More Night') and sturdy production. Pass, friend.

IAN MacCULLOCH: Pity the solo career didn't develop – a fine version of Maxwell Anderson/Kurt Weill's 'September Song' was a perfect start. Oh well, back to the Bunnymen ...

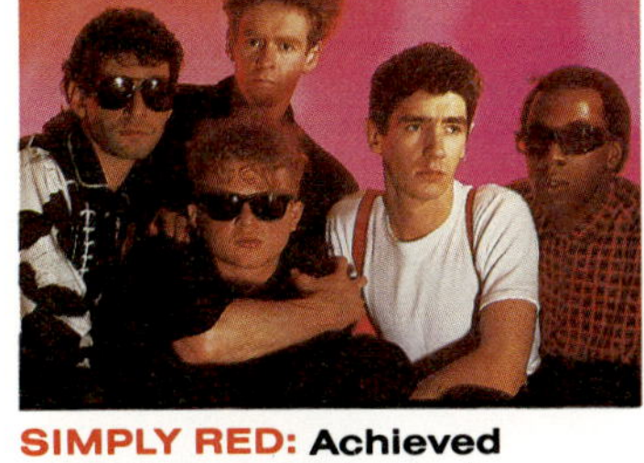

SIMPLY RED: Achieved what the much touted Prince Charles couldn't with a fine version of 'Money's Too Tight To Mention' *and* gave James Brown a run for his money live – an awesome start.

PET SHOP BOYS: When pop journalists make pop records, it usually underlines the old truism that those who can, do; those who can't, write about it. Neil Tennant manages both in quite irksomely stylish fashion, damn him.

SCRITTI POLITTI: His hair may be getting dangerously long but he's still the master at making the tastiest cake out of the lightest of ingredients. *Cupid & Psyche 85* was sweet satisfaction.

DEAD OR ALIVE: I'm sorry, but there is absolutely nothing wrong with 'You Spin Me Round' – quite clearly the reason why God gave us vinyl. Long overdue success for a determined talent.

THE AVENGERS: Still the best TV series ever produced – these repeats will be welcome any time.

EVERYTHING BUT THE GIRL: Tracey Thorn could take on the world with those lyrics and that voice alone; despite Ben Watt's irritatingly lightweight presence, a bittersweet delight.

CHAKA KHAN: Well maybe *she* didn't think much of it, but I certainly thought her wonderfully uplifting 'I Feel For You' was one of the year's best singles.

GILBERTO GIL: When everybody's finished absorbing African music overnight, how about starting on Latin music? *Raça Humana* and 'Indigo Blue' provided new delights from the beautiful Brazilian beat merchant.

NICK DRAKE: Thanks to the Dream Academy's 'Life In A Northern Town' for the interest it aroused in this great neglected talent from the heyday of the singer/songwriter. A rare beauty.

XTC: Enduring and endearing, XTC are one of the great unappreciated talents of our time. For further proof that Andy Partridge is genius at work, see *The Big Express*.

SQUEEZE: Reunions are usually the last refuge of the creatively bankrupt – Squeeze were the exception that proved the rule. A rare sophistication in pop talent.

FINE YOUNG CANNIBALS: Who would have dared think it – *two* fine bands from the ashes of the much loved and sadly missed Beat? Roland Gift is an important vocal find.

THE COCTEAU TWINS: Defensive and prickly in interviews about their instinctive explorations, they complain that no one ever just says thank you for the music. Thank you for the music.

CHINA CRISIS: A gift for gentle melody, some intriguing images and a pleasingly poseless stance made *Flaunt The Imperfection* easily their best yet. Real people in a world of robots.

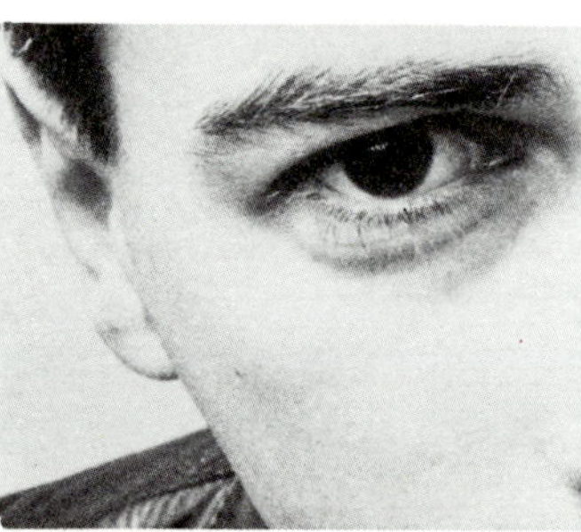

PAUL MORLEY/ZTT: They came, they saw, they marketed. Whether Morley's verbal sleights of hand actually *changed* anything is open to question, but how dull the year would have been without them.

TEARS FOR FEARS: Why is it that anyone not indulging in macho posturing or wanton preening is deemed a wimp? Take a bow, chaps, for some fine moments on *Songs From The Big Chair*.

PROPAGANDA: Nothing startlingly original perhaps, but a strong alliance of good tunes, some strong lyrics and excellent production made their presence very welcome.

MARC ALMOND: The flower in the dustbin, the fly in the ointment – a genuine original and the perfect antidote to pre-packaged pop and the New Authenticity alike.

ALISON MOYET: Still a long way short of achieving her potential, but a respectful tip of the hat to a great singer and a commendably down-to-earth person.

THE BLUE NILE: Literate lyrics, wonderful melodies, modern arrangements without any fuss, singing with passion – great music is still being made.

JOOLZ: Not only is the Bradford wordsmith simply the sharpest social commentator of the lot, she's devastatingly funny with it. *Never Never Land* is an essential purchase.

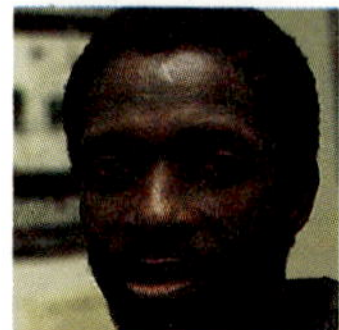

TONY ALLEN: Looking for that elusive key to that African music you feel you ought to be enjoying so much? Fela Kuti's former drummer provides it with 'NEPA (Never Expect Power Always)' on Earthworks – one of the joys of the year.

SPITTING IMAGE: Now that the scripts are finally getting as vicious as the puppet caricatures, this show is one of the few good reasons for possessing a television.

ONYEKA: This Nigerian singer and journalist is evidently a force to be reckoned with on any level. Her 'Trina Four' single on Mother Africa was one of the year's more esoteric delights – reggae meets bagpipes and everybody wins.

SOMETHING ON THE AIR TONIGHT

Ian Cranna turns the dial in search of Radio One's finest

Standards seemed to be the main concern of all at Radio One this year – lowering them, that is.

The principal effect of the ill-advised relegation of Peter Powell to the backwater of Saturday morning can now be seen to have been the closure of the main outlet for new talents to the nation's airwaves as the BBC slipped almost imperceptibly back to being virtually a playlist station (Top Forty or oldies only) during the day.

Symptomatically, Powell's replacement – the dreadful Bruno Brookes, a man whose desire to impress was such that his first call to arms was inviting listeners to send in reasons why women go to the toilet in pairs – is one of the new generation of inane natterers currently favoured by Radio One. But why?

Evidently one of the reasons for the BBC's new conservatism is that it feels obliged to compete with pirates like Laser 558. Laser's lowest common denominator formula of playing only recognizable hits by DJs with the IQ of a stick insect has indeed proved popular with the cab drivers of this world, but even with them Laser becomes so numbingly mindless that even smarmy Gary 'medallion man' Davies seems preferable.

Sadly the day of the informed music fan on the national station seems to be well in retreat. John Peel is still there, although cruelly truncated to a three-day week in favour of – of all things – the pompous Tommy Vance and his rock dinosaurs. Is this the BBC's idea of progress? Peel, if nothing else, is a supremely entertaining man to listen to and his choice of material from African music to European experimentalists, from reggae to bluegrass and other pleasingly non-commercially oriented musics denied airtime elsewhere is never less than interesting. Do any of the man's ill-informed critics actually *listen* to his show?

Peel's early evening predecessor, Janice Long, is often criticized for apparently indiscriminate enthusiasm over new acts but at least – like Powell – she comes across as a genuine person more interested in the music than the sound of her own voice. Her show also grants precious airtime to the hilariously irreverent John Walters, whose perceptive and witty half-hour slots on the music press and his own arts week (aided by his supreme gift for sound effects) are the highlights of the listening week.

Away from the more considered evening shows, intelligent fans of the music they play are hard to find. Robbie Vincent's knowledgeable and discerning two hours of jazz-funk actually manage to transcend their patently token status into good radio. Anne Nightingale's personable request show usually does the same and Mike Read's morning spot just about qualifies since the man can be amusing and interesting, despite an alarming tendency towards creeping smugness and conceit – a disease that seems to affect any DJ who holds this slot for any length of time. Someone really should take him on one side and administer a sharp clip round the back of the head about that wretched guitar of his.

Strangely enough (or perhaps not in the current climate), one of the best of the lot has yet to gain a regular daily show. Richard Skinner is a skilful interviewer and a moderately humorous man with good taste in music; both he and his eminently listenable *Saturday Live* magazine show are worthy of better hours.

The two main slots of the day –morning and afternoon – are the exceptions that prove the rule about the ratio of chat to music. Despite signs that his hits and headlines formula is getting stuck in something of a rut and an eagerness to provide the latest gossip that verges on the fawning, Simon Bates remains the jewel in Radio One's crown. A supremely accomplished broadcaster, Bates is also wickedly funny and frequently gets away with murder under his seemingly innocuously jovial presentation. He also sounds as if he's actually enjoying himself up there, as opposed to dispensing official government fun.

Steve Wright is a bizarre mixture of the brilliant and the barbaric: often extremely funny, some of his attempts at humour on politically sensitive topics like gays and women are, whether intended to provoke or not, quite simply beyond the pale and in danger of becoming a vanguard for the unthinking New Right. His array of guest characters is similarly variable – the excellent Mr Angry has now passed into the nation's consciousness but others are desperately thin. Still, at least he has the true personality to make you want to tune in, unlike the sorry lot of also-rans who comprise the rest of the BBC's crew.

Alas, the prospect of improvement seems remote. Janice Long's phone-in interview with her new boss at Radio One, Johnny Bierling, made depressing listening. "Why don't you play more reggae?" asked one frustrated listener. "Oh but we do play reggae," replied Bierling, citing two freak crossover hits of the day and ignoring – either deliberately or through ignorance – the main thrust of the question. But at least we now have the ex-pirate Miss P with her ghettoized Sunday night hour, though the wide variety of styles played only underlines how pitifully under-represented reggae (like most minority interests) remains.

So yet another stage of American cultural colonization appears to have taken place – the ratings battle made official policy. Whatever happened to the Reithian ethic of quality of broadcast before quantity of listeners? When you hear a Radio One DJ enthusing about a "beautiful new record from Foreigner", you know something somewhere has gone terribly wrong.

● JOHN PEEL

● SIMON BATES

● JANICE LONG

● MIKE READ

BEAT OF THE BOX

Tony Parsons thumbs his nose at the state of music programmes on British television.

Sometimes it's hard to tell a seasonal break from a death sentence. I really *miss* — well, remember with a vague affection — those shockingly sensitive, in-depth interviews that "Little" Nicky Horne used to do on *Earsay*. They were always done in this hushed, darkened room, with the solitary camera always positioned a couple of millimetres away from the hairs of the subject's left nostril — this was *such* great television — and they always ended in tears. Even Marc Almond came across as a sympathetic character. Lemmy, for God's sake, came across as a sympathetic character! But where is *Earsay* now that we need it a little bit? A seasonal break for a pop programme is so often a kindly executioner's song. They come and then they go. Ah, but that's what they're like — don't get involved with them. They're all the same.

Almost.

Two of them are on infinitely solid ground now, two of them will always be with us. The rest of them are on *very* shaky ground and their air of breezy confidence does nothing to disguise the fact that the hapless presenters of this doomed revelry have absolutely no idea where their next contract is coming from. Channel 4 has come right out of the closet. TV programmers since the dawn of time — since the release date of 'Twenty Flight Rock' at least — have had this thought and at last the dirty finks have had the guts to come right out and say it. They know what to do with music on Channel 4 — shove it in a ghetto. The only people who could possibly sit through the entire *Friday Zone* are (a) those who are being paid for it and (b) those who have the IQ of a geranium.

ECT, which is *The Price is Right* to the imaginary Flying-V guitar brigade, is like *Spinal Tap* without the laughs. No, that's not strictly true — it's like *Spinal Tap with* the laughs. It has great dialogue ("See you at the Rock Garden on Sunday, reet?"), young gentlemen who, at the end of every song, open their mouths, shake their fists and nod, young ladies in various stages of undress who stand crooning with their legs alarming apart and, to boot, a most unusual presentation. The bands go on stage, play a couple of numbers live and go. God, the presentation is pretentious.

From the touchingly brainless to the sick-makingly cerebral — *Paintbox* is music without feeling, images without meaning. Coming as it does after ECT, *Paintbox* seems almost like a letter of apology for the sweaty antics of the very metal mob. While I am quite sure that the pictures on *Paintbox* are all highly symbolic of something or other, I found some of the images a mite strong for viewing at this hour. *Paintbox* is unsuitable viewing at teatime. In fact, *Paintbox* is unsuitable, period. The outer limits of the *Friday Zone*'s ghetto walls, though, are really quite beautiful. *Soul Train* wipes the dancefloor with its American counterpart and at long last Malcolm McLaren's dream has been realized — here is an audience that looks better than the performers.

The Tube — which like poverty and *Top of the Pops* will always be with us — works for a lot of reasons. Mostly it works because it is impossible to tell where the programme ends and its commercials start and because Jools Holland quite clearly doesn't give a toss. As a presenter of a music programme, old Jools is touched with genius — because it is strikingly clear that this is not what he wants to be. A pop show presenter who doesn't believe he has arrived in the Promised Land! It . . . it . . . it's revolutionary. The light that Jools Holland gets in his eyes when he sits on a piano stool is quite possibly the most moving thing that you will ever see on Channel 4 between five thirty and seven on a Friday night.

The Max Headroom Show is about as low as it goes. Hopefully before the passing of many moons this insipid abomination will have taken a seasonal break that will see us all out. The worst thing about *The Max Headroom Show* is not even the cornball android-talking-head jape — it probably seemed like a great idea at the time — but all those *videos*. It's only a little promotional device, the video, it's not some kind of ultimate state-of-the-art statement. The absolute worst thing about *The* so-called *Max Headroom Show* is that it believes MTV to be something to aspire to.

But at least Channel 4 — that Palestine for all us minority groups such as people who are off-white and people who like music — is trying. ITV — the most popular station in fair Albion — would be more palatable if it totally banned the beat from the box. I mean, during the week I wrote this ITV offered just three things (not including the imaginatively named "Pop Video" slot at 7.54 every *Good Morning Britain*, which is invariably reviewed by Wincey the weatherperson with an astute, "Good that, innit?") Two of the things ITV offered were *In Concert* and *Portrait of a Legend*. Now both of these little gems go out just before the epilogue and both of them feature people who anybody under twenty-five never knew existed and everybody over twenty-five thought was dead. *In Concert* was horrible enough — Kris Kristofferson and Anne Murray — but *Portrait of a Legend... Portrait of a Legend — Bobby Vinton.* Bobby *Vinton? A Legend?* They should call it *Portrait of Somebody Who's Name Vaguely Rings a Bell.*

The only other thing ITV has in the way of something you can tap your toes to is *Razzmatazz*, which I have ambivalent feelings about. It's nice to see all those ankle-biters' sticky little faces light up with joy at having some popular crooner in their midst but one can't help but feel the brake-pads coming on against total pleasure. It's difficult not to feel slightly ludicrous about watching some snotty-nosed brat of around ten or eleven picking up a Razz stuffed toy if you are slightly above the age of ten or eleven yourself and, try as you may, cannot see any intrinsic value in owning a Razz stuffed toy. The monosyllabic inanity of the interviews on *Razzmatazz* are highly watchable, though — everybody that appears on the show comes across like a Ramone.

I can't quite see the *raison d'etre* of BBC2's *Off the Record, which features some bald, middle-aged punk encouraging some obese soap-opera star — Eddie Yates of Coronation Street* and Simple Benny of *Crossroads* seem to appear on alternate weeks — to rifle through his collection of Barclay James Harvest bootlegs and reminisce emotionally about the seventies. *Off the Record* seems to exist to make the programme that follows look good.

I don't know quite what has happened to *The Old Grey Whistle Test*. It's got very modern, that's for sure. Calling itself simply *WHISTLE TEST*, well, that's not the half of it. Bob Harris has shaved off his beard, got glasses and lightened up a bit. Richard Williams has lost his moustache, started attempting *bon mots* and lightened up a bit. Gary Crowley has been brought in — stuff *The Other Side of the Tracks* and *Eight Days a Week*, bring back *Earsay* — and forced to wear clogs as a penance for dropping his aitches for so long. Everyone has put on a ludicrous amount of weight. But they all look like mere slips of boys when compared to an angry young poet with a crew cut who poses many provocative, controversial questions every week — most notably, why are the current crop of poets so fat? Aren't poets meant to be thin and beautiful and doomed-looking? Well, *Whistle Test* is a little too modern for me, I'm afraid! What with its computer "graphics" and video "phone-ins" and chats with American musicians so tiresome that their presence in this country makes Cruise seem like a welcome guest. With *The Tube* around, *Whistle Test* has got a lot of nerve. What I dislike most about it is when

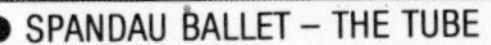

● SPANDAU BALLET – THE TUBE

● WARRIOR – E.C.T.

● WARRIOR – E.C.T.

● CHAKA KHAN –THE TUBE

● THE AUDIENCE – E.C.T.

● NICKY HORN – EARSAY

● LESLEY-ANN JONES – EARSAY

● JEFFREY DANIEL – SOUL TRAIN

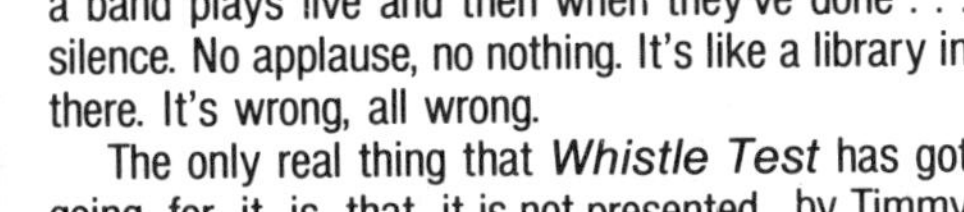

a band plays live and then when they've done . . . silence. No applause, no nothing. It's like a library in there. It's wrong, all wrong.

The only real thing that *Whistle Test* has got going for it is that it is not presented by Timmy Mallett. Timmy has the crawling conceit necessary for a successful career in television and he has it in abundance. I'm not sure what his day job is — an early morning DJ for Radio Blackburn or something — but this cretinously exuberant personality somehow manages to force his way on screen whenever a bit of rogue pop music starts to play. He presents pop items on stray bits of independent breakfast television — I seem to see Timmy's inane, bespectacled face leering at me every time I look up from my cornflakes. He presents the *Oxford Road Show* and the guest star co-presenters (always musicians, always surprisingly *nervous* in front of the camera until they are given the chance to strum and croon) always abuse, ridicule and humiliate poor Tim at every opportunity. This bullying of Timmy would seem like loutish behaviour if the wretch did not completely deserve it. Indeed, I strongly hope that in the next series of the *Oxford Road Show* the guest star co-presenters will pull no punches. If you really want to know what is wrong with popular music on TV, then tune in to Timmy.

What is right with popular music on TV is *Top of the Pops*. It is easy to sneer at this British institution, easy to heap scorn on the aural hacks shipped in to present from Radio 1 (they look so *grateful*), the prancing bimbos desperately soliciting the camera every time it is pointed remotely in their direction, easy — and very wrong — to sneer at the old warhorse for being a vehicle for pap.

It is nothing less than the people's choice. If the masses don't buy it then it will not be shown; if it doesn't get shown it won't get known. How democratic can you get? The only thing that is a bigger deal for a band than appearing on *Top of the Pops* is being a band who get *banned* from going on *Top of the Pops*. And when that band — Sex Pistols, Sex Frankies — eventually arrive in that studio, the studio that towers over the entire record industry like a colossus, it is always a magical moment, one to cherish forever (well, until you get a bit bored with the single at least).

The people's choice is all powerful. You can hate it if you want, but it is as pointless as hating God.

FINDING VIRTUE IN VICE

Mark Coleman defends MIAMI VICE as the most successful use of pop music on US television

The Birds, The Bees And The Monkees

Elvis' hip movements censored on *The Ed Sullivan Show*; Mick Jagger and James Brown going head-to-head on *The T.A.M.I. Show*; Iggy Pop going into the audience armed only with a jar of peanut butter during the nationally televised Cincinnati Pop Festival; David Bowie going to Mars and back on the *1980 Floor Show:* traditionally rock 'n' roll on television results in confrontation, a cultural rout. In the sixties and seventies pop music was, for the most part, a world unto itself and attempts to render even a taste of that on TV were either clumsy (musical variety) or hopelessly square (pop sitcom/drama). And in between those moments of confrontation came long periods of boredom relieved only by semi-intentional humour. But it was worth suffering through Paul Revere and the Raiders every afternoon on *Where the Action Is* just to catch a glimpse of Mary Wells, and to David Cassidy fans it hardly mattered that the Partridge Family always played to tables of families in what looked like a posh strip club. The most memorable thing about the made-for-TV Monkees wasn't their accidental development into an interesting group, but the fact that even good singles didn't help once the ratings started to slide. Even the most fervent teenybopper could tell the difference between television and the real thing.

You Get What You Need

"I WANT MY MTV!" declares Pete Townshend in the adverts seen by everybody who can't get it. It doesn't matter who you are or how loudly you shout: cable technology isn't available to just anybody. According to Arbitron, in February of 1985 44 per cent of television households (37,175,300) in the US were hooked up to some form of cable. Sure, MTV is a basic staple of virtually every cable service but that still means the majority of American viewers have to live without the 24-hour music video channel. For most Americans, pop music on network television means catch-as-catch-can viewing at its dodgiest. If you like videos, *ABC Rocks* and *Friday Night Videos* present nothing but, introduced by disembodied robot-like voices amid video-game graphics. Most cities have a few locally-based clipshows as well, which are run at odd hours and often utilize some rather unusual on-air "talent". "It's Friday Night at the Roxy Disco and we're paaaartyying!" bellows *New York Hot Tracks* host Carlos DeJesus from the apex of a human pyramid of shapely female models. *Hot Tracks*, with its inventive mix of video clips, live interviews, teenage dancers and unrehearsed fun ("we're waiting here on the runway, live, to meet Rick James' plane") recalls the glory days of pop variety shows like *American Bandstand* and *Soul Train*. Both those shows are still on the air and holding their own, thanks. That's as much a tribute to their venerable hosts as to the tried-and-true lip synch/interview/audience dance format. Dick Clark, the man who survived payola and Public Image Ltd with his hairdo intact, is a Saturday morning fixture, spinning singles for camera-shy kids who know a good dance record when they hear it. And dandy Don Cornelius still stands like a hulking guru behind *Soul Train*'s dancefloor of teenaged contortionists. He seems more at ease chatting with old friends like the Temptations than Whodini and the Fat Boys, but both Don and Dick have managed to keep abreast of the changing beats without losing their, er, dignity.

Nobody has ever accused *Solid Gold* of being dignified, and that may well explain its popularity. It's one of the most popular of all syndicated (non-network) shows, reaching 6,130,000 TV households by Arbitron's February 1985 tally. (For the same period *American Bandstand* reached 3,217,000 and *Friday Night Videos*, 2,300,003.) The secret of *Solid Gold*? It's not the live lip-synching by everyone from Olivia Neutron Bomb to Prince, not the catfight duets between co-hosts Marilyn McCoo and John 'Dukes of Hazzard' Schnieder, and certainly not the hideous ventriloquist's dummy and charity-case comedians who fill up the show's odd moments. No, it's the Solid Gold Dancers who make *Solid Gold* what it is. Watching this nimble troupe interpret each week's Top Ten songs is like witnessing a bizarre melange of belly dancing, disco aerobics and a wet T-shirt contest. For a while this programme let the occasional convincing musical performance slip by, but lately *Solid Gold* has ascended to the level of high camp. However, the SG Dancers now have some stiff competition in that department from *Puttin' On The Hits*, a ghastly half-hour in which the "contestants" imitate the stars in a sort of televised version of a Japanese *Karoke* bar. An unexpected success in its initial season, *POTH* seems healthy in comparison to the creepy freakshow of a video clip, 'Yo Little Brother' by Nolan Thomas. When innocent midgets start impersonating Ric Ocasek, you know things are getting out of hand.

Five Things To Do While Watching MTV

1. Houshold Chores. MTV was made for those annoying tasks where subliminal hum and the occasional distraction come as a relief – washing dishes, dusting furniture, mopping and sweeping, sorting laundry. You've got to be careful though; video can make some jobs downright dangerous. Nobody should witness one of the "exclusive" interviews between the "VJs" and the likes of REO Speedwagon while, say, polishing Dad's pistol collection. The life of your set could be reduced by as much as half. And if one of REO's videos comes on, suicide may suddenly seem attractive.

2. Talking on the Telephone. Once upon a time watching TV with someone on the horn was considered the height of rudeness. But as in many other aspects of life, MTV has changed conversation etiquette for ever. Pop songs, commercials, patter, and more commercials are just as easy to tune out visually as they are aurally, and when a good one pops up your correspondent doesn't even have to be watching to enjoy.

3. Homework. JULIE, WHAT ABOUT YOUR MATH PROBLEMS? Mom, Simon's about to get strapped in the torture wheel again. YOUNG LADY, YOU KNOW WHAT WE DECIDED ABOUT STUDYING WITH THE TELEVISION ON. But Mom, I'm not watching television – it's MTV! Anyway, I'm just looking at the good ones. Oh, God, it's Brewce Springsteen. I'm going back to my room, WELL, JUST LEAVE IT ON . . .

4. Eat. Hell, sometimes videos can really enhance a meal – looking up from a plate of Hamburger Helper and seeing Dee Snider is an experience every meat-eater should undergo. Somehow, the prospect of Howard Jones, Morrissey, frozen Lean Cuisine and mung bean sprouts isn't as inspiring.

5. Making Love. Let's face it, MTV is a great aid to seduction. It's nominally diverting entertainment without the tentacles of a progress-impeding plot and, after giving you something to talk about, provides background music of a sort (at least you don't have to get up to change the record). But if you find it working as an aphrodisiac either you're a leather 'n' lace fetishist or you subconsciously have a crush on one of the VJs. The only moments on MTV itself that approach passion come when the dimpled and diminutive VJ Martha Quinn gets anywhere near David Lee Roth – check the look in her eyes as she innocently asks Diamond Dave about the details of his latest video casting call. If they did it, would MTV *Music News* report it the next day?

Like A Record, Baby, Round And Round

MTV doesn't compare to traditional pop music programmes because people don't watch MTV with the attention devoted to even *Solid Gold* or *Soul Train*, and fifteen mellow minutes of the new "adult contemporary" video channel Video Hits 1 (VH-1) proves that boring is an extremely relative term. Oddly enough, perhaps the most progressive pop-music show that's ever been on US television was a situation comedy about a radio station.

When *WKRP in Cincinnati* was on the air in the late seventies, it was dismissed by most as an amusing but obvious clone of the *Mary Tyler Moore Show*. Like WJM-TV, WKRP-FM was that station with the lowest ratings in town, staffed by a regular crew who were endearingly eccentric and absolutely incompetent. The burned-out overlord of this decaying manor was Dr Johnny Fever (played by Howard Hesseman), a man so zapped by drugs and music-biz hype he had his current pseudonym embossed on a coffee mug as a constant reminder of

● MTV VIDEO JOCKS (L to R Alan Hunter, Martha Quinn, Mark Goodman, Nina Blackwood, J.J. Jackson)

● DICK CLARK

● "SOLID GOLD" DANCERS

his identity. Yet for all his shady past and wasted gaffes, Johnny Fever was a shrewd dude who came to life when he was in front of that mike. Strong writing and character acting made *WKRP* a rare bird – an intelligent sitcom. And the imaginary station's use of pop music made it unique. Johnny didn't like Journey but as a DJ he'd put up with it so he could slip in Bob Marley and Chuck Berry, while overnight announcer/love-man Venus Flytrap read Kahil Gibrahn over Grover Washington Jr tracks and programme director/college jock Andy always used to complain: "This is a playlist. Do you understand? These are the songs you're supposed to play." When the camera would scan a Clash poster in the DJ's booth, it was both cool and caustic, since no radio programmer in his right mind was playing punk rock in 1978. Rather than appropriating pop as commercial hook or gimmick, *WKRP* heightened its dramatic effect by placing music in a real-life context. And it was funny. Not until 1985 and *Miami Vice* would pop music figure so heavily in a prime-time programme. And so far, the main difference between *WKRP in Cincinnati* and *Miami Vice* has been the overwhelming success of the latter.

Miami Vice is so slick it scares people. All that neon-lit pastel flash and scalpel-sharp editing is a little intimidating, and it somewhat obscures the soundtrack's primary contribution to this show's electrifying impact. Jan Hammer's synthesized original scores each week provide much of the throbbing pulse, underscoring the action with a deftness and subtlety unheard of on television (ever listened to the music on *Dynasty*?). Pop songs are deployed strategically throughout the hour-long show, and more often than not they actually enhance what's going on. And they're not always obvious hits; a drug deal stake-out in an abandoned parking lot went down to the eerie strains of JA dubmaster Augustus Pablo's melodica. The show has been attacked as a vacuous vid-clip stretched out to incorporate commercials, but I think that's unfair. Occasionally scenes get stolen by the scenery but despite wildly inconsistent writing, even the weakest episode has attempted to tell a story. (And surprisingly, the show based on Glenn Frey's 'Smuggler's Blues', which guest-starred the ex-Eagle, was one of the most dramatically satisfying.) Co-stars Don Johnson (Sonny Crockett) and Michael Philip Thomas (Rico Tubbs) both have LPs in the works and a new *Miami Vice* theme song is being penned by Robert Palmer and Chic's Bernard Edwards, to be sung by Chaka Khan. Nobody will go broke betting that those three records will land in the charts. After a honeymoon like *Miami Vice*, the marriage between pop music and prime-time television should bear even more bizarre (and entertaining) fruit.

● GLENN FREY

● NOLAN THOMAS AND THE VID KIDS

BEHIND THE TIMES

Simon Frith argues that the old guard of the British music press, overtaken by the eighties, is struggling to find a way forward

The thing to remember about the British music press is that pop writers take themselves very seriously and no one else takes them at all seriously. When I was writing for *Melody Maker* at the end of the seventies, its publishers IPC commissioned a market research company to find out who read (and didn't read) *MM* and why and how they read it. Their report was salutary. Most people read music papers for their tour and record news; they didn't care who wrote the features; they noticed record reviews after they'd made up their minds and not before. I came to two conclusions. First, music papers' relative sales figures are accidental – in a market in which casual newsagent demand is more important than regular subscription, cover pictures (and free offers) are the most significant sales point and brand loyalty is as irrational as it is with washing powders. Second, the music press always follows trends, never initiates them.

Music papers flourish when the people buying music are the same as the people wanting to read about music are the same as the people music advertisers want to reach – hence the success of *Melody Maker* in the late sixties and *NME* in the mid-seventies, with their sales peaks of 300,000 plus. In the eighties the equation has meant the rise of a new pop press, *Smash Hits* and its imitators (*No 1*, the revamped *Record Mirror*), and the decline of the rock weeklies (*NME, Sounds* and *Melody Maker*). Phil Collins and Dire Straits outsell Howard Jones and Tears For Fears, but there are far more people who want to read about the latter; the Smiths and New Order don't command the sheer pin-up appeal of Duran Duran and Wham! And, anyway, in the current economic climate, pre-teens' spending power is more interesting to advertisers than their older sisters' and brothers' student grants and YTS pay-outs.

1985 meant a consolidation of this pattern: *Smash Hits* now has over half a million sales every fortnight, *No 1* a quarter of a million a week, while *NME* has stabilized at around 120,000, *Melody Maker* at less than 70,000. But for the music papers' long-term development, what mattered more was what was happening to music coverage elsewhere. *Smash Hits*' tone of voice – cynical, fawning, mocking, up-to-the-minute – now fuels the *Mirror*'s and the *Sun*'s obsessive pursuit of young readers, while its publishers' version of a young woman's magazine, *Just Seventeen*, has been successful enough to call forth instant copies (like IPC's *Mizz*). Teenage girls' spending power isn't limitless and the increased competition for their attention, the increased use of pop stars as advertising agents, will, eventually, bust the market.

The "serious" music papers face a new sort of competition too: there are more news/reviews/interview programmes on national and local radio and television now than ever. The most telling media event of 1985 came when promoter Harvey Goldsmith announced the long-awaited details of Bruce Springsteen's British dates on the revivified *Whistle Test*, thus neatly missing that week's music press deadlines. *NME* wrote an angry attack on Goldsmith's ploy but they missed both the point – *Whistle Test* reaches far more Springsteen fans than *NME* does – and the really worrying question: what, these days, is the rock press for?

The dearth of reading rock fans is obvious in the monthly market too. The two glossy fanzines that have kept going, the dire *Zig-Zag* and the well-meaning *Jamming*, lurk on WH Smith's shelves like scruffy, boys' versions of all the poster mags. The good music journals now are specialist, hard-to-find, "minority" publications, like Anthony Wood's enterprising jazz monthly, *The Wire*, and Tony Russell's *Old Time Music*, or hobby papers like the various equipment and musicians' journals and the excellent *Record Collector*.

The anomaly in this pattern is *The Face*, which celebrated its fifth anniversary with monthly sales figures of 80,000 (and a successful imitator, *Blitz*). But *The Face* (this is the secret of its success) has long since ceased to be a music magazine. It's a style sheet, a marketing manual, packaging pop in among the clothes and furnishing, treating music as just another source of popular imagery, alongside sport and film and fashion. Whatever its origins, *The Face* now has much more in common with a lifestyle magazine like *Harpers and Queen* than it does with the music weeklies.

These last have reacted to the changed market circumstances in different ways. *New Musical Express*, under editor Neil Spencer (who left this year), has become more and more of a general interest paper. It carries extensive film coverage, a good books page, political stories – CND, the Youth Training Scheme, Neil Kinnock, Ireland, heroin, sport; its cassette offers are the best available introductions to popular music history; it has printed colour fashion pull-out booklets. *NME* already had a tradition of wide-ranging cultural coverage, reflecting its seventies writers' roots in the underground press, but ex-teacher Spencer shifted its focus from hippie interests (drugs/sci-fi/comix) to an odd mixture of metropolitan mod-about-town and youth worker socialist realism.

The problem for *NME* is, ironically, how to fit music into its social concerns. Its ideal readership, the smart and dishevelled underclass, isn't its actual readership, which is, judging by annual poll results, drawn from serious rock's traditional clientele – sixth-formers, students, suburban fantasists, followers of the Smiths and Cocteau Twins. *NME* is still the most readable British music paper, the most intelligent, the funniest, the best designed, but this is, increasingly, despite its music coverage. Its record and concert reviews are, year by year, more incomprehensible, its interviews less revealing, its news sense more erratic. The paper no longer represents any sort of pop or rock vanguard and, since Paul Morley left, has lost even that buzz that comes from writers who are out clubbing every night, listening obsessively to any new sound that comes along. *NME*, in short, no longer fulfils the central role of a music weekly – to be a reliable guide to what's happening.

Sounds (whose editor, Eric Fuller, also left this year) continues as if its readers were still living in the seventies, when the paper's alliance of metal, garage rock and punk fans was first put together. This is a sensible strategy in some ways. *Sounds* does read as the music paper which best understands its audience, best services them with advice and news and flattery – its writers are, on the whole, enthusiastic and unpretentious, clearly on the consumers' side. *Sounds*' problem is that the seventies tastes it still meets are now so dull and clichéd. What was once an exciting celebration of proletarian noise – *Sounds*, not *NME*, had the earliest and best appreciation of punk – has degenerated, via oi, into a formula yobbishness. *Sounds* (whose sales briefly overtook *NME*'s early in the eighties) is in danger of becoming the tabloid version of *Kerrang!*, a heavy metal cult paper with a (diminishing) cult following. It will be interesting to see what changes a new editor makes.

Melody Maker has faced a sales decline for much longer than its rivals and has, as a result, made the most serious attempt to adapt itself to eighties market patterns. This has had some odd effects. I never could take *MM* seriously as a teeny-bop outlet, all those interminable, inky features on Wham! followed by pages of musicians' small ads. And it was a serious misjudgement to end sixty years of jazz coverage when a) you had Brian Case, one of Britain's best jazz writers, and b) jazz itself was just becoming part of the thinking dancer's background music. Case was shifted to the film/book/video page but *MM* has never had *NME*'s credibility with non-musical matters.

On the other hand, the 1985 revival of "roots" music, the new cult of Authenticity, the regrowing interest in American musics of all sorts put *MM* in a good position – it had taken these things seriously already. I found myself reading it again – it has the best gossip column, the most trustworthy reviews, the most interesting interviews. *Melody Maker*'s problem now is to shake off its stodgy reputation – a reputation still encouraged, unfortunately, by a dull design, colourless, apolitical prose, a heavy, beery sense of humour. *MM* seems a rather thin read; it lacks *NME*'s variety. Still, the tastes of the reading music public do seem to be shifting back from pop to rock and my bet is that within five years *MM*'s and *NME*'s relative sales positions will be reversed.

Everything else being equal, that is, and here I'm less sure. Is there still room in the leisure market for Britain's remarkable number of music magazines? They are, in the end, all dependent on the industry which they service, and while the weeklies do have individual styles and voices, what's most striking is how similar they are, how much their coverage – in terms of both form and content – is determined by that week's press office activity. Shifts in the music business – the declining importance of records, the increasing tie-up of music and other forms of entertainment – will affect the music press (as consumer interests change, as patterns of advertising expenditure are altered) regardless of their editorial flair.

What I find most depressing about Britain's music press is that you wouldn't know much about these changes from reading it. These days music writers are critics not reporters, more concerned to foster their own myths than to dig, anonymously, behind other people's. It's ironic, for example, that *NME* should run a "real", newspaper-type story on private detective agencies, while it has virtually no investigative interest in the music business. Who knows, from reading the music press, how ZTT or Blanco y Negro really work? What was involved in the Island/Stiff merger? Who made what money out of the Bruce Springsteen visit?

The music weeklies take what "dirt" and money-talk they do carry from other sources – *Billboard* and *Music Week*, Dave Marsh's *Rock 'n' Roll Confidential*; they rarely discover such stories for themselves. They're quick to voice opinions – on home-taping, say – slow to gather fresh information to support such opinions. The weeklies would, in fact, be in a strong position to perform their own home-taping surveys, to discover who records what and why, to influence legislation even. That they don't reflects their writers' idleness, their publishers' meanness (music papers are produced *very* cheaply) and their place, despite the usual protestations, at the heart of a sales machine.

And this is the essential paradox of the British music press. In material terms it is parasitical on a sophisticated industry; in ideological terms it is – post-hippie and post-punk – naively anti-commercial. The contradiction could be fruitful. Most of the time, though, it gives the music weeklies an odour of hypocrisy (which is why *Smash Hits* can claim, tongue out of cheek, to be *more* honest). The only paper with a solution to the problem is *NME*. It ends every week with Lowry's and Benyon's cartoon strips, cutting through all the crap that's gone before.

RAH RAH AMERICA

Tim Sommer berates the US music press for its xenophobic support of "Reaganite rock'n'roll".

The American rock press has always been misleading. They've consistently provided a selective picture of what's been going on, a bizarre yet highly predictable view of American rock that frequently omits the most interesting stuff while hyping and re-hyping the most tired and saturated dross. But in the last year or two, the press has been instrumental in creating a *myth* – a pure and ultimately destructive fiction. That's the myth of the American roots rock revival.

There are more deceptive critical hypes currently being perpetrated (f'rinstance, the DC go-go music scene, which plain and simple *does not exist* on the streets and outside the feeble-yet-eager imaginations of some rock critics and record publicists). But the American rock press has *never* been more unified than they are now in their constant and vociferous support of this American roots rock thing.

Basically, and this isn't even touching on its aesthetic and ideological defects, this myth is full of holes. American rock has been healthy and active for a long time – since the new wave dawn and the vicious energy and spirit of seventies west coast punk and post-punk. In earlier years it was ignored by the scribes, that's all, but it existed nonetheless. Secondly, for most of the musicians capitalizing on it, roots rock is just another goddamn trend, and that's important to keep in mind. In fact, it's probably the most thoroughly saturated and embraced trend to hit America since '77.

In general, the strength of the roots rock revival indicates that American rock is taking a few large, unhealthy steps backward. To most of these musicians, it's a denial of the advances – both musically and philosophically – of the last ten years. We're back to the gang-of-boys plod-rock attitude of the early seventies. A lot of these musicians failed to get contracts or critical note by jumping on any number of trends that have surfaced (and sunk) in the last seven or eight years; now, they've returned to delivering the predictable, macho twang that they (or their older brothers) were doling out ten years ago.

A band like New York's Del Lords typifies this movement (perhaps it's unfair to single them out, but their journeymen good-'ol-boys-playing-good-'ol-music style and sound personifies the whole thing). The Del Lords approach rock'n'roll as if it were a dull and dusty old photo album – a photo album with no new pictures to be added and no new angles to be explored. They are dumb without dumb charm (à la the Ramones or AC/DC), roots obsessed without being perverse or raunchy (as the '62-'65 Brits were when they tackled American roots rock). Even Springsteen spices his 1-3-5 plaints with passion and soul, but there's none of that anywhere in sight when it comes to the vastly predictable and contrived sound of the Del Lords, Del Fuegos, Green On Red, Dream Syndicate, Long Ryders, etc.

Conformity – and the belief that modern white urban rock culture *can* fit into American redneck anti-urban culture – is at the heart of the roots revival. And yes, there is plenty of genuine American roots music that proves that rock and R&B and country etc *are* indigenous American folk forms; but *who needs* a bevy of former punks, synth players and ska supporters suddenly wearing check shirts and cowboy boots, and suddenly claiming to conform to the great American reactionary anti-art-school, anti-homosexual, anti-foreign, and anti-change and innovation scheme of things.

And the British have fallen for it, too. Witness any number of recent swooning British weekly essays on R.E.M. or the Long Ryders, all full of leaden prose on the glory and the mystery of the American South and the simmering shock waves of the American Civil War.

Yes, R.E.M. (who remain a constantly reassuring example that American rock *can* be a fascinating, innovative, and non-sexist forum) are from the South, and yes, they are deserving of all the attention they've received; but in their formative days and years they were the *outcasts* in this romantic South, fixated on British music (for years, R.E.M. guitarist Peter Buck has been saying that the Soft Boys were a far bigger influence on him than the Byrds were), and called *fags* and (worse yet) art students in their native land. They were teased for their appearance and inability to conform in this humid Dixie clime.

The American roots rock revival is perfect for the Reagan era. This is reactionary, jingoistic, xenophibic rock 'n' roll, and its continued hyping is deceptive in an obvious way, and hateful and dangerous just under the surface. The fact that critics have fallen so uniformly and so wholeheartedly for this nonsense makes you distrust everything they might have to say.

I've devoted this much space to discussing the roots rock phenomenon because it is such a dominant concern of the rock press. It's an excellent example of how completely and passionately scribes can wander *miles* off base.

But, as they say, in other news . . .

The "Riffs" section in New York's weekly *Village Voice*, the carefully watched old warhorse of American rock criticism, underwent a major change when Robert Christgau, the feared/benevolent/highly opinionated dean of American rock criticism, gave up his editorship of it. Formerly, the Riffs section personified American rock criticism – it was highly misleading and almost laughably out of touch, self-important, largely ignored by the general public . . . yet the body of American rock critics and aspiring rock critics watched it with hawk-like intensity, scrutinizing every nuance and taking its stance at any given moment as gospel.

Tom Carson, formerly a first-rate television analyst for the *Voice* (and not a bad rock critic, either), replaced Christgau as editor of the Riffs section, and within six months, even rock critics weren't bothering to read it. Perhaps Carson lacked Christgau's authority, but more probably, he further cemented and encouraged the existing relationship between Riffs and the rest of the world: more ossified and predictable opinions, and an almost unreal paranoia of music that utilised instrumental or structural innovation, especially if it was British.

The brightest point in the last year may have been the emergence of *Spin* magazine, a monthly glossy mag published by Bob Guccione Jr, the son of the man behind *Penthouse*. *Spin* offers the most straightforward, loving, and investigative rock criticism going. They write about interesting things, new things, and different things in an unpretentious and highly readable manner. They also write about *old* things in precisely the same caring way. Add to this a modern and striking graphic sense, worthy of European fashion mags and architectural digests, and you've got the best high visibility rock publication now available. *Spin* was probably intended to compete with *Rolling Stone*, but they're already miles ahead of that useless, hateful and ugly industry-and-coke dictated rag. *Spin* is a clear and simple magazine; the staff genuinely likes music (more than it likes the music industry, which is a great sign), and it shows. Pretence, smugness, and attitude may come in time, but they're not evident yet.

Matter began upgrading itself from first class fanzine to thorough and glossy mag; they seem to be attempting to fill the void created by the disappearance of the *NY Rocker*, the industry-orientation of *US Rock* (formerly *Boston Rock*), and the Brit music press's consistent inability to get the story straight on what is going on in the States. *Matter* tries real hard, but aside from some striking writing, they've fallen prey to the rah-rah American syndrome. Their Anglophobia, though in some ways an understandable reaction to the rampant Anglophilia of the past decade or so, often borders on xenophobic hysteria; and reviews of the Smiths, f'rinstance, accompanies this ever present Anglophobia with a disturbing and pronounced homophobia (it seems that gays – not to mention feminists – and American roots rock really don't mix). Smithsphobia was very common in American fanzines in 1985.

Two fanzines, however, that caught the eye and made consistently on-target observations about what was really going on in the States were *The Big Takeover* and *Conflict*. Both are highly opinionated, but at least their opinions are original. And both are very supportive of the music that the editors believe in, regardless of the rest of the industry's stance on those groups or artists. If I had to recommend any place to *start* getting the real score on the States, I would probably recommend *Spin* (which, unlike *Rolling Stone* or the great body of the American rock media, isn't afraid of – dreaded words – innovators! Blacks! Sensitive Men! Free-thinking Women!) and *The Big Takeover* (c/o 249 Eldridge St., Apt. 14, NY, NY10002.)

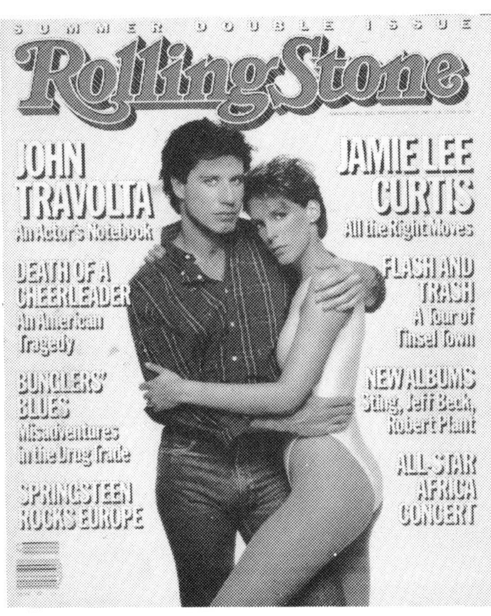

BOOKS

■ Reviewed by sundry readers

BIOGRAPHIES

ACCOMPANYING THE POLICE Mick St. Michael *(Proteus)*

Whether the omnipresent split stories are true or not, it's been over two years since the Police released an album and not much less since they played together live. With Sting's re-emergence as a solo artist, this is a timely reminder of the making of one of the world's finest pop/rock bands to emerge since a certain Merseyside combo in the sixties. Coincidentally, the book begins by recounting the Police's appearance before 67,000 people at New York's Shea Stadium in August 1983, a milestone in the threesome's career which saw them reach the same pinnacle as had the Beatles nearly two decades earlier. And if the comparison is laid to rest in subsequent chapters, the point has still been made, with the author's readable and concise style leading you to similar conclusions. All three Policemen get roughly equal coverage, with plenty of detail on their individual ventures. All in all a worthy tribute – and one good enough to serve as a eulogy should those rumours prove true. (MH)

BEATLE! THE PETE BEST STORY Pete Best & Patrick Doncaster *(Plexus)*
THE LIFE AND TIMES OF LITTLE RICHARD Charles White *(Pan)*
JAGGER Carey Schofield *(Futura)*

The Beatles story is as famous as that of the Nativity by now, and has been told by all disciples from wives to road managers to one-night-stands to people who were once in an elevator with Brian Epstein's chaffeur.

The ignoble name of Pete Best has become not so much a name as a plight; "He was the Pete Best of such and such," people say to denote someone dumped unceremoniously just before the combo in question hit the big time. Now he has "broken a twenty-year silence and becomes the first Beatle to tell the full story of his experiences in those early years."

We learn that John Lennon could be offensive when drunk and that the Reeperbahn is full of tarts. If we did not already know these banal facts as well as our two times table, there might be some point in telling them – but not much. Altogether, *Beatle!* is as lucid, original and gripping as any given drunk singing 'My Way' at closing time.

The Little Richard book, though, is a revved up revelation; telling you everything you ever suspected about the tooting fruity (his major vices being cocaine – "My nose got big enough to back a diesel truck in, unload it and drive it right out again" – and boys – "I had this boy with fifteen inches. I tried to have sex with him in my rectum. I think I know how women feel when they are having a baby"). He beats Albert Goldman to the draw, leaving no stone unturned whether talking about Buddy Holly ("He was huge! I've never seen anybody that big in my life!"), his masturbation habits (eight times a day batting average: talk about a sticky wicket), his voyeurism (adds new realms to the phrase "just looking") or orgies that really do sound like something to write home (or to *Forum*) about as opposed to the dreary and furtive Hamburg legovers the Beatles went in for.

Little Richard's monologues are in the rambling, poetic, half-mad, repetitive style of the best Baptist call and response preaching; he is sharp about the decision made to defuse the sexual threat of the black man – a process repeated successfully today with Prince and Jackson. "We decided my image should be crazy and way out, so the adults would think I was harmless." He is also well aware of the poetry and emotion of poverty in motion – pulling wood off the family home to feed the dying fire in deepest Georgia winter.

While the Richard papers are lively and fluent, Charles White's text is almost indecently rapturous. Little Richard is "an uncontrollable genius whose influence on Western culture has been incalculable", his story "epitomizes man's crucial struggle – the battle between the good and evil that exists in all of us." Pompous rubbish; Little Richard was a big bright demented firework and little more. When Mr White is not being contrary, he is being confused. One minute Little Richard is being pushed as a victim of and a crusader against repressive racist America and then before you can say "Awapbopaloobopalopbamboom" Mr White is claiming "Little Richard IS America."

Guilt and sexual incontinence finally forced Little Richard into the arms of the final great dark man, God; he now says that rock'n'roll is "demonic. A lot of the beats in today's music are taken from voodoo, from the voodoo drums." Which is exactly what the North Alabama White Citizens Council said thirty years ago when they first heard his records. If Little Richard had listened to them, he could have saved an awful lot of time and energy. There's lots about de Devil towards the end; some transcripts of his sermons (mostly gabble about the evils of homosexuality and a woman's place) and lots of testimonies from the sublime – Muhammad Ali – to the ridiculous – Kenny Everett – to the effect that Little Richard is perfect. Graven idols, anyone?

Mick Jagger emerges from Carey Schofield's book as a pouting Sphinx without a riddle; really just a cipher that any big silly bratty ism – Satanism, Maoism, mysticism, capitalism – could momentarily occupy and colour, the Centrepoint of pop. The birds, the booze, the Mars bars; also lots about Mr Jagger's legendary stinginess and lachrymosity. Along with Bobby Charlton, Jagger is one of the great weepers of our time – weeps when he first sees his performance in films, weeps when busted, weeps when arrested. When he was in jail for a couple of weeks on account of a phial of Italian pep pills, Marianne Faithfull visited him whereupon he began, yes, to weep. She told him to pull himself together; when *Marianne Faithfull* tells *you* to pull yourself together, you know you're a suitable case for treatment.

Carey Schofield's writing is fluent, frivolous and feisty – some would say bitchy. Minimal respect is given to the subject, and minimal lyric analysis indulged in. A common mistake in recent years is to believe that everything means something; the fact is that many things mean nothing, and Mick Jagger is one of them. What is most interesting about him are his girlfriends. Realizing this, Miss Schofield has made sure that her book reads like one long gossip column. Of course those afflicted with the reverent, quiet-in-the-library respect for pop won't approve, but this really is something like the perfect pop biography. (JB)

BEATLEMANIA: The History of the Beatles on Film. An Illustrated Filmography (The Beatles, Volume 4) Bill Harry *(Virgin)*

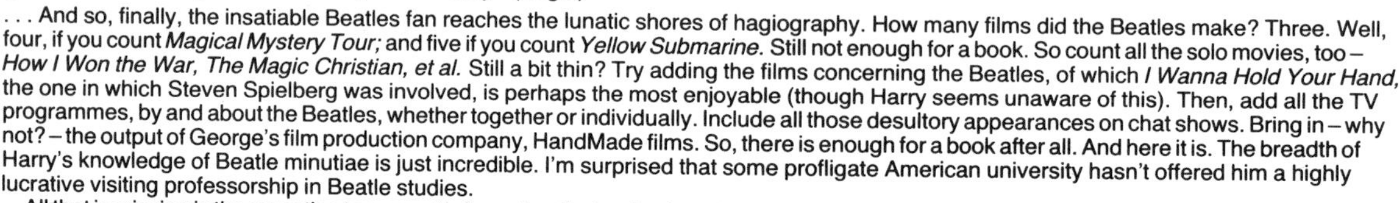

. . . And so, finally, the insatiable Beatles fan reaches the lunatic shores of hagiography. How many films did the Beatles make? Three. Well, four, if you count *Magical Mystery Tour;* and five if you count *Yellow Submarine.* Still not enough for a book. So count all the solo movies, too – *How I Won the War, The Magic Christian, et al.* Still a bit thin? Try adding the films concerning the Beatles, of which *I Wanna Hold Your Hand,* the one in which Steven Spielberg was involved, is perhaps the most enjoyable (though Harry seems unaware of this). Then, add all the TV programmes, by and about the Beatles, whether together or individually. Include all those desultory appearances on chat shows. Bring in – why not? – the output of George's film production company, HandMade films. So, there is enough for a book after all. And here it is. The breadth of Harry's knowledge of Beatle minutiae is just incredible. I'm surprised that some profligate American university hasn't offered him a highly lucrative visiting professorship in Beatle studies.

All that is missing is the expertise to present information that varies from the all-too-familiar (the Beatles' first film was *A Hard Day's Night*) to the dismally recondite (a promotional video of 'Mary Had A Little Lamb' was broadcast on *The Flip Wilson Show* in the US on 12 October 1972) in a lively and readable manner. Everything is imparted without one felicitous phrase or a single shaft of wit. Dull? The book is the quintessence of dullness. Every true Beatle fan should recoil in horror. We loved the Beatles precisely because they banished dullness from our lives. Perhaps Harry needed a co-author. As it stands, this would have rated only two stars in his previous book. (BW)

PAPERBACK WRITERS: The History of the Beatles in Print. An Illustrated Bibliography (The Beatles, Volume 3) Bill Harry *(Virgin)*

There has indeed been an awful lot written about the Beatles, the first two volumes in this series included. Here, every little published thing is listed, assessed and rated, on a scale of from one to five stars, by the genial Bill Harry. The problem is that, considering the surfeit of lamentable literature that's come out, he's never as trenchant as he ought to be. The result is that the handful of genuinely good books – the Carr/Tyler *Illustrated Record,* Nicholas Schaffner's *The Beatles Forever,* Michael Braun's *Love Me Do,* Philip Norman and Hunter Davies, of course, and a few others – do not stand out, as they should, like electricity pylons at the North Pole. The cutting edge of constructive criticism is missing. Twenty years' worth of books and magazines are listed in order of publication (1964-84). The information is exhaustive, the commentaries exhausting. (BW)

BOY GEORGE Scott Cohen *(Corgi)*
BOY GEORGE Merle Ginsberg *(New English Library)*
PRINCE Steven Ivory *(Bantam)*

Three scanty "biographies" angled around "image" and not a lot else: two alarmingly similar books about "the sensation of the eighties" and one about, er, "the sensation of the eighties". The first "sensation of the eighties" is a man called Boy George. But *is* he a man? Who knows? Certainly not this pair of authors who use the word "outrageous" quite a lot, dwell on the "gender-bender" phenomenon with hefty and indescribably boring passages on frocks and make-up, and scoff haughtily at the reactions of the tabloid press to G O'Dowd. The filth! The fury! So *what*? From the soaraway *Sun,* the *Star,* the *National Enquirer* and others, one learns nothing more than that Boy George was a geezer who got famous by wearing frocks. From Cohen and Ginsberg one learns it all over gain at greater, more boring length with ghastly blurry black-and-white photos which – in books that talk about nothing but "style'n'image" – seems a trifle batty.

The second "sensation of the eighties" is a man called Prince. But *is* he a man? Who knows? He used to do obscene things in knickers on stage but he doesn't any more. What does *this* prove? Steven Ivory, according to the back-cover blurb, will help one to "Unravel The Shroud Of Mystery Surrounding Prince And Discover . . ." Discover what? Absolutely nothing, of course. Ivory does lots of "exclusive interviews" with Prince's "closest associates" who spill such earth-shattering beans as the fact that Prince – gasp! – "seems kinda lonely". Don't we all? . . . (TH)

ELVIS COSTELLO: The Illustrated Disco/Biography Geoff Parkyn *(Omnibus)*

Did you know that Costello had released seventy-nine singles and twenty-two albums? And that's not including the fifteen compilations on which his work appears. The assiduous collector of the complete Costello catalogue will want to know about all of them; the absolutely assiduous collector of the c.C.c. could not possibly bear to be without the thirty-two bootlegs either . . .

An indispensable guide for indefatigable devotees. (BW)

ERIC CLAPTON: A Biography John Pidgeon *(Vermillion)*

A thorough, efficient, tidily-written biography, originally published in 1976 and now updated. Meticulous research and illuminating assessments of the records; the book does, however, deserve an index. (BW)

ERIC CLAPTON: The Illustrated Disco/Biography Marc Roberty & Chris Welch *(Omnibus Press)*

Diligently listed herein is every scrap of vinyl of which it could truly be said that EC was here; as well as a few bits – these are classified as "rumours" – where he might, perhaps, not have been here after all. (BW)

CROSBY, STILLS & NASH Dave Zimmer *(Omnibus Press)*

The back cover offers a quote from Graham Nash: "This book is as close to the truth as you're going to get." It doesn't say how close to the truth it is, of course, and I suppose it would be asking too much to get the full story or at least contradictions of the rumours. On the negative side, there isn't enough here about Neil Young, without any doubt a more fascinating character than any of the trio with whom he occasionally linked up; but to balance that omission (and Young's story has been pretty well covered by last year's Johnny Rogan epic), there is some heartfelt stuff about David Crosby and his trials and tribulations. If you care about these relics of the early seventies you'll enjoy this book which at least chooses subjects with some depth and history. Certainly worth perusing if you still play 'Suite: Judy Blue Eyes'. (JT)

DARYL HALL/JOHN OATES – DANGEROUS DANCES Nick Tosches *(St Martin's Press)*

The jacket is drab, the enormous number of pictures (some possibly very interesting) are rarely captioned and there are numerous drawings by Daryl Hall which for the most part aren't captioned either. The story itself is curiously meaningless to a Briton, largely because Hall & Oates really don't mean that much here, and the approach by the author is somewhat less analytical than might have been expected. Having said that, the splendid Nick Tosches does from time to time make the reader feel the need to play a track by H & O and that's the mark of a good writer. There are some interesting items, like the fact that Hall actually got to know the Temptations and was himself in a band known as the Temptones; that the duo knew John Belushi; that Hall values a first edition of Aleister Crowley (fetch the garlic, please), and so on. Their transition from being produced to producing themselves is well observed, and there's a certain amount of interesting personal fax and info, but little on Gulliver (Hall was in this group), Elvis Costello (Hall duetted with EC and with Diana Ross – how did these collaborations occur?), or the ratio of Hall:Oates vis à vis songwriting, singing lead, whether the duo play more than one instrument. It is, however, nice to know which albums the duo don't like. Not bad, but a touch disappointing, possibly due to the comparative drabness of the subject matter. (JT)

THE DECADE OF THE WHO: "My Generation". A History in Music and Photographs
Introduction and notes on the songs by Pete Townshend *(Wise Publications)*

The unwieldy title almost says it all. Herein is contained the music to forty Who songs. Townshend has contributed background notes on several of them together with a brief introduction which, suspiciously, seems to have been written seven years prior to the book's publication. There are also a number of fascinating period photographs. (BW)

DURAN DURAN LIVE Philip Kamin and Peter Goddard *(St Martin's Press)*
DURAN DURAN: The First Four Years of the Fab Five Neil Gaiman *(Proteus Books)*

Definitely the worst of the brace is the Kamin/Goddard effort. Kamin, the photographer, tops the bill, and provides . . . um . . . a lot of pictures, from which we learn that even pretty boys, taken live, have shiny noses, spots, gloopy expressions and ratty hair (these rather suit Andy Taylor); also that Simon Le Bon and Roger Taylor have bad teeth. All this is quite reassuring, if not very attractive on a full colour (sort of pinko-grey) life-size double spread. From the words we learn very little, except that the rock and jazz critic of the *Toronto Star* doesn't know how to spell Suzie (*sic*) and the Banshees, quotes from a paper called the *London Daily Star* (ever heard of it?) and does a nice line in portentous one-sentence paragraphs: "This is where it all began"; "Le Bon was waiting for them" – that sort of thing. We also learn (from Nick Rhodes) that "black musicians have his huge sense of rhythm"; from John Taylor that *Seven And The Ragged Tiger* is the funkiest a white band have ever been, and from Goddard himself that Duran Duran are Verdi to Phil Spector's "Wagnerisms". On reflection this must be worth ten dollars.

Too many misprints for nigh on six quid in Neil Gaiman's book, and we don't need to have it explained that Brighton is a "South coast seaside resort" – but let's be charitable, everybody wants to crack America. Still, is Nick Rhodes' young lady called Julie Anne Friedman or Juliana Freedman? Both on page seventeen – I think we should be told. Otherwise Gaiman gives us a lot of interesting biographical trivia – the Ladybird book of Duran Duran, good for beginners – and coins a great word, Jamesbondian. The intellectual analysis of the videos suffers by having no stills to illustrate it (they're all in last year's *The Book of Words*) but reveals that Sri Lankan extras in "native costume" were paid for their appearance in the videos with a ball-point each. Ho hum. The rest of the book is conveniently chronological, with no confusing hopping about, and provides pictures of everybody's wedding except Andy Taylor's. Also, Gaiman says that the girls don't scream at Andy as much as they do at the others, which is a great shame. He was beginning to grow on me. (LY)

DYLAN Text by Jonathan Cott *(Vermillion)*

Although Cott supplies the commentary on Dylan's life and art (and thus gets his name on the spine) he'd no doubt admit that this is really the ultimate picture book (and like all classy picture books it doesn't come cheap – £20). Produced in a large format on the best paper, it's a tribute to Rolling Stone's photo researchers, appropriately captioned and impeccably designed. All the Dylans are here: the chubby Minnesota kid making his first record; the cool ruler of *Highway 61* in the suede jacket and shades; the blinking family man of Big Pink and *Nashville Skyline;* these and many others dramatically emphasize how this curious-looking individual has been a far greater influence on "style" than any number of Boy Georges. Robbie Robertson's pretty cool, too. (DH)

ELVIS AND GLADYS Elaine Dundy *(Weidenfeld & Nicolson)*
KING! WHEN ELVIS ROCKED THE WORLD Pete Nelson *(Proteus)*
ELVIS: THE GOLDEN ANNIVERSARY TRIBUTE Richard Peters *(Souvenir Press)*

Elvis Presley is still fascinating: not simply because of the nature and scale of his achievement but because he existed in such isolation that very few of the millions of words written about him have succeeded in evoking a substantial human being behind the smokescreen of myth. Elaine Dundy's painstaking research in Tennessee and Mississippi has radically redefined the accepted picture of Presley's roots, childhood and early career. As the title implies, the book re-examines standard assumptions concerning Presley's relationship with his mother Gladys, and rejects the usual simplistic, stereotyped notion of her as a classic Freudian smotherer. In the process, the slippery, manipulative Colonel Tom Parker emerges as a more hideous and ruthless figure than ever: no previous Presley biographer has gone nearly as far in order to explain the nature of the methods by which the ol' Colonel controlled his client. Compassionate, insightful and at times downright chilling, *Elvis And Gladys* is unquestionably the definitive account of the early stages of Presley's career, the period when he produced most of his most crucial work. Pete Nelson's lavishly illustrated treatment of the Presley fifties cannot hope to compete, and Richard Peters' fannish drivel is literally not worth reading. (CSM)

EURYTHMICS: Sweet Dreams Johnny Waller & Steve Rapport *(Virgin Books)*

This "definitive" biography takes the reader through the bewildering maze of Dave 'n' Annie's visual styles, musical wiles and passionate trials in a highly readable fashion. It does a fair job, in other words, of explaining the long-term origins of overnight success. The story is helped along by the fact that Dave's a bit of a card and Annie's a bit of a one. Photographer/researcher Rapport provides something more than the usual photographic fare and designer Laurence Stevens (who is also responsible for the group's LP covers) designs sympathetically. Dave 'n' Annie have looked and sounded like a pair of kippers before now, but they also make excellent pop records – this book tells you why. (Pete Clark)

FLEETWOOD MAC Steve Clarke *(Proteus)*

There appears to be a feeling among rock book publishers that major record sales equate with major book sales. Unfortunately, save for the case of hard rock bands whose fans will buy just about anything connected with their favourite act, this is largely inaccurate, mostly because many of the biggest selling rock stars are rather colourless people who have often led mundane lives. And so it is with this F Mac biog. There's nothing about Mick Fleetwood's alleged bankruptcy, no mention of the foul rumour that his African LP was recorded at the Manor Studio in Oxfordshire, which was supposedly booked without staff for a week. Peter Green's rather curious views of his years of fame are certainly mentioned, although hardly expanded into the good story they actually make, and overall there's precious little in the way of anything unsavoury. If this had been an authorized biography, the lack of controversy would be understandable; as it is, there is little here that an averagely interested student of rock doesn't already know. Shame really. (JT)

FRANKIE SAY – THE RISE OF FRANKIE GOES TO HOLLYWOOD Danny Jackson *(Omnibus Press)*

Just when we thought the complete history of the Frankies had been written on T-shirts, here's the "first in-depth study" to put us right. Mr Jackson bravely takes his machete to the undergrowth of hype and promptly disappears from critical view, muttering "it's all in the music". It had certainly better be, for outside the music lies a grim territory of pouting buttocks, good old scallywaggery and Morley's book of other people's sayings. The pictures do nothing to relieve the gloom, being composed of endless publicity mug shots and a selection of murky real-life snaps. Clocking in at three singles, the discography must rate as the shortest on record (*sic*). (Pete Clark)

BILLY JOEL: An Illustrated Biography Debbie Geller & Tom Hibbert *(Virgin)*

An early entrant in the Joel stakes, which tells those who want to know about the Hassles and Attila (Joel's pre-solo recording groups). It doesn't really confirm the long-held rumour that the immortal Shadow Morton used a young Joel as a session pianist on several Shangri-La's hits, unfortunately, but maybe that isn't as important as Joel's up-and-down career, his being managed by his wife, and such topics as his relationship with Christie Brinkley. There's a certain amount of investigation of the meaning of some of the songs (perhaps not enough) and a lot of pictures of Joel doing nothing much except looking rather like he looks in all the other pictures. Pretty much your average rock biography, really – no enormous revelations, no major controversy. If you enjoy Billy Joel's music, you'll probably be happy with the basics, but if anyone expects to gain any new insights from this book, they're in for a let-down, as its subject, in spite of an undoubted talent as a singer/songwriter of distinction, is really not much more exciting a person than the bloke next door. (JT)

JOY DIVISION & NEW ORDER – PLEASURES AND WAYWARD DISTRACTIONS
Brian Edge *(Omnibus Press)*

Joy Division's biographers to date have both adopted the same formula – lots of white space, the odd bold capital among the headings, strictly geometrical design and lots of little postage-stamp-sized pictures dotted about the place. And no – definitely *no* – colour. If you, like Omnibus's earnest blurb writer, truly believe that Joy Division and New Order are "the two most important and influential groups to have emerged in the UK since the Sex Pistols", you'll probably already own this: Wham! fans and cynics are unlikely to be converted either by the grey, unimaginative concept or Mr Edge's po-faced text. (MH)

THE KINKS: The Official Biography Jon Savage *(Faber & Faber)*
THE KINKS: The Sound and the Fury Johnny Rogan *(Elm Tree)*

Biographies share one characteristic with buses: they often tend to arrive in pairs. Jon Savage's authorized volume was disowned by Ray Davies at the last minute but it's difficult to see why, since the author is almost appallingly discreet. Savage is an uncommonly acute observer, but here he seems to tiptoe round the edges of the more sensitive areas of the Kinks' career, treating the Davies' family life, the long-running quarrels within the band and the relationship between Ray and Dave Davies with the kind of deadpan respect brought to *Telegraph* reports of Cabinet dissension. These are exactly the topics which interest Johnny Rogan who, unencumbered by any desire to please Mr Davies, steams in with fists flying. Savage writes far more elegant prose than Rogan, and he is a far more sophisticated critic of both social and musical issues than Rogan can ever hope to be, but the excellent vintage photos and copious lyrical quotations in his book cannot conceal the fact that large chunks of the story appear to have been positively vetted. Rogan's book has a photo section that is scarcely more than a token, but by way of compensation he provides an exceptionally thorough discography. Read back-to-back, the two books combine to suggest that Ray and Dave will be continuing their adolescent scrapping until they're playing 'You Really Got Me' in their wheelchairs. (CSM)

BOB MARLEY: The Illustrated Disco/Biography Observer Station *(Omnibus Press)*

To attempt to catalogue every release from any Jamaican recording artist who has more than a quarter of an hour or so of professional history is a job few would envy, so to chronicle Bob Marley and his offshoots – solo Wailers, individual I-Threes, Tuff Gong Productions etc – over twenty years, through myriad dodgy domestic deals and two terms at Island requires dedication verging on fixation. Thankfully, by approaching his task with the wide-eyed zeal of the true obsessive, *NME's* Observer Station has saved many a nervous breakdown. Inevitably there are a few omissions, but what is there is much more than could be imagined. This meticulous listing is attractive and infinitely interesting – a must for anyone who has ever flirted with the legend that is Bob Marley. (LB)

MADONNA – LUCKY STAR Michael McKenzie *(Columbus Books)*

If you're one of those perverse people who, like me, delights in noting the unusually high incidence of left-handed guitarists in the more shoddily designed species of rock books you'll enjoy the spectacle of Madonna's beauty spot flitting from under one nostril to the other. And, truthfully, that's about the height of excitement this slim little volume offers. Did I say slim? How exactly they managed to stretch the life story of disco's latest diva to ninety-six pages is still beyond me – the extended remix, perhaps? – but a few blank pages and some dodgy design certainly helps. When Madonna, the lucky star, disappears down the inevitable black hole after her fifteen minutes of fame this book deserves to go with her. (MH)

MOTHER! IS THE STORY OF FRANK ZAPPA Michael Gray *(Proteus)*

Not the most covered subject (only *No Commercial Potential* by David Walley and *Zappalog* by a continental European whose name momentarily escapes me, before this), there is obviously room for more literature on Zappa, one of the most prolific LP makers of the last twenty years. Michael Gray, who was press officer for the label which released the *200 Motels* soundtrack, is a better choice than most to write it; but I suspect that the book was written some years ago, Gray updating it when he finally found a publisher. The early stuff is excellent, but coverage of more recent years (when admittedly less extra-musical newsworthy activity occurred) relies heavily on detailing FZ's music and lacks a certain amount of enthusiasm. However, since we have no ready comparative tome, it's difficult to know whether criticism is in order. What can certainly be criticised is the unaccountable assertion by Gray that Helsinki is in Iceland, especially unforgivable since Gray has been to Iceland. Quibbles apart, this is not a bad read if you have a faint interest in the subject and although it didn't make me want to dust off any FZ albums, at least it's not a Prince or Michael Jackson book. (JT)

THE MOTOWN STORY *(Orbis)*
MARVIN GAYE Sharon Davis *(Proteus)*
LIONEL RICHIE David Nathan *(Virgin)*

The Motown Story is, in fact, merely a collection of the essays which appeared in Orbis's part-work the *History of Rock* between the years 1981-83. The pieces are generally well researched and well written though some of the errors which appeared in the original texts have not been corrected. The piece on the Jacksons, for instance, repeats the myth that Diana Ross discovered them. She did not. Gladys Knight did. Ross was merely used to launch them because she was more popular in the white pop market and had a TV special to boot. I'd also suggest that four pages on the Four Seasons (yes, Seasons not Tops) somewhat exaggerates their importance in the grand scheme of Motown. Sharon Davis was for many years a Motown press officer but her brief biography of Gaye is wholly unrevealing, only mentions the fact that he was shot dead by his father in the introduction and with the publication in America of a Gaye biog by David Ritz has been made utterly redundant. Nor can I see much reward in toiling through Nathan's thin script of the life of Lionel, who despite his propensity for writing extremely commercial ballads and pop songs, comes over as a singularly ordinary – not to say downright dull – fellow. In all cases, stick to their recordings. (GB)

SIMON AND GARFUNKEL: A Musical Biography John Swenson *(WH Allen)*

The judicious book-buyer will have somewhat conservative expectations of this. What is the sub-title – a *musical* biography – other than a veiled admission that the author has done no first-hand research? Even on its own limited terms, however, the book is a crashing failure because Swenson has nothing of interest to say about the music. He does, admittedly, offer a comparison between the versions of 'The Big Bright Green Pleasure Machine' which appear on *Parsley, Sage, Rosemary & Thyme* and *The Paul Simon Songbook.* ("This was hardly one of the better songs on *Songbook,* but here it sounds great"). This is fascinating stuff, though only because 'Big Bright etc' didn't appear at all on *Songbook.*

The book compares poorly with Patrick Humphries' 1982 biography (*Bookends,* Proteus). Humphries provides interesting insights about the time Simon spent in England – producing an album for Jackson C Frank, for example – of which Swenson apparently knows nothing. Swenson blandly describes Kathy, the muse of much early Simon material, as "the mysterious Kathy". A journalist who'd done his job properly, like Humphries, would have been able to offer the admittedly prosaic information that she was a secretary from Hornchurch in Essex; proving, I suppose, that muses do live at the end of the District line.

Simon and Garfunkel does, however, have an excellent index. This allows the reader to check that the first reference to studio engineer Roy Halee ("from the beginning we sensed that he was very much on our side . . . we requested that [he] engineer again") is contradicted by the second one ("he was a young engineer . . . we didn't pay much attention to him").

Swenson also plumbs fresh depths in critical timidity. "*Bookends*," he writes, "is very arguably the finest Simon & Garfunkel album", Wow! The presence in a text of the word "arguably" indicates that the journalist is making a tendentious statement which he can't really justify, so he'd better qualify it. This unprecedented use of the phrase "very arguably" indicates either that the writer is making a statement he doesn't actually think is true, but which he's damned well determined to make anyway; or that he's lost contact with the basics of the English language. An appalling book. (BW)

SIMPLE MINDS – THE RACE IS THE PRIZE Alfred Bos *(Virgin)*

The second official Minds biography: the first was written by *Melody Maker's* Adam Sweeting, but never made it into print. So try this on for size . . . "Hope. Hope is a fly's turd on an empty page. Simple Minds are that empty page." That was on page one hundred and something: long before then, you get the sneaking suspicion that someone somewhere, backed the wrong horse. Design-wise, *Race* takes up where *The New Gold Dream* album left off – all illuminated lettering and biblical rubrics. But if you're looking for revelations, don't look here: the verbose Alfred, a native of Amsterdam, writes in a style only marginally more comprehensible than a Peter O'Sullevan commentary and about half as entertaining. Despite being in a field of one (who *did* nobble the opposition?), *The Race Is the Prize* remains a pretentious non-runner. (MH)

FRANK SINATRA: An American Classic John Rockwell *(Elm Tree)*

Frank Sinatra occupies a unique position on the cultural map of America: he is one of the century's most influential entertainers, he has been the confidant of Presidents and hoods alike, he is one of the few people to combine legitimate careers as actor and vocalist, and he has elevated the art of pop balladeers to heights inconceivable before he entered the field and proceeded to redefine it to his own specifications. John Rockwell is the first author to tackle the subject of Frank Sinatra from the perspective of someone who grew up during the rock'n'roll era, and he combines the critical disciplines of pop, rock, jazz and classical criticism to assess his subject both musically and socially. He presents a picture of a man who has merged the functions of popular artist and power broker, a man for whom elegance and power are indivisible. The book positively overflows with both colour and monochrome photographs – Sinatra already looked like Sinatra when he was nine-years-old – and the illustrations are a tribute to the man's unfaltering sense of visual style, just as the text is an eloquent testimonial to Sinatra's qualities as an artist and public figure, and his ability to stand naked when he sings or acts while living behind a mask. As such, the book is well-nigh flawless; unfortunately, it is also well-nigh unaffordable and will remain so until its emergence in paperback. A perfect gift for your Godfather. (CSM)

SPRINGSTEEN: No Surrender Kate Lynch *(Proteus)*
SPRINGSTEEN LIVE Philip Kamin & Peter Goddard *(New English Library)*

There's only one Springsteen book worth investing cash in and neither of these is it. Dave Marsh's *Born To Run* recounts the story and indulges in interpretation sparingly. Kate Lynch, on the other hand, had no access to her subject (a problem this) and finds herself forced between cannibalising Marsh's firsthand account and telling us at great length what Springsteen's songs are all about. This seems increasingly absurd. Here's an artist who goes to enormous lengths to prune his lyrics to the bone and then has to stand back and watch in horror as critics queue up to append copious footnotes at the end of each verse. Then they have the bloody front to applaud his brevity! *Springsteen Live* is comparatively painless. It's a photo-souvenir of the 1984-85 tour of America, interspersed with some amusing and readable observations on Springsteen's life, language and lore. Were it not designed in the most annoying possible fashion (pics upright and text on its side) I'd recommend it to anyone who couldn't get a ticket and wants to know what all the fuss was about. (DH)

BRUCE SPRINGSTEEN Peter Gambaccini *(Omnibus Press)*

An updated version of an earlier book which takes us up to the *Born In The USA* LP and international tour. A marvellously uncritical author takes the reader through every tune 'The Boss' has committed to vinyl, both lyrically and musically – exhaustive or exhausting, depending on your viewpoint. A sketchy life story is offered up in the gaps between amazing albums, but to be fair to the author, there doesn't seem to be all that much to Bruce except a monstrous decency. The book also features several million pictures of our hero (all b/w) and a discography. Needless to say, the reasons for the potentially disastrous three-year gap in his recording career are scarcely touched upon. (Pete Clark)

SPRINGSTEEN: Blinded By The Light Patrick Humphries and Chris Hunt *(Plexus)*

Another tome on the bosslike figure of Bruce Frederick Joseph Springsteen, the Italian Irishman with the Dutch moniker. The first part of the book gives the story to date (does this man ever go on a bender?) and ends up concentrating on the lyrics. The second part is a riot of Brucefax: list upon list of every gig played (sometimes which songs were sung), career milestones and TV appearances, songs composed, bootlegs, foreign releases, other peoples' songs covered etc, right down to the identity of the man who hand-tools those bosslike vests! Pleasantly designed in glorious black and white, this effort comes as near to being interesting as it is possible to be without being totally blinded by the bosslike luminescence. (Pete Clark)

THE THOMPSON TWINS – AN ODD COUPLE Rose Rouse *(Virgin)*

An official biography of the group which offers the usual advantages and disadvantages: to wit, access to the members and an almost complete lack of critical distance. The book tells the story from the beginning, when the seven-piece Thompsons peddled a distinctly difficult brand of angular dance music, to the hyper-successful eighties, when the music was smoothly tailored to fit.

Rose Rouse asks a series of sensible, saucy and idiotic questions and gets a corresponding set of answers. The Thompson Twins come across as beings with an occasional penchant for tub-thumping – ie. not desparately interesting. The photos, which comprise a large percentage of the book, consist of a seemingly endless series of dire poses, a handicap which the startlingly pedestrian layout does nothing to alleviate. Includes a discography. (Pete Clark)

U2 – STORIES FOR BOYS Dave Thomas *(Proteus)*

A solid if unexciting tome about a solid and unexciting band. Sensibly its author doesn't really attempt to justify the sensational jacket copy (*War* being one of the most influential albums of the past decade, etc), preferring instead to provide an obviously well-researched account of the clean-living Irish quartet's rise from fourth division bar-band obscurity to their current stadium status. Bono's sole presence on the cover betrays the sad fact that U2 don't score too highly in the visual appeal stakes – and no line-up changes in their eight years together makes captions for the team photos pretty much optional too – so even if the look of the book singularly fails to match its worthy text, then that's hardly Mr Thomas's fault. But as Everton found last season the double isn't easy to accomplish – and despite Proteus's usual mispaced passes (spelling errors, etc) and a positive own-goal of a title, scarf-waving U2 fans will find this package if not a convincing winner, certainly worth extra time. (MH)

WALK RIGHT BACK: The Story of the Everly Brothers Roger White *(Plexus)*

Few acts merit a thorough biography as much as the Everly Brothers. This, on the whole, is it. From their early days in the Kentucky coal-mining belt, to the much-publicized reunion as concert artists (hugely successful) and recording ones (comparatively unsuccessful), this book diligently covers all aspects of the careers of Don and Phil.

The family background is particularly interesting. Their father, Ike, was a local celebrity and minor country music name. Such work, however, was poorly rewarded. Ike and his wife, Margaret, endured considerable privation to ensure that neither the upbringing nor the education of their sons ever suffered. "They moved out of their house into an apartment where, to make ends meet, Ike was the caretaker and Margaret cleaned the stairs and hallways." Nevertheless, the family did know Chet Atkins, a contact who unlocked the door to Nashville for Don and Phil. After a difficult time in 1956, it was all systems go in the years following the release of 'Bye Bye Love' in May 1957. White carefully documents the world wide acclaim and the subsequent period of exasperating failure. The incident on the British tour in October 1962, when Don was flown home suffering from what a reticent press described as "nervous exhaustion" and Phil had to go it alone, is properly explained here: "Don had tried to commit suicide by taking drug overdoses." This presaged the beginning of their eclipse. Their stature as recording artists never recovered. White is sympathetic, but never sycophantic (though he is a little too indulgent of some of the less inspired music). He charts the growing distance between the brothers in the sixties – with Don inclining more to the rock environment, and Phil more to Las Vegas – right up to the absolute nadir, their "last" concert in 1973 at Knotts Berry Farm in Buena Park, California. And, of course, the happy postscript: reunion in 1983 and 1984.

One solitary blemish. The reader is told on page 67 that "they followed Elvis into the night-club circuit of Las Vegas, playing there for the first time in the summer of 1961"; and on page 100, by which time the narrative has moved on to 1969, "they had never played Las Vegas".

The book contains many interesting illustrations, a complete discography and a number of heartfelt tributes, foremost among which is Bob Dylan's: "We owe these guys everything." (BW)

WHAM! YOUNG AND GUNNING Barry Grant *(Zomba Books)*

The touching story of two young bloods from Bushey, Hertfordshire, who met when they were twelve and are still together; Georgious Panayatiou (nick-named "Yog") and Andrew Ridgeley (called simply "bastard" by Georgious). Georgious used to be very fat, had steel-rimmed glasses and one very bushy eyebrow "that went right across, although he plucks the middle of it now", reveals Andrew. Georgious changed his looks and his name to George Michael, and shortly afterwards became a sex symbol. "Call them opportunists – they weren't. Call them lucky – they weren't" protests Barry Grant (a mite too much) before detailing how the boys scrapped a ska band they were in called the Executives and released 'Wham Rap' in the wake of 'The Message'. Young and cunning, they left all that behind and we discover that "the sun-tanned Wham! are the real Wham!". George emerges as likeably arrogant, while Andrew has a penchant for observations like "No one can define creativity. If you don't have it, you can't be expected to understand it". We get to hear about Andrew's nose-job and how the boys wind up the gutter press about their love lives, but Barry Grant is apparently an old mate from Bushey and sheds little light on the Wham! phenomenon. (Peter Culshaw)

STEVIE WONDER – The Illustrated Disco/Biography Rick Taylor *(Omnibus Press)*

Compared with the Bob Marley lists, this one has the edge. Presumably Motown Records write things down. Counting re-issues and re-packages, few artists can have racked up the sheer volume of titles Stevie Wonder has, yet they are all here. Details of track listings and timings, and many line-ups and chart placings, are displayed for every song the man has written, recorded, not recorded, deleted, produced or played on since he was twelve – all that is missing is a chapter entitled Projects Thought About For A Long Time. Even the short preface describing Wonder's thirty-five years turns up some surprises. Buy this book to discover all you ever wanted to know about the works of Stevie Wonder, or simply to win a fortune in your local by betting on what his real name is – it's *not* Steveland Morris. (LB)

PAUL YOUNG Garry Johnson *(Proteus)*

At thirty-two pages, not so much a book as a magazine – but then its subject had only one solo LP to his name at the time it was written. Talking of magazines, the design of this rather anorexic publication inevitably brings to mind *Smash Hits,* the teen mag whose art department has unwittingly played a large part in shaping the style of record sleeves and rivals alike in the past five or six years. But what *Smash Hits* – and those of its rivals that still survive – realized early on in the game was that patronising one's teenage readership is a recipe for disaster. And frankly a book that fails to identify Paul's backing musicians correctly in photo captions and confuses clothes designer Antony Price with songwriter Anthony Moore (composer of Young's 'No Parlez') won't score too many points with the man's youthful fans – who will have better things to do with their money than buy this. When you consider that *Smash Hits* gives you nearly twice as many pages at around one quarter the cost, you don't need O'Level Maths to conclude that it just doesn't add up. (MH)

AUTOBIOGRAPHIES

TONY BLACKBURN – THE LIVING LEGEND: An Autobiography (as told to Cheryl Garnsey) *(WH Allen)*

In which T Blackburn confirms what we all knew or strongly suspected: that disc jockeys are the most charmless of people. The rugby club-type romps aboard the pirate ships (no "poofters" pur*lease!*), Tone's sizzlin' nites of sin with "leggy blondes" (who, he confesses, he doesn't really "care about"), the supermarket openings . . . Our ex-public schoolboy hero's marriage goes awry and he ends up hooked on Valium without – it seems – very many (or *any*) friends apart from his soul records. In this "autobiography", Blackburn emerges as a shallow and rather pathetic figure hiding behind some awful jokes ("This boat's listing to one side. I did say listing." (?)) and a towering conceit. It's all very sad. (TH)

PICTORIAL

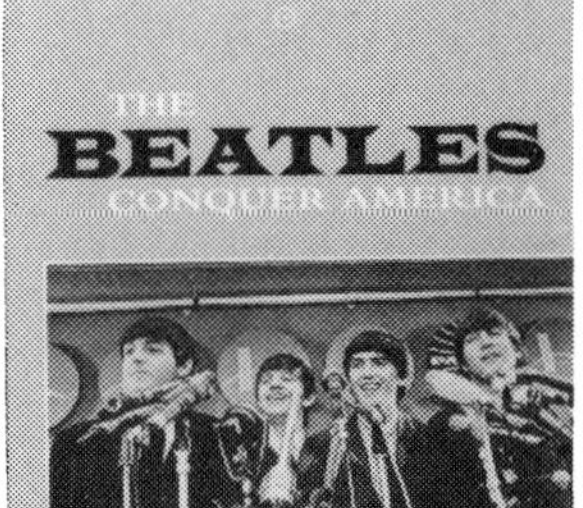

THE BEATLES CONQUER AMERICA   Dezo Hoffmann *(Virgin)*

The pictures (all black and white) in this book were taken during the Beatles' first American tour in early 1964 and their little-documented Paris dates preceding it. Hoffmann was the Beatles "official" photographer up till 1965 and has clearly put this detailed and witty account of the Fab Four at their youthful best together with great affection. The photographs record literally every moment, on and off stage, from their first appearance on the Ed Sullivan show to Ringo drying out his money after falling into a Miami canal. Each picture is painstakingly explained together with a really entertaining and personal account of the whole tour. Captivating. (KL)

GENESIS? FROM ONE FAN TO ANOTHER   Armando Gallo *(Omnibus Press)*

Apart from the terrible cover, this is as comprehensive a pictorial biography as any fanatical (and I believe they usually are) follower of Genesis could wish for. Every year in the life of the band, from the first demo made at school in 1966 up to their most recent performances in 1984, is documented with spectacular, mostly live photographs, album sleeves and early tour programmes, accompanied by a month-by-month account of major events in quotes and brief extracts from the author's 1980 biography *Genesis: I Know What I Like*. Well produced and interesting. (KL)

INTERFERENCE   Nick Rhodes *(Michael Joseph)*

In his introduction, "A Monologue Between You And I" (excuse me, but a monologue between two people is impossible; it's a dialogue), Nick explains that his "images represent a journey through time and space; utilizing the ubiquitous tube of culture . . ." Translation: a collection of polaroids taken from television sets around the world. Fine; people have been taking snaps off the box for years, but no one has yet had the gall to publish a whole book of them. The pictures themselves, with the help of some deft graphics, look like early seventies LP sleeves and make a colourful enough little package but do not, as the blurb on the back cover says, result in a "a new generation of photographic art". Could even the most devoted Duran Duran fan take such titles as "She Was Niagara", "Vertigo In Children" and "Gadgets That Are Good" seriously? I doubt it. (KL)

HIT PARADE   Harry Hammond & Gered Mankowitz *(Plexus)*

Taken from the exhibition Pop People that was held at the London Photographers' Gallery in 1981, this book records in full page portraits the changing face of the pop performer from the early fifties. Harry Hammond's marvellous black-and-white publicity shots take us up to 1963 and include Johnnie Ray, Paul Anka and most other major Brylcreem users of the day in suitably square-jawed poses. Gered Mankowitz's pictures span the mid-sixties up to the present day and show the change in approach to photographing pop stars that occurred when bands established themselves as characters rather than crooners. From the wide-angle leers of Free and Jimi Hendrix through platform soles up to Adam Ant and ABC, it's as much a history of fashion as of music. A bit pricy (£12) since you'll have to buy a coffee table to put it on as well. (KL)

SPRINGSTEEN   Lynn Goldsmith *(Sidgwick & Jackson)*

Ninety well-presented pages (no text) of colour photos taken by the tousle-haired hero's ex-girlfriend around the time of his fourth album *Darkness On The Edge Of Town* – although he looks exactly the same now. Straightforward but excellent pictures feature the man live, at home and in "urban landscape" situations but don't tell you anything you didn't already know, ie Bruce leaps about a lot on stage, doesn't shave very often and appears to wear his jeans even in bed. Assuming there isn't much else to know, then good value for fans. (KL)

THE ROLLING STONES   Dezo Hoffmann *(Vermillion)*

Similar to he Beatles book, but with minimal text, this chronicles ten years of the Stones' activities from one of their first nights at London's Crawdaddy Club in 1963 onwards. Loads of portraits and informal shots taken at parties and recording sessions, together with coverage of their early appearances on *Ready Steady Go!* up to the infamous Hyde Park concert after Brian Jones' death in 1969. Always fascinating to see chubby-chopped boys change into wasted rock stars, it's a thorough and exciting history. Excellent value. (KL)

SATISFACTION: The Rolling Stones 1965-1967   Gered Mankowitz *(St Martins Press)*

An interesting comparison to Dezo Hoffmann's work, it's a much grittier collection of photographs that really capture the sullen intensity of the Rolling Stones at the most significant period of their career. Starting with their first American tour, it includes many behind-the-scenes pictures and some sadly pathetic shots of the Stones at their most dissipated, while recording *Their Satanic Majesties*. Gered Mankowitz's brittle acocunt of his relationship with the band is enlightening and finally almost distressing. Very well put together and worth having. (KL)

HEAVY METAL

BENATAR   Doug Magee *(Proteus)*

A surprisingly interesting effort by American freelancer Magee who, it appears, preceded this work with a book on Michael Jackson and two volumes about Stateside jurisprudence. His style is fast but he only seems to know about two other songstresses – Judy Garland and Janis Joplin – or at least these are the only comparisons he seems to use to La Benatar. Her private life isn't anywhere near as interesting as those two ladies, thank God for her sake, but Magee delves well enough into her early life, her relationship with her opera-singing mother, her band, manager and family and devotes a goodly chunk of space to a critical appraisal of the body of her work, not to mention the workings of her body. Magee does well enough with an only fairly interesting subject. (BH)

DEF LEPPARD – An Illustrated Biography   Chris Welch *(Omnibus Press)*

I was amazed when I saw this because it seemed that Leppard had only been round for about five minutes and hadn't really done very much. Having read it my opinion hasn't changed too much. Yes, I know their third album *Pyromania* went berserk in the American charts and established them as an international act, but then how many other international acts are there around at the moment who don't have too much to commend them above anyone else? Leppard always struck me as sparky, talkative and opinionated blokes but here they come across like any other bunch of old bores. It's author Welch who is at fault; he describes several tracks from *Pyromania* in this book as "sturdy and workmanlike" and the same applies to his performance, but with "stolid" substituted for "sturdy". It is, in short, boring – he's certainly capable of much better than this race-against-the-clock hackwork. (BH)

HAMMER OF THE GODS: The Led Zeppelin Saga   Stephen Davis *(Sidgwick & Jackson)*
LED ZEPPELIN: The Book   Chris Welch *(Proteus)*

Led Zeppelin were the band that professionalised rock 'n' roll: they had the best-recorded guitar and drum sound of their era and they played the most relentlessly phallocentric rock that ever existed. Two books emerge based on their history. Chris Welch tells the story of four nice lads who played wonderful music, made a lot of money and gave endless enjoyment to millions despite going off the rails a bit and falling victim to some extremely bad luck. Stephen Davis' tale deals with two cynical music-biz veterans and a heavy manager who pick up an eager, gormless drummer and vocalist and terrorize the world with black magic, drugs, debauchery and sheer, vicious savagery. Both writers bend over backwards to make their respective points; Stephen Davis' account is both far more melodramatic and far better written, while Welch's reluctance to examine the darker side of the band combines with his resentment of most post-'76 pop to preclude him saying anything particularly interesting. The last chapter of each book is entitled 'Coda'. (CSM)

IRON MAIDEN – Running Free   Garry Bushell and Ross Halfin *(Zomba Books)*

This is one of the best, if not the *best*, rock biographies ever. It's an official biog and it's obvious from the mass of detail – both from intimate and public domain – that Bushell was given full access by Maiden, manager Rod Smallwood and, seemingly, just about everyone else who ever had anything to do or say about them. But, better than that, Bushell's style is passionate, witty and outrageous, not unlike Maiden's, thinking about it. Halfin's pix are excellent too – about twenty-five pages of full colour and a ton of black and whites, onstage, offstage, backstage and all over the shop. A brilliant piece of work. (BH)

MASTERS OF METAL Lee Martyn *(Zomba Books)*

In the ever-pliable history of rock 'n' roll, particularly the hyperbole-laden land of metal, every single bit of documentation contradicts itself. Take six different items – a contemporary interview, a historical one, an album sleeve note, a record company biography, the reminiscence of the artist's manager and a letter from the A&R man who first signed him or her – and they'll give six different dates for the artist's first date. Anyone who takes this kind of thing on deserves a medal. Aside from covering forty-eight bands in detail – including old chums like AC/DC, Black Sabbath and ZZ Top – Martyn gives a general rundown on Euro-metal, as invented by *Sounds*. There's no unnecessary detail, a welcome lack of that breathy kind of "Gee, what a great band they are" filler material, and an equally welcome attention to lesser known bands. An index would have been useful though. (BH)

OZZY OSBOURNE Garry Johnson *(Proteus)*

Ozzy could well be the best-known HM/hard rock artist in the world – not least because of his innate sense of self-publicity, his genuine affection for punters and his startling ability as a raconteur. There are plenty of people who take an instant dislike to him, but just for once, to quote Phil Spector, "to know him is to love him". Johnson tries occasionally to take an objective look at the Oz but mostly, with good grace and style, he gives in to the wizardly wildman's spell. Osbourne's story is packed with incidents, and Johnson captures most if not all of them. My personal favourite is the one about Ozzy shooting a cat sitting on his car bonnet. Why? "The cat cost 35p, the car cost six grand – no contest". (BH)

STATUS QUO – Rockin' All Over The World Neil Jeffries *(Proteus)*

A genuine fan's book which reads as though the author really did want to write it and wasn't forced to because the mortgage payment was due. Jeffries says he's been following Quo for the last twelve years and it's easy to believe, if only through looking at the discography which, for a pleasant change, is exhaustive and informative. Delightfully, Jeffries sideswipes Pye Records for taking compilations to the point of overkill, while ignoring tracks they have the rights to and which Quo fans would give their cardboard guitars for. The familiar Quo story is told well enough – although Jeffries pays some interesting attention to record company relations which makes for novel reading. Some great pictures too, including fabbo old ones of Quo in their psychedelic days. (BH)

SLADE FEEL THE NOIZE! Chris Charlesworth *(Omnibus Press)*

We're talking Rolls-Royce here, in a race normally run by patched up Buicks and clapped out Minis. Charlesworth's book is lavishly illustrated, beautifully presented, well written and extremely well researched. It also helps that the Slade story, unlike most, is a genuinely interesting one: a classic tragedy complete with hubris, downfall, catharsis and regeneration. Charlesworth follows them all in detail. Perhaps the best section concerns the moment when the band, dead and gone as far as most people are concerned, steal the show at the 1980 Reading Festival. Charlesworth captures every little moment, from arriving and having to pay to leave their van in a public car-park, through having to argue to get past security, to the triumph of their show and the hideous time Def Leppard had following them. Charlesworth should be proud to have this one on his bookshelf – and so should you. (BH)

TWISTED SISTER – The First Official Book Gary Bushell and Mark Weiss *(Zomba)*

At last – the first official book on "sultans of shock rock" Twisted Sister and their followers the SMF (Sick Mother Fuckers). Everything you could possibly want to know, and more, in a mercifully short book, enlivened by the unique literary style of Bushell: "By Mohammed and Ali! Do not forsake me or my barmaid!" You probably thought Twisted Sister were camper than Baden-Powell, but Bushell reveals that underneath the lorry-loads of make-up they are in fact real tuff guys. When heavy metal band Hanoi Rocks insult them, singer Dee Snider challenges them to a "physical confrontation". "They wanna debate – we're going to debate on their faces," snarles Snider. Wimpish Hanoi Rocks don't even turn up to the rumble. Fascinating, but boys will be boys (sigh). (Peter Culshaw)

VAN HALEN – Jumpin' For The Dollar John Shearlaw *(Zomba Books)*

Possibly the only thing more embarrassing than Shearlaw's style in this scanty, flimsy piece of work, is the standard of the picture caption writing. It brings to mind nothing so much as those old Victorian paintings of doggies, chambermaids or urchins, which always had to have a twee title. Thus a picture of bass-player Michael Anthony not doing very much is captioned "I think therefore I play". Shearlaw puffs and pants his way through what is essentially a bowl of very thin gruel. In fact this kind of diet could induce terminal starvation were it not for the roughage of motormouth Dave Lee Roth's endless stream of quotes. The best chapter is the one given over to the sayings of Roth and of various critics world wide. An average issue of *Kerrang* would provide more information and better entertainment. (BH)

GENERAL

THE DOORS CONCISE COMPLETE *(Omnibus Press)*

Subtitled "Music and Lyrics 1965-1971", this book is exactly that: the words and notation for 59 songs. Provided you can read it, the music speaks for itself. The lyrics, particularly those of the more "thought-provoking" songs, deal a deathly blow to Morrison's reputation as a poet while at the same time confirming him as an exceptional rock lyricist. For fans with plans only. (Pete Clark)

HOT SAUCES: Reggae and Latin Pop Billy Bergman *(Blandford Paperbacks))*

The first in a series which aims to examine musical categories that have moved from insignificant to influential during the last few years, *Hot Sauces* deals with the sound of the Carribbean and bits of South America in eight short essays. Apart from the obvious problems of trying to cover such a vast subject range in 140 pages and waiting until so many detailed works have already appeared on the topics, Bergman undermines his own efforts by using five different writers. This ensures that the various chapters – reggae, soca, rara, salsa, R & B and latin international – remain as eclectic as possible, devastating his "roots and branches" claims of the introductions and so removing any advantages a geographical analysis would have. Apart from the piece on rara (the music of Haiti), which is frustratingly the shortest in the book, there is little here that anyone with a passing acquaintance with the UK music press is unaware of. The series title is *Planet Rock,* and so many people have heard that before. (LB)

NOWHERE TO RUN Gerri Hirshey *(Pan)*

Good books about popular music are rare; excellent ones are extremely few and far between. This one (subtitled, accurately enough *The Story of Soul Music*) is, quite simply, one of the finest books written about any Western popular form as well as being the definitive essay on the theory and practice of soul. Hirshey's book has been accused of being a series of magazine features strung together, but the thread of continuity that runs through her encounters with James Brown, Wilson Pickett, Aretha Franklin, Diana Ross, Martha Reeves, Michael Jackson, Solomon Burke, Ben E King, Sam and Dave, Isaac Hayes, Screamin' Jay Hawkins, Jerry Butler, Steve Cropper, the Temptations, the Four Tops, Mary Wells, Junior Walker, Irma Thomas and many, many others gives the lie to that accusation. The book places the music within its context; it stresses the vital importance of soul's gospel roots, traces the sometimes uneasy relationships between soul and the pop mainstream, and tells the stories of the rise and fall of Stax and the rise and rise of Motown. Deceased greats like Jackie Wilson, Sam Cooke and Otis Redding are remembered, and Hirshey's credentials as an interviewer are demonstrated by the simple fact that she manages to get Michael Jackson to talk sense. There is no excuse whatsoever for not owning a copy of this book. It tells you what you need to know, and does so beautifully. *Nowhere to Run* is one of the most spectacular achievements in the short history of rock criticism. (CSM)

THE LORDS – THE NEW CREATURES: The Only Published Poetry Of Jim Morrison
(Omnibus Press)

Good lyricists are not necessarily good poets; the most facile pop lyric can achieve a kind of power within the context of a song, but once printed its banality becomes painfully obvious. Morrison's blurred vision is that perennial Romantic idealization of the Primitive – "We have been metamorphosed from a mad body dancing on hillsides to a pair of eyes staring in the dark" (one of the better lines) – and its undisciplined free-verse approach touches on esoteric subjects ranging from Shamanism to Alchemists – "who picture love affairs of chemicals and stars". Then there's pseudo-profound nonsense like "When play dies it becomes the Game/When sex dies it becomes Climax", while a curious section on "The Passengers" was obviously borrowed uncredited by Iggy Pop for 'The Passenger' on *Lust For Life*. This substandard collection will do nothing to help Morrison's aura of misunderstood visionary. (Peter Culshaw)

SIGNED, SEALED AND DELIVERED Sue Steward and Sheryl Garratt *(Pluto Press)*

An intelligent, well researched and only occasionally sermonising book on "women in pop". Inevitably, in covering such a vast range from Ivy Benson's All-Girl Dance Band in the forties to Beki Bondage and Sade in the eighties, points are skimmed over and left undeveloped. While showing what a rough deal women get in the music biz by unearthing women in every field, from producing (Ann Dudley) to running a label (Carol Wilson), the overall effect is optimistic – it *is* possible for women to be a success in any area of the wonderful world of pop, though some of the propaganda is laid on *too* thick. "You have to be twice as smart, twice as good as the men just to get to the bottom of the rank where you can eat and pay your rent," says Carol Colman, bass player with Kid Creole and the Coconuts. I'd like to have seen more discussion of class, as the lot of a woman working in a record-pressing plant is utterly different to more middle-class areas like publishing and journalism, while the feminist complaint that women singers are preferred if they are thin and beautiful applies to boys too. If Duran Duran were bald, middle-aged navvies they would hardlıy have been quite so successful; in any case, Helen Terry and Alison Moyet are Big in both senses of the word. Still, the book is a labour of love and is recommended for its abundance of information. (Peter Culshaw).

THE DEATH AND RESURRECTION SHOW Rogan Taylor *(Blond)*

This is that rarity among "rock" books – one which spends its time constructing and illustrating an interesting theory of "why", rather than spraying forth enervating eulogies over "what" and "when". Rogan Taylor's theory is that modern show business (aka rock 'n' roll) has an unmistakable ritual element, wherein the great stars of the day commune on a mystic level with their audience: any photograph of a large concert audience immediately illustrates that the greater proportion are not quite right in the head.

The author traces this strange phenomenom back to the "shamans" of olden days, the weirdly-garbed medicine men whose metaphorical (or even actual) death and resurrection endowed them with benevolent, but frightening, spiritual powers. He then follows their entertaining descendants through the centuries via a gallery of fools, clowns, escape artists, comedians and, finally, rock stars. The book is clearly and intelligently written, although the absence of Jim Morrison, self-confessed shaman, is a mite puzzling. Try a little mental exercise (and at £15, try the library). (Peter Clark)

THE RAP ATTACK: African Jive To New York Hip Hop David Toop *(Pluto Press)*

The rattling subway ride through the history of hip hop is a potentially hazardous venture. A writer's minefield, fraught with the callings of an imaginative social conscience, Staggerlee romanticism or simple macho envy – most UK journalists have tinged their words with one or the other. Toop deftly avoids such wooing. He tackles the rap with a workmanlike thoroughness kept lively by a fan's enthusiasm and occasional flashes of wry humour. He neither looks up to or down on the B Boys and Girls, yet never assumes to be on a par. Like the mixers he talks of, he keeps the beat sweet from somewhere in the backgroud, throwing in another flashbacked reference just when you thought you had it sussed, and stripping away any superfluous theorizing or creative connections.

Such a readable, informative, comprehensive outing that if there are no other books written about hip hop it won't matter. (LB)

THE TRUE ADVENTURES OF THE ROLLING STONES Stanley Booth *(Heinemann)*

Booth toured America with the Stones in 1969 with a view to writing the book. Here it is sixteen years later. Booth claims that had he published this account of debauchery on the grand scale any earlier the Feds would have hauled him away before his first signing session. Certainly the main characters – of whom the author is generally one – seem perpetually engaged in ingesting the entire chemical output of the Third World. What emerges is a vivid picture of five men in suspended adolescence: flirting with the low life, burning their fingers at Altamont, sniffing for that Funky Thang at Muscle Shoals, taking their punishment in London courtrooms and generally being the major league smartasses their fans have always willed them to be. Booth's attempts to place them in the blues tradition of his Deep South background occasionally strain the patience but as a portrait of the chilling emptiness of Rock Fame it's unlikely to be surpassed before someone writes the Michael Jackson book in sixteen years time. (DH)

REFERENCE

ROCKIN' REELS Jan Stacy & Ryder Syvertsen *(Columbus)*

A hefty but meagrely-filled tome, providing cast listings, plots, and various bits of trivia regarding some rock movies. "It's hard to find a question on rock films that this book doesn't answer" claims an accompanying handout. Not so difficult. How about "Whatever happened to Dylan's *Renaldo and Clara,* any films featuring music by Curtis Mayfield (*Short Eyes* and *Superfly*) or maybe Taylor Hackford's *The Idolmaker*?" In fact, whatever happened to the 800 movies featuring rock stars either as actors or music makers? Skip this one and try to pick up copies of Ehrenstein and Reed's *Rock on Film* or *The NME Guide to Rock Cinema,* both of which are more Oscar-worthy. (FD)

ROLLING STONE ROCK ALMANAC *(Papermac)*

Not actually your complete day-by-day chronology of rock as claimed by the cover blurb, but, nevertheless, an engrossing stab at listing many of the events and non-events that have figured in old man Rock's diary since 4 January 1954, when Elvis Presley first met Sun Records' Sam Phillips. Additionally, weekly charts of number one UK and US singles and albums are included, along with an extensive list of birthdates and cemetary appointments. The compilers have performed a sterling task in documenting even the minor (and often more interesting) happenings, such as the day the Treniers recorded 'Say Hey', with the help of New York Giants centrefield man Willie Mays and 21-year-old producer Quincy Jones. Ultimately though, it's the guy who got saddled with providing the mind-blowing index who really deserves mention in the New Year's Honours List. (FD)

THE BILLBOARD BOOK OF TOP 40 SINGLES Joel Whitburn *(Guinness)*

All of America's Top Forty singles from January 1955 through to December 1984. Whitburn is *the* US chart ace and has been fashioning such books for so many years that he's perfected the format down to the last comma. He's compiled books of country charts, jazz charts, Hot One Hundred entries, top albums and even one that lists 4,000 hits that simply bubbled under Billboard's Hot One Hundred. Little wonder then that this Guinness publication reeks of know-how. Indispensable. (FD)

BRITISH HIT SINGLES Tim and Jo Rice, Paul Gambaccini & Mike Read *(Guinness)*

Now up to its fifth edition. An essential buy for chart freaks, listing over 10,000 hits and nearly 3,000 hitmakers, and though each bi-yearly edition comes beset with added problems due to the increase in facts and figures, the book remains well laid out and easy to refer to. (FD)

RARE ROCK – A COLLECTOR'S GUIDE Tony Rees *(Blandford Press)*

Down in the nether regions of pop fandom lurks a sad breed of eternally unsatisfied wraiths. They are called "completists" because they are damned by some inner demon to seek out the complete works of their chosen "faves" – not only the regular releases, you understand, but every last purple, pop-up Taiwanese promo flexi-demo – that's the one where the lead guitarist accidentally de-tuned top E with a Marlboro and thus played a significantly different solo. If you know one of these people (or, God forbid, if you are one), you might be interested in this labour of love, which collects a mass of information on non-standard (but *not* bootleg) releases and arranges them in order of artist. "A" for effort. (Pete Clark)

ROCK'N'ROLL CONFIDENTIAL Penny Stallings *(Vermillion)*

The trashy introduction suggests the very worst: "Rock stars burn brightest when most tarnished. They must live and die by the outlaw code. Their love lives [must be] sinful, their drug use suicidal, their demise, if possible, tragically premature . . ." Oh gawd, one thinks, not another book about fat old rock goats, disgusting drugs, grisly "groupies", life in the so-called "fast lane" – eg totally obnoxious behaviour that we common folk are supposed to find so titillating and/or seductive. With dread one begins to turn the pages . . .

Well, yes. Stallings *can't* write for toffee. The text – clumsily-linked anecdotes of seedy "horror", ghastly and sordid goings-on in rock'n'roll's potting shed that everyone knows about already, stumpy inanities that don't raise a hoot – is best avoided. But the *pictures* tell another story altogether. After the prurient glooping is out of the way, one can wallow in a scintillating collage of pop at its most charmingly *inept*. Long-forgotten and absolutely *essential* visual items on such giants of stupid popular music as the Chipmunks, the Goofers, Elvis Presley ("artist's impression"); the most glorious symbol of unfettered womanhood in world history, Annette Funicello; advertisements for Ed 'Kookie' Byrnew's combs! All these are presented in pictorial splendour within these pages. Yes! Everything is trash! (Except for Frankie Avalon.) (TH)

■ THE YEAR IN VIDEO

Adam Sweeting finds little to celebrate in the rise and rise of music video

According to TV and video producer Peter Wagg, "Since 'Vienna', the pop promo has come of age, with more productions, larger budgets and happily more opportunities for them to be seen. But with this, the creative freedom has gone and, all too often, so has the fun."

On the other hand, you heard a different story from Kevin Godley who, with his partner Lol Creme, has made some of the best-known pop videos for acts such as Duran Duran, Frankie Goes To Hollywood, Yes, Culture Club and the Police. According to Kevin: "The great thing about working in the video medium is the speed with which everything has to be done. It's all based on adrenalin, unlike commercials which are very, very detailed, where they do research before the storyboard is done and before anything is shot they're sure about everything. Whereas video leaves you a lot of room to experiment. It's the only area left in film-making where experimental film-makers can be commercial film-makers."

Perhaps Wagg and Godley have different ideas about what "creative" and "experimental" mean. One of 1985's more talked-about promo videos was Godley and Creme's effort for their own hit single 'Cry'. Simplicity carried the day in a medium not noted for restraint or (very often) taste. 'Cry' was simply a perpetually evolving sequence of faces mouthing along to the song, parts of the image overlapping at different speeds to produce strange and unsettling changes of sex, age, expression and apparent emotional intention. Allied to the unhurried melodic lilt of the song, the video generated curious power.

The efficacy of video in reaching a wider audience has now been accepted by just about everybody, even artists who were once hostile to the very idea of acting in their own charades. Bruce Springsteen appeared in a video for the first time with 'Dancing In The Dark', and was rewarded with a massive hit for his trouble. He followed it up with a so-called "conceptual" clip for 'I'm On Fire', winning more plaudits in the process.

Also going rampantly audio-visual were Tom Petty, who teamed up with Eurythmic Dave Stewart for the trippy 'Don't Come Around Here No More' (weird but memorable), and even John Fogerty, back from a decade or more of silence and invisibility. You didn't have to be old or American, though. Jesse Rae married armour, a kilt, and a claymore with a long background doing funk sessions in the US to create video singles like 'Over The Sea'. Robyn Hitchcock, English eccentric, made videos for 'I Often Dream Of Trains' and 'The Man With The Lightbulb Head' on the cheap, and found the Americans were clamouring for more. And the Cocteau Twins teamed up with director John Scarlett-Davis to create the lingering pleasures of 'Aikea Guinea'.

Nevertheless, Peter Wagg's point is this – while the increasing acceptance of video as part and parcel of pop has brought greater readiness to invest in it, this same process has brought the imposition of corporate ideas of taste and acceptability. MTV has been steadily reshaping the way America thinks about music since its inception in 1981, and though people no longer accuse the channel of racist bias so often, it is nonetheless true that MTV's bread and butter is the record company promo for the group the record company wants to plug.

● *PETER WAGG*

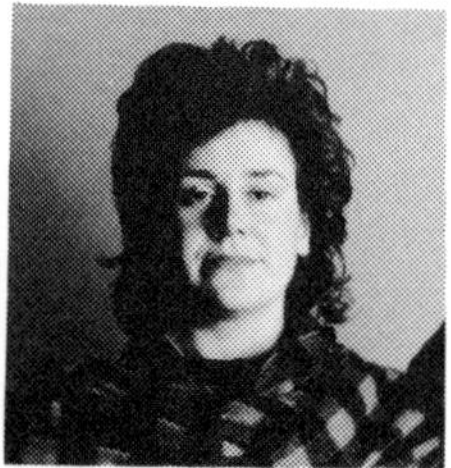

● *ANNABEL JANKEL*

● *ROCKY MORTON*

● *GODLEY & CREME*

● *JESSE RAE*

● *JOHN SCARLETT-DAVIS*

While it wasn't MTV's *fault* that Americans seem to love Bryan Adams or Toto, the station did ram home its chart-dominating formula to ever-greater audiences. It now reaches twenty million American homes (as does its rival *Night Flight* on USA Network cable TV), while NBC's *Friday Night Video* is watched by an amazing fifty million people.

No record company accountant argues with figures like these. He just has to use them to his own ends. Wall Street financial analyst Mark Reily has predicted that the American video industry will be turning over some $5 billion by 1988, with a quarter of that figure being generated solely by music video. Record and tape turnover, on the basis of his calculations, will be left trailing behind. As pictures take over, is this the day the music died?

Britain, meanwhile, had yet to receive the full force of "music television" on the American model. *Top of the Pops* still relied on its absurd but loveable miming formula with a few videos thrown in as a sop to the force of destiny – though producer Michael Hurll deserved to be shot for the number of times the programme aired Foreigner's disgustingly sententious clip for 'I Want To Know What Love Is', while the promo for Andrew Lloyd-Webber's 'Pie Jesu', which seemed to rely on the aftermath of an air raid for its exploitative effect, was in appalling taste, yet slipped through the moral watchdog net presumably by virtue of its sanctified lyric.

Meanwhile, *The Tube* remained flippantly critical of the videos it showed. *Whistle Test* was highly selective. *Saturday Superstore* aired a few but at an unsociable hour, and the only thing anyone can remember about *ORS '85* is that they wanted to tread on the presenter.

That left *Max Headroom*. Max has been the gate-crasher at the video party, a computer-generated smartass with an unstable arsenal of pre-programmed one-liners. Peter Wagg produced the programme, which is more coincidental than anything else. The show burst on to British TV screens in April '85 with an hour-long pilot, a slightly futuristic saga of a crumbling world dominated by rival TV networks. Max Headroom, cloned by computer from the brain of investigative reporter Edison Carter, finds himself accidentally installed as presenter of pop videos for a fly-blown pirate TV station.

The film was directed by Annabel Jankel and Rocky Morton, already well known from their work with their film/video production company, Cucumber. Morton and Jankel have a reputation for making the best animated promos going – they were responsible for Elvis Costello's 'Accidents Will Happen', Donald Fagen's 'New Frontier' and Tom Tom Club's 'Genius Of Love', among others. "We felt the time was right to develop into directing live-action dialogue and narrative fiction," said Annabel Jankel.

The context they had devised for the tale of Max Headroom and his wallpaper-blur of non-stop pop promos felt a little bit alien and quite a lot familiar. Filthy, tattered tramps huddled around miserable bonfires in the middle of derelict sites, watching pop promos on old TV sets abandoned on rubbish tips. In sky-high boardrooms, TV moguls went way beyond the law and morality to secure ever-higher ratings. Background music was provided by Midge Ure and Chris Cross of Ultravox, themselves no strangers to producing videos, either for themselves or for other artists such as Bananarama and Fun Boy Three. This was the future . . . and it was already *here*.

In Max Headroom, who went on to act as anchorman for a Channel 4 promo-clip show, Morton and Jankel had provided their own tongue-in-cheek critique of the video milieu. In between picking out promos apparently on his own whim, Max made jokes about President Reagan, mocked the idea of TV presenters and even his own show, and would then get locked into a randomly-sampled electronic nervous tic. Smooth, mid-Atlantic and fatally flawed, Headroom proved that information technology had already done away with people. Somewhere, there were already enough promos to provide programming until the end of time.

Behind the *Headroom* concept was the realization that video need do no more than exist. MTV has demonstrated that people who meet the right criteria to be termed "adult" will sit and watch an unending stream of appalling promo clips in the hope that a

● *MAX HEADROOM*

good one will come up next. Dee Snider of Twisted Sister confessed to the press that his band never bothered themselves much about the quality of a video, since excellence would be a bonus, but if it was lousy it would be just another among many.

The independent sector of music video failed to mount a serious challenge to the inexorable growth of mainstream product, though Manchester's Ikon F.C.L. made intrepid efforts to bamboozle and/or educate the populace with their bizarre William Burroughs double-pack *The Final Academy Documents* plus the ominous movie *Feverhouse*.

It came as no real surprise to learn cash-flow was the main stumbling block for many independent operators. Doublevision, who once released the kaleidoscopic *TV Wipeout*, went into a long hibernation while planning a comeback with new material from the Residents, Cabaret Voltaire and Tuxedomoon. New releases may also be expected from the Ink and Jungle labels, while Films At Work owe it to everybody to follow up their Redskins cassette and its successor, *Learning on the Line*, a provocative documentary about the political lessons of the miners' strike. John Benson's Jettisoundz in Lancashire continued to release low-budget, minority-interest punk extravaganzas.

Companies like these will hopefully receive a boost if the independent retailers in the Cartel distribution network are able to implement their plan to stock independent video releases, cross-referencing them with record releases where possible.

At the other end of the market, the British charts began to reflect one particular trend brought on by the American fixation with "picture music" – the hit record from the movie soundtrack. Promo whizzkid Steve Barron (Michael Jackson, Human League) made *Electric Dreams* which generated its own batch of hit singles. *Footloose* did likewise. Eurythmics' soundtrack for Michael Radford's film of *Nineteen Eighty Four* became a source of hit singles, in the form of 'Julia' and 'Sex Crime'. *Flashdance* was virtually one long promotional clip, while Prince's blockbusting *Purple Rain* cunningly leap-frogged several stages on the traditional route to stardom by incorporating the rising star in a celluloid framework depicting . . . his own rise to stardom.

It also became something of a misnomer to describe these proliferating money-spinners as "spin-offs". Glenn Frey's hit single with 'The Heat Is On', from the Eddie Murphy vehicle *Beverly Hills Cop*, no doubt prolonged the movie's longevity with a young rock-orientated audience, while Frey's record was certainly helped by a promo clip featuring Eddie Murphy. The same goes for the low-budget hit *The Breakfast Club*, which at last gave Simple Minds a sizeable hit single in 'Don't You (Forget About Me)' with accompanying silly video; and Duran Duran's stock must have risen incalculably with *A View To A Kill*, the fruit of a prestigious liaison with James Bond producer Cubby Broccoli. Shame about the song . . .

Largely thanks to America's widespread adoption of cable television, this cross-feeding process between music, TV and movies increased rapidly. Nevertheless, the British remained a nation of VTR owners (or renters), with approximately one third of UK households now believed to contain a machine. While partly accounting for the dilapidated state of British cinema, this also meant that British viewers were well placed to take advantage of the increasingly swift release of feature films on video cassette. *Purple Rain* looks as though it may be in with a chance of giving Vestron's *Making Michael Jackson's 'Thriller'* cassette a run for its money, though the latter's freakish sales (150,000 in the UK *alone*) will probably remain a record for some time to come.

When Virgin released *Nineteen Eighty Four* on cassette, the importance now being attached to this end of the market became apparent when a small fortune was spent on promotional back-up – cardboard cutouts of Big Brother, plus '1984' T-shirts, coffee mugs and badges. Shades of ZTT's surreal Frankie marketing. *Electric Dreams* went out on cassette too, as did Alex Cox's left-field hit movie *Repo Man*, which includes a soundtrack by numerous LA punk bands and even the evergreen Iggy Pop. (Cox has also made a move into pop video by directing the Pogues' 'A Pair Of Brown Eyes'.)

The MTV mentality began to inform broadcast TV too, perhaps most conspicuously in the American import, *Miami Vice*. Market research in the States found a close correlation between the show's audience and MTV's viewer profile. *Miami Vice* costs about $1 million per episode to make, with $50,000 of that dedicated to purchasing rights for a bunch of current chart (and MTV) hit records, which are incorporated into the show's experimental stereo soundtrack. Add to all this the programme's quickfire hip dialogue, designer clothes for men and state-of-the-art personal firearms and maybe you have some insight into the current state of the American (electric) Dream. It was perhaps not surprising that a member of the *Miami Vice* team was arrested for dealing cocaine to an undercover cop.

With audio-visual information streaming in from a variety of sources, and heading in loosely the same direction, it would be ironic if the information revolution merely led to standardization of taste, audience and (worst of all) intellectual content. When Britain is finally, belatedly "cabled-up", cable owners will immediately be able to avail themselves of *Sky Channel* and *Music Box*, both beamed across Europe by Satellite. *Sky Channel* provides some music programming, while *Music Box* is all music on the MTV pattern.

● *ELECTRIC DREAMS*

● *STEVE BARRON*

I have been taken to task in the past for making disparaging remarks about *Music Box*, so suffice it to say that programme quality tends to devolve towards the level of the average pop promo. This is, of course, a source of fast, cheap programming, and it isn't only cable operators who are cottoning on to the fact. Christmas TV viewing in 1984 was dominated to an unprecedented degree by pop video. Duran Duran appeared twice in hour-long programmes, as did Culture Club. On Christmas Day itself, ITV broadcast *Top Pop Videos of 1984*, a straight dose of promos only slightly diluted by the occasional vacuous link from one of the featured stars.

With TV no longer the envied "licence to print money" it was once held to be, the insertion of an hour-long segment of pop promos into a programming schedule cut costs miraculously and aimed squarely for the coveted "young people" whom TV researchers talk so much about and understand so inadequately. But, perhaps due to some residual Reithian ethic, British TV kept its distance from full-tilt promomania.

Even a series like Channel 4's *Mirror Image* – in which groups as disparate as Orange Juice (RIP), the Violent Femmes and Barclay James Harvest were presented in concert with additional video effects and indigestible lumps of interview – at least paid some attention to the idea that groups can still exist as living, breathing entities which play live to an audience of paying customers. They are not, in other words, merely ghosts in some corporate machine, summoned by gibbering "veejays".

Mirror Image also broke new ground in following up its broadcast programmes by releasing slightly different versions of them on cassette, more or less simultaneously. The reasoning here seemed to be that the double punch would help both Channel 4's ratings and Polygram Video's sales. Interestingly, the cassettes featured more music and no interview, perhaps registering the perception that the paying punter regards all talk as lies.

The difference between market conditions in Britain and America also produced strange disparities – and even stranger correspondences – in chart activity. While the holier-than-thou British regarded it as only right and proper that the American Top Forty should be chock-full of UK acts – albeit of the Thompson Twins, Wham! and Go West ilk (designed by computer, hand-built by robots, consumed by Americans) – they themselves seemed only too keen to embrace the suffocating AOR of Chicago, Foreigner or Bryan Adams received in return.

As the common language of TV and video spreads ever wider, music will probably eventually be much the same everywhere.

For the time being though, while the promo clip became as much a part of America's daily routine as destroying European cultures and currencies, for the British it still retained a certain amount of novelty value. While British TV exercised some quality control over the videos it showed, Americans could watch them indiscriminately on assorted cable and broadcast channels as well as in the video clubs which have burgeoned across the continent.

Ed Steinberg's RockAmerica, for instance, is the nation's largest supplier of material to video clubs, and it publishes its own monthly magazine with a regional breakdown of the most popular videos alongside features and reviews. Video clubs offer the opportunity for groups to make somewhat more risqué products, perhaps the most celebrated example of this being Duran Duran's unexpurgated version of 'Girls On Film' (directed by Godley and Creme). EMI Picture Music even released a cassette called 'Sexy Shorts' featuring mildly titillating videos from artists as diverse as Duran Duran, Queen and Dwight Twilley. This does not, on the whole, seem to be a particularly healthy trend, a kind of *Charlie's Angels* approach to selling music (a pair of naked breasts being worth any number of quotes from famous movies).

On the other hand, even though video clubs doubtless encourage the making of all kinds of video atrocities, they also allow groups like Bronski Beat, Art Of Noise or even the Smiths to get their audio-visual point across. The Smiths, so avowedly anti-video, have evidently made one for 'How Soon Is Now' for US consumption.

The crucial transatlantic difference is that while Americans might see a video clip six times a day every day of the week, even a big hit record in Britain is unlikely to have its accompanying video shown more than half a dozen times in total, and even then bits have probably been removed at either end. Consequently the audio-visual idiom is second nature to the American viewer/listener – simply the new language of what was once only a business of music. The Brits pick and choose and expect the medium to mean more than it usually does.

Indeed, while a video offers immediate basic information about an act – how many of them there are, what colour their hair is, which one plays the euphonium etc – the medium's codified presentation (with its frequently neutral sense of locale) actually tells you *less* about the true nature of the artist than does attentive listening to their records. Pick any example . . . does Hitlist's 'Into The Fire' clip, with its flashes from old Hollywood films interspersed with cutaways to the group watching them in assorted imitative postures, mean anything more than that the

● *LLOYD COLE & THE COMMOTIONS ON MIRROR IMAGE*

● *QUEEN*

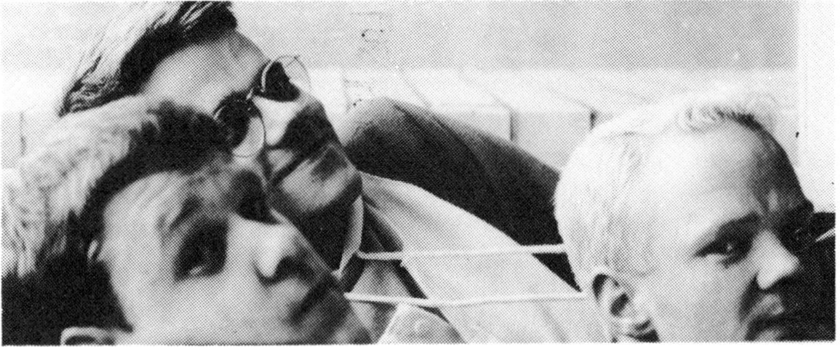

● *BRONSKI BEAT*

video is funny and the record isn't? When you see ABC's clip for 'Be Near Me', what do those jerky bits of pixillation tell you? That the group are dummies or toys? Is it funny – or mocking? Does the humour belong to Martin Fry, or the video director? Is the song heartfelt or does it deride the pre-MTV idea of "love"? If the record isn't a hit – or even if it is – do you care?

In a magazine called *Jump Cut*, Deborah H Holdstein wrote an amusingly pretentious piece about pop video called 'Messages and Structures'. To reinforce her theory that, for some artists, video can be used to create and perpetuate an image and persona comparable to those of the great movie stars of the thirties and forties, she analysed some key promo clips – Michael Jackson's 'Beat It', Bowie's 'Let's Dance' and Donna Summer's 'She Works Hard For The Money'. Few things are more comical than the application of academic apparatus to completely unsuitable topics, and Ms Holdstein sprung any number of traps. While Bob Giraldi's 'Beat It' clip is indeed a virtuoso performance, it hardly stands comparison with *West Side Story*, *An American In Paris* or, indeed, the entire weight of the American film-musical tradition.

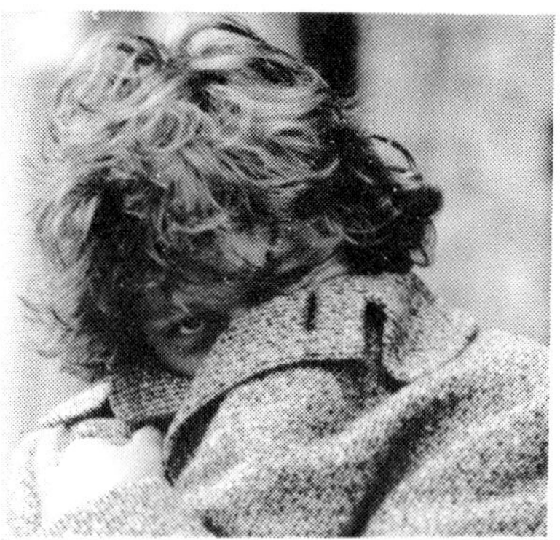
● *RUSSELL MULCAHY*

● *THE STARS OF MOTOWN*

However, she did help to prove one thing, that music video is a sub-literary form. Frankly, it is never going to be a feasible proposition to compare (for instance) the collected video works of the Cars with the *oeuvre* of Orson Welles, nor to contrast the lifetime's work of Russell Mulcahy, video director, with that of Francis Coppola. Yet we read in Michael Shore's *Rolling Stone Book Of Rock Video*, an excellent and thorough volume in many ways, that Steve Barron's promo for Human League's 'Don't You Want Me' "happened to be one of rock video's most sublime movie homages (in this case, Truffaut's *Day For Night*) . . . " Good video, maybe, but . . .

In most other media, blatant plagiarism is often regarded as actionable, yet here we had Queen lifting chunks of *Metropolis* for 'Radio Ga Ga', and Paul McCartney employing Rupert Bear in a Walt Disney setting for 'We All Stand Together'. When Palace wanted to assemble a clip for Elvis Costello's 'Watching The Detectives' for a compilation tape, one was spliced together from old detective movies. In the age of the Fairlight computer-synthesizer, when music can be created from noises plundered from other people's records and then recycled, perhaps we shouldn't go round looking these wonderful gift horses in the mouth. We'd only find they had someone else's teeth.

The increasing spread of the video currency has also revolutionized musical home entertainment. On the one hand there were straightforward compilations of promos of the 'Now That's What I Call Music' or 'Don't Watch That, Watch This' variety. Then there was the standard band-in-concert genre (everyone from Lloyd Cole to Jimi Hendrix and vintage sixties footage of the Beatles or the stars of Motown). Or the biog-style programme – in the case of the Doors, you could have Warner Home Video's 'Tribute To Jim Morrison', first shown on BBC2, or a new American compilation of allegedly stunning quality called 'Dance On Fire' (MCA). Or the increasingly popular video EP format, maybe half a dozen tracks by one group retailing for about £12, with hi-fi sound.

● *JIM MORRISON*

Rock movies, too, were all there in the racks at your local newsagent – *200 Motels*, all the Elvis Presley films, *The Last Waltz*, *Rainbow Bridge* and the great *Spinal Tap*, which came to bury rock 'n' roll and profit from it. My favourite video moment of the year came from Lionel Richie on his *All Night Long* tape. Recalling how the ghastly promo clip for 'Hello' came to be made, Lionel described how director Bob Giraldi had come up with the idea: "Giraldi said 'why don't we do something different? Why don't we make her blind?' "

For the future, it seems likely that the clip-with-talkover option will continue gaining ground. If you thought it couldn't get worse than Phil Collins and Philip Bailey trying to be funny and spontaneous in front of a camera crew – and let's face it, even video-wizards Eurythmics nearly came unstuck with the storyline intro of 'Would I Lie To You' – just wait.

Ex-Monkee turned video-maker Mike Nesmith may not have been completely wrong when he said: "The music-only phenomenon is now history." But history does have a way of repeating itself.

● *SPINAL TAP*

LABOUR OF LOVE

Ian Cranna talks to UB40's Brian Travers about the group's unique video achievement

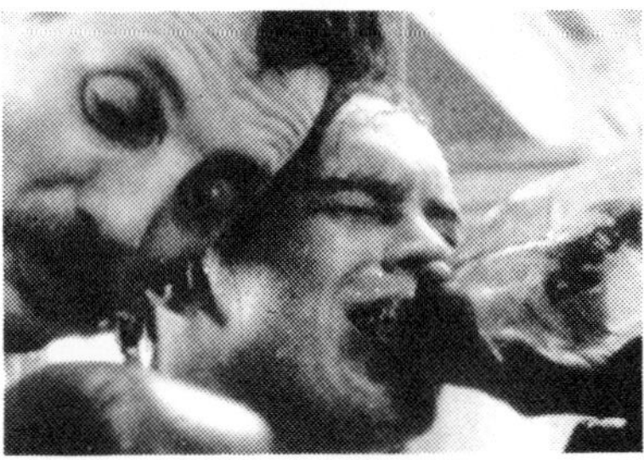

Amongst all the brainless beach fantasies, tedious travelogues and assorted escapist extravanganza thrown up by the year's promo clips, one video stood head and shoulders above the rest. It was grittily (as in working class) realistic, shot in glorious black and white, thirty-one minutes long, and by turns tough, tender and very funny indeed. This was the unassuming integrity of UB40's *Labour of Love*.

Perhaps it isn't strictly accurate to call *Labour of Love* a pop video at all – it's more of a short film with music (nine out of the ten tracks from the LP of the same name). Described by its makers as a cross between *Seven Brides for Seven Brothers* and *On the Waterfront,* it's set in inner city Birmingham and opens in startling fashion with two members of the group attempting to break into a parked car. From there it proceeds as a fairly conventional love story – a battle between two guys (Robin and Ali Campbell) over the girl, building up to a trial by strength in a boxing match. The supporting action and local colour is provided by the rest of the band appearing as minor characters in the workplace and club scenes – the kind of people and places informed by the band's own firsthand experience. The action culminates in a brutally realistic run-in with the police, though the end is left intriguingly open.

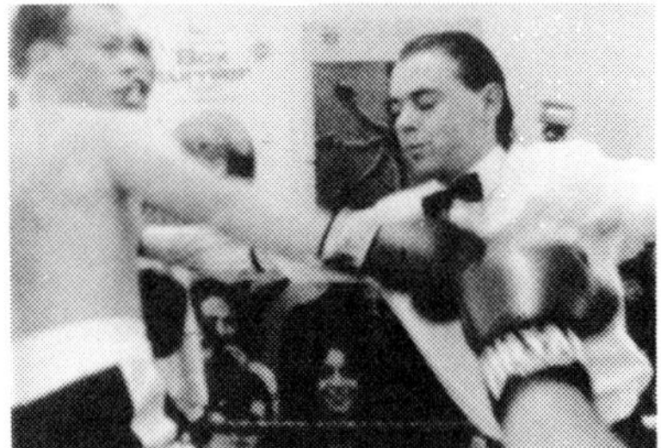

Labour of Love was produced by Brian Travers, UB40's sax player – a highly likeable man with a droll, self-effacing sense of humour and as down to earth as the rest of this frank and singularly unpretentious band.

"It's quite a classic film," Travers offers of its structure. "The hero and the anti-hero, winning and losing and the emotional aspects of it – that's what really sold it, I think. It's really quite delicate in its rough teenage way, where you're not allowed to cry or put your arm around your mates. It's all about status – being the hardest, who can be the biggest crook, the most dangerous – because all the girls like the most dangerous ones, the excitement of it. I'm sure quite a lot of people will see it as quite an affront – quite sexist to a certain degree and reinforcing the stereotyped idea of the girl hanging about for the guy, getting pregnant, getting married off. But of course it's not like that – it's just a story."

While occasionally pointed, *Labour of Love* scores heavily by not attempting to lionize or moralize about the kind of hard life it portrays, simply letting the action speak for itself.

"It wasn't supposed to be a film to promote positive thinking," Travers continues. "It was supposed to be a teenage *On the Waterfront* or an English *West Side Story.* I know that sounds a bit grandiose but that's what we had in mind."

UB40 had made videos before in their own disorganized fashion – a lot of money had been spent to little effect and the band had in fact stopped making them until Travers – worried about the strength of the *Labour of Love* album – decided to take matters in hand.

"I'm pretty concerned about the way the band is portrayed publicly," he admits, "not so much the specific image but the way the band is received. I just got involved – somebody had to – just because I was concerned that we'd have bigger hits."

Funded by UB40 themselves on a minimal budget, *Labour of Love* grew out of the band's attempt to make their own promo clip for 'Red Red Wine'. Despite having no experience himself, Travers chose as director Bernard Rose, who has since worked with Frankie Goes To Hollywood and Bronski Beat but was then just "this kid from film school who'd never made a video ever. I said 'Think you can make the best video that's ever been made?' and he said 'Yeah'. A lot of people went 'Err. . .err' so I hung up on them – I didn't tell them who I was."

Together they wrote the film, Rose knocking it into dramatic shape and a shootable film, Travers taking care of locations, props and casting ("just everybody from our neighbourhood, all having a laugh and drinking lots of beer").

One of the film's great successes is the natural, unselfconscious way in which the band themselves play their parts, with Ali Campbell standing out in the lead role of the cocky street kid. The secret?

"There wasn't a script as such," Travers reveals. "We'd write the scene and then explain what we wanted so we could get into the next scene. So rather than Ali saying lines that I might say, he'd say the lines he'd actually say himself. I think that's why it worked – because there were no actors being all Shakespearean and projecting themselves."

The finished film, made on a single 16mm camera over a period of months, was first shown in the interval at UB40's own concerts – the audience for whom it was intended.

"It wasn't made for the West End," Travers shrugs, "or the intelligentsia or any of these people – it was for teenagers. I wasn't interested in impressing any of these people with Art and because we didn't, I figure we got quite a fine piece of art, really quite unique. A bit tatty, a bit gritty, but it worked; a good start as well which installed a lot of confidence in our little record company."

So are there any lessons in *Labour of Love* for other ambitious independents?

"Most definitely. Take it in hand – ask how much every single thing costs. Use your initiative, learn to say fuck off at regular intervals and remind everybody how useless they are at what you're doing. It's absolute intimidation – it's either that or be turned over!"

Adam Sweeting asks a question

DOES FLASHY VIDEO = HIT RECORD?

. . . and gets many answers but no solutions

● *ANDY MORAHAN*

● *THE ART OF NOISE*

● *BRUCE SPRINGSTEEN*

The $64,000 question was put to Andy Morahan of Big Features, who has made a number of memorable pop promo clips — Lloyd Cole's 'Rattlesnakes', King's 'Love And Pride', Nick Heyward's 'Warning Sign', Art Of Noise's 'Close (To The Edit)': Andy, are you only as good as your last video?

Morahan chortled nervously. "Most bands are as bad as their next video," he finally riposted. "I think it's the record, myself," he went on. "It's a combination of things really. I think video can sell a record but . . . Wham! will have a Top Five record anyway" (Morahan's clip for Wham's 'Everything She Wants' was at number four in America at the time).

And what about the Art Of Noise? "The video made the record," he asserted, pointing out that Art Of Noise had no clear visual identity before the video imposed one on them.

What about Bruce Springsteen? The 'Dancing In The Dark' video definitely boosted sales of the record.

"He looks like he wants to have a crap," growled Morahan. "It probably re-established in people's minds that he was a big live attraction. The video was helpful for the record, but detrimental to his image."

Simple question, lots of answers. While video has been touted as the solution to all the problems of the music industry worldwide, the situation has already changed since MTV began in 1981. As Spandau Ballet's manager Steve Dagger pointed out, when the channel commenced broadcasting there weren't vast numbers of promo clips available to show. Among the best were British-made clips, in Spandau's case those made for 'Musclebound' or 'Chant No 1' by Russell Mulcahy. These, plus others by Duran, "got a belting", in Dagger's words.

As the industry caught on to the potential of video, it was inevitable that American financial muscle would start to dominate. Soon MTV was crammed full of corporate AOR acts of the Journey/Foreigner variety. These were the groups also familiar from FM radio, itself a medium which fell into a pomp-rockist rut despite its "progressive" intentions. But the changes wrought in the music business by shifts in musical taste and style, and by the rapid turnover of artists encouraged by video where pictures speak louder than music, meant that FM radio declined in influence as the emphasis swung back towards Top Forty records. MTV and its competitors now echo this trend in their programming, and as a result many English groups with hit records are getting heavy video exposure.

Nevertheless, money often still talks loudest. Howard Klein, president of the American independent label 415, told *Rock America* magazine: "Videos are growing more and more clichéd, safe, formulaic and artistically bland. The creative edge the new 'arty' groups once had in the video world over big groups like Journey, Chicago and REO Speedwagon has been blotted out by money (I mean 'production value') and worse yet, by the homogenous attitude demanded by those who control the making of videos."

There is no definitive yes/no answer to the question of whether flashy video equals hit record. The investment of large sums of corporate cash in an expensive promo is, happily, still no guarantee that the record will be a hit. Indeed, there are still some optimistic souls who believe that trusty old talent will win the day, with or without that coveted video exposure. Video makers Godley and Creme, for example.

Lol Creme: "People with big record companies that are prepared to give the bands videos are the ones that are making it. But a band like the Smiths haven't even used video in England — seeing them on *Top of the Pops* has done all they've needed. They make great music, they've got a good image, and they're with a small record company as well. Wonderful. It can happen."

Well, it *can* happen, but of course it doesn't always. Kevin Godley: "I think it's quite possible to enhance a bad song to such an extent that the product becomes attractive with the pictures that you put to it. There are a lot of vacuous crappy records out there with maybe really good videos. If we get a lousy record and do a really good job with the video, we feel we've actually achieved something."

In Godley and Creme's case, their naughty uncensored version of Duran Duran's 'Girls On Film' demonstrably played a major part in Duran's breakthrough in America. The risqué version of the clip wasn't shown on MTV and wasn't intended to be. Instead, it was aimed at the rapidly spreading video clubs, where it generated swift and effective word-of-mouth reports.

● *JAZZIN' FOR BLUE JEAN*

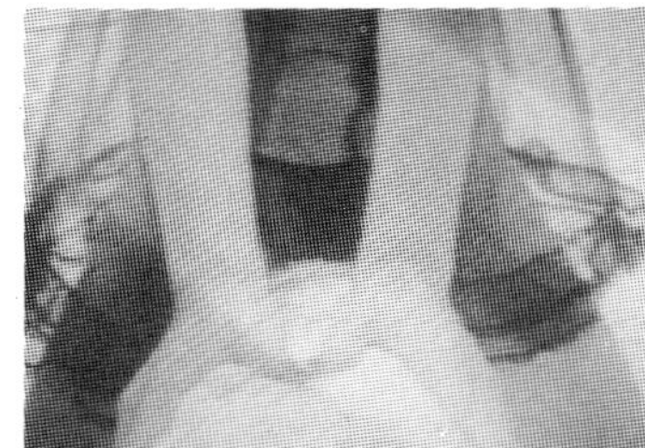

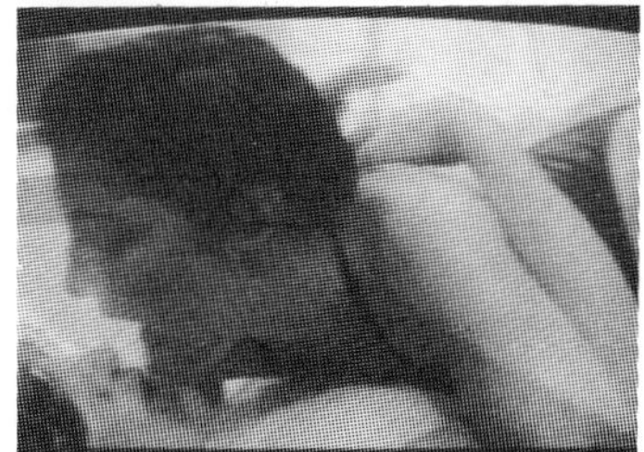

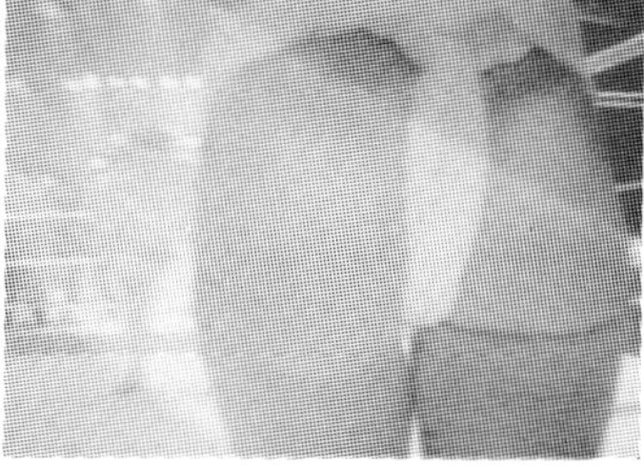

GIRLS ON FILM ●

But then, who can quantify the effect of a video clip such as the one Julien Temple made for the Rolling Stones' 'Undercover' single? Temple wrote the storyline himself and was surprised that the Stones agreed to go with it. The result, a violent, atmospheric evocation of a Central American country in the grip of terrorism and military repression, suggested Costa Gavras' chilling political thriller *Missing.* More to the point, it created a media brouhaha, and at the end of it the Stones appeared, like Frankie Goes To Hollywood, to be making a political statement. Not everybody thought they were qualified to do so, and Mick Jagger claimed that the 'Undercover' video had in fact caused the Stones to lose record sales.

Julien Temple is a film-maker who often works in pop video. He made the Sex Pistols' film *The Great Rock'n'Roll Swindle,* he made the impressive 20-minute film for Bowie's 'Jazzin' For Blue Jean', and he's worked with Culture Club, the (English) Beat and ABC. One day he might finish the film version of *Absolute Beginners.* Meanwhile, the Kinks were always his favourite band.

"I'm not interested in selling records," he told *NME.* "I'm interested in learning how to tell stories. If I can work with someone like Ray Davies, I jump at it because he's a character who is not only a good actor, but a part of a view of British history that, to me, is very interesting . . . even if he no longer sells records to the current record buying public."

Temple's particular vision is best seen in the video he made for the Kinks' 'Come Dancing', an affectionate and nostalgic look back at an era of ballrooms, spivs and a slightly sweaty hedonism. It was a perfect match for Ray Davies' gentle musical evocations. Temple is unusual in pop video because he has a clear picture of the story he wants to tell and the means he intends to use. He is not, as a rule, seduced into expensive but meaningless imagery of the kind which runs riot throughout the promo industry.

Thus, he has avoided typecasting both himself and the artists with whom he works. The alternative might be, according to video director Simon Milne (Duran Duran, Marillion, Kajagoogoo, Kim Carnes to name but a few), something like this: "With Duran, we have created a very powerful image which involves glamour, fashion, exotic locations and split screens. These are now Duran clichés — and something they are very aware of, but it is also a mould which they have settled into very quickly and one which they are irrevocably associated with. And like most bands, it is an image they will have great difficulty in moving away from."

Therefore, an image created for an act by video can be a powerful commercial tool, but might end up as a televisual albatross of disastrous proportions. At a time when groups as awful as Chicago can rejuvenate themselves in the eyes of a vast TV audience by making videos which borrow freely from Indiana Jones and Bogart movies, Duran might discover that the relentless super-glamour of their promos looks suddenly tired and repetitive, far too much of a once-good thing.

Bruce Springsteen, of all rock's superstars, has been one of the most reluctant to become involved with video. In Springsteen's case, his extraordinary reputation as a live performer and his unique cultural status probably render him impervious to many of the market factors which bind the common-or-garden pop star. But the fact remains that, despite his reservations, he made the move into video with 'Dancing In The Dark' and 'I'm On Fire', and has benefited accordingly.

Probably, it comes down to making the right video at the right time. It seems now that a record is unlikely to be a hit in America without radio play, and radio play spurs the TV operators to show the video. Steve Dagger points out that Spandau Ballet's 'True' was already in *Billboard's* Top Twenty before the video was put into "heavy rotation" on MTV.

Dagger likens the impact of video for a group in America to the combined effects in Britain of exposure on Radio 1, *Top of the Pops* and in pop magazines like *No1* or *Smash Hits.* Video has given America a nation-wide medium for the dissemination of pop music for the *first time,* since the country still has no national music press on the British model. It is also noteworthy that Spandau Ballet's public reception was noticeably warmer in areas where MTV was available than in those where it wasn't. And, given Spandau Ballet's inability to produce a follow-up of the calibre of 'True', while video might assist a band into the Big League, in itself it is no guarantee that the group will stay there — no matter how many exotic foreign locations are used — if the new songs themselves aren't up to scratch.

Now that everybody's at it, perhaps the video bubble will burst, or at least grow smaller. Perhaps, as Springsteen says, promos have taken the place of cartoons for kids. Perhaps there are unexpected side-effects — maybe the recent upsurge in the number of powerful new American groups from all over the nation has come about partly as a reaction to the force-fed pap of MTV and similar stations.

For now, video is a crucial component in the marketing of pop music. One day, there may be a stratification between "video-music" (chart fodder) and a new strain of what was once called "progressive" or "underground" music, listened to seriously and relying on a live audience. Happily it still looks as if the song will be the decisive factor at the end of the day.

Dessa Fox passes judgement on a selection of the year's VIDEOS

BANANARAMA. And That's Not All (PolyGram)
All the hits, plus the most recent single 'Wild Life'. Interestingly, the look the Narns helped make popular – a sort of dandelions-in-baggy-trousers chic – has since died the death. Today's fashion female wears jewels all the way to the boardroom; *ergo*, these ten videos have gone speedily out of date. You'll just have to enjoy them for the vocals, which seems a dangerous topic to introduce.

BAND AID. Do They Know Its Christmas?: The Band Aid Video EP (PolyGram)
Criticism doesn't come into it. Buy it, and then don't put away your chequebook. **(proceeds to the Band Aid Trust)**

THE BEACH BOYS. An American Band (Vestron)
There is an unnervingly hilarious sequence in this very entertaining retrospective, and it involves Brian Wilson. Up until this point we're shown the Brian we all recognize: as one of the boys Murray Wilson Senior had sacrificed his business for (and who promptly received an "F" in music at Hawthorne High); as the tall, motionless guy in early TV appearances, surrounded by studio sand, studio palms, and missile-breasted girls doing the frug; as the man forever entranced by vocal harmonies ("The Four Freshman taught me everything"); and as the Brian of reclusive habits, lying doped for days in a huge clamshell of a bed. But a Brian Wilson with a sense of humour?? Without warning, we get a loony gem of a scene: the blank-era Brian is lying cocooned in his bedroom when in burst John Belushi and Danny Ayckroyd, dressed in California Patrol outfits. Briskly, they cite Bri for "failure to surf". Ayckroyd grasps a Wilson arm and barks "Let's go surfin' now"; Belushi takes the other arm with "Everyone's learnin' how. Let's move it." The hapless Brian is bundled up and escorted down to the beach.

'An American Band' contains a vast amount of similarly priceless material, not least tracks from film and television archives. Among others, there's 'Surfin' USA' and 'I Get Around' (TV studios, 1964), 'Help Me Rhonda' and 'In My Room' (with the Boys dressed as Harvard students), 'Wouldn't It Be Nice' (acquiring long hair and flares) and 'California Girls' from the film *Girls on the Beach* (featuring Jack Benny wisecracking to Bob Hope "I can hardly wait to get out there and hang ten"). As the Boys pass from wistfulness to psychedelia to the fractured seventies to the Reagan-sanctioned eighties, the visual record-keeping is superb. Watch the 'Pet Sounds' promo film, or Mike Love's increasingly embarrassing Jagger mannerisms, or the middle-aged Boys harmonizing 'Surfer Girl' around a piano. Recommended.

BLANCMANGE. Hello Good Evening (PolyGram)
Recorded live at the Hammersmith Palais, 'Hello' is deep-pepped with a kind of spangled likeableness (smiles galore on Neil and Arthur, playpen outfits on the back-up girls, day-glo splashes on the walls) until director Mike Mansfield declares an art emergency. Awful, intrusive stock footage of bombed cities and goose-stepping armies are these days the very nerve centre of art-video cliché. Only industrial gloomster bands could ever render this stuff interesting, and in 1985 they're finding fewer and fewer willing to watch. Between the grim gaffes are 'Living On The Ceiling', 'Blind Vision', 'Waves', and 'Don't Tell Me.'

A COLLECTION OF BLOOD GROUPS. Blood On The Cats (Jettisoundz)
'Cats' features seventeen clots of ghastlybillies, among them Bone Orchard, Folk Devils, the Stingrays, Guana Batz, Screaming Lord Sutch (in his living room), Inca Babies and Alien Sex Fiend. Unlike, say, this month's chart-toppers, the Blood bands don't need money to look comfortable. Stylistically speaking, the Guana Batz are face down on the carpet from the word go, which spares them the indignity of Wrinkle Erase filters or having to beg for Julien Temple's phone number. Ausgang have only a mangy fox tail to work with, and the Jazz Butchers two squares of cardboard and an eyeliner pencil.

Still, as every cheapie horror fan knows, the Book of Gnash is best writ with a shaky, starving hand. Everyone here bites as many ankles as possible on a next-to-zero budget, which is fine by this viewer.

MARC BOLAN. Marc On Video (Videoform)
A love library. This 19-track video was assembled by two Marc devotees, and fans always care enough to send the very best. Probably only a fan could wrestle the obscure 'Buick McKane' video from Warner Brothers, or love-pummel the West Germans into contributing dusty slews of Marc on the *Beat Club*. Marc himself is the way we always remembered him – born under a mandrake root the night Morticia Addams ran into Alan Ladd. In his earliest and best videos – 'Ride A White Swan', 'Metal Guru', 'Get It On' – he looks batty and sly; later he looks batty, sly, and dissipated ('Telegram Sam' and 'Dreamy Lady'). But no matter how much paunch crept behind the boas or how tedious his back-up became, Bolan never looked abandoned by talent. History of Video note: visual psychedelia fans – seekers of splodges, day-glo beehives, and mandalas with motion sickness – need look no further than 'Jewel'.

DAVID BOWIE. Jazzin' For Blue Jean (PMI)

This 21-minute short was released for cinemas in tandem with the film *Company of Wolves*. Format-wise, 'Jazzin'' is what the video industry dubs a "long-form" project – ie a combination of talkie and promo. 'Jazzin'' is a surprisingly durable bit of glitter, chiefly because there's a send-up in every scene. Bowie plays two roles; the wide-boy labourer Vic and the clapped-out lizard king Screamin' Lord Byron, a hilariously paranoid spectre who needs a stretch in an oxygen tent before he goes on stage. The plot follows the adventures of Vic trying to persuade a girl that he's a friend of the famous Screamin'.

The easy action is in the script: it's full of spot-on little digs at everything pop – the name-dropping jetsetters (Vic to girl: "David Hockney introduced me to Screamin'"), the usual liggers' lines at the concert door ("I'm not on that list, I'm on the manager's list.") and Great Clichés of the Bowie Era (Vic yelling after Screamin': "Your record sleeves are better than your songs.") Plus there's a Bryan Ferry satire and some brilliant turns from Bowie as Screamin'. Director Julien Temple even sends up the send-up: at the very end, Bowie walks off the set in a raging sulk: "Look, Julie, it's my song, my concept, my act". Caveats: 'Jazzin''s polish sometimes veers close to smugness, and does the girl have to be such a dimbulb?

DAVID BOWIE. David Bowie Live (Videoform)

This one looks suspiciously like remainders from the Serious Moonlight tour video of last year, swept from the cutting-room floor, injected with a few freeze frames and committed to video tape.

It's also pointedly un-fun, principally because the first one wasn't fun and volume one had all the best songs. 'Live' contains lesser lights like 'Station To Station', 'Scary Monsters', 'Cracked Actor' and a colourless version of 'White Light, White Heat', all given chugging rock-riff treatment by guitarist Earl Slick. The close-ups of Bowie are discouraging; there's nothing flickering here, no zing, pep, tang, or wit. Even worse is the complete abscence of style in the stage set, which looks like a Greek temple designed by Steven Spielberg. And if only Bowie would lay off those stage props – in 'Fame', he staggers around bearing a plastic globe on his shoulders. The more you see concerts like this, the more you understand the rise of Springsteenism.

BRONSKI BEAT. The First Chapter (PolyGram)

'The First Chapter' should be committed to memory by every recently-signed band in the country, because it illustrates how easily videos go astray when the profits roll in. The initial 'Smalltown Boy' was made for next to nothing and achieved almost everything, being both beautifully photographed and rich in feeling. After the gold rush, however, time got tight, the sets got huge, party pals dropped in for bit roles and videos two and three turned out to be expensive mules. 'Why?' is so crowded that Jimmy bobs up only briefly, a champagne cork at someone else's social event. Fortunately, the 'I Feel Love' medley falls backwards into sensibleness; the only thing that goes over the top is Marc Almond's groaning.

LLOYD COLE AND THE COMMOTIONS. Lloyd Cole And The Commotions (PolyGram)

'Lloyd Cole' is too young to be useful; plainly put, one LP is not enough. Bands with maybe twelve songs behind them are asking a lot from videotape – not only are we prevented from enjoying the march of time (new clothes, new audiences, new singles), but nobody in the Commotions looks prematurely visionary to begin with; stripling tornadoes they're not.

'The Commotions' is just the LP *Rattlesnakes* filmed live at the Marquee. It's all right – 'Speedboat' in particular raises a fine mist – but it's short on experience wattage. History has yet to pass through Lloydsville, and it shows.

ELVIS COSTELLO. The Best Of Elvis Costello: The Man (Palace)

Pop video – you can go for weeks without seeing any adults. 'The Man' is immaculately titled; guaranteed free of numbskull tantrums, excessive attention to clothing manufacturers, dry ice and wet ideas. You're going to like it.

These twenty-two videos range from 1978's 'Pump It Up' to last year's 'The Only Flame In Town'. In between are memory banks from *Top of the Pops*: 'Oliver's Army', 'I Can't Stand Up (For Falling Down)', 'New Lace Sleeves', 'Accidents Will Happen', etc. This is an unconditionally brilliant tape, not least because you get to watch both EC and Music Video grow up in public.

In the early days, video produced Piltdown punk, not the real thing but convincing enough to do the job. Untold thousands of bands came over all knock-kneed and deranged in little white studios, exactly like 'Pump It Up' or 'Radio Radio'. Costello was without equal when it came to the spittle stuff, but looks miles more convincing in the Madness-era travelogues (such as the Chuck Statler-directed 'I Can't Stand Up'), which allowed him to exercise a bit and flash the humour. After 1980 comes the style dispersal: jazz flirtations, a host of night-club settings, and the inevitable embarrassing soft-focus drama ('You Little Fool', which is probably how everyone addressed the director).

And so to 1983, and one of the best promos ever made: 'I Wanna Be Loved'. Glowing, elegant, and full of low-key majesties, your thirteen pounds will never find a more gorgeous destination.

THE DOORS. The Doors: A Tribute To Jim Morrison (Warner Home Video)

Assuming Jim Morrison *was* a poet – since this is the way a lot of people want to remember him – what kind of eulogies are these? Here's Ray Manzarek sporting a jacuzzi-punk haircut: "He was possessed, man. To make art." Paul Rothchild, producer: "He was a Renaissance man of the mind." Someone else: "He had a burning fire to create", and (repeated *ad infinitum* over the cover of Danny Sugerman's cheesefile bio 'No One Gets Out Of Here Alive') "He lived life on the edge, for all of us". Too bad they didn't interview any women, else someone might have blurted the word *trousers*.

Not only is this California pseuds' documentary full of ghastly *Rolling Stone*-speak, but it also manages to commit crimes in the editing room. The classic 'People Are Strange' clip from the *Ed Sullivan Show* is here *cut in half* by a rock critic in a luau shirt going on about what a seminal performer Morrison was. Very good footage is actually quite thin on the ground: there are only three TV segments and a single, dozy interview with Morrison. The rest of it is much too fond of Danny Sugerman, starchy descent-into-madness theories, and those worshipful stills zooms that spell Deity Ahead.

DURAN DURAN. Dancing On The Valentine EP (PMI)

Three brilliantly executed but conceptually damp promos: 'The Reflex', 'New Moon On Monday', and 'Union Of The Snake'. The first of these goes by very quickly, the second features female "revolutionaries" not doing much of anything unless being kissed on the breasts by backlit stormtroopers, and the third aims to be – what's the word? – *heavy*. 'Union Of The Snake' sprouts mystical stuff all over the place: serpents, swords, stars, trees, etc. Imbued with the wisdom of centuries, Nick Rhodes flips through a parchment scroll. Elsewhere in this fantastic kingdom, a mime juggles, little girls dolled up like Etruscan Brooke Shieldses dart towards the offscreen catering tables, and *all the umbrellas are upside down*. Jung wept.

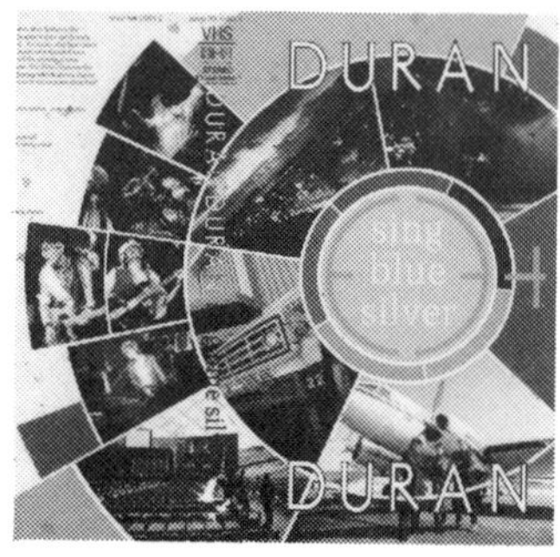

DURAN DURAN. Sing Blue Silver (PMI)

This feature-length tour documentary is as truthful and contentious as a cashmere sweater: it looks great, it conceals more than it displays, and people will probably think you have limited taste if you put it on all the time. 'Silver' is of course very costly and very elegant. Some luxuriant particulars: *Best Camera Cliché* – hand-held trailing of roadies into the dressing room; *Best Rockspeak* – "That was a brilliant vibe onstage" (back-up sax aide); *Best Facial Expressions* – the imploded, worn-out looks on the Taylors as they realize they're going to have to make speeches to Coca-Cola executives; *Number Of Breakdancers* – two.

ECHO & THE BUNNYMEN. Pictures On My Wall (Warner Music Video)

This one is mysteriously free of interviews from the mouthy McCulloch. No one demands an out-and-out stripping of mystique, but for Mac not to utter one offstage word is flatly disappointing. For this reason, the 'Porcupine'-oriented first half – a visual fleabag of a section to begin with – is made even worse by sheer absence of personality. There's a lot of jerkily zoomed buses and Holiday Inns, a scalped version of 'Promise' (no intro) and a pack of frosty clichés (shots of broken windows).

The concert footage, however, is excellent, principally due to Bunny genius and Tyne Tees's handling of the Crystal Day evening in St George's Hall. 'Thorn Of Crowns' and 'Porcupine' come close to the mystic rub of actually being there. Still, at the end of it all Mac remains all lips and no quips.

JIMI HENDRIX. Jimi Plays Berkeley (Palace)

The only documentary video centred around Hendrix, Mitch Mitchell and Billy Cox was shot on Memorial Day 1970 at the Berkeley Community Centre, California. Tracks featured are 'Johnny B Goode', 'Star Spangled Banner' (which Hendrix ends with a disgusted "Big deal!"), 'Purple Haze', 'Machine Gun', and 'Voodoo Chile'. Aside from the performances – and even burning type couldn't do this *incendiary* music justice – other points of interest are the grainy sequences of student protest. They look odd in the yuppie eighties – who could imagine Days of Rage in the Prince era?

ELTON JOHN. The Night Time Concert (Vestron)

Viewed from the air – and this is one of those videos that opens with a fleet of helicopters taking pictures – a seventy-thousand strong Wembley stadium looks exactly like a huge bowl of caviar. This seems entirely appropriate for the likeable Elt, performer with first-class tastes but an uncannily common touch.

Here, Elton and band razz gently through all the hits, from 'Blue Eyes' to a closing Beatles medley. Everyone is satisfied except for director Mike Mansfield, who couldn't resist painting in a special-effects yellow brick road during the you-guessed-it song.

KOOL AND THE GANG. Live In Concert (Embassy)

This is a recent hour of the Kools in New Orleans, and it's very, very smoochy. It's also one of the few videos where you'll witness genuine audience rapport – it's worth keeping in mind that the Kools' publishing company is called Delightful Music Ltd. Watch that buoyant crowd, and you'll see delight all the way to the back seats.

Some of the raptures herein are the happy-footed devilment of Kools Michael Ray and J T Taylor; the modest, precision-timed camerawork; and the girls going wild over 'Ladies Night', 'Celebration', 'Joanna', and 'Let's Go Dancing (Ooh La La La)'. By the end of it you realize that 'Live In Concert' has packaged the party quite nicely; it *is* like actually being there.

MADONNA. Madonna (Warner Home Video)

So what if she looks and acts like an excommunicated swizzle stick; Virginia Woolf never made it big in America anyway. The key idea here is in fact making it big in America. All that this entails is revealed in the promos 'Like A Virgin', 'Borderline', 'Lucky Star', and 'Burning Up'.

GARY MOORE. Emerald Aisles (Virgin)

This one begins on a note of blushing shyness. Here is an interviewee who avoided the cutting-room floor by saying: "Jimi Hendrix was the greatest thing I'd ever seen, and then I saw Gary Moore". Testimonials like this abound, together with bizarre tourist shots of stately Irish castles. This one is definitely made for the American market, with jig-and-reel music being played over hearty pints of Guinness and narrator Kid Jensen being forced to say things like "Dublin is a city steeped in historical tradition." In the true spirit of rock wunderkinds Gary, of course, "picked up a battered acoustic guitar at the age of eight". Many years and several pints of Guinness later, one of Gary's sidemen avows, "Gary Moore can make the guitar laugh, and he can make it cry." He can also make it sound like a tortured rasberry, as you will discover in 'Out In The Fields', 'Empty Rooms, 'Parisienne Walkways' (with Phil Lynott) and the inevitable 'Shapes Of Things'.

THE SOUNDS OF MOTOWN. A Ready Steady Go! Special (PMI)

These twenty-one heart-stoppingly modest bravuras were recorded in March 1965. Motown effectively arrived in Britain with this revue: Smokey Robinson and the Miracles ('Oo Baby Baby'), Stevie Wonder ('Kiss Me Baby'), the Supremes ('Stop! In The Name Of Love'), Martha and the Vandellas ('Nowhere To Run'), the Temptations ('My Girl'), and Marvin Gaye ('How Sweet It Is To Be Loved By You'). Each one of these people – including hysterically happy MC Dusty Springfield – manages to look sharp, snappy, and brimful of mystic professionalism. Check out the Temptations' natty suits, the rapture from the bleachers, and the celestial talent that was Marvin Gaye.

WILLIE NELSON AND FAMILY. In Concert (CBS Fox)

With Bobbie Nelson on piano, Bee Spears on bass and Jody Payne on guitar, Nelson and Family skip the interviews and glide through twenty-eight exceptionally well photographed hits. The cumulative effect, though, is like being lashed below the doom spinnakers. It is worth remembering that Nelson wrote one of the all time best knell-of-despair songs (for Faron Young), 'Hello Walls'.

YOKO ONO. Then And Now (Videoform)

'Then And Now' features 'Imagine', 'Give Peace A Chance' (Toronto version), 'Thin Ice', 'Watching The Wheels' and 'Beautiful Boy'; an even-handed mixture of old and new. This hour-long documentary does an appealing job of illuminating Ono's life (with and without *him*), and excels when it comes to her misrepresentation by Beatle worshippers, the press and the other three Fab Four. A reflective Paul McCartney puts his finger on it: "Back then, we thought she was hard and calculating. She wasn't; she was just honest."

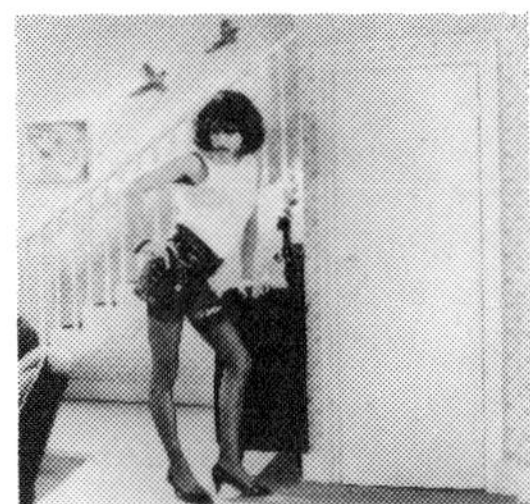

QUEEN. The Works EP (PMI)

"*This is a tricky situation*" sings Freddie Mercury, surveying the scene below. He's right, since there are seventeen plastic eyeballs glued to Fred's chest, and Fred's chest has to make it intact through a mass of courtiers, jugglers and other baroque boobytraps. But if anyone can do this Fred can. Grandly he descends the staircase, his wig askew but *proud*. You just have to love him; I don't know why. The three tracks here are 'Radio Ga-Ga', 'I Want To Break Free' and the aforementioned 'It's A Hard Life'.

READY STEADY GO! Volume III (PMI)

Ready Steady Go! videos are like electronic jewel boxes; there's always bits of classic sparkle to enjoy on a rainy day. Somehow, MC Keith Fordyce's smooth-guy charm never wears thin, nor those uncomplicatedly happy audiences, nor *those singers*. Here, the highlights are Marvin Gaye's radiant 'How Sweet It Is To Be Loved By You', and the Rolling Stones shrugging through 'Off The Hook' and 'Little Red Rooster'. The latter is a brilliant piece of preening, so lasciviously cocky that your average Prince single looks like a disco ostrich by comparison. Other dividends include Martha and the Vandellas ('Heat Wave'), Jerry Lee Lewis ('High Heel Sneakers'), four Beatles numbers and several deliciously hokey old adverts.

OTIS REDDING. Otis Redding Live: A Ready Steady Go! Special Edition (PMI)

The little details make up the picture: dim lights, pockets of cheers from the seats, a blocky stage, old-fashioned videotape that confers a million nimbi around the drum kit, and then the man in the four button sports jacket twists into view and flatly breaks your heart. This live performance was recorded in 1966 at the RSG studios, with guests Eric Burdon and Chris Farlow. Burdon rants like a hotheaded postbox (a compliment) while Farlow looks plainly out of his depth. The tracks are some kind of miracle, including 'Respect', 'My Girl', 'This Is A Man's World', 'Shake', and 'Land Of A 1000 Dances'.

THE ROLLING STONES. Rewind: The Rolling Stones Great Video Hits (Vestron)

Ah, the Rolling Stones collection – a few diamonds, a few zircons, and one sparkler ('Undercover') of such dubious origins you'll wish they'd peddle that thing somewhere else.

This made-for-home-video compilation features twelve promos, ranging from the 'Sticky Fingers' era to just preceding the Jagger solo LP. Tracks include 'Start Me Up', 'Brown Sugar', 'Neighbours', 'Angie', 'It's Only Rock 'N' Roll', 'Miss You', and 'Waiting On A Friend'. The connecting material – with Jagger and Wyman as exhibit and exhibit-keeper larking around in a deserted rock museum – was written and directed by Julien Temple. Part of Temple's genius lies in his ability to squeeze (subtly) the daylights out of a dramatic situation. Thus the plotline allows Jagger and Wyman to trade in-jokes with each other ("Let's open Mama Cass's fridge") and also leads them to places where it makes sense to zoom in on a promo (TVs, computer screens, and a microwave oven).

With some of the more recent promos, however, Temple plus Stones equals a funny smell from the TV corner. Temple is a supremely talented editor and scenarist, but if he's not working with someone like Ray Davies his brilliance tends to look cutting and cool. 'She Was Hot' is brilliant, funny, and cold; 'Too Much Blood' is brilliant, inventive, and cold. Jagger doesn't help matters by contributing his usual spunky chicken routine, all popping eyes and "sexiness" and not an ounce of conviction in sight. 'Undercover' is the ugly peak of all this: Jagger probably insisted on looking the very picture of hip martyrdom (complete with beautiful native girl) and Temple probably couldn't help handing him the perfect frame. *Ergo* 'Undercover', a promo that is a gilded disgrace.

STATUS QUO. More From The Road '84 (Videoform)

It's 1985, and women everywhere are struggling to be heard; Francis Rossi has *great legs*. Possibly also the Big Rockist In The Sky thinks so too, for this outdoor concert is blessed with spectacularly gorgeous weather. The sunset is a cameraman's dream, and this – together with a devoted, packed-to-the-rafters Milton Keynes crowd – lends 'End Of The Road' a sort of epic feel. Speaking of epic feels, can I mention Francis Rossi again? (*spare us – Ed.*) Thirteen hits are here, plus a 'Mystery Song' medley.

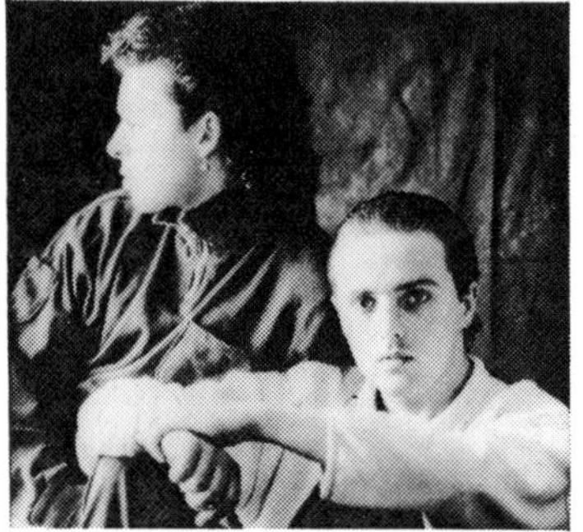

TEARS FOR FEARS. In My Mind's Eye (PolyGram)

'Eye' is a sixty-minute concert tape that just has to cop 1985's Most Deadly Editing Effects award. We find at the controls director Mike Mansfield, who has been exhibiting these disturbing tendencies all year (perhaps he's been working too hard).

The way the stage has been treated at the Hammersmith Palais looks more or less all right, the lighting is fine, the songs are fine, and Orzabal and Smith might be fine if we could see beyond the flying electro cubes bisecting the scenery. Or the split screens, or the superimpositions, or the colour effects, or any other device known to the grid-like warrens of video editing suites. It makes you long for the old hickory-smoked visual era in pop, when people only had wide-angle lenses and a couple of sheets of foil. Includes tracks from the LP *The Hurting*.

THE THOMPSON TWINS. Into The Gap Live (Virgin/Arista)

Another travel documentary that begins with dull fanfare – ie shots of American tour buses flapping their tiny wings in underground parking garages. The music swells, fans buy T-shirts outside stadiums, and somehow you feel you're going to get a sequence in which the band explains how unreal tour life is, just as someone else staggers in the door with a crate of Sardinian strawberries.

All the customary fillips are here: interviews, giggly fans, halo-eyed views of the live dates, etc. Watching the music, it becomes apparent that this band's house is built upon sand. Currie and Leeway have little to do on stage, and no amount of canary-birding around in lumpen fashionwear will disguise something remarkable; deep in the darkness, several session players are doing most of the work.

ULTRAVOX. The Collection (Chrysalis)

'The Collection' is twelve chronologically ordered blocks of floss, from 'Passing Strangers' to 'Love's Great Adventure'. Of course they're grandiose, and of course the band eventually recognized what viewers knew all along – namely, that overblown epics make musicians look humourless and slightly balding in the imagination area. *Ergo*, latter-day Ultravox videos made occasional attempts at wit and warmth. But the changes came in all the wrong places: Midge Ure's wheezing pause in the safari-like 'Adventure' incites a friendly ripple until you realize that black actors are *still* being asked to do mambo routines like jump out of bushes and rattle spears. 'Dancing With Tears In My Eyes' is even worse; ostensibly anti-war, the pretty-pretty production design ends up romanticizing everything nuclear. Spotless blasts, dewy last cuddles, and views of Warren Cann dressed as a priest are not the stuff of dissent; they're the stuff of star trips.

VARIOUS. Blues Alive (RCA)
The sleeve is hideous, and the general Van Wrinkledness of the project might seem off-putting, but at least these people don't look like they spend all day at the hairdressers. In 1982 ex-members of John Mayall's Bluesbreakers somehow converged in New Jersey: the former Rolling Stone Mick Taylor (who herein plays a genuinely affecting slide guitar), ex-Fleetwood Mac bassist John McVie, Rod Stewart sideman Colin Allen on drums, and Mayall himself. They were joined by five blues greats: Buddy Guy, Junior Wells, Albert King, Etta James, and Sippie Wallace. This tape succeeds because it achieves what most others like to proclaim in their press releases – ie letting the music speak for itself. There are twelve fervent tracks, among them 'The Dark Side Of Midnight', 'Why Are You So Mean To Me?', the foolproof 'Born Under A Bad Sign', and 'Call It Stormy Monday'. The highlight is Sippie Wallace, an extremely ancient lady who looks sweet as heck in a feathered hat; watch her slug down the beer before launching into 'Shorty George'.

VARIOUS. Don't Watch That – Watch This Vols I & II (Chrysalis)
Volume I contains twenty-three videos; Volume II has twenty-four. The former's attractions include Bronski Beat/'Smalltown Boy', Lloyd Cole and the Commotions/'Perfect Skin', Swans Way/'Soul Train', and the Frank Chickens/'We Are Ninja', a little-exposed masterpiece of space and time and huge scaly paws. Volume II is slightly drippier, lacking the usual graces of director Tim Pope and really only offering the wonderful Billy Mackenzie (in the Associates' 'Breakfast').

VARIOUS. The Other Side Of Nashville (MGM/UA Home Video)
'Nashville' is 112 minutes of interviews, concert footage, and archive material from middling-to-great country music stars, among them Kenny Rogers, Johnny Cash, Charlie Daniels, Hank Williams, Hank Williams Jr, Emmylou Harris and Kris Kristofferson. The history side of things is a slightly speedy backwards travelogue: quickly, we see the origins of the Grande Ole Opry, the importance of rival stations WSM (country) and WLAC (blues), a short skid into rockabilly (Elvis, Vincent, Carl Perkins explaining how he couldn't spell "suede") a stellar sequence devoted to Hank Williams, and a final dash to the Austin City Limits rebels.

But the bulk of this tape is taken up with worries. Most of the younger interviewees are aware that the prime impetus in country music is fast disappearing; next to no one comes from the farm anymore. As Gail Davies says, "It's kinda silly for me to write a song about trains when there are hardly any left." Yet Nashville's fanatical worship of all things dead and miserable means that newer artists must continually re-chew old symbols. The smarter ones – like Waylon and Willie – bring old feelings to new objects; they're haunted by air-conditioning units.

VARIOUS. Rock And Roll: The Early Days (RCA/Columbia)
The back cover proclaims the birth of rock 'n' roll "as it really happened", which probably means that Kenneth Anger can sleep through this one undisturbed. And lo: the thirteen-year-old Frankie Lymon appears singing 'I'm Not A Juvenile Delinquent', but the ironies of kid star Lymon ending his short life broke and wasted remain massively unexplored.

True, 'The Early Days' skirts the weird side of the pop pram, but the healthy stuff on display is a treat. Tracing as it does the careers of Presley, Jerry Lee Lewis, Chuck Berry and Little Richard, this cassette contains classic renditions of 'Tutti Frutti', 'Sweet Little Sixteen', 'Great Balls Of Fire', 'Hound Dog', 'Great Balls Of Fire' etc, plus Carl Perkins looking like he wished he'd stayed home with the hens, and other, bigger hens swooning over Fabian records. The omissions are a toss-up: Sam Cooke isn't here, but then neither is Dick Clark.

KIM WILDE. The Video EP (PMI)
Kim is always getting herself involved in "threatening" situations, the kind peculiar to tacky pop videos. In 'Cambodia' there are silly shots of Oriental water torture, in 'Chequered Love' it's yawnsome views of broken glass, in 'View From A Bridge' we have the classic fondle-the-blood-red-curtains routine, and in 'Child Come Away' someone (it's not clear who) tops themselves as a result of a malicious video review.

PAUL YOUNG. The Video Singles (CBS Fox)
Four fairly bubonic promos, with Young looking understandably stricken throughout. It's all here: the naff narratives, the venetian blinds, the light falling facewards like pink hamburger grease. Particularly ghastly is that Fear-of-Set-Design look in Paul's eyes, a look which tells you the artist is signed to CBS Records. CBS videos are unmistakable; someone up there likes ballerinas, and wants to look at them through a wet box of Kleenex.

In 'Every Time You Go Away' Paul is last seen slugging patiently through a forest of gaudy trees, blinded by an artificial hailstorm. Behind him are the glowing eyes of hungry ballerinas. Next time, Paul, grasp those camera mounts and pull the house down.

ROCK ON FILM

● STOP MAKING SENSE

● REPO MAN

● STREETS OF FIRE

● SPINAL TAP

1985 was the year when the music/film crossover finally clicked. The success of MTV in America opened up the eyes of the movie moguls to the potential of rock music as a means of getting through to the market they ill-understand but know they need, the 15-25-year-olds. It also spawned a more visually orientated form of music. In 1985 videos became more like movies and movies became more like videos.

The most obvious meeting point was the "long-form" video, like David Bowie's 'Jazzin' For Blue Jean' (directed by Julien Temple) which followed the format established by Michael Jackson's 'Thriller' – still based around a song but with extended narrative and spoken dialogue.

From the long-form it's only one step to the full feature-length promo, and that step was inevitably taken by the crowned head of the MTV generation, Prince. *Purple Rain*, all loneliness of the long-distance egotist, moist-lipped poppettes and macho juvenilia with an extended variation on the Marx Brothers' password sketch thrown in for good measure, was like half-a-dozen long-forms stuck together. Any random twenty minutes would have gone down just fine on MTV. It didn't pull the masses expected, though, perhaps because it revealed the Minnesota midget as the tedious preening narcissist he is. There's also the question of how fifty per cent of the audience might have felt about images of women being slung in garbage skips, even in the context of the film's cod psychology.

Many producers found it more successful and less problematic to use music and pop stars as motifs, little hooks to snag the audience. Thus Ray Parker Jr's insanely catchy, not to mention remarkably derivative (see Lawsuits In Motion Dept.), *Ghostbusters* theme was used to implant a name in the mind of the movie-going public before the product release date. More recently the *Mad Max III* soundtrack saw Tina Turner on *Top of the Pops* dressed in full mutant warrior gear, standing legs astride in front of tantalizing clips of the movie.

This conceptual linking of star and movie theme took its cue from *Electric Dreams* which used two noted electro-pop pioneers (Oakey and Moroder) for the soundtrack single to hint at the nature of its technological fantasy. "A cute little electro-acoustic parable for our times" *NME* called it at the time. Nor is it going to stop there. Frankie Goes To Hollywood appear in Brian de Palma's forthcoming satire of sleaze *Body Double*, although by the time it sees the light of day their suitably oozing reading of 'Relax' may be looking a trifle crusty.

The other easy thing to do with rock stars is parody them, which is precisely what *Spinal Tap* did. The fact that it disappeared almost without trace in Britain was probably due to its out-dated idea of the rock 'n' roll band, inevitable from a bunch of middle-aged Americans. The *Bad News Tour* TV programme produced by the Comic Strip a couple of years back had already done the same thing far more acutely.

On the documentary front a lot of attention was garnered by Jonathan Demme's *Stop Making Sense* which managed to redefine the live footage movie. What Demme realized is that no matter how many camera angles you employ, the sight of a band on stage is basically fairly boring. By manipulating props and settings and by building from a solo Byrne to a full band, he imposed a further dimension of pacing.

Released on video this year was the superb *This Is Elvis*, one of the few rock star documentaries not to try to soften its subject matter or squeeze it into a more convenient form of fiction. Using mainly original material of Elvis, from TV shows, home movies and films, plastering over the joins with a lookalike only where strictly necessary, *This Is Elvis* speaks volumes between the lines. From a country boy hanging around the old-time blues singers, to the snake-hipped greasy hipster apparently unaware of his own sexual danger, to the newly shorn Private Presley brought firmly into line, to the bloated dead whale beached on a Las Vegas stage, it's the most frighteningly frank and dispassionate observation of the degeneration of a man and the birth of a legend.

The Golden Jellyfish award for Flop Of The Year went to Paul McCartney for the intolerably smug *Give My Regards To Broad Street*. The problem was that McCartney's audience is housewives and they don't go to the cinema. Nobody else seemed vaguely interested in a cosy attempt to recreate the wild wackiness of the Beatles' films, and who can blame them?

The surprise success of the year, on the other hand, was the immaculately contemporary *Repo Man*, which was snappy, aware and anything *but* smug. It had a demon soundtrack by Iggy Pop, the Plugz and the Circle Jerks but above all, however surreal it got, it drew its material from modern day reality, not the sort of messy amalgam of rock 'n' roll myths as peddled by cynical efforts like *Streets of Fire* and *Eddie and the Cruisers*. It showed an America where good credit is true salvation, where sustenance for the soul comes from multi-media, mega-buck religion and where food is stuff in generic tins marked FOOD. It was witty, imaginative and (just like America) perpetually bordering on insanity. Director Cox, a Liverpudlian-born spiky top, relished his role as punk upstart of the movie-business and his continued disruptions will be eagerly anticipated in '86.

Don Watson

VIDEO INCORPORATED

Jon Savage lays the blame for promo mediocrity firmly at record company doors

We had half an hour to fill, so we took refuge in a nondescript Chelsea pub. I'd been in there about six months before; then, it was dim and dowdy, hinting at a kind of bored violence. But on this evening, it was transformed: "It's A Budweiser Kind Of Day" decor, packed with casuals and all the other accoutrements of the theme pub experience. In the corner winked a video jukebox, monitor high up on the wall. What it told me, as I sat unwillingly hypnotised by the Eurythmics, Tears For Fears, David Grant and Jaki Graham, Bruce Springsteen, Phil Collins and Philip Bailey, was that the pop video had now become as standardized as any other form of advertisement, its format as rigidly patrolled as any nightly *News at Ten*.

What irritated me was not so much the fact that pop video had become formularized — for which there are several very good reasons — but how these particular examples reflected the MTV-ization of the world, how the infinite possibilities of image and music had been reduced to series of stock "rock" signifiers. Once you've twigged the formula — 16-19-year-old Midwesterner — you can predict every shot change, every cut as they occur. *CUT TO THE BEAT* Tears For Fears — a REAL ROCK GROUP — performing 'Everybody Wants To Rule The World' in a studio *CUT TO THE BEAT* Curt Smith (the CUTE ONE) in a carefully picked OLD CAR (Austin Healey 3000) tooling down the FREEWAY with the WIND BLOWING IN HIS HAIR *CUT TO THE BEAT* Eurythmics playing in another studio LEATHER JACKET AND LEAPS now a REAL ROCK GROUP not a pervy synth-pop duo *CUT TO THE BEAT* CLOSE UP of the BLACK BACKING SINGERS in TONIK SUITS CLICKING THEIR FINGERS *CUT TO THE BEAT* Phil and Phil SWAPPING A FEW JOKES — yes, they're BUDDIES — before they get down to the SERIOUS BUSINESS of performing 'Easy Lover' in a TELEVISION STUDIO *CUT* . . . After all those beautifully filmed lies, the tawdry, chromakeyed mess of Dead Or Alive's 'Lover Come Back To Me' came as refreshing relief: beware pop when it has delusions of quality!

The standardization of music videos that has occurred since 1983 — still the high water mark of creative interest, lavish budgets, newsworthiness and public appreciation — has made it quite clear that the real changes are not aesthetic but industrial. Consider: the recent crop of pop videos — more often than not — use classic advertising techniques: pack shots of the product (ie the group) in a "realistic" situation, intercut at regular intervals with extra details to give placing and fantasy orientation. Thus Tears For Fears are presented playing "live" — to prove that they are real, and to shake off those synth-pop associations not considered smart in the Midwest — with additional material that presents them as swingin' but arty: a bit of flash, a bit of surrealism. It's very effective — the single went to number one in the US — but doesn't add anything to the visual language of advertising, itself a form, as definitions of postmodernism will tell you, intricately involved with the aesthetic. So what is new about pop videos?

In its current form, pop video began almost as a joke and ended up as an industry staple almost by accident. The actual idea of making short visual clips to promote songs is nothing new: black jazz artists were making them from the late twenties onwards and

● *EVERYBODY WANTS TO RULE THE WORLD*

● *LOVER COME BACK TO ME*

● *WOULD I LIE TO YOU?*

●*EASY LOVER*

●*BOHEMIAN RHAPSODY*

●*MIND OF A TOY*

multi-national sixties pop groups like the Beatles or the Rolling Stones made them to send around the world. The bands couldn't be everywhere at once but the film could. Yet despite its attractiveness — some of those mid-sixties films, particularly Peter Whitehead's 'Have You Seen Your Mother, Baby ?' for the Rolling Stones in 1966, remain among the most successful marriage of sound and vision to date — the form did not take off. Up until the mid-seventies, pop videos — or films — were little seen and regarded as imperfect substitutes for the "real" thing: the performer in the TV studio.

Bruce Gowers' 'Bohemian Rhapsody' for Queen in 1975 is now notorious as the first current pop video. The aesthetic reasons for this are quite clear, but bear repeating: the video's repeated exposure on *Top of the Pops* dazzled Britain and ensured that 'Bohemian Rhapsody' stayed at the top of the charts for nine weeks, the first song to do so for over eighteen years. It broke with previous conventions of "realism" and presented a highly stylised, glamorous package using to the hilt the emergent video technology still as yet unfamiliar to the public. 'Bohemian Rhapsody' was not only a breakthrough in ways of presenting music, but also the harbinger of profound changes in both hardware and software: 1975 was the year that the domestic video recorder was introduced which coincided with a gradual shift, by the television industry in particular, away from film towards video, as evidenced by greater use of Electronic News Gathering equipment whose results are now ubiquitous on our TV screens.

Despite the historical correctness of its timing, it took a while for 'Bohemian Rhapsody's influence to be felt in full. Part of the problem was punk rock: not a malleable medium, and not one immediately attractive to TV producers, although the Sex Pistols, to avoid fuss, allowed themselves to be filmed "authentically" in 'Pretty Vacant' and, in appearing like a "classic rock'n'roll band", sealed their fate as pop's untameable demons. The music industry couldn't see the attraction of investing money in pop videos because the outlets weren't there: the maximum exposure you could hope for was a lucky break on *Top of the Pops* and that was that. Until the early 1980s, pop videos were either the province of the very successful — who could afford such indulgencies — or the terminally arty, Video Art being a big thing around that time.

What happened in the early eighties was that pop changed and the outlets started appearing. Pop video was made for, and made, that clutch of pop groups that emerged from 1980 onwards, whom, for the sake of argument, we'll call New Romantics. Posing and Pop became both commercially and ideologically sound. Two crucial promos, Russell Mulcahy's 'Vienna' for Ultravox and Godley and Creme's 'Mind Of A Toy' for Visage (both 1981) caught the surprised yet arrogant stare endemic then and which — as an extension of fashion photography — has since become endemic throughout pop video. 'Mind Of A Toy' in particular displayed all the New Romantic hallmarks; in twenty years time, it'll be key research material on "History of Eighties Pop" courses. What also happened at this time was that the television industry began to fragment, both in Britain and in the US. In the UK, the previously monolithic duopoly of the BBC and the ITV network was being extended (and, you could add with hindsight, threatened) by the introduction in 1982/83 of both Breakfast Television and Channel 4. In the States, MTV had already started operations, playing pop videos twenty-four hours a day, in September 1981. The final piece of the jigsaw was set in place: so much time, so little programming to fill it with.

It is now clear that the real interest in pop video comes from its central placing as a vector between three hitherto separate industries: the film industry, the TV industry and the music industry. Pop video is important to the TV industry because it provides high quality programming at a minimal price for formats which, stretched by lack of resources, are gasping for airtime. It also provides an easy way into that elusive "youth" market, so much patronized but so little catered for by most corporate TV folk. Pop people — in the person of music industry execs — have become important to the TV industry by virtue of the fact that they have a lot of money to throw around. At a time when most major

TV companies are cutting back to basics because of falls in advertising revenue and years of mismanagement, you need outside finance even to think of making a programme that goes beyond the basics. So the two are getting closer: *Mirror Image* and *Max Headroom,* funded by Polygram and Chrysalis respectively, are the first of many such joint-venture programmes.

Pop video has also become very important to the film industry. In the UK, the production of pop videos has provided a new industrial space for a variety of companies to open up and operate. Some specialize in making videos only, some plan to move into commercials, some plan to move into feature films or TV documentaries. Some pop video directors have used the kudos surrounding pop video to make their feature film debuts: Russell Mulcahy, Steve Barron and Julien Temple to name but three. For many people, it provides an acceptable stopgap in an unreliable industry; for others it has provided a sound base from which to expand. Pop video is also frequently integrated into the marketing process of the feature film itself: note the trailering in the UK of *Ghostbusters* through Ray Parker's hit tune, of *The Falcon and the Snowman* by David Bowie's and Pat Metheny's 'This Is Not America' and of the new Bond movie through Duran Duran's 'A View To A Kill'. Note too the films — *Flashdance* for one — and the TV shows — *Miami Vice* to name another — directly influenced by pop video in their form.

On the music industry itself the pop video has had an incalculable effect. Record company executives are being forced to look outside their previously myopic confines in order to be able to communicate and work with people from a film and TV background. The days of pop being a place for children to play, unheeded in the dirt, is now over; it has become enmeshed as never before in a sophisticated, sometimes vertically integrated, media industrial agglomerate. The whole funding of pop music has now changed: executives now have to consider an entirely new level of capital investment in breaking a new group or keeping a successful one up to scratch. The nature of the music itself has also been changed, as the tail begins to wag the dog — pop videos are now no longer a means to an end but, because of their enmeshing in the corporate structure, an end in themselves. Nobody has quite worked out how to market these products properly, but forethought is, unfortunately, not a generic music industry trait. The music and the musicians, therefore, have to work within a whole new section of restraints: Will we look good on video? Can we afford to look good on video? Will MTV show it? Will we get our money back? No wonder pop is boring at the moment: nobody can afford to TAKE RISKS. Truly is this the age of Corp-pop.

●*MAX HEADROOM*

Pop video thus presents itself as a perfect postmodern. Both industrially and culturally, it presents itself as the product of a new era of production and consumption, "a new type of social life and a new economic order – what is often euphemistically called . . . post-industrial or consumer society, the society of the media or the spectacle, or multinational capitalism" (Frederic Jameson 1982). Typically, pop video is hamstrung by its industrial importance: Audio-Visual (formerly Music) executives may sit and bitch about MTV's idiot view of the world, but that's still where they need to get their product shown. Pop videos too obviously reflect corporate demands: like the pop they exhibit, they show too nakedly the need to satisfy inter-office politicking and the demands of the balance-sheet.

Yet it's worth bitching about videos that lie and insult your intelligence: I still believe that pop music can survive without video and that the video itself, if freed in part from its advertising function, can change into something more than an advert for potato crisps or shampoo. The problem that pop video has, in relation to the industrial agglomerate of which it is the tip of the iceberg, is the same as that of postmodernism in our society. As Jameson states in *Postmodern Culture* (Pluto 1985), "We have seen that there is a way in which postmodernism replicates or reproduces — reinforces — the logic of consumer capitalism; the more significant question is whether there is also a way in which it resists that logic."

JON SAVAGE FINDS MUCH TO LOWER THE SPIRIT WHEN COMPILING THE BEST AND WORST

VIDEOS

OF THE YEAR

A short while ago, videos used to be on the dividing line of Art and Commerce. Now they're just Commerce, and it shows. This results in a far greater proportion of Bad Videos to Good Videos: we shall start, therefore, with the Horrors.

The year was encapsulated by one particular shot: hundreds of monitors, stuck in theatre seats repeating endless images of . . . Bryan Adams: a paradigm of the current form/content imbalance. The examples of drivel mentioned below exhibit the daily violence committed on the public's sensibilities as private fantasies are co-opted into a lowest common consumerist denominator. One more point: any sexist imagery automatically makes the shit list – that means about fifty per cent of videos.

THE WORST

● *GET IT ON*

● *19*

● *CALL ME*

● *LOVING THE ALIEN*

● *WOULD I LIE TO YOU?*

POWER STATION: Get It On

Sexist drivel. A great song murdered in every conceivable way, both musical and visual. Nice one, "lads".

PAUL HARDCASTLE: 19

Scratchist drivel. A classic example of an exciting new form (see FIVE BEST) ruined by the customary lack of politics, lack of sensitivity and motive confusion. What attempts to be a critique ends up as a celebration, with its splatter-splatter crescendoes.

GO WEST: Call Me

Mid-American drivel. The MTV principle finds its lowest common denominator. High budget, low audience esteem: every possible Main Street cliché trotted out and topped up with the usual "buddy buddy" mix. Sinclair Lewis would turn in his grave: 85's "hottest new band".

DAVID BOWIE: Loving The Alien

Surrealist drivel. Appalling Art Damage – those De Chirico sets! –confused by David's simultaneous desire to appear aloof and "real". The Disappointment Value – from 'Ashes To Ashes' to this in five short years! –really hurts.

EURYTHMICS: Would I Lie To You?

Quality drivel. A handy example – not the worst by any means, but deeply symptomatic – of the simultaneous drive towards "quality" videos on the part of the music industry and towards a greater ethnocentricity on the part of previously synthetic pop groups. Beware pop groups with horns and black backing singers; beware the music industry when it attempts to apply standards of technical excellence.

THE BEST (in alphabetical order): The best are chosen with the thought: Beyond Music Video.

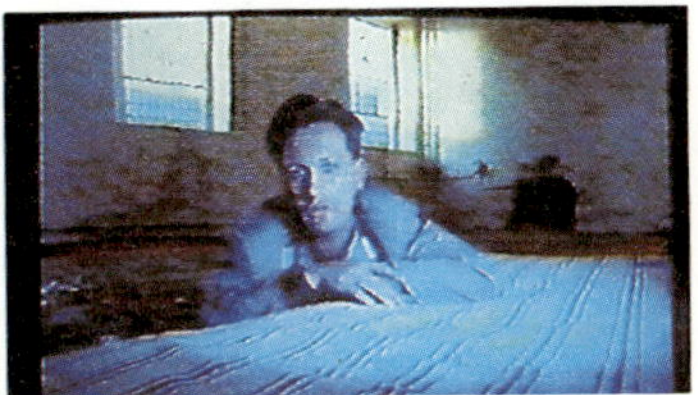

CABARET VOLTAIRE: Sensoria

The year's high-wire act between Art and Commerce. The full flowering of Cabaret Voltaire and Peter Care in a narrative of rare power and psychic disturbance.

THE DUVET BROTHERS: Blue Monday

Song visualization as a political record of the year: Greenham Common, the miners' strike, Mrs Thatcher, Lady Di, Cruise, American colonization. An exemplary scratch: how '19' should have been.

GORILLA TAPES/LUTON 33: Secret Love

Malcolm McLaren and the Shangri-Las; Thatcher and Reagan cut up and cursed. Anger as a source of humour; video images as redirected violence. "The individual talks back to television". Another exemplary scratch.

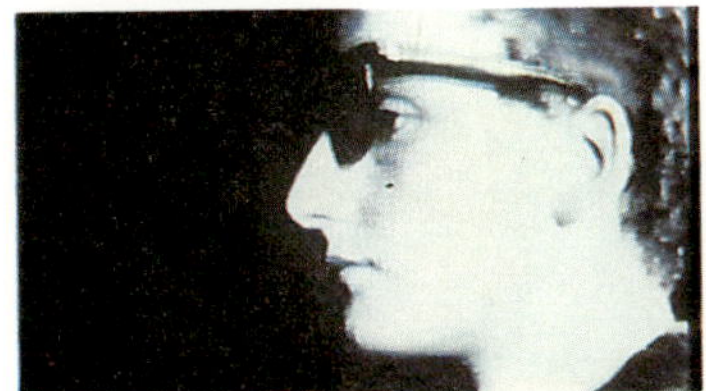

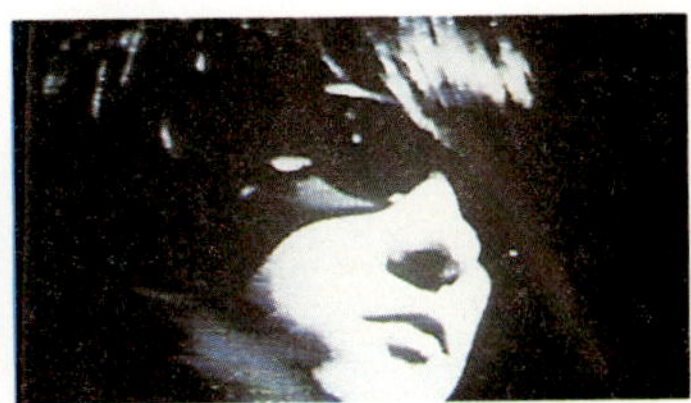

JESUS AND MARY CHAIN: Never Understand

One of the year's best records. An accompanying video of rare restraint and aptness: the group's stylistic disjunctions matched visually with slo-mo, stills and simple lack of synch. Even the Warhol references are permissible.

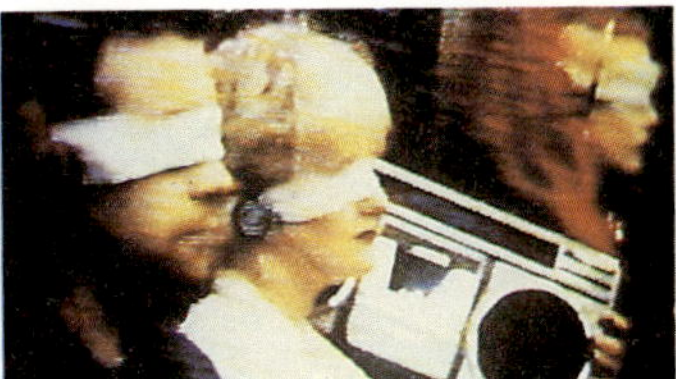

THE POGUES: A Pair Of Brown Eyes

Lullaby turned into an acid (taste, not drug) version of a future fascist Britain. A few good Irish jokes about the British, a bit of Bataille, a lot of Alex Cox, and a Northern Line location. What more could you ask for?

CH...CH...CHANGES

Bev Hillier and Cath Murphy take a backwards look at street fashions and remind us of the time when Dad's underpants were worth pinching.

The turnover gets quicker: fashion changes faster than the blonde on Rod Stewart's arm these days. Over the past year alone we've seen tartan, patent shoes, clashing checks, brocade, labels, crumpled shirts and now dare we say the return of polo necks, flares and platform shoes (arghhh). Dedicated followers of fashion definitely had their work cut out this year – keeping up with current trends suddenly became a full time job.

● Late last year everyone had a label. We're not talking *Delaware* or *Winfield* either but *Lacoste*, *Fila*, *Tacchini* and *Armani*. Saving up for that £38 T-shirt was an arduous task but we all managed it and went out sporting, as proud as peacocks. You'll need your calculator to total up the cost of this little lot.

● It ain't what you wear . . . it's the way that you wear it. This was the case 99 per cent of the time. The mark of a "casual" started right at the bottom. If the trainers weren't *Nike* or the *Lois* jeans unripped, forget about it. Was this the start of the eighties flare?

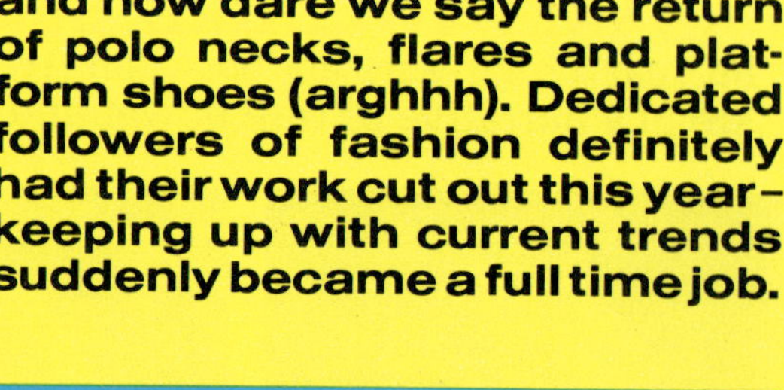

● Ford Escorts weren't the only things that got customised – Walkmans, watches and tapes caught the eye of budding graffiti artists. Note the tartan shirt.

● Everything the complete breakdancer could ask for. *Nike* anorak with hood up over *Lacoste* sun visor. The specs were worn regardless of the sun's rays. If you couldn't move like this then there was no point carrying a copy of *Electro 4*.

● While "Frankie Say . . .", "Choose Wham!" and Katharine Hamnett "Save The World" T-shirts became a thing of the past, the plain white baggy variety made their entry. Nobody forgot those important braces – worn back to front of course.

● Still mourning the death of comedian Tommy Cooper, the fez took on a whole new image in November '84. Leather ones, straw ones and tartan ones hit the streets – Steve Strange gave us all a giggle when he was seen wearing one. Baggy white shirts and a brooch were a must at this time. In London's *very* trendy Do-do's club you couldn't move for either.

The winter of '84 not only brought us a lot of snow on the ground but plenty of winter whites in the fashion department. Hair, make-up, nails – the whole look took on a whiter perspective. Matched with bold crumpled brights and a string of pearls, some folk took it that little bit too far – as you can see, their cleaning bill wasn't the only thing that suffered. Has this man tried *Spotoway*?

When fashion-conscious females had disposed of their long skirts, big shirts, waistcoats and brooches, they took men's clothing one step further than underwear and nicked their suits as well. Hunting around thrift shops on a Saturday afternoon became very important. But did it turn the men on? It's rumoured that Mark O'Toole of Frankie Goes To Hollywood got a little hot under the collar about it. Down boy!

Were Strawberry Switchblade to blame for the sudden surge of spots? Oh no – striped polo necks and thick-soled shoes; could this mean a seventies revival? Dig out those platforms!

After the chintzes and brocades of last November (did you spot Spandau Ballet's effort?), we looked forward to a summer of florals. Tough luck if you suffered from hay fever!

Those people responsible for Spandau Ballet's artwork (The Cloth) brought us more baggy T-shirts and vests – but just who was responsible for Dad's underwear getting into this? Is Calvin Klein the man to blame? The craze even found its way onto the shelves of *Marks & Spencer's* with big pants and boxer shorts being bought by women world-wide.

Just when you thought it was safe to throw out your mini-skirts, Beatle suits and love beads, the sixties found their way into '85. Peace, love and harmony – very psychedelic, man!

Whether you needed them or not, National Health specs became an essential item among young professional trendies.

IN

- Sleeveless polo necks
- Flares
- Platforms
- Short haircuts
- Kilt pins
- Keys worn as accessories
- White leggings and white minis
- Hats
- Black and white clothes
- Italian rucksacks
- Fringed jackets
- Knitwear
- Customised denim jackets
- Body painting
- Junk jewellery (esp. fake gems)
- *Marks & Spencer* clothes

OUT

- Crumpled shirts, especially Katharine Hamnett
- Tartan
- Checks
- Labelled clothes
- Worded T-shirts
- Brocade
- Long skirts
- Black clothes (but okay if worn with white)
- Fluorescents
- Patent shoes
- Plastic briefcases
- Diamanté jewellery
- White lipstick
- Tracksuits

Photographs courtesy of *Just Seventeen* magazine

DRESSED TO CONFORM

● **GIRLS (or should I say "Women In Rock"?)** Sorry to lump them all together, but there are so few of them, and unless they're *very* brilliant singers (eg Alison Moyet), they rely almost entirely on their image anyway. I mean, look at Madonna, Sade and Strawberry Switchblade. None of them can sing for toffee, but because they look the part – temptress, sultry sophisticate and dolly-birds respectively – they've got where they are (which in Strawberry Switchblade's case isn't that far). Still, it's not their fault; they're forced to act out the clichéd roles expected of them by the music business if they want any success at all. And at least they're not "rock chicks" or "foxy ladies" . . .

● **HOWARD JONES.** Until embarrassingly recently a Keith Emerson look-alike, Howard engineered a deft change of image courtesy of a somewhat receding cockatoo coiffure, home-made outfits, and giant shaggy sweaters knitted by his sister-in-law. The result, despite being alarmingly reminiscent of a decomposing parsnip, at least had an endearing homespun simplicity at odds with the vile "designerist" pretensions of most other big-league popsters. Yet, horror of horrors! Even this saintly character is not immune to the temptations of conspicuous consumption – he now has very expensive outfits designed for him by none other than Jeff Banks.

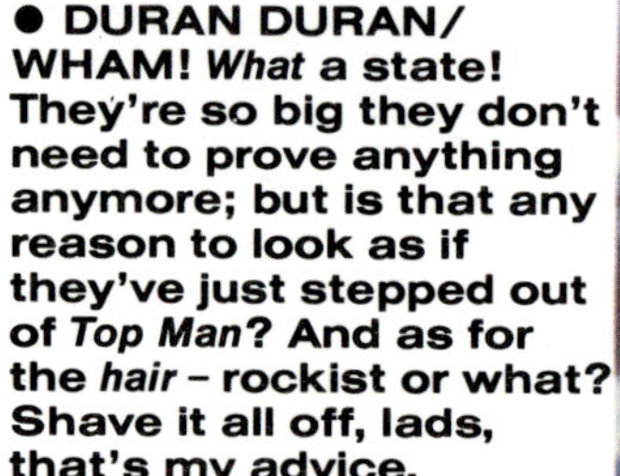

● **DURAN DURAN/ WHAM!** *What* a state! They're so big they don't need to prove anything anymore; but is that any reason to look as if they've just stepped out of *Top Man*? And as for the *hair* – rockist or what? Shave it all off, lads, that's my advice.

● **BRONSKI BEAT/BILLY BRAGG.** Life's simple if you're a committed gay commie pinko lefty, etc etc – you just bung on a pair of jeans and hey presto! Instant street-cred.

"Give them enough rope and they'll probably make cummerbunds out of it," as Julie Burchill once said. Vici MacDonald finds the popsters still sporting cummerbands, but these days they're more likely to have cost a couple of hundred quid from *Jean Paul Gaultier*.

Talk about fashion in pop, and you're talking about image – as Joe Strummer once said, "Like trousers, like brain". That was back when musicians used to choose their *own* clothes, of course. These days, what with "corporate pop" and "image styling", you never know *whose* brains are behind the trousers. The result is that both style and imagination have gone completely down the dumper . . .

As recently as 1983, when the charts were still vital and imaginative, Britain's fave popsters were a pretty diverse bunch sartorially. OK, so people like Adam Ant, Marc Almond and the Human League undoubtedly looked a bit *naff*, but that was all part of their charm. At least it was good old home-grown eccentricity, and there was plenty of leeway for quirky individuality and experimentation.

Not so today, however. As the music industry becomes ever more monolithic and stagnant, so individuality has been all but squeezed out. Most new groups look as if they've been designed by a committee – and usually they have.

Pop is pre-packaged as it never has been before, and the choice of images is becoming appallingly limited – there's an increasing polarization between dressing up and dressing down. In other words, either you're a "real", "committed" rock performer, who wears denim and leather and attempts to look "streetwise"; or you're an "entertainer", who sports the latest overpriced designer-label uniform, looks pretty and hopes to appear on *Wogan*. There's not a lot of ground in between, and apart from various superannuated Batcave refugees, only the Smiths have straddled the line with any wit or ingenuity.

Play it safe, that's the motto these days. The only trouble is, it doesn't *work*. I mean, what stylist would ever come up with an image as bizarre as Gary Numan's? Take a balding, pudgy-looking little geezer, paint his lips blue, dress him up like Mad Max and bung him in an aeroplane . . . it'd *never* work. And can you imagine what would happen to Boy George were he to walk into a record company office tomorrow – a big hairy bruiser in six inches of make-up and a dress? They'd cut his hair, wash his face, stuff him into a *Jean Paul Gaultier* waistcoat, and we'd never hear of him again.

Nevertheless, spurred on by Paul Morley's success with Frankie Goes To Hollywood (who did have a couple of good tunes to their name, after all), record companies continue to try to impose their will. As a result, stylists like XL Design have had a field day, whilst being perfectly well aware (and, to be fair, never denying) that an image is only as good as the record it's promoting. Take the oft-quoted examples of the Roaring Boys and Spelt Like This – two incredibly bland groups, malleable and compliant, a perfect canvas for record company pretensions. Vast sums of money were spent on providing the acceptable gloss of expensive suits and pretty videos, and what happened? Absolutely nothing. Their records were crap, and that was that. Compare them with Wham! in their early days – young and spunky, with loads of energy, good ideas and great pop songs. Nobody "styled" them; they had the intelligence and ability to handle their *own* image. And surely that's the crux of the matter – if you're not clever enough (or not allowed) even to choose your own *clothes*, ultimately you're *bound* to be bland.

So where does that leave new groups? Basically, either they conform to one of the current stereotypes delineated by the major record companies, and squander vast amounts of their advance on becoming bland and boring like everybody else, or they follow their own convictions and become consigned to the arid hinterlands of the independent world. Meanwhile the new "supergroups" – Duran Duran, Spandau, Wham! etc – grow richer and more decadent by the day, aping rockist seventies values for all they're worth and indulging in vulgar and tasteless displays of conspicuous consumption that wouldn't have disgraced Led Zeppelin or the Stones in their heyday.

Somewhere along the line, things like "music" and "spontaneity" have been left behind; pretty depressing, really. As they say, it's like punk never happened . . .

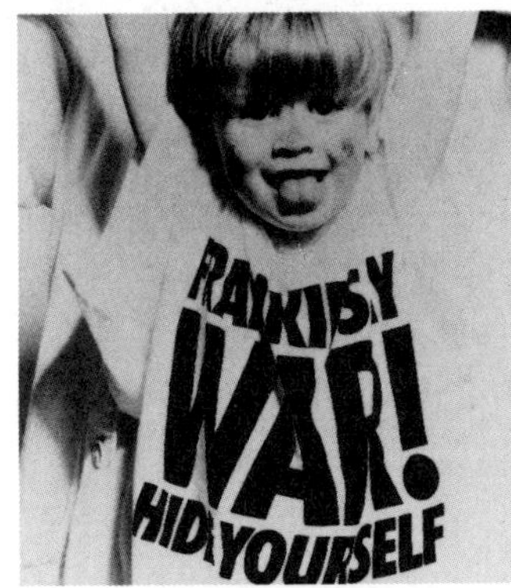

● **FRANKIE GOES TO HOLLYWOOD.** Frankie were the only group to influence fashion in any way, thanks to Paul Morley, who skilfully hijacked Katharine Hamnett's "message" T-shirts to disseminate his own brand of pop propaganda. Entire cotton plantations were razed to the ground to provide the vehicle for a zillion sub-"Frankie Say" rip-offs, the remnants of which are still being unloaded on hapless tourists the length and breadth of Carnaby Street. The ironic thing is that the group, apart from initial publicity shots, didn't actually wear the things themselves; that they ever sported "Jean Genet Boxer Shorts" or "Edith Sitwell Duffle Bags" is equally in doubt . . .

● **MORRISSEY**'s one of those rare beings in the pop world – a man with *style*. Look at the raw material: *Evans* oversize shirts, manky old gladioli, National Health specs and, Heaven forfend, a *hearing aid*. Not since Johnny Ray has one man done so much with so little. Still, as the ancient Chinese proverb states: one hearing aid is worth a trillion *J P Gaultier* brocade waistcoats. Eat your heart out, Gary Kemp . . .

● **SPANDAU BALLET.** Fashion victims to a man, this lot. They seem to have embarked on a contest to see who can spend the most enormous amount of money on looking a complete prat. Nothing new about that, of course – remember when they all wore kilts? The only difference is that as they get older, they lavish more and more dosh on achieving precisely the same effect. Some people *never* learn.

THE BOY GEORGE WELCOMING COMMITTEE

Not everything that happened during the year was deadly serious. On the lighter side of life, Guru Weirdbrain and his fellow conspirators spent an enjoyable few months winding up the establishment. It could only have happened in Ireland . . . .

Boy George's dad gives visit thumbs up

SOME DOUBLE!

ARTS NEWS

Thurles less than mad about the Boy

'HE WOULDN'T WANT V.I.P. TREATMENT!'

There were those who had scoffed when, months earlier, Ballyporeen publican John O'Farrell changed the name of his establishment to the Ronald Reagan Lounge. But now, at last, The Great One was about to visit "The Town of the Small Potatoes", birthplace of his great-grandfather! As advance teams of presidential advisers descended on the village so too did representatives of the world's media, installing tons of electronic equipment and interviewing everyone in sight. As the fever spread, local inhabitants began practising their fiddle and bodhran skills with wild abandon, telephones went automatic, footpaths were widened and the town's curate began promoting his Reagan Ancestry Souvenir Brochure.

Amid the mounting hysteria, somebody down the road in Bohernanave casually suggested that perhaps their local council could lay on a civic reception for another famous descendent of Tipperary — Boy George.

Thurles' councillors were less than enthusiastic. With a confidence born of years on the hustings, one politician asserted that it would be pointless bringing the singing star to the county because, as he put it, "there's no jobs in Boy George." Another elected representative suggested sagely: "The fact that he wears dresses and women's make-up would come against him." Yet another good burgher considered it inappropriate to invite George to Thurles since the Archbishop lived in the town!

But when a Sunday newspaper ran the front page exclusive — "Irish Home Town Snubs Boy George" — it sparked a debate which was to command headlines long after the departure of the Presidential Emmigrant.

First to make his voice heard on the issue was one Jeremiah O'Dowd, whose letter to the local TIPPERARY STAR was an emotional time-bomb. Eloquent and folksy, it touched many a heart in a country where protest groups were questioning a Tourist and his Nuclear Alert Code Activator. The Reagan Reception Committee was staging Rock Against Reagan gigs. The Munster Campaign Against Reagan's Visit was organizing meetings and the Reagan Protest Committee was working with South American refugees. Against this backdrop of public concern, Mr O'Dowd's fatherly reaction to the rebuke to his son spelt out some akward home truths. "The exile does not expect, or want, the red-carpet treatment, for he sees the red carpet as the instrument that represents the imperial misfortune of his country and birthright."

He then tapped many a private paranoia when he went on: "While the town councillors of Thurles prepare for the impending visit by the President of the USA, I may ask what kind of new industry the town councillors are expecting the President to provide for the town of Thurles? Could it be that they are expecting a devastating legacy that, in time, no one will be alive to remember?" An air of Celtic mysticism confirmed the family's Irish roots. "When an Irishman goes home he is made welcome by the turf fires . . . the mystery of the mountains . . . by the recognition of the very stones on the roads that he once trod . . ." In defence of his flamboyant son he added: "Should my son ever visit Thurles it will only be to call in and say hello to the kinsfolk and, perhaps, have a few old jars." The epistle closed on a final master-stroke as Mr O'Dowd displayed a genuine affection for both his son and things Irish by describing himself as "the boyo's father."

Immediately, a new pressure group was formed. It was The Boy George Welcoming Committee. Chief organizers were writer and critic Joe Ambrose, himself a native of Tipperary, and former Horslip Eamon Carr, both fans of Boy George. Their first public statement was straight and to the point. "A visit by Boy George would be welcomed by the majority of Irish people. He preaches peace, understanding and equality. It is obvious that he is the very kind of foreign dignitary that we need."

For weeks it seemed not a day went by without a headline like "Boy George Gets Cold Shoulder, "Tipp Snub For Boy George" and "Thurles Less Than Mad About The Boy". Investigative journalists soon began to introduce the public to George's closest Tipperary relatives. One aged cousin, Johnny Boyle, spoke out from his Thurles home: "I used to play the chromatic accordion years ago down in Hayes Hotel at weddings and I visited Boy George's father, Jer, in England years ago. I do not know that I ever met Boy George. But I would greet him. He is only entertaining people." As the roots craze spread we discovered that the Tipperary connection went back to the superstar's grandmother, Maggie Boyle O'Dowd, who left Ireland when she was 18. It came as no surprise to learn from Johnny Boyle that the pretty lass had been musically gifted: "As far as I can remember she was a fine mouth-organ player."

Around this time the people of Ireland began to show their true colours. A spokesperson for the Boy George Welcoming Committee announced that they had been in touch with the O'Dowd family in London. "We explained our belief that the vast majority of Irish people didn't share the old-fashioned views of a few begrudging councillors in Tipperary and we promised Boy George a wholehearted Irish welcome should he arrive here later this year." By this time the Committee had grown to take on board the ex-manager of Johnny Thunders and DJ B.P. Fallon, Irish TV GLENROE soap-opera star Mary 'Biddy' McEvoy, IN DUBLIN magazine editor Ferdia McAnna and Robert Fredericks, manager of Dublin band Light A Big Fire.

The bureaucratic tide began to turn when a former Urban District Council Chairman, Martin Kennedy, told the press: "The Boy is a world celebrity and should be honoured and hosted in his hometown. He is one of us." Worried that the comments of his fellow councillors would "alienate youth from politics", he expressed a desire for Boy George to do a concert in a large field near the town. His colleague, Martin Ryan, agreed. "I feel he should be honoured by the town. At least he covers himself with long dresses, not like some of the girls in town during the sunny weather lately."

Shortly before the mid-June meeting of Thurles' UDC an anonymous council source indicated the possibility of a "U-turn" on the matter. "We gave a reception to a racehorse, Quare Times, in 1955 so why not a pop star? I do know the Boy is very very big, especially in America." Aware that they were now under the spotlight of the world's media and because one delegate felt they had "been made to look rather silly over the whole affair", the Council voted to discuss the issue behind closed doors. The result of their deliberations was contained in a terse statement which claimed that the town clerk had received no intimation of any visit by Boy George. However, they would consider holding a reception for a prominent industrialist who had recently retired from the local sugar factory. It was also pointed out that they would give a warm welcome to anyone who would visit the town.

The TIPPERARY STAR then devoted a front-page editorial to the vexed question in which they hit out at certain sections of the media who they felt were "representing the people of the area as either being priest-ridden or a community of morons without minds of their own, and blissfully ignorant of events around them." Concluding the full-length comment, boldly headed "Boy George", they remarked: "It must be said that one cannot but feel sympathy, too, for Boy George and the members of his family who, whatever publicity they may seek, were unwitting pawns in the unseemly wrangle that has arisen and of which, we hope, we have heard the last."

But the question refused to go away. A short time later, newspapers carried the story of how the Welcoming Committee's anthem, 'A Hundred Thousand Welcomes For Boy George', had run into trouble. Recorded with a cast of hundreds — including members of various bands, fans, friends and committee members, the disc's release was postponed by the record company following discussions with Chairperson of Thurles' UDC, undertaker Frank Dwan. "The situation is too confused," said company executive, Dermot Brady. "Mr Dwan appeared most upset at the 'twisted' manner in which his statements are being presented by the media. Not wishing to become embroiled in controversy we've decided to shelve plans for the release of the Committee's disc."

Listeners to Irish national radio could not have been surprised to hear the debate spread to the airwaves. Jeremiah O'Dowd explained his position to broadcaster Pat Kenny: "My grandfather's cottage is still standing in Thurles and there's a Boyle still in it so obviously we didn't need rebukes from any town councillors. I felt we belong there." Of his son's dress sense Mr O'Dowd sanely observed: "It's the lack of tolerance the world over that's caused so much trouble." Thurles' Councillor, Frank Dwan was next up. "The town's motto is 'FLEADH AGUS FAILTE' — feast and welcome," he argued; "And anybody who comes to Thurles is always welcome." Stopping short of extending an official invitation to Boy George he added: "If a visit were taking place we would see what could be done." When Committee Organizer Joe Ambrose was asked if he was not taking things a little too seriously because, after all, Boy George was not Ronald Reagan, he replied: "I think there should be a proper Irish reception for a guy who represents peace and equality. A more peaceful and gentle star than Boy George there never has been."

Within days, 'A Hundred Thousand Welcomes For Boy George', credited to the Saints and Scholars and described as "a sure-fire foot-tapper", was released on the Hotwire label. The NME described it as "very silly", MELODY MAKER pronounced it "utter rubbish" and Hot Press reckoned it was "something like Dr Strangely Strange on amyl meeting the Pogues".

It's said that Boy George's hectic schedule prevented him from visiting Thurles. But on long dark nights, when the good folk of Tipperary gather round their videos, a song is often sung. A song that will be kept alive forever — thanks to the Boy George Welcoming Committee.

A Hundred Thousand Welcomes For Boy George

There's a welcome on the hillsides/There's a welcome in our hearts
There's a welcome on the air/And there's a welcome in the charts
There's a welcome in each cottage/There's a welcome on the mat
There's a welcome down the disco/So's you know where we're at

Hand me down my paisley shirt/Hand down my dancing shoes
I'm going to tell the neighbours/I'm off to spread the news
Hand me down my old guitar/Let us all sing a toast
To that peaceful shining star/The one we love the most

There's a hundred thousand welcomes for Boy George
There's a hundred thousand welcomes and every one is true
There's a hundred thousand welcomes just for you, Boy George
There's a hundred thousand welcomes just for you

Your feet have walked on Broadway/In LA and Hong Kong
But no welcome will sound better/Than in the place where you come from
And so we say it loud and clear/For all to understand
Let "CEAD MILE FAILTE"/Be heard throughout the land

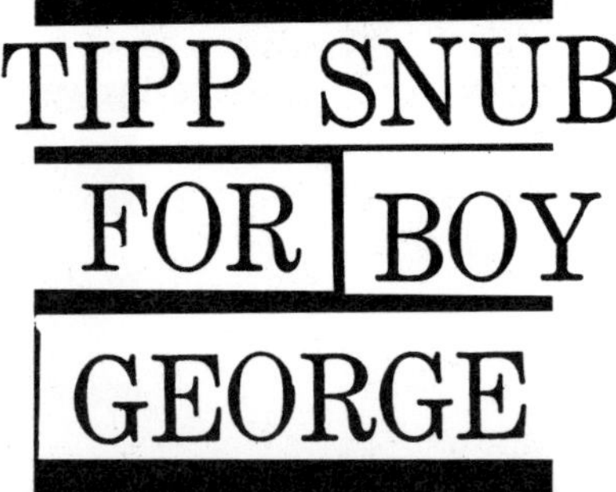
TIPP SNUB FOR BOY GEORGE

The Boy George Sure-fire Foot-tapper

Civic-welcome anthem for Boy George shelved

COUSIN GEORGE IS A REAL BROTH OF A BOY

..but Boy George gets cold shoulder

IN MEMORIAM

DAVID BYRON
Died aged 38, 28 February 1985, nr Maidenhead, Berks
With Mick Box he formed a group called Spice, which evolved into Uriah Heep in 1971. After making ten albums with the very 'umble, very 'eavy Heep, vocalist Byron was sacked in July 1976. Oddly, on three previous occasions he had threatened to leave the band but each time was implored to stay on. "The unfortunate thing about Heep," he once said, "was that we didn't know what success meant. All we did was order another limo and another twelve bottles of champagne." He recorded solo albums for Bronze and Arista in the late seventies and in '82, headed the Byron Band (Byron, Robin George, Mel Collins and John Shearer) which cut an album for Creole. But his band-leading days were adjudged over when he collapsed during a London Marquee gig, after which it seemed only a matter of time before he became yet another rock casualty.

TASHA THOMAS
Died aged 34, 15 October 1984, New York
Alaskan-born session singer who appeared on scores of records by such artists as Stevie Wonder, Luther Allison, Al Kooper, Diana Ross, Rick Derringer, Kiss, Johnny Winter, Carly Simon and many others. Thomas was also in the Broadway production of *The Wiz*.

WELLS KELLY
Died aged 35, 29 October 1984, London, England
Meat Loaf's American-born drummer was found dead on the steps of the London house in which the band was staying. He'd been to a party and had been driven home in a taxi which the band heard pull up outside the house. But Kelly never made it to the door, collapsing on the steps where he choked on his own vomit, his body being discovered the following morning. Drummer with Orleans from 1975-80, Kelly also recorded with Ian Hunter, Boffalongo, King Harvest, Mike Love's Celebration, Al Kooper, John Martyn, Bonnie Raitt, Todd Rundgren and others.

JAMES C PETRILLO
Died aged 92, 23 October 1984, Chicago
The man who negotiated British and US band exchanges – before 1956 American bands were not allowed to play concerts in the UK and vice versa – one-time trumpet-player Petrillo was the President of the American Federation of Musicians from 1940-1958. A man who defied the Mafia – his home was bombed twice by gangsters – he called a strike against the recording industry in 1942, during which no musicians recorded for over a year, the strike finally ending in late 1944 when RCA and CBS agreed to pay the union a royalty on every record sold.

JEANINE DECKERS
Died aged 52, 23 March 1985, Wavre, Belgium
Perhaps the most famous of all one-hit wonders, Deckers, known as Sister Luc-Gabrielle, recorded 'Dominique' as the Singing Nun in 1963, and claimed the number one spot in the US for ten weeks in a row. Later, she left the convent and for the latter part of her life lived in poverty. She and a female companion ended their lives in a suicide pact.

BUMPS BLACKWELL
Died aged 66, 9 March 1985, Whittier, California
An ace black music producer and songwriter, Blackwell once headed a teenage band that included two kids named Quincy Jones and Ray Charles. Later he moved to Los Angeles and began making records with Lloyd Price, Guitar Slim and others, eventually becoming A&R man at Specialty Records where he produced all of Little Richard's early hits, some of which he co-wrote. Blackwell was also the man who helped turn gospel singer Sam Cooke into one of the all-time soul greats. An A&R man with Mercury during the early sixties – once more resuming a relationship with Quincy Jones – he also helped create soundtrack songs for films like *The Girl Can't Help It* and was an influence on the careers of many leading rock acts, including those of Jimi Hendrix, Bobby Womack, the Chambers Brothers, Clydie King and Sly Stone.

MATT MONRO
Died aged 54, 7 February 1985, Cambridge, England
One of the rags-to-riches merchants, Monro, once Terry Parsons, a London bus driver on the No. 27 route between Highgate and Teddington, became an in-demand singer on radio during the fifties. But real fame came following a Peter Sellers session on which George Martin asked him to impersonate Frank Sinatra, using the name Fred Flange. During the early sixties, he provided a steady flow of hits, including 'Portrait Of My Love' (1960), 'My Kind Of Girl' (1961), 'Softly As I Leave You' (1962), 'From Russia With Love' (1963) and 'Yesterday' (1965). He also sang the Oscar-nominated title song to the movie *Born Free* (1965) and thereafter gained constant bookings on the ritzy US hotel and night-club circuit. However, his records failed to sell in high numbers in later years, his last hit of any size coming in '73. He appeared to be making something of a UK comeback during '84, via appearances on the *Russell Harty* and *Jimmy Tarbuck* TV shows. But during a liver transplant op in early '85 it was discovered that he had widespread cancer.

NORMAN PETTY
Died aged 57, 15 August 1984, Lubbock, Texas
Once the organ-playing leader of an instrumental trio that had hits with 'Mood Indigo' in '54 and 'Almost Paradise' in '57, Petty logged his right to rock fame as producer of Buddy Knox's classic 'Party Doll', Jimmy Bowen's 'I'm Sticking With You' and, more importantly, all Buddy Holly's early successes.

It was in Petty's own Clovis, New Mexico, studio that Holly cut such singles as, 'Maybe Baby', 'Peggy Sue', 'Not Fade Away', 'Oh Boy', 'Rave On' and the hit remake of 'That'll Be The Day' following the singer's abortive attempts to gain hits out of sides recorded at various Nashville sessions. But relations between the producer and Holly soured and it was rumoured that Petty was about to sue Holly at the time of the latter's fatal plane crash. Afterwards, Petty did help on further hit records, including the Stringalongs' 'Wheels' (1961) and Jimmy Gilmer and the Fireballs' 'Sugar Shack' (1963), but in later years he had little chart success and spent much of his time running a Clovis radio station.

ERNEST TUBB
Died aged 70, 6 September 1984, Nashville, Tennessee
Known as 'The Texas Troubadour', honky-tonk singer Tubb was one of the early stars of the Grand Ole Opry and the man who brought some sort of dignity to country music by insisting that the record industry drop the derogatory term "hillbilly". He wrote such hits as 'Walking The Floor Over You' and 'Waltz Across Texas', the latter a favourite of bands such as Joe Ely's, and also instigated the Midnight Jamboree radio show, which is still broadcast from one of Tubb's Nashville record shops. Among the entertainers who gained attention through appearances on the Jamboree was Elvis Presley, earlier spurned by the Opry management.

MARCUS PRICE
Died 24 September 1984, age unknown, Memphis
Shot while leaving a rehearsal studio. Price was, at the time of his death, guitarist with the ill-fated Bar Kays, the Stax band that suffered four fatalities in the plane crash that killed Otis Redding.

WILLIE MAE (BIG MAMA) THORNTON
Died aged 57, 25 July 1984, Los Angeles
One of seven children, Big Mama Thornton, from Montgomery, Alabama, began her blues-wailing career with the Hot Harlem Revue (actually from Atlanta, Georgia) during the forties. In the early fifties she based herself in Texas and began touring with Johnny Otis' Rhythm and Blues Caravan, in 1953 gaining commercial success with 'Hound Dog', a song that later brought kudos and even more loot to an up-and-coming Elvis Presley. A cigar-puffing, mouth-harp-totin' blues queen who could also wield an effective drumstick, she played the Monterey and Newport Jazz Festivals, the Ann Arbour and Chicago Blues Festivals and also toured Europe as part of the 1965 American Blues Festival package. During '68, Thornton's 'Ball And Chain' became part of Janis Joplin's staple repertoire and in '71, following an appearance at Carnegie Hall, she contributed the Segarini and Bishop song 'Dear Jesus God' to the soundtrack of the film *Vanishing Point*. A gutsy, earthy singer, Thornton continued blues-belting throughout the seventies and early eighties but looked seriously ill by the time she made her appearance in *Legends of Rhythm and Blues*, a programme in the Channel 4 TV series *Repercussions*, which was shot in LA during May '83. When she died, just over a year later, she was living in poverty, which caused anger among the blues community, Etta James claiming: "Willie Mae's face was on every blues package, tape or video. There are pirates all around, they've pirated her music and she died without a penny."

IN MEMORIAM

JOHN HALEY 'ZOOT' SIMS
Died aged 59, 23 March 1985, New York
One of the great jazz sax stylists, Sims established his reputation with Benny Goodman before gaining legendary status as a member of Woody Herman's Four Brothers line-up (with Stan Getz, Serge Chaloff, Herbie Steward and, later, Al Cohn) during the late forties. A player with a distinctive tone who owed much to Lester Young in his early days, he also played with Jazz At The Philharmonic, Stan Kenton, Miles Davis and Bill Evans but is probably best remembered by jazzers for his productive partnership with Al Cohn.

KEITH HUDSON
Died aged 38, 14 November 1984, New York
A reggae experimentalist, Hudson first came to prominence as a producer, fashioning hits for Ken Boothe, John Holt, Delroy Wilson, U Roy, Dennis Alcapone, Big Youth and others. An innovative but erratic singer his first strong-selling album was *Entering The Dragon*, a previous offering, *Class And Subject*, having been totally ignored. But it was his albums for Atra, such as *Flesh Of My Skin*, *Torch Of Freedom* and the classic dub set *Pick A Dub*, that confirmed Hudson's genius. A synthireggae pioneer, working in that area long before such sounds came into vogue, he's been hailed as "a producer virtually without peer" (Penny Reel *NME*) and "a man who ploughed individual furrows in reggae's sometimes predictable field" (Danny Kelly *NME*.) His death followed a long battle against cancer.

NICHOLAS DINGLEY
Died aged 24, 8 December 1984, Southern California
English-born, 'Razzle' Dingley, the drummer with Hanoi Rocks, was killed in a head-on car crash while a passenger in a vehicle driven by Motley Crue singer Vincent Neil Wharton, the latter escaping injury. As a result of the tragedy, Hanoi Rocks projected Christmas tour of the UK had to be cancelled. Dingley, who hailed from the Isle of Wight, also briefly worked with the Dark after a two year stint with what Gary Bushell once termed "a legendary if well peculiar semi-freak, semi-pathetique outfit called the Fuck Pigs."

BARBARA COWSILL
Died aged 56, 31 January 1985, Tempe, Arizona
Main lady with the Cowsills, a Rhode Island family band that provided the inspiration for TV's *Partridge Family*, Cowsill, her hubby, five sons and daughter made it out of the New York club scene during the mid-sixties. Not nearly as twee as they might have been, the Cowsills made some excellent pop singles and were rewarded with a US number two hit in 'The Rain The Park And Other Things' in 1967. The hits continued throughout the sixties but the group disbanded in the early seventies, the sons re-forming as a country band some years later but without success.

SHELLY MANNE
Died aged 64, 26 September 1984, Los Angeles
One of the last great drummers to come out of the big band era – Manne worked with Stan Kenton, Les Brown and Woody Herman, later becoming a prime mover among the West Coast's cool school of the fifties. A frequent poll-winner, his *My Fair Lady* album, featuring André Previn, proved a massive seller in 1958. More often than not, he could be found playing with small groups often comprised of fellow ex-Herman and Kenton sidekicks but he was also a much in-demand TV and film studio musician, composing the scores for films such as *Young Billy Young* and the *Daktari* TV series. At trivia level, he also achieved some degree of fame as the man who tutored Frank Sinatra for the drumming scenes in *Man with the Golden Arm.*

ALBERTA HUNTER
Died aged 89, 17 October 1984, New York
Legendary blues singer whose recording career began in 1921. She worked with King Oliver and Louis Armstrong, replaced Bessie Smith in a musical show, played overseas tours to troops during World War II, was understudy to Eartha Kitt in the 1953 show *Mrs Patterson* and, after quitting music to take up nursing, made a spectacular comeback in 1977, making a memorable appearance at the Newport Jazz Festival the following year. Also in 1978 she provided the soundtrack to the Geraldine Chaplin-starring movie *Remember My Name*, writing and performing all the material.

KENNY 'KLOOK' CLARKE
Died aged 71, 26 January 1985, Montreuil-Sous-Bois, France
The Bop era drummer, Clarke virtually rewrote the book on jazz drumming, changing the way of thinking of percussionists from 52nd Street and beyond. An early Dizzy Gillespie sideman, he was also a founder member of the Modern Jazz Quartet, leaving in the mid-fifties to settle in France, where he lived for the rest of his life, co-leading a formidable big band with Belgian pianist Francy Boland during the sixties. "He forgot more than most drummers will ever know about moving and shaping music." (*Downbeat*)

WILLIE MABON
Died aged 59, 19 April 1985, Paris, France
Born in Hollyood, Tennessee, singer-pianist Mabon was one of the leading R&B stars of the fifties, and the man responsible for such Chess hits as 'I Don't Know', 'I'm Mad' and 'Poison Ivy'. During the seventies he played frequent dates in Europe and eventually settled down in Paris, where he was resident act at the Trois Mailletz Club. His death followed a long illness.

PERCY MAYFIELD
Died aged 63, 11 August 1984, Los Angeles
Called "probably the most consistent good blues writer" by *Blues Unlimited*, Mayfield, who recorded for Specialty, Chess, Cash, Imperial, RCA, Atlantic, Tangerine etc, was a fine blues-inspired vocalist and pianist. But doubtless he'll be remembered best for the years he spent working with Ray Charles, providing the latter with such songs as 'Hit The Road, Jack', 'Danger Zone', 'Hide Nor Hair', all hits in the early sixties, though the most endearing Mayfield song remains 'Please Send Me Someone To Love', a chart record for the Moonglows in 1957.

COLLIN WALCOTT
Died aged 39, 8 November 1984, Magdeburg, West Germany
"Walcott's restrained command of the subtly random scope of the sitar and tabla complete a moist impeccable sound that goes beyond the merely fascinating" (Paul Morley, 1978). Sitar and tabla player with Oregon since 1974, Walcott also recorded with Larry Coryell, the Paul Winter Consort, Codona, John Abercrombie, David Liebman and others. His death followed injuries sustained in a car accident.

JULES BIHARI
Died aged 72, 17 November 1984, Los Angeles
Bihari brothers Jules, Joe, Lester and Saul formed Modern Records in 1947, the first indie to own its own pressing plant. The Biharis also set up such labels as RPM, Crown and Kent and were responsible for aiding the careers of scores of major black artists including B.B. King, Ike and Tina Turner, Pee Wee Crayton, John Lee Hooker, Etta James and Elmore James.

STEVE GOODMAN
Died aged 36, 20 September 1984, Seattle, Washington
From Chicago, Goodman began his career as a creator of advertising jingles, but also gradually edged his way into the folk club scene, befriending John Prine. The twosome were signed to major labels following a recommendation from Kris Kristofferson, Buddah notching Goodman whose first real album was produced by Kristofferson, in Nashville. Some success ensued when Arlo Guthrie recorded Goodman's 'City Of New Orleans' in 1972, gaining a US Top Twenty hit. But Goodman, though the creator of what Prine hailed as "the greatest damn train song of 'em all", never really made a major breakthrough. By '73 he was still living in a $145-a-month apartment, even though he could boast that Bob Dylan had appeared on one of his records. A fine entertainer, whose appearance at the '72 Cambridge Festival blew the place apart, Goodman spent the last fifteen years of his life knowing that he was likely to lose out to leukemia, his death resulting from kidney and liver failure after a bone marrow transplant made in an effort to combat the disease. At the time of Goodman's death, Willie Nelson's single of 'City Of New Orleans' was high in the country music charts, his album of the same name reaching number one.

THE US BUSINESS YEAR

In the United States, the national pastime of baseball is currently giving a lot of credence to Earl Weaver's theory of The Big Inning. Weaver, a manager for the Baltimore Orioles, compiled the game's best record over ten years by directing his game strategies towards scoring a lot of runs in one at-bat instead of piling them up slowly over the course of a game's nine innings. Hence, The Big Inning tag.

The American record industry also subscribes to the Big Inning Theory. But in the last year it has become an obsession, with the stakes higher and the rewards greater for those who reach the top of the charts. Mega-hits have come back in a big way: just a few years ago, John Cougar's *American Fool* became the biggest selling album of the year while notching just under three million units; in the last two years, Bruce Springsteen, Lionel Richie, Prince and Michael Jackson have had albums that have sold seven, eight, ten and twenty million copies respectively. But to reach those bigger numbers, the American record companies have all but abandoned the artists who produce steady but smaller sales for cores of faithful followers. If an artist does not have what the labels consider multi-million selling potential, the chances are he/she will find it harder than ever to get a deal. And if they're with a major label, they may have to prove themselves with several singles before they gain the attention of their label, as happened with Madonna, whose first few dance hits happened in pite of Warner Bros almost complete isinterest.

In hard figures 1984 shipments totalled ,4.5 billion – a higher dollar volume than even the boom days of *Saturday Night Fever* – on the smallest number of new LP and cassette releases in many years. There were nearly twenty-five per cent fewer album titles released than in 1983, with the Recording Industry Association of American (RIAA) tallying just 1,740 new releases. It was the sixth year in a row the number of new titles had decreased, and 1985 is virtually guaranteed to extend that run. In human and artistic terms, mainstays like Van Morrison, Graham Parker and Heart found themselves shopping for new labels.

To celebrate the new measure of success, the RIAA instituted a new higher plateau of sales recognition: the multi-platinum album award, signifying sales of two million or more units. Although the gloved one's *Thriller* immediately set the highwater mark, Cyndi Lauper showed that newcomers can be high-stake players in the mega-platinum game by selling over four million copies of her debut album, *She's So Unusual*.

In part, the narrowing of the music field can be laid to the strength of reverse crossover music in the preceding year. Although black radio programmers had remained more open to playing whatever fit their format – ask Hall & Oates – rock 'n' roll radio became increasingly isolated in the seventies until there were virtually no black records played on so-called "alternative" stations by the start of the eighties. But the success of Prince, Jackson, Richie and other black artists with white listeners made it increasingly difficult for rock radio stations to continue their programming policies and retain their listeners. Just how far rock radio was from understanding the growing similarity in black and white music was shown when rock radio got behind Huey Lewis and the News' 'I Want A New Drug', but ignored the later and even more successful 'Ghostbusters' of Ray Parker Jr. The records sounded so similar that a copyright infringement suit was filed against Parker claiming he'd stolen the Lewis tune. Yet for some reason, rock radio felt only one of these records – Lewis's – sounded right for their stations.

Obviously this apartheid of the airwaves couldn't last, especially when it didn't reflect listeners' tastes. What replaced it was an old format with a new name: Contemporary Hit Radio, formerly called Top Forty. It signalled a return to the limited playlists and heavy rotation of hits that were popular in the sixties. And like that earlier form, in which records by the Supremes and the Beatles were programmed side by side, a hit is a hit whether it's black or white. The hit format proved so powerful that most black stations moved towards the middle with their white counterparts, with "urban" style stations that played rap, hip hop and hard core funk becoming increasingly scarce. A more homogeneous market, with bigger hits and less variety.

Another reason for the higher stakes is the increased cost of promotion, owing in large part to music video expenses. Within two

● *HUEY LEWIS & THE NEWS*

● *LIONEL RICHIE*

● *MICHAEL JACKSON*

years the cost of clips has soared by as much as 300 per cent and even more in the case of artists with a lot of clout. With MTV having tightened its grip on the cable broadcast market by laughing off the Discovery network and buying out the even less successful Ted Turner music channel, record companies lined up to sign exclusivity pacts with the cable network that would guarantee airtime for artists of the labels' selection and pay the labels for clip use. CBS Records got a firsthand lesson in what it means to lose under the Big Inning theory when a high-priced Barbra Streisand album went nowhere, its expensive video bombed – and ate up a lot of the label's guaranteed time on MTV – and several other Christmas blockbusters failed to materialize. It was a rude awakening for a company lulled into believing itself invincible in the armour of mega-hits from Jackson, Culture Club, Lauper and Springsteen.

At the same time CBS was cooling, the Los Angeles-based Warner labels were getting hotter and hotter thanks in large part to Phil Collins, Prince and Madonna. The collapse of the proposed Warner/PolyGram merger, which came to naught when a federal appeals court rejected the deal in April of '84, never engendered for the former the serious loss of momentum that it meant for PolyGram.

One area where all labels seemed to be able to glean some success was soundtracks. Once the backbone of the album business along with theatrical show recordings, the cast album and soundtracks' glory days were laid to rest in the sixties by the rise of the LP as the dominant conceptual configuration of rock. But the more recent success of various artist compilations for films like *Flashdance* and *Footloose* has unleashed a virtual torrent of rock soundtracks. Several of them including *Beverly Hills Cop* and *Purple Rain* as well as *Flashdance* and *Footloose* have reached mega-platinum by following the same formula of multi-hits that are helping super-selling artists reach the top. With the exception of *Purple Rain*, the formula has been almost cynically similar: a track for black radio, one for rock and one for the slightly older thirty-five-plus audience, all performed by established artists.

Perhaps ultimately more significant than the success of the soundtracks is the eager symbiosis developing between the record and film business. Many of the music-oriented films, *Flashdance* and *Footloose* in particular, have made no pretence of hiding the pattern they've taken from music videos. And the success of *Purple Rain* obviously owed very little to Prince's thespian abilities and everything to the fact that he can shake that thang and look exciting in front of a band.

For record companies, films have become an increasingly attractive way to get their music and artists exposed to the public. Even when an artist doesn't appear in the film, if their music is featured prominently or even featured in the advertising for the film, it can be a promotional bonanza.

But the negative side of the Big Inning theory appears to be looming right behind the large numbers that the industry announced last year. When CBS Records notched their six-month financial report at the end of June, they had to confess to a nearly forty per cent decrease in profits during the second quarter. The company's explanation included noting a scarcity of new product from established hit artists – a dire warning that they've probably bet a bit too heavily on proven talent instead of developing more new artists and expanding the base of mid-level acts.

It seems almost inevitable that the American record business will enter another downward cycle similar to the post-disco fall off. A decline in MTV's ratings suggest that music videos have a boredom factor no matter how elaborate or sophisticated they become. The dependence on film soundtrack and tie-ins are bringing vast numbers of casual album buyers into record stores, but they remain casual buyers rather than vinyl junkies, who have always been the bread-and-butter customer.

● *PRINCE*

Although rock radio was cited as a culprit in the record industry recession of the early eighties, the record industry's willingness to hew to the popularity of the contemporary "hits" format of the moment makes it seem that nothing was learned last time. Then executives at labels said the mistake was trying too hard to make records to fit the popular radio format regardless of whether that format reflected sales or consumer tastes. It might be argued that stations are now playing the hits, but the eagerness to follow, rather than lead, radio has the tail wagging the dog again.

If conservative A&R policies are stunting future growth, the industry is certainly looking to technology to provide a re-invigorated marketplace through the compact disc.

At the mid-year mark the new configuration accounted for just four per cent of all pre-recorded music sales in the US. But with prices dropping fast on hardware and software, dealers were saying that the move from an audiophile to mass market is going to be much quicker than anybody predicted, with the LP being supplanted as the dominant delivery system within as little as five years. With several manufacturers offering CD players for under $200, record retailers expected kids to take earnings from summer jobs and sink them into new players by the autumn.

Although the industry took great pains and pride in pointing out that the new disc is a unified configuration – one on which everyone has agreed on the standards instead of creating their own as happened with 78s, 45s and LPs – it seems things couldn't stay agreed for long. Packaging became a major issue, with PolyGram and CBS favouring a clear "clamshell" case and Warner Bros championing a cardboard wrapper with different dimensions that made it hard for retailers to display everything together. A unified package was eventually agreed upon, but not without the requisite chest-thumping and ego-salving.

The physical manufacturing of the disc itself also proved more difficult than had been anticipated, especially for CBS, who operate the only CD plant in the US in partnership with Sony. That plant, which was expected to produce 300,000 discs a month within six months of going on line, was plagued by a rejection rate that was rumoured to have been as high as ninety per cent. As a result, the company was forced to cancel all work it had contracted from other labels, kill all back-orders and start from scratch with orders filled from plants in Japan.

The swelling needs of American labels for overseas press time – mounting due to both CBS's problems and the increasing demand from the expanding number of CD buyers – placed pressure on the manufacturing facilities in Japan and Europe. In Germany, Phillips responded by getting special permission from the government to operate extra Sunday shifts. In Japan, where the manufacturing technology has been more successfully disseminated, the availability of press time was also pushed to the limit. The companies to suffer the most seemed to be the smaller American independent labels without the clout of their larger competitors. Small labels

● *FLASHDANCE*

manufacturing their CD's in Japan had been used to waiting a month for delivery. By the beginning of 1985, they had to wait three months for press time, and by mid-year, it was five to six months. Not surprisingly, they blamed the large American labels for muscling them off the presses.

By late spring, CBS seemed to have hammered out many of its production problems, but was still short of its initial projections. Yet it seemed just a matter of time until they mastered the process, and other companies began investigating licensing CD manufacturing technology from Sony and Phillips.

While the industry was looking to the CD as a boon to its traditional business of music, others in the industry were suggesting that record companies go even further. Retailers were pleased with having a third configuration to complement cassette and LP sales, but at least one record company executive, Stan Cornyn of Warner Communications, suggested that the record industry's real growth lay in "taking a bite out of our neighbours".

Toward that end, Cornyn suggested at a national record retailers' convention in Miami that the compact disc be developed as a visual storage system to compete with computer floppy discs. His presentation demonstrated that the CD is versatile enough as a storage system to hold the United States phonebook on one disc, and could be used for interactive games. A CD unit with a terminal could be used as a map and tour guide when mounted in a car.

● *FOOTLOOSE*

Perhaps because business was up, record companies stopped lobbying the government for action that would have placed a special tax on tape recorders and blank tape. In the last few years, the home taping war had been the industry's special crusade, but the campaign wound down as albums once again racked up big numbers. Instead, the RIAA turned its attention to "dub deck" players, demanding that manufactures curtail their lines, especially from Japan. While the Association's activities have yet to produce a reverse in production, it was clearly cheered by the film industry's lobby group, the Motion Picture Association of American, and its victory in getting an effective ban against the import of Japanese-made double well video players.

The import issue continues to be an explosive one for record retailers too. Under a section of the US Copyright Laws, the major American record labels have been stemming the flow of imported records by claiming they have exclusive ownership to musical copyrights, and therefore are the sole determinants of when and how a record will be made available in the US marketplace. Terming imports of their properties "parallel product", the majors, led by CBS, have taken several import houses and retailers to court to stop them from bringing records from other countries into the US. Hardest hit has been the collectors' market, which relied heavily on imported, unavailable B-sides. And as a result, import companies like Jem, Important, Dutch East and Greenworld have turned increasingly to recording their own albums and developing rosters for new domestic labels.

To make matters even bleaker for the importers, the Harry Fox Agency, which collects and administers mechanical royalties for music publishers, entered the fray. Its claim is that publishers are hurt by imports since royalty rates paid overseas are less than those paid at home and any imported albums cost publishers a hefty portion of their income.

If the domestic market's heavyweights wanted to isolate themselves from the outside world, the same couldn't be said for the artists. Following the lead of Bob Geldof, American musicians made their most eloquent gesture with USA For Africa's 'We Are The World' benefit for African hunger victims. Snapped up by record buyers, it demonstrated a concern and generosity among rock musicians and their fans unequalled by any other art form. Clearly, in an era of almost unparalleled commercialism for rock 'n' roll, the spirit of change and challenge that fuelled the music burned brighter than ever. The massive, world-wide telecast that hooked up an American show with the UK's Wembley Stadium concert was living, breathing proof that rock is a power that *can* change the world.

Fred Goodman

THE UK BUSINESS YEAR

If the British music business resented the fact that the most prodigiously successful one-off idea it had ever hatched took money out of the industry, then it had the grace (or the good sense) not to show it. 1984/5 will obviously be chiefly remembered for Band Aid, the genuinely altruistic response of the rock fraternity to the Ethiopian famine. Band Aid was, in business terms too, the story of the year – whether it concerned the remarkably efficient pressing and distribution of 'Do They Know It's Christmas?', so that the single was on sale throughout the UK within days of being recorded, or the quite unanticipated smoothness with which the marathon Live Aid Wembley concert functioned.

Whether or not they were browbeaten into it by the indefatigable Bob Geldof, all sections of the industry rendered magnanimous assistance. There were complaints, however from isolated retailers, whose bone of contention was not that they had been required to forsake their profit margins, but that they had been virtually drummed into doing so.

The Band Aid phenomenon did raise unspoken questions that might one day require answering. As a rule, distributors and retailers know that forty per cent of their annual business will be concentrated in the final quarter of the year; and that they can generally reckon on the emergence of one spectacularly successful Christmas record which boosts profits all round and perhaps even helps to turn a borderline operation into a commercially viable one. This year they were all working overtime handling the biggest selling 45 in the history of the UK business. Over three million copies were sold – yet retailers were unable to profit from it. So did 'Do They Know It's Christmas?' bring into the business revenue that would not otherwise have been there? Or did its heady success inhibit the commercial potential of records released at the same time?

In fact, this particular year was undoubtedly exceptional, and the Band Aid single was greeted with unsuspected reserves of public good will. The fact that no objections were raised from inside the industry can be attributed partly to the fact that everyone had been so distressed by the newsreel from the stricken regions of East Africa, and partly to the fact that the record industry was itself enjoying a year that was somewhat better than it cared to admit.

During 1984, six singles sold over a million copies, something that had never previously happened. Two of them, 'Relax' and 'Two Tribes', were contributed by Frankie Goes To Hollywood, who just about got in before Band Aid to ensure that they registered the first hat-trick of number ones with initial singles since Gerry and the Pacemakers in 1964. Their double album, *Welcome To The Pleasuredome,* was equally successful: it shipped double platinum, having achieved advance orders of 700,000, the highest level since Abba's *Super Trouper*.

Not that sales of 'Relax' and 'Two Tribes' were, by the standards of the year, prodigious. They were surpassed not only by Band Aid, but also by both George Michael's 'Careless Whisper' and Stevie Wonder's 'I Just Called To Say I Love You', the latter notching up astonishing sales of 1.8 million. The sixth million-seller of the year was 'Last Christmas' by Wham!, which became the first single for almost a quarter of a century to sell in such quantities and yet fail to reach number one.

Altogether, then, the British record industry could be reasonably satisfied with its level of business during the year. The total turnover of £329 million was the equivalent of a volume rise of fourteen per cent. Over the Christmas period, in particular, sales were buoyant, with forty-nine per cent more singles being sold than during the corresponding period in the previous year. Although thirty-seven per cent of this increase was felt to be directly attributable to Band Aid, it was nevertheless a heartening trend.

Over the year as a whole, singles were up by four per cent and although long-playing records had dropped by ten per cent, this reflected not waning interest, but increasing diversification of consumer tastes, since combined LP, cassette and compact disc (CD) sales actually increased by eleven per cent.

Small wonder, then, that everyone could afford to applaud Band Aid and set aside private misgivings. In a year in which the record business was contracting, it might be different. Sections of the industry could be less co-operative about future ventures. A foretaste of such problems arose over the recording made by the US equivalent of Band Aid, USA For Africa. Many retailers did express public annoyance at the fact that it was taken for granted that they would all be prepared to offer the same facilities to this all-star famine-relief effort as they had done to the original one.

Band Aid, though, certainly set a conspicuous example to others, and there was even a third charity number one during this period. An *ad hoc* assembly of somewhat more seasoned show-business celebrities came together as the Crowd to raise money for the dependants of the victims of the Bradford City Football Club fire. Another appeal record, Marti Webb's 'Ben', made in memory of Ben Hardwick, the small child whose fight for life had been featured on Esther Rantzen's *That's Life*, also reached the Top Ten. It was a very good year for good causes.

As far as individual record companies were concerned, CBS maintained a convincing lead over all-comers in both the albums and singles lists of 1984. Buttressed by the talents of Bruce Springsteen, Alison Moyet, Paul Young and Sade – artists as dependable as they were fashionable – the company won market shares of 17.2 and sixteen per cent for, respectively, albums and singles. Its nearest competitor in albums was EMI (12.9 per cent), and in singles a resurgent WEA (11.1 per cent). The latter benefited particularly from the emergence of major new artists like Howard Jones, though it also astutely re-marketed dormant Sister Sledge material, and accordingly was able to generate huge sales on the group's newer recordings.

The leading UK company, Thorn-EMI, continued to be dogged by a mixture of misfortune and mismanagement. In March, one of its own acts brought a significant court case against the company. Ray Jackson, once one of Lindisfarne, had been signed by EMI as a solo artist at the beginning of the eighties. In court, he claimed that the company had been negligent in its handling of his career.

And he won. Mr Justice Davies declared that, "Ray Jackson was a very impressive and fair witness with a burning conviction that he had been let down by a great company which he trusted". Thorn-EMI was probably less embarrassed by the amount of damages – the judge ordered the company to pay Jackson compensation of £24,000, together with costs which were estimated at £40,000 – than by the fact that one of its own witnesses called during the trial, producer Glyn Johns, had stated that he knew that in the early eighties the company was "a shambles".

Thus, while Jackson's test-case was of immense significance for other, similarly neglected acts, it was also important for the entire future of EMI. In 1979 the company had been taken over by Thorn, but had for some time retained its pre-eminent position in the UK music business. By 1984, however, it was trailing, and the debacle of the court case no doubt further eroded corporate confidence.

One of EMI's problems is that although it has long been a company of many and diverse interests, the music, however marginal its contributions to overall profits, remains important as a barometer of the well-being of the whole outfit. During 1984/5 the record side was again depressed – and so, equally, was the company. In July 1985, Peter Laister resigned as chairman and chief executive, a position he had held for only fifteen months. During that time he had made an impressively bold, but unhappily thwarted, bid for British Aerospace; but he had completed some business with the government by purchasing the microchip manufacturer, Inmos. By summer 1985, however, overall profits declined sharply from £87 to £33 million, and Laister departed.

With its flagship in such disrepair, the British record industry had perhaps done well to keep foreign companies at bay as much as it had. The three smaller companies – Virgin, Island and Chrysalis – all remained buoyant; though the staggering success that had been Virgin's in 1983, largely thanks to Culture Club, now belonged to Island, thanks to its tie-up with Trevor Horn's ZTT label and Frankie Goes To Hollywood. In the summer of 1984, the company's publishing subsidiary was collecting songwriting royalties on four of the Top Five records in the chart – 'Relax' and 'Two Tribes', neil's, Hole In My Shoe', and Prince's 'When Doves Cry'.

Chrysalis underwent drastic re-shaping. The company had mushroomed out of a booking agency launched in 1968 by Chris Wright and Terry Ellis. This turned into a management company (Ten Years After, Jethro Tull, Procol Harum) and then into a recording one. In January 1985, however, the eighteen year partnership of the two men was sundered. Ellis wanted to diversify into film and video production; Wright wanted to keep the company in its existing state and was opposed to investment in film projects (although the company was at this stage financing Channel 4's popular *Max Headroom* programme). With renewed success in the US charts – from US signings Huey Lewis & the News and Pat Benatar, and the British singer Billy Idol – Wright was able to do that. Ellis left the company, which acquired his stake in it for £17.3 million. Wright, with a ninety-three per cent shareholding, was left firmly in the saddle.

A merger was then agreed with MAM,

● *PETER LAISTER EX CHAIRMAN OF THORN-EMI*

● *CHRIS WRIGHT*

the management agency started by Gordon Mills which represented Tom Jones and Engelbert Humperdinck. Plans were laid to go public (a move which would theoretically have made Wright a millionaire twenty-five times over), and to raise £6.75 million on the stock exchange to finance development in Australia and Canada.

In the event, the amalgamation of Chrysalis's rock roster with MAM's middle-of-the-road one seemed not to appeal. No stockbrokers were killed in the rush to buy shares. Only 240,000 of the 4.3 million on offer were taken up.

In 1984 EMI and Virgin had joined forces to move into the market for TV-advertised hit compilation albums which had previously been dominated by specialist companies like K-Tel. This proved so successful that MCA and Chrysalis joined together in opposition. Unfair opposition, according to EMI and Virgin, who had used the title *Now That's What I Call Music* for their albums. They took MCA and Chrysalis to court, arguing that their alternative title – *Out Now* – infringed the copyright of EMI and Virgin.

It must have been an extraordinary case, since the judge was virtually being asked to restrict to EMI and Virgin the use of the word 'Now'. This he quite sensibly refused to do; and the Court of Appeal agreed with him. *Out Now* and *Now That's What . . .* were soon vying for chart supremacy, the consumers apparently unconfused.

On the whole, a large number of lawyers were able to turn an honest penny or two supporting the actions of rock industry plaintiffs in the high court. Elton John and Bernie Taupin sued Dick James, for whose organization they had originally written and recorded. There was legal action concerning further allegations of chart hyping; a buying-in team was alleged to have charged £15,000 for its services.

Far more potentially serious was the surprising confiscation by the local police of a number of albums from Spectrum Records, a shop in Northwich, Cheshire. The Dead Kennedys, Crass and Icons Of Filth were amongst those whose work was seized.

The shop owners were taken to court and prosecuted successfully under the Obscene Publications Act. This could have had devastating repercussions for the UK industry. Fortunately, wiser counsels prevailed. British justice was reasserted when the verdict was overturned on appeal. The judge observed that the records to which he had listened – no doubt with great care – were "crude, vulgar and consist to a large extent of abusive rubbish, but they don't tend to deprave and corrupt".

No mention of the courts would, of course, be complete without a reference to the Beatles, who are now almost as famous for their litigation as they were for their recordings. In December 1984, in yet another blow for EMI, the company lost a court case to the Beatles, whose lawyers argued that the group members had been paid insufficient royalties in the early seventies. Mr Justice Gibson agreed, and granted Apple Corps Ltd an order so that a statement could be drawn up of the monies due to the group.

The main technical story of the year concerned the ever-increasing market penetration of compact discs. Appreciated at the end of 1983 only by the most discerning ears, CDs became a taste acquired by hundreds of thousands during 1984. Trade deliveries rose 220 per cent, from 250,000 to 800,000. This looked like the start of a major, long-term breakthrough. Certainly, it was another of the factors which helped to keep the market buoyant throughout 1984/5. One report commissioned for the financial institutions of the City in the summer of 1984 concluded that the CD system would soon become "an obligatory household item". It was, it went on, no longer a question of whether or not CD would replace the conventional stereo equipment ("outdated vinyl product", according to the report), but when it would do so.

There was a rush, not just in the UK but throughout the world, to create new manufacturing capacity. At the start of 1985, there were only eleven plants in production world-wide. Nimbus, the main UK factory sited in Monmouth, Gwent, started producing CDs in August 1984, which was actually a month before the US had any production capacity of its own. (For some time, Germany and Japan had been leading the world in CD production). By the time that EMI announced, in July 1985, that it would build a CD plant in Swindon, there were two others already under construction in the UK.

Initially, of course, the main problem lay in persuading consumers to purchase CD equipment (whether for the home or the car). To this end, PolyGram and Philips jointly launched an £800,000 promotional campaign in October 1984. Once a sufficient number had made the initial commitment, then the CD boom would really begin. Record-buyers would soon start purchasing fresh CD copies of favourite albums they already possessed as conventional LPs: a vision, perhaps, to soothe the jangled nerves of the most harassed record company executive. To sell a recording to a customer once is good business; to sell it to him twice is sheer heaven.

But it wasn't quite that simple. The mandarins of the music industry unfailingly spotted black clouds in the bluest sky, and conceived dire presentiments about the CD boom. CDs were high quality recordings which were resistant to wear-and-tear and consequently lasted a long time. Wasn't this true? And wasn't it also true that they were easily portable being so . . . well, compact?

Yes, of course – wasn't that the whole point? Apparently not. Music industry executives were soon knitting their brows in contemplation of the development of the CD market, imagining the mushrooming of mail order facilities for the hire of CDs, and of rental clubs and libraries. CDs seemed the salvation of the industry one minute; and a whopping potential embarrassment the next.

Those running the industry constantly suspected the public of doing unspeakable, shameless things with their own records – like lending them to a friend, for example. The campaign against what the industry, in ever-increasing flights of hyperbole, sometimes referred to as the ravages of home taping gathered momentum throughout the year. This was largely because the record industry spent a great deal of money in the cause; and partly because it engaged a top firm of parliamentary lobbyists – GJW (Gifford, Jeger and Weeks) – to act on its behalf in Westminster.

The upshot was that a Green Paper – a consultation document – on audio and video copyright material was published at the end of February 1985. This reversed the position taken by a government Green Paper four years earlier. It reached the cautious opinion that "a levy should be introduced on blank audio and video tape to remunerate copyright owners for private recording". Although the cautionary note was struck from the outset – "the government recognizes that an element of inequity is inherent in such a scheme" – the tenor of the report was nevertheless music to the ears of the record industry.

The details of the Green Paper were not quite so encouraging, however. A levy on tapes of ten per cent was advocated. If this was accepted, then the levy would raise an annual sum of £5 million. This fell some distance short of £320 million, the preposterous sum which the British Phonographic Industry (BPI) claimed was being lost each year. The plan outlined was for a collecting agency representing the copyright owners to take in the levy and redistribute the proceeds of it.

Such a levy would have the effect of introducing the principle that a reasonably efficient industry (that of cassette manufacture) should subsidise a frequently inefficient one (the UK record business); the principle is not only iniquitous, but also, oddly, inherently anti-Thatcherite.

For all the millions it has spent on its campaign, the BPI has never put forward tenable evidence to support its thesis that people tape records instead of buying them. On the contrary, there is every reason to believe that the opposite applies: that people tape records instead of not buying them – ie they buy those records which they particularly want, and tape the ones they are undecided about. This does not inhibit the sale of records. It simply allows people to perform in their own homes the service which record shops once offered, of providing listening booths or headphones to give customers the opportunity to test-drive records.

The last year has provided sales indications which refute the BPI's wall of prejudice and publicity about home taping. Retail sales of records and tapes increased, at well above the level of inflation, to £550 million. If home taping really influenced consumer purchasing habits, then one would expect to see more titles being sold, but with the top selling records shifting relatively fewer copies. Instead, the reverse trend is apparent. The best selling records are selling ever more prodigiously and the successes scored by the industry during 1984/5 adequately refuted its claims that its failures of recent times were attributable to home taping.

Bob Woffinden

● *PARLIAMENTARY LOBBYISTS WILF WEEKS, JENNY JEGERS AND ANDREW GIFFORD OF GJW.*

THE BPI CERTIFIED AWARDS

The qualifying sales levels for BPI gold and platinum awards are, respectively, 500,000 units and one million units (singles); 100,000 and 300,000 units (albums). To qualify for either of the two new awards, double and triple platinum, a single or an album must have been released since January 1985 or have appeared in the Gallup charts since then if it was released earlier.
An asterisk denotes that the BPI was not notified of a record's sales in that category but was notified of its sales in a higher category.

GOLD Singles

AUGUST 1984
BLACK LACE
Agadoo (Flair)
GEORGE MICHAEL
Careless Whisper (Epic)

SEPTEMBER 1984
STEVIE WONDER
I Just Called To Say I Love You (Motown)

OCTOBER 1984
RAY PARKER JR
Ghostbusters (Arista)

NOVEMBER 1984
WHAM!
Freedom (CBS)
CHAKA KHAN
I Feel For You (Warner Bros)

DECEMBER 1984
BAND AID
Do They Know It's Christmas? (Mercury)
FRANKIE GOES TO HOLLYWOOD
The Power Of Love (ZTT/Island)
WHAM!
Last Christmas (Epic)

JANUARY 1985
MADONNA
Like A Virgin (Warner Bros)
PAUL McCARTNEY
We All Stand Together (Parlophone)
FOREIGNER
I Want To Know What Love Is (Atlantic)

FEBRUARY 1985
KING
Love And Pride (CBS)

MARCH 1985
DEAD OR ALIVE
You Spin Me Round (Epic)
ELAINE PAIGE AND BARBARA DICKSON
I Know Him So Well (RCA)
ASHFORD AND SIMPSON
Solid (Capitol)

APRIL 1985
PHILIP BAILEY AND PHIL COLLINS
Easy Lover (CBS)

MAY 1985
PAUL HARDCASTLE
19 (Chrysalis)
PHYLLIS NELSON
Move Closer (PRT)

JULY 1985
SISTER SLEDGE
Frankie (Atlantic/WEA)

Albums

AUGUST 1984
ECHO AND THE BUNNYMEN
Ocean Rain (Korova)
SADE
Diamond Life (Epic)
TINA TURNER
Private Dancer (Capitol)
VARIOUS ARTISTS
Breakdance (Polydor)
VARIOUS ARTISTS
Now That's What I Call Music Vol 3 (EMI/Virgin)

SEPTEMBER 1984
POINTER SISTERS
Breakout (Planet)
ZZ TOP
Eliminator (Warner Bros)
VAN HALEN
1984 (Warner Bros)
PRINCE
Purple Rain (Warner Bros)
LEVEL 42
Standing In The Light (Polydor)
SISTER SLEDGE
We Are Family (Cotillion)

OCTOBER 1984
STEVIE WONDER
Woman In Red (Motown)

SHIRLEY BASSEY
I Am What I Am (Towerbell)
RANDY CRAWFORD
Miss Randy Crawford – Greatest Hits (K-Tel)
ELAINE PAIGE
Cinema (K-Tel)
DAVID BOWIE
Tonight (Capitol)
BIG COUNTRY
Steeltown (Mercury)
BRONSKI BEAT
The Age Of Consent (London)
VARIOUS ARTISTS
Hits Hits Hits (Telstar)
BARBRA STREISAND
Emotion (CBS)
VARIOUS ARTISTS
All By Myself (K-Tel)
ORCHESTRAL MANOEUVRES
Junk Culture (Virgin)
CULTURE CLUB
Waking Up With The House On Fire (Virgin)

NOVEMBER 1984

ECHO AND THE BUNNYMEN
Porcupine (Korova)
ULTRAVOX
The Collection (Chrysalis)
MEAT LOAF
Bad Attitude (Arista)
WHAM!
Make It Big (CBS)
ALISON MOYET
Alf (CBS)
ART GARFUNKEL
The Art Garfunkel Album (CBS)
PAUL McCARTNEY
Give My Regards To Broad Street (Parlophone)
ANDY WILLIAMS
Greatest Love Classics (EMI)
THE CARPENTERS
Yesterday Once More (EMI/A&M)
NIK KERSHAW
The Riddle (MCA)
THE SMITHS
Hat Full Of Hollow (Rough Trade)
STATUS QUO
12 Gold Bars Vol 2 (Vertigo)
DEEP PURPLE
Perfect Strangers (Polydor)
VARIOUS ARTISTS
Night Moves (K-Tel)
DURAN DURAN
Arena (Parlophone)

DECEMBER 1984

MARILLION
Script For A Jesters Tear (EMI)
VARIOUS ARTISTS
The Hits Album (WEA/CBS)*
VARIOUS ARTISTS
Now That's What I Call Music Vol 4 (EMI/Virgin)*
DES O'CONNOR
Des O'Connor Now (Telstar)
FOSTER AND ALLEN
The Very Best Of Foster And Allen (Spartan)
THE FUREYS
Golden Days (K-Tel)
CHAS AND DAVE
Greatest Hits (Towerbell)
EDDY GRANT
All The Hits (K-Tel)
YES
Close To The Edge (Atlantic)
SHAKIN' STEVENS
Greatest Hits (Epic)
ELKIE BROOKS
Screen Gems (EMI/A&M)
IRON MAIDEN
Powerslave (EMI)
CHAKA KHAN
I Feel For You (Warner Bros)
ECHO AND THE BUNNYMEN
Crocodiles (Korova)
BLACK LACE
Party Party (Telstar)
STEVIE WONDER
Love Songs (Telstar)
VARIOUS ARTISTS
Hooked On No 1's (K-Tel)
EURYTHMICS
1984 (Virgin)
HOWARD JONES
The 12" Howard Jones Mixes (WEA)
JOHN DENVER
The John Denver Collection (Telstar)

JANUARY 1985

YES
90125 (Atlantic)
RICHARD CLAYDERMAN
The Music Of Love (Delphine)
VARIOUS ARTISTS
Ghostbusters (Arista)
VARIOUS ARTISTS
Love Songs (Telstar)
DURAN DURAN
Arena (Parlophone)
MADONNA
Like A Virgin (Sire)
FOREIGNER
Agent Provocateur (Atlantic)
CHRIS DE BURGH
The Very Best Of Chris De Burgh (Telstar)
BLANCMANGE
Mange Tout (London)

FEBRUARY 1985

MEAT LOAF
Hits Out Of Hell (Epic)
BARBARA DICKSON
Barbara Dickson Song Book (K-Tel)
VARIOUS ARTISTS
Modern Love (K-Tel)
GEORGE BENSON
20/20 (Warner Bros)
THE SMITHS
Meat Is Murder (Rough Trade)
PHIL COLLINS
No Jacket Required (Virgin)

MARCH 1985

TEARS FOR FEARS
Songs From The Big Chair (Mercury)
VARIOUS ARTISTS
Chess (RCA)
KING
Steps In Time (CBS)
HOWARD JONES
Dream Into Action (WEA)
IRON MAIDEN
Iron Maiden (EMI)
JEAN MICHEL JARRE
The Concerts In China (Polydor)
ERIC CLAPTON
Time Pieces (RSO)

APRIL 1985

PAUL YOUNG
The Secret of Association (CBS)
ANDREW LLOYD-WEBBER
Requiem (HMV/EMI)
PRINCE AND THE REVOLUTION
Around The World (Warner Bros)
BILLY BRAGG
Life's A Riot (Go! Discs/Chrysalis)
MIKE OLDFIELD
5 Miles Out (Virgin)
BRYAN ADAMS
Reckless (A&M)

MAY 1985

FREDDIE MERCURY
Mr Bad Guy (CBS)
DEAD OR ALIVE
Youthquake (Epic)
VARIOUS ARTISTS
Now Dance (EMI/Virgin)
BRENDA LEE
The Very Best Of (MCA)
GO WEST
Go West (Chrysalis)

JUNE 1985

CLANNAD
Legend (RCA)
THE STYLE COUNCIL
Our Favourite Shop (PolyGram)
MARC BOLAN
20th Century Boy (K-Tel)
BRYAN FERRY
Boys And Girls (PolyGram)
YES
90125 (Atlantic)
DOORS
LA Woman (Elektra)
EURYTHMICS
Be Yours Tonight (RCA)

JULY 1985

BILLY OCEAN
Suddenly (Zomba)
MARILLION
Fugazi (EMI)
MARILLION
Real To Reel (EMI)
MARILLION
Misplaced Childhood (EMI)*
SCRITTI POLITTI
Cupid & Psyche (Virgin)
CYNDI LAUPER
She's So Unusual (Portrait/CBS)

PLATINUM Singles

JULY 1984

FRANKIE GOES TO HOLLYWOOD
Two Tribes (Island)

SEPTEMBER 1984

GEORGE MICHAEL
Careless Whisper (Epic)
STEVIE WONDER
I Just Called To Say I Love You (RCA)

DECEMBER 1984

BAND AID
Do They Know It's Christmas? (Mercury)

JANUARY 1985

WHAM!
Last Christmas (Epic)

Albums

AUGUST 1984

VARIOUS ARTISTS
Now That's What I Call Music Vol 3 (EMI/Virgin)

OCTOBER 1984

NIK KERSHAW
Human Racing (MCA)
SPANDAU BALLET
Parade (Chrysalis)
SADE
Diamond Life (Epic)
CULTURE CLUB
Waking Up With The House On Fire (Virgin)

NOVEMBER 1984

WHAM!
Make It Big (CBS)
ZZ TOP
Eliminator (Warner Bros)
ULTRAVOX
The Collection (Chrysalis)
ALISON MOYET
Alf (CBS)

DECEMBER 1984

VARIOUS ARTISTS
Now That's What I Call Music Vol 4 (EMI/Virgin)
VARIOUS ARTISTS
The Hits Album (WEA/CBS)
YES
Close To The Edge (Atlantic)
THE CARPENTERS
Yesterday Once More (EMI/A&M)
PAUL McCARTNEY
Give My Regards To Broad Street (Parlophone)
TINA TURNER
Private Dancer (Capitol)
SHAKIN' STEVENS
Greatest Hits (Epic)
NIK KERSHAW
The Riddle (MCA)
BLACK LACE
Party Party (Telstar)

JANAURY 1985

THOMPSON TWINS
Quick Step And Side Kick (Arista)
ELAINE PAIGE
Cinema (K-Tel)

FEBRUARY 1985

STEVIE WONDER
Woman In Red (Soundtrack) (Motown)
TEARS FOR FEARS
The Hurting (Mercury)
DIRE STRAITS
Alchemy (Vertigo)
BRUCE SPRINGSTEEN
Born In The USA (CBS)

MARCH 1985

BRONSKI BEAT
The Age Of Consent (Forbidden Fruit)
PHIL COLLINS
No Jacket Required (Virgin)
DURAN DURAN
Arena (EMI)

APRIL 1985

PAUL YOUNG
The Secret Of Association (CBS)
TEARS FOR FEARS
Songs From The Big Chair (Mercury)
PRINCE
Purple Rain (Warner Bros)

MAY 1985

FOREIGNER
Agent Provocateur (Atlantic)
DIRE STRAITS
Brothers In Arms (Vertigo)

JUNE 1985

VARIOUS ARTISTS
Out Now (Chrysalis)
CHAS AND DAVE
Greatest Hits (Towerbell)

JULY 1985

BRUCE SPRINGSTEEN
Born To Run (CBS)

DOUBLE PLATINUM Albums

MARCH 1985

THOMPSON TWINS
Into The Gap (Arista)

APRIL 1985

ELAINE PAIGE
Stages (K-Tel)
ZZ TOP
Eliminator (Warner Bros)
ULTRAVOX
The Collection (Chrysalis)*
FLEETWOOD MAC
Rumours (Warner Bros)*
VARIOUS
The Hits Album (Warner Bros)*
WHAM!
Fantastic (Innervision)
ALISON MOYET
Alf (CBS)*
BILLY JOEL
An Innocent Man (CBS)*
PAUL YOUNG
No Parlez (CBS)*
MICHAEL JACKSON
Thriller (Epic)*
SADE
Diamond Life (Epic)*
WHAM!
Make It Big (Epic)*
TINA TURNER
Private Dancer (Capitol)
VARIOUS ARTISTS
The Hits Album Vol 2 (WEA/CBS)
PHIL COLLINS
Face Value (Virgin)
CULTURE CLUB
Colour By Numbers (Virgin)
THE HUMAN LEAGUE
Dare (Virgin)

MAY 1985

PHIL COLLINS
No Jacket Required (Virgin)
BRUCE SPRINGSTEEN
Born In The USA (CBS)
FRANKIE GOES TO HOLLYWOOD
Welcome To The Pleasuredome (ZTT)*
BOB MARLEY
Legend (Island)*

TRIPLE PLATINUM Albums

APRIL 1985

FLEETWOOD MAC
Rumours (Warner Bros)
VARIOUS ARTISTS
The Hits Album (Warner Bros)
ULTRAVOX
The Collection (Chrysalis)
ALISON MOYET
Alf (CBS)
BILLY JOEL
An Innocent Man (CBS)
PAUL YOUNG
No Parlez (CBS)
WHAM!
Make It Big (Epic)
SADE
Diamond Life (Epic)
MICHAEL JACKSON
Thriller (Epic)
CULTURE CLUB
Colour By Numbers (Virgin)
HUMAN LEAGUE
Dare (Virgin)

MAY 1985

QUEEN
Greatest Hits (EMI)
MICHAEL JACKSON
Thriller (Epic)
VARIOUS
Now That's What I Call Music Vol 4 (EMI/Virgin)
FRANKIE GOES TO HOLLYWOOD
Welcome To The Pleasuredome (ZTT)
BOB MARLEY
Legend (Island)

THE RIAA CERTIFIED AWARDS

The qualifying sales levels for RIAA gold and platinum awards are, respectively, one million and two million units (singles); 500,000 and one million units (albums). To qualify for the new multi-platinum award, which certifies successive million-level sales, an album or single must have been released on or after 1 January 1976. The figures at the end of the multi-platinum entries indicate the million level reached.

GOLD Singles

AUGUST 1984

THE JACKSONS
State of Shock (Epic)
RAY PARKER JR
Ghostbusters (Arista)
TINA TURNER
What's Love Got To Do With It (Capitol)

OCTOBER 1984

BILLY OCEAN
Caribbean Queen (Jive)

NOVEMBER 1984

STEVIE WONDER
I Just Called To Say I Love You (Motown)
PRINCE
Let's Go Crazy (Warner Bros)
CHAKA KHAN
I Feel For You (Warner Bros)

DECEMBER 1984

BAND AID
Do They Know It's Christmas? (Columbia)
PRINCE AND THE REVOLUTION
Purple Rain (Warner Bros)

JANUARY 1985

NEW EDITION
Cool It Now (MCA)
MADONNA
Like A Virgin (Sire/Warner Bros)

MARCH 1985

WHAM!
Careless Whisper (Columbia)
PHILIP BAILEY AND PHIL COLLINS
Easy Lover (Columbia)
FOREIGNER
I Want To Know What Love Is (Atlantic)

APRIL 1985

USA FOR AFRICA
We Are The World (Columbia)

JULY 1985

MADONNA
Crazy For You (Geffen/Warner Bros)
VARIOUS ARTISTS
The Hobbit (Disneyland)
VARIOUS ARTISTS
Mother Goose Rhymes (Disneyland)
VARIOUS ARTISTS
The Wizard Of Oz (Disneyland)
VARIOUS ARTISTS
Winnie The Pooh And The Blustery Day (Disneyland)
VARIOUS ARTISTS
Brer Rabbit And The Tar Baby (Disneyland)

Albums

AUGUST 1984

HANK WILLIAMS JR
Greatest Hits (Curb)
TWISTED SISTER
Stay Hungry (Atlantic)
ROD STEWART
Camouflage (Warner Bros)
BRUCE SPRINGSTEEN
Born In The USA (Columbia)
SOUNDTRACK
Eddie and the Cruisers (Scotti Bros)
SOUNDTRACK
Ghostbusters (Arista)
PRINCE AND THE REVOLUTION
Purple Rain (Warner Bros)
LUCIANO PAVAROTTI
O Sole Mio (London)
THE JACKSONS
Victory (Epic)
LAURA BRANIGAN
Branigan (Atlantic)
LAURA BRANIGAN
Self Control (Atlantic)

SEPTEMBER 1984

BERLIN
Pleasure Victim (Geffen)
CHICAGO
17 (Full Moon)
DIO
Holy Diver (Warner Bros)
DIO
The Last In Line (Warner Bros)
ELTON JOHN
Breaking Hearts (Geffen)
MÖTLEY CRÜE
Too Fast For Love (Elektra)
TEDDY PENDERGRASS
Love Language (Asylum)
QUIET RIOT
Condition Critical (Pasha)

SCANDAL
Warrior (Columbia)
TIME
Ice Cream Castle (Warner Bros)
JOHN WAITE
No Brakes (EMI America)

OCTOBER 1984

RICKY SCAGGS
Don't Cheat In Our Home (Epic)
BILLY SQUIER
Signs Of Life (Capitol)
BILLY OCEAN
Suddenly (Jive)
JULIO IGLESIAS
1100 Bel Air Place (Columbia)
THE FIXX
Phantoms (MCA)
SHEENA EASTON
You Could Have Been With Me (EMI America)
NEIL DIAMOND
Primitive (Columbia)
THE BEATLES
20 Greatest Hits (Capitol)

NOVEMBER 1984

DAVID BOWIE
Tonight (EMI America)
CANDLE
Bullfrogs And Butterflies (Birdwing)
SHEENA EASTON
Private Heaven (EMI America)
SAMMY HAGAR
VOA (Geffen)
SAM HARRIS
Sam Harris (Motown)
IRON MAIDEN
Powerslave (Capitol)
OAK RIDGE BOYS
Greatest Hits 2 (MCA)
DIANA ROSS
Swept Away (RCA)
SOUNDTRACK
The Woman In Red (Motown)
SOUNDTRACK
Teachers (Capitol)
GEORGE STRAIT
Right Or Wrong (MCA)

DECEMBER 1984

GEORGE WINSTON
December (Windham Hill)
WHAM!
Make It Big (Columbia)
U2
The Unforgettable Fire (Island)
VARIOUS ARTISTS
Disney's Christmas Favourites (Disneyland)
BARBRA STREISAND
Emotion (Columbia)
RUN D.M.C.
Run D.M.C. (Profile)
KENNY ROGERS AND DOLLY PARTON
Once Upon A Christmas (RCA)
KENNY ROGERS
What About Me (RCA)
JEFFREY OSBORNE
Don't Stop (A&M)
NEW EDITION
New Edition (MCA)
WILLIE NELSON
City Of New Orleans (Columbia)
PAUL McCARTNEY
Give My Regards To Broad Street (Columbia)
KROKUS
The Blitz (Arista)
KISS
Animalize (Mercury)
CHAKA KHAN
I Feel For You (Warner Bros)
THE HONEYDRIPPERS
Vol 1 (Atlantic)
HALL & OATES
Big Bam Boom (RCA)
CULTURE CLUB
Waking Up With The House On Fire (Virgin)

JANUARY 1985

JULIAN LENNON
Valotte (Atlantic)
PAT BENATAR
Tropico (Chrysalis)
HANK WILLIAMS JR
Major Moves (Warner Bros)
SHEILA E
The Glamorous Life (Warner Bros)
DURAN DURAN
Arena (Capitol)
JEFFERSON STARSHIP
Nuclear Furniture (Grunt/RCA)
BARRY MANILOW
2:00 am Paradise Cafe (Arista)
DEEP PURPLE
Perfect Strangers (Mercury/PolyGram)
MORMON TABERNACLE CHOIR
Mormon Tabernacle Choir Sings Christmas Carols (CBS Masterworks)
MORMON TABERNACLE CHOIR
Joy To The World (CBS Masterworks)
MIDNIGHT STAR
Planetary Invasion (Elektra)
LINDA RONSTADT
Lush Life (Elektra)
MADONNA
Like A Virgin (Sire/Warner Bros)
WHODINI
Escape (Jive/Arista)
DON HENLEY
Building The Perfect Beast (Geffen/Warner Bros)
HANK WILLIAMS JR
Man Of Steel (Warner Bros)

FEBRUARY 1985

BRYAN ADAMS
Reckless (A&M)
FOREIGNER
Agent Provocateur (Atlantic)
SOUNDTRACK
Beverly Hills Cop (MCA)
LEE GREENWOOD
You've Got A Good Love Comin' (MCA)
TOTO
Isolation (Columbia)

MARCH 1985

TALKING HEADS
Stop Making Sense (Sire/Warner Bros)
KOOL AND THE GANG
Emergency (De-Lite/PolyGram)
FRANKIE GOES TO HOLLYWOOD
Welcome To The Pleasuredome (Island/Atlantic)
ASHFORD AND SIMPSON
Solid (Capitol)
PHILIP BAILEY
Chinese Wall (Columbia)
SURVIVOR
Vital Signs (Scotti Bros)
REO SPEEDWAGON
Wheels Are Turnin' (Epic)
JOHN FOGERTY
Centerfield (Warner Bros)
COMMODORES
All The Great Hits (Motown)
ANNE MURRAY
A Little Good News (Capitol)

APRIL 1985

USA FOR AFRICA
We Are The World (Columbia)
TEENA MARIE
Starchild (Epic)
AUTOGRAPH
Sign In Please (RCA)
ALABAMA
40 Hour Week (RCA)
DAVID LEE ROTH
Crazy From The Heat (Warner Bros)
GEORGE WINSTON
Autumn (Windam Hill)
THE JUDDS
Why Not Me (RCA)
GEORGE STRAIT
Does Fort Worth Ever Cross Your Mind (MCA)
SOUNDTRACK
Vision Quest (Warner Bros)
THE FIRM
The Firm (Atlantic)
PHIL COLLINS
No Jacket Required (Atlantic)

MAY 1985

AMY GRANT
Straight Ahead (Myrrh/Word Inc)
FAT BOYS
Fat Boys (Sutra Records)
SADE
Diamond Life (Portrait)
MICK JAGGER
She's The Boss (Columbia)
COMMODORES
Nightshift (Motown)
DeBARGE
Rhythm Of The Night (Motown)
TEARS FOR FEARS
Songs From The Big Chair (Mercury)
LUTHER VANDROSS
The Night I Fell In Love (Epic)
THE POWER STATION
Power Station (Capitol)
TOM PETTY AND THE HEARTBREAKERS
Southern Accents (MCA)
HANK WILLIAMS JR
Rowdy (Curb/Warner)

JUNE 1985

RUN D.M.C.
King Of Rock (Profile)
SPYRO GYRA
Catching The Sun (MCA)
MAZE FEATURING FRANKIE BEVERLY
Can't Stop The Love (Capitol)
SOUNDTRACK
The Breakfast Club (A&M)
ANNE MURRAY
Heart Over Mind (Capitol)
RICK SPRINGFIELD
Tao (RCA)
HOWARD JONES
Dream Into Action (Elektra)
SOUNDTRACK
More Songs From The Big Chill (Motown)
MARY JANE GIRLS
Only Four You (Motown)
WHITNEY HOUSTON
Whitney Houston (Arista)
SANDI PATTI
More Than Wonderful (Impact/The Benson Co)

JULY 1985

PRINCE AND THE REVOLUTION
Around The World In A Day (Paisley Park/Warner Bros)
EURYTHMICS
Be Yourself Tonight (RCA)
SOUNDTRACK
Visionquest (Geffen/Warner Bros)
ROBERT PLANT
Shaken 'N' Stirred (Es Paranza/Atlantic)
VARIOUS ARTISTS
Best of Disney Vol II (Disneyland)
NIGHT RANGER
7 Wishes (MCA)
DIRE STRAITS
Brothers In Arms (Warner Bros)
FREDDIE JACKSON
Rock Me Tonight (Capitol)

PLATINUM Singles

AUGUST 1984

PRINCE
When Doves Cry (Warner Bros)

NOVEMBER 1984

VARIOUS ARTISTS
Star Wars (Disneyland)

APRIL 1985

USA FOR AFRICA
We Are The World (Columbia)

Albums

AUGUST 1984

MERLE AND WILLIE HAGGARD
Poncho & Lefty (Epic)
JULIO IGLESIAS
Julio (Columbia)
THE JACKSONS
Victory (Epic)
MADONNA
Madonna (Sire)
POLICE
Outlandos D'Amour (A&M)
PRINCE AND THE REVOLUTION
Purple Rain (Warner Bros)
RATT
Out Of The Cellar (Atlantic)
SOUNDTRACK
Ghostbusters (Arista)
TINA TURNER
Private Dancer (Capitol)
HANK WILLIAMS JR
Greatest Hits (Curb)
BRUCE SPRINGSTEEN
Born In The USA (Columbia)

SEPTEMBER 1984

QUIET RIOT
Condition Critical (Pasha)

OCTOBER 1984

CHICAGO
17 (Full Moon)
NEIL DIAMOND
12 Greatest Hits Vol 2 (Columbia)
EURYTHMICS
Touch (RCA)
JULIO IGLESIAS
1100 Bel Air Place (Columbia)
POINTER SISTERS
Break Out (Planet)
SOUNDTRACK
Eddie and the Cruisers (Scotti Bros)
BILLY SQUIER
Signs Of Life (Jive)
THOMPSON TWINS
Into The Gap (Arista)

NOVEMBER 1984

SOUNDTRACK
The Woman In Red (Motown)
DAVID BOWIE
Tonight (EMI America)

DECEMBER 1984

CULTURE CLUB
Waking Up With The House On Fire (Virgin)
HALL & OATES
Big Bam Boom (RCA)
THE HONEYDRIPPERS
Vol 1 (Atlantic)
CHAKA KHAN
I Feel For You (Warner Bros)
KISS
Animalize (Mercury)
KENNY ROGERS
What About Me (RCA)
KENNY ROGERS AND DOLLY PARTON
Once Upon A Christmas (RCA)
BARBRA STREISAND
Emotion (A&M)
WHAM!
Make It Big (Columbia)

JANUARY 1985

LUTHER VANDROSS
Busybody (Epic)
BILLY OCEAN
Suddenly (Jive)
DURAN DURAN
Duran Duran (Capitol)
PAT BENATAR
Tropico (Chrysalis)
THE TIME
Ice Cream Castle (Warner Bros)
PRINCE
Controversy (Warner Bros)
LINDA RONSTADT
Lush Life (Elektra)
NEW EDITION
New Edition (MCA)
LARRY ELGART
Hooked On Swing (RCA)
MADONNA
Like A Virgin (Sire)

FEBRUARY 1985

BRYAN ADAMS
Reckless (A&M)
U2
The Unforgettable Fire (Island/Atlantic)
FOREIGNER
Agent Provocateur (Atlantic)
U2
War (Island/Atlantic)

MARCH 1985

REO SPEEDWAGON
Wheels Are Turnin' (Epic)
JOHN FOGERTY
Centerfield (Warner Bros)
JULIAN LENNON
Valotte (Atlantic)
PHIL COLLINS
Hello, I Must Be Going (Atlantic)
SHEENA EASTON
A Private Heaven (EMI America)

APRIL 1985

ALABAMA
40 Hour Week (RCA)
SOUNDTRACK
Beverly Hills Cop (MCA)
DEEP PURPLE
Perfect Strangers (Mercury)
DON HENLEY
Building The Perfect Beast (Geffen)
SCANDAL FEATURING PATTI SMYTH
Warrior (Columbia)
EDDIE MURPHY
Comedian (Columbia)
USA FOR AFRICA
We Are The World (Columbia)
PHIL COLLINS
No Jacket Required (Atlantic)

MAY 1985

SADE
Diamond Life (Portrait)
LUTHER VANDROSS
The Night I Fell In Love (Epic)

JUNE 1985

DAVID LEE ROTH
Crazy From The Heat (Warner Bros)
AMY GRANT
Age To Age (Myrrh/Word Inc)
MICK JAGGER
She's The Boss (Columbia)
SURVIVOR
Vital Signs (Scotti Bros)
TEARS FOR FEARS
Songs From The Big Chair (Mercury)

JULY 1985

KOOL AND THE GANG
Emergency (De Lite/PolyGram)
U2
Under A Blood Red Sky (Island/Atlantic)
PRINCE AND THE REVOLUTION
Around The World In A Day (Paisley Park/Warner Bros)

MULTI-PLATINUM Singles

APRIL 1985

USA FOR AFRICA
We Are The World (Columbia) (4m)

Albums

OCTOBER 1984

AC/DC
Black In Black (Atlantic) (5m)
AC/DC
Dirty Deeds Done Dirt Cheap (Atlantic) (2m)
AC/DC
For Those About To Rock (We Salute You) (Atlantic) (2m)
AC/DC
Highway To Hell (Atlantic) (2m)
AEROSMITH
Rocks (Columbia) (2m)
ALABAMA
The Closer We Get To You (RCA) (3m)

ALABAMA
Feels So Right (RCA) (3m)
ALABAMA
Mountain Music (RCA) (3m)
ALABAMA
Roll On (RCA) (2m)
ASIA
Asia (Geffen) (3m)
GEORGE BENSON
Breezin' (Warner Bros) (3m)
THE BLUES BROTHERS
Briefcase Full Of Blues (Atlantic) (2m)
THE CARS
Heartbeat City (Elektra) (2m)
JOHN COUGAR MELLENCAMP
Uh Huh (Riva) (2m)
JOHN COUGAR
American Fool (Riva) (2m)
CHRISTOPHER CROSS
Christopher Cross (Warner Bros) (4m)
DEF LEPPARD
Pyromania (Mercury) (6m)
NEIL DIAMOND
You Don't Bring Me Flowers (Columbia) (2m)
DOOBIE BROTHERS
The Best Of (Warner Bros) (5m)
DOOBIE BROTHERS
Minute By Minute (Warner Bros) (3m)
EARTH, WIND & FIRE
All 'n' All (Columbia) (2m)
EARTH, WIND & FIRE
Spirit (Columbia) (2m)
EARTH, WIND & FIRE
The Best Of, Vol 1 (Arc) (2m)
EARTH, WIND & FIRE
I Am (Arc) (2m)
FLEETWOOD MAC
Mirage (Warner Bros) (2m)
FLEETWOOD MAC
Rumours (Warner Bros) (12m)
FLEETWOOD MAC
Tusk (Warner Bros) (2m)
FOGHAT
Foghat Live (Bearsville) (2m)
JANE FONDA
Jane Fonda's Workout Album (Columbia) (2m)
FOREIGNER
Double Vision (Atlantic) (5m)
FOREIGNER
4 (Atlantic) (5m)
FOREIGNER
Head Games (Atlantic) (2m)
JULIO IGLESIAS
1100 Bel Air Place (Columbia) (2m)
MICHAEL JACKSON
Thriller (Epic) (20m)
THE JACKSONS
Victory (Epic) (2m)
BILLY JOEL
An Innocent Man (Columbia) (4m)
BILLY JOEL
52nd Street (Columbia) (5m)
BILLY JOEL
Glass Houses (Columbia) (5m)
BILLY JOEL
The Stranger (Columbia) (6m)
JOURNEY
Escape (Columbia) (6m)
JOURNEY
Evolution (Columbia) (2m)
JOURNEY
Frontiers (Columbia) (3m)
JOURNEY
Infinity (Columbia) (2m)
CYNDI LAUPER
She's So Unusual (Portrait) (2m)
LED ZEPPELIN
In Through The Out Door (Swan Song) (3m)
LED ZEPPELIN
The Song Remains The Same (Swan Song) (2m)
JOHN LENNON AND YOKO ONO
Double Fantasy (Geffen) (3m)
LOVERBOY
Get Lucky (Columbia) (3m)
MEN AT WORK
Business As Usual (Columbia) (4m)
MEN AT WORK
Cargo (Columbia) (2m)
MICKEY MOUSE
Mickey Mouse Disco (Disneyland) (2m)
WILLIE NELSON
Always On My Mind (Columbia) (3m)
WILLIE NELSON
Stardust (Columbia) (3m)
OLIVIA NEWTON-JOHN
Greatest Hits (MCA) (2m)
OLIVIA NEWTON-JOHN
Greatest Hits Vol 2 (MCA) (2m)
OLIVIA NEWTON-JOHN
Physical (MCA) (2m)
OLIVIA NEWTON-JOHN
Xanadu (MCA) (2m)
STEVIE NICKS
Bella Donna (Modern) (3m)
OAK RIDGE BOYS
Fancy Free (MCA) (2m)
TOM PETTY AND THE HEARTBREAKERS
Damn The Torpedoes (Backstreet) (2m)
PINK FLOYD
Animals (Columbia) (2m)
PINK FLOYD
The Wall (Columbia) (4m)
PRINCE
1999 (Warner Bros) (2m)
LIONEL RICHIE
Can't Slow Down (Motown) (8m)
LIONEL RICHIE
Lionel Richie (Motown) (4m)
ROLLING STONES
Some Girls (Rolling Stones) (4m)
ROLLING STONES
Tattoo You (Rolling Stones) (3m)
LINDA RONSTADT
What's New (Asylum) (2m)
RUSH
Moving Pictures (Mercury) (2m)
BOZ SCAGGS
Silk Degrees (Columbia) (4m)
SCORPIONS
Love At First Sting (Polydor/PolyGram) (2m)
SOUNDTRACK
Footlose (Columbia) (5m)
SOUNDTRACK
Flashdance (Casablanca) (5m)
BRUCE SPRINGSTEEN
Born In The USA (Columbia) (3m)
ROD STEWART
A Night On The Town (Warner Bros) (2m)
ROD STEWART
Blondes Have More Fun (Warner Bros) (3m)
ROD STEWART
Footloose & Fancy Free (Warner Bros) (3m)
BARBRA STREISAND AND KRIS KRISTOFFERSON
A Star Is Born (Columbia) (4m)
BARBRA STREISAND
Greatest Hits Vol 2 (Columbia) (4m)
BARBRA STREISAND
Guilty (Columbia) (4m)
BARBRA STREISAND
Memories (Columbia) (2m)
JAMES TAYLOR
Greatest Hits (Warner Bros) (2m)
TOTO
Toto IV (Columbia) (2m)
VAL HALEN
Diver Down (Warner Bros) (2m)
VAN HALEN
1984 (Warner Bros) (4m)
VAN HALEN
Van Halen (Warner Bros) (5m)
VAN HALEN
Van Halen II (Warner Bros) (3m)
VAN HALEN
Women And Children First (Warner Bros) (2m)
ZZ TOP
Eliminator (Warner Bros) (4m)

NOVEMBER 1984

PAT BENATAR
Crimes of Passion (Chrysalis) (4m)
PAT BENATAR
Precious Time (Chrysalis) (2m)
FOREIGNER
Foreigner (Atlantic) (4m)
PETER FRAMPTON
Frampton Comes Alive (A&M) (6m)
GO-GOS
Beauty And The Beat (IRS) (2m)
HUEY LEWIS AND THE NEWS
Sports (Chrysalis) (5m)
CHUCK MANGIONE
Feels So Good (A&M) (2m)
POLICE
Ghost In The Machine (A&M) (2m)
POLICE
Synchronicity (A&M) (4m)
PRINCE
Purple Rain (Warner Bros) (8m)
SOUNDTRACK
Grease (RSO) (8m)
SOUNDTRACK
Saturday Night Fever (RSO) (11m)
STYX
Cornerstone (A&M) (2m)
STYX
The Grand Illusion (A&M) (3m)
STYX
Paradise Theater (A&M) (3m)
STYX
Pieces Of Eight (A&M) (3m)
SUPERTRAMP
Breakfast In America (A&M) (4m)

DECEMBER 1984

CHICAGO
17 (Full Moon) (2m)
MADONNA
Madonna (Sire) (2m)
RATT
Out Of The Cellar (Atlantic) (2m)

JANUARY 1985

MÖTLEY CRÜE
Shout At The Devil (Elektra) (2m)
BILLY IDOL
Rebel Yell (Chrysalis) (2m)
PRINCE AND THE REVOLUTION
Purple Rain (Warner Bros) (9m)
WAYLON JENNINGS
The Outlaws (RCA) (2m)
WAYLON JENNINGS
Greatest Hits (RCA) (3m)
WAYLON JENNINGS AND WILLIE NELSON
Waylon & Willie (RCA) (2m)
VAN HALEN
1984 (Warner Bros) (5m)
MADONNA
Like A Virgin (Sire) (2m)

FEBRUARY 1985

MIDNIGHT STAR
No Parking On The Dance Floor
(Solar/Elektra) (2m)

TINA TURNER
Private Dancer (Capitol) (3m)

DURAN DURAN
Arena (Capitol) (2m)

MADONNA
Like A Virgin (Sire) (3m)

CHICAGO
17 (Full Moon) (3m)

POINTER SISTERS
Break Out (Planet) (2m)

MARCH 1985

CYNDI LAUPER
She's So Unusual (Portrait) (4m)

TWISTED SISTER
Stay Hungry (Atlantic) (2m)

APRIL 1985

HALL & OATES
H2O (RCA) (2m)

HALL & OATES
Big Bam Boom (RCA) (2m)

HALL & OATES
Rock'n'Soul Part I (RCA) (2m)

USA FOR AFRICA
We Are The World (Columbia) (2m)

MADONNA
Like A Virgin (Sire) (4m)

MAY 1985

BRUCE SPRINGSTEEN
Born In The USA (Columbia) (6m)

FOREIGNER
Agent Provocateur (Atlantic) (2m)

JUNE 1985

PHIL COLLINS
No Jacket Required (Atlantic) (2m)

TINA TURNER
Private Dancer (Capitol) (4m)

USA FOR AFRICA
We Are The World (Columbia) (3m)

MICHAEL JACKSON
Off The Wall (Epic) (5m)

JULY 1985

PRINCE AND THE REVOLUTION
Around The World In A Day
(Paisley Park/Warner Bros) (2m)

WHAM!
Make It Big (Columbia) (3m)

BRUCE SPRINGSTEEN
Born In The USA (Columbia) (7m)

THE CARS
Heartbeat City (Elektra) (2m)

ZZ TOP
Eliminator (Warner Bros) (5m)

PRINCE
1999 (Warner Bros) (3m)

MADONNA
Like A Virgin (Sire) (5m)

● JOHN LENNON & YOKO ONO

● WAYLON JENNINGS

● PHIL COLLINS

● TOM PETTY

CHART ROUND UP

Alan Jones looks beyond the numbers and tries to make sense of the UK and US chart movements

The first thing to notice about the British charts in 1985 is that the much-ballyhooed renaissance of American rock impressed the average record buyer much less than the average critic. Springsteen was the notable exception, selling out concerts in Newcastle, London and Leeds, to bring his 1985 tour gross to a staggering £37 million. For a while, all seven Springsteen albums – including the previously uncharted *Greetings From Asbury Park N J* (1974) – were in the Top Sixty at the same time; the best haul since David Bowie had ten albums in the chart at the time of his Serious Moonlight tour in 1983. Lone Justice, Green On Red, Rain Parade, and other new heroes of the guitar made a much smaller impact.

Indeed, as always, the best way for an American to succeed in Britain was to be black and recording dance records. In a typical week, black American acts outnumbered their white counterparts by a margin of three to one. Sometimes the ratio in favour of blacks rose as high as seven to one; a remarkable triumph considering that, in the American population as a whole, it's whites who outnumber blacks by seven to one.

This apparent reverse discrimination reflects Britain's preference for the more inventive, technology-minded rock produced indigenously over the more traditional American variety, and the high esteem in which American disco/dance music is held in Britain. The latter is especially true in London, which typically accounts for about twenty-five per cent of all singles sales, but returns a figure twice as high for black music.

Apart from a surfeit of soundtrack albums – MCA released twelve in one month alone in America – one of the year's most noticeable phenomena was the charity record. Following Band Aid's enormous success in raising cash for Ethiopia, a steady stream of charity records dotted the release schedules throughout the year, their success or failure depending largely on public empathy of the causes they espoused rather than any intrinsic musical merit. USA For Africa and the Crowd (supporting Ethiopia and the Bradford Disaster Fund) both raced to number one, Marti Webb had a Top Five hit for the Ben Hardwick Fund, though records in support of Muscular Dystrophy, the RSCPA, Greenpeace, Animus and numerous other worthy causes made less impact.

Twelve-inch singles now being obligatory, and picture discs apparently heading for the same status, record companies had to find new and even more expensive methods of "creative marketing" in order to gain advantage over their rivals. Twinpacks (two singles in a gatefold sleeve) – both 7″ and 12″ – and poster bags increased in frequency, as did shaped discs. And some bright spark decreed that it was no longer enough to release one 12″, or even two, and the third generation remix came into being. It was most effectively used by Chrysalis to prolong the career of Paul Hardcastle's '19', and was also used well by Island to boost Skipworth and Turner's magnificent 'Thinking About Your Love' which, in its final remix, had the original male vocal track completely removed and replaced by the soulfully wailing diva, Helena Springs.

Despite all the hype the magic formula for having a hit remains simple: make a good record. It worked for Denise LaSalle who, at the age of 51, became the oldest woman to make her chart debut with a splendid version of Rockin' Sydney's cajun hit 'My Toot Toot'. And for Roy Orbison, who returned to the chart, albeit briefly, for the first time in fifteen years with the moody 'Wild Hearts'. And for Kool and the Gang, who first hit the charts in 1979 with 'Ladies Night' and haven't missed since. Their string of eighties' hits, eighteen at the time of writing, is rivalled only by Shakin' Stevens.

The British singles chart remains the most accurate, fast-moving, intriguing and keenly contested in the world. Every week brings a new contingent of chart-makers, some with long and distinguished careers, others with only one hit in them. The continuing battle for chart honours is a 33-year-old soap opera which delights, disappoints and intrigues millions each week. For them at least, it's number one.

Last year, the American singles chart celebrated its forty-fifth birthday, and in its middle age it seemed to cast off some of the conservatism that has blighted its recent past. It still reflects, in almost equal measure, the attitudes of radio programmers (without whom very little can or does become a hit) and record buyers. The former have for several years stifled new talent by imposing heavily formated and constantly diminishing playlists on the airwaves, but have recently become considerably more adventurous.

The new era of enlightenment largely benefited British acts; not just the risqué and the political – Frankie Goes To Hollywood, Dead Or Alive, Paul Hardcastle – but also groups like Depeche Mode, Tears For Fears, Go West and King as Top Forty radio realized there was life beyond Night Ranger and Survivor. Indeed, British acts had a banner year, though American rock institutions like Hall & Oates, Huey Lewis, Kenny Loggins and Bruce Springsteen continued to prosper. Springsteen, in particular, had a great year. His *Born In The USA* album sold over seven million copies, and spawned five Top Ten singles, a feat previously attained only by Michael Jackson (seven hits from *Thriller*) and Lionel Richie (five from *Can't Slow Down*).

If there was a loser, it was black music. Consistently the most creative and interesting sector of the American business, it has never been particularly well-served by the Hot One Hundred chart system, many of its more precious gems remaining in the ghetto of the specialist "black music" charts, undiscovered by whites, but selling in huge quantities to the black population. If anything, Top Forty radio has become even *less* interested in black music in the eighties. To right this imbalance, black records have to sell far more copies than rock records to attain equal status in the all-important Top Forty. The injustice of this system was clearly shown in 1981, when Frankie Smith, a little known black artist, sold more than two million copies of his single 'Double Dutch Bus'. It was one of only five singles to go double platinum in America that year. The other four, all by whites, reached number one. 'Double Dutch Bus' peaked at number thirty-one.

The only black artists regularly gaining admittance to the Top Forty are mainstream acts like Lionel Richie, Prince, Michael Jackson, Tina Turner, Diana Ross and Aretha Franklin. The sort of success recently enjoyed by "harder" acts like Mary Jane Girls and Patti LaBelle is unusual, and most likely temporary. Ironically, *black* radio stations are opening their airwaves to more blue-eyed soulsters than ever before, and played an important part in the success of Howard Jones, Wham!, Sting, Paul Young and Phil Collins, amongst others.

In the constantly shifting landscape of the charts, the appeal of heavy metal appears to be undiminished, as proved by the enormous success of AC/DC, Ratt, Mötley Crüe, the Scorpions and many others including the Japanese band Loudness. Indeed there is a slight but discernible shift from the softer AOR rock of REO Speedwagon, Supertramp and myriad others back to the more unrestrained, cruder noises made by the metallurgists.

Summing up, America had its healthiest and most liveliest chart scene for years. It will be interesting to see what direction it takes in the next twelve months.

THE YEAR'S CHARTS

August 1984 – July 1985

Featuring the *Billboard* and *Music Week* charts

WEEK ENDING AUGUST 4 1984

UK

SINGLES		ALBUMS
TWO TRIBES — FRANKIE GOES TO HOLLYWOOD (ZTT/ISLAND)	1	LEGEND — BOB MARLEY AND THE WAILERS (ISLAND)
HOLE IN MY SHOE — NEIL (WEA)	2	DIAMOND LIFE — SADE (EPIC)
RELAX — FRANKIE GOES TO HOLLYWOOD (ZTT/ISLAND)	3	PRIVATE DANCER — TINA TURNER (CAPITOL)
WHEN DOVES CRY — PRINCE (WARNER BROS)	4	CAN'T SLOW DOWN — LIONEL RICHIE (MOTOWN)
WHAT'S LOVE GOT TO DO WITH IT — TINA TURNER (CAPITOL)	5	THE WORKS — QUEEN (EMI)
IT'S A HARD LIFE — QUEEN (EMI)	6	AN INNOCENT MAN — BILLY JOEL (CBS)
WHITE LINES — GRANDMASTER AND MELLE MEL (SUGARHILL)	7	PARADE — SPANDAU BALLET (CHRYSALIS)
TIME AFTER TIME — CYNDI LAUPER (PORTRAIT)	8	THRILLER — MICHAEL JACKSON (EPIC)
DOWN ON THE STREET — SHAKATAK (POLYDOR)	9	HUMAN RACING — NIK KERSHAW (MCA)
EVERYBODY'S LAUGHING — PHIL FEARON AND GALAXY (ENSIGN)	10	BREAKOUT — POINTER SISTERS (PLANET)
YOUNG AT HEART — BLUEBELLS (LONDON)	11	INTO THE GAP — THOMPSON TWINS (ARISTA)
CARELESS WHISPER — GEORGE MICHAEL (EPIC)	12	PRIMITIVE — NEIL DIAMOND (CBS)
WHATEVER I DO — HAZELL DEAN (PROTO)	13	VICTORY — JACKSONS (EPIC)
LOVE RESURRECTION — ALISON MOYET (CBS)	14	BREAKDANCE — ORIGINAL SOUNDTRACK (POLYDOR)
CLOSEST THING TO HEAVEN — KANE GANG (KITCHENWARE)	15	BREAKING HEARTS — ELTON JOHN (ROCKET)
YOU THINK YOU'RE A MAN — DIVINE (PROTO)	16	SHE'S SO UNUSUAL — CYNDI LAUPER (PORTRAIT)
I WON'T LET THE SUN GO DOWN — NIK KERSHAW (MCA)	17	AMERICAN HEARTBEAT — VARIOUS (EPIC)
EYES WITHOUT A FACE — BILLY IDOL (CHRYSALIS)	18	PURPLE RAIN — PRINCE AND THE REVOLUTION (WARNER BROS)
AGADOO — BLACK LACE (FLAIR)	19	THE LAST IN LINE — DIO (VERTIGO)
ON THE WINGS OF LOVE — JEFFREY OSBORNE (A&M)	20	HUMAN'S LIB — HOWARD JONES (WEA)

US

SINGLES		ALBUMS
WHEN DOVES CRY — PRINCE (WARNER BROS)	1	PURPLE RAIN — PRINCE AND THE REVOLUTION (WARNER BROS)
GHOSTBUSTERS — RAY PARKER JR (ARISTA)	2	BORN IN THE USA — BRUCE SPRINGSTEEN (COLUMBIA/CBS)
STATE OF SHOCK — JACKSONS/MICK JAGGER (EPIC)	3	SPORTS — HUEY LEWIS AND THE NEWS (CHRYSALIS)
DANCING IN THE DARK — BRUCE SPRINGSTEEN (COLUMBIA/CBS)	4	VICTORY — JACKSONS (EPIC)
WHAT'S LOVE GOT TO DO WITH IT — TINA TURNER (CAPITOL)	5	CAN'T SLOW DOWN — LIONEL RICHIE (MOTOWN)
INFATUATION — ROD STEWART (WARNER BROS)	6	HEARTBEAT CITY — THE CARS (ELEKTRA)
SAD SONGS (SAY SO MUCH) — ELTON JOHN (GEFFEN)	7	OUT OF THE CELLAR — RATT (ATLANTIC)
STUCK ON YOU — LIONEL RICHIE (MOTOWN)	8	GHOSTBUSTERS — SOUNDTRACK (ARISTA)
THERE'S NO STOPPING US — OLLIE & JERRY (POLYDOR)	9	BREAKIN' — SOUNDTRACK (POLYDOR)
I CAN DREAM ABOUT YOU — DAN HARTMAN (MCA)	10	1984 — VAN HALEN (WARNER BROS)
EYES WITHOUT A FACE — BILLY IDOL (CHRYSALIS)	11	REBEL YELL — BILLY IDOL (CHRYSALIS)
LEGS — ZZ TOP (WARNER BROS)	12	ELIMINATOR — ZZ TOP (WARNER BROS)
JUMP (FOR MY LOVE) — POINTER SISTERS (PLANET)	13	PRIVATE DANCER — TINA TURNER (CAPITOL)
DOCTOR! DOCTOR! — THOMPSON TWINS (ARISTA)	14	FOOTLOOSE — SOUNDTRACK (COLUMBIA/CBS)
IF EVER YOU'RE IN MY ARMS AGAIN — PEABO BRYSON (ELEKTRA)	15	MIDNIGHT MADNESS — NIGHT RANGER (CAMEL/MCA)
PANAMA — VAN HALEN (WARNER BROS)	16	BREAK OUT — POINTER SISTERS (PLANET)
SUNGLASSES AT NIGHT — COREY HART (EMI AMERICA)	17	SEVEN AND THE RAGGED TIGER — DURAN DURAN (CAPITOL)
ALMOST PARADISE — RENO/WILSON (COLUMBIA/CBS)	18	BEAT STREET — SOUNDTRACK (ATLANTIC)
ROUND AND ROUND — RATT (ATLANTIC)	19	LOVE AT FIRST STING — SCORPIONS (MERCURY)
MAGIC — THE CARS (ELEKTRA)	20	CAMOUFLAGE — ROD STEWART (WARNER BROS)

WEEK ENDING AUGUST 11 1984

UK

SINGLES		ALBUMS
TWO TRIBES — FRANKIE GOES TO HOLLYWOOD (ZTT/ISLAND)	1	NOW THAT'S WHAT I CALL MUSIC 3 — VARIOUS (EMI/VIRGIN)
CARELESS WHISPER — GEORGE MICHAEL (EPIC)	2	LEGEND — BOB MARLEY AND THE WAILERS (ISLAND)
WHAT'S LOVE GOT TO DO WITH IT — TINA TURNER (CAPITOL)	3	DIAMOND LIFE — SADE (EPIC)
AGADOO — BLACK LACE (FLAIR)	4	PRIVATE DANCER — TINA TURNER (CAPITOL)
WHEN DOVES CRY — PRINCE (WARNER BROS)	5	CAN'T SLOW DOWN — LIONEL RICHIE (MOTOWN)
RELAX — FRANKIE GOES TO HOLLYWOOD (ZTT/ISLAND)	6	THE WORKS — QUEEN (EMI)
HOLE IN MY SHOE — NEIL (WEA)	7	THRILLER — MICHAEL JACKSON (EPIC)
WHATEVER I DO — HAZELL DEAN (PROTO)	8	AN INNOCENT MAN — BILLY JOEL (CBS)
IT'S A HARD LIFE — QUEEN (EMI)	9	BREAKOUT — POINTER SISTERS (PLANET)
WHITE LINES — GRANDMASTER AND MELLE MEL (SUGARHILL)	10	INTO THE GAP — THOMPSON TWINS (ARISTA)
EVERYBODY'S LAUGHING — PHIL FEARON AND GALAXY (ENSIGN)	11	HUMAN RACING — NIK KERSHAW (MCA)
CLOSEST THING TO HEAVEN — KANE GANG (KITCHENWARE)	12	BREAKDANCE — ORIGINAL SOUNDTRACK (POLYDOR)
SELF CONTROL — LAURA BRANIGAN (ATLANTIC)	13	PARADE — SPANDAU BALLET (CHRYSALIS)
DOWN ON THE STREET — SHAKATAK (POLYDOR)	14	PURPLE RAIN — PRINCE AND THE REVOLUTION (WARNER BROS)
ON THE WINGS OF LOVE — JEFFREY OSBORNE (A&M)	15	BREAKING HEARTS — ELTON JOHN (ROCKET)
TIME AFTER TIME — CYNDI LAUPER (PORTRAIT)	16	PRIMITIVE — NEIL DIAMOND (CBS)
YOUNG AT HEART — BLUEBELLS (LONDON)	17	SHE'S SO UNUSUAL — CYNDI LAUPER (PORTRAIT)
YOU THINK YOU'RE A MAN — DIVINE (PROTO)	18	AMERICAN HEARTBEAT — VARIOUS (EPIC)
EYES WITHOUT A FACE — BILLY IDOL (CHRYSALIS)	19	VICTORY — JACKSONS (EPIC)
TOSSING AND TURNING — WINDJAMMER (MCA)	20	NOW THAT'S WHAT I CALL MUSIC 2 — VARIOUS (EMI/VIRGIN)

US

SINGLES		ALBUMS
GHOSTBUSTER — RAY PARKER JR (ARIST)	1	PURPLE RAIN — PRINCE AND THE REVOLUTION (WARNER BROS)
WHEN DOVES CRY — PRINCE (WARNER BROS)	2	SPORTS — HUEY LEWIS AND THE NEWS (CHRYSALIS)
STATE OF SHOCK — JACKSONS/MICK JAGGER (EPIC)	3	BORN IN THE USA — BRUCE SPRINGSTEEN (COLUMBIA/CBS)
WHAT'S LOVE GOT TO DO WITH IT — TINA TURNER (CAPITOL)	4	VICTORY — JACKSONS (EPIC)
SAD SONGS (SAY SO MUCH) — ELTON JOHN (GEFFEN)	5	HEARTBEAT CITY — THE CARS (ELEKTRA)
STUCK ON YOU — LIONEL RICHIE (MOTOWN)	6	CAN'T SLOW DOWN — LIONEL RICHIE (MOTOWN)
DANCING IN THE DARK — BRUCE SPRINGSTEEN (COLUMBIA)	7	OUT OF THE CELLAR — RATT (ATLANTIC)
I CAN DREAM ABOUT YOU — DAN HARTMAN (MCA)	8	GHOSTBUSTERS — SOUNDTRACK (ARISTA)
INFATUATION — ROD STEWART (WARNER BROS)	9	PRIVATE DANCER — TINA TURNER (CAPITOL)
SUNGLASSES AT NIGHT — COREY HART (EMI AMERICA)	10	REBEL YELL — BILLY IDOL (CHRYSALIS)
THERE'S NO STOPPING US — OLLIE & JERRY (POLYDOR)	11	1984 — VAN HALEN (WARNER BROS)
MISSING YOU — JOHN WAITE (EMI AMERICA)	12	ELIMINATOR — ZZ TOP (WARNER BROS)
IF EVER YOU'RE IN MY ARMS AGAIN — PEABO BRYSON (ELEKTRA)	13	BREAKIN' — SOUNDTRACK (POLYDOR)
LEGS — ZZ TOP (WARNER BROS)	14	FOOTLOOSE — SOUNDTRACK (COLUMBIA/CBS)
PANAMA — VAN HALEN (WARNER BROS)	15	MIDNIGHT MADNESS — NIGHT RANGER (CAMEL/MCA)
EYES WITHOUT A FACE — BILLY IDOL (CHRYSALIS)	16	BREAK OUT — POINTER SISTERS (PLANET)
ROUND AND ROUND — RATT (ATLANTIC)	17	SEVEN AND THE RAGGED TIGER — DURAN DURAN (CAPITOL)
JUMP (FOR MY LOVE) — POINTER SISTERS (PLANET)	18	CAMOUFLAGE — ROD STEWART (WARNER BROS)
IF THIS IS IT — HUEY LEWIS AND THE NEWS (CHRYSALIS)	19	LOVE AT FIRST STING — SCORPIONS (MERCURY)
SHE BOP — CYNDI LAUPER (PORTRAIT)	20	BREAKING HEARTS — ELTON JOHN (GEFFEN)

WEEK ENDING AUGUST 18 1984

UK

SINGLES		ALBUMS
CARELESS WHISPER GEORGE MICHAEL (EPIC)	1	NOW THAT'S WHAT I CALL MUSIC 3 VARIOUS (VIRGIN/EMI)
AGADOO BLACK LACE (FLAIR)	2	DIAMOND LIFE SADE (EPIC)
TWO TRIBES FRANKIE GOES TO HOLLYWOOD (ZTT/ISLAND)	3	LEGEND BOB MARLEY AND THE WAILERS (ISLAND)
WHATEVER I DO HAZELL DEAN (PROTO)	4	PRIVATE DANCER TINA TURNER (CAPITOL)
WHAT'S LOVE GOT TO DO WITH IT TINA TURNER (CAPITOL)	5	CAN'T SLOW DOWN LIONEL RICHIE (MOTOWN)
SELF CONTROL LAURA BRANIGAN (ATLANTIC)	6	THE WORKS QUEEN (EMI)
RELAX FRANKIE GOES TO HOLLYWOOD (ZTT/ISLAND)	7	THRILLER MICHAEL JACKSON (EPIC)
WHEN DOVES CRY PRINCE (WARNER BROS)	8	AN INNOCENT MAN BILLY JOEL (CBS)
WHITE LINES GRANDMASTER AND MELLE MEL (SUGARHILL)	9	BREAKOUT POINTER SISTERS (PLANET)
LIKE TO GET TO KNOW YOU WELL HOWARD JONES (WEA)	10	BREAKDANCE SOUNDTRACK VARIOUS (POLYDOR)
ON THE WINGS OF LOVE JEFFREY OSBORNE (A&M)	11	PURPLE RAIN PRINCE AND THE REVOLUTION (WARNER BROS)
IT'S A HARD LIFE QUEEN (EMI)	12	INTO THE GAP THOMPSON TWINS (ARISTA)
HOLE IN MY SHOE NEIL (WEA)	13	HUMAN RACING NIK KERSHAW (MCA)
CLOSEST THING TO HEAVEN THE KANE GANG (KITCHENWARE)	14	BREAKING HEARTS ELTON JOHN (ROCKET)
STUCK ON YOU TREVOR WALTERS (I&S PRODUCTIONS)	15	PARADE SPANDAU BALLET (CHRYSALIS)
EVERYBODY'S LAUGHING PHIL FEARON AND GALAXY (ENSIGN)	16	HUMAN'S LIB HOWARD JONES (WEA)
DOWN ON THE STREET SHAKATAK (POLYDOR)	17	SHE'S SO UNUSUAL CYNDI LAUPER (PORTRAIT)
TOSSING AND TURNING WINDJAMMER (MCA)	18	BREAKDANCE, YOU CAN DO IT VARIOUS (K-TEL)
SUNGLASSES TRACEY ULLMAN (STIFF)	19	AMERICAN HEARTBEAT VARIOUS (EPIC)
SOME GUYS HAVE ALL THE LUCK ROD STEWART (WARNER)	20	NOW THAT'S WHAT I CALL MUSIC 2 VARIOUS (VIRGIN/EMI)

US

SINGLES		ALBUMS
GHOSTBUSTERS RAY PARKER JR (ARISTA)	1	PURPLE RAIN PRINCE AND THE REVOLUTION (WARNER BROS)
WHAT'S LOVE GOT TO DO WITH IT TINA TURNER (CAPITOL)	2	BORN IN THE USA BRUCE SPRINGSTEEN (COLUMBIA/CBS)
STATE OF SHOCK JACKSONS/MICK JAGGER (EPIC)	3	SPORTS HUEY LEWIS AND THE NEWS (CHRYSALIS)
WHEN DOVES CRY PRINCE (WARNER BROS)	4	VICTORY JACKSONS (EPIC)
STUCK ON YOU LIONEL RICHIE (MOTOWN)	5	HEARTBEAT CITY THE CARS (ELEKTRA)
I CAN DREAM ABOUT YOU DAN HARTMAN (MCA)	6	GHOSTBUSTERS SOUNDTRACK (ARISTA)
MISSING YOU JOHN WAITE (EMI AMERICA)	7	CAN'T SLOW DOWN LIONEL RICHIE (MOTOWN)
SAD SONGS (SAY SO MUCH) ELTON JOHN (GEFFEN)	8	PRIVATE DANCER TINA TURNER (CAPITOL)
SUNGLASSES AT NIGHT COREY HART (EMI AMERICA)	9	OUT OF THE CELLAR RATT (ATLANTIC)
IF EVER YOU'RE IN MY ARMS AGAIN PEABO BRYSON (ELEKTRA)	10	ELIMINATOR ZZ TOP (WARNER BROS)
INFATUATION ROD STEWART (WARNER BROS)	11	1984 VAN HALEN (WARNER BROS)
DANCING IN THE DARK BRUCE SPRINGSTEEN (COLUMBIA/CBS)	12	REBEL YELL BILLY IDOL (CHRYSALIS)
PANAMA VAN HALEN (WARNER BROS)	13	BREAKIN' SOUNDTRACK (POLYDOR)
ROUND AND ROUND RATT (ATLANTIC)	14	BREAK OUT POINTER SISTERS (PLANET)
SHE BOP CYNDI LAUPER (PORTRAIT)	15	CONDITION CRITICAL QUIET RIOT (PASHA)
IF THIS IS IT HUEY LEWIS AND THE NEWS (CHRYSALIS)	16	SHE'S SO UNUSUAL CYNDI LAUPER (PORTRAIT)
THE WARRIOR SCANDAL WITH PATTI SMYTH (COLUMBIA/CBS)	17	MIDNIGHT MADNESS NIGHT RANGER (CAMEL/MCA)
LIGHTS OUT PETER WOLF (EMI AMERICA)	18	CAMOUFLAGE ROD STEWART (WARNER BROS)
ROCK ME TONIGHT BILLY SQUIER (CAPITOL)	19	SIGNS OF LIFE BILLY SQUIER (CAPITOL)
SEXY GIRL GLENN FREY (MCA)	20	BREAKING HEARTS ELTON JOHN (GEFFEN)

WEEK ENDING AUGUST 25 1984

UK

SINGLES		ALBUMS
CARELESS WHISPER GEORGE MICHAEL (EPIC)	1	NOW THAT'S WHAT I CALL MUSIC 3 VARIOUS (VIRGIN/EMI)
AGADOO BLACK LACE (FLAIR)	2	LEGEND BOB MARLEY AND THE WAILERS (ISLAND)
I JUST CALLED TO SAY I LOVE YOU STEVIE WONDER (MOTOWN)	3	CAN'T SLOW DOWN LIONEL RICHIE (MOTOWN)
LIKE TO GET TO KNOW YOU WELL HOWARD JONES (WEA)	4	PRIVATE DANCER TINA TURNER (CAPITOL)
TWO TRIBES FRANKIE GOES TO HOLLYWOOD (ZTT/ISLAND)	5	DIAMOND LIFE SADE (EPIC)
SELF CONTROL LAURA BRANIGAN (ATLANTIC)	6	THE WORKS QUEEN (EMI)
WHATEVER I DO HAZELL DEAN (PROTO)	7	THRILLER MICHAEL JACKSON (EPIC)
WHAT'S LOVE GOT TO DO WITH IT TINA TURNER (CAPITOL)	8	PARADE SPANDAU BALLET (CHRYSALIS)
STUCK ON YOU TREVOR WALTERS (SANITY)	9	PHIL FEARON AND GALAXY PHIL FEARON AND GALAXY (ENSIGN)
WHITE LINES GRANDMASTER AND MELLE MEL (SUGARHILL)	10	BREAKOUT POINTER SISTERS (PLANET)
2 MINUTES TO MIDNIGHT IRON MAIDEN (EMI)	11	AN INNOCENT MAN BILLY JOEL (CBS)
RELAX FRANKIE GOES TO HOLLYWOOD (ZTT/ISLAND)	12	HUMAN'S LIB HOWARD JONES (WEA)
ON THE WINGS OF LOVE JEFFREY OSBORNE (A&M)	13	BREAKING HEARTS ELTON JOHN (ROCKET)
WHEN DOVES CRY PRINCE (WARNER BROS)	14	INTO THE GAP THOMPSON TWINS (ARISTA)
PASSENGERS ELTON JOHN (ROCKET)	15	PURPLE RAIN PRINCE AND THE REVOLUTION (WARNER BROS)
DR BEAT MIAMI SOUND MACHINE (EPIC)	16	NOW THAT'S WHAT I CALL MUSIC 2 VARIOUS (VIRGIN/EMI)
IT'S A HARD LIFE QUEEN (EMI)	17	HUMAN RACING NIK KERSHAW (MCA)
SUNGLASSES TRACEY ULLMAN (STIFF)	18	BREAKDANCE ORIGINAL SOUNDTRACK (POLYDOR)
SOME GUYS HAVE ALL THE LUCK ROD STEWART (WARNER BROS)	19	BREAKDANCE, YOU CAN DO IT VARIOUS (K-TEL)
CLOSEST THING TO HEAVEN THE KANE GANG (KITCHENWARE)	20	BORN IN THE USA BRUCE SPRINGSTEEN (CBS)

US

SINGLES		ALBUMS
GHOSTBUSTERS RAY PARKER JR (ARISTA)	1	PURPLE RAIN PRINCE AND THE REVOLUTION (WARNER BROS)
WHAT'S LOVE GOT TO DO WITH IT TINA TURNER (CAPITOL)	2	SPORTS HUEY LEWIS AND THE NEWS (CHRYSALIS)
STUCK ON YOU LIONEL RICHIE (MOTOWN)	3	BORN IN THE USA BRUCE SPRINGSTEEN (COLUMBIA/CBS)
WHEN DOVES CRY PRINCE (WARNER BROS)	4	PRIVATE DANCER TINA TURNER (CAPITOL)
MISSING YOU JOHN WAITE (EMI AMERICA)	5	HEARTBEAT CITY THE CARS (ELEKTRA)
I CAN DREAM ABOUT YOU DAN HARTMAN (MCA)	6	GHOSTBUSTERS SOUNDTRACK (ARISTA)
STATE OF SHOCK JACKSONS/MICK JAGGER (EPIC)	7	VICTORY JACKSONS (EPIC)
SUNGLASSES AT NIGHT COREY HART (EMI AMERICA)	8	CAN'T SLOW DOWN LIONEL RICHIE (MOTOWN)
SHE BOP CYNDI LAUPER (PORTRAIT)	9	OUT OF THE CELLAR RATT (ATLANTIC)
IF EVER YOU'RE IN MY ARMS PEABO BRYSON (ELEKTRA)	10	BREAK OUT POINTER SISTERS (PLANET)
IF THIS IS IT HUEY LEWIS AND THE NEWS (CHRYSALIS)	11	1984 VAN HALEN (WARNER BROS)
ROUND AND ROUND RATT (ATLANTIC)	12	SIGNS OF LIFE BILLY SQUIER (CAPITOL)
THE WARRIOR SCANDAL WITH PATTI SMYTH (COLUMBIA/CBS)	13	ELIMINATOR ZZ TOP (WARNER BROS)
SAD SONGS (SAY SO MUCH) ELTON JOHN (GEFFEN)	14	REBEL YELL BILLY IDOL (CHRYSALIS)
LIGHTS OUT PETER WOLF (EMI AMERICA)	15	CONDITION CRITICAL QUIET RIOT (PASHA)
LET'S GO CRAZY PRINCE AND THE REVOLUTION (WARNER BROS)	16	SHE'S SO UNUSUAL CYNDI LAUPER (PORTRAIT)
ROCK ME TONIGHT BILLY SQUIER (CAPITOL)	17	MIDNIGHT MADNESS NIGHT RANGER (CAMEL/MCA)
DRIVE THE CARS (ELEKTRA)	18	STAY HUNGRY TWISTED SISTER (ATLANTIC)
DANCING IN THE DARK BRUCE SPRINGSTEEN (COLUMBIA/CBS)	19	BREAKIN' SOUNDTRACK (POLYDOR)
SEXY GIRL GLENN FREY (MCA)	20	BREAKING HEARTS ELTON JOHN (GEFFEN)

WEEK ENDING SEPTEMBER 1 1984

UK

SINGLES		ALBUMS
CARELESS WHISPER GEORGE MICHAEL (EPIC)	1	NOW THAT'S WHAT I CALL MUSIC 3 VARIOUS (VIRGIN/EMI)
I JUST CALLED TO SAY I LOVE YOU STEVIE WONDER (MOTOWN)	2	PRIVATE DANCER TINA TURNER (CAPITOL)
AGADOO BLACK LACE (FLAIR)	3	CAN'T SLOW DOWN LIONEL RICHIE (MOTOWN)
LIKE TO GET TO KNOW YOU WELL HOWARD JONES (WEA)	4	LEGEND BOB MARLEY AND THE WAILERS (ISLAND)
SELF CONTROL LAURA BRANIGAN (ATLANTIC)	5	DIAMOND LIFE SADE (EPIC)
PASSENGERS ELTON JOHN (ROCKET/PHONOGRAM)	6	THE WORKS QUEEN (EMI)
DR BEAT MIAMI SOUND MACHINE (EPIC)	7	PARADE SPANDAU BALLET (CHRYSALIS)
WHATEVER I DO HAZELL DEAN (PROTO)	8	PHIL FEARON AND GALAXY PHIL FEARON AND GALAXY (ENSIGN)
TWO TRIBES FRANKIE GOES TO HOLLYWOOD (ZTT/ISLAND)	9	HUMAN'S LIB HOWARD JONES (WEA)
STUCK ON YOU TREVOR WALTERS (I&S PRODUCTIONS)	10	THRILLER MICHAEL JACKSON (EPIC)
I'LL FLY FOR YOU SPANDAU BALLET (CHRYSALIS)	11	BREAKING HEARTS ELTON JOHN (ROCKET)
WHAT'S LOVE GOT TO DO WITH IT TINA TURNER (CAPITOL)	12	BREAK OUT POINTER SISTERS (PLANET)
WHITE LINES GRANDMASTER AND MELLE MEL (SUGARHILL)	13	AN INNOCENT MAN BILLY JOEL (CBS)
2 MINUTES TO MIDNIGHT IRON MAIDEN (EMI)	14	NOW THAT'S WHAT I CALL MUSIC 2 VARIOUS (EMI/VIRGIN)
SOME GUYS HAVE ALL THE LUCK ROD STEWART (WARNER BROS)	15	PURPLE RAIN PRINCE AND THE REVOLUTION (WARNER BROS)
ON THE WINGS OF LOVE JEFFREY OSBORNE (A&M)	16	1100 BEL AIR PLACE JULIO IGLESIAS (CBS)
MOTHERS TALK TEARS FOR FEARS (MERCURY)	17	DOWN ON THE STREET SHAKATAK (POLYDOR)
GHOSTBUSTERS RAY PARKER JR (ARISTA)	18	HUMAN RACING NIK KERSHAW (MCA)
WHEN DOVES CRY PRINCE (WARNER BROS)	19	BORN IN THE USA BRUCE SPRINGSTEEN (CBS)
RELAX FRANKIE GOES TO HOLLYWOOD (ZTT/ISLAND)	20	INTO THE GAP THOMPSON TWINS (ARISTA)

US

SINGLES		ALBUMS
WHAT'S LOVE GOT TO DO WITH IT TINA TURNER (CAPITOL)	1	PURPLE RAIN PRINCE AND THE REVOLUTION (WARNER BROS)
MISSING YOU JOHN WAITE (EMI AMERICA)	2	BORN IN THE USA BRUCE SPRINGSTEEN (COLUMBIA/CBS)
STUCK ON YOU LIONEL RICHIE (MOTOWN)	3	SPORTS HUEY LEWIS AND THE NEWS (CHRYSALIS)
GHOSTBUSTERS RAY PARKER JR (ARISTA)	4	PRIVATE DANCER TINA TURNER (CAPITOL)
WHEN DOVES CRY PRINCE (WARNER BROS)	5	HEARTBEAT CITY THE CARS (ELEKTRA)
SHE BOP CYNDI LAUPER (PORTRAIT)	6	GHOSTBUSTERS SOUNDTRACK (ARISTA)
SUNGLASSES AT NIGHT COREY HART (EMI AMERICA)	7	CAN'T SLOW DOWN LIONEL RICHIE (MOTOWN)
LET'S GO CRAZY PRINCE AND THE REVOLUTION (WARNER BROS)	8	OUT OF THE CELLAR RATT (ATLANTIC)
IF THIS IS IT HUEY LEWIS AND THE NEWS (CHRYSALIS)	9	VICTORY JACKSONS (EPIC)
IF EVER YOU'RE IN MY ARMS PEABO BRYSON (ELEKTRA)	10	BREAK OUT POINTER SISTERS (PLANET)
THE WARRIOR SCANDAL WITH PATTI SMYTH (COLUMBIA/CBS)	11	SIGNS OF LIFE BILLY SQUIER (CAPITOL)
I CAN DREAM ABOUT YOU DAN HARTMAN (MCA)	12	1984 VAN HALEN (WARNER BROS)
LIGHTS OUT PETER WOLF (EMI AMERICA)	13	SHE'S SO UNUSUAL CYNDI LAUPER (PORTRAIT)
DRIVE THE CARS (ELEKTRA)	14	NO BRAKES JOHN WAITE (EMI AMERICA)
ROUND AND ROUND RATT (ATLANTIC)	15	CONDITION CRITICAL QUIET RIOT (PASHA)
THE GLAMOROUS LIFE SHEILA E (WARNER BROS)	16	ELIMINATOR ZZ TOP (WARNER BROS)
ROCK ME TONIGHT BILLY SQUIER (CAPITOL)	17	REBEL YELL BILLY IDOL (CHRYSALIS)
STATE OF SHOCK MICHAEL JACKSON/MICK JAGGER (EPIC)	18	STAY HUNGRY TWISTED SISTER (ATLANTIC)
ALL OF YOU JULIO IGLESIAS & DIANA ROSS (COLUMBIA/CBS)	19	MIDNIGHT MADNESS NIGHT RANGER (CAMEL/MCA)
DYNAMITE JERMAINE JACKSON (ARISTA)	20	BREAKING HEARTS ELTON JOHN (GEFFEN)

WEEK ENDING SEPTEMBER 8 1984

UK

SINGLES		ALBUMS
I JUST CALLED TO SAY I LOVE YOU STEVIE WONDER (MOTOWN)	1	NOW THAT'S WHAT I CALL LOVE VARIOUS (VIRGIN/EMI)
CARELESS WHISPER GEORGE MICHAEL (EPIC)	2	PRIVATE DANCER TINA TURNER (CAPITOL)
AGADOO BLACK LACE (FLAIR)	3	DIAMOND LIFE SADE (EPIC)
LIKE TO GET TO KNOW YOU WELL HOWARD JONES (WEA)	4	CAN'T SLOW DOWN LIONEL RICHIE (MOTOWN)
PASSENGERS ELTON JOHN (ROCKET)	5	LEGEND BOB MARLEY AND THE WAILERS (ISLAND)
GHOSTBUSTERS RAY PARKER JR (ARISTA)	6	PARADE SPANDAU BALLET (CHRYSALIS)
DR BEAT MIAMI SOUND MACHINE (EPIC)	7	THILLER MICHAEL JACKSON (EPIC)
SELF CONTROL LAURA BRANIGAN (ATLANTIC)	8	THE WORKS QUEEN (EMI)
I'LL FLY FOR YOU SPANDAU BALLET (CHRYSALIS)	9	HUMAN'S LIB HOWARD JONES (WEA)
WHATEVER I DO HAZELL DEAN (PROTO)	10	BREAKING HEARTS ELTON JOHN (ROCKET)
BIG IN JAPAN ALPHAVILLE (WEA)	11	PHIL FEARON AND GALAXY PHIL FEARON AND GALAXY (ENSIGN)
MASTER AND SERVANT DEPECHE MODE (MUTE)	12	ELIMINATOR ZZ TOP (WARNER BROS)
TWO TRIBES FRANKIE GOES TO HOLLYWOOD (ZTT/ISLAND)	13	BREAKOUT POINTER SISTERS (PLANET)
MOTHERS TALK TEAR FOR FEARS (MERCURY)	14	1100 BEL AIR PLACE JULIO IGLESIAS (CBS)
MADAM BUTTERFLY MALCOLM McLAREN (CHARISMA)	15	PURPLE RAIN PRINCE AND THE REVOLUTION (WARNER BROS)
STUCK ON YOU TREVOR WALTERS (SANITY)	16	AN INNOCENT MAN BILLY JOEL (CBS)
WILLIAM IT WAS REALLY NOTHING SMITHS (ROUGH TRADE)	17	NOW THAT'S WHAT I CALL MUSIC 2 VARIOUS (VIRGIN/EMI)
WHITE LINES GRANDMASTER AND MELLE MEL (SUGARHILL)	18	SELF CONTROL LAURA BRANIGAN (ATLANTIC)
WHAT'S LOVE GOT TO DO WITH IT TINA TURNER (CAPITOL)	19	INTO THE GAP THOMPSON TWINS (ARISTA)
SOME GUYS HAVE ALL THE LUCK ROD STEWART (WARNER BROS)	20	HUMAN RACING NIK KERSHAW (MCA)

US

SINGLES		ALBUMS
WHAT'S LOVE GOT TO DO WITH IT TINA TURNER (CAPITOL)	1	PURPLE RAIN PRINCE AND THE REVOLUTION (WARNER BROS)
MISSING YOU JOHN WAITE (EMI AMERICA)	2	BORN IN THE USA BRUCE SPRINGSTEEN (COLUMBIA/CBS)
SHE BOP CYNDI LAUPER (PORTRAIT)	3	SPORTS HUEY LEWIS AND THE NEWS (CHRYSALIS)
GHOSTBUSTERS RAY PARKER JR (ARISTA)	4	PRIVATE DANCER TINA TURNER (CAPITOL)
STUCK ON YOU LIONEL RICHIE (MOTOWN)	5	HEARTBEAT CITY THE CARS (ELEKTRA)
LET'S GO CRAZY PRINCE AND THE REVOLUTION (WARNER BROS)	6	CAN'T SLOW DOWN LIONEL RICHIE (MOTOWN)
IF THIS IS IT HUEY LEWIS AND THE NEWS (CHRYSALIS)	7	OUT OF THE CELLAR RATT (ATLANTIC)
THE WARRIOR SCANDAL WITH PATTI SMYTH (COLUMBIA/CBS)	8	VICTORY JACKSONS (EPIC)
SUNGLASSES AT NIGHT COREY HART (EMI AMERICA)	9	GHOSTBUSTERS SOUNDTRACK (ARISTA)
DRIVE THE CARS (ELEKTRA)	10	1100 BEL AIR PLACE JULIO IGLESIAS (COLUMBIA)
WHEN DOVES CRY PRINCE (WARNER BROS)	11	SIGNS OF LIFE BILLY SQUIER (CAPITOL)
LIGHTS OUT PETER WOLF (EMI AMERICA)	12	BREAK OUT POINTERS SISTERS (PLANET)
THE GLAMOROUS LIFE SHEILA E (WARNER BROS)	13	SHE'S SO UNUSUAL CYNDI LAUPER (PORTRAIT)
IF EVER YOU'RE IN MY ARMS AGAIN PEABO BRYSON (ELEKTRA)	14	NO BRAKES JOHN WAITE (EMI AMERICA)
ROCK ME TONIGHT BILLY SQUIER (CAPITOL)	15	1984 VAN HALEN (WARNER BROS)
I CAN DREAM ABOUT YOU DAN HARTMAN (MCA)	16	STAY HUNGRY TWISTED SISTER (ATLANTIC)
COVER ME BRUCE SPRINGSTEEN (COLUMBIA/MCA)	17	REBEL YELL BILLY IDOL (CHRYSALIS)
CRUEL SUMMER BANANARAMA (LONDON)	18	MIDNIGHT MADNESS NIGHT RANGER (CAMEL/MCA)
ALL OF YOU JULIO IGLESIAS & DIANA ROSS (COLUMBIA/CBS)	19	MADONNA MADONNA (SIRE)
DYNAMITE JERMAINE JACKSON (ARISTA)	20	BREAKING HEARTS ELTON JOHN (GEFFEN)

WEEK ENDING SEPTEMBER 15 1984

UK

SINGLES	UK	ALBUMS
I JUST CALLED TO SAY I LOVE YOU STEVIE WONDER (MOTOWN)	1	NOW THAT'S WHAT I CALL MUSIC 3 VARIOUS (VIRGIN/EMI)
CARELESS WHISPER GEORGE MICHAEL (EPIC)	2	POWERSLAVE IRON MAIDEN (EMI)
GHOSTBUSTERS RAY PARKER JR (ARISTA)	3	DIAMOND LIFE SADE (EPIC)
AGADOO BLACK LACE (FLAIR)	4	PRIVATE DANCER TINA TURNER (CAPITOL)
LIKE TO GET TO KNOW YOU WELL HOWARD JONES (WEA)	5	PARADE SPANDAU BALLET (CHRYSALIS)
PASSENGERS ELTON JOHN (ROCKET)	6	CAN'T SLOW DOWN LIONEL RICHIE (MOTOWN)
DR BEAT MIAMI SOUND MACHINE (EPIC)	7	ELIMINATOR ZZ TOP (WARNER BROS)
PRIDE (IN THE NAME OF LOVE) U2 (ISLAND)	8	THE WORKS QUEEN (EMI)
BIG IN JAPAN ALPHAVILLE (WEA)	9	LEGEND BOB MARLEY AND THE WAILERS (ISLAND)
SELF CONTROL LAURA BRANIGAN (ATLANTIC)	10	PURPLE RAIN PRINCE AND THE REVOLUTION (WARNER BROS)
MASTER AND SERVANT DEPECHE MODE (MUTE)	11	THRILLER MICHAEL JACKSON (EPIC)
I'LL FLY FOR YOU SPANDAU BALLET (CHRYSALIS)	12	HUMAN'S LIB HOWARD JONES (WEA)
MADAM BUTTERFLY MALCOM McLAREN (CHARISMA)	13	BREAKING HEARTS ELTON JOHN (ROCKET)
LOST IN MUSIC SISTER SLEDGE (COTILLION)	14	NO REMORSE MOTORHEAD (BRONZE)
TALKING IN YOUR SLEEP BUCKS FIZZ (RCA)	15	BREAKOUT POINTER SISTERS (PLANET)
WHATEVER I DO HAZELL DEAN (PROTO)	16	1100 BELL AIR PLACE JULIO IGLESIAS (CBS)
TWO TRIBES/WAR FRANKIE GOES TO HOLLYWOOD (ZTT/ISLAND)	17	SELF CONTROL LAURA BRANIGAN (ATLANTIC)
MOTHER'S TALK TEARS FOR FEARS (MERCURY)	18	UNDER WRAPS JETHRO TULL (CHRYSALIS)
HOT WATER LEVEL 42 (POLYDOR)	19	AN INNOCENT MAN BILLY JOEL (CBS)
WHITE LINES GRANDMASTER AND MELLE MEL (SUGARHILL)	20	PHIL FEARON AND GALAXY PHIL FEARON AND GALAXY (ENSIGN)

US

SINGLES	US	ALBUMS
WHAT'S LOVE GOT TO DO WITH IT TINA TURNER (CAPITOL)	1	PURPLE RAIN PRINCE AND THE REVOLUTION (WARNER BROS)
MISSING YOU JOHN WAITE (EMI AMERICA)	2	BORN IN THE USA BRUCE SPRINGSTEEN (COLUMBIA/CBS)
SHE BOP CYNDI LAUPER (PORTRAIT)	3	SPORTS HUEY LEWIS AND THE NEWS (CHRYSALIS)
LET'S GO CRAZY PRINCE AND THE REVOLUTION (WARNER BROS)	4	PRIVATE DANCER TINA TURNER (CAPITOL)
STUCK ON YOU LIONEL RICHIE (MOTOWN)	5	HEARTBEAT CITY THE CARS (ELEKTRA)
IF THIS IS IT HUEY LEWIS AND THE NEWS (CHRYSALIS)	6	CAN'T SLOW DOWN LIONEL RICHIE (MOTOWN)
DRIVE THE CARS (ELEKTRA)	7	OUT OF THE CELLAR RATT (ATLANTIC)
THE WARRIOR SCANDAL WITH PATTI SMYTH (COLUMBIA/CBS)	8	1100 BEL AIR PLACE JULIO IGLESIAS (COLUMBIA/CBS)
GHOSTBUSTERS RAY PARKER JR (ARISTA)	9	GHOSTBUSTERS SOUNDTRACK (ARISTA)
THE GLAMOROUS LIFE SHEILA E (WARNER BROS)	10	VICTORY JACKSONS (EPIC)
SUNGLASSES AT NIGHT COREY HART (EMI AMERICA)	11	SIGNS OF LIFE BILLY SQUIER (CAPITOL)
LIGHTS OUT PETER WOLF (EMI AMERICA)	12	BREAK OUT POINTER SISTERS (PLANET)
CRUEL SUMMER BANANARAMA (LONDON)	13	SHE'S SO UNUSUAL CYNDI LAUPER (PORTRAIT)
COVER ME BRUCE SPRINGSTEEN (COLUMBIA/CBS)	14	NO BRAKES JOHN WAITE (EMI AMERICA)
DYNAMITE JERMAINE JACKSON (ARISTA)	15	STAY HUNGRY TWISTED SISTER (ATLANTIC)
ROCK ME TONIGHT BILLY SQUIER (CAPITOL)	16	MADONNA MADONNA (SIRE)
WHEN DOVES CRY PRINCE (WARNER BROS)	17	1984 VAN HALEN (WARNER BROS)
I JUST CALLED TO SAY I LOVE YOU STEVIE WONDER (MOTOWN)	18	MIDNIGHT MADNESS NIGHT RANGER (CAMEL/MCA)
WHEN YOU CLOSE YOUR EYES NIGHT RANGER (CAMEL/MCA)	19	SOUNDTRACK EDDIE AND THE CRUISERS (SCOTTI BROS)
HARD HABIT TO BREAK CHICAGO (FULL MOON/WARNER BROS)	20	ELIMINATOR ZZ TOP (WARNER BROS)

WEEK ENDING SEPTEMBER 22 1984

UK

SINGLES	UK	ALBUMS
I JUST CALLED TO SAY I LOVE YOU STEVIE WONDER (MOTOWN)	1	NOW THAT'S WHAT I CALL MUSIC 3 VARIOUS (VIRGIN/EMI)
GHOSTBUSTERS RAY PARKER JR (ARISTA)	2	WOMAN IN RED ORIGINAL SOUNDTRACK STEVIE WONDER & DIONNE WARWICK (MOTOWN)
CARELESS WHISPER GEORGE MICHAEL (EPIC)	3	DIAMOND LIFE SADE (EPIC)
PRIDE (IN THE NAME OF LOVE) U2 (ISLAND)	4	POWERSLAVE IRON MAIDEN (EMI)
AGADOO BLACK LACE (FLAIR)	5	ELIMINATOR ZZ TOP (WARNER BROS)
DR BEAT MIAMI SOUND MACHINE (EPIC)	6	PRIVATE DANCER TINA TURNER (CAPITOL)
LOST IN MUSIC SISTER SLEDGE (COTILLION)	7	CAN'T SLOW DOWN LIONEL RICHIE (MOTOWN)
BIG IN JAPAN ALPHAVILLE (WEA)	8	PARADE SPANDAU BALLET (CHRYSALIS)
MASTER AND SERVANT DEPECHE MODE (MUTE)	9	THE WORKS QUEEN (EMI)
PASSENGERS ELTON JOHN (ROCKET)	10	LEGEND BOB MARLEY AND THE WAILERS (ISLAND)
A LETTER TO YOU SKAKIN' STEVENS (EPIC)	11	THRILLER MICHAEL JACKSON (EPIC)
LIKE TO GET TO KNOW YOU WELL HOWARD JONES (WEA)	12	PURPLE RAIN PRINCE AND THE REVOLUTION (WARNER BROS)
MADAM BUTTERFLY MALCOLM McLAREN (CHARISMA)	13	HUMAN'S LIB HOWARD JONES (WEA)
SELF CONTROL LAURA BRANIGAN (ATLANTIC)	14	BREAKING HEARTS ELTON JOHN (ROCKET)
I'LL FLY FOR YOU SPANDAU BALLET (CHRYSALIS)	15	1100 BEL AIR PLACE JULIO IGLESIAS (CBS)
TALKING IN YOUR SLEEP BUCKS FIZZ (RCA)	16	SELF CONTROL LAURA BRANIGAN (ATLANTIC)
BLUE JEAN DAVID BOWIE (EMI AMERICA)	17	BREAKOUT POINTER SISTERS (PLANET)
HOT WATER LEVEL 42 (POLYDOR)	18	NO REMORSE MOTORHEAD (BRONZE)
HAMMER TO FALL QUEEN (EMI)	19	AN INNOCENT MAN BILLY JOEL (CBS)
HUMAN RACING NIK KERSHAW (MCA)	20	UNDER WRAPS JETHRO TULL (CHRYSALIS)

US

SINGLES	US	ALBUMS
MISSING YOU JOHN WAITE (EMI AMERICA)	1	PURPLE RAIN PRINCE AND THE REVOLUTION (WARNER BROS)
LET'S GO CRAZY PRINCE AND THE REVOLUTION (WARNER BROS)	2	BORN IN THE USA BRUCE SPRINGSTEEN (COLUMBIA/CBS)
SHE BOP CYNDI LAUPER (PORTRAIT)	3	SPORTS HUEY LEWIS AND THE NEWS (CHRYSALIS)
WHAT'S LOVE GOT TO DO WITH IT TINA TURNER (CAPITOL)	4	PRIVATE DANCER TINA TURNER (CAPITOL)
DRIVE THE CARS (ELEKTRA)	5	HEARTBEAT CITY THE CARS (ELEKTRA)
IF THIS IS IT HUEY LEWIS AND THE NEWS (CHRYSALIS)	6	1100 BEL AIR PLACE JULIO IGLESIAS (COLUMBIA/CBS)
THE WARRIOR SCANDAL WITH PATTI SMYTH (COLUMBIA/CBS)	7	CAN'T SLOW DOWN LIONEL RICHIE (MOTOWN)
THE GLAMOROUS LIFE SHEILA E (WARNER BROS)	8	OUT OF THE CELLAR RATT (ATLANTIC)
I JUST CALLED TO SAY I LOVE YOU STEVIE WONDER (MOTOWN)	9	GHOSTBUSTERS SOUNDTRACK (ARISTA)
CRUEL SUMMER BANANARAMA (LONDON)	10	BREAK OUT POINTER SISTERS (PLANET)
COVER ME BRUCE SPRINGSTEEN (COLUMBIA/CBS)	11	NO BRAKES JOHN WAITE (EMI AMERICA)
STUCK ON YOU LIONEL RICHIE (MOTOWN)	12	SIGNS OF LIFE BILLY SQUIER (CAPITOL)
GHOSTBUSTERS RAY PARKER JR (ARISTA)	13	SOUNDTRACK EDDIE AND THE CRUISERS (SCOTTI BROS)
HARD HABIT TO BREAK CHICAGO (FULL MOON/WARNER BROS)	14	VICTORY JACKSONS (EPIC)
DYNAMITE JERMAINE JACKSON (ARISTA)	15	STAY HUNGRY TWISTED SISTER (ATLANTIC)
LUCKY STAR MADONNA (SIRE)	16	MADONNA MADONNA (SIRE)
WHEN YOU CLOSE YOUR EYES NIGHT RANGER (CAMEL/MCA)	17	MIDNIGHT MADNESS NIGHT RANGER (CAMEL/MCA)
LIGHTS OUT PETER WOLF (EMI AMERICA)	18	SHE'S SO UNUSUAL CYNDI LAUPER (PORTRAIT)
TORTURE JACKSONS (EPIC)	19	WARRIOR SCANDAL WITH PATTI SMYTH (COLUMBIA/CBS)
SUNGLASSES AT NIGHT COREY HART (EMI AMERICA)	20	ELIMINATOR ZZ TOP (WARNER BROS)

WEEK ENDING SEPTEMBER 29 1984

UK

SINGLES		ALBUMS
I JUST CALLED TO SAY I LOVE YOU STEVIE WONDER (MOTOWN)	1	NOW THAT'S WHAT I CALL MUSIC 3 VARIOUS (EMI/VIRGIN)
GHOSTBUSTERS RAY PARKER JR (ARISTA)	2	WOMAN IN RED STEVIE WONDER/DIONNE WARWICK (MOTOWN)
PRIDE (IN THE NAME OF LOVE) U2 (ISLAND)	3	DIAMOND LIFE SADE (EPIC)
LOST IN MUSIC SISTER SLEDGE (COTILLION)	4	ELIMINATOR ZZ TOP (WARNER BROS)
CARELESS WHISPER GEORGE MICHAEL (EPIC)	5	THE WORKS QUEEN (EMI)
BLUE JEAN DAVID BOWIE (EMI AMERICA)	6	PRIVATE DANCER TINA TURNER (CAPITOL)
WHY? BRONSKI BEAT (FORBIDDEN FRUIT)	7	CAN'T SLOW DOWN LIONEL RICHIE (MOTOWN)
AGADOO BLACK LACE (FLAIR)	8	POWERSLAVE IRON MAIDEN (EMI)
BIG IN JAPAN ALPHAVILLE (WEA)	9	PURPLE RAIN PRINCE AND THE REVOLUTION (WARNER BROS)
A LETTER TO YOU SHAKIN' STEVENS (EPIC)	10	LEGEND BOB MARLEY AND THE WAILERS (ISLAND)
DR BEAT MIAMI SOUND MACHINE (EPIC)	11	PARADE SPANDAU BALLET (CHRYSALIS)
LOVE KILLS FREDDIE MERCURY (CBS)	12	THRILLER MICHAEL JACKSON (EPIC)
HAMMER TO FALL QUEEN (EMI)	13	HUMAN'S LIB HOWARD JONES (WEA)
MASTER AND SERVANT DEPECHE MODE (MUTE)	14	KNIFE AZTEC CAMERA (WEA)
APOLLO 9 ADAM ANT (CBS)	15	WE ARE FAMILY SISTER SLEDGE (COTILLION)
PURPLE RAIN PRINCE (WARNER BROS)	16	BREAKOUT POINTER SISTERS (PLANET)
IF IT HAPPENS AGAIN UB40 (DEP INTERNATIONAL)	17	UNDER A BLOOD RED SKY U2 (ISLAND)
MADAM BUTTERFLY MALCOLM McLAREN (CHARISMA)	18	HUMAN RACING NIK KERSHAW (MCA)
HUMAN RACING NIK KERSHAW (MCA)	19	BREAKING HEARTS ELTON JOHN (ROCKET)
LIKE TO GET TO KNOW YOU WELL HOWARD JONES (WEA)	20	SELF CONTROL LAURA BRANIGAN (ATLANTIC)

US

SINGLES		ALBUMS
LET'S GO CRAZY PRINCE AND THE REVOLUTION (WARNER BROS)	1	PURPLE RAIN PRINCE AND THE REVOLUTION (WARNER BROS)
MISSING YOU JOHN WAITE (EMI AMERICA)	2	BORN IN THE USA BRUCE SPRINGSTEEN (COLUMBIA/CBS)
DRIVE THE CARS (ELEKTRA)	3	PRIVATE DANCER TINA TURNER (CAPITOL)
SHE BOP CYNDI LAUPER (PORTRAIT)	4	SPORTS HUEY LEWIS AND THE NEWS (CHRYSALIS)
I JUST CALLED TO SAY I LOVE YOU STEVIE WONDER (MOTOWN)	5	HEARTBEAT CITY THE CARS (ELEKTRA)
WHAT'S LOVE GOT TO DO WITH IT TINA TURNER (CAPITOL)	6	1100 BEL AIR PLACE JULIO IGLESIAS (COLUMBIA/CBS)
THE WARRIOR SCANDAL WITH PATTI SMYTH (COLUMBIA/CBS)	7	CAN'T SLOW DOWN LIONEL RICHIE (MOTOWN)
THE GLAMOROUS LIFE SHEILA E (WARNER BROS)	8	OUT OF THE CELLAR RATT (ATLANTIC)
CRUEL SUMMER BANANARAMA (LONDON)	9	BREAK OUT POINTER SISTERS (PLANET)
COVER ME BRUCE SPRINGSTEEN (COLUMBIA/CBS)	10	NO BRAKES JOHN WAITE (EMI AMERICA)
IF THIS IS IT HUEY LEWIS AND THE NEWS (CHRYSALIS)	11	SIGNS OF LIFE BILLY SQUIER (CAPITOL)
HARD HABIT TO BREAK CHICAGO (FULL MOON/WARNER BROS)	12	MADONNA MADONNA (SIRE)
LUCKY STAR MADONNA (SIRE)	13	SOUNDTRACK EDDIE AND THE CRUISERS (SCOTTI BROS)
WHEN YOU CLOSE YOUR EYES NIGHT RANGER (CAMEL/MCA)	14	GHOSTBUSTERS SOUNDTRACK (ARISTA)
CARIBBEAN QUEEN BILLY OCEAN (JIVE)	15	STAY HUNGRY TWISTED SISTER (ATLANTIC)
DYNAMITE JERMAINE JACKSON (ARISTA)	16	SHE'S SO UNUSUAL CYNDI LAUPER (PORTRAIT)
TORTURE JACKSONS (EPIC)	17	MIDNIGHT MADNESS NIGHT RANGER (CAMEL/MCA)
STUCK ON YOU LIONEL RICHIE (MOTOWN)	18	VICTORY JACKSONS (EPIC)
GHOSTBUSTERS RAY PARKER JR (ARISTA)	19	WARRIOR SCANDAL WITH PATTI SMYTH (COLUMBIA/CBS)
THE LUCKY ONE LAURA BRANIGAN (ATLANTIC)	20	PHANTOMS THE FIXX (MCA)

WEEK ENDING OCTOBER 6 1984

UK

SINGLES		ALBUMS
I JUST CALLED TO SAY I LOVE YOU STEVIE WONDER (MOTOWN)	1	TONIGHT DAVID BOWIE (EMI AMERICA)
GHOSTBUSTERS RAY PARKER JR (ARISTA)	2	WOMAN IN RED STEVIE WONDER/DIONNE WARWICK (MOTOWN)
THE WAR SONG CULTURE CLUB (VIRGIN)	3	DIAMOND LIFE SADE (EPIC)
PRIDE (IN THE NAME OF LOVE) U2 (ISLAND)	4	NOW THAT'S WHAT I CALL MUSIC 3 VARIOUS (EMI/VIRGIN)
LOST IN MUSIC SISTER SLEDGE (COTILLION)	5	SOME GREAT REWARD DEPECHE MODE (MUTE)
WHY? BRONSKI BEAT (FORBIDDEN FRUIT)	6	ELIMINATOR ZZ TOP (WARNER BROS)
BLUE JEAN DAVID BOWIE (EMI AMERICA)	7	WE ARE FAMILY SISTER SLEDGE (COTILLION)
PURPLE RAIN PRINCE (WARNER BROS)	8	PRIVATE DANCER TINA TURNER (CAPITOL)
IF IT HAPPENS AGAIN UB40 (DEP INTERNATIONAL)	9	PURPLE RAIN PRINCE AND THE REVOLUTION (WARNER BROS)
LOVE KILLS FREDDIE MERCURY (CBS)	10	THE WORKS QUEEN (EMI)
CARELESS WHISPER GEORGE MICHAEL (EPIC)	11	ANIMALIZE KISS (VERTIGO)
A LETTER TO YOU SHAKIN' STEVENS (EPIC)	12	HOW MEN ARE HEAVEN 17 (VIRGIN)
APOLLO 9 ADAM ANT (CBS)	13	CAN'T SLOW DOWN LIONEL RICHIE (MOTOWN)
BIG IN JAPAN ALPHAVILLE (WEA)	14	PARADE SPANDAU BALLET (CHRYSALIS)
DRIVE THE CARS (ELEKTRA)	15	KNIFE AZTEC CAMERA (WEA)
AGADOO BLACK LACE (FLAIR)	16	LEGEND BOB MARLEY AND THE WAILERS (ISLAND)
EAST OF EDEN BIG COUNTRY (MERCURY)	17	STREET SOUNDS ELECTRO 5 VARIOUS (STREETSOUNDS)
DR BEAT MIAMI SOUND MACHINE (EPIC)	18	HUMAN RACING NIK KERSHAW (MCA)
HAMMER TO FALL QUEEN (EMI)	19	THRILLER MICHAEL JACKSON (EPIC)
HUMAN RACING NIK KERSHAW (MCA)	20	NIGHT MOVES VARIOUS (K-TEL)

US

SINGLES		ALBUMS
LET'S GO CRAZY PRINCE AND THE REVOLUTION (WARNER BROS)	1	PURPLE RAIN PRINCE AND THE REVOLUTION (WARNER BROS)
I JUST CALLED TO SAY I LOVE YOU STEVIE WONDER (MOTOWN)	2	BORN IN THE USA BRUCE SPRINGSTEEN (COLUMBIA/CBS)
DRIVE THE CARS (ELEKTRA)	3	SPORTS HUEY LEWIS AND THE NEWS (CHRYSALIS)
MISSING YOU JOHN WAITE (EMI AMERICA)	4	PRIVATE DANCER TINA TURNER (CAPITOL)
SHE BOP CYNDI LAUPER (PORTRAIT)	5	HEARTBEAT CITY THE CARS (ELEKTRA)
HARD HABIT TO BREAK CHICAGO (FULL MOON/WARNER BROS)	6	1100 BEL AIR PLACE JULIO IGLESIAS (COLUMBIA/CBS)
THE GLAMOROUS LIFE SHEILA E (WARNER BROS)	7	CAN'T SLOW DOWN LIONEL RICHIE (MOTOWN)
LUCKY STAR MADONNA (SIRE)	8	BREAK OUT POINTER SISTERS (PLANET)
THE WARRIOR SCANDAL WITH PATTI SMYTH (COLUMBIA/CBS)	9	SOUNDTRACK EDDIE AND THE CRUISERS (SCOTTI BROS)
COVER ME BRUCE SPRINGSTEEN (COLUMBIA/CBS)	10	MADONNA MADONNA (SIRE)
CARIBBEAN QUEEN BILLY OCEAN (JIVE)	11	NO BRAKES JOHN WAITE (EMI AMERICA)
CRUEL SUMMER BANANARAMA (LONDON)	12	SIGNS OF LIFE BILLY SQUIER (CAPITOL)
WHAT'S LOVE GOT TO DO WITH IT TINA TURNER (CAPITOL)	13	OUT OF THE CELLAR RATT (ATLANTIC)
IF THIS IS IT HUEY LEWIS AND THE NEWS (CHRYSALIS)	14	SHE'S SO UNUSUAL CYNDI LAUPER (PORTRAIT)
I'M SO EXCITED POINTER SISTERS (PLANET)	15	MIDNIGHT MADNESS NIGHT RANGER (CAMEL/MCA)
ON THE DARK SIDE JOHN CAFFERTY (SCOTTI BROS)	16	GHOSTBUSTERS SOUNDTRACK (ARISTA)
TORTURE JACKSONS (EPIC)	17	WARRIOR SCANDAL WITH PATTI SMYTH (COLUMBIA/CBS)
WHEN YOU CLOSE YOUR EYES NIGHT RANGER (CAMEL/MCA)	18	WOMAN IN RED STEVIE WONDER (MOTOWN)
ARE WE OURSELVES? THE FIXX (MCA)	19	STAY HUNGRY TWISTED SISTER (ATLANTIC)
THE LUCKY ONE LAURA BRANIGAN (ATLANTIC)	20	PHANTOMS THE FIXX (MCA)

WEEK ENDING OCTOBER 13 1984

UK

	SINGLES		ALBUMS
1	I JUST CALLED TO SAY I LOVE YOU	STEVIE WONDER (MOTOWN)	THE UNFORGETTABLE FIRE	U2 (ISLAND)
2	THE WAR SONG	CULTURE CLUB (VIRGIN)	DIAMOND LIFE	SADE (EPIC)
3	FREEDOM	WHAM! (EPIC)	TONIGHT	DAVID BOWIE (EMI AMERICA)
4	GHOSTBUSTERS	RAY PARKER JR (ARISTA)	WOMAN IN RED	STEVIE WONDER/DIONNE WARWICK (MOTOWN)
5	DRIVE	CARS (ELEKTRA)	NOW THAT'S WHAT I CALL MUSIC 3	VARIOUS (EMI/VIRGIN)
6	NO MORE LONELY NIGHTS	PAUL McCARTNEY (PARLOPHONE)	ELIMINATOR	ZZ TOP (WARNER BROS)
7	WHY?	BRONSKI BEAT (FORBIDDEN FRUIT)	WE ARE FAMILY	SISTER SLEDGE (COTILLION)
8	PRIDE (IN THE NAME OF LOVE)	U2 (ISLAND)	SOME GREAT REWARD	DEPECHE MODE (MUTE)
9	TOGETHER IN ELECTRIC DREAMS	GIORGIO MORODER/PHILIP OAKEY (VIRGIN)	PRIVATE DANCER	TINA TURNER (CAPITOL)
10	PURPLE RAIN	PRINCE (WARNER BROS)	PURPLE RAIN	PRINCE AND THE REVOLUTION (WARNER BROS)
11	LOST IN MUSIC	SISTER SLEDGE (COTILLION)	THE WORKS	QUEEN (EMI)
12	IF IT HAPPENS AGAIN	UB40 (DEP INTERNATIONAL)	CAN'T SLOW DOWN	LIONEL RICHIE (MOTOWN)
13	SHOUT TO THE TOP	STYLE COUNCIL (POLYDOR)	ALL BY MYSELF	VARIOUS (K-TEL)
14	LOVE KILLS	FREDDIE MERCURY (CBS)	TRUE COLOURS	LEVEL 42 (POLYDOR)
15	APOLLO 9	ADAM ANT (CBS)	NIGHT MOVES	VARIOUS (K-TEL)
16	MISSING YOU	JOHN WAITE (EMI AMERICA)	HITS HITS HITS	VARIOUS (TELSTAR)
17	BLUE JEAN	DAVID BOWIE (EMI AMERICA)	THRILLER	MICHAEL JACKSON (EPIC)
18	CARELESS WHISPER	GEORGE MICHAEL (EPIC)	LEGEND	BOB MARLEY AND THE WAILERS (ISLAND)
19	A LETTER TO YOU	SHAKIN' STEVENS (EPIC)	HOW MEN ARE	HEAVEN 17 (VIRGIN)
20	. . . TEAR YOUR PLAYHOUSE DOWN	PAUL YOUNG (CBS)	PARADE	SPANDAU BALLET (CHRYSALIS)

US

	SINGLES		ALBUMS	
1	I JUST CALLED TO SAY I LOVE YOU	STEVIE WONDER (MOTOWN)	PURPLE RAIN	PRINCE AND THE REVOLUTION (WARNER BROS)
2	LET'S GO CRAZY	PRINCE AND THE REVOLUTION (WARNER BROS)	BORN IN THE USA	BRUCE SPRINGSTEEN (COLUMBIA/CBS)
3	DRIVE	THE CARS (ELEKTRA)	PRIVATE DANCER	TINA TURNER (CAPITOL)
4	HARD HABIT TO BREAK	CHICAGO (FULL MOON/WARNER BROS)	SPORTS	HUEY LEWIS AND THE NEWS (CHRYSALIS)
5	LUCKY STAR	MADONNA (SIRE)	HEARTBEAT CITY	THE CARS (ELEKTRA)
6	CARIBBEAN QUEEN	BILLY OCEAN (JIVE)	1100 BEL AIR PLACE	JULIO IGLESIAS (COLUMBIA/CBS)
7	MISSING YOU	JOHN WAITE (EMI AMERICA)	CAN'T SLOW DOWN	LIONEL RICHIE (MOTOWN)
8	COVER ME	BRUCE SPRINGSTEEN (COLUMBIA/CBS)	BREAK OUT	POINTER SISTERS (PLANET)
9	THE GLAMOROUS LIFE	SHEILA E (WARNER BROS)	SOUNDTRACK	EDDIE AND THE CRUISERS (SCOTTI BROS)
10	SHE BOP	CYNDI LAUPER (PORTRAIT)	MADONNA	MADONNA (SIRE)
11	THE WARRIOR	SCANDAL WITH PATTI SMYTH (COLUMBIA/CBS)	SHE'S SO UNUSUAL	CYNDI LAUPER (PORTRAIT)
12	ON THE DARK SIDE	JOHN CAFFERTY (SCOTTI BROS)	WOMAN IN RED	STEVIE WONDER (MOTOWN)
13	I'M SO EXCITED	POINTER SISTERS (PLANET)	OUT OF THE CELLAR	RATT (ATLANTIC)
14	CRUEL SUMMER	BANANARAMA (LONDON)	NO BRAKES	JOHN WAITE (EMI AMERICA)
15	WHAT'S LOVE GOT TO DO WITH IT	TINA TURNER (CAPITOL)	MIDNIGHT MADNESS	NIGHT RANGER (CAMEL/MCA)
16	ARE WE OURSELVES?	THE FIXX (MCA)	SIGNS OF LIFE	BILLY SQUIER (CAPITOL)
17	SOME GUYS HAVE ALL THE LUCK	ROD STEWART (WARNER BROS)	WARRIOR	SCANDAL WITH PATTI SMYTH (COLUMBIA/CBS)
18	PURPLE RAIN	PRINCE (WARNER BROS)	STAY HUNGRY	TWISTED SISTER (ATLANTIC)
19	IF THIS IS IT	HUEY LEWIS AND THE NEWS (CHRYSALIS)	17	CHICAGO (FULL MOON/WARNER BROS)
20	BLUE JEAN	DAVID BOWIE (EMI AMERICA)	PHANTOMS	THE FIXX (MCA)

WEEK ENDING OCTOBER 20 1984

UK

	SINGLES		ALBUMS	
1	FREEDOM	WHAM! (EPIC)	THE UNFORGETTABLE FIRE	U2 (ISLAND)
2	I JUST CALLED TO SAY I LOVE YOU	STEVIE WONDER (MOTOWN)	DIAMOND LIFE	SADE (EPIC)
3	THE WAR SONG	CULTURE CLUB (VIRGIN)	GEFFERY MORGAN	UB40 (DEP INTERNATIONAL/VIRGIN)
4	NO MORE LONELY NIGHTS	PAUL McCARTNEY (PARLOPHONE)	THE AGE OF CONSENT	BRONSKI BEAT (FORBIDDEN FRUIT)
5	TOGETHER IN ELECTRIC DREAMS	GIORGIO MORODER/PHILIP OAKEY (VIRGIN)	TONIGHT	DAVID BOWIE (EMI AMERICA)
6	DRIVE	THE CARS (ELEKTRA)	HITS HITS HITS	VARIOUS (TELSTAR)
7	SHOUT TO THE TOP	STYLE COUNCIL (POLYDOR)	WOMAN IN RED	STEVIE WONDER/DIONNE WARWICK (MOTOWN)
8	GHOSTBUSTERS	RAY PARKER JR (ARISTA)	NOW THAT'S WHAT I CALL MUSIC 3	VARIOUS (EMI/VIRGIN)
9	. . . TEAR YOUR PLAYHOUSE DOWN	PAUL YOUNG (CBS)	ELIMINATOR	ZZ TOP (WARNER BROS)
10	MISSING YOU	JOHN WAITE (EMI AMERICA)	ALL BY MYSELF	VARIOUS (K-TEL)
11	WHY?	BRONSKI BEAT (FORBIDDEN FRUIT)	PURPLE RAIN	PRINCE AND THE REVOLUTION (WARNER BROS)
12	ALL CRIED OUT	ALISON MOYET (CBS)	WE ARE FAMILY	SISTER SLEDGE (COTILLION)
13	PRIDE (IN THE NAME OF LOVE)	U2 (ISLAND)	RATTLESNAKES	LLOYD COLE AND THE COMMOTIONS (POLYDOR)
14	PURPLE RAIN	PRINCE (WARNER BROS)	CAN'T SLOW DOWN	LIONEL RICHIE (MOTOWN)
15	SKIN DEEP	STRANGLERS (EPIC)	PRIVATE DANCER	TINA TURNER (CAPITOL)
16	IF IT HAPPENS AGAIN	UB40 (DEP INTERNATIONAL/VIRGIN)	BREWING UP WITH BILLY BRAGG	BILLY BRAGG (GO! DISCS)
17	LOST IN MUSIC	SISTER SLEDGE (COTILLION)	THE WORKS	QUEEN (EMI)
18	LOVE KILLS	FREDDIE MERCURY (CBS)	GREATEST HITS	RANDY CRAWFORD (K-TEL)
19	SMOOTH OPERATOR	SADE (EPIC)	TRUE COLOURS	LEVEL 42 (POLYDOR)
20	CARELESS WHISPER	GEORGE MICHAEL (EPIC)	SOME GREAT REWARD	DEPECHE MODE (MUTE)

US

	SINGLES		ALBUMS	
1	I JUST CALLED TO SAY I LOVE YOU	STEVIE WONDER (MOTOWN)	PURPLE RAIN	PRINCE AND THE REVOLUTION (WARNER BROS)
2	CARIBBEAN QUEEN	BILLY OCEAN (JIVE)	BORN IN THE USA	BRUCE SPRINGSTEEN (COLUMBIA/CBS)
3	HARD HABIT TO BREAK	CHICAGO (FULL MOON/WARNER BROS)	PRIVATE DANCER	TINA TURNER (CAPITOL)
4	LUCKY STAR	MADONNA (SIRE)	SPORTS	HUEY LEWIS AND THE NEWS (CHRYSALIS)
5	LET'S GO CRAZY	PRINCE AND THE REVOLUTION (WARNER BROS)	HEARTBEAT CITY	THE CARS (ELEKTRA)
6	DRIVE	THE CARS (ELEKTRA)	1100 BEL AIR PLACE	JULIO IGLESIAS (COLUMBIA/CBS)
7	COVER ME	BRUCE SPRINGSTEEN (COLUMBIA/CBS)	WOMAN IN RED	STEVIE WONDER (MOTOWN)
8	ON THE DARK SIDE	JOHN CAFFERTY (SCOTTI BROS)	MADONNA	MADONNA (SIRE)
9	PURPLE RAIN	PRINCE (WARNER BROS)	CAN'T SLOW DOWN	LIONEL RICHIE (MOTOWN)
10	I'M SO EXCITED	POINTER SISTERS (PLANET)	SOUNDTRACK	EDDIE AND THE CRUISERS (SCOTTI BROS)
11	THE GLAMOROUS LIFE	SHIELA E (WARNER BROS)	BREAK OUT	POINTER SISTERS (PLANET)
12	MISSING YOU	JOHN WAITE (EMI AMERICA)	SHE'S SO UNUSUAL	CYNDI LAUPER (PORTRAIT)
13	WAKE ME UP BEFORE YOU GO GO	WHAM! (COLUMBIA/CBS)	17	CHICAGO (FULL MOON/WARNER BROS)
14	SOME GUYS HAVE ALL THE LUCK	ROD STEWARD (WARNER BROS)	OUT OF THE CELLAR	RATT (ATLANTIC)
15	ARE WE OURSELVES?	THE FIXX (MCA)	NO BRAKES	JOHN WAITE (EMI AMERICA)
16	BLUE JEAN	DAVID BOWIE (EMI AMERICA)	MIDNIGHT MADNESS	NIGHT RANGER (CAMEL/MCA)
17	SHE BOP	CYNDI LAUPER (PORTRAIT)	WARRIOR	SCANDAL WITH PATTI SMYTH (COLUMBIA/CBS)
18	WHO WEARS THESE SHOES?	ELTON JOHN (GEFFEN)	STAY HUNGRY	TWISTED SISTER (ATLANTIC)
19	DESERT MOON	DENNIS DE YOUNG (A&M)	PHANTOMS	THE FIXX (MCA)
20	BOP 'TIL YOU DROP	RICK SPRINGFIELD (RCA)	SUDDENLY	BILLY OCEAN (JIVE)

WEEK ENDING OCTOBER 27 1984

SINGLES	UK	ALBUMS
FREEDOM WHAM! (EPIC)	1	STEELTOWN BIG COUNTRY (MERCURY)
NO MORE LONELY NIGHTS PAUL McCARTNEY (PARLOPHONE)	2	THE UNFORGETTABLE FIRE U2 (ISLAND
TOGETHER IN ELECTRIC DREAMS GIORGIO MORODER/PHILIP OAKEY (VIRGIN)	3	DIAMOND LIFE SADE (EPIC)
I JUST CALLED TO SAY I LOVE YOU STEVIE WONDER (MOTOWN)	4	THE AGE OF CONSENT BRONSKI BEAT (FORBIDDEN FRUIT)
I FEEL FOR YOU CHAKA KHAN (WARNER BROS)	5	GEFFERY MORGAN UB40 (DEP INTERNATIONAL/VIRGIN)
THE WAR SONG CULTURE CLUB (VIRGIN)	6	HITS HITS HITS VARIOUS (TELSTAR)
DRIVE THE CARS (ELEKTRA)	7	ALL BY MYSELF VARIOUS (K-TEL)
ALL CRIED OUT ALISON MOYET (CBS)	8	NOW THAT'S WHAT I CALL MUSIC 3 VARIOUS (EMI/VIRGIN)
MISSING YOU JOHN WAITE (EMI AMERICA)	9	ELIMINATOR ZZ TOP (WARNER BROS)
SHOUT TO THE TOP STYLE COUNCIL (POLYDOR)	10	WOMAN IN RED STEVIE WONDER/DIONNE WARWICK (MOTOWN)
. . . TEAR YOUR PLAYHOUSE DOWN PAUL YOUNG (CBS)	11	TONIGHT DAVID BOWIE (EMI AMERICA)
TOO LATE FOR GOODBYES JULIAN LENNON (CHARISMA)	12	CAN'T SLOW DOWN LIONEL RICHIE (MOTOWN)
LOVE'S GREAT ADVENTURE ULTRAVOX (CHRYSALIS)	13	YESTERDAY ONCE MORE CARPENTERS (EMI/A&M)
GHOSTBUSTERS RAY PARKER JR (ARISTA)	14	GREATEST HITS RANDY CRAWFORD (K-TEL)
HIGHLY STRUNG SPANDAU BALLET (CHRYSALIS)	15	EMOTION BARBRA STREISAND (CBS)
WHY? BRONSKI BEAT (FORBIDDEN FRUIT)	16	RATTLESNAKES LLOYD COLE AND THE COMMOTIONS (POLYDOR)
MODERN GIRL MEAT LOAF (ARISTA)	17	PARADE SPANDAU BALLET (CHRYSALIS)
SKIN DEEP STRANGLERS (EPIC)	18	WE ARE FAMILY SISTER SLEDGE (COTILLION)
PRIDE (IN THE NAME OF LOVE) U2 (ISLAND)	19	THE WORKS QUEEN (EMI)
SMOOTH OPERATOR SADE (EPIC)	20	PURPLE RAIN PRINCE AND THE REVOLUTION (WARNER BROS)

SINGLES	US	ALBUMS
I JUST CALLED TO SAY I LOVE YOU STEVIE WONDER (MOTOWN)	1	PURPLE RAIN PRINCE AND THE REVOLUTION (WARNER BROS)
CARIBBEAN QUEEN BILLY OCEAN (JIVE)	2	BORN IN THE USA BRUCE SPRINGSTEEN (COLUMBIA/CBS)
HARD HABIT TO BREAK CHICAGO (FULL MOON/WARNER BROS)	3	PRIVATE DANCER TINA TURNER (CAPITOL)
PURPLE RAIN PRINCE AND THE REVOLUTION (WARNER BROS)	4	SPORTS HUEY LEWIS AND THE NEWS (CHRYSALIS)
LUCKY STAR MADONNA (SIRE)	5	1100 BEL AIR PLACE JULIO IGLESIAS (COLUMBIA/CBS)
WAKE ME UP BEFORE YOU GO GO WHAM! (COLUMBIA/CBS)	6	HEARTBEAT CITY THE CARS (ELEKTRA)
ON THE DARK SIDE JOHN CAFFERTY (SCOTTI BROS)	7	WOMAN IN RED STEVIE WONDER (MOTOWN)
LET'S GO CRAZY PRINCE AND THE REVOLUTION (WARNER BROS)	8	MADONNA MADONNA (SIRE)
I'M SO EXCITED POINTER SISTERS (PLANET)	9	SOUNDTRACK EDDIE AND THE CRUISERS (SCOTT BROS)
SOME GUYS HAVE ALL THE LUCK ROD STEWART (WARNER BROS)	10	CAN'T SLOW DOWN LIONEL RICHIE (MOTOWN)
COVER ME BRUCE SPRINGSTEEN (COLUMBIA/CBS)	11	BREAK OUT POINTER SISTERS (PLANET)
DRIVE THE CARS (ELEKTRA)	12	17 CHICAGO (FULL MOON/WARNER BROS)
BLUE JEAN DAVID BOWIE (EMI AMERICA)	13	SHE'S SO UNUSUAL CYNDI LAUPER (PORTRAIT)
DESERT MOON DENNIS DE YOUNG (A&M)	14	OUT OF THE CELLAR RATT (ATLANTIC)
I FEEL FOR YOU CHAKA KHAN (WARNER BROS)	15	NO BRAKES JOHN WAITE (EMI AMERICA)
BETTER BE GOOD TO ME TINA TURNER (CAPITOL)	16	SUDDENLY BILLY OCEAN (JIVE/ARISTA)
WHO WEARS THESE SHOES? ELTON JOHN (GEFFEN)	17	MIDNIGHT MADNESS NIGHT RANGER (CAMEL/MCA)
STRUT SHEENA EASTON (EMI AMERICA)	18	STAY HUNGRY TWISTED SISTER (ATLANTIC)
SWEPT AWAY DIANA ROSS (RCA)	19	PHANTOMS THE FIXX (MCA)
OUT OF TOUCH HALL & OATES (RCA)	20	ANIMALIZE KISS (MERCURY)

WEEK ENDING NOVEMBER 3 1984

SINGLES	UK	ALBUMS
FREEDOM WHAM! (EPIC)	1	GIVE MY REGARDS TO BROAD STREET PAUL McCARTNEY (PARLOPHONE)
I FEEL FOR YOU CHAKA KHAN (WARNER BROS)	2	WAKING UP WITH THE HOUSE ON FIRE CULTURE CLUB (VIRGIN)
NO MORE LONELY NIGHTS PAUL McCARTNEY (PARLOPHONE)	3	DIAMOND LIFE SADE (EPIC)
TOGETHER IN ELECTRIC DREAMS GIORGIO MORODER/PHILIP OAKEY (VIRGIN)	4	ELIMINATOR ZZ TOP (WARNER BROS)
THE WILD BOYS DURAN DURAN (EMI)	5	STEELTOWN BIG COUNTRY (MERCURY)
TOO LATE FOR GOODBYES JULIAN LENNON (CHARISMA)	6	THE UNFORGETTABLE FIRE U2 (ISLAND)
THE WANDERER STATUS QUO (VERTIGO)	7	THE AGE OF CONSENT BRONSKI BEAT (FORBIDDEN FRUIT)
ALL CRIED OUT ALISON MOYET (CBS)	8	NOW THAT'S WHAT I CALL MUSIC 3 VARIOUS (EMI/VIRGIN)
I JUST CALLED TO SAY I LOVE YOU STEVIE WONDER (MOTOWN)	9	CAN'T SLOW DOWN LIONEL RICHIE (MOTOWN)
MISSING YOU JOHN WAITE (EMI AMERICA)	10	GREATEST HITS RANDY CRAWFORD (K-TEL)
DRIVE THE CARS (ELEKTRA)	11	HITS HITS HITS VARIOUS (TELSTAR)
CARIBBEAN QUEEN BILLY OCEAN (JIVE)	12	ALL BY MYSELF VARIOUS (K-TEL)
LOVE'S GREAT ADVENTURE ULTRAVOX (CHRYSALIS)	13	GEFFERY MORGAN UB40 (DEP INTERNATIONAL/VIRGIN)
THE WAR SONG CULTURE CLUB (VIRGIN)	14	WOMAN IN RED STEVIE WONDER/DIONNE WARWICK (MOTOWN)
GIMME ALL YOUR LOVIN' ZZ TOP (WARNER BROS)	15	YESTERDAY ONCE MORE CARPENTERS (EMI/A&M)
SHOUT TO THE TOP STYLE COUNCIL (POLYDOR)	16	TONIGHT DAVID BOWIE (EMI AMERICA)
MODERN GIRL MEAT LOAF (ARISTA)	17	CINEMA ELAINE PAGE (K-TEL)
PENNY LOVER LIONEL RICHIE (MOTOWN)	18	EMOTION BARBRA STREISAND (CBS)
GHOSTBUSTERS RAY PARKER JR (ARISTA)	19	I FEEL FOR YOU CHAKA KHAN (WARNER BROS)
THE NEVER ENDING STORY LIMAHL (EMI)	20	VALOTTE JULIAN LENNON (CHARISMA)

SINGLES	US	ALBUMS
CARIBBEAN QUEEN BILLY OCEAN (JIVE)	1	PURPLE RAIN PRINCE AND THE REVOLUTION (WARNER BROS)
I JUST CALLED TO SAY I LOVE YOU STEVIE WONDER (MOTOWN)	2	BORN IN THE USA BRUCE SPRINGSTEEN (COLUMBIA/CBS)
PURPLE RAIN PRINCE AND THE REVOLUTION (WARNER BROS)	3	PRIVATE DANCER TINA TURNER (CAPITOL)
HARD HABIT TO BREAK CHICAGO (FULL BREAK/WARNER BROS)	4	SPORTS HUEY LEWIS AND THE NEWS (CHRYSALIS)
WAKE ME UP BEFORE YOU GO GO WHAM! (COLUMBIA/CBS)	5	1100 BEL AIR PLACE JULIO IGLESIAS (COLUMBIA/CBS)
LUCKY STAR MADONNA (SIRE)	6	WOMAN IN RED STEVIE WONDER (MOTOWN)
ON THE DARK SIDE JOHN CAFFERTY (SCOTTI BROS)	7	HEARTBEAT CITY THE CARS (ELEKTRA)
BLUE JEAN DAVID BOWIE (EMI AMERICA)	8	MADONNA MADONNA (SIRE)
BETTER BE GOOD TO ME TINA TURNER (CAPITOL)	9	SOUNDTRACK EDDIE AND THE CRUISERS (SCOTTI BROS)
I FEEL FOR YOU CHAKA KHAN (WARNER BROS)	10	CAN'T SLOW DOWN LIONEL RICHIE (MOTOWN)
DESERT MOON DENNIS DE YOUNG (A&M)	11	BREAK OUT POINTER SISTERS (PLANET)
OUT OF TOUCH HALL & OATES (RCA)	12	17 CHICAGO (FULL MOON/WARNER BROS)
I'M SO EXCITED POINTER SISTERS (PLANET)	13	SHE'S SO UNUSUAL CYNDI LAUPER (PORTRAIT)
SOME GUYS HAVE ALL THE LUCK ROD STEWART (WARNER BROS)	14	SUDDENLY BILLY OCEAN (JIVE/ARISTA)
STRUT SHEENA EASTON (EMI AMERICA)	15	NO BRAKES JOHN WAITE (EMI AMERICA)
WHO WEARS THESE SHOES? ELTON JOHN (GEFFEN)	16	BIG BAM BOOM HALL & OATES (RCA)
LET'S GO CRAZY PRINCE AND THE REVOLUTION (WARNER BROS)	17	THE UNFORGETTABLES FIRE U2 (ISLAND)
PENNY LOVER LIONEL RICHIE (RCA)	18	OUT OF THE CELLAR RATT (ATLANTIC)
SWEPT AWAY DIANA ROSS (RCA)	19	PHANTOMS THE FIXX (MCA)
ALL THROUGH THE NIGHT CYNDI LAUPER (PORTRAIT)	20	ANIMALIZE KISS (MERCURY)

WEEK ENDING NOVEMBER 10 1984

UK

SINGLES	Artist (Label)	No.	ALBUMS	Artist (Label)
I FEEL FOR YOU	CHAKA KHAN (WARNER BROS)	1	WELCOME TO THE PLEASUREDOME	FRANKIE GOES TO HOLLYWOOD (ZTT/ISLAND)
FREEDOM	WHAM! (EPIC)	2	THE COLLECTION	ULTRAVOX (CHRYSALIS)
THE WILD BOYS	DURAN DURAN (EMI)	3	GIVE MY REGARDS TO BROAD STREET	PAUL McCARTNEY (PARLOPHONE)
NO MORE LONELY NIGHTS	PAUL McCARTNEY (PARLOPHONE)	4	ELIMINATOR	ZZ TOP (WARNER BROS)
TOGETHER IN ELECTRIC DREAMS	GIORGIO MORODER/PHILIP OAKEY (VIRGIN)	5	PERFECT STRANGERS	DEEP PURPLE (POLYDOR)
TOO LATE FOR GOODBYES	JULIAN LENNON (CHARISMA)	6	DIAMOND LIFE	SADE (EPIC)
THE WANDERER	STATUS QUO (VERTIGO)	7	WAKING UP WITH THE HOUSE ON FIRE	CULTURE CLUB (VIRGIN)
ALL CRIED OUT	ALISON MOYET (CBS)	8	BAD ATTITUDE	MEAT LOAF (ARISTA)
CARIBBEAN QUEEN	BILLY OCEAN (JIVE)	9	THE UNFORGETTABLE FIRE	U2 (ISLAND)
THE NEVER ENDING STORY	LIMAHL (EMI)	10	STEELTOWN	BIG COUNTRY (MERCURY)
GIMME ALL YOUR LOVIN'	ZZ TOP (WARNER BROS)	11	GREATEST HITS	RANDY CRAWFORD (K-TEL)
LOVE'S GREAT ADVENTURE	ULTRAVOX (CHRYSALIS)	12	CAN'T SLOW DOWN	LIONEL RICHIE (MOTOWN)
I SHOULD HAVE KNOWN BETTER	JIM DIAMOND (A&M)	13	THE AGE OF CONSENT	BRONSKI BEAT (FORBIDDEN FRUIT/LONDON)
I JUST CALLED TO SAY I LOVE YOU	STEVIE WONDER (MOTOWN)	14	YESTERDAY ONCE MORE	CARPENTERS (EMI/A&M)
MISSING YOU	JOHN WAITE (EMI AMERICA)	15	NOW THAT'S WHAT I CALL MUSIC 3	VARIOUS (EMI/VIRGIN)
I'M SO EXCITED	POINTER SISTERS (PLANET)	16	EMOTION	BARBRA STREISAND (CBS)
DRIVE	THE CARS (ELEKTRA)	17	WOMAN IN RED	STEVIE WONDER/DIONNE WARWICK (MOTOWN)
PENNY LOVER	LIONEL RICHIE (MOTOWN)	18	I FEEL FOR YOU	CHAKA KHAN (WARNER BROS)
MODERN GIRL	MEAT LOAF (ARISTA)	19	HITS HITS HITS	VARIOUS (TELSTAR)
ACES HIGH	IRON MAIDEN (EMI)	20	GEFFERY MORGAN	UB40 (DEP INTERNATIONAL/VIRGIN)

US

SINGLES	Artist (Label)	No.	ALBUMS	Artist (Label)
CARIBBEAN QUEEN	BILLY OCEAN (JIVE)	1	PURPLE RAIN	PRINCE AND THE REVOLUTION (WARNER BROS)
I JUST CALLED TO SAY I LOVE YOU	STEVIE WONDER (MOTOWN)	2	BORN IN THE USA	BRUCE SPRINGSTEEN (COLUMBIA/CBS)
PURPLE RAIN	PRINCE AND THE REVOLUTION (WARNER BROS)	3	PRIVATE DANCER	TINA TURNER (CAPITOL)
WAKE ME UP BEFORE YOU GO GO	WHAM! (COLUMBIA/CBS)	4	WOMAN IN RED	STEVIE WONDER (MOTOWN)
I FEEL FOR YOU	CHAKA KHAN (WARNER BROS)	5	SPORTS	HUEY LEWIS AND THE NEWS (CHRYSALIS)
OUT OF TOUCH	HALL & OATES (RCA)	6	1100 BEL AIR PLACE	JULIO IGLESIAS (COLUMBIA/CBS)
BETTER BE GOOD TO ME	TINA TURNER (CAPITOL)	7	HEARTBEAT CITY	THE CARS (ELEKTRA)
BLUE JEAN	DAVID BOWIE (EMI AMERICA)	8	CAN'T SLOW DOWN	LIONEL RICHIE (MOTOWN)
HARD HABIT TO BREAK	CHICAGO (FULL MOON/WARNER BROS)	9	SOUNDTRACK	EDDIE AND THE CRUISERS (SCOTTI BROS)
DESERT MOON	DENNIS DE YOUNG (A&M)	10	SHE'S SO UNUSUAL	CYNDI LAUPER (PORTRAIT)
STRUT	SHEENA EASTON (EMI AMERICA)	11	BIG BAM BOOM	HALL & OATES (RCA)
ALL THROUGH THE NIGHT	CYNDI LAUPER (PORTRAIT)	12	17	CHICAGO (FULL MOON/WARNER BROS)
PENNY LOVER	LIONEL RICHIE (MOTOWN)	13	BREAK OUT	POINTER SISTERS (PLANET)
ON THE DARK SIDE	JOHN CAFFERTY (SCOTT BROS)	14	SUDDENLY	BILLY OCEAN (JIVE/ARISTA)
I'M SO EXCITED	POINTER SISTERS (PLANET)	15	THE UNFORGETTABLE FIRE	U2 (ISLAND)
SOME GUYS HAVE ALL THE LUCK	ROD STEWART (WARNER BROS)	16	MADONNA	MADONNA (SIRE)
LUCKY STAR	MADONNA (SIRE)	17	TONIGHT	DAVID BOWIE (EMI AMERICA)
WHAT ABOUT ME?	KENNY ROGERS/KIM CARNES/JAMES INGRAM (RCA)	18	VOLUME ONE	THE HONEYDRIPPERS (COLUMBIA/CBS)
NO MORE LONELY NIGHTS	PAUL McCARTNEY (COLUMBIA/CBS)	19	EMOTION	BARBRA STREISAND (COLUMBIA/CBS)
THE WAR SONG	CULTURE CLUB (VIRGIN/EPIC)	20	ANIMALIZE	KISS (MERCURY)

WEEK ENDING NOVEMBER 17 1984

UK

SINGLES	Artist (Label)	No.	ALBUMS	Artist (Label)
I FEEL FOR YOU	CHAKA KHAN (WARNER BROS)	1	MAKE IT BIG	WHAM! (EPIC)
THE WILD BOYS	DURAN DURAN (EMI)	2	WELCOME TO THE PLEASUREDOME	FRANKIE GOES TO HOLLYWOOD (ZTT/ISLAND)
I SHOULD HAVE KNOWN BETTER	JIM DIAMOND (A&M)	3	ALF	ALISON MOYET (CBS)
FREEDOM	WHAM! (EPIC)	4	THE COLLECTION	ULTRAVOX (CHRYSALIS)
THE NEVER ENDING STORY	LIMAHL (EMI)	5	DIAMOND LIFE	SADE (EPIC)
CARIBBEAN QUEEN	BILLY OCEAN (JIVE)	6	ELIMINATOR	ZZ TOP (WARNER BROS)
THE WANDERER	STATUS QUO (VERTIGO)	7	GIVE MY REGARDS TO BROAD STREET	PAUL McCARTNEY (PARLOPHONE)
ALL CRIED OUT	ALISON MOYET (CBS)	8	REAL TO REEL	MARILLION (EMI)
TOO LATE FOR GOODBYES	JULIAN LENNON (CHARISMA)	9	PERFECT STRANGERS	DEEP PURPLE (POLYDOR)
GIMME ALL YOUR LOVIN'	ZZ TOP (WARNER BROS)	10	BAD ATTITUDE	MEAT LOAF (ARISTA)
HARD HABIT TO BREAK	CHICAGO (FULL MOON)	11	YESTERDAY ONCE MORE	CARPENTERS (EMI/A&M)
LOVE'S GREAT ADVENTURE	ULTRAVOX (CHRYSALIS)	12	THE UNFORGETTABLE FIRE	U2 (ISLAND)
NO MORE LONELY NIGHTS	PAUL McCARTNEY (PAROPHONE)	13	CAN'T SLOW DOWN	LIONEL RICHIE (MOTOWN)
I'M SO EXCITED	POINTER SISTERS (PLANET)	14	AURAL SCULPTURE	STRANGLERS (EPIC)
TOGETHER IN ELECTRIC DREAMS	GIORGIO MORODER/PHILIP OAKEY (VIRGIN)	15	I FEEL FOR YOU	CHAKA KHAN (WARNER BROS)
BLASPHEMOUS RUMOURS/SOMEBODY	DEPECHE MODE (MUTE)	16	WAKING UP WITH THE HOUSE ON FIRE	CULTURE CLUB (VIRGIN)
THE RIDDLE	NIK KERSHAW (MCA)	17	NOW THAT'S WHAT I CALL MUSIC 3	VARIOUS (EMI/VIRGIN)
GOTTA GET YOU HOME TONIGHT	EUGENE WILDE (FOURTH & BROADWAY)	18	GREATEST HITS	SKAKIN' STEVENS (EPIC)
I JUST CALLED TO SAY I LOVE YOU	STEVIE WONDER (MOTOWN)	19	GREATEST HITS	RANDY CRAWFORD (K-TEL)
MISSING YOU	JOHN WAITE (EMI AMERICA)	20	CINEMA	ELAINE PAIGE (K-TEL)

US

SINGLES	Artist (Label)	No.	ALBUMS	Artist (Label)
WAKE ME UP BEFORE YOU GO GO	WHAM! (COLUMBIA/CBS)	1	PURPLE RAIN	PRINCE AND THE REVOLUTION (WARNER BROS)
PURPLE RAIN	PRINCE AND THE REVOLUTION (WARNER BROS)	2	BORN IN THE USA	BRUCE SPRINGSTEEN (COLUMBIA/CBS)
CARIBBEAN QUEEN	BILLY OCEAN (JIVE)	3	PRIVATE DANCER	TINA TURNER (CAPITOL)
I FEEL FOR YOU	CHAKA KHAN (WARNER BROS)	4	WOMAN IN RED	STEVIE WONDER (MOTOWN)
I JUST CALLED TO SAY I LOVE YOU	STEVIE WONDER (MOTOWN)	5	SPORTS	HUEY LEWIS AND THE NEWS (CHRYSALIS)
OUT OF TOUCH	HALL & OATES (RCA)	6	CAN'T SLOW DOWN	LIONEL RICHIE (MOTOWN)
BETTER BE GOOD TO ME	TINA TURNER (CAPITOL)	7	1100 BEL AIR PLACE	JULIO IGLESIAS (COLUMBIA/CBS)
STRUT	SHEENA EASTON (EMI AMERICA)	8	VOLUME ONE	THE HONEYDRIPPERS (ES PARANZA)
ALL THROUGH THE NIGHT	CYNDI LAUPER (PORTRAIT)	9	HEARTBEAT CITY	THE CARS (ELEKTRA)
PENNY LOVER	LIONEL RICHIE (MOTOWN)	10	SHE'S SO UNUSUAL	CYNDI LAUPER (PORTRAIT)
BLUE JEAN	DAVID BOWIE (EMI AMERICA)	11	BIG BAM BOOM	HALL & OATES (RCA)
DESERT MOON	DENNIS DE YOUNG (A&M)	12	SOUNDTRACK	EDDIE AND THE CRUISERS (SCOTTI BROS)
HARD HABIT TO BREAK	CHICAGO (FULL MOON/WARNER BROS)	13	BREAK OUT	POINTER SISTERS (PLANET)
NO MORE LONELY NIGHTS	PAUL McCARTNEY (COLUMBIA/CBS)	14	SUDDENLY	BILLY OCEAN (JIVE/ARISTA)
WHAT ABOUT ME?	KENNY ROGERS/KIM CARNES/JAMES INGRAM (RCA)	15	THE UNFORGETTABLE FIRE	U2 (ISLAND)
COOL IT NOW	NEW EDITION (MCA)	16	MADONNA	MADONNA (SIRE)
THE WAR SONG	CULTURE CLUB (VIRGIN/EPIC)	17	TONIGHT	DAVID BOWIE (EMI AMERICA)
SEA OF LOVE	HONEYDRIPPERS (ES PARANZA)	18	17	CHICAGO (FULL MOON/WARNER BROS)
THE WILD BOYS	DURAN DURAN (CAPITOL)	19	EMOTION	BARBRA STREISAND (COLUMBIA/CBS)
I CAN'T HOLD BACK	SURVIVOR (SCOTTI BROS)	20	ANIMALIZE	KISS (MERCURY)

WEEK ENDING NOVEMBER 24 1984

UK

SINGLES	UK	ALBUMS
I FEEL FOR YOU CHAKA KHAN (WARNER BROS)	1	MAKE IT BIG WHAM! (EPIC)
I SHOULD HAVE KNOWN BETTER JIM DIAMOND (A&M)	2	THE COLLECTION ULTRAVOX (CHRYSALIS)
THE WILD BOYS DURAN DURAN (EMI)	3	ALF ALISON MOYET (CBS)
THE NEVER ENDING STORY LIMAHL (EMI)	4	WELCOME TO THE PLEASUREDOME FRANKIE GOES TO HOLLYWOOD (ZTT/ISLAND)
THE RIDDLE NIK KERSHAW (MCA)	5	DIAMOND LIFE SADE (EPIC)
CARIBBEAN QUEEN BILLY OCEAN (JIVE)	6	ARENA DURAN DURAN (EMI)
SEXCRIME (1984) EURYTHMICS (VIRGIN)	7	HATFUL OF HOLLOW SMITHS (ROUGH TRADE)
HARD HABIT TO BREAK CHICAGO (FULL MOON/WEA)	8	ELIMINATOR ZZ TOP (WARNER BROS)
FREEDOM WHAM! (EPIC)	9	GIVE MY REGARDS TO BROAD STREET PAUL McCARTNEY (PARLOPHONE)
THE WANDERER STATUS QUO (VERTIGO)	10	GREATEST HITS SHAKIN' STEVENS (EPIC)
I'M SO EXCITED POINTER SISTERS (PLANET)	11	YESTERDAY ONCE MORE CARPENTERS (EMI)
TREAT HER LIKE A LADY TEMPTATIONS (MOTOWN)	12	REAL TO REEL MARILLION (EMI)
ALL CRIED OUT ALISON MOYET (CBS)	13	BAD ATTITUDE MEAT LOAF (ARISTA)
LET IT ALL BLOW DAZZ BAND (MOTOWN)	14	CAN'T SLOW DOWN LIONEL RICHIE (MOTOWN)
GIMME ALL YOUR LOVIN' ZZ TOP (WARNER BROS)	15	THE ART GARFUNKEL ALBUM ART GARFUNKEL (CBS)
LOVE'S GREAT ADVENTURE ULTRAVOX (CHRYSALIS)	16	CINEMA ELAINE PAIGE (K-TEL)
BLASPHEMOUS RUMOURS/SOMEBODY DEPECHE MODE (MUTE)	17	NOW THAT'S WHAT I CALL MUSIC 3 VARIOUS (EMI/VIRGIN)
I WON'T RUN AWAY ALVIN STARDUST (CHRYSALIS)	18	THE UNFORGETTABLE FIRE U2 (ISLAND)
TOO LATE FOR GOODBYES JULIAN LENNON (CHARISMA)	19	GREATEST HITS RANDY CRAWFORD (K-TEL)
ALL JOIN HANDS SLADE (RCA)	20	I FEEL FOR YOU CHAKA KHAN (WARNER BROS)

US

SINGLES	US	ALBUMS
WAKE ME UP BEFORE YOU GO GO WHAM! (COLUMBIA/CBS)	1	PURPLE RAIN PRINCE AND THE REVOLUTION (WARNER BROS)
PURPLE RAIN PRINCE AND THE REVOLUTION (WARNER BROS)	2	BORN IN THE USA BRUCE SPRINGSTEEN (COLUMBIA/CBS)
I FEEL FOR YOU CHAKA KHAN (WARNER BROS)	3	PRIVATE DANCER TINA TURNER (CAPITOL)
OUT OF TOUCH HALL & OATES (RCA)	4	WOMAN IN RED STEVIE WONDER (MOTOWN)
BETTER BE GOOD TO ME TINA TURNER (CAPITOL)	5	VOLUME ONE THE HONEYDRIPPERS (ES PARANZA)
CARIBBEAN QUEEN BILLY OCEAN (JIVE)	6	BIG BAM BOOM HALL & OATES (RCA)
STRUT SHEENA EASTON (EMI AMERICA)	7	SPORTS HUEY LEWIS AND THE NEWS (CHRYSALIS)
ALL THROUGH THE NIGHT CYNDI LAUPER (PORTRAIT/EPIC)	8	CAN'T SLOW DOWN LIONEL RICHIE (MOTOWN)
PENNY LOVER LIONEL RICHIE (MOTOWN)	9	SUDDENLY BILLY OCEAN (JIVE/ARISTA)
I JUST CALLED TO SAY I LOVE YOU STEVIE WONDER (MOTOWN)	10	SHE'S SO UNUSUAL CYNDI LAUPER (PORTRAIT)
NO MORE LONELY NIGHTS PAUL McCARTNEY (COLUMBIA/CBS)	11	TONIGHT DAVID BOWIE (EMI AMERICA)
THE WILD BOYS DURAN DURAN (CAPITOL)	12	THE UNFORGETTABLE FIRE U2 (ISLAND)
SEA OF LOVE HONEYDRIPPERS (ES PARANZA)	13	BREAK OUT POINTER SISTERS (PLANET)
COOL IT NOW NEW EDITION (MCA)	14	17 CHICAGO (FULL MOON/WARNER BROS)
DESERT MOON DENNIS DE YOUNG (A&M)	15	1100 BEL AIR PLACE JULIO IGLESIAS (COLUMBIA/CBS)
BLUE JEAN DAVID BOWIE (EMI AMERICA)	16	I FEEL FOR YOU CHAKA KHAN (WARNER BROS)
I CAN'T HOLD BACK SURVIVOR (SCOTTI BROS)	17	HEARTBEAT CITY THE CARS (ELEKTRA)
THE WAR SONG CULTURE CLUB (VIRGIN/EPIC)	18	SOUNDTRACK EDDIE AND THE CRUISERS (SCOTTI BROS)
WE BELONG PAT BENATAR (CHRYSALIS)	19	EMOTION BARBRA STREISAND (COLUMBIA/CBS)
HARD HABIT TO BREAK CHICAGO (FULL MOON/WARNER BROS)	20	ANIMALIZE KISS (MERCURY)

WEEK ENDING DECEMBER 1 1984

UK

SINGLES	UK	ALBUMS
I SHOULD HAVE KNOWN BETTER JIM DIAMOND (A&M)	1	THE HITS ALBUM VARIOUS (CBS/WEA)
I FEEL FOR YOU CHAKA KHAN (WARNER BROS)	2	MAKE IT BIG WHAM! (EPIC)
THE POWER OF LOVE FRANKIE GOES TO HOLLYWOOD (ZTT/ISLAND)	3	THE COLLECTION ULTRAVOX (CHRYSALIS)
THE RIDDLE NIK KERSHAW (MCA)	4	ALF ALISON MOYET (CBS)
THE NEVER ENDING STORY LIMAHL (EMI)	5	WELCOME TO THE PLEASUREDOME FRANKIE GOES TO HOLLYWOOD (ZTT/ISLAND)
SEXCRIME (1984) EURYTHMICS (VIRGIN)	6	DIAMOND LIFE SADE (EPIC)
TEARDROPS SHAKIN' STEVENS (EPIC)	7	ARENA DURAN DURAN (EMI)
HARD HABIT TO BREAK CHICAGO (FULL MOON)	8	THE RIDDLE NIK KERSHAW (MCA)
THE WILD BOYS DURAN DURAN (EMI)	9	GREATEST HITS SHAKIN' STEVENS (EPIC)
CARIBBEAN QUEEN BILLY OCEAN (JIVE)	10	ELIMINATOR ZZ TOP (WARNER BROS)
I WON'T RUN AWAY ALVIN STARDUST (CHRYSALIS)	11	HATFUL OF HOLLOW SMITHS (ROUGH TRADE)
LET IT ALL BLOW DAZZ BAND (MOTOWN)	12	CINEMA ELAINE PAIGE (K-TEL)
TREAT HER LIKE A LADY TEMPTATIONS (MOTOWN)	13	YESTERDAY ONCE MORE CARPENTERS (EMI)
LOUISE HUMAN LEAGUE (VIRGIN)	14	GIVE MY REGARDS TO BROAD STREET PAUL McCARTNEY (PARLOPHONE)
ALL JOIN HANDS SLADE (RCA)	15	THE ART GARFUNKEL ALBUM ART GARFUNKEL (CBS)
I'M SO EXCITED POINTER SISTERS (PLANET)	16	TWELVE GOLD BARS VOL 1 & 2 STATUS QUO (VERTIGO)
ONE NIGHT IN BANGKOK MURRAY HEAD (RCA)	17	CAN'T SLOW DOWN LIONEL RICHIE (MOTOWN)
THE WANDERER STATUS QUO (VERTIGO)	18	VERY BEST OF FOSTER AND ALLEN FOSTER AND ALLEN (RITZ)
FRESH KOOL AND THE GANG (DE-LITE)	19	BAD ATTITUDE MEAT LOAF (ARISTA)
FREEDOM WHAM! (EPIC)	20	GREATEST HITS CHAS AND DAVE (ROCKNEY)

US

SINGLES	US	ALBUMS
WAKE ME UP BEFORE YOU GO GO WHAM! (COLUMBIA/CBS)	1	PURPLE RAIN PRINCE AND THE REVOLUTION (WARNER BROS)
OUT OF TOUCH HALL & OATES (RCA)	2	BORN IN THE USA BRUCE SPRINGSTEEN (COLUMBIA/CBS)
I FEEL FOR YOU CHAKA KHAN (WARNER BROS)	3	PRIVATE DANCER TINA TURNER (CAPITOL)
PURPLE RAIN PRINCE AND THE REVOLUTION (WARNER BROS)	4	VOLUME ONE THE HONEYDRIPPERS (ES PARANZA)
BETTER BE GOOD TO ME TINA TURNER (CAPITOL)	5	BIG BAM BOOM HALL & OATES (RCA)
ALL THROUGH THE NIGHT CYNDI LAUPER (PORTRAIT)	6	WOMAN IN RED STEVIE WONDER (MOTOWN)
THE WILD BOYS DURAN DURAN (CAPITOL)	7	CAN'T SLOW DOWN LIONEL RICHIE (MOTOWN)
PENNY LOVER LIONEL RICHIE (MOTOWN)	8	SPORTS HUEY LEWIS AND THE NEWS (CHRYSALIS)
STRUT SHEENA EASTON (EMI AMERICA)	9	SUDDENLY BILLY OCEAN (JIVE)
NO MORE LONELY NIGHTS PAUL McCARTNEY (COLUMBIA/CBS)	10	17 CHICAGO (FULL MOON/WARNER BROS)
SEA OF LOVE HONEYDRIPPERS (ES PARANZA)	11	TONIGHT DAVID BOWIE (EMI AMERICA)
CARIBBEAN QUEEN BILLY OCEAN (JIVE)	12	THE UNFORGETTABLE FIRE U2 (ISLAND)
COOL IT NOW NEW EDITION (MCA)	13	BREAK OUT POINTER SISTERS (PLANET)
WE BELONG PAT BENATAR (CHRYSALIS)	14	I FEEL FOR YOU CHAKA KHAN (WARNER BROS)
I CAN'T HOLD BACK SURVIVOR (SCOTTI BROS)	15	SHE'S SO UNUSUAL CYNDI LAUPER (PORTRAIT)
I JUST CALLED TO SAY I LOVE YOU STEVIE WONDER (MOTOWN)	16	1100 BEL AIR PLACE JULIO IGLESIAS (COLUMBIA/CBS)
IT AIN'T ENOUGH COREY HART (EMI AMERICA)	17	HEARTBEAT CITY THE CARS (ELEKTRA)
VALOTTE JULIAN LENNON (ATLANTIC)	18	SOUNDTRACK EDDIE AND THE CRUISERS (SCOTTI BROS)
WALKING ON A THIN LINE HUEY LEWIS AND THE NEWS (CHRYSALIS)	19	ANIMALIZE KISS (MERCURY)
DESERT MOON DENNIS DE YOUNG (A&M)	20	VALOTTE JULIAN LENNON (ATLANTIC)

WEEK ENDING DECEMBER 8 1984

UK

SINGLES	UK	ALBUMS
THE POWER OF LOVE FRANKIE GOES TO HOLLYWOOD (ZTT/ISLAND)	1	THE HITS ALBUM VARIOUS (CBS/WEA)
I SHOULD HAVE KNOWN BETTER JIM DIAMOND (A&M)	2	NOW THAT'S WHAT I CALL MUSIC 4 VARIOUS (EMI VIRGIN)
THE RIDDLE NIK KERSHAW (MCA)	3	MAKE IT BIG WHAM! (EPIC)
SEXCRIME (1984) EURYTHMICS (VIRGIN)	4	THE COLLECTION ULTRAVOX (CHRYSALIS)
TEARDROPS SHAKIN' STEVENS (EPIC)	5	ALF ALISON MOYET (CBS)
I FEEL FOR YOU CHAKA KHAN (WARNER BROS)	6	WELCOME TO THE PLEASUREDOME FRANKIE GOES TO HOLLYWOOD (ZTT/ISLAND)
I WON'T RUN AWAY ALVIN STARDUST (CHRYSALIS)	7	DIAMOND LIFE SADE (EPIC)
LIKE A VIRGIN MADONNA (SIRE)	8	GREATEST HITS SHAKIN' STEVENS (EPIC)
WE ALL STAND TOGETHER PAUL McCARTNEY & FROG CHORUS (PARLOPHONE)	9	ARENA DURAN DURAN (EMI)
THE NEVER ENDING STORY LIMAHL (EMI)	10	GIVE MY REGARDS TO BROAD STREET PAUL McCARTNEY (PARLOPHONE)
HARD HABIT TO BREAK CHICAGO (FULL MOON)	11	YESTERDAY ONCE MORE CARPENTERS (EMI)
FRESH KOOL AND THE GANG (DE-LITE)	12	THE RIDDLE NIK KERSHAW (MCA)
LOUISE HUMAN LEAGUE (VIRGIN)	13	THE ART GARFUNKEL ALBUM ART GARFUNKEL (CBS)
LET IT ALL BLOW DAZZ BAND (MOTOWN)	14	CINEMA ELAINE PAIGE (K-TEL)
DO THE CONGA BLACK LACE (FLAIR)	15	ELIMINATOR ZZ TOP (WARNER BROS)
ONE NIGHT IN BANGKOK MURRAY HEAD (RCA)	16	TWELVE GOLD BARS VOL 1 & 2 STATUS QUO (VERTIGO)
CARIBBEAN QUEEN BILLY OCEAN (JIVE)	17	GOLDEN DAYS FUREYS (K-TEL)
TREAT HER LIKE A LADY TEMPTATIONS (MOTOWN)	18	GREATEST HITS CHAS AND DAVE (ROCKNEY)
THE WILD BOYS DURAN DURAN (EMI)	19	THE 12" ALBUM HOWARD JONES (WEA)
ALL JOIN HANDS SLADE (RCA)	20	LOVE SONGS STEVIE WONDER (TELSTAR)

US

SINGLES	US	ALBUMS
OUT OF TOUCH HALL & OATES (RCA)	1	PURPLE RAIN PRINCE AND THE REVOLUTION (WARNER BROS)
WAKE ME UP BEFORE YOU GO GO WHAM! (COLUMBIA/CBS)	2	BORN IN THE USA BRUCE SPRINGSTEEN (COLUMBIA/CBS)
I FEEL FOR YOU CHAKA KHAN (WARNER BROS)	3	PRIVATE DANCER TINA TURNER (CAPITOL)
THE WILD BOYS DURAN DURAN (CAPITOL)	4	VOLUME ONE THE HONEYDRIPPERS (EX PARANZA)
ALL THROUGH THE NIGHT CYNDI LAUPER (PORTRAIT)	5	BIG BAM BOOM HALL & OATES (RCA)
NO MORE LONELY NIGHTS PAUL McCARTNEY (COLUMBIA/CBS)	6	WOMAN IN RED STEVIE WONDER (MOTOWN)
SEA OF LOVE HONEYDRIPPERS (ES PARANZA)	7	CAN'T SLOW DOWN LIONEL RICHIE (MOTOWN)
PENNY LOVER LIONEL RICHIE (MOTOWN)	8	SPORTS HUEY LEWIS AND THE NEWS (CHRYSALIS)
COOL IT NOW NEW EDITION (MCA)	9	ARENA DURAN DURAN (CAPITOL)
WE BELONG PAT BENATAR (CHRYSALIS)	10	LIKE A VIRGIN MADONNA (SIRE)
LIKE A VIRGIN MADONNA (SIRE)	11	SUDDENLY BILLY OCEAN (JIVE/ARISTA)
BETTER BE GOOD TO ME TINA TURNER (CAPITOL)	12	THE UNFORGETTABLE FIRE U2 (ISLAND)
I CAN'T HOLD BACK SURVIVOR (SCOTTI BROS)	13	SHE'S SO UNUSUAL CYNDI LAUPER (PORTRAIT)
STRUT SHEENA EASTON (EMI AMERICA)	14	I FEEL FOR YOU CHAKA KHAN (WARNER BROS)
PURPLE RAIN PRINCE AND THE REVOLUTION (WARNER BROS)	15	17 CHICAGO (FULL MOON/WARNER BROS)
VALOTTE JULIAN LENNON (ATLANTIC)	16	HEARTBEAT CITY THE CARS (ELEKTRA)
IT AIN'T ENOUGH COREY HART (EMI AMERICA)	17	1100 BEL AIR PLACE JULIO IGLESIAS (COLUMBIA/CBS)
WALKING ON A THIN LINE HUEY LEWIS AND THE NEWS (CHRYSALIS)	18	RECKLESS BRYAN ADAMS (A&M)
CARIBBEAN QUEEN BILLY OCEAN (JIVE)	19	VALOTTE JULIAN LENNON (ATLANTIC)
ALL I NEED JACK WAGNER (QWEST)	20	TROPICO PAT BENATAR (CHRYSALIS)

WEEK ENDING DECEMBER 15 1984

UK

SINGLES	UK	ALBUMS
DO THEY KNOW IT'S CHRISTMAS? BAND AID (MERCURY)	1	THE HITS ALBUM VARIOUS (CBS/WEA)
LAST CHRISTMAS WHAM! (EPIC)	2	NOW THAT'S WHAT I CALL MUSIC 4 VARIOUS (EMI/VIRGIN)
THE POWER OF LOVE FRANKIE GOES TO HOLLYWOOD (ZTT/ISLAND)	3	MAKE IT BIG WHAM! (EPIC)
WE ALL STAND TOGETHER PAUL McCARTNEY & FROG CHORUS (PARLOPHONE)	4	THE COLLECTION ULTRAVOX (CHRYSALIS)
LIKE A VIRGIN MADONNA (SIRE)	5	WELCOME TO THE PLEASUREDOME FRANKIE GOES TO HOLLYWOOD (ZTT/ISLAND)
I SHOULD HAVE KNOWN BETTER JIM DIAMOND (A&M)	6	ALF ALISON MOYET (CBS)
TEARDROPS SHAKIN' STEVENS (EPIC)	7	PARTY PARTY BLACK LACE (TELSTAR)
THE RIDDLE NIK KERSHAW (MCA)	8	GREATEST HITS SHAKIN' STEVENS (EPIC)
SEXCRIME (1984) EURYTHMICS (VIRGIN)	9	DIAMOND LIFE SADE (EPIC)
I WON'T RUN AWAY ALVIN STARDUST (CHRYSALIS)	10	ARENA DURAN DURAN (PARLOPHONE)
FRESH KOOL AND THE GANG (DE-LITE)	11	YESTERDAY ONCE MORE CARPENTERS (EMI)
ONE NIGHT IN BANGKOK MURRAY HEAD (RCA)	12	TWELVE GOLD BARS VOL 1 & 2 STATUS QUO (VERTIGO)
DO THE CONGA BLACK LACE (FLAIR)	13	GIVE MY REGARDS TO BROAD STREET PAUL McCARTNEY (PARLOPHONE)
I FEEL FOR YOU CHAKA KHAN (WARNER BROS)	14	THE RIDDLE NIK KERSHAW (MCA)
LOUISE HUMAN LEAGUE (VIRGIN)	15	THE ART GARFUNKEL ALBUM ART GARFUNKEL (CBS)
NELLIE THE ELEPHANT TOY DOLLS (VOLUME)	16	CINEMA ELAINE PAIGE (K-TEL)
EVERYTHING MUST CHANGE PAUL YOUNG (CBS)	17	ELIMINATOR ZZ TOP (WARNER BROS)
THE NEVER ENDING STORY LIMAHL (EMI)	18	GOLDEN DAYS FUREYS (K-TEL)
ROUND AND ROUND SPANDAU BALLET (CHRYSALIS)	19	GREATEST HITS CHAS AND DAVE (ROCKNEY)
LAY YOUR HANDS ON ME THOMPSON TWINS (ARISTA)	20	VERY BEST OF FOSTER AND ALLEN FOSTER AND ALLEN (RITZ)

US

SINGLES	US	ALBUMS
OUT OF TOUCH HALL & OATES (RCA)	1	PURPLE RAIN PRINCE AND THE REVOLUTION (WARNER BROS)
THE WILD BOYS DURAN DURAN (CAPITOL)	2	BORN IN THE USA BRUCE SPRINGSTEEN (COLUMBIA/CBS)
LIKE A VIRGIN MADONNA (SIRE)	3	PRIVATE DANCER TINA TURNER (CAPITOL)
I FEEL FOR YOU CHAKA KHAN (WARNER BROS)	4	LIKE A VIRGIN MADONNA (SIRE)
SEA OF LOVE HONEYDRIPPERS (ES PARANZA)	5	VOLUME ONE THE HONEYDRIPPERS (ES PARANZA)
NO MORE LONELY NIGHTS PAUL McCARTNEY (COLUMBIA/CBS)	6	BIG BAM BOOM HALL & OATES (RCA)
COOL IT NOW NEW EDITION (MCA)	7	ARENA DURAN DURAN (CAPITOL)
WAKE ME UP BEFORE YOU GO GO WHAM! (COLUMBIA/CBS)	8	WOMAN IN RED STEVIE WONDER (MOTOWN)
WE BELONG PAT BENATAR (CHRYSALIS)	9	CAN'T SLOW DOWN LIONEL RICHIE (MOTOWN)
ALL THROUGH THE NIGHT CYNDI LAUPER (PORTRAIT)	10	SPORTS HUEY LEWIS AND THE NEWS (CHRYSALIS)
PENNY LOVER LIONEL RICHIE (MOTOWN)	11	17 CHICAGO (FULL MOON/WARNER BROS)
VALOTTE JULIAN LENNON (ATLANTIC)	12	RECKLESS BRYAN ADAMS (A&M)
I CAN'T HOLD BACK SURVIVOR (SCOTTI BROS)	13	SHE'S SO UNUSUAL CYNDI LAUPER (PORTRAIT)
ALL I NEED JACK WAGNER (QWEST)	14	I FEEL FOR YOU CHAKA KHAN (WARNER BROS)
BORN IN THE USA BRUCE SPRINGSTEEN (COLUMBIA/CBS)	15	TROPICO PAT BENATAR (CHRYSALIS)
RUN TO YOU BRYAN ADAMS (A&M)	16	HEARTBEAT CITY THE CARS (ELEKTRA)
STRUT SHEENA EASTON (EMI AMERICA)	17	SUDDENLY BILLY OCEAN (JIVE/ARISTA)
WALKING ON A THIN LINE HUEY LEWIS AND THE NEWS (CHRYSALIS)	18	VALOTTE JULIAN LENNON (ATLANTIC)
DO WHAT YOU DO JERMAINE JACKSON (ARISTA)	19	THE UNFORGETTABLE FIRE U2 (ISLAND)
BETTER BE GOOD TO ME TINA TURNER (CAPITOL)	20	BREAK OUT POINTER SISTER (PLANET)

WEEK ENDING DECEMBER 22 1984

UK

SINGLES	UK	ALBUMS
DO THEY KNOW IT'S CHRISTMAS? BAND AID (MERCURY)	1	THE HITS ALBUM VARIOUS (CBS/WEA)
LAST CHRISTMAS WHAM! (EPIC)	2	NOW THAT'S WHAT I CALL MUSIC 4 VARIOUS (EMI/VIRGIN)
WE ALL STAND TOGETHER PAUL McCARTNEY & FROG CHORUS (PARLOPHONE)	3	MAKE IT BIG WHAM! (EPIC)
LIKE A VIRGIN MADONNA (SIRE)	4	PARTY PARTY BLACK LACE (FLAIR)
THE POWER OF LOVE FRANKIE GOES TO HOLLYWOOD (ZTT/ISLAND)	5	THE COLLECTION ULTRAVOX (CHRYSALIS)
NELLIE THE ELEPHANT TOY DOLLS (VOLUME)	6	WELCOME TO THE PLEASUREDOME FRANKIE GOES TO HOLLYWOOD (ZTT/ISLAND)
ANOTHER ROCK 'N' ROLL CHRISTMAS GARY GLITTER (ARISTA)	7	ALF ALISON MOYET (CBS)
THE RIDDLE NIK KERSHAW (MCA)	8	GREATEST HITS SHAKIN' STEVENS (EPIC)
EVERYTHING MUST CHANGE PAUL YOUNG (CBS)	9	DIAMOND LIFE SADE (EPIC)
DO THE CONGA BLACK LACE (FLAIR)	10	YESTERDAY ONCE MORE CARPENTERS (EMI)
TEARDROPS SHAKIN' STEVENS (EPIC)	11	THE RIDDLE NIK KERSHAW (MCA)
FRESH KOOL AND THE GANG (DE-LITE)	12	THE ART GARFUNKEL ALBUM ART GARFUNKEL (CBS)
SHOUT TEARS FOR FEARS (MERCURY)	13	TWELVE GOLD BARS VOL 1 & 2 STATUS QUO (VERTIGO)
ONE NIGHT IN BANGKOK MURRAY HEAD (RCA)	14	GIVE MY REGARDS TO BROAD STREET PAUL McCARTNEY (PARLOPHONE)
GHOSTBUSTERS RAY PARKER JR (ARISTA)	15	ARENA DURAN DURAN (PARLOPHONE)
I WON'T RUN AWAY ALVIN STARDUST (CHRYSALIS)	16	GREATEST HITS CHAS AND DAVE (ROCKNEY)
SEXCRIME (1984) EURYTHMICS (A&M)	17	CINEMA ELAINE PAIGE (K-TEL)
I SHOULD HAVE KNOWN BETTER JIM DIAMOND (A&M)	18	GOLDEN DAYS FUREYS (K-TEL)
ROUND AND ROUND SPANDAU BALLET (CHRYSALIS)	19	ELIMINATOR ZZ TOP (WARNER BROS)
LAY YOUR HANDS ON ME THOMPSON TWINS (ARISTA)	20	THE JOHN DENVER COLLECTION JOHN DENVER (TELSTAR)

US

SINGLES	US	ALBUMS
LIKE A VIRGIN MADONNA (SIRE)	1	PURPLE RAIN PRINCE AND THE REVOLUTION (WARNER BROS)
THE WILD BOYS DURAN DURAN (CAPITOL)	2	BORN IN THE USA BRUCE SPRINGSTEEN (COLUMBIA/CBS)
OUT OF TOUCH HALL & OATES (RCA)	3	LIKE A VIRGIN MADONNA (SIRE)
SEA OF LOVE THE HONEYDRIPPERS (ES PARANZA)	4	PRIVATE DANCER TINA TURNER (CAPITOL)
COOL IT NOW NEW EDITION (MCA)	5	ARENA DURAN DURAN (CAPITOL)
WE BELONG PAT BENATAR (CHRYSALIS)	6	BIG BAM BOOM HALL & OATES (RCA)
I FEEL FOR YOU CHAKA KHAN (WARNER BROS)	7	VOLUME ONE THE HONEYDRIPPERS (ES PARANZA)
NO MORE LONELY NIGHTS PAUL McCARTNEY (COLUMBIA/CBS)	8	WOMAN IN RED STEVIE WONDER (MOTOWN)
ALL I NEED JACK WAGNER (QWEST)	9	17 CHICAGO (FULL MOON/WARNER BROS)
VALOTTE JULIAN LENNON (ATLANTIC)	10	CAN'T SLOW DOWN LIONEL RICHIE (MOTOWN)
WAKE ME UP BEFORE YOU GO GO WHAM! (COLUMBIA/CBS)	11	SPORTS HUEY LEWIS AND THE NEWS (CHRYSALIS)
RUN TO YOU BRYAN ADAMS (A&M)	12	RECKLESS BRYAN ADAMS (A&M)
ALL THROUGH THE NIGHT CYNDI LAUPER (PORTRAIT)	13	SHE'S SO UNUSUAL CYNDI LAUPER (PORTRAIT)
BORN IN THE USA BRUCE SPRINGSTEEN (COLUMBIA/CBS)	14	TROPICO PAT BENATAR (CHRYSALIS)
YOU'RE THE INSPIRATION CHICAGO (FULL MOON/WARNER BROS)	15	LUSH LIFE LINDA RONSTADT (ASYLUM)
I CAN'T HOLD BACK SURVIVOR (SCOTTI BROS)	16	THE UNFORGETTABLE FIRE U2 (ISLAND)
DO WHAT YOU DO JERMAINE JACKSON (ARISTA)	17	I FEEL FOR YOU CHAKA KHAN (WARNER BROS)
PENNY LOVER LIONEL RICHIE (MOTOWN)	18	VALOTTE JULIAN LENNON (ATLANTIC)
UNDERSTANDING BOB SEGER/THE SILVER BULLET BAND (CAPITOL)	19	HEARTBEAT CITY THE CARS (ELEKTRA)
HELLO AGAIN THE CARS (ELEKTRA)	20	SUDDENLY BILLY OCEAN (JIVE/ARISTA)

WEEK ENDING DECEMBER 29 1984

UK

SINGLES	UK	ALBUMS
DO THEY KNOW IT'S CHRISTMAS? BAND AID (MERCURY)	1	THE HITS ALBUM VARIOUS (CBS/WEA)
LAST CHRISTMAS WHAM! (EPIC)	2	NOW THAT'S WHAT I CALL MUSIC 4 VARIOUS (EMI/VIRGIN)
WE ALL STAND TOGETHER PAUL McCARTNEY & FROG CHORUS (PARLOPHONE)	3	MAKE IT BIG WHAM! (EPIC)
NELLIE THE ELEPHANT TOY DOLLS (VOLUME)	4	PARTY PARTY BLACK LACE (TELSTAR)
LIKE A VIRGIN MADONNA (SIRE)	5	THE COLLECTION ULTRAVOX (CHRYSALIS)
THE POWER OF LOVE FRANKIE GOES TO HOLLYWOOD (ZTT/ISLAND)	6	WELCOME TO THE PLEASUREDOME FRANKIE GOES TO HOLLYWOOD (ZTT/ISLAND)
GHOSTBUSTERS RAY PARKER JR (ARISTA)	7	ALF ALISON MOYET (CBS)
ANOTHER ROCK 'N' ROLL CHRISTMAS GARY GLITTER (ARISTA)	8	GREATEST HITS SHAKIN' STEVENS (EPIC)
EVERYTHING MUST CHANGE PAUL YOUNG (CBS)	9	DIAMOND LIFE SADE (EPIC)
SHOUT TEARS FOR FEARS (MERCURY)	10	GREEN VELVET VARIOUS (TELSTAR)
I WANT TO KNOW WHAT LOVE IS FOREIGNER (ATLANTIC)	11	ARENA DURAN DURAN (PARLOPHONE)
THE RIDDLE NIK KERSHAW (MCA)	12	THE ART GARFUNKEL ALBUM ART GARFUNKEL (CBS)
FRESH KOOL AND THE GANG (DE-LITE)	13	YESTERDAY ONCE MORE CARPENTERS (EMI)
DO THE CONGA BLACK LACE (FLAIR)	14	PRIVATE DANCER TINA TURNER (CAPITOL)
ONE NIGHT IN BANGKOK MURRAY HEAD (RCA)	15	ELIMINATOR ZZ TOP (WARNER BROS)
TEARDROPS SHAKIN' STEVENS (EPIC)	16	TWELVE GOLD BARS VOL 1 & 2 STATUS QUO (VERTIGO)
SEXCRIME (1984) EURYTHMICS (VIRGIN)	17	THE RIDDLE NIK KERSHAW (K-TEL)
I WON'T RUN AWAY ALVIN STARDUST (CHRYSALIS)	18	CINEMA ELAINE PAIGE (K-TEL)
LAY YOUR HANDS ON ME THOMPSON TWINS (ARISTA)	19	GREATEST HITS CHAS AND DAVE (ROCKNEY)
I SHOULD HAVE KNOWN BETTER JIM DIAMOND (A&M)	20	GIVE MY REGARDS TO BROAD STREET PAUL McCARTNEY (PARLOPHONE)

SINGLES US ALBUMS

NO US CHARTS PUBLISHED

WEEK ENDING JANUARY 5 1985

UK

SINGLES		ALBUMS
DO THEY KNOW IT'S CHRISTMAS? BAND AID (MERCURY)	1	THE HITS ALBUM VARIOUS (CBS/WEA)
EVERYTHING SHE WANTS WHAM! (EPIC)	2	NOW THAT'S WHAT I CALL MUSIC 4 VARIOUS (EMI/VIRGIN)
WE ALL STAND TOGETHER PAUL McCARTNEY & FROG CHORUS (PARLOPHONE)	3	MAKE IT BIG WHAM! (EPIC)
LIKE A VIRGIN MADONNA (SIRE)	4	THE COLLECTION ULTRAVOX (CHRYSALIS)
NELLIE THE ELEPHANT TOY DOLLS (VOLUME)	5	WELCOME TO THE PLEASUREDOME FRANKIE GOES TO HOLLYWOOD (ZTT/ISLAND)
GHOSTBUSTERS RAY PARKER JR (ARISTA)	6	ALF ALSION MOYET (CBS)
THE POWER OF LOVE FRANKIE GOES TO HOLLYWOOD (ZTT/ISLAND)	7	PARTY PARTY BLACK LACE (TELSTAR)
SHOUT TEARS FOR FEARS (MERCURY)	8	DIAMOND LIFE SADE (EPIC)
EVERTHING MUST CHANGE PAUL YOUNG (CBS)	9	ARENA DURAN DURAN (PARLOPHONE)
I WANT TO KNOW WHAT LOVE IS FOREIGNER (ATLANTIC)	10	GREATEST HITS SHAKIN' STEVENS (EPIC)
THE RIDDLE NIK KERSHAW (MCA)	11	ELIMINATOR ZZ TOP (WARNER BROS)
ANOTHER ROCK 'N' ROLL CHRISTMAS GARY GLITTER (ARISTA)	12	THE RIDDLE NIK KERSHAW (MCA)
DO THE CONGA BLACK LACE (FLAIR)	13	PARADE SPANDAU BALLET (CHRYSALIS)
FRESH KOOL AND THE GANG (DE-LITE)	14	PRIVATE DANCER TINA TURNER (CAPITOL)
ONE NIGHT IN BANGKOK MURRAY HEAD (RCA)	15	YESTERDAY ONCE MORE CARPENTERS (EMI)
LAY YOUR HANDS ON ME THOMPSON TWINS (ARISTA)	16	GIVE MY REGARDS TO BROAD STREET PAUL McCARTNEY (PAROLOPHONE)
SEXCRIME (1984) EURYTHMICS (VIRGIN)	17	CAN'T SLOW DOWN LIONEL RICHIE (MOTOWN)
ROUND AND ROUND SPANDAU BALLET (CHRYSALIS)	18	THE 12" ALBUM HOWARD JONES (WEA)
I SHOULD HAVE KNOWN BETTER JIM DIAMOND (A&M)	19	TWELVE GOLD BARS VOL 1 & 2 STATUS QUO (VERTIGO)
TEARDROPS SHAKIN' STEVENS (EPIC)	20	LOVE SONGS VARIOUS (TELSTAR)

US

SINGLES		ALBUMS
LIKE A VIRGIN MADONNA (SIRE)	1	PURPLE RAIN PRINCE AND THE REVOLUTION (WARNER BROS)
THE WILD BOYS DURAN DURAN (CAPITOL)	2	LIKE A VIRGIN MADONNA (SIRE)
SEA OF LOVE THE HONEYDRIPPERS (ES PARANZA)	3	BORN IN THE USA BRUCE SPRINGSTEEN (COLUMBIA/CBS)
COOL IT NOW NEW EDITION (MCA)	4	ARENA DURAN DURAN (CAPITOL)
WE BELONG PAT BENATAR (CHRYSALIS)	5	PRIVATE DANCER TINA TURNER (CAPITOL)
ALL I NEED JACK WAGNER (QWEST)	6	VOLUME ONE THE HONEYDRIPPERS (ES PARANZA)
OUT OF TOUCH HALL & OATES (RCA)	7	BIG BAM BOOM HALL & OATES (RCA)
RUN TO YOU BRYAN ADAMS (A&M)	8	17 CHICAGO (FULL MOON/WARNER BROS)
YOU'RE THE INSPIRATION CHICAGO (FULL MOON/WARNER BROS)	9	SHE'S SO UNUSUAL CYNDI LAUPER (PORTRAIT)
VALOTTE JULIAN LENNON (ATLANTIC)	10	RECKLESS BRYAN ADAMS (A&M)
BORN IN THE USA BRUCE SPRINGSTEEN (COLUMBIA/CBS)	11	SPORTS HUEY LEWIS AND THE NEWS (CHRYSALIS)
I FEEL FOR YOU CHAKA KHAN (WARNER BROS)	12	CAN'T SLOW DOWN LIONEL RICHIE (MOTOWN)
DO WHAT YOU DO JERMAINE JACKSON (ARISTA)	13	LUSH LIFE LINDA RONSTADT (ASYLUM)
I WANT TO KNOW WHAT LOVE IS FOREIGNER (ATLANTIC)	14	TROPICO PAT BENATAR (CHRYSALIS)
NO MORE LONELY NIGHTS PAUL McCARTNEY (COLUMBIA/CBS)	15	WOMAN IN RED STEVIE WONDER (MOTOWN)
EASY LOVER PHILIP BAILEY (COLUMBIA/CBS)	16	THE UNFORGETTABLE FIRE U2 (ISLAND)
UNDERSTANDING BOB SEGER/THE SILVER BULLET BAND (CAPITOL)	17	NEW EDITION NEW EDITION (MCA)
JAMIE RAY PARKER JR (ARISTA)	18	VALOTTE JULIAN LENNON (ATLANTIC)
THE BOYS OF SUMMER DON HENLEY (GEFFEN)	19	MAKE IT BIG WHAM! (COLUMBIA/CBS)
WAKE ME UP BEFORE YOU GO GO WHAM! (COLUMBIA/CBS)	20	SUDDENLY BILLY OCEAN (JIVE/ARISTA)

WEEK ENDING JANUARY 12 1985

UK

SINGLES		ALBUMS
DO THEY KNOW IT'S CHRISTMAS? BAND AID (MERCURY)	1	THE HITS ALBUM VARIOUS (CBS/WEA)
EVERYTHING SHE WANTS WHAM! (EPIC)	2	NOW THAT'S WHAT I CALL MUSIC 4 VARIOUS (EMI/VIRGIN)
LIKE A VIRGIN MADONNA (SIRE)	3	ALF ALISON MOYET (CBS)
I WANT TO KNOW WHAT LOVE IS FOREIGNER (ATLANTIC)	4	MAKE IT BIG WHAM! (EPIC)
WE ALL STAND TOGETHER PAUL McCARTNEY & FROG CHORUS (PARLOPHONE)	5	THE COLLECTION ULTRAVOX (CHRYSALIS)
NELLIE THE ELEPHANT TOY DOLLS (VOLUME)	6	WELCOME TO THE PLEASUREDOME FRANKIE GOES TO HOLLYWOOD (ZTT/ISLAND)
SHOUT TEARS FOR FEARS (MERCURY)	7	ARENA DURAN DURAN (EMI)
GHOSTBUSTERS RAY PARKER JR (ARISTA)	8	DIAMOND LIFE SADE (EPIC)
EVERYTHING MUST CHANGE PAUL YOUNG (CBS)	9	PARTY PARTY BLACK LACE (TELSTAR)
THE POWER OF LOVE FRANKIE GOES TO HOLLYWOOD (ZTT/ISLAND)	10	ELIMINATOR ZZ TOP (WARNER BROS)
STEP OFF GRANDMASTER MELLE MEL (SUGARHILL)	11	PRIVATE DANCER TINA TURNER (CAPITOL)
FRESH KOOL AND THE GANG (DE-LITE	12	THE RIDDLE NIK KERSHAW (MCA)
LAY YOUR HANDS ON ME THOMPSON TWINS (ARISTA)	13	PARADE SPANDAU BALLET (CHRYSALIS)
THE RIDDLE NIK KERSHAW (MCA)	14	GREATEST HITS SHAKIN' STEVENS (EPIC)
POLICE OFFICER SMILEY CULTURE (FASHION)	15	THE 12" ALBUM HOWARD JONES (WEA)
ONE NIGHT IN BANGKOK MURRAY HEAD (RCA)	16	THE AGE OF CONSENT BRONSKI BEAT (FORBIDDEN FRUIT)
SAN DAMIANO (HEART AND SOUL) SAL SOLO (MCA)	17	AGENT PROVOCATEUR FOREIGNER (ATLANTIC)
DO THE CONGA BLACK LACE (FLAIR)	18	CAN'T SLOW DOWN LIONEL RICHIE (MOTOWN)
IT AIN'T NECESSARILY SO BRONSKI BEAT (FORBIDDEN FRUIT)	19	THE UNFORGETTABLE FIRE U2 (ISLAND)
ROUND AND ROUND SPANDAU BALLET (CHRYSALIS)	20	STEELTOWN BIG COUNTRY (MERCURY)

US

SINGLES		ALBUMS
LIKE A VIRGIN MADONNA (SIRE)	1	PURPLE RAIN PRINCE AND THE REVOLUTION (WARNER BROS)
ALL I NEED JACK WAGNER (QWEST)	2	BORN IN THE USA BRUCE SPRINGSTEEN (COLUMBIA/CBS)
THE WILD BOYS DURAN DURAN (CAPITOL)	3	LIKE A VIRGIN MADONNA (SIRE)
SEA OF LOVE THE HONEYDRIPPERS (ES PARANZA)	4	ARENA DURAN DURAN (CAPITOL)
WE BELONG PAT BENATAR (CHRYSALIS)	5	PRIVATE DANCER TINA TURNER (CAPITOL)
YOU'RE THE INSPIRATION CHICAGO (FULL MOON/WARNER BROS)	6	VOLUME ONE THE HONEYDRIPPERS (ES PARANZA)
RUN TO YOU BRYAN ADAMS (A&M)	7	17 CHICAGO (FULL MOON/WARNER BROS)
COOL IT NOW NEW EDITION (MCA)	8	BIG BAM BOOM HALL & OATES (RCA)
VALOTTE JULIAN LENNON (ATLANTIC)	9	SHE'S SO UNUSUAL CYNDI LAUPER (PORTRAIT)
BORN IN THE USA BRUCE SPRINGSTEEN (COLUMBIA/CBS)	10	RECKLESS BRYAN ADAMS (A&M)
I WANT TO KNOW WHAT LOVE IS FOREIGNER (ATLANTIC)	11	SPORTS HUEY LEWIS AND THE NEWS (CHRYSALIS)
OUT OF REACH HALL & OATES (RCA)	12	CAN'T SLOW DOWN LIONEL RICHIE (MOTOWN)
EASY LOVER PHILIP BAILEY (COLUMBIA/CBS)	13	LUSH LIFE LINDA RONSTADT (ASYLUM)
DO WHAT YOU DO JERMAINE JACKSON (ARISTA)	14	TROPICO PAT BENATAR (CHRYSALIS)
WAKE ME UP BEFORE YOU GO GO WHAM! (COLUMBIA/CBS)	15	NEW EDITION NEW EDITION (MCA)
THE BOYS OF SUMMER DON HENLEY (GEFFEN)	16	THE UNFORGETTABLE FIRE U2 (ISLAND)
UNDERSTANDING BOB SEGER/THE SILVER BULLET BAND (CAPITOL)	17	MAKE IT BIG WHAM! (COLUMBIA/CBS)
JAMIE RAY PARKER JR (ARISTA)	18	VALOTTE JULIAN LENNON (ATLANTIC)
I WOULD DIE 4 U PRINCE AND THE REVOLUTION (WARNER BROS)	19	WOMAN IN RED STEVIE WONDER (MOTOWN)
DO THEY KNOW IT'S CHRISTMAS BAND AID (COLUMBIA/CBS)	20	SUDDENLY BILLY OCEAN (JIVE/ARISTA)

WEEK ENDING JANUARY 19 1985

UK

SINGLES		ALBUMS
I WANT TO KNOW WHAT LOVE IS FOREIGNER (ATLANTIC)	1	ALF ALISON MOYET (CBS)
DO THEY KNOW IT'S CHRISTMAS? BAND AID (FEED THE WORLD)	2	THE COLLECTION ULTRAVOX (CHRYSALIS)
EVERYTHING SHE WANTS WHAM! (EPIC)	3	MAKE IT BIG WHAM! (EPIC)
LIKE A VIRGIN MADONNA (SIRE)	4	THE HITS ALBUM/THE HITS TAPE VARIOUS (CBS/WEA)
SHOUT TEARS FOR FEARS (MERCURY)	5	AGENT PROVOCATEUR FOREIGNER (ATLANTIC)
I KNOW HIM SO WELL ELAINE PAIGE/BARBARA DICKSON (RCA)	6	NOW THAT'S WHAT I CALL MUSIC 4 VARIOUS (EMI/VIRGIN)
GHOSTBUSTERS RAY PARKER JR (ARISTA)	7	ELIMINATOR ZZ TOP (WARNER BROS)
STEP OFF GRANDMASTER MELLE MEL (SUGARHILL)	8	WELCOME TO THE PLEASUREDOME FRANKIE GOES TO HOLLYWOOD (ZTT/ISLAND)
EVERYTHING MUST CHANGE PAUL YOUNG (CBS)	9	THE AGE OF CONSENT BRONSKI BEAT (FORBIDDEN FRUIT)
SINCE YESTERDAY STRAWBERRY SWITCHBLADE (KOROVA)	10	DIAMOND LIFE SADE (EPIC)
WE ALL STAND TOGETHER PAUL McCARTNEY & FROG CHORUS (PARLOPHONE)	11	ARENA DURAN DURAN (EMI)
POLICE OFFICER SMILEY CULTURE (FASHION)	12	PRIVATE DANCER TINA TURNER (CAPITOL)
1999/LITTLE RED CORVETTE PRINCE (WARNER BROS)	13	LIKE A VIRGIN MADONNA (SIRE)
NELLIE THE ELEPHANT TOY DOLLS (VOLUME)	14	PARADE SPANDAU BALLET (CHRYSALIS)
SAN DAMIANO (HEART AND SOUL) SAL SOLO (MCA)	15	BORN IN THE USA BRUCE SPRINGSTEEN (CBS)
IT AIN'T NECESSARILY SO BRONSKI BEAT (FORBIDDEN FRUIT)	16	PARTY PARTY BLACK LACE (TELSTAR)
FRIENDS AMII STEWART (RCA)	17	THE 12" ALBUM HOWARD JONES (WEA)
ATMOSPHERE RUSS ABOTT (SPIRIT)	18	THE BARBARA DICKSON SONGBOOK BARBARA DICKSON (K-TEL)
SAY YEAH LIMIT (PORTRAIT)	19	THE UNFORGETTABLE FIRE U2 (ISLAND)
THE POWER OF LOVE FRANKIE GOES TO HOLLYWOOD (ZTT/ISLAND)	20	VERY BEST OF CHRIS DE BURGH CHRIS DE BURGH (TELSTAR)

US

SINGLES		ALBUMS
LIKE A VIRGIN MADONNA (SIRE)	1	BORN IN THE USA BRUCE SPRINGSTEEN (COLUMBIA/CBS)
ALL I NEED JACK WAGNER (QWEST)	2	PURPLE RAIN PRINCE AND THE REVOLUTION (WARNER BROS)
YOU'RE THE INSPIRATION CHICAGO (FULL MOON/WARNER BROS)	3	LIKE A VIRGIN MADONNA (SIRE)
I WANT TO KNOW WHAT LOVE IS FOREIGNER (ATLANTIC)	4	ARENA DURAN DURAN (CAPITOL)
EASY LOVER PHILIP BAILEY (COLUMBIA/CBS)	5	17 CHICAGO (FULL MOON/WARNER BROS)
RUN TO YOU BRYAN ADAMS (A&M)	6	PRIVATE DANCER TINA TURNER (CAPITOL)
THE WILD BOYS DURAN DURAN (CAPITOL)	7	BIG BAM BOOM HALL & OATES (RCA)
WE BELONG PAT BENATAR (CHRYSALIS)	8	RECKLESS BRYAN ADAMS (A&M)
BORN IN THE USA BRUCE SPRINGSTEEN (COLUMBIA/CBS)	9	VOLUME ONE THE HONEYDRIPPERS (ES PARANZA)
CARELESS WHISPER GEORGE MICHAEL (COLUMBIA/CBS)	10	SHE'S SO UNUSUAL CYNDI LAUPER (PORTRAIT)
SEA OF LOVE THE HONEYDRIPPERS (ES PARANZA)	11	NEW EDITION NEW EDITION (MCA)
THE BOYS OF SUMMER DON HENLEY (GEFFEN)	12	SPORTS HUEY LEWIS AND THE NEWS (CHRYSALIS)
DO THEY KNOW IT'S CHRISTMAS? BAND AID (COLUMBIA/CBS)	13	MAKE IT BIG WHAM! (COLUMBIA/CBS)
I WOULD DIE 4 U PRINCE AND THE REVOLUTION (WARNER BROS)	14	AGENT PROVOCATEUR FOREIGNER (ATLANTIC)
COOL IT NOW NEW EDITION (MCA)	15	LUSH LIFE LINDA RONSTADT (ASYLUM)
LOVER BOY BILLY OCEAN (JIVE/ARISTA)	16	CAN'T SLOW DOWN LIONEL RICHIE (MOTOWN)
JAMIE RAY PARKER JR (ARISTA)	17	SUDDENLY BILLY OCEAN (JIVE/ARISTA)
DO WHAT YOU DO JERMAINE JACKSON (ARISTA)	18	TROPICO PAT BENETAR (CHRYSALIS)
VALOTTE JULIAN LENNON (ATLANTIC)	19	WOMAN IN RED STEVIE WONDER (MOTOWN)
NEUTRON DANCE POINTER SISTERS (PLANET)	20	VALOTTE JULIAN LENNON (ATLANTIC)

WEEK ENDING JANUARY 26 1985

UK

SINGLES		ALBUMS
I WANT TO KNOW WHAT LOVE IS FOREIGNER (ATLANTIC)	1	AGENT PROVOCATEUR FOREIGNER (ATLANTIC)
1999/LITTLE RED CORVETTE PRINCE (WARNER BROS)	2	ALF ALISON MOYET (CBS)
I KNOW HIM SO WELL ELAINE PAIGE/BARBARA DICKSON (RCA)	3	ELIMINATOR ZZ TOP (WARNER BROS)
SHOUT TEARS FOR FEARS (MERCURY)	4	THE COLLECTION ULTRAVOX (CHRYSALIS)
SINCE YESTERDAY STRAWBERRY SWITCHBLADE (KOROVA)	5	MAKE IT BIG WHAM! (EPIC)
LOVE AND PRIDE KING (CBS)	6	THE HITS ALBUM/THE HITS TAPE VARIOUS (CBS/WEA)
LIKE A VIRGIN MADONNA (SIRE)	7	HITS OUT OF HELL MEAT LOAF (EPIC)
EVERYTHING SHE WANTS WHAM! (EPIC)	8	NOW THAT'S WHAT I CALL MUSIC 4 VARIOUS (EMI/VIRGIN)
DO THEY KNOW IT'S CHRISTMAS? BAND AID (FEED THE WORLD)	9	THE AGE OF CONSENT BRONSKI BEAT (FORBIDDEN FRUIT)
ATMOSPHERE RUSS ABBOTT (SPIRIT)	10	BORN IN THE USA BRUCE SPRINGSTEEN (CBS)
STEP OFF GRANDMASTER MELLE MEL (SUGARHILL)	11	VERY BEST OF CHRIS DE BURGH CHRIS DE BURGH (TELSTAR)
FRIENDS AMII STEWART (RCA)	12	WELCOME TO THE PLEASUREDOME FRANKIE GOEST TO HOLLYWOOD (ZTT/ISLAND)
SOLID ASHFORD AND SIMPSON (CAPITOL)	13	20/20 GEORGE BENSON (WARNER BROS)
EVERYTHING MUST CHANGE PAUL YOUNG (CBS)	14	ARENA DURAN DURAN (EMI)
POLICE OFFICER SMILEY CULTURE (FASHION)	15	DIAMOND LIFE SADE (EPIC)
GHOSTBUSTERS RAY PARKER JR (ARISTA)	16	THE BARBARA DICKSON SONGBOOK BARBARA DICKSON (K-TEL)
SAY YEAH LIMIT (PORTRAIT)	17	LIKE A VIRGIN MADONNA (SIRE)
THIS IS MY NIGHT CHAKA KHAN (WARNER BROS)	18	PARADE SPANDAU BALLET (CHRYSALIS)
SAN DAMIANO (HEART AND SOUL) SAL SOLO (MCA)	19	PRIVATE DANCER TINA TURNER (CAPITOL)
DANCING IN THE DARK BRUCE SPRINGSTEEN (CBS)	20	THE 12" ALBUM HOWARD JONES (WEA)

US

SINGLES		ALBUMS
LIKE A VIRGIN MADONNA (SIRE)	1	BORN IN THE USA BRUCE SPRINGSTEEN (COLUMBIA/CBS)
I WANT TO KNOW WHAT LOVE IS FOREIGNER (ATLANTIC)	2	LIKE A VIRGIN MADONNA (SIRE)
YOU'RE THE INSPIRATION CHICAGO (FULL MOON/WARNER BROS)	3	PURPLE RAIN PRINCE AND THE REVOLUTION (WARNER BROS)
EASY LOVER PHILIP BAILEY (COLUMBIA/CBS)	4	17 CHICAGO (FULL MOON/WARNER BROS)
CARELESS WHISPER GEORGE MICHAEL (COLUMBIA/CBS)	5	ARENA DURAN DURAN (CAPITOL)
ALL I NEED JACK WAGNER (QWEST)	6	RECKLESS BRYN ADAMS (A&M)
RUN TO YOU BRYAN ADAMS (A&M)	7	BIG BAM BOOM HALL & OATES (RCA)
THE BOYS OF SUMMER DON HENLEY (GEFFEN)	8	PRIVATE DANCER TINA TURNER (CAPITOL)
LOVER BOY BILLY OCEAN (JIVE/ARISTA)	9	AGENT PROVOCATEUR FOREIGNER (ATLANTIC)
I WOULD DIE 4 U PRINCE AND THE REVOLUTION (WARNER BROS)	10	MAKE IT BIG WHAM! (COLUMBIA/CBS)
BORN IN THE USA BRUCE SPRINGSTEEN (WARNER BROS)	11	NEW EDITION NEW EDITION (MCA)
METHOD OF MODERN LOVE HALL & OATES (RCA)	12	SHE'S SO UNUSUAL CYNDI LAUPER (PORTRAIT)
NEUTRON DANCE POINTER SISTERS (PLANET)	13	VOLUME ONE THE HONEYDRIPPERS (ES PARANZA)
JAMIE RAY PARKER JR (ARISTA)	14	SPORTS HUEY LEWIS AND THE NEWS (CHRYSALIS)
THE WILD BOYS DURAN DURAN (CAPITOL)	15	SUDDENLY BILLY OCEAN (JIVE/ARISTA)
WE BELONG PAT BENATAR (CHRYSALIS)	16	CAN'T SLOW DOWN LIONEL RICHIE (MOTOWN)
DO THEY KNOW IT'S CHRISTMAS? BAND AID (COLUMBIA/CBS)	17	WOMAN IN RED STEVIE WONDER (MOTOWN)
COOL IT NOW NEW EDITION (MCA)	18	BREAK OUT POINTER SISTERS (PLANET)
DO WHAT YOU DO JERMAINE JACKSON (ARISTA)	19	TROPICO PAT BENATAR (CHRYSALIS)
LOVE LIGHT IN FLIGHT STEVIE WONDER (MOTOWN)	20	A PRIVATE HEAVEN SHEENA EASTON (EMI AMERICA)

WEEK ENDING FEBRUARY 2 1985

UK

SINGLES		ALBUMS
I WANT TO KNOW WHAT LOVE IS FOREIGNER (ATLANTIC)	1	AGENT PROVOCATEUR FOREIGNER (ATLANTIC)
I KNOW HIM SO WELL ELAINE PAIGE/BARBARA DICKSON (RCA)	2	ALF ALISON MOYET (CBS)
LITTLE RED CORVETTE/1999 PRINCE (WARNER BROS)	3	HITS OUT OF HELL MEAT LOAF (EPIC)
LOVE AND PRIDE KING (CBS)	4	BORN IN THE USA BRUCE SPRINGSTEEN (CBS)
SHOUT TEARS FOR FEARS (MERCURY)	5	THE AGE OF CONSENT BRONSKI BEAT (FORBIDDEN FRUIT)
SOLID ASHFORD AND SIMPSON (CAPITOL)	6	VERY BEST OF CHRIS DE BURGH CHRIS DE BURGH (TELSTAR)
SINCE YESTERDAY STRAWBERRY SWITCHBLADE (KOROVA)	7	ELIMINATOR ZZ TOP (WARNER BROS)
ATMOSPHERE RUSS ABBOTT (SPIRIT)	8	THE COLLECTION ULTRAVOX (CHRYSALIS)
LIKE A VIRGIN MADONNA (SIRE)	9	MAKE IT BIG WHAM! (EPIC)
DANCING IN THE DARK BRUCE SPRINGSTEEN (CBS)	10	THE BARBARA DICKSON SONGBOOK BARBARA DICKSON (K-TEL)
EVERYTHING SHE WANTS WHAM! (EPIC)	11	20/20 GEORGE BENSON (WARNER BROS)
YAH MO BE THERE JAMES INGRAM/MICHAEL McDONALD (QWEST)	12	THE HITS ALBUM/THE HITS TAPE VARIOUS (CBS/WEA)
FRIENDS AMII STEWART (RCA)	13	WELCOME TO THE PLEASUREDOME FRANKIE GOES TO HOLLYWOOD (ZTT/ISLAND)
THIS IS MY NIGHT CHAKA KHAN (WARNER BROS)	14	DIAMOND LIFE SADE (EPIC)
STEP OFF GRANDMASTER MELLE MEL (SUGARHILL)	15	NOW THAT'S WHAT I CALL MUSIC 4 VARIOUS (EMI/VIRGIN)
LOVERBOY BILLY OCEAN (JIVE)	16	ARENA DURAN DURAN (PARLOPHONE)
DO THEY KNOW IT'S CHRISTMAS? BAND AID (FEED THE WORLD)	17	CAN'T SLOW DOWN LIONEL RICHIE (MOTOWN)
RUN TO YOU BRYAN ADAMS (A&M)	18	LIKE A VIRGIN MADONNA (SIRE)
SUSSUDIO PHIL COLLINS (VIRGIN)	19	THE 12" ALBUM HOWARD JONES (WEA)
GHOSTBUSTERS RAY PARKER JR (ARISTA)	20	PRIVATE DANCER TINA TURNER (CAPITOL)

US

SINGLES		ALBUMS
I WANT TO KNOW WHAT LOVE IS FOREIGNER (ATLANTIC)	1	BORN IN USA BRUCE SPRINGSTEEN (COLUMBIA/CBS)
EASY LOVER PHILIP BAILEY (COLUMBIA/CBS)	2	LIKE A VIRGIN MADONNA (SIRE)
CARELESS WHISPER GEORGE MICHAEL (COLUMBIA/CBS)	3	PURPLE RAIN PRINCE AND THE REVOLUTION (WARNER BROS)
YOU'RE THE INSPIRATION CHICAGO (FULL MOON/WARNER BROS)	4	AGENT PROVOCATEUR FOREIGNER (ATLANTIC)
LOVER BOY BILLY OCEAN (JIVE/ARISTA)	5	17 CHICAGO (FULL MOON/WARNER BROS)
THE BOYS OF SUMMER DON HENLEY (GEFFEN)	6	MAKE IT BIG WHAM! (COLUMBIA/CBS)
LIKE A VIRGIN MADONNA (SIRE)	7	RECKLESS BRYAN ADAMS (A&M)
I WOULD DIE 4 U PRINCE AND THE REVOLUTION (WARNER BROS)	8	PRIVATE DANCER TINA TURNER (CAPITOL)
METHOD OF MODERN LOVE HALL & OATES (RCA)	9	BIG BAM BOOM HALL & OATES (RCA)
NEUTRON DANCE POINTER SISTERS (PLANET)	10	NEW EDITION NEW EDITION (MCA)
ALL I NEED JACK WAGNER (QWEST)	11	ARENA DURAN DURAN (CAPITOL)
RUN TO YOU BRYAN ADAMS (A&M)	12	SHE'S SO UNUSUAL CYNDI LAUPER (PORTRAIT)
THE HEAT IS ON GLENN FREY (MCA)	13	SUDDENLY BILLY OCEAN (JIVE/ARISTA)
SOLID ASHFORD AND SIMPSON (CAPITOL)	14	CAN'T SLOW DOWN LIONEL RICHIE (MOTOWN)
CALL TO THE HEART GUIFFRIA (CAMEL/MCA)	15	A PRIVATE HEAVEN SHEENA EASTON (EMI AMERICA)
JAMIE RAY PARKER JR (ARISTA)	16	BUILDING THE PERFECT BEAST DON HENLEY (GEFFEN)
LOVE LIGHT IN FLIGHT STEVIE WONDER (MOTOWN)	17	VOLUME ONE THE HONEYDRIPPERS (ES PARANZA)
OPERATOR MIDNIGHT STAR (SOLAR)	18	BREAK OUT POINTER SISTERS (PLANET)
SUGAR WALLS SHEENA EASTON (EMI AMERICA)	19	PERFECT STRANGERS DEEP PURPLE (MERCURY)
FOOLISH HEART STEVE PERRY (COLUMBIA/CBS)	20	SPORTS HUEY LEWIS AND THE NEWS (CHRYSALIS)

WEEK ENDING FEBRUARY 9 1985

UK

SINGLES		ALBUMS
I KNOW HIM SO WELL ELAINE PAIGE/BARBARA DICKSON (RCA)	1	AGENT PROVOCATEUR FOREIGNER (ATLANTIC)
LOVE AND PRIDE KING (CBS)	2	HITS OUT OF HELL MEAT LOAF (EPIC)
I WANT TO KNOW WHAT LOVE IS FOREIGNER (ATLANTIC)	3	BORN IN THE USA BRUCE SPRINGSTEEN (CBS)
SOLID ASHFORD AND SIMPSON (CAPITOL)	4	ALF ALISON MOYET (CBS)
LITTLE RED CORVETTE/1999 PRINCE (WARNER BROS)	5	THE BARBARA DICKSON SONGBOOK BARBARA DICKSON (K-TEL)
DANCING IN THE DARK BRUCE SPRINGSTEEN (CBS)	6	ELIMINATOR ZZ TOP (WARNER BROS)
ATMOSPHERE RUSS ABBOTT (SPIRIT)	7	MAKE IT BIG WHAM! (EPIC)
SHOUT TEARS FOR FEARS (MERCURY)	8	THE AGE OF CONSENT BRONSKI BEAT (FORBIDDEN FRUIT)
SINCE YESTERDAY STRAWBERRY SWITCHBLADE (CBS)	9	20/20 GEORGE BENSON (WARNER BROS)
CLOSE (TO THE EDIT) ART OF NOISE (ZTT/ISLAND)	10	VERY BEST OF CHRIS DE BURGH CHRIS DE BURGH (TELSTAR)
RUN TO YOU BRYAN ADAMS (A&M)	11	THE COLLECTION ULTRAVOX (CHRYSALIS)
SUSSUDIO PHIL COLLINS (VIRGIN)	12	THE HITS ALBUM/THE HITS TAPE VARIOUS (CBS/WEA)
A NEW ENGLAND KIRSTY MacCOLL (STIFF)	13	STEPS IN TIME KING (CBS)
YAH MO B THERE JAMES INGRAM/MICHAEL McDONALD (QWEST)	14	DIAMOND LIFE SADE (EPIC)
LIKE A VIRGIN MADONNA (SIRE)	15	NOW THAT'S WHAT I CALL MUSIC 4 VARIOUS (EMI/VIRGIN)
LOVER BOY BILLY OCEAN (JIVE)	16	WELCOME TO THE PLEASUREDOME FRANKIE GOES TO HOLLYWOOD (ZTT/ISLAND)
THINKING OF YOU COLOURFIELD (CHRYSALIS)	17	THE 12" ALBUM HOWARD JONES (WEA)
THINGS CAN ONLY GET BETTER HOWARD JONES (WEA)	18	LIKE A VIRGIN MADONNA (SIRE)
NIGHTSHIFT COMMODORES (MOTOWN)	19	CAN'T SLOW DOWN LIONEL RICHIE (MOTOWN)
FRIENDS AMII STEWART (RCA)	20	ARENA DURAN DURAN (PARLOPHONE)

US

SINGLES		ALBUMS
I WANT TO KNOW WHAT LOVE IS FOREIGNER (ATLANTIC)	1	LIKE A VIRGIN MADONNA (SIRE)
EASY LOVER PHILIP BAILEY (COLUMBIA/CBS)	2	BORN IN THE USA BRUCE SPRINGSTEEN (COLUMBIA/CBS)
CARELESS WHISPER GEORGE MICHAEL (COLUMBIA/CBS)	3	MAKE IT BIG WHAM! (COLUMBIA/CBS)
LOVER BOY BILLY OCEAN (JIVE/ARISTA)	4	AGENT PROVOCATEUR FOREIGNER (ATLANTIC)
THE BOYS OF SUMMER DON HENLEY (GEFFEN)	5	PURPLE RAIN PRINCE AND THE REVOLUTION (WARNER BROS)
YOU'RE THE INSPIRATION CHICAGO (FULL MOON/WARNER BROS)	6	17 CHICAGO (FULL MOON/WARNER BROS)
METHOD OF MODERN LOVE HALL & OATES (RCA)	7	NEW EDITION NEW EDITION (MCA)
NEUTRON DANCE POINTER SISTERS (PLANET)	8	RECKLESS BRYAN ADAMS (A&M)
LIKE A VIRGIN MADONNA (SIRE)	9	PRIVATE DANCER TINA TURNER (CAPITOL)
I WOULD DIE 4 U PRINCE AND THE REVOLUTION (WARNER BROS)	10	CENTERFIELD JOHN FOGERTY (WARNER BROS)
THE HEAT IS ON GLENN FREY (MCA)	11	BIG BAM BOOM HALL & OATES (RCA)
SOLID ASHFORD AND SIMPSON (CAPITOL)	12	SUDDENLY BILLY OCEAN (JIVE/ARISTA)
CALIFORNIA GIRLS DAVID LEE ROTH (WARNER BROS)	13	SHE'S SO UNUSUAL CYNDI LAUPER (PORTRAIT)
SUGAR WALLS SHEENA EASTON (EMI AMERICA)	14	BUILDING THE PERFECT BEAST DON HENLEY (GEFFEN)
CALL TO THE HEART GUIFFRIA (CAMEL/MCA)	15	A PRIVATE HEAVEN SHEENA EASTON (EMI AMERICA)
CAN'T FIGHT THIS FEELING REO SPEEDWAGON (EPIC)	16	ARENA DURAN DURAN (CAPITOL)
THE OLD MAN DOWN THE ROAD JOHN FOGERTY (WARNER BROTHERS)	17	PERFECT STRANGERS DEEP PURPLE (MERCURY)
OPERATOR MIDNIGHT STAR (SOLAR)	18	VOLUME ONE THE HONEYDRIPPERS (ES PARANZA)
FOOLISH HEART STEVE PERRY (COLUMBIA/CBS)	19	CAN'T SLOW DOWN LIONEL RICHIE (MOTOWN)
MISLED KOOL AND THE GANG (DE-LITE)	20	BEVERLY HILLS COP SOUNDTRACK (MCA)

WEEK ENDING FEBRUARY 16 1985

UK

SINGLES		ALBUMS
I KNOW HIM SO WELL ELAINE PAIGE/BARBARA DICKSON (RCA)	1	BORN IN THE USA BRUCE SPRINGSTEEN (CBS)
LOVE AND PRIDE KING (CBS)	2	ALF ALISON MOYET (CBS)
SOLID ASHFORD AND SIMPSON (CAPITOL)	3	AGENT PROVOCATEUR FOREIGNER (ATLANTIC)
DANCING IN THE DARK BRUCE SPRINGSTEEN (CBS)	4	HITS OUT OF HELL MEAT LOAF (EPIC)
I WANT TO KNOW WHAT LOVE IS FOREIGNER (ATLANTIC)	5	THE BARBARA DICKSON SONGBOOK BARBARA DICKSON (K-TEL)
LITTLE RED CORVETTE/1999 PRINCE (WARNER BROS)	6	STEPS IN TIME KING (CBS)
THINGS CAN ONLY GET BETTER HOWARD JONES (WEA)	7	ELIMINATOR ZZ TOP (WARNER BROS)
ATMOSPHERE RUSS ABBOTT (SPIRIT)	8	VERY BEST OF CHRIS DE BURGH CHRIS DE BURGH (TELSTAR)
CLOSE (TO THE EDIT) ART OF NOISE (ZTT/ISLAND)	9	THE AGE OF CONSENT BRONSKI BEAT (FORBIDDEN FRUIT)
A NEW ENGLAND KIRSTY MacCOLL (STIFF)	10	MAKE IT BIG WHAM! (EPIC)
RUN TO YOU BRYAN ADAMS (A&M)	11	CHESS VAROUS (RCA)
SUSSUDIO PHIL COLLINS (VIRGIN)	12	THE COLLECTION ULTRAVOX (CHRYSALIS)
THINKING OF YOU COLOURFIELD (CHRYSALIS)	13	20/20 GEORGE BENSON (WARNER BROS)
THIS IS NOT AMERICA DAVID BOWIE (EMI AMERICA)	14	SECRETS, SECRETS JOAN ARMATRADING (A&M)
LOVER BOY BILLY OCEAN (JIVE)	15	DIAMOND LIFE SADE (EPIC)
SHOUT TEARS FOR FEARS (MERCURY)	16	THE HITS ALBUM/THE HITS TAPE VARIOUS (CBS/WEA)
NIGHTSHIFT COMMODORES (MOTOWN)	17	NOW THAT'S WHAT I CALL MUSIC 4 VARIOUS (EMI/VIRGIN)
SINCE YESTERDAY STRAWBERRY SWITCHBLADE (KOROVA)	18	THE 12" ALBUM HOWARD JONES (WEA)
YOU SPIN ME ROUND DEAD OR ALIVE (EPIC)	19	HATFUL OF HOLLOW SMITHS (ROUGH TRADE)
YOU'RE THE INSPIRATION CHICAGO (FULL MOON)	20	CAN'T SLOW DOWN LIONEL RICHIE (MOTOWN)

US

SINGLES		ALBUMS
CARELESS WHISPER GEORGE MICHAEL (COLUMBIA/CBS)	1	LIKE A VIRGIN MADONNA (SIRE)
I WANT TO KNOW WHAT LOVE IS FOREIGNER (ATLANTIC)	2	BORN IN THE USA BRUCE SPRINGSTEEN (COLUMBIA/CBS)
EASY LOVER PHILIP BAILEY (COLUMBIA/CBS)	3	MAKE IT BIG WHAM! (COLUMBIA/CBS)
LOVER BOY BILLY OCEAN (JIVE/ARISTA)	4	AGENT PROVOCATEUR FOREIGNER (ATLANTIC)
METHOD OF MODERN LOVE HALL & OATES (RCA)	5	CENTERFIELD JOHN FOGERTY (WARNER BROS)
NEUTRON DANCE POINTER SISTERS (PLANET)	6	17 CHICAGO (FULL MOON/WARNER BROS)
CAN'T FIGHT THIS FEELING REO SPEEDWAGON (EPIC)	7	PURPLE RAIN PRINCE AND THE REVOLUTION (WARNER BROS)
THE HEAT IS ON GLENN FREY (MCA)	8	RECKLESS BRYAN ADAMS (A&M)
THE BOYS OF SUMMER DON HENLEY (GEFFEN)	9	NEW EDITION NEW EDITION (MCA)
CALIFORNIA GIRLS DAVID LEE ROTH (WARNER BROS)	10	BIG BAM BOOM HALL & OATES (RCA)
SUGAR WALLS SHEENA EASTON (EMI AMERICA)	11	PRIVATE DANCER TINA TURNER (CAPITOL)
SOLID ASHFORD AND SIMPSON (CAPITOL)	12	SUDDENLY BILLY OCEAN (JIVE/ARISTA)
YOU'RE THE INSPIRATION CHICAGO (FULL MOON/WARNER BROS)	13	SHE'S SO UNUSUAL CYNDI LAUPER (PORTRAIT)
THE OLD MAN DOWN THE ROAD JOHN FOGERTY (WARNER BROS)	14	BUILDING THE PERFECT BEAST DON HENLEY (GEFFEN)
MR TELEPHONE MAN NEW EDITION (COLUMBIA/MCA)	15	BEVERLY HILLS COP SOUNDTRACK (MCA)
MISLED KOOL AND THE GANG (DE-LITE)	16	ARENA DURAN DURAN (CAPITOL)
LIKE A VIRGIN MADONNA (SIRE)	17	PERFECT STRANGERS DEEP PURPLE (MERCURY)
FOOLISH HEART STEVE PERRY (COLUMBIA/CBS)	18	A PRIVATE HEAVEN SHEENA EASTON (EMI AMERICA)
I WOULD DIE 4 U PRINCE AND THE REVOLUTION (WARNER BROS)	19	CAN'T SLOW DOWN LIONEL RICHIE (MOTOWN)
OPERATOR MIDNIGHT STAR (SOLAR)	20	BREAK OUT POINTER SISTERS (PLANET)

WEEK ENDING FEBRUARY 23 1985

UK

SINGLES		ALBUMS
I KNOW HIM SO WELL ELAINE PAIGE/BARBARA DICKSON (RCA)	1	MEAT IS MURDER SMITHS (ROUGH TRADE)
LOVE AND PRIDE KING (CBS)	2	BORN IN THE USA BRUCE SPRINGSTEEN (CBS)
SOLID ASHFORD AND SIMPSON (CAPITOL)	3	ALF ALISON MOYET (CBS)
DANCING IN THE DARK BRUCE SPRINGSTEEN (CBS)	4	DIAMOND LIFE SADE (EPIC)
YOU SPIN ME ROUND DEAD OR ALIVE (EPIC)	5	AGENT PROVOCATEUR FOREIGNER (ATLANTIC)
THINGS CAN ONLY GET BETTER HOWARD JONES (WEA)	6	THE AGE OF CONSENT BRONSKI BEAT (FORBIDDEN FRUIT)
A NEW ENGLAND KIRSTY MacCOLL (STIFF)	7	THE BARBARA DICKSON SONGBOOK BARBARA DICKSON (K-TEL)
CLOSE (TO THE EDIT) ART OF NOISE (ZTT/ISLAND)	8	STEPS IN TIME KING (CBS)
NIGHTSHIFT COMMODORES (MOTOWN)	9	HITS OUT OF HELL MEAT LOAF (EPIC)
LITTLE RED CORVETTE/1999 PRINCE (WARNER BROS)	10	MAKE IT BIG WHAM! (EPIC)
RUN TO YOU BRYAN ADAMS (A&M)	11	VERY BEST OF CHRIS DE BURGH CHRIS DE BURGH (TELSTAR)
I WANT TO KNOW WHAT LOVE IS FOREIGNER (ATLANTIC)	12	CHESS VARIOUS (RCA)
THINKING OF YOU COLOURFIELD (CHRYSALIS)	13	ELIMINATOR ZZ TOP (WARNER BROS)
YOU'RE THE INSPIRATION CHICAGO (FULL MOON)	14	20/20 GEORGE BENSON (WARNER BROS)
ATMOSPHERE RUSS ABBOTT (SPIRIT)	15	WELCOME TO THE PLEASUREDOME FRANKIE GOES TO HOLLYWOOD (ZTT/ISLAND)
LOVER BOY BILLY OCEAN (JIVE)	16	THE COLLECTION ULTRAVOX (CHRYSALIS)
THIS IS NOT AMERICA DAVID BOWIE (EMI AMERICA)	17	THE 12" ALBUM HOWARD JONES (WEA)
SUSSUDIO PHIL COLLINS (VIRGIN)	18	SECRET SECRETS JOAN ARMATRADING (A&M)
LOVE LIKE BLOOD KILLING JOKE (EG)	19	PRIVATE DANCER TINA TURNER (CAPITOL)
CHANGE YOUR MIND SHARPE AND NUMAN (POLYDOR)	20	HATFUL OF HOLLOW SMITHS (ROUGH TRADE)

US

SINGLES		ALBUMS
CARELESS WHISPER GEORGE MICHAEL (COLUMBIA/CBS)	1	LIKE A VIRGIN MADONNA (SIRE)
LOVER BOY BILLY OCEAN (JIVE/ARISTA)	2	MAKE IT BIG WHAM! (COLUMBIA/CBS)
EASY LOVER PHILIP BAILEY (COLUMBIA/CBS)	3	BORN IN THE USA BRUCE SPRINGSTEEN (COLUMBIA/CBS)
CAN'T FIGHT THIS FEELING REO SPEEDWAGON (EPIC)	4	CENTERFIELD JOHN FOGERTY (WARNER BROS)
I WANT TO KNOW WHAT LOVE IS FOREIGNER (ATLANTIC)	5	AGENT PROVOCATEUR FOREIGNER (WARNER BROS)
NEUTRON DANCE POINTER SISTERS (PLANET)	6	NEW EDITION NEW EDITION (MCA)
THE HEAT IS ON GLENN FREY (MCA)	7	PURPLE RAIN PRINCE AND THE REVOLUTION (WARNER BROS)
CALIFORNIA GIRLS DAVID LEE ROTH (WARNER BROS)	8	RECKLESS BRYAN ADAMS (A&M)
METHOD OF MODERN LOVE HALL & OATES (RCA)	9	17 CHICAGO (FULL MOON/WARNER BROS)
SUGAR WALLS SHEENA EASTON (EMI AMERICA)	10	PRIVATE DANCER TINA TURNER (CAPITOL)
THE OLD MAN DOWN THE ROAD JOHN FOGERTY (WARNER BROS)	11	BIG BAM BOOM HALL & OATES (RCA)
MR TELEPHONE MAN NEW EDITION (COLUMBIA/MCA)	12	BEVERLY HILLS COP SOUNDTRACK (MCA)
MISLED KOOL AND THE GANG (DE-LITE)	13	SUDDENLY BILLY OCEAN (JIVE/ARISTA)
SOLID ASHFORD AND SIMPSON (CAPITOL)	14	BUILDING THE PERFECT BEAST DON HENLEY (GEFFEN)
THE BOYS OF SUMMER DON HENLEY (GEFFEN)	15	WHEELS ARE TURNING REO SPEEDWAGON (EPIC)
LOVERGIRL TEENA MARIE (EPIC)	16	SHE'S SO UNUSUAL CYNDI LAUPER (PORTRAIT)
TOO LATE FOR GOODBYES JULIAN LENNON (ATLANTIC)	17	VALOTTE JULIAN LENNON (ATLANTIC)
PRIVATE DANCER TINA TURNER (CAPITOL)	18	BREAK OUT POINTER SISTERS (PLANET)
YOU'RE THE INSPIRATION CHICAGO (FULL MOON/WARNER BROS)	19	CAN'T SLOW DOWN LIONEL RICHIE (MOTOWN)
JUNGLE LOVE THE TIME (WARNER BROS)	20	PERFECT STRANGERS DEEP PURPLE (MERCURY)

WEEK ENDING MARCH 2 1985

UK

SINGLES		ALBUMS
I KNOW HIM SO WELL ELAINE PAIGE/BARBARA DICKSON (RCA)	1	NO JACKET REQUIRED PHIL COLLINS (VIRGIN)
YOU SPIN ME ROUND DEAD OR ALIVE (EPIC)	2	BORN IN THE USA BRUCE SPRINGSTEEN (CBS)
LOVE AND PRIDE KING (CBS)	3	MEAT IS MURDER SMITHS (ROUGH TRADE)
SOLID ASHFORD AND SIMPSON (CAPITOL)	4	ALF ALISON MOYET (CBS)
DANCING IN THE DARK BRUCE SPRINGSTEEN (CBS)	5	HITS OUT OF HELL MEAT LOAF (EPIC)
NIGHTSHIFT COMMODORES (MOTOWN)	6	MAKE IT BIG WHAM! (EPIC)
THINGS CAN ONLY GET BETTER HOWARD JONES (WEA)	7	RECKLESS BRYAN ADAMS (A&M)
A NEW ENGLAND KIRSTY MacCOLL (STIFF)	8	DIAMOND LIFE SADE (EPIC)
LET'S GO CRAZY PRINCE AND THE REVOLUTION (WARNER BROS)	9	ELIMINATOR ZZ TOP (WARNER BROS)
CLOSE (TO THE EDIT) ART OF NOISE (ZTT/ISLAND)	10	CHESS VARIOUS (RCA)
RUN TO YOU BRYAN ADAMS (A&M)	11	AGENT PROVOCATEUR FOREIGNER (ATLANTIC)
THINKING OF YOU COLOURFIELD (CHRYSALIS)	12	STEPS IN TIME KING (CBS)
THE BOYS OF SUMMER DON HENLEY (GEFFEN)	13	THE AGE OF CONSENT BRONSKI BEAT (FORBIDDEN FRUIT)
YOU'RE THE INSPIRATION CHICAGO (FULL MOON)	14	THE BARBARA DICKSON SONGBOOK BARBARA DICKSON (K-TEL)
LITTLE RED CORVETTE/1999 PRINCE (WARNER BROS)	15	THE FIRM THE FIRM (ATLANTIC)
LOVE LIKE BLOOD KILLING JOKE (EG)	16	THE 12" ALBUM HOWARD JONES (WEA)
CHANGE YOUR MIND SHARPE AND NUMAN (POLYDOR)	17	HATFUL OF HOLLOW SMITHS (ROUGH TRADE)
LOVER BOY BILLY OCEAN (JIVE)	18	VERY BEST OF CHRIS DE BURGH CHRIS DE BURGH (TELSTAR)
SHAFT EDDY AND THE SOUL BAND (CLUB)	19	THE HITS ALBUM/THE HITS TAPE VARIOUS (CBS/WEA)
ATMOSPHERE RUSS ABBOTT (SPIRIT)	20	PRIVATE DANCER TINA TURNER (CAPITOL)

US

SINGLES		ALBUMS
CARELESS WHISPER GEORGE MICHAEL (COLUMBIA/CBS)	1	MAKE IT BIG WHAM! (COLUMBIA/CBS)
CAN'T FIGHT THIS FEELING REO SPEEDWAGON (EPIC)	2	LIKE A VIRGIN MADONNA (SIRE)
CALIFORNIA GIRLS DAVID LEE ROTH (WARNER BROS)	3	BORN IN THE USA BRUCE SPRINGSTEEN (COLUMBIA/CBS)
THE HEAT IS ON GLENN FREY (MCA)	4	CENTERFIELD JOHN FOGERTY (WARNER BROS)
LOVER BOY BILLY OCEAN (JIVE/ARISTA)	5	AGENT PROVOCATEUR FOREIGNER (ATLANTIC)
NEUTRON DANCE POINTER SISTERS (PLANET)	6	NEW EDITION NEW EDITION (MCA)
I WANT TO KNOW WHAT LOVE IS FOREIGNER (ATLANTIC)	7	RECKLESS BRYAN ADAMS (A&M)
EASY LOVER PHILIP BAILEY (COLUMBIA/CBS)	8	BEVERLY HILLS COP SOUNDTRACK (MCA)
SUGAR WALLS SHEENA EASTON (EMI AMERICA)	9	PRIVATE DANCER TINA TURNER (CAPITOL)
THE OLD MAN DOWN THE ROAD JOHN FOGERTY (WARNER BROS)	10	17 CHICAGO (FULL MOON/WARNER B)
METHOD OF MODERN LOVE HALL & OATES (RCA)	11	PURPLE RAIN PRINCE AND THE REVOLUTION (WARNER BROS)
MR TELEPHONE MAN NEW EDITION (MCA)	12	WHEELS ARE TURNING REO SPEEDWAGON (EPIC)
MISLED KOOL AND THE GANG (DE-LITE)	13	SUDDENLY BILLY OCEAN (JIVE/ARISTA)
LOVERGIRL TEENA MARIE (EPIC)	14	BUILDING THE PERFECT BEAST DON HENLEY (GEFFEN)
TOO LATE FOR GOODBYES JULIAN LENNON (ATLANTIC)	15	BIG BAM BOOM HALL & OATES (RCA)
PRIVATE DANCER TINA TURNER (CAPITOL)	16	CRAZY FROM THE HEAT DAVID LEE ROTH (WARNER BROS)
SOLID ASHFORD AND SIMPSON (CAPITOL)	17	VALOTTE JULIAN LENNON (ATLANTIC)
MATERIAL GIRL MADONNA (SIRE)	18	BREAK OUT POINTER SISTERS (PLANET)
RELAX FRANKIE GOES TO HOLLYWOOD (ZTT/ISLAND)	19	CAN'T SLOW DOWN LIONEL RICHIE (MOTOWN)
ONLY THE YOUNG JOURNEY (GEFFEN)	20	A PRIVATE HEAVEN SHEENA EASTON (EMI AMERICA)

WEEK ENDING MARCH 9 1985

UK

SINGLES		ALBUMS
YOU SPIN ME ROUND DEAD OR ALIVE (EPIC)	1	NO JACKET REQUIRED PHIL COLLINS (VIRGIN)
I KNOW HIM SO WELL ELAINE PAIGE/BARBARA DICKSON (RCA)	2	SONG FROM THE BIG CHAIR TEARS FOR FEARS (MERCURY)
NIGHTSHIFT COMMODORES (MOTOWN)	3	BORN IN THE USA BRUCE SPRINGSTEEN (CBS)
KISS ME STEPHEN TIN TIN DUFFY (10 RECORDS)	4	HITS OUT OF HELL MEAT LOAF (EPIC)
MATERIAL GIRL MADONNA (SIRE)	5	ALF ALISON MOYET (CBS)
SOLID ASHFORD AND SIMPSON (CAPITOL)	6	MEAT IS MURDER SMITHS (ROUGH TRADE)
LET'S GO CRAZY PRINCE AND THE REVOLUTION (WARNER BROS)	7	RECKLESS BRYAN ADAMS (A&M)
LOVE AND PRIDE KING (CBS)	8	ELIMINATOR ZZ TOP (WARNER BROS)
DANCING IN THE DARK BRUCE SPRINGSTEEN (CBS)	9	PURPLE RAIN PRINCE AND THE REVOLUTION (WARNER BROS)
THINGS CAN ONLY GET BETTER HOWARD JONES (WEA)	10	DIAMOND LIFE SADE (EPIC)
THE LAST KISS DAVID CASSIDY (ARISTA)	11	NIGHT TIME KILLING JOKE (EG)
THE BOYS OF SUMMER DON HENLEY (GEFFEN)	12	PRIVATE DANCER TINA TURNER (CAPITOL)
SHAFT EDDY AND THE SOUL BAND (CLUB)	13	MODERN LOVE VARIOUS (K-TEL)
A NEW ENGLAND KIRSTY MacCOLL (STIFF)	14	THE AGE OF CONSENT BRONSKI BEAT (FORBIDDEN FRUIT)
BREAKING UP MY HEART SHAKIN' STEVENS (EPIC)	15	MAKE IT BIG WHAM! (EPIC)
LEGS ZZ TOP (WARNER BROS)	16	BUILDING THE PERFECT BEAST DON HENLEY (GEFFEN)
RUN TO YOU BRYAN ADAMS (A&M)	17	CHESS VARIOUS (RCA)
DO WHAT YOU DO JERMAINE JACKSON (ARISTA)	18	THE BARBARA DICKSON SONGBOOK BARBARA DICKSON (K-TEL)
LOVE LIKE BLOOD KILLING JOKE (EG)	19	STEPS IN TIME KING (CBS)
EASY LOVER PHILIP BAILEY/PHIL COLLINS (CBS/VIRGIN)	20	NIGHTSHIFT COMMODORES (MOTOWN)

US

SINGLES		ALBUMS
CAN'T FIGHT THIS FEELING REO SPEEDWAGON (EPIC)	1	MAKE IT BIG WHAM! (COLUMBIA/CBS)
CARELESS WHISPER GEORGE MICHAEL (COLUMBIA/CBS)	2	CENTERFIELD JOHN FOGERTY (WARNER BROS)
THE HEAT IS ON GLENN FREY (MCA)	3	LIKE A VIRGIN MADONNA (SIRE)
CALIFORNIA GIRLS DAVID LEE ROTH (WARNER BROS)	4	BORN IN THE USA BRUCE SPRINGSTEEN (COLUMBIA/CBS)
MATERIAL GIRL MADONNA (SIRE)	5	AGENT PROVOCATEUR FOREIGNER (ATLANTIC)
TOO LATE FOR GOODBYES JULIAN LENNON (ATLANTIC)	6	BEVERLY HILLS COP SOUNDTRACK (MCA)
NEURTRON DANCE POINTER SISTERS (PLANET)	7	NEW EDITION NEW EDITION (MCA)
I WANT TO KNOW WHAT LOVE IS FOREIGNER (ATLANTIC)	8	WHEELS ARE TURNING REO SPEEDWAGON (EPIC)
SUGAR WALLS SHEENA EASTON (EMI AMERICA)	9	PRIVATE DANCER TINA TURNER (CAPITOL)
MISLED KOOL AND THE GANG (DE-LITE)	10	RECKLESS BRYAN ADAMS (A&M)
LOVER BOY BILLY OCEAN (JIVE/ARISTA)	11	PURPLE RAIN PRINCE AND THE REVOLUTION (WARNER BROS)
LOVERGIRL TEENA MARIE (EPIC)	12	17 CHICAGO (FULL MOON/WARNER BROS)
THE OLD MAN DOWN THE ROAD JOHN FOGERTY (WARNER BROS)	13	SUDDENLY BILLY OCEAN (JIVE/ARISTA)
ONE MORE NIGHT PHIL COLLINS (ATLANTIC)	14	BUILDING THE PERFECT BEAST DON HENLEY (GEFFEN)
PRIVATE DANCER TINA TURNER (CAPITOL)	15	BIG BAM BOOM HALL & OATES (WARNER BROS)
EASY LOVER PHILIP BAILEY (COLUMBIA/CBS)	16	CRAZY FROM THE HEAT DAVID LEE ROTH (WARNER BROS)
RELAX FRANKIE GOES TO HOLLYWOOD (ZTT/ISLAND)	17	BREAK OUT POINTER SISTERS (PLANET)
ONLY THE YOUNG JOURNEY (GEFFEN)	18	A PRIVATE HEAVEN SHEENA EASTON (EMI AMERICA)
MR TELEPHONE MAN NEW EDITION (MCA)	19	VALOTTE JULIAN LENNON (ATLANTIC)
METHOD OF MODERN LOVE HALL & OATES (RCA)	20	CAN'T SLOW DOWN LIONEL RICHIE (MOTOWN)

WEEK ENDING MARCH 16 1985

UK

SINGLES		ALBUMS
YOU SPIN ME ROUND DEAD OR ALIVE (EPIC)	1	NO JACKET REQUIRED PHIL COLLINS (VIRGIN)
EASY LOVER PHILIP BAILEY/PHIL COLLINS (CBS/VIRGIN)	2	SONGS FROM THE BIG CHAIR TEARS FOR FEARS (MERCURY)
MATERIAL GIRL MADONNA (SIRE)	3	BORN IN THE USA BRUCE SPRINGSTEEN (CBS)
KISS ME STEPHEN TIN TIN DUFFY (10 RECORDS)	4	HITS OUT OF HELL MEAT LOAF (EPIC)
NIGHTSHIFT COMMODORES (MOTOWN)	5	ALF ALISON MOYET (CBS)
THE LAST KISS DAVID CASSIDY (ARISTA)	6	SHE'S THE BOSS MICK JAGGER (CBS)
DO WHAT YOU DO JERMAINE JACKSON (ARISTA)	7	PURPLE RAIN PRINCE AND THE REVOLUTION (WARNER BROS)
I KNOW HIM SO WELL ELAINE PAIGE/BARBARA DICKSON (RCA)	8	ELIMINATOR ZZ TOP (WARNER BROS)
EVERY TIME YOU GO AWAY PAUL YOUNG (CBS)	9	DIAMOND LIFE SADE (EPIC)
LET'S GO CRAZY PRINCE AND THE REVOLUTION (WARNER BROS)	10	LIKE A VIRGIN MADONNA (SIRE)
THAT OLE DEVIL CALLED LOVE ALISON MOYET (CBS)	11	RECKLESS BRYAN ADAMS (A&M)
SOLID ASHFORD AND SIMPSON (CAPITOL)	12	PRIVATE DANCER TINA TURNER (CAPITOL)
DANCING IN THE DARK BRUCE SPRINGSTEEN (CBS)	13	NIGHTSHIFT COMMODORES (MOTOWN)
BREAKING UP MY HEART SHAKIN' STEVENS (EPIC)	14	BUILDING THE PERFECT BEAST DON HENLEY (GEFFEN)
WIDE BOY NIK KERSHAW (MCA)	15	NIGHT TIME KILLING JOKE (EG)
WE CLOSE OUR EYES GO WEST (CHRYSALIS)	16	MEAT IS MURDER SMITHS (ROUGH TRADE)
LOVE AND PRIDE KING (CBS)	17	MAKE IT BIG WHAM! (EPIC)
LEGS ZZ TOP (WARNER BROS)	18	MODERN LOVE VARIOUS (K-TEL)
THINGS CAN ONLY GET BETTER HOWARD JONES (WEA)	19	THE AGE OF CONSENT BRONSKI BEAT (FORBIDDEN FRUIT)
THE BOYS OF SUMMER DON HENLEY (GEFFEN)	20	CHESS VARIOUS (RCA)

US

SINGLES		ALBUMS
CAN'T FIGHT THIS FEELING REO SPEEDWAGON (EPIC)	1	MAKE IT BIG WHAM! (COLUMBIA/CBS)
THE HEAT IS ON GLENN FREY (MCA)	2	CENTERFIELD JOHN FOGERTY (WARNER BROS)
MATERIAL GIRL MADONNA (SIRE)	3	BORN IN THE USA BRUCE SPRINGSTEEN (COLUMBIA/CBS)
CALIFORNIA GIRLS DAVID LEE ROTH (WARNER BROS)	4	LIKE A VIRGIN MADONNA (SIRE)
ONE MORE NIGHT PHIL COLLINS (ATLANTIC)	5	BEVERLY HILLS COP SOUNDTRACK (MCA)
TOO LATE FOR GOODBYES JULIAN LENNON (ATLANTIC)	6	AGENT PROVOCATEUR FOREIGNER (ATLANTIC)
CARELESS WHISPER GEORGE MICHAEL (COLUMBIA/CBS)	7	WHEELS ARE TURNING REO SPEEDWAGON (EPIC)
LOVERGIRL TEENA MARIE (EPIC)	8	NO JACKET REQUIRED PHIL COLLINS (ATLANTIC)
PRIVATE DANCER TINA TURNER (CAPITOL)	9	PRIVATE DANCER TINA TURNER (CAPITOL)
RELAX FRANKIE GOES TO HOLLYWOOD (ZTT/ISLAND)	10	RECKLESS BRYAN ADAMS (A&M)
ONLY THE YOUNG JOURNEY (GEFFEN)	11	NEW EDITION NEW EDITION (MCA)
NEUTRON DANCE POINTER SISTERS (PLANET)	12	BREAK OUT POINTER SISTERS (PLANET)
MISLED KOOL AND THE GANG (DE-LITE)	13	BULDING THE PERFECT BEAST DON HENLEY (GEFFEN)
HIGH ON YOU SURVIVOR (SCOTTI BROS)	14	BIG BAM BOOM HALL & OATES (RCA)
I WANT TO KNOW WHAT LOVE IS FOREIGNER (ATLANTIC)	15	CRAZY FROM THE HEAT DAVID LEE ROTH (WARNER BROS)
SAVE A PRAYER DURAN DURAN (CAPITOL)	16	17 CHICAGO (FULL MOON/WARNER BROS)
SUGAR WALLS SHEENA EASTON (EMI AMERICA)	17	SUDDENLY BILLY OCEAN (JIVE/ARISTA)
JUST ANOTHER NIGHT MICK JAGGER (COLUMBIA/CBS)	18	PURPLE RAIN PRINCE AND THE REVOLUTION (WARNER BROS)
THE OLD MAN DOWN THE ROAD JOHN FOGERTY (WARNER BROS)	19	A PRIVATE HEAVEN SHEENA EASTON (EMI AMERICA)
LOVER BOY BILLY OCEAN (JIVE/ARIST)	20	VALOTTE JULIAN LENNON (ATLANTIC)

WEEK ENDING MARCH 23 1985

UK

SINGLES		ALBUMS
EASY LOVER PHILIP BAILEY/PHIL COLLINS (CBS/VIRGIN)	1	NO JACKET REQUIRED PHIL COLLINS (VIRGIN)
THAT OLE DEVIL CALLED LOVE ALISON MOYET (CBS)	2	DREAM INTO ACTION HOWARD JONES (WEA)
MATERIAL GIRL MADONNA (SIRE)	3	ALF ALISON MOYET (CBS)
EVERY TIME YOU GO AWAY PAUL YOUNG (CBS)	4	SONGS FROM THE BIG CHAIR TEARS FOR FEARS (MERCURY)
KISS ME STEPHEN TIN TIN DUFFY (10 RECORDS)	5	BORN IN THE USA BRUCE SPRINGSTEEN (CBS)
YOU SPIN ME ROUND DEAD OR ALIVE (EPIC)	6	PRIVATE DANCER TINA TURNER (CAPITOL)
DO WHAT YOU DO JERMAINE JACKSON (ARISTA)	7	HITS OUT OF HELL MEAT LOAF (EPIC)
THE LAST KISS DAVID CASSIDY (ARISTA)	8	BEHIND THE SUN ERIC CLAPTON (DUCK)
WE CLOSE OUR EYES GO WEST (CHRYSALIS)	9	ELIMINATOR ZZ TOP (WARNER BROS)
I KNOW HIM SO WELL ELAINE PAIGE/BARBARA DICKSON (RCA)	10	LIKE A VIRGIN MADONNA (SIRE)
NIGHTSHIFT COMMODORES (MOTOWN)	11	ANDREW LLOYD WEBBER REQUIEM DOMINGO/BRIGHTMAN/MAAZEL/ECO (HMV)
WIDE BOY NIK KERSHAW (MCA)	12	PURPLE RAIN PRINCE AND THE REVOLUTION (WARNER BROS)
DANCING IN THE DARK BRUCE SPRINGSTEEN (CBS)	13	DIAMOND LIFE SADE (EPIC)
PIE JESU SARAH BRIGHTMAN/PAUL MILES-KINGSTON (EMI)	14	FIRST AND LAST AND ALWAYS SISTERS OF MERCY (MERCIFUL RELEASE)
BETWEEN THE WARS EP BILLY BRAGG (GO! DISCS)	15	MAKE IT BIG WHAM! (EPIC)
LET'S GO CRAZY PRINCE AND THE REVOLUTION (WARNER BROS)	16	BUILDING THE PERFECT BEAST DON HENLEY (GEFFEN)
SOME LIKE IT HOT POWER STATION (PARLOPHONE)	17	THE BARBARA DICKSON SONGBOOK BARBARA DICKSON (K-TEL)
THE BELLE OF ST MARK SHEILA E (WARNER BROS)	18	NIGHTSHIFT COMMODORES (MOTOWN)
MR TELEPHONE MAN NEW EDITION (MCA)	19	RECKLESS BRYAN ADAMS (A&M)
HANGIN' ON A STRING LOOSE ENDS (VIRGIN)	20	SHE'S THE BOSS MICK JAGGER (CBS)

US

SINGLES		ALBUMS
CAN'T FIGHT THIS FEELING REO SPEEDWAGON (EPIC)	1	CENTERFIELD JOHN FOGERTY (WARNER BROS)
MATERIAL GIRL MADONNA (SIRE)	2	NO JACKET REQUIRED PHIL COLLINS (ATLANTIC)
ONE MORE NIGHT PHIL COLLINS (ATLANTIC)	3	BORN IN THE USA BRUCE SPRINGSTEEN (COLUMBIA/CBS)
THE HEAT IS ON GLENN FREY (MCA)	4	MAKE IT BIG WHAM! (COLUMBIA/CBS)
TOO LATE FOR GOODBYES JULIAN LENNON (ATLANTIC)	5	BEVERLY HILLS COP SOUNDTRACK (MCA)
LOVERGIRL TEENA MARIE (EPIC)	6	PRIVATE DANCER TINA TURNER (CAPITOL)
PRIVATE DANCER TINA TURNER (CAPITOL)	7	LIKE A VIRGIN MADONNA (SIRE)
HIGH ON YOU SURVIVOR (SCOTTI BROS)	8	WHEELS ARE TURNING REO SPEEDWAGON (EPIC)
ONLY THE YOUNG JOURNEY (GEFFEN)	9	AGENT PROVOCATEUR FOREIGNER (ATLANTIC)
RELAX FRANKIE GOES TO HOLLYWOOD (ZTT/ISLAND)	10	RECKLESS BRYAN ADAMS (A&M)
CALIFORNIA GIRLS DAVID LEE ROTH (WARNER BROS)	11	NEW EDITION NEW EDITION (MCA)
CARELESS WHISPER GEORGE MICHAEL (COLUMBIA/CBS)	12	BREAK OUT POINTER SISTERS (PLANET)
JUST ANOTHER NIGHT MICK JAGGER (COLUMBIA/CBS)	13	BUILDING THE PERFECT BEAST DON HENLEY (GEFFEN)
SOMEBODY BRYAN ADAMS (A&M)	14	17 CHICAGO (FULL MOON/WARNER BROS)
NIGHTSHIFT COMMODORES (MOTOWN)	15	CRAZY FROM THE HEAT DAVID LEE ROTH (WARNER BROS)
SAVE A PRAYER DURAN DURAN (CAPITOL)	16	SHE'S THE BOSS MICK JAGGER (COLUMBIA)
I'M ON FIRE BRUCE SPRINGSTEEN (COLUMBIA/CBS)	17	SUDDENLY BILLY OCEAN (JIVE/ARISTA)
KEEPING THE FAITH BILLY JOEL (COLUMBIA/CBS)	18	PURPLE RAIN PRINCE AND THE REVOLUTION (WARNER BROS)
MISSING YOU DIANA ROSS (RCA)	19	CAN'T SLOW DOWN LIONEL RICHIE (MOTOWN)
CRAZY FOR YOU MADONNA (SIRE)	20	BIG BAM BOOM HALL & OATES (RCA)

WEEK ENDING MARCH 30 1985

SINGLES	UK	ALBUMS
EASY LOVER PHILIP BAILEY/PHIL COLLINS (CBS/VIRGIN)	1	NO JACKET REQUIRED PHIL COLLINS (VIRGIN)
THAT OLE DEVIL CALLED LOVE ALISON MOYET (CBS)	2	DREAM INTO ACTION HOWARD JONES (WEA)
PIE JESU SARAH BRIGHTMAN/PAUL MILES-KINGSTON (EMI)	3	SONGS FROM THE BIG CHAIR TEARS FOR FEARS (MERCURY)
EVERY TIME YOU GO AWAY PAUL YOUNG (CBS)	4	ALF ALISON MOYET (CBS)
WELCOME TO THE PLEASUREDOME FRANKIE GOES TO HOLLYWOOD (ZTT/ISLAND)	5	ANDREW LLOYD WEBBER REQUIEM DOMINGO/BRIGHTMAN/MAAZEL/ECO (HMV)
DO WHAT YOU DO JERMAINE JACKSON (ARISTA)	6	BORN IN THE USA BRUCE SPRINGSTEEN (CBS)
MATERIAL GIRL MADONNA (SIRE)	7	PRIVATE DANCER TINA TURNER (CAPITOL)
WE CLOSE OUR EYES GO WEST (CHRYSALIS)	8	LIKE A VIRGIN MADONNA (SIRE)
KISS ME STEPHEN TIN TIN DUFFY (10 RECORDS)	9	BEHIND THE SUN ERIC CLAPTON (DUCK)
WIDE BOY NIK KERSHAW (MCA)	10	RECKLESS BRYAN ADAMS (A&M)
THE LAST KISS DAVID CASSIDY (ARISTA)	11	HITS OUT OF HELL MEAT LOAF (EPIC)
YOU SPIN ME ROUND DEAD OR ALIVE (EPIC)	12	ELIMINATOR ZZ TOP (WARNER BROS)
HANGIN' ON A STRING LOOSE ENDS (VIRGIN)	13	PURPLE RAIN PRINCE AND THE REVOLUTION (WARNER BROS)
SOME LIKE IT HOT POWER STATION (PARLOPHONE)	14	WELCOME TO THE PLEASUREDOME FRANKIE GOES TO HOLLYWOOD (ZTT/ISLAND)
BETWEEN THE WARS EP BILLY BRAGG (GO! DISCS)	15	MAKE IT BIG WHAM! (EPIC)
EVERYBODY WANTS TO RULE . . . TEARS FOR FEARS (MERCURY)	16	DIAMOND LIFE SADE (EPIC)
NIGHTSHIFT COMMODORES (MOTOWN)	17	BUILDING THE PERFECT BEAST DON HENLEY (GEFFEN)
COVER ME BRUCE SPRINGSTEEN (CBS)	18	NO PARLEZ PAUL YOUNG (CBS)
MOVE CLOSER PHYLLIS NELSON (CARRERE)	19	SHE'S THE BOSS MICK JAGGER (CBS)
MR TELEPHONE MAN NEW EDITION (MCA)	20	VERY BEST OF BRENDA LEE BRENDA LEE (MCA)

SINGLES	US	ALBUMS
ONE MORE NIGHT PHIL COLLINS (ATLANTIC)	1	NO JACKET REQUIRED PHIL COLLINS (ATLANTIC)
MATERIAL GIRL MADONNA (SIRE)	2	CENTERFIELD JOHN FOGERTY (WARNER BROS)
CAN'T FIGHT THIS FEELING REO SPEEDWAGON (EPIC)	3	BORN IN THE USA BRUCE SPRINGSTEEN (COLUMBIA/CBS)
LOVERGIRL TEENA MARIE (EPIC)	4	BEVERLY HILLS COP SOUNDTRACK (MCA)
WE ARE THE WORLD USA FOR AFRICA (COLUMBIA)	5	PRIVATE DANCER TINA TURNER (CAPITOL)
TOO LATE FOR GOODBYES JULIAN LENNON (ATLANTIC)	6	LIKE A VIRGIN MADONNA (SIRE)
PRIVATE DANCER TINA TURNER (CAPITOL)	7	MAKE IT BIG WHAM! (COLUMBIA/CBS)
HIGH ON YOU SURVIVOR (SCOTTI BROS)	8	WHEELS ARE TURNING REO SPEEDWAGON (EPIC)
CRAZY FOR YOU MADONNA (SIRE)	9	AGENT PROVOCATEUR FOREIGNER (ATLANTIC)
NIGHTSHIFT COMMODORES (MOTOWN)	10	RECKLESS BRYAN ADAMS (A&M)
THE HEAT IS ON GLENN FREY (MCA)	11	NEW EDITION NEW EDITION (MCA)
JUST ANOTHER NIGHT MICK JAGGER (COLUMBIA/CBS)	12	BREAK OUT POINTER SISTERS (PLANET)
SOMEBODY BRYAN ADAMS (A&M)	13	BUILDING THE PERFECT BEAST DON HENLEY (GEFFEN)
I'M ON FIRE BRUCE SPRINGSTEEN (COLUMBIA/CBS)	14	SHE'S THE BOSS MICK JAGGER (COLUMBIA/CBS)
MISSING YOU DIANA ROSS (RCA)	15	CRAZY FROM THE HEAT DAVID LEE ROTH (WARNER BROS)
ONLY THE YOUNG JOURNEY (GEFFEN)	16	17 CHICAGO (FULL MOON/WARNER BROS)
CARELESS WHISPER GEORGE MICHAEL (COLUMBIA/CBS)	17	CAN'T SLOW DOWN LIONEL RICHIE (MOTOWN)
RHYTHM OF THE NIGHT DEBARGE (GORDY)	18	VALOTTE JULIAN LENNON (ATLANTIC)
OBSESSION ANIMOTION (MERCURY)	19	BIG BAM BOOM HALL & OATES (RCA)
RELAX FRANKIE GOES TO HOLLYWOOD (ZTT/ISLAND)	20	THE FIRM THE FIRM (ATLANTIC)

WEEK ENDING APRIL 6 1985

SINGLES	UK	ALBUMS
EASY LOVER PHILIP BAILEY/PHIL COLLINS (CBS/VIRGIN)	1	THE SECRET OF ASSOCIATION PAUL YOUNG (CBS)
WELCOME TO THE PLEASUREDOME FRANKIE GOES TO HOLLYWOOD (ZTT/ISLAND)	2	NO JACKET REQUIRED PHIL COLLINS (VIRGIN)
PIE JESU SARAH BRIGHTMAN/PAUL MILES-KINGSTON (EMI)	3	SONGS FROM THE BIG CHAIR TEARS FOR FEARS (MERCURY)
THAT OLE DEVIL CALLED LOVE ALISON MOYET (CBS)	4	ANDREW LLOYD WEBBER REQUIEM DOMINGO/BRIGHTMAN/MAAZEL/ECO (HMV)
EVERYBODY WANTS TO RULE . . . TEARS FOR FEARS (MERCURY)	5	ALF ALISON MOYET (CBS)
WE CLOSE OUR EYES GO WEST (CHRYSALIS)	6	DREAM INTO ACTION HOWARD JONES (WEA)
EVERY TIME YOU GO AWAY PAUL YOUNG (CBS)	7	BORN IN THE USA BRUCE SPRINGSTEEN (CBS)
DO WHAT YOU DO JERMAINE JACKSON (ARISTA)	8	PRIVATE DANCER TINA TURNER (CAPITOL)
WIDE BOY NIK KERSHAW (MCA)	9	WELCOME TO THE PLEASUREDOME FRANKIE GOES TO HOLLYWOOD (ZTT/ISLAND)
KISS ME STEPHEN TIN TIN DUFFY (10 RECORDS)	10	LIKE A VIRGIN MADONNA (SIRE)
MATERIAL GIRL MADONNA (SIRE)	11	RECKLESS BRYAN ADAMS (A&M)
COULD IT BE I'M FALLING IN LOVE DAVID GRANT AND JAKI GRAHAM (CHRYSALIS)	12	THE POWER STATION POWER STATION (PARLOPHONE)
HANGIN' ON A STRING LOOSE ENDS (VIRGIN)	13	HITS OUT OF HELL MEAT LOAF (EPIC)
MOVE CLOSER PHYLLIS NELSON (CARRERE)	14	BEHIND THE SUN ERIC CLAPTON (DUCK)
SOME LIKE IT HOT POWER STATION (PARLOPHONE)	15	ELIMINATOR ZZ TOP (WARNER BROS)
COVER ME BRUCE SPRINGSTEEN (CBS)	16	VERY BEST OF BRENDA LEE BRENDA LEE (MCA)
THE HEAT IS ON GLENN FREY (MCA)	17	DIAMOND LIFE SADE (EPIC)
SPEND THE NIGHT COOL NOTES (ABSTRACT DANCE)	18	MAKE IT BIG WHAM! (EPIC)
THE LAST KISS DAVID CASSIDY (ARISTA)	19	THE NIGHT I FELL IN LOVE LUTHER VANDROSS (EPIC)
YOU SPIN ME ROUND DEAD OR ALIVE (EPIC)	20	PURPLE RAIN PRINCE AND THE REVOLUTION (WARNER BROS)

SINGLES	US	ALBUMS
ONE MORE NIGHT PHIL COLLINS (ATLANTIC)	1	NO JACKET REQUIRED PHIL COLLINS (ATLANTIC)
WE ARE THE WORLD USA FOR AFRICA (COLUMBIA/CBS)	2	CENTERFIELD JOHN FOGERTY (WARNER BROS)
MATERIAL GIRL MADONNA (SIRE)	3	BORN IN THE USA BRUCE SPRINGSTEEN (COLUMBIA/CBS)
CRAZY FOR YOU MADONNA (SIRE)	4	BEVERLY HILLS COP SOUNDTRACK (MCA)
LOVERGIRL TEENA MARIE (EPIC)	5	PRIVATE DANCER TINA TURNER (CAPITOL)
CAN'T FIGHT THIS FEELING REO SPEEDWAGON (EPIC)	6	LIKE A VIRGIN MADONNA (SIRE)
NIGHTSHIFT COMMODORES (MOTOWN)	7	MAKE IT BIG WHAM! (COLUMBIA/CBS)
I'M ON FIRE BRUCE SPRINGSTEEN (COLUMBIA/CBS)	8	WHEELS ARE TURNING REO SPEEDWAGON (EPIC)
RHYTHM OF THE NIGHT DEBARGE (GORDY)	9	AGENT PROVOCATEUR FOREIGNER (ATLANTIC)
TOO LATE FOR GOODBYES JULIAN LENNON (ATLANTIC)	10	RECKLESS BRYAN ADAMS (A&M
SOMEBODY BRYAN ADAMS (A&M)	11	BREAK OUT POINTER SISTERS (PLANET)
JUST ANOTHER NIGHT MICK JAGGER (COLUMBIA/CBS)	12	NEW EDITION NEW EDITION (MCA)
MISSING YOU DIANA ROSS (RCA)	13	BUILDING THE PERFECT BEAST DON HENLEY (GEFFEN)
OBSESSION ANIMOTION (MERCURY)	14	SHE'S THE BOSS MICK JAGGER (COLUMBIA/CBS)
HIGH ON YOU SURVIVOR (SCOTTI BROS)	15	17 CHICAGO (FULL MOON/WARNER BROS)
PRIVATE DANCER TINA TURNER (CAPITOL)	16	VISION QUEST SOUNDTRACK (GEFFEN)
THE HEAT IS ON GLENN FREY (MCA)	17	CRAZY FROM THE HEAT DAVID LEE ROTH (WARNER BROS)
DON'T YOU (FORGET ABOUT ME) SIMPLE MINDS (A&M)	18	THE FIRM THE FIRM (ATLANTIC)
ONE NIGHT IN BANGKOK MURRAY HEAD (RCA)	19	VALOTTE JULIAN LENNON (ATLANTIC)
ALL SHE WANTS TO DO IS DANCE DON HENLEY (GEFFEN)	20	DIAMOND LIFE SADE (PORTRAIT)

WEEK ENDING APRIL 13 1985

UK

SINGLES		ALBUMS
EASY LOVER PHILIP BAILEY/PHIL COLLINS (CBS/VIRGIN)	1	HITS 2 VARIOUS (CBS/WEA)
WELCOME TO THE PLEASUREDOME FRANKIE GOES TO HOLLYWOOD (ZTT)	2	THE SECRET OF ASSOCIATION PAUL YOUNG (CBS)
EVERYBODY WANT TO RULE . . . TEARS FOR FEARS (MERCURY)	3	NO JACKET REQUIRED PHIL COLLINS (VIRGIN)
PIE JESU SARAH BRIGHTMAN/PAUL MILES-KINGSTON (EMI)	4	SONGS FROM THE BIG CHAIR TEARS FOR FEARS (MERCURY)
WE CLOSE OUR EYES GO WEST (CHRYSALIS)	5	ANDREW LLOYD WEBBER REQUIEM DOMINGO/BRIGHTMAN/MAAZEL/ECO (HMV)
THAT OLE DEVIL CALLED LOVE ALISON MOYET (CBS)	6	BORN IN THE USA BRUCE SPRINGSTEEN (CBS)
WE ARE THE WORLD USA FOR AFRICA (CBS)	7	ALF ALISON MOYET (CBS)
MOVE CLOSER PHYLLIS NELSON (CARRERE)	8	DREAM INTO ACTION HOWARD JONES (WEA)
EVERY TIME YOU GO AWAY PAUL YOUNG (CBS)	9	WELCOME TO THE PLEASUREDOME FRANKIE GOES TO HOLLYWOOD (ZTT)
COULD IT BE I'M FALLING IN LOVE DAVID GRANT/JAKI GRAHAM (CHRYSALIS)	10	GO WEST GO WEST (CHRYSALIS)
WIDE BOY NIK KERSHAW (MCA)	11	PRIVATE DANCER TINA TURNER (CAPITOL)
DO WHAT YOU DO JERMAINE JACKSON (ARISTA)	12	MAKE IT BIG WHAM! (EPIC)
SPEND THE NIGHT COOL NOTES (ABSTRACT DANCE)	13	THE POWER STATION POWER STATION (PARLOPHONE)
THE HEAT IS ON GLENN FREY (MCA)	14	RECKLESS BRYAN ADAMS (A&M)
KISS ME STEPHEN TIN TIN DUFFY (10 RECORDS)	15	PURPLE RAIN PRINCE AND THE REVOLUTION (WARNER BROS)
MATERIAL GIRL MADONNA (SIRE)	16	LIKE A VIRGIN MADONNA (SIRE)
HANGIN' ON A STRING LOOSE ENDS (VIRGIN)	17	ELIMINATOR ZZ TOP (WARNER BROS)
CLOUDS ACROSS THE MOON RAH BAND (RCA)	18	VERY BEST OF BRENDA LEE BRENDA LEE (MCA)
CAN'T FIGHT THIS FEELING REO SPEEDWAGON (EPIC)	19	BEHIND THE SUN ERIC CLAPTON (DUCK)
COVER ME BRUCE SPRINGSTEEN (CBS)	20	THE HITS ALBUM/THE HITS TAPE VARIOUS (CBS/WEA)

US

SINGLES		ALBUMS
WE ARE THE WORLD USA FOR AFRICA (COLUMBIA/CBS)	1	NO JACKET REQUIRED PHIL COLLINS (ATLANTIC)
ONE MORE NIGHT PHIL COLLINS (ATLANTIC)	2	CENTERFIELD JOHN FOGERTY (WARNER BROS)
CRAZY FOR YOU MADONNA (GEFFEN)	3	BORN IN THE USA BRUCE SPRINGSTEEN (COLUMBIA/CBS)
NIGHTSHIFT COMMODORES (MOTOWN)	4	BEVERLY HILLS COP SOUNDTRACK (MCA)
MATERIAL GIRL MADONNA (SIRE)	5	PRIVATE DANCER TINA TURNER (CAPITOL)
I'M ON FIRE BRUCE SPRINGSTEEN (COLUMBIA/CBS)	6	LIKE A VIRGIN MADONNA (SIRE)
RHYTHM OF THE NIGHT DEBARGE (GORDY)	7	MAKE IT BIG WHAM! (COLUMBIA/CBS)
LOVERGIRL TEENA MARIE (EPIC)	8	WHEELS ARE TURNING REO SPEEDWAGON (EPIC)
OBSESSION ANIMOTION (MERCURY)	9	AGENT PROVOCATEUR FOREIGNER (ATLANTIC)
MISSING YOU DIANA ROSS (RCA)	10	RECKLESS BRYAN ADAMS (A&M)
DON'T YOU (FORGET ABOUT ME) SIMPLE MINDS (A&M)	11	BREAK OUT POINTER SISTERS (PLANET)
JUST ANOTHER NIGHT MICK JAGGER (COLUMBIA/CBS)	12	DIAMOND LIFE SADE (PORTRAIT)
CAN'T FIGHT THIS FEELING REO SPEEDWAGON (EPIC)	13	BUILDING THE PERFECT BEAST DON HENLEY (GEFFEN)
SOMEBODY BRYAN ADAMS (A&M)	14	SHE'S THE BOSS MICK JAGGER (COLUMBIA/CBS)
ALL SHE WANTS TO DO IS DANCE DON HENLEY (GEFFEN)	15	VISION QUEST SOUNDTRACK (GEFFEN)
ONE NIGHT IN BANGKOK MURRAY HEAD (RCA)	16	NEW EDITION NEW EDITION (MCA)
SOME LIKE IT HOT POWER STATION (CAPITOL)	17	THE FIRM THE FIRM (ATLANTIC)
ALONG COMES A WOMAN CHICAGO (FULL MOON/WARNER BROS)	18	17 CHICAGO (FULL MOON/WARNER BROS)
HIGH ON YOU SURVIVOR (SCOTTI BROS)	19	VALOTTE JULIAN LENNON (ATLANTIC)
TOO LATE FOR GOODBYES JULIAN LENNON (ATLANTIC)	20	NIGHTSHIFT COMMODORES (MOTOWN)

WEEK ENDING APRIL 20 1985

UK

SINGLES		ALBUMS
WE ARE THE WORLD USA FOR AFRICA (CBS)	1	HITS 2 VARIOUS (CBS/WEA)
EVERBODY WANTS TO RULE . . . TEARS FOR FEARS (MERCURY)	2	THE SECRET OF ASSOCIATION PAUL YOUNG (CBS)
EASY LOVER PHILIP BAILEY/PHIL COLLINS (CBS/VIRGIN)	3	SONGS FROM THE BIG CHAIR TEARS FOR FEARS (MERCURY)
MOVE CLOSER PHYLLIS NELSON (CARRERE)	4	NO JACKET REQUIRED PHIL COLLINS (VIRGIN)
WELCOME TO THE PLEASUREDOME FRANKIE GOES TO HOLLYWOOD (ZTT)	5	ANDREW LLOYD WEBBER REQUIEM DOMINGO/BRIGHTMAN/MAAZEL/ECO (HMV)
WE CLOSE OUR EYES GO WEST (CHRYSALIS)	6	BORN IN THE USA BRUCE SPRINGSTEEN (CBS)
COULD IT BE I'M FALLING IN LOVE DAVID GRANT/JAKI GRAHAM (CHRYSALIS)	7	WELCOME TO THE PLEASUREDOME FRANKIE GOES TO HOLLYWOOD (ZTT)
ONE MORE NIGHT PHIL COLLINS (VIRGIN)	8	ALF ALISON MOYET (CBS)
CLOUDS ACROSS THE MOON RAH BAND (RCA)	9	DREAM INTO ACTION HOWARD JONES (WEA)
PIE JESU SARAH BRIGHTMAN/PAUL MILES-KINGSTON (EMI)	10	GO WEST GO WEST (CHRYSALIS)
SPEND THE NIGHT COOL NOTES (ABSTRACT DANCE)	11	MAKE IT BIG WHAM! (EPIC)
THE HEAT IS ON GLENN FREY (MCA)	12	THE POWER STATION POWER STATION (PARLOPHONE)
EVERY TIME YOU GO AWAY PAUL YOUNG (CBS)	13	SO WHERE ARE YOU LOOSE ENDS (VIRGIN)
THAT OLE DEVIL CALLED LOVE ALISON MOYET (CBS)	14	PRIVATE DANCER TINA TURNER (CAPITOL)
LIFE IN A NORTHERN TOWN DREAM ACADEMY (BLANCO Y NEGRO)	15	RECKLESS BRYAN ADAMS (A&M)
CAN'T FIGHT THIS FEELING REO SPEEDWAGON (EPIC)	16	LIKE A VIRGIN MADONNA (SIRE)
LOVE IS A BATTLEFIELD PAT BENATAR (CHRYSALIS)	17	PURPLE RAIN PRINCE AND THE REVOLUTION (WARNER BROS)
WIDE BOY NIK KERSHAW (MCA)	18	ELIMINATOR ZZ TOP (WARNER BROS)
BLACK MAN RAY CHINA CRISIS (VIRGIN)	19	THE HITS ALBUM/THE HITS TAPE VARIOUS (CBS/WEA)
LOOK MAMA HOWARD JONES (WEA)	20	DIAMOND LIFE SADE (EPIC)

US

SINGLES		ALBUMS
WE ARE THE WORLD USA FOR AFRICA (COLUMBIA/CBS)	1	NO JACKET REQUIRED PHIL COLLINS (ATLANTIC)
CRAZY FOR YOU MADONNA (GEFFEN)	2	BORN IN THE USA BRUCE SPRINGSTEEN (COLUMBIA/CBS)
NIGHTSHIFT COMMODORES (MOTOWN)	3	BEVERLY HILLS COP SOUNDTRACK (MCA)
RHYTHM OF THE NIGHT DEBARGE (GORDY)	4	CENTERFIELD JOHN FOGERTY (WARNER BROS)
ONE MORE NIGHT DEBARGE (GORDY)	5	PRIVATE DANCER TINA TURNER (CAPITOL)
I'M ON FIRE BRUCE SPRINGSTEEN (COLUMBIA/CBS)	6	LIKE A VIRGIN MADONNA (SIRE)
OBSESSION ANIMOTION (MERCURY)	7	MAKE IT BIG WHAM! (COLUMBIA/CBS)
DON'T YOU (FORGET ABOUT ME) SIMPLE MINDS (A&M)	8	WHEELS ARE TURNING REO SPEEDWAGON (EPIC)
JUST ANOTHER NIGHT MICK JAGGER (COLUMBIA/CBS)	9	USA FOR AFRICA WE ARE THE WORLD (COLUMBIA)
MISSING YOU DIANA ROSS (MCA)	10	DIAMOND LIFE SADE (PORTRAIT)
ALL SHE WANTS TO DO IS DANCE DON HENLEY (GEFFEN)	11	AGENT PROVOCATEUR FOREIGNER (ATLANTIC)
SOME LIKE IT HOT POWER STATION (CAPITOL)	12	RECKLESS BRYAN ADAMS (A&M)
MATERIAL GIRL MADONNA (SIRE)	13	SHE'S THE BOSS MICK JAGGER (COLUMBIA/CBS)
ALONG COMES A WOMAN CHICAGO (FULL MOON/WARNER BROS)	14	VISION QUEST SOUNDTRACK (GEFFEN)
LOVERGIRL TEENA MARIE (EPIC)	15	SOUTHERN ACCENTS TOM PETTY/HEARTBREAKERS (MCA)
SMOOTH OPERATOR SADE (PORTRAIT)	16	BUILDING THE PERFECT BEAST DON HENLEY (GEFFEN)
THAT WAS YESTERDAY FOREIGNER (ATLANTIC)	17	THE FIRM THE FIRM (ATLANTIC)
SOMEBODY BRYAN ADAMS (A&M)	18	BREAK OUT POINTER SISTERS (PLANET)
EVERYTHING SHE WANTS WHAM! (COLUMBIA/CBS)	19	NEW EDITION NEW EDITION (MCA)
DON'T COME AROUND TOM PETTY/HEARTBREAKERS (MCA)	20	NIGHTSHIFT COMMODORES (MOTOWN)

WEEK ENDING APRIL 27 1985

UK

SINGLES	UK	ALBUMS
WE ARE THE WORLD USA FOR AFRICA (CBS)	1	HITS 2 VARIOUS (CBS/WEA)
EVERYBODY WANTS TO RULE . . . TEARS FOR FEARS (MERCURY)	2	SONGS FROM THE BIG CHAIR TEARS FOR FEARS (MERCURY)
MOVE CLOSER PHYLLIS NELSON (CARRERE)	3	NO JACKET REQUIRED PHIL COLLINS (VIRGIN)
ONE MORE NIGHT PHIL COLLINS (VIRGIN)	4	THE SECRET OF ASSOCIATION PAUL YOUNG (CBS)
COULD IT BE I'M FALLING IN LOVE DAVID GRANT AND JAKI GRAHAM (CHRYSALIS)	5	BORN IN THE USA BRUCE SPRINGSTEEN (CBS)
CLOUDS ACROSS THE MOON RAH BAND (RCA)	6	DREAM INTO ACTION HOWARD JONES (WEA)
I FEEL LOVE BRONSKI BEAT/MARC ALMOND (FORBIDDEN FRUIT)	7	ANDREW LLOYD WEBBER REQUIEM DOMINGO/BRIGHTMAN/MAAZEL/ECO (HMV)
DON'T YOU (FORGET ABOUT ME) SIMPLE MINDS (VIRGIN)	8	ALF ALSION MOYET (CBS)
WE CLOSE OUR EYES GO WEST (CHRYSALIS)	9	GO WEST GO WEST (CHRYSALIS)
LOOK MAMA HOWARD JONES (WEA)	10	LOVE NOT MONEY EVERYTHING BUT THE GIRL (BLANCO Y NEGRO)
LOVER COME BACK TO ME DEAD OR ALIVE (EPIC)	11	PRIVATE DANCER TINA TURNER (CAPITOL)
WELCOME TO THE PLEASUREDOME FRANKIE GOES TO HOLLYWOOD (ZTT)	12	RECKLESS BRYAN ADAMS (A&M)
EASY LOVER PHILIP BAILEY/PHIL COLLINS (CBS/VIRGIN)	13	WELCOME TO THE PLEASUREDOME FRANKIE GOES TO HOLLYWOOD (ZTT)
BLACK MAN RAY CHINA CRISIS (VIRGIN)	14	SO WHERE ARE YOU LOOSE ENDS (VIRGIN)
LIFE IN A NORTHERN TOWN DREAM ACADEMY (BLANCO Y NEGRO)	15	LEGEND CLANNAD (RCA)
SPEND THE NIGHT COOL NOTES (ABSTRACT DANCE)	16	MAKE IT BIG WHAM! (EPIC)
LOVE IS A BATTLEFIELD PAT BENATAR (CHRYSALIS)	17	LIKE A VIRGIN MADONNA (SIRE)
THE HEAT IS ON GLENN FREY (MCA)	18	THE POWER STATION POWER STATION (PARLOPHONE)
EYE TO EYE CHAKA KHAN (WARNER BROS)	19	DIAMOND LIFE SADE (EPIC)
FEEL SO REAL STEVE ARRINGTON (ATLANTIC)	20	ELIMINATOR ZZ TOP (WARNER BROS)

US

SINGLES	US	ALBUMS
WE ARE THE WORLD USA FOR AFRICA (COLUMBIA/CBS)	1	WE ARE THE WORLD USA FOR AFRICA (COLUMBIA/CBS)
CRAZY FOR YOU MADONNA (GEFFEN)	2	NO JACKET REQUIRED PHIL COLLINS (ATLANTIC)
RHYTHM OF THE NIGHT DEBARGE (GORDY)	3	BORN IN THE USA BRUCE SPRINGSTEEN (COLUMBIA/CBS)
NIGHTSHIFT COMMODORES (MOTOWN)	4	BEVERLY HILLS COP SOUNDTRACK (MCA)
DON'T YOU (FORGET ABOUT ME) SIMPLE MINDS (A&M)	5	CENTERFIELD JOHN FOGERTY (WARNER BROS)
ONE NIGHT IN BANGKOK MURRAY HEAD (RCA)	6	LIKE A VIRGIN MADONNA (SIRE)
OBSESSION ANIMOTION (MERCURY)	7	PRIVATE DANCER TINA TURNER (CAPITOL)
SOME LIKE IT HOT POWER STATION (CAPITOL)	8	DIAMOND LIFE SADE (PORTRAIT)
I'M ON FIRE BRUCE SPRINGSTEEN (COLUMBIA/CBS)	9	MAKE IT BIG WHAM! (COLUMBIA/CBS)
ALL SHE WANTS TO DO IS DANCE DON HENLEY (GEFFEN)	10	SOUTHERN ACCENTS TOM PETTY/HEARTBREAKERS (MCA)
ONE MORE NIGHT PHIL COLLINS (ATLANTIC)	11	AGENT PROVOCATEUR FOREIGNER (ATLANTIC)
SMOOTH OPERATOR SADE (PORTRAIT)	12	NIGHTSHIFT COMMODORES (MOTOWN)
MISSING YOU DIANA ROSS (RCA)	13	WHEELS ARE TURNING REO SPEEDWAGON (GEFFEN)
ALONG COMES A WOMAN CHICAGO (FULL MOON/WARNER BROS)	14	VISION QUEST SOUNDTRACK (GEFFEN)
THAT WAS YESTERDAY FOREIGNER (ATLANTIC)	15	RECKLESS BRYAN ADAMS (A&M)
EVERYTHING SHE WANTS WHAM! (COLUMBIA/CBS)	16	BUILDING THE PERFECT BEAST DON HENLEY (GEFFEN)
DON'T COME AROUND TOM PETTY/HEARTBREAKERS (MCA)	17	SHE'S THE BOSS MICK JAGGER (COLUMBIA/CBS)
EVERYBODY WANTS TO RULE . . . TEARS FOR FEARS (MERCURY)	18	CRAZY FROM THE HEAT DAVID LEE ROTH (WARNER BROS)
SOME THINGS ARE BETTER HALL & OATES (RCA)	19	17 CHICAGO (FULL MOON/WARNER BROS)
ROCK AND ROLL GIRLS JOHN FOGERTY (WARNER BROS)	20	BREAK OUT POINTER SISTERS (PLANET)

WEEK ENDING MAY 4 1985

UK

SINGLES	UK	ALBUMS
MOVE CLOSER PHYLLIS NELSON (CARRERE)	1	HITS 2 VARIOUS (CBS/WEA)
WE ARE THE WORLD USA FOR AFRICA (CBS)	2	NO JACKET REQUIRED PHIL COLLINS (VIRGIN)
EVERYBODY WANTS TO RULE . . . TEARS FOR FEARS (MERCURY)	3	SONGS FROM THE BIG CHAIR TEARS FOR FEARS (MERCURY)
19 PAUL HARDCASTLE (CHRYSALIS)	4	THE SECRET OF ASSOCIATION PAUL YOUNG (CBS)
I FEEL LOVE BRONSKI BEAT/MARC ALMOND (FORBIDDEN FRUIT)	5	AROUND THE WORLD IN A DAY PRINCE AND THE REVOLUTION (WARNER BROS)
ONE MORE NIGHT PHIL COLLINS (VIRGIN)	6	BORN IN THE USA BRUCE SPRINGSTEEN (CBS)
DON'T YOU (FORGET ABOUT ME) SIMPLE MINDS (VIRGIN)	7	DREAM INTO ACTION HOWARD JONES (WEA)
THE UNFORGETTABLE FIRE U2 (ISLAND)	8	ALF ALISON MOYET (CBS)
CLOUDS ACROSS THE MOON RAH BAND (RCA)	9	VOICES FROM THE HOLY LAND BBC WELSH CHORUS (BBC)
COULD IT BE I'M FALLING IN LOVE DAVID GRANT AND JAKI GRAHAM (CHRYSALIS)	10	GO WEST GO WEST (CHRYSALIS)
FEEL SO REAL STEVE ARRINGTON (ATLANTIC)	11	ANDREW LLOYD WEBBER REQUIEM DOMINGO/BRIGHTMAN/MAAZEL/ECO (HMV)
LOVER COME BACK TO ME DEAD OR ALIVE (EPIC)	12	VIRGINS AND PHILISTINES COLOURFIELD (CHRYSALIS)
LOOK MAMA HOWARD JONES (WEA)	13	LOVE NOT MONEY EVERYTHING BUT THE GIRL (BLANCO Y NEGRO)
I WAS BORN TO LOVE YOU FREDDIE MERCURY (CBS)	14	RECKLESS BRYAN ADAM (A&M)
BLACK MAN RAY CHINA CRISIS (VIRGIN)	15	BEST OF ELVIS COSTELLO ELVIS COSTELLO (TELSTAR)
EYE TO EYE CHAKA KHAN (WARNER BROS)	16	PRIVATE DANCER TINA TURNER (CAPITOL)
RHYTHM OF THE NIGHT DEBARGE (GORDY)	17	THE AGE OF CONSENT BRONSKI BEAT (FORBIDDEN FRUIT)
WE CLOSE OUR EYES GO WEST (CHRYSALIS)	18	WELCOME TO THE PLEASUREDOME FRANKIE GOES TO HOLLYWOOD (ZTT)
EASY LOVER PHILIP BAILEY/PHIL COLLINS (CBS/VIRGIN)	19	SO WHERE ARE YOU LOOSE ENDS (VIRGIN)
SO FAR AWAY DIRE STRAITS (VERTIGO)	20	MAKE IT BIG WHAM! (EPIC)

US

SINGLES	US	ALBUMS
WE ARE THE WORLD USA FOR AFRICA (COLUMBIA/CBS)	1	WE ARE THE WORLD USA FOR AFRICA (COLUMBIA/CBS)
CRAZY FOR YOU MADONNA (GEFFEN)	2	NO JACKET REQUIRED PHIL COLLINS (ATLANTIC)
RHYTHM OF THE NIGHT DEBARGE (GORDY)	3	BORN IN THE USA BRUCE SPRINGSTEEN (COLUMBIA/CBS)
NIGHTSHIFT COMMODORES (MOTOWN)	4	BEVERLY HILLS COP SOUNDTRACK (MCA)
DON'T YOU (FORGET ABOUT ME) SIMPLE MINDS (A&M)	5	LIKE A VIRGIN MADONNA (SIRE)
ONE NIGHT IN BANGKOK MURRAY HEAD (RCA)	6	DIAMOND LIFE SADE (PORTRAIT)
OBSESSION ANIMOTION (MERCURY)	7	CENTERFIELD JOHN FOGERTY (WARNER BROS)
SOME LIKE IT HOT POWER STATION (CAPITOL)	8	PRIVATE DANCER TINA TURNER (CAPITOL)
I'M ON FIRE BRUCE SPRINGSTEEN (COLUMBIA/CBS)	9	SOUTHERN ACCENTS TOM PETTY/HEARTBREAKERS (MCA)
ALL SHE WANTS TO DO IS DANCE DON HENLEY (GEFFEN)	10	MAKE IT BIG WHAM! (COLUMBIA/CBS)
ONE MORE NIGHT PHIL COLLINS (ATLANTIC)	11	VISION QUEST SOUNDTRACK (GEFFEN)
SMOOTH OPERATOR SADE (PORTRAIT)	12	NIGHTSHIFT COMMODORES (MOTOWN)
MISSING YOU DIANA ROSS (RCA)	13	WHEELS ARE TURNING REO SPEEDWAGON (EPIC)
ALONG COMES A WOMAN CHICAGO (FULL MOON/WARNER BROS)	14	AGENT PROVOCATEUR FOREIGNER (ATLANTIC)
THAT WAS YESTERDAY FOREIGNER (ATLANTIC)	15	RECKLESS BRYAN ADAMS (A&M)
EVERYTHING SHE WANTS WHAM! (COLUMBIA/CBS)	16	BUILDING THE PERFECT BEAST DON HENLEY (GEFFEN)
DON'T COME AROUND TOM PETTY/HEARTBREAKERS (MCA)	17	THE POWER STATION POWER STATION (CAPITOL)
EVERYBODY WANTS TO RULE . . . TEARS FOR FEARS (MERCURY)	18	SONGS FROM THE BIG CHAIR TEARS FOR FEARS (MERCURY)
SOME THINGS ARE BETTER HALL & OATES (RCA)	19	BREAK OUT POINTER SISTERS (PLANET)
ROCK AND ROLL GIRLS JOHN FOGERTY (WARNER BROS)	20	CRAZY FROM THE HEAT DAVID LEE ROTH (WARNER BROS)

WEEK ENDING MAY 11 1985

UK

SINGLES		ALBUMS
19 — PAUL HARDCASTLE (CHRYSALIS)	1	HITS 2 — VARIOUS (CBS/WEA)
MOVE CLOSER — PHYLLIS NELSON (CARRERE)	2	NO JACKET REQUIRED — PHIL COLLINS (VIRGIN)
I FEEL LOVE — BRONSKI BEAT/MARC ALMOND (FORBIDDEN FRUIT)	3	SONGS FROM THE BIG CHAIR — TEARS FOR FEARS (MERCURY)
EVERYBODY WANTS TO RULE . . . — TEARS FOR FEARS (MERCURY)	4	BE YOURSELF TONIGHT — EURYTHMICS (RCA)
WE ARE THE WORLD — USA FOR AFRICA (CBS)	5	THE SECRET OF ASSOCIATION — PAUL YOUNG (CBS)
THE UNFORGETTABLE FIRE — U2 (ISLAND)	6	MR BAD GUY — FREDDIE MERCURY (CBS)
FEEL SO REAL — STEVE ARRINGTON (ATLANTIC)	7	BORN IN THE USA — BRUCE SPRINGSTEEN (CBS)
DON'T YOU (FORGET ABOUT ME) — SIMPLE MINDS (VIRGIN)	8	VOICES FROM THE HOLY LAND — BBC WELSH CHORUS (BBC)
RHYTHM OF THE NIGHT — DEBARGE (GORDY)	9	FLAUNT THE IMPERFECTION — CHINA CRISIS (VIRGIN)
ONE MORE NIGHT — PHIL COLLINS (VIRGIN)	10	AROUND THE WORLD IN A DAY — PRINCE AND THE REVOLUTION (WARNER BROS)
I WAS BORN TO LOVE YOU — FREDDIE MERCURY (CBS)	11	DREAM INTO ACTION — HOWARD JONES (WEA)
CLOUDS ACROSS THE MOON — RAH BAND (CBS)	12	BEST OF ELVIS COSTELLO — ELVIS COSTELLO (TELSTAR)
WALLS COME TUMBLING DOWN — STYLE COUNCIL (POLYDOR)	13	ALF — ALISON MOYET (CBS)
LOVER COME BACK TO ME — DEAD OR ALIVE (EPIC)	14	PRIVATE DANCER — TINA TURNER (CAPITOL)
COULD IT BE I'M FALLING IN LOVE — DAVID GRANT AND JAKI GRAHAM (CHRYSALIS)	15	GO WEST — GO WEST (CHRYSALIS)
I WANT YOUR LOVIN' — CURTIS HAIRSTON (LONDON)	16	ANDREW LLOYD WEBBER REQUIEM — DOMINGO/BRIGHTMAN/MAAZEL/ECO (HMV)
WOULD I LIE TO YOU — EURYTHMICS (RCA)	17	THE AGE OF CONSENT — BRONSKI BEAT (FORBIDDEN FRUIT)
LOOK MAMA — HOWARD JONES (WEA)	18	WELCOME TO THE PLEASUREDOME — FRANKIE GOES TO HOLLYWOOD (ZTT)
CRY — GODLEY AND CREME (POLYDOR)	19	THE POWER STATION — POWER STATION (PARLOPHONE)
LOVE DON'T LIVE HERE ANYMORE — JIMMY NAIL (VIRGIN)	20	MAKE IT BIG — WHAM! (EPIC)

US

SINGLES		ALBUMS
CRAZY FOR YOU — MADONNA (GEFFEN)	1	WE ARE THE WORLD — USA FOR AFRICA (COLUMBIA/CBS)
WE ARE THE WORLD — USA FOR AFRICA (COLUMBIA/CBS)	2	NO JACKET REQUIRED — PHIL COLLINS (ATLANTIC)
DON'T YOU (FORGET ABOUT ME) — SIMPLE MINDS (A&M)	3	BORN IN THE USA — BRUCE SPRINGSTEEN (COLUMBIA/CBS)
RHYTHM OF THE NIGHT — DEBARGE (GORDY)	4	BEVERLY HILLS COP — SOUNDTRACK (MCA)
ONE NIGHT IN BANGKOK — MURRAY HEAD (RCA)	5	LIKE A VIRGIN — MADONNA (SIRE)
SOME LIKE IT HOT — POWER STATION (CAPITOL)	6	DIAMOND LIFE — SADE (PORTRAIT)
SMOOTH OPERATOR — SADE (PORTRAIT)	7	SOUTHERN ACCENTS — TOM PETTY/HEARTBREAKERS (MCA)
EVERYTHING SHE WANTS — WHAM! (COLUMBIA/CBS)	8	CENTERFIELD — JOHN FOGERTY (WARNER BROS)
OBSESSION — ANIMOTION (MERCURY)	9	MAKE IT BIG — WHAM! (COLUMBIA/CBS)
EVERYBODY WANTS TO RULE . . . — TEARS FOR FEARS (MERCURY)	10	PRIVATE DANCER — TINA TURNER (CAPITOL)
ALL SHE WANTS TO DO IS DANCE — DON HENLEY (GEFFEN)	11	RECKLESS — BRYAN ADAMS (A&M)
AXEL F — HAROLD FALTERMEYER (MCA)	12	NIGHTSHIFT — COMMODORES (MOTOWN)
NIGHTSHIFT — COMMODORES (MOTOWN)	13	THE POWER STATION — POWER STATION (CAPITOL)
DON'T COME AROUND — TOM PETTY/HEARBREAKERS (MCA)	14	AROUND THE WORLD IN A DAY — PRINCE (PAISLEY PARK)
THAT WAS YESTERDAY — FOREIGNER (ATLANTIC)	15	VISION QUEST — SOUNDTRACK (GEFFEN)
SUDDENLY — BILLY OCEAN (JIVE/ARISTA)	16	WHEELS ARE TURNING — REO SPEEDWAGON (EPIC)
NEW ATTITUDE — PATTI LABELLE (MCA)	17	SONGS FROM THE BIG CHAIR — TEARS FOR FEARS (MERCURY)
FRESH — KOOL AND THE GANG (DE-LITE)	18	CRAZY FROM THE HEAT — DAVID LEE ROTH (WARNER BROS)
THINGS CAN ONLY GET BETTER — HOWARD JONES (ELEKTRA)	19	AGENT PROVOCATEUR — FOREIGNER (ATLANTIC)
IN MY HOUSE — MARY JANE GIRLS (GORDY)	20	BREAK OUT — POINTER SISTERS (PLANET)

WEEK ENDING MAY 18 1985

UK

SINGLES		ALBUMS
19 — PAUL HARDCASTLE (CHRYSALIS)	1	HITS 2 — VARIOUS (CBS/WEA)
MOVE CLOSER — PHYLLIS NELSON (CARRERE)	2	NO JACKET REQUIRED — PHIL COLLINS (VIRGIN)
I FEEL LOVE — BRONSKI BEAT/MARC ALMOND (FORBIDDEN FRUIT)	3	BE YOURSELF TONIGHT — EURYTHMICS (RCA)
RHYTHM OF THE NIGHT — DEBARGE (GORDY)	4	SONGS FROM THE BIG CHAIR — TEARS FOR FEARS (MERCURY)
FEEL SO REAL — STEVE ARRINGTON (ATLANTIC)	5	THE SECRET OF ASSOCIATION — PAUL YOUNG (CBS)
WALLS COME TUMBLING DOWN — STYLE COUNCIL (POLYDOR)	6	MR BAD GUY — FREDDIE MERCURY (CBS)
A VIEW TO A KILL — DURAN DURAN (PARLOPHONE)	7	BORN IN THE USA — BRUCE SPRINGSTEEN (CBS)
LOVE DON'T LIVE HERE ANYMORE — JIMMY NAIL (VIRGIN)	8	BEST OF ELVIS COSTELLO — ELVIS COSTELLO (TELSTAR)
EVERYBODY WANTS TO RULE . . . — TEARS FOR FEARS (MERCURY)	9	BEST OF THE 20TH CENTURY BOY — MARC BOLAN AND T REX (K-TEL)
DON'T YOU (FORGET ABOUT ME) — SIMPLE MINDS (VIRGIN)	10	FLAUNT THE IMPERFECTION — CHINA CRISIS (VIRGIN)
I WAS BORN TO LOVE YOU — FREDDIE MERCURY (CBS)	11	VOICES FROM THE HOLY LAND — BBC WELSH CHORUS (BBC)
THE UNFORGETTABLE FIRE — U2 (ISLAND)	12	STREET SOUNDS ELECTRO 7 — VARIOUS (STREETSOUNDS)
I WANT YOUR LOVIN' — CURTIS HAIRSTON (LONDON)	13	ALF — ALISON MOYET (CBS)
SLAVE TO LOVE — BRYAN FERRY (EG)	14	THE AGE OF CONSENT — BRONSKI BEAT (FORBIDDEN FRUIT)
KAYLEIGH — MARILLION (EMI)	15	AROUND THE WORLD IN A DAY — PRINCE AND THE REVOLUTION (WARNER BROS)
ONE MORE NIGHT — PHIL COLLINS (VIRGIN)	16	BEST OF EAGLES — EAGLES (ASYLUM)
WE ARE THE WORLD — USA FOR AFRICA (CBS)	17	GO WEST — GO WEST (CHRYSALIS)
WOULD I LIE TO YOU — EURYTHMICS (RCA)	18	DREAM INTO ACTION — HOWARD JONES (WEA)
CRY — GODLEY AND CREME (POLYDOR)	19	THE POWER STATION — POWER STATION (PARLOPHONE)
MAGIC TOUCH — LOOSE ENDS (VIRGIN)	20	PRIVATE DANCER — TINA TURNER (CAPITOL)

US

SINGLES		ALBUMS
DON'T YOU (FORGET ABOUT ME) — SIMPLE MINDS (A&M)	1	NO JACKET REQUIRED — PHIL COLLINS (ATLANTIC)
CRAZY FOR YOU — MADONNA (GEFFEN)	2	WE ARE THE WORLD — USA FOR AFRICA (COLUMBIA/CBS)
ONE NIGHT IN BANGKOK — MURRAY HEAD (RCA)	3	BEVERLY HILLS COP — SOUNDTRACK (MCA)
EVERYTHING SHE WANTS — WHAM! (COLUMBIA/CBS)	4	BORN IN THE USA — BRUCE SPRINGSTEEN (COLUMBIA/CBS)
SMOOTH OPERATOR — SADE (PORTRAIT)	5	AROUND THE WORLD IN A DAY — PRINCE AND THE RLVOLUTION (PAISLEY PARK)
SOME LIKE IT HOT — POWER STATION (CAPITOL)	6	DIAMOND LIFE — SADE (PORTRAIT)
RHYTHM OF THE NIGHT — DEBARGE (GORDY)	7	SOUTHERN ACCENTS — TOM PETTY/HEARTBREAKERS (MCA)
WE ARE THE WORLD — USA FOR AFRICA (COLUMBIA/CBS)	8	LIKE A VIRGIN — MADONNA (SIRE)
EVERYBODY WANTS TO RULE . . . — TEARS FOR FEARS (MERCURY)	9	MAKE IT BIG — WHAM! (COLUMBIA/CBS)
AXEL F — HAROLD FALTERMEYER (MCA)	10	CENTERFIELD — JOHN FOGERTY (WARNER BROS)
SUDDENLY — BILLY OCEAN (JIVE/ARISTA)	11	RECKLESS — BRYAN ADAMS (A&M)
OBSESSION — ANIMOTION (MERCURY)	12	SONGS FROM THE BIG CHAIR — TEARS FOR FEARS (MERCURY)
DON'T COME AROUND — TOM PETTY/HEARTBREAKERS (MCA)	13	THE POWER STATION — POWER STATION (CAPITOL)
ALL SHE WANTS TO DO IS DANCE — DON HENLEY (GEFFEN)	14	NIGHTSHIFT — COMMODORES (MOTOWN)
THINGS CAN ONLY GET BETTER — HOWARD JONES (ELEKTRA)	15	PRIVATE DANCER — TINA TURNER (CAPITOL)
IN MY HOUSE — MARY JANE GIRLS (GORDY)	16	CRAZY FROM THE HEAT — DAVID LEE ROTH (WARNER BROS)
FRESH — KOOL AND THE GANG (DE-LITE)	17	THE BREAKFAST CLUB — SOUNDTRACK (A&M)
JUST A GIGOLO/I AIN'T NOBODY — DAVID LEE ROTH (WARNER BROS)	18	WHEELS ARE TURNING — REO SPEEDWAGON (EPIC)
NEW ATTITUDE — PATTI LABELLE (MCA)	19	BREAK OUT — POINTER SISTERS (PLANET)
HEAVEN 'LIVE' — BRYAN ADAMS (A&M)	20	AGENT PROVOCATEUR — FOREIGNER (ATLANTIC)

WEEK ENDING MAY 25 1985

UK

	SINGLES		ALBUMS
1	19 / PAUL HARDCASTLE (CHRYSALIS)	1	BROTHERS IN ARMS / DIRE STRAITS (VERTIGO)
2	A VIEW TO A KILL / DURAN DURAN (PARLOPHONE)	2	OUT NOW / VARIOUS (CHRYSALIS/MCA)
3	LOVE DON'T LIVE HERE ANYMORE / JIMMY NAIL (VIRGIN)	3	HITS 2 / VARIOUS (CBS/WEA)
4	MOVE CLOSER / PHYLLIS NELSON (CARRERE)	4	NO JACKET REQUIRED / PHIL COLLINS (VIRGIN)
5	I FEEL LOVE / BRONSKI BEAT/MARC ALMOND (FORBIDDEN FRUIT)	5	SONGS FROM THE BIG CHAIR / TEARS FOR FEARS (MERCURY)
6	RHYTHM OF THE NIGHT / DEBARGE (GORDY)	6	BE YOURSELF TONIGHT / EURYTHMICS (RCA)
7	KAYLEIGH / MARILLION (EMI)	7	LOW LIFE / NEW ORDER (FACTORY)
8	FEEL SO REAL / STEVE ARRINGTON (ATLANTIC)	8	BEST OF THE 20TH CENTURY BOY / MARC BOLAN AND T REX (K-TEL)
9	WALLS COME TUMBLING DOWN / STYLE COUNCIL (POLYDOR)	9	YOUTHQUAKE / DEAD OR ALIVE (EPIC)
10	WE ALL FOLLOW MAN UNITED / MANCHESTER UNITED (COLUMBIA)	10	BEST OF ELVIS COSTELLO / ELVIS COSTELLO (TELSTAR)
11	SLAVE TO LOVE / BRYAN FERRY (EG)	11	THE SECRET OF ASSOCIATION / PAUL YOUNG (CBS)
12	I WAS BORN TO LOVE YOU / FREDDIE MERCURY (CBS)	12	BEST OF EAGLES / EAGLES (ASYLUM)
13	DON'T YOU (FORGET ABOUT ME) / SIMPLE MINDS (VIRGIN)	13	BORN IN THE USA / BRUCE SPRINGSTEEN (CBS)
14	HERE WE GO / EVERTON 1985 (COLUMBIA)	14	MR BAD GUY / FREDDIE MERCURY (CBS)
15	EVERYBODY WANTS TO RULE . . . / TEARS FOR FEARS (MERCURY)	15	GO WEST / GO WEST (CHRYSALIS)
16	MAGIC TOUCH / LOOSE ENDS (VIRGIN)	16	FLAUNT THE IMPERFECTION / CHINA CRISIS (VIRGIN)
17	CALL ME / GO WEST (CHRYSALIS)	17	THE AGE OF CONSENT / BRONSKI BEAT (FORBIDDEN FRUIT)
18	OUT IN THE FIELDS / GARY MOORE/PHIL LYNOTT (10 RECORDS)	18	VOICES FROM THE HOLY LAND / BBC WELSH CHORUS (BBC)
19	RAGE TO LOVE / KIM WILDE (MCA)	19	WEST SIDE STORY / BERNSTEIN/TE KANAWA/CARRERAS (DEUTSCHE)
20	WALKING ON SUNSHINE / KATRINA AND THE WAVES (CAPITOL)	20	BROTHER WHERE YOU BOUND / SUPERTRAMP (A&M)

US

	SINGLES		ALBUMS
1	EVERYTHING SHE WANTS / WHAM! (COLUMBIA/CBS)	1	NO JACKET REQUIRED / PHIL COLLINS (ATLANTIC)
2	DON'T YOU (FORGET ABOUT ME) / SIMPLE MINDS (A&M)	2	AROUND THE WORLD IN A DAY / PRINCE AND THE REVOLUTION (PAISLEY PARK)
3	EVERYBODY WANTS TO RULE . . . / TEARS FOR FEARS (MERCURY)	3	BEVERLY HILLS COP / SOUNDTRACK (MCA)
4	AXEL F / HAROLD FALTERMEYER (MCA)	4	BORN IN THE USA / BRUCE SPRINGSTEEN (COLUMBIA/CBS)
5	SMOOTH OPERATOR / SADE (PORTRAIT)	5	WE ARE THE WORLD / USA FOR AFRICA (COLUMBIA/CBS)
6	CRAZY FOR YOU / MADONNA (GEFFEN)	6	DIAMOND LIFE / SADE (PORTRAIT)
7	ONE NIGHT IN BANGKOK / MURRAY HEAD (RCA)	7	LIKE A VIRGIN / MADONNA (SIRE)
8	SUDDENLY / BILLY OCEAN (JIVE/ARISTA)	8	MAKE IT BIG / WHAM! (COLUMBIA/CBS)
9	SOME LIKE IT HOT / POWER STATION (CAPITOL)	9	SONGS FROM THE BIG CHAIR / TEARS FOR FEARS (MERCURY)
10	THINGS CAN ONLY GET BETTER / HOWARD JONES (ELEKTRA)	10	SOUTHERN ACCENTS / TOM PETTY/HEARTBREAKERS (MCA)
11	FRESH / KOOL AND THE GANG (DE-LITE)	11	RECKLESS / BRYAN ADAMS (A&M)
12	HEAVEN 'LIVE' / BRYAN ADAMS (A&M)	12	THE POWER STATION / POWER STATION (CAPITOL)
13	IN MY HOUSE / MARY JANE GIRLS (GORDY)	13	CENTERFIELD / JOHN FOGERTY (WARNER BROS)
14	WE ARE THE WORLD / USA FOR AFRICA (COLUMBIA/CBS)	14	DREAM INTO ACTION / HOWARD JONES (ELEKTRA)
15	JUST A GIGOLO/I AIN'T GOT NOBODY / DAVID LEE ROTH (WARNER BROS)	15	CRAZY FROM THE HEAT / DAVID LEE ROTH (WARNER BROS)
16	RHYTHM OF THE NIGHT / DEBARGE (GORDY)	16	PRIVATE DANCER / TINA TURNER (CAPITOL)
17	WALKING ON SUNSHINE / KATRINA AND THE WAVES (CAPITOL)	17	THE BREAKFAST CLUB / SOUNDTRACK (A&M)
18	DON'T COME AROUND / TOM PETTY/HEARTBREAKERS (MCA)	18	SUDDENLY / BILLY OCEAN (JIVE/ARISTA)
19	ANGEL / MADONNA (SIRE)	19	NIGHTSHIFT / COMMODORES (MOTOWN)
20	ONE LONELY NIGHT / REO SPEEDWAGON (EPIC)	20	BUILDING THE PERFECT BEAST / DON HENLEY (GEFFEN)

WEEK ENDING JUNE 1 1985

UK

	SINGLES		ALBUMS
1	19 / PAUL HARDCASTLE (CHRYSALIS)	1	BROTHERS IN ARMS / DIRE STRAITS (VERTIGO)
2	A VIEW TO A KILL / DURAN DURAN (PARLOPHONE)	2	OUT NOW / VARIOUS (CHRYSALIS/MCA)
3	LOVE DON'T LIVE HERE ANYMORE / JIMMY NAIL (VIRGIN)	3	NOW DANCE / VARIOUS (EMI/VIRGIN)
4	KAYLEIGH / MARLLION (EMI)	4	SONGS FROM THE BIG CHAIR / TEARS FOR FEARS (MERCURY)
5	RHYTHM OF THE NIGHT / DEBARGE (GORDY)	5	BEST OF THE 20TH CENTURY BOY / MARC BOLAN AND T REX (K-TEL)
6	MOVE CLOSER / PHYLLIS NELSON (CARRERE)	6	NO JACKET REQUIRED / PHIL COLLINS (VIRGIN)
7	I FEEL LOVE / BRONSKI BEAT/MARC ALMOND (FORBIDDEN FRUIT)	7	HITS 2 / VARIOUS (CBS/WEA)
8	OUT IN THE FIELDS / GARY MOORE/PHIL LYNOTT (10 RECORDS)	8	BE YOURSELF TONIGHT / EURYTHMICS (RCA)
9	WALKING ON SUNSHINE / KATRINA AND THE WAVES (CAPITOL)	9	LOW LIFE / NEW ORDER (FACTORY)
10	SLAVE TO LOVE / BRYAN FERRY (EG)	10	BEST OF EAGLES / EAGLES (ASYLUM)
11	FEEL SO REAL / STEVE ARRINGTON (ATLANTIC)	11	GO WEST / GO WEST (CHRYSALIS)
12	OBSESSION / ANIMOTION (MERCURY)	12	BEST OF ELVIS COSTELLO / ELVIS COSTELLO (TELSTAR)
13	CALL ME / GO WEST (CHRYSALIS)	13	THE SECRET OF ASSOCIATION / PAUL YOUNG (CBS)
14	WE ALL FOLLOW MAN UNITED / MANCHESTER UNITED (COLUMBIA)	14	BORN IN THE USA / BRUCE SPRINGSTEEN (CBS)
15	THE WORD GIRL / SCRITTI POLITTI (VIRGIN)	15	SHAMROCK DIARIES / CHRIS REA (MAGNET)
16	WALLS COME TUMBLING DOWN / STYLE COUCIL (POLYDOR)	16	YOUTHQUAKE / DEAD OR ALIVE (EPIC)
17	MAGIC TOUCH / LOOSE ENDS (VIRGIN)	17	MR BAD GUY / FREDDIE MERCURY (CBS)
18	I WAS BORN TO LOVE YOU / FREDDIE MERCURY (CBS)	18	THE AGE OF CONSENT / BRONSKI BEAT (FORBIDDEN FRUIT)
19	SUDDENLY / BILLY OCEAN (JIVE)	19	SHAKEN AND STIRRED / ROBERT PLANT (ES PARANZA)
20	ICING ON THE CAKE / STEPHEN TIN TIN DUFFY (10 RECORDS)	20	THE POWER STATION / POWER STATION (PARLOPHONE)

US

	SINGLES		ALBUMS
1	EVERYTHING SHE WANTS / WHAM! (COLUMBIA/CBS)	1	AROUND THE WORLD / PRINCE AND THE REVOLUTION (PAISLEY PARK)
2	EVERYBODY WANTS TO RULE . . . / TEARS FOR FEARS (MERCURY)	2	NO JACKET REQUIRED / PHIL COLLINS (ATLANTIC)
3	AXEL F / HAROLD FALTERMEYER (MCA)	3	BORN IN THE USA / BRUCE SPRINGSTEEN (COLUMBIA/CBS)
4	DON'T YOU (FORGET ABOUT ME) / SIMPLE MINDS (A&M)	4	BEVERLY HILLS COP / SOUNDTRACK (MCA)
5	SUDDENLY / BILLY OCEAN (JIVE/ARISTA)	5	DIAMOND LIFE / SADE (PORTRAIT)
6	SMOOTH OPERATOR / SADE (PORTRAIT)	6	SONGS FROM THE BIG CHAIR / TEARS FOR FEARS (MERCURY)
7	HEAVEN 'LIVE' / BRYAN ADAMS (A&M)	7	LIKE A VIRGIN / MADONNA (SIRE)
8	THINGS CAN ONLY GET BETTER / HOWARD JONES (ELEKTRA)	8	MAKE IT BIG / WHAM! (COLUMBIA/CBS)
9	IN MY HOUSE / MARY JANE GIRLS (GORDY)	9	WE ARE THE WORLD / USA FOR AFRICA (COLUMBIA/CBS)
10	FRESH / KOOL AND THE GANG (DE-LITE)	10	RECKLESS / BRYAN ADAMS (A&M)
11	WALKING ON SUNSHINE / KATRINA AND THE WAVES (CAPITOL)	11	SOUTHERN ACCENTS / TOM PETTY/HEARTBREAKERS (MCA)
12	JUST A GIGOLO/I AIN'T GOT NOBODY / DAVID LEE ROTH (WARNER BROS)	12	THE POWER STATION / POWER STATION (CAPITOL)
13	CRAZY FOR YOU / MADONNA (GEFFEN)	13	CENTERFIELD / JOHN FOGERTY (WARNER BROS)
14	ANGEL / MADONNA (SIRE)	14	DREAM INTO ACTION / HOWARD JONES (ELEKTRA)
15	ONE NIGHT IN BANGKOK / MURRAY HEAD (RCA)	15	SUDDENLY / BILLY OCEAN (JIVE/ARISTA)
16	SOME LIKE IT HOT / POWER STATION (CAPTIOL)	16	CRAZY FROM THE HEAT / DAVID LEE ROTH (WARNER BROS)
17	SUSSUDIO / PHIL COLLINS (ATLANTIC)	17	BUILDING THE PERFECT BEAST / DON HENLEY (GEFFEN)
18	SMUGGLER'S BLUES / GLENN FREY (MCA)	18	PRIVATE DANCER / TINA TURNER (CAPITOL)
19	ONE LONELY NIGHT / REO SPEEDWAGON (EPIC)	19	RHYTHM OF THE NIGHT / DEBARGE (GORDY)
20	NEVER ENDING STORY / LIMAHL (EMI AMERICA)	20	THE NIGHT I FELL IN LOVE / LUTHER VANDROSS (EPIC)

WEEK ENDING JUNE 8 1985

UK

SINGLES	UK	ALBUMS
19 — PAUL HARDCASTLE (CHRYSALIS)	1	OUR FAVOURITE SHOP — STYLE COUNCIL (POLYDOR)
A VIEW TO A KILL — DURAN DURAN (PARLOPHONE)	2	OUT NOW — VARIOUS (CHRYSALIS/MCA)
KAYLEIGH — MARILLION (EMI)	3	BROTHERS IN ARMS — DIRE STRAITS (VERTIGO)
YOU'LL NEVER WALK ALONE — CROWD (SPARTAN)	4	NOW DANCE — VARIOUS (EMI/VIRGIN)
OUT IN THE FIELDS — GARY MOORE/PHIL LYNOTT (10 RECORDS)	5	BEST OF THE 20TH CENTURY BOY — MARC BOLAN AND T REX (K-TEL)
OBSESSION — ANIMOTION (MERCURY)	6	SONGS FROM THE BIG CHAIR — TEARS FOR FEARS (MERCURY)
LOVE DON'T LIVE HERE ANYMORE — JIMMY NAIL (VIRGIN)	7	HITS 2 — VARIOUS (CBS/WEA)
WALKING ON SUNSHINE — KATRINA AND THE WAVES (CAPITOL)	8	NO JACKET REQUIRED — PHIL COLLINS (VIRGIN)
SUDDENLY — BILLY OCEAN (JIVE)	9	BORN IN THE USA — BRUCE SPRINGSTEEN (CBS)
THE WORD GIRL — SCRITTI POLITTI (VIRGIN)	10	BE YOURSELF TONIGHT — EURYTHMICS (RCA)
RHYTHM OF THE NIGHT — DEBARGE (GORDY)	11	GO WEST — GO WEST (CHRYSALIS)
CALL ME — GO WEST (CHRYSALIS)	12	VOICES FROM THE HOLY LAND — BBC WELSH CHORUS (BBC)
SLAVE TO LOVE — BRYAN FERRY (EG)	13	LOW LIFE — NEW ORDER (FACTORY)
ICING ON THE CAKE — STEPHEN TIN TIN DUFFY (10 RECORDS)	14	BEST OF EAGLES — EAGLES (ASYLUM)
I FEEL LOVE — BRONSKI BEAT/MARC ALMOND (FORBIDDEN FRUIT)	15	THE SECRET OF ASSOCIATION — PAUL YOUNG (CBS)
HISTORY — MAI TAI (VIRGIN)	16	SHAMROCK DIARIES — CHRIS REA (MAGNET)
MOVE CLOSER — PHYLLIS NELSON (CARRERE)	17	BEST OF ELVIS COSTELLO — ELVIS COSTELLO (TELSTAR)
SHAKE THE DISEASE — DEPECHE MODE (MUTE)	18	FLAUNT THE IMPERFECTION — CHINA CRISIS (VIRGIN)
ALL FALL DOWN — FIVE STAR (TENT)	19	MR BAD GUY — FREDDIE MERCURY (CBS)
FEEL SO REAL — STEVE ARRINGTON (ATLANTIC)	20	THE POWER STATION — POWER STATION (PARLOPHONE)

US

SINGLES	US	ALBUMS
EVERYBODY WANTS TO RULE . . — TEARS FOR FEARS (MERCURY)	1	AROUND THE WORLD — PRINCE AND THE REVOLUTION (PAISLEY PARK)
EVERYTHING SHE WANTS — WHAM! (COLUMBIA/CBS)	2	NO JACKET REQUIRED — PHIL COLLINS (ATLANTIC)
AXEL F — HAROLD FALTERMEYER (MCA)	3	BEVERLY HILLS COP — SOUNDTRACK (MCA)
SUDDENLY — BILLY OCEAN (JIVE/ARISTA)	4	BORN IN THE USA — BRUCE SPRINGSTEEN (COLUMBIA/CBS)
HEAVEN 'LIVE' — BRYAN ADAMS (A&M)	5	DIAMOND LIFE — SADE (PORTRAIT)
THINGS CAN ONLY GET BETTER — HOWARD JONES (ELEKTRA)	6	SONGS FROM THE BIG CHAIR — TEARS FOR FEARS (MERCURY)
IN MY HOUSE — MARY JANE GIRLS (GORDY)	7	MAKE IT BIG — WHAM! (COLUMBIA/CBS)
DON'T YOU (FORGET ABOUT ME) — SIMPLE MINDS (A&M)	8	RECKLESS — BRYAN ADAMS (A&M)
FRESH — KOOL AND THE GANG (DE-LITE)	9	LIKE A VIRGIN — MADONNA (SIRE)
WALKING ON SUNSHINE — KATRINA AND THE WAVES (CAPITOL)	10	SOUTHERN ACCENTS — TOM PETTY/HEARTBREAKERS (MCA)
ANGEL — MADONNA (SIRE)	11	WE ARE THE WORLD — USA FOR AFRICA (COLUMBIA/CBS)
SUSSUDIO — PHIL COLLINS (ATLANTIC)	12	THE POWER STATION — POWER STATION (CAPITOL)
SMOOTH OPERATOR — SADE (PORTRAIT)	13	DREAM INTO ACTION — HOWARD JONES (ELEKTRA)
SMUGGLER'S BLUES — GLENN FREY (MCA)	14	SUDDENLY — BILLY OCEAN (JIVE/ARISTA)
A VIEW TO A KILL — DURAN DURAN (CAPITOL)	15	CENTERFIELD — JOHN FOGERTY (WARNER BROS)
THE SEARCH IS OVER — SURVIVOR (SCOTTI BROS)	16	CRAZY FROM THE HEAT — DAVID LEE ROTH (WARNER BROS)
RASPBERRY BERET — PRINCE AND THE REVOLUTION (PAISLEY PARK)	17	BUILDING THE PERFECT BEAT — DON HENLEY (GEFFEN)
NEVER ENDING STORY — LIMAHL (EMI AMERICA)	18	PRIVATE DANCER — TINA TURNER (CAPITOL)
JUST A GIGOLO/I AIN'T GOT NOBODY — DAVID LEE ROTH (WARNER BROS)	19	RHYTHM OF THE NIGHT — DEBARGE (GORDY)
WOULD I LIE TO YOU? — EURYTHMICS (RCA)	20	THE NIGHT I FELL IN LOVE — LUTHER VANDROSS (EPIC)

WEEK ENDING JUNE 15 1985

UK

SINGLES	UK	ALBUMS
YOU'LL NEVER WALK ALONE — CROWD (SPARTAN)	1	BOYS AND GIRLS — BRYAN FERRY (EG)
KAYLEIGH — MARILLION (EMI)	2	OUT NOW — VARIOUS (CHRYSALIS/MCA)
19 — PAUL HARDCASTLE (CHRYSALIS)	3	NOW DANCE — VARIOUS (EMI/VIRGIN)
SUDDENLY — BILLY OCEAN (JIVE)	4	BROTHERS IN ARMS — DIRE STRAITS (VERTIGO)
OBSESSION — ANIMOTION (MERCURY)	5	BORN IN THE USA — BRUCE SPRINGSTEEN (CBS)
A VIEW TO A KILL — DURAN DURAN (PARLOPHONE)	6	OUR FAVOURITE SHOP — STYLE COUNCIL (POLYDOR)
OUT IN THE FIELDS — GARY MOORE/PHIL LYNOTT (10 RECORDS)	7	BEST OF THE 20TH CENTURY BOY — MARC BOLAN AND T REX (K-TEL)
THE WORD GIRL — SCRITTI POLITTI (VIRGIN)	8	NO JACKET REQUIRED — PHIL COLLINS (VIRGIN)
CRAZY FOR YOU — MADONNA (GEFFEN)	9	SONGS FROM THE BIG CHAIR — TEARS FOR FEARS (MERCURY)
HISTORY — MAI TAI (VIRGIN)	10	HITS 2 — VARIOUS (CBS/WEA)
FRANKIE — SISTER SLEDGE (ATLANTIC)	11	GO WEST — GO WEST (CHRYSALIS)
WALKING ON SUNSHINE — KATRINA AND THE WAVES (CAPITOL)	12	BE YOURSELF TONIGHT — EURYTHMICS (RCA)
CHERISH — KOOL AND THE GANG (DE-LITE)	13	BEST OF EAGLES — EAGLES (ASYLUM)
ICING ON THE CAKE — STEPHEN TIN TIN DUFFY (10 RECORDS)	14	VOICES FROM THE HOLY LAND — BBC WELSH CHORUS (BBC)
ALL FALL DOWN — FIVE STAR (TENT)	15	SHAMROCK DIARIES — CHRIS REA (MAGNET)
JOHNNY COME HOME — FINE YOUNG CANNIBALS (LONDON)	16	THE SECRET OF ASSOCIATION — PAUL YOUNG (CBS)
CALL ME — GO WEST (CHRYSALIS)	17	FLAUNT THE IMPERFECTION — CHINA CRISIS (VIRGIN)
LOVE DON'T LIVE HERE ANYMORE — JIMMY NAIL (VIRGIN)	18	WEST SIDE STORY — BERNSTEIN/TE KANAWA/CARRERAS (DEUTSCHE)
LOVING THE ALIEN — DAVID BOWIE (EMI AMERICA)	19	LOW LIFE — NEW ORDER (FACTORY)
BEN — MARTI WEBB (STARBLEND)	20	ROMANCE — DAVID CASSIDY (ARISTA)

US

SINGLES	US	ALBUMS
EVERYBODY WANTS TO RULE . . . — TEARS FOR FEARS (MERCURY)	1	AROUND THE WORLD — PRINCE AND THE REVOLUTION (PAISLEY PARK)
HEAVEN 'LIVE' — BRYAN ADAMS (A&M)	2	NO JACKET REQUIRED — PHIL COLLINS (ATLANTIC)
AXEL F — HAROLD FALTERMEYER (MCA)	3	BEVERLY HILLS COP — SOUNDTRACK (MCA)
SUDDENLY — BILLY OCEAN (JIVE/ARISTA)	4	SONGS FROM THE BIG CHAIR — TEARS FOR FEARS (MERCURY)
THINGS CAN ONLY GET BETTER — HOWARD JONES (ELEKTRA)	5	BORN IN THE USA — BRUCE SPRINGSTEEN (COLUMBIA/CBS)
SUSSUDIO — PHIL COLLINS (ATLANTIC)	6	MAKE IT BIG — WHAM! (COLUMBIA/CBS)
IN MY HOUSE — MARY JANE GIRLS (GORDY)	7	RECKLESS — BRYAN ADAMS (A&M)
EVERYTHING SHE WANTS — WHAM! (COLUMBIA/CBS)	8	DIAMOND LIFE — SADE (PORTRAIT)
ANGEL — MADONNA (SIRE)	9	LIKE A VIRGIN — MADONNA (SIRE)
WALKING ON SUNSHINE — KATRINA AND THE WAVES (CAPITOL)	10	THE POWER STATION — POWER STATION (CAPITOL)
RASPBERRY BERET — PRINCE AND THE REVOLUTION (PAISLEY PARK)	11	SOUTHERN ACCENTS — TOM PETTY/HEARTBREAKERS (MCA)
A VIEW TO A KILL — DURAN DURAN (CAPITOL)	12	SUDDENLY — BILLY OCEAN (JIVE/ARISTA)
THE SEARCH IS OVER — SURVIVOR (SCOTTI BROS)	13	DREAM INTO ACTION — HOWARD JONES (ELEKTRA)
SMUGGLER'S BLUES — GLENN FREY (MCA)	14	WE ARE THE WORLD — USA FOR AFRICA (COLUMBIA/CBS)
FRESH — KOOL AND THE GANG (DE-LITE)	15	CENTERFIELD — JOHN FOGERTY (WARNER BROS)
WOULD I LIE TO YOU? — EURYTHMICS (RCA)	16	CRAZY FROM THE HEAT — DAVID LEE ROTH (WARNER BROS)
NEVER ENDING STORY — LIMAHL (EMI AMERICA)	17	EMERGENCY — KOOL AND THE GANG (DE-LITE)
DON'T YOU (FORGET ABOUT ME) — SIMPLE MINDS (A&M)	18	BE YOURSELF TONIGHT — EURYTHMICS (RCA)
VOICES CARRY — 'TIL TUESDAY (EPIC)	19	THE NIGHT I FELL IN LOVE — LUTHER VANDROSS (EPIC)
YOU GIVE GOOD LOVE — WHITNEY HOUSTON (ARISTA)	20	ONLY FOR YOU — MARY JANE GIRLS (GORDY)

WEEK ENDING JUNE 22 1985

SINGLES	UK	ALBUMS
YOU'LL NEVER WALK ALONE CROWD (SPARTAN)	1	BOYS AND GIRLS BRYAN FERRY (EG)
FRANKIE SISTER SLEDGE (ATLANTIC)	2	BORN IN THE USA BRUCE SPRINGSTEEN (CBS)
CRAZY FOR YOU MADONNA (GEFFEN)	3	BROTHERS IN ARMS DIRE STRAITS (VERTIGO)
KAYLEIGH MARILLION (EMI)	4	OUT NOW VARIOUS (CHRYSALIS/MCA)
SUDDENLY BILLY OCEAN (JIVE)	5	CUPID AND PSYCHE 85 SCRITTI POLITTI (VIRGIN)
THE WORD GIRL SCRITTI POLITTI (VIRGIN)	6	NOW DANCE VARIOUS (EMI/VIRGIN)
CHERISH KOOL AND THE GANG (DE-LITE)	7	BEST OF THE 20TH CENTURY BOY MARC BOLAN AND T REX (K-TEL)
OBSESSION ANIMOTION (MERCURY)	8	SONGS FROM THE BIG CHAIR TEARS FOR FEARS (MERCURY)
HISTORY MAI TAI (VIRGIN)	9	OUR FAVOURITE SHOP STYLE COUNCIL (POLYDOR)
AXEL F HAROLD FALTERMEYER (MCA)	10	NO JACKET REQUIRED PHIL COLLINS (VIRGIN)
A VIEW TO A KILL DURAN DURAN (PARLOPHONE)	11	EMPIRE BURLESQUE BOB DYLAN (CBS)
BEN MARTI WEBB (STARBLEND)	12	HITS 2 VARIOUS (CBS/WEA)
I'M ON FIRE/BORN IN THE USA BRUCE SPRINGSTEEN (CBS)	13	GO WEST GO WEST (CHRYSALIS)
19 PAUL HARDCASTLE (CHRYSALIS)	14	BEST OF EAGLES EAGLES (ASYLUM)
JOHNNY COME HOME FINE YOUNG CANNIBALS (LONDON)	15	SUDDENLY BILLY OCEAN (JIVE)
OUT IN THE FIELDS GARY MOORE/PHIL LYNOTT (10 RECORDS)	16	VOICES FROM THE HOLY LAND BBC WELSH CHORUS (BBC)
WALKING ON SUNSHINE KATRINA AND THE WAVES (CAPITOL)	17	THE SECRET OF ASSOCIATION PAUL YOUNG (CBS)
ALL FALL DOWN FIVE STAR (TENT)	18	WEST SIDE STORY BERNSTEIN/TE KANAWA/CARRERAS (DEUTSCHE)
LOVING THE ALIEN DAVID BOWIE (EMI AMERICA)	19	FLAUNT THE IMPERFECTION CHINA CRISIS (VIRGIN)
ICING ON THE CAKE STEPHEN TIN TIN DUFFY (10 RECORDS)	20	BE YOURSELF TONIGHT EURYTHMICS (RCA)

SINGLES	US	ALBUMS
HEAVEN BRYAN ADAMS (A&M)	1	BEVERLY HILLS COP SOUNDTRACK (MCA)
SUSSUDIO PHIL COLLINS (ATLANTIC)	2	AROUND THE WORLD IN A DAY PRINCE AND THE REVOLUTION (PAISLEY PARK)
EVERYBODY WANTS TO RULE . . . TEARS FOR FEARS (MERCURY)	3	NO JACKET REQUIRED PHIL COLLINS (ATLANTIC)
RASPBERRY BERET PRINCE AND THE REVOLUTION (PAISLEY PARK)	4	SONGS FROM THE BIG CHAIR TEARS FOR FEARS (MERCURY)
A VIEW TO A KILL DURAN DURAN (CAPITOL)	5	BORN IN THE USA BRUCE SPRINGSTEEN (COLUMBIA/CBS)
ANGEL MADONNA (SIRE)	6	RECKLESS BRYAN ADAMS (A&M)
IN MY HOUSE MARY JANE GIRLS (GORDY)	7	MAKE IT BIG WHAM! (COLUMBIA/CBS)
THINGS CAN ONLY GET BETTER HOWARD JONES (ELEKTRA)	8	LIKE A VIRGIN MADONNA (SIRE)
WALKING ON SUNSHINE KATRINA AND THE WAVES (CAPITOL)	9	THE POWER STATION POWER STATION (CAPITOL)
THE SEARCH IS OVER SURVIVOR (SCOTTI BROS)	10	DIAMOND LIFE SADE (PORTRAIT)
SUDDENLY BILLY OCEAN (JIVE/ARISTA)	11	DREAM INTO ACTION HOWARD JONES (ELEKTRA)
SMUGGLER'S BLUES GLENN FREY (MCA)	12	SUDDENLY BILLY OCEAN (JIVE/ARISTA)
EVERYTHING SHE WANTS WHAM! (COLUMBIA/CBS)	13	SOUTHERN ACCENTS TOM PETTY/HEARTBREAKERS (MCA)
WOULD I LIE TO YOU? EURYTHMICS (RCA)	14	BY YOURSELF TONIGHT EURYTHMICS (RCA)
AXEL F HAROLD FALTERMEYER (MCA)	15	EMERGENCY KOOL AND THE GANG (DE-LITE)
VOICES CARRY 'TIL TUESDAY (EPIC)	16	CENTERFIELD JOHN FOGERTY (WARNER BROS)
YOU GIVE GOOD LOVE WHITNEY HOUSTON (ARISTA)	17	CRAZY FROM THE HEAT DAVID LEE ROTH (WARNER BROS)
FRESH KOOL AND THE GANG (DE-LITE)	18	ONLY FOR YOU MARY JANE GIRLS (GORDY)
THE GOONIES 'R' GOOD ENOUGH CYNDI LAUPER (PORTRAIT)	19	THE NIGHT I FELL IN LOVE LUTHER VANDROSS (EPIC)
EVERYTIME YOU GO AWAY PAUL YOUNG (COLUMBIA/CBS)	20	WE ARE THE WORLD USA FOR AFRICA (COLUMBIA/CBS)

WEEK ENDING JUNE 29 1985

SINGLES	UK	ALBUMS
FRANKIE SISTER SLEDGE (ATLANTIC)	1	MISPLACED CHILDHOOD MARILLION (EMI)
CRAZY FOR YOU MADONNA (GEFFEN)	2	BORN IN THE USA BRUCE SPRINGSTEEN (CBS)
YOU'LL NEVER WALK ALONE CROWD (SPARTAN)	3	THE DREAM OF THE BLUE TURTLES STING (A&M)
AXEL F HAROLD FALTERMEYER (MCA)	4	BOYS AND GIRLS BRYAN FERRY (EG)
CHERISH KOOL AND THE GANG (DE-LITE)	5	CUPID AND PSYCHE 85 SCRITTI POLITTI (VIRGIN)
SUDDENLY BILLY OCEAN (JIVE)	6	BROTHERS IN ARMS DIRE STRAITS (VERTIGO)
KAYLEIGH MARILLION (EMI)	7	ALL THROUGH THE NIGHT ALED JONES (BBC)
HISTORY MAI TAI (VIRGIN)	8	OUT NOW VARIOUS (CHRYSALIS/MCA)
BEN MARTI WEBB (STARBLEND)	9	SONGS FROM THE BIG CHAIR TEARS FOR FEARS (MERCURY)
THE WORD GIRL SCRITTI POLITTI (VIRGIN)	10	LITTLE CREATURES TALKING HEADS (EMI)
I'M ON FIRE/BORN IN THE USA BRUCE SPRINGSTEEN (CBS)	11	VOICES FROM THE HOLY LAND BBC WELSH CHORUS (BBC)
JOHNNY COME HOME FINE YOUNG CANNIBALS (LONDON)	12	NOW DANCE VARIOUS (EMI/VIRGIN)
OBSESSION ANIMOTION (MERCURY)	13	CRUSH ORCHESTRAL MANOEUVRES (VIRGIN)
HEAD OVER HEELS TEARS FOR FEARS (MERCURY)	14	BEST OF THE 20TH CENTURY BOY MARC BOLAN AND T REX (K-TEL)
A VIEW TO A KILL DURAN DURAN (PARLOPHONE)	15	NO JACKET REQUIRED PHIL COLLINS (VIRGIN)
19 PAUL HARDCASTLE (CHRYSALIS)	16	SUDDENLY BILLY OCEAN (JIVE)
TOMB OF MEMORIES PAUL YOUNG (CBS)	17	OUR FAVOURITE SHOP STYLE COUNCIL (POLYDOR)
PAISLEY PARK PRINCE (WARNER BROS)	18	THE RIVER BRUCE SPRINGSTEEN (CBS)
KING IN A CATHOLIC STYLE CHINA CRISIS (VIRGIN)	19	THE SECRET OF ASSOCIATION PAUL YOUNG (CBS)
OUT IN THE FIELDS GARY MOORE/PHIL LYNOTT (10 RECORDS)	20	EMPIRE BURLESQUE BOB DYLAN (CBS)

SINGLES	US	ALBUMS
HEAVEN BRYAN ADAMS (A&M)	1	BEVERLY HILLS COP SOUNDTRACK (MCA)
SUSSUDIO PHIL COLLINS (ATLANTIC)	2	NO JACKET REQUIRED PHIL COLLINS (ATLANTIC)
A VIEW TO A KILL DURAN DURAN (CAPITOL)	3	SONGS FROM THE BIG CHAIR TEARS FOR FEARS (MERCURY)
RASPBERRY BERET PRINCE AND THE REVOLUTION (PAISLEY PARK)	4	AROUND THE WORLD PRINCE AND THE REVOLUTION (PAISLEY PARK)
ANGEL MADONNA (SIRE)	5	BORN IN THE USA BRUCE SPRINGSTEEN (COLUMBIA/CBS)
THE SEARCH IS OVER SURVIVOR (SCOTTI BROS)	6	RECKLESS BRYAN ADAMS (A&M)
EVERYBODY WANTS TO RULE . . . TEARS FOR FEARS (MERCURY)	7	MAKE IT BIG WHAM! (COLUMBIA/CBS)
WOULD I LIE TO YOU? EURYTHMICS (RCA)	8	LIKE A VIRGIN MADONNA (SIRE)
THINGS CAN ONLY GET BETTER HOWARD JONES (ELEKTRA)	9	THE POWER STATION POWER STATION (CAPITOL)
IN MY HOUSE MARY JANE GIRLS (GORDY)	10	DREAM INTO ACTION HOWARD JONES (ELEKTRA)
WALKING ON SUNSHINE KATRINA AND THE WAVES (CAPITOL)	11	SOUTHERN ACCENTS TOM PETTY/HEARTBREAKERS (MCA)
VOICES CARRY 'TIL TUESDAY (EPIC)	12	BE YOURSELF TONIGHT EURYTHMICS (RCA)
YOU GIVE GOOD LOVE WHITNEY HOUSTON (ARISTA)	13	SUDDENLY BILLY OCEAN (JIVE/ARISTA)
EVERYTIME YOU GO AWAY PAUL YOUNG (COLUMBIA/CBS)	14	7 WISHES NIGHT RANGER (CAMEL/MCA)
THE GOONIES 'R' GOOD ENOUGH CYNDI LAUPER (PORTRAIT)	15	DIAMOND LIFE SADE (PORTRAIT)
SMUGGLER'S BLUES GLENN FREY (MCA)	16	CENTERFIELD JOHN FOGERTY (WARNER BROS)
GLORY DAYS BRUCE SPRINGSTEEN (COLUMBIA/CBS)	17	EMERGENCY KOOL AND THE GANG (DE-LITE)
SUDDENLY BILLY OCEAN (JIVE/ARISTA)	18	ONLY FOR YOU MARY JANE GIRLS (GORDY)
IF YOU LOVE SOMEBODY STING (A&M)	19	THE NIGHT I FELL IN LOVE LUTHER VANDROSS (EPIC)
SENTIMENTAL STREET NIGHT RANGER (CAMEL/MCA)	20	VITAL SIGNS SURVIVOR (SCOTTI BROS)

WEEK ENDING JULY 6 1985

UK

SINGLES	Artist		ALBUMS	Artist
FRANKIE	SISTER SLEDGE (ATLANTIC)	1	BORN IN THE USA	BRUCE SPRINGSTEEN (CBS)
AXEL F	HAROLD FLATERMEYER (MCA)	2	MISPLACED CHILDHOOD	MARILLION (EMI)
CRAZY FOR YOU	MADONNA (GEFFEN)	3	ALL THROUGH THE NIGHT	ALED JONES (BBC)
CHERISH	KOOL AND THE GANG (DE-LITE)	4	THE DREAM OF THE BLUE TURTLES	STING (A&M)
BEN	MARTI WEBB (STARBLEND)	5	BROTHERS IN ARMS	DIRE STRAITS (VERTIGO)
YOU'LL NEVER WALK ALONE	CROWD (SPARTAN)	6	CUPID AND PSYCHE 85	SCRITTI POLITTI (VIRGIN)
SUDDENLY	BILLY OCEAN (JIVE)	7	SONGS FROM THE BIG CHAIR	TEARS FOR FEARS (MERCURY)
I'M ON FIRE/BORN IN THE USA	BRUCE SPRINGSTEEN (CBS)	8	BOYS AND GIRLS	BRYAN FERRY (EG)
HISTORY	MAI TAI (VIRGIN)	9	SUDDENLY	BILLY OCEAN (JIVE)
KAYLEIGH	MARILLION (EMI)	10	OUT NOW	VARIOUS (CHRYSALIS/MCA)
JOHNNY COME HOME	FINE YOUNG CANNIBALS (LONDON)	11	VOICES FROM THE HOLY LAND	BBC WELSH CHORUS (BBC)
HEAD OVER HEELS	TEARS FOR FEARS (MERCURY)	12	NOW DANCE	VARIOUS (EMI/VIRGIN)
N-N-NINETEEN (NOT OUT)	COMMENTATORS (OVAL)	13	THE SECRET OF ASSOCIATION	PAUL YOUNG (CBS)
LIFE IN ONE DAY	HOWARD JONES (WEA)	14	BEST OF THE 20TH CENTURY BOY	MARC BOLAN AND T REX (K-TEL)
THE WORD GIRL	SCRITTI POLITTI (VIRGIN)	15	NO JACKET REQUIRED	PHIL COLLINS (VIRGIN)
TOMB OF MEMORIES	PAUL YOUNG (CBS)	16	LITTLE CREATURES	TALKING HEADS (EMI)
MY TOOT TOOT	DENISE LASALLE (EPIC)	17	CRUSH	ORCHESTRAL MANOEUVRES (VIRGIN)
OBSESSION	ANIMOTION (MERCURY)	18	WORLD WIDE LIVE	SCORPIONS (HARVEST)
IN TOO DEEP	DEAD OR ALIVE (EPIC)	19	WHEN THE BOYS MEET THE GIRLS	SISTER SLEDGE (ATLANTIC)
KING IN A CATHOLIC STYLE	CHINA CRISIS (VIRGIN)	20	GO WEST	GO WEST (CHRYSALIS)

US

SINGLES	Artist		ALBUMS	Artist
SUSSUDIO	PHIL COLLINS (ATLANTIC)	1	NO JACKET REQUIRED	PHIL COLLINS (ATLANTIC)
A VIEW TO A KILL	DURAN DURAN (CAPITOL)	2	SONGS FROM THE BIG CHAIR	TEARS FOR FEARS (MERCURY)
RASPBERRY BERET	PRINCE AND THE REVOLUTION (PAISLEY PARK)	3	BEVERLY HILLS COP	SOUNDTRACK (MCA)
HEAVEN	BRYAN ADAMS (A&M)	4	AROUND THE WORLD	PRINCE AND THE REVOLUTION (PAISLEY PARK)
THE SEARCH IS OVER	SURVIVOR (SCOTTI BROS)	5	RECKLESS	BRYAN ADAMS (A&M)
WOULD I LIE TO YOU?	EURYTHMICS (RCA)	6	BORN IN THE USA	BRUCE SPRINGSTEEN (COLUMBIA/CBS)
YOU GIVE GOOD LOVE	WHITNEY HOUSTON (ARISTA)	7	MAKE IT BIG	WHAM! (COLUMBIA/CBS)
EVERYTIME YOU GO AWAY	PAUL YOUNG (COLUMBIA/CBS)	8	THE POWER STATION	POWER STATION (CAPITOL)
VOICES CARRY	'TIL TUESDAY (EPIC)	9	LIKE A VIRGIN	MADONNA (SIRE)
ANGEL	MADONNA (SIRE)	10	BE YOURSELF TONIGHT	EURYTHMICS (RCA)
GLORY DAYS	BRUCE SPRINGSTEEN (COLUMBIA/CBS)	11	DREAM INTO ACTION	HOWARD JONES (ELEKTRA)
THE GOONIES 'R' GOOD ENOUGH	CYNDI LAUPER (PORTRAIT)	12	SOUTHERN ACCENTS	TOM PETTY/HEARTBREAKERS (MCA)
IF YOU LOVE SOMEBODY . . .	STING (A&M)	13	7 WISHES	NIGHT RANGER (CAMEL/MCA)
EVERYBODY WANTS TO RULE . . .	TEARS FOR FEARS (MERCURY)	14	SUDDENLY	BILLY OCEAN (JIVE/ARISTA)
SENTIMENTAL STREET	NIGHT RANGER (CAMEL/MCA)	15	INVASION OF YOUR PRIVACY	RATT (ATLANTIC)
THINGS CAN ONLY GET BETTER	HOWARD JONES (ELEKTRA)	16	WHITNEY HOUSTON	WHITNEY HOUSTON (ARISTA)
CRAZY IN THE NIGHT	KIM CARNES (EMI AMERICA)	17	CENTERFIELD	JOHN FOGERTY (WARNER BROS)
SMUGGLER'S BLUES	GLENN FREY (MCA)	18	VITAL SIGNS	SURVIVOR (SCOTTI BROS)
WALKING ON SUNSHINE	KATRINA AND THE WAVES (CAPITOL)	19	EMERGENCY	KOOL AND THE GANG (DE-LITE)
IN MY HOUSE	MARY JANE GIRLS (GORDY)	20	DIAMOND LIFE	SADE (PORTRAIT)

WEEK ENDING JULY 13 1985

UK

SINGLES	Artist		ALBUMS	Artist
FRANKIE	SISTER SLEDGE (ATLANTIC)	1	BORN IN THE USA	BRUCE SPRINGSTEEN (CBS)
AXEL F	HAROLD FALTERMEYER (MCA)	2	MISPLACED CHILDHOOD	MARILLION (EMI)
CRAZY FOR YOU	MADONNA (GEFFEN)	3	SONGS FROM THE BIG CHAIR	TEARS FOR FEARS (MERCURY)
CHERISH	KOOL AND THE GANG (DE-LITE)	4	BROTHERS IN ARMS	DIRE STRAITS (VERTIGO)
I'M ON FIRE/BORN IN THE USA	BRUCE SPRINGSTEEN (CBS)	5	THE DREAM OF THE BLUE TURTLES	STING (A&M)
BEN	MARTI WEBB (STARBLEND)	6	ALL THROUGH THE NIGHT	ALED JONES (BBC)
MY TOOT TOOT	DENISE LASALLE (EPIC)	7	FLY ON THE WALL	AC/DC (ATLANTIC)
JOHNNY COME HOME	FINE YOUNG CANNIBALS (LONDON)	8	CUPID AND PSYCHE 85	SCRITTI POLITTI (VIRGIN)
HISTORY	MAI TAI (VIRGIN)	9	BOYS AND GIRLS	BRYAN FERRY (EG)
THERE MUST BE AN ANGEL	EURYTHMICS (RCA)	10	OUT NOW	VARIOUS (CHRYSALIS/MCA)
SUDDENLY	BILLY OCEAN (JIVE)	11	SUDDENLY	BILLY OCEAN (JIVE)
HEAD OVER HEELS	TEARS FOR FEARS (MERCURY)	12	VOICES FROM THE HOLY LAND	BBC WELSH CHORUS (BBC)
KAYLEIGH	MARILLION (EMI)	13	THE SECRET OF ASSOCIATION	PAUL YOUNG (CBS)
IN TOO DEEP	DEAD OR ALIVE (EPIC)	14	BE YOURSELF TONIGHT	EURYTHMICS (RCA)
LIVE IS LIFE	OPUS (POLYDOR)	15	NO JACKET REQUIRED	PHIL COLLINS (VIRGIN)
N-N-NINETEEN (NOT OUT)	COMMENTATORS (OVAL)	16	A SECRET WISH	PROPAGANDA (ZTT)
LIFE IN ONE DAY	HOWARD JONES (WEA)	17	THE RIVER	BRUCE SPRINGSTEEN (CBS)
TURN IT UP	CONWAY BROTHERS (10 RECORDS)	18	NOW DANCE	VARIOUS (EMI/VIRGIN)
YOU'LL NEVER WALK ALONE	CROWD (SPARTAN)	19	WHEN THE BOYS MEET THE GIRLS	SISTER SLEDGE (ATLANTIC)
TOMB OF MEMORIES	PAUL YOUNG (CBS)	20	LITTLE CREATURES	TALKING HEADS (EMI)

US

SINGLES	Artist		ALBUMS	Artist
A VIEW TO A KILL	DURAN DURAN (CAPITOL)	1	SONGS FROM THE BIG CHAIR	TEARS FOR FEARS (MERCURY)
SUSSUDIO	PHIL COLLINS (ATLANTIC)	2	NO JACKET REQUIRED	PHIL COLLINS (ATLANTIC)
RASPBERRY BERET	PRINCE AND THE REVOLUTION (PAISLEY PARK)	3	AROUND THE WORLD IN A DAY	PRINCE AND THE REVOLUTION (PAISLEY PARK)
THE SEARCH IS OVER	SURVIVOR (SCOTTI BROS)	4	RECKLESS	BRYAN ADAMS (A&M)
WOULD I LIE TO YOU?	EURYTHMICS (RCA)	5	BEVERLY HILLS COP	SOUNDTRACK (MCA)
EVERYTIME YOU GO AWAY	PAUL YOUNG (COLUMBIA/CBS)	6	BORN IN THE USA	BRUCE SPRINGSTEEN (COLUMBIA/CBS)
YOU GIVE GOOD LOVE	WHITNEY HOUSTON (ARISTA)	7	THE POWER STATION	POWER STATION (CAPITOL)
VOICES CARRY	'TIL TUESDAY (EPIC)	8	MAKE IT BIG	WHAM! COLUMBIA/CBS
GLORY DAYS	BRUCE SPRINGSTEEN (COLUMBIA/CBS)	9	LIKE A VIRGIN	MADONNA (SIRE)
THE GOONIES 'R' GOOD ENOUGH	CYNDI LAUPER (PORTRAIT)	10	BE YOURSELF TONIGHT	EURYTHMICS (RCA)
IF YOU LOVE SOMEBODY . . .	STING (A&M)	11	INVASION OF YOUR PRIVACY	RATT (ATLANTIC)
HEAVEN	BRYAN ADAMS (A&M)	12	7 WISHES	NIGHT RANGER (CAMEL/MCA)
SENTIMENTAL STREET	NIGHT RANGER (CAMEL/MCA)	13	WHITNEY HOUSTON	WHITNEY HOUSTON (ARISTA)
SHOUT	TEARS FOR FEARS (MERCURY)	14	DREAM INTO ACTION	HOWARD JONES (ELEKTRA)
ANGEL	MADONNA (SIRE)	15	SOUTHERN ACCENTS	TOM PETTY/HEARTBREAKERS (MCA)
CRAZY IN THE NIGHT	KIM CARNES (EMI AMERICA)	16	VITAL SIGNS	SURVIVOR (SCOTTI BROS)
19	PAUL HARDCASTLE (CHRYSALIS)	17	SUDDENLY	BILLY OCEAN (JIVE/ARISTA)
GET IT ON	POWER STATION (CAPITOL)	18	BROTHERS IN ARMS	DIRE STRAITS (WARNER BROS)
JUST AS I AM	AIR SUPPLY (ARISTA)	19	EMERGENCY	KOOL AND THE GANG (DE-LITE)
NEVER SURRENDER	COREY HART (EMI AMERICA)	20	SHAKEN 'N' STIRRED	ROBERT PLANT (ES PARANZA/WARNER BROS)

WEEK ENDING JULY 20 1985

UK

SINGLES		ALBUMS
FRANKIE SISTER SLEDGE (ATLANTIC)	1	BORN IN THE USA BRUCE SPRINGSTEEN (CBS)
AXEL F HAROLD FLATERMEYER (MCA)	2	ALL THROUGH THE NIGHT ALED JONES (BBC)
THERE MUST BE AN ANGEL EURYTHMICS (RCA)	3	BROTHERS IN ARMS DIRE STRAITS (VERTIGO)
CHERISH KOOL AND THE GANG (DE-LITE)	4	SONGS FROM THE BIG CHAIR TEARS FOR FEARS (MERCURY)
CRAZY FOR YOU MADONNA (GEFFEN)	5	BE YOURSELF TONIGHT EURYTHMICS (RCA)
MY TOOT TOOT DENISE LASALLE (EPIC)	6	VOICES FROM THE HOLY LAND BBC WELSH CHORUS (BBC)
I'M ON FIRE/BORN IN THE USA BRUCE SPRINGSTEEN (CBS)	7	GREATEST HITS VOL 1 AND 2 BILLY JOEL (CBS)
LIVE IS LIFE OPUS (POLYDOR)	8	MISPLACED CHILDHOOD MARILLION (EMI)
JOHNNY COME HOME FINE YOUNG CANNIBALS (LONDON)	9	THE DREAM OF THE BLUE TURTLES STING (A&M)
BEN MARTI WEBB (STARBLEND)	10	FLY ON THE WALL AC/DC (ATLANTIC)
TURN IT UP CONWAY BROTHERS (10 RECORDS)	11	BOYS AND GIRLS BRYAN FERRY (EG)
ROUND AND AROUND JAKI GRAHAM (EMI)	12	THE RIVER BRUCE SPRINGSTEEN (CBS)
MONEY'S TOO TIGHT (TO MENTION) SIMPLY RED (ELEKTRA)	13	SUDDENLY BILLY OCEAN (JIVE)
HEAD OVER HEELS TEARS FOR FEARS (MERCURY)	14	CUPID AND PSYCHE 85 SCRITTI POLITTI (VIRGIN)
IN YOUR CAR COOL NOTES (ABSTRACT DANCE)	15	NO JACKET REQUIRED PHIL COLLINS (VIRGIN)
IN TOO DEEP DEAD OR ALIVE (EPIC)	16	THE SECRET OF ASSOCIATION PAUL YOUNG (CBS)
HISTORY MAI TAI (VIRGIN)	17	BORN TO RUN BRUE SPRINGSTEEN (CBS)
LIVING ON VIDEO TRANS X (BOILING POINT)	18	OUT NOW VARIOUS (CHRYSALIS/MCA)
SHE SELLS SANCTUARY CULT (BEGGARS BANQUET)	19	LIKE A VIRGIN MADONNA (SIRE)
SUDDENLY BILLY OCEAN (JIVE)	20	NOW DANCE VARIOUS (EMI/VIRGIN)

US

SINGLES		ALBUMS
A VIEW TO A KILL DURAN DURAN (CAPITOL)	1	SONGS FROM THE BIG CHAIR TEARS FOR FEARS (MERCURY)
RASPBERRY BERET PRINCE AND THE REVOLUTION (PAISLEY PARK)	2	NO JACKET REQUIRED PHIL COLLINS (ATLANTIC)
EVERYTIME YOU GO AWAY PAUL YOUNG (COLUMBIA/CBS)	3	RECKLESS BRYAN ADAMS (A&M)
YOU GIVE GOOD LOVE WHITNEY HOUSTON (ARISTA)	4	AROUND THE WORLD IN A DAY PRINCE AND THE REVOLUTION (PAISLEY PARK)
SUSSUDIO PHIL COLLINS (ATLANTIC)	5	BORN IN THE USA BRUCE SPRINGSTEEN (COLUMBIA/CBS)
THE SEARCH IS OVER SURVIVOR (SCOTTI BROS)	6	BEVERLY HILLS COP SOUNDTRACK (MCA)
IF YOU LOVE SOMEBODY . . . STING (A&M)	7	THE POWER STATION POWER STATION (CAPITOL)
GLORY DAYS BRUCE SPRINGSTEEN (COLUMBIA/CBS)	8	LIKE A VIRGIN MADONNA (SIRE)
SHOUT TEARS FOR FEARS (MERCURY)	9	BE YOURSELF TONIGHT EURYTHMICS (RCA)
WOULD I LIE TO YOU? EURYTHMICS (RCA)	10	INVASION OF YOUR PRIVACY RATT (ATLANTIC)
VOICES CARRY 'TIL TUESDAY (EPIC)	11	MAKE IT BIG WHAM! (COLUMBIA/CBS)
SENTIMENTAL STREET NIGHT RANGER (CAMEL/MCA)	12	7 WISHES NIGHT RANGER (CAMEL/MCA)
NEVER SURRENDER COREY HART (EMI AMERICA)	13	WHITNEY HOUSTON WHITNEY HOUSTON (ARISTA)
GET IT ON POWER STATION (CAPITOL)	14	THE DREAM OF THE BLUE TURTLES STING (A&M)
19 PAUL HARDCASTLE (CHRYSALIS)	15	DREAM INTO ACTION HOWARD JONES (ELEKTRA)
THE GOONIES 'R' GOOD ENOUGH CYNDI LAUPER (PORTRAIT)	16	VITAL SIGNS SURVIVOR (SCOTTI BROS)
WHO'S HOLDING DONNA NOW? DEBARGE (GORDY)	17	BROTHERS IN ARMS DIRE STRAITS (WARNER BROS)
PEOPLE ARE PEOPLE DEPECHE MODE (SIRE)	18	THEATRE OF PAIN MOTELY CRUE (ELEKTRA)
JUST AS I AM AIR SUPPLY (ARISTA)	19	SOUTHERN ACCENTS TOM PETTY/HEARTBREAKERS (MCA)
HEAVEN BRYAN ADAMS (A&M)	20	SHAKEN 'N' STIRRED ROBERT PLANT (ES PARANZA/WARNER BROS)

WEEK ENDING JULY 27 1985

UK

SINGLES		ALBUMS
THERE MUST BE AN ANGEL EURYTHMICS (RCA)	1	BORN IN THE USA BRUCE SPRINGSTEEN (CBS)
FRANKIE SISTER SLEDGE (ATLANTIC)	2	BROTHERS IN ARMS DIRE STRAITS (VERTIGO)
AXEL F HAROLD FALTERMEYER (MCA)	3	BE YOURSELF TONIGHT EURYTHMICS (RCA)
INTO THE GROOVE MADONNA (SIRE)	4	SONGS FROM THE BIG CHAIR TEARS FOR FEARS (MERCURY)
CHERISH KOOL AND THE GANG (DE-LITE)	5	THE SECRET OF ASSOCIATION PAUL YOUNG (CBS)
CRAZY FOR YOU MADONNA (GEFFEN)	6	NO JACKET REQUIRED PHIL COLLINS (VIRGIN)
LIVE IS LIFE OPUS (POLYDOR)	7	ALL THROUGH THE NIGHT ALED JONES (BBC)
MY TOOT TOOT DENISE LASALLE (EPIC)	8	GREATEST HITS VOL 1 AND 2 BILLY JOEL (CBS)
ROUND AND AROUND JAKI GRAHAM (EMI)	9	THE DREAM OF THE BLUE TURTLES STING (A&M)
LIVING ON VIDEO TRANS X (BOILING POINT)	10	LIKE A VIRGIN MADONNA (SIRE)
WE DON'T NEED ANOTHER HERO TINA TURNER (CAPITOL)	11	PHANTASMAGORIA DAMNED (MCA)
I'M ON FIRE/BORN IN THE USA BRUCE SPRINGSTEEN (CBS)	12	THE UNFORGETTABLE FIRE U2 (ISLAND)
IN YOUR CAR COOL NOTES (ABSTRACT DANCE)	13	VOICES FROM THE HOLY LAND BBC WELSH CHORUS (BBC)
MONEY'S TOO TIGHT (TO MENTION) SIMPLY RED (ELEKTRA)	14	BOYS AND GIRLS BRYAN FERRY (EG)
MONEY FOR NOTHING DIRE STRAITS (VERTIGO)	15	MISPLACED CHILDHOOD MARILLION (EMI)
JOHNNY COME HOME FINE YOUNG CANNIBALS (LONDON)	16	UNDER A BLOOD RED SKY U2 (ISLAND)
TURN IT UP CONWAY BROTHERS (10 RECORDS)	17	QUEEN GREATEST HITS QUEEN (EMI)
WHITE WEDDING BILLY IDOL (CHRYSALIS)	18	OUT NOW VARIOUS (CHRYSALIS/MCA)
SHE SELLS SANCTUARY CULT (BEGGARS BANQUET)	19	CUPID AND PSYCHE 85 SCRITTI POLITTI (VIRGIN)
ALL NIGHT HOLIDAY RUSS ABBOTT (SPIRIT)	20	SUDDENLY BILLY OCEAN (JIVE)

US

SINGLES		ALBUMS
EVERY TIME YOU GO AWAY PAUL YOUNG (COLUMBIA/CBS)	1	SONGS FROM THE BIG CHAIR TEARS FOR FEARS (MERCURY)
SHOUT TEARS FOR FEARS (MERCURY)	2	NO JACKET REQUIRED PHIL COLLINS (ATLANTIC)
YOU GIVE GOOD LOVE WHITNEY HOUSTON (ARISTA)	3	RECKLESS BRYAN ADAMS (A&M)
A VIEW TO A KILL DURAN DURAN (CAPITOL)	4	BORN IN THE USA BRUCE SPRINGSTEEN (COLUMBIA/CBS)
IF YOU LOVE SOMEBODY . . . STING (A&M)	5	AROUND THE WORLD IN A DAY PRINCE AND THE REVOLUTION (PAISLEY PARK)
GLORY DAYS BRUCE SPRINGSTEEN (COLUMBIA/CBS)	6	THE POWER STATION POWER STATION (CAPTIOL)
RASPBERRY BERET PRINCE AND THE REVOLUTION (PAISLEY PARK)	7	INVASION OF YOUR PRIVACY RATT (ATLANTIC)
SENTIMENTAL STREET NIGHT RANGER (CAMEL/MCA)	8	BEVERLY HILLS COP SOUNDTRACK (MCA)
NEVER SURRENDER COREY HART (EMI AMERICA)	9	THE DREAM OF THE BLUE TURTLES STING (A&M)
GET IT ON POWER STATION (CAPITOL)	10	7 WISHES NIGHT RANGER (CAMEL/MCA)
THE SEARCH IS OVER SURVIVOR (SCOTTI BROS)	11	LIKE A VIRGIN MADONNA (SIRE)
VOICES CARRY 'TIL TUESDAY (EPIC)	12	THEATRE OF PAIN MOTLEY CRUE (ELEKTRA)
SUSSUDIO PHIL COLLINS (ATLANTIC)	13	WHITNEY HOUSTON WHITNEY HOUSTON (ARISTA)
WHO'S HOLDING DONNA NOW? DEBARGE (GORDY)	14	BE YOURSELF TONIGHT EURYTHMICS (RCA)
19 PAUL HARDCASTLE (CHRYSALIS)	15	MAKE IT BIG WHAM! (COLUMBIA/CBS)
POWER OF LOVE HUEY LEWIS AND THE NEWS (CHRYSALIS)	16	VITAL SIGNS SURVIVOR (SCOTTI BROS)
PEOPLE ARE PEOPLE DEPECHE MODE (SIRE)	17	BROTHERS IN ARMS DIRE STRAITS (WARNER BROS)
WOULD I LIE TO YOU? EURYTHMICS (RCA)	18	DREAM INTO ACTION HOWARD JONES (ELEKTRA)
FREEWAY OF LOVE ARETHA FRANKLIN (ARISTA)	19	VOICES CARRY 'TIL TUESDAY (EPIC)
YOU SPIN ME ROUND DEAD OR ALIVE (EPIC)	20	LITTLE CREATURES TALKING HEADS (SIRE)

● RECORD COMPANIES

● A&M Records
(01) 736 3311, 136-140 New Kings Road, London SW6 4LZ
Labels: Piggy Bank, Windham Hill.

● Abstract Records
(01) 969 4018, 35 Kempe Road, London NW6 6SP

● Ace Records
(01) 453 1311, 48-50 Steele Road, London NW10

● Albion Records Ltd
(01) 243 0011, 119-121 Freston Road, London W11 4BD

● Anagram Records
(01) 727 0346, 53 Kensington Gardens Square, London W2 4BA

● Arista Records
(01) 580 5566, 3 Cavendish Square, London W1

● Aura Records And Music Ltd
(01) 486 5288, 1 Kendall Place, London W1H 3AG

● Backs Recording Company Ltd
(0603) 26221, St Mary's Works, St Mary's Plain, Norwich NR3 3AF

● Bam-Caruso Records
(0727) 32109, 9 Ridgmont Road, St Albans, Herts

● BBC Records And Tapes
(01) 580 4468, The Langham, Portland Place, London W1A 1AA

● Beggars Banquet/ Situation 2/4AD
(01) 870 9912, 17-19 Alma Road, London SW18.
Labels: Coda, Ark, Paradox

● Big Bear Records
(021) 454 7020, 190 Monument Road, Birmingham B16 8UU

● Bright Records
(01) 408 0288, 34-36 Maddox Street, London W1R 9PD

● Bronze Records
(01) 267 4499, 100 Chalk Farm Road, London NW1 8EH

● Carrere Records
(01) 437 7581, 3rd Floor, Mutual House, 193-197 Regent Street, London W1

● CBS
(01) 734 8181, 17-19 Soho Square, London W1.
Labels: Burning Rome, Epic, Geffen, Portrait, Full Moon, Kitchenware, Monument, Philadelphia International, Tabu, Caribou, Unlimited Gold, Blue Sky, Scotti Bros.

● Charly Records Ltd
(01) 639 8603/4/5/6, 156-166 Ilderton Road, London SE15 1NT

● Cherry Red Records
(01) 229 8854/5, 53 Kensington Gardens Square, London W2 4BA

● Chrysalis
(01) 408 2355, 12 Stratford Place, London W1N 9AF.
Labels: Two Tone, Reformation, Air

● Clay Records Ltd
(0782) 273324/261990, 26 Hope Street, Stoke-on-Trent

● Cocteau Records
(01) 398 6413, P.O. Box 134A, Thames Ditton, Surrey

● Compact-Organization
(01) 580 1617, Compact House, 31 Riding House Street, London W1P 7PG

● Crass Records
(01) 888 8949, 10 Myddleton Road, London N22 4NS

● Creole Records Ltd
(01) 965 9223, 91-93 High Street, Harlesden, London NW10
Labels: Dynamic, Ecstasy, Replay, AMFM, Cactus, Blast From The Past, Silver Screen, Timeless Treasures, Rhino, Review, Mix Factory, Street Level.

● Demon Records
(01) 847 2481, Western House, Harlequin Avenue, Great West Road, Brentford, Middlesex TW8 9EW

● DEP International
(021) 643 1321, 92 Fazeley Street, Digbeth, Birmingham B5 5RD

● DJM Records
(01) 242 6886, James House, 5-11 Theobalds Road, London WC1X 8SE

● Don't Fall Off The Mountain
(01) 870 9912, 17-19 Alma Road, Wandsworth, London SW18

● EG Records
(01) 730 2162, 63a Kings Road, London SW3 4NT

● EMI Records
(01) 486 4488, 20 Manchester Square, London W1A 1ES.
Labels: Harvest, Parlophone, Columbia, Rolling Stones, Capitol, Liberty, HMV, EMI, America, MFP, LFP CFP, Sunset, Zonophone, Starline, Blue Note.

● Ensign Records Ltd
(01) 727 0527, 3 Monmouth Place, London W2 5SH

● Factory Communications Limited
(061) 434 3876, 86 Palatine Road, Manchester 20

● **Fast Forward**
(031) 226 4616 21a Alva Street, Edinburgh EH2 4PS.
Label: Disposable

● **F-Beat**
(01) 847 2481, Western House, Harlequin Avenue, Great West Road, Brentford, Middlesex TW8 9EW

● **Flicknife**
(01) 743 9412, 1st Floor, The Metrostore, 5/10 Eastman Road, Acton, London W3 7YG

● **Glass Records**
(01) 740 9628, The Metrostore, 231 The Vale, Acton, London W3

● **Go! Discs**
(01) 743 3845/3919, Go! Mansions, 8 Wendell Road, London W12

● **Greensleeves Records Ltd**
(01) 749 3277/8, Unit 7, Goldhawk Industrial Estate, 2A Brackenbury Road, London W6

● **Hannibal Records**
(01) 370 6166, 3 Logan Place, London W8

● **Heartbeat Productions**
(0272) 730458, 14c Lansdowne Place, Clifton, Bristol BS8 3AF

● **Ice Record Company**
(01) 730-7291, P.O. Box 212, London SW1 4PU

● **Illuminated Records**
(01) 381 1393, 452 Fulham Road, London SW6

● **IRS (International Recording Syndicate)**
(01) 727 0734, 194 Kensington Park Road, London W11 2ES.
Label: Illegal

● **Island Records**
(01) 741 1511, 22 St Peter's Square, London W6 9NW.
Labels: Ensign, Mango, Ze, Zang Tuum Tumb, Stiff, Taxi, Fourth & Broadway, Tommy Boy, Philly World, TTED.

● **Jet**
(01) 637 2111, 35 Portland Place, London W1N 3AG

● **Kitchenware Records**
(0632) 618036, 62 Clayton Street, Newcastle-upon-Tyne 1

● **K-Tel International Ltd**
(01) 992 8055, K-Tel House, 620 Western Avenue, London W3 0TU

● **Lamborghini Records**
(01) 262 1695/6/7, 138 Gloucester Place, London NW1 6DT

● **Lightning Records**
(01) 969 5255, 841 Harrow Road, London NW10 5N4

● **London Records**
(01) 491 4600, 15 St George Street, London W1

● **MCA**
(01) 437 9797, 72-74 Brewer Street, London W1.
Labels: MCA, ABC, Coral, Curt, Loose End, Panther, Solar.

● **Magnet Records**
(01) 486 8151, Magnet House, 22 York Street, London W1H 1FD

● **Music For Nations**
(01) 437 4688, 8 Carnaby Street, London W1V 1PG

● **Music For Pleasure**
(01) 561 8722, 1-3 Uxbridge Road, Hayes, Middlesex UB4 0SY

● **Mute Records**
(01) 221 4840, 49-53 Kensington Gardens Square, London W2

● **Neat Records**
(091) 262 4999, 71 High Street, East Wallsend, Tyne And Wear NE28 7RJ.
Labels: Wudwink, Rigid, Completely Different, Floating World.

● **Oily Records**
(0224) 632749/630120, 6 Cedar Place, Aberdeen

● **Old Gold Records**
(01) 884 2220, Unit 1, Langhedge Lane Industrial Estate, Edmonton N18 2TQ

● **Oval Records**
(01) 622 0111, 11 Liston Road, London SW4

● **People Unite Musicians Co-op And Publications**
(01) 574 1718/1453 2a Dudley Road, Southall, Middlesex

● **Phonogram Ltd**
(01) 491 4600, 50 New Bond Street, London W1Y 9HA.
Labels: Mercury, Vertigo, Phillips, De-Lite, Casablanca, Some Bizarre, Rockets, Neutron, Club, Fontana, 20th Century.

● **Pickwick International Inc. Ltd**
(01) 200 7000, The Hyde Industrial Estate, The Hyde, London NW9 6JU.
Labels: Hallmark, Contour, Camden, Contour Classics, Spot, Ditto, Scoop, Tell-A-Tale, Pickwick, Imp.

● **Polydor**
(01) 499 8686, 13-14 St George Street, London W1R 9DE.
Labels: RSO, MGM, Verve, Fiction, Kudi, Obscure, Dreamland, Wonderland, 21 Records, Capricorn, Track, Montage, Deutsche Gramophone, Ambient.

● **President Records Ltd**
(01) 839 4672/5, Broadmead House, 21 Panton Street, London SW1 4DR.
Labels: Bulldog, Crystal, Dart, Energy, Enterprise, Gemini, Jayboy, Joy, Max's, Kansas City, New World, Rhapsody, Seville, Spiral.

● **Probe Records**
(051) 227 5646, 8-12 Rainford Gardens, Liverpool 2

● **PRT Records**
(01) 262 8040, ACC House, 17 Great Cumberland Place, London W1A 1AG.
Labels: Blueprint, Caliber, Caliber/Plus, Collector, Flashback, Golden House, Golden Guinea, Precision, Piccadilly, Spotlight, Top Brass, Becket, Compleat, GNP Crescendo, Sunnyview, Personal, Teresa, Hi-Cream.

● **Radicalchoice**
(01) 853 5899, 17 Nelson Road, London SE1

● **RAK Records**
(01) 586 2012, 42 Charlbert Street, London NW8

● **RCA/Motown**
(01) 636 8311, 1 Bedford Avenue, London WC1.
Labels: Ice, Regard, Salsoul, KR Records, Red Seal, Total Experience, F-Beat, Tamla Motown, Gordy, Morocco, Prelude.

● **Reachout International Records (Europe)**
(01) 274 2025, 1 Clarence House, Rushcroft Road, London SW2

● **Red Flame**
(01) 743 0006, The Metrostore, 231 The Vale, Acton, London W3 7QS

● **Red Lightnin' Records Blues And R&B Specialists**
(0379) 88693, The White House, North Lopham, Diss Norfolk

● **The Rocket Record Company Ltd**
(01) 938 1741, 125 Kensington High Street, London W8 5SN

● **Ronco Teleproducts**
(01) 274 7761, Ellerslie Park, 11 Lyham Road, London SW2

● **Rough Trade Records**
(01) 833 2133/2561/2/3, 61-71 Collier Street, London N1

● **Safari Records**
(01) 723 8464, 44 Seymour Place, London W1.
Label: Singing Dog Records

● **Saga Records Ltd**
(01) 969 6651, 326 Kensal Road, London W10 5BL.
Labels: Trojan, B&C, Mooncrest

● **Satril Records Ltd**
(01) 435 8065, 444 Finchley Road, London NW2
Labels: Crash, Topaz, Service

● **Shout Records**
(01) 740 0680, The Metrostore, 231 The Vale, London W3 7QS

● **Siren Records**
(01) 727 8070, 2-4 Vernon Yard, 119 Portobello Road, London W11

● **Solid Gold Records**
(01) 734 3251, 14 New Burlington Street, London W1X 2LR

● **Small Wonder Records Ltd**
(0787) 76026, PO Box 23. Sudbury, Suffolk

● **Some Bizarre**
(01) 734 9411, St Anne's Court, Wardour Street, London W1

● **Sonet Records**
(01) 229 7267, 121 Ledbury Road, London W11.
Labels: Speciality, Alligator, Kicking Mule, Red Stripe, Titanic, Stone

● **Statik Records**
(01) 381 0116, 385 0567, 1a Normand Gardens, Greyhound Road, London W14

● **Stiff Records**
(01) 741 1511, 22 St Peters Square, London W6 9NW

● **Towerbell Records**
(01) 328 1787, Iverson Road, London NW6.
Labels: Rockney, Shelf, Cockerel

● **Upright Records**
(01) 833 3456, 61/71 Collier Street, London N1 9BE

● **Virgin Records**
(01) 968 6688, Kensal House, 533/579 Harrow Road, London W10.
Labels: Caroline, Charisma, Paladin, DEP International, Statik, Beggars Banquet, WMOT, 10/Virgin, Siren

● **WEA Records Ltd**
(01) 434 3232, 20 Broadwick Street, London W1V 2BH.
Labels: Asylum, Atlantic, Elektra, Reprise, Warner Brothers, Sire, Cotillion, Korova.

● **Zang Tumb Tuum Records**
(01) 229 1229, ZTT Building, 8-10 Basing Street, London W11 1ET

● **Zomba Productions Ltd**
(01) 459 8899, Zomba House, 165-167 Willesden High Road, London NW10 2SG.
Labels: Jive, Afrika, Jive Electro.

● MUSIC PUBLISHERS

● **Albion Music Ltd**
(01) 243 0011, 119/121 Freston Road, London W11 4BD

● **Ambassador Music Ltd**
(01) 836 5996, 22 Denmark Street, London WC2

● **Ash Music Publishers**
(0623) 752448, Cropwell House, Salmon Lane, Kirkby-in-Ashfield, Notts

● **ASL Publishing**
(0633) 856327, 5 Ogmore Crescent, Bettws, Newport, Gwent NPT 6SP

● **Asterisk Music**
(01) 397 8957/390 3711, PO Box 18F, Chessington, Surrey KT9 1UZ

● **ATV Music Ltd**
(01) 409 2211, 19 Upper Brook Street, London W1Y 1PD

● **Balgier Ltd**
(021) 643 7727, Room 32, Princess Chambers, 6 Coronation Street, Birmingham B2 4RN

● **Banks Music Publications**
(0904) 21818, 139 Holgate Road, York YO2 4DF

● **Barn Publishing**
(01) 935 8323, 12 Thayer Street, London W1

● **Beadle Music Ltd**
(0444) 412284, Suite D, The Priory, Haywards Heath, Sussex

● **Belsize Music Ltd**
(01) 499 2014/409 0287, 38 North Row, London W1R 1DH

● **Big Ben Music Ltd**
(01) 723 4499, 18 Lancaster Mews, London W2 3QE

● **Big Secret Music**
(0734) 213623, Havoc House, Cods Hill, Beenham Berkshire

● **Black Sheep Music Ltd UK**
(02816) 2143/2109, Fulmer Gardens House, Fulmer, Bucks

● **Bocu Music Ltd**
(01) 402 7433/4/5, 1 Wyndham Yard, Wyndham Place, London W1H 1AR

● **Bourne Music Ltd**
(01) 493 6412, 34/36 Maddox Street, London W1R 9PD

● **Sydney Bron Music Co. Ltd**
(01) 267 4499, 100 Chalk Farm Road, London NW1 8EH

● **Brothers Music**
(01) 794 9177, 5 Hollycroft Avenue, London NW3 7QG

● **BTW (Music) Ltd**
(01) 888 6655, 125 Myddleton Road, Wood Green, London N22 4NG

● **Bullseye Music Ltd**
(0388) 814632, AIR House, Spennymoor, Co. Durham DL16 7SE

● **Burlington Music Co. Ltd**
(01) 499 0067, 129 Park Street, London W1

● **Carlin Music Corporation**
(01) 734 3251, 14 New Burlington Street, London W1X 2LR

● **CBS Songs**
(01) 637 5831, 3-5 Rathbone Place, London W1V SDG

● **Chappell Music Ltd**
(01) 629 7600, 129 Park Street, London W1Y 3FA

● **Charly Publishing Ltd**
(01) 732 5647, 46-47 Pall Mall, London SW1 5JG

● **Cherry Music**
(01) 437 7418/9, 49 Greek Street, London W1

● **Chevron Music Publishing Ltd**
(0532) 438283, The Television Centre, Leeds LS3 1JS

● **Christabel Music Ltd**
(0532) 694105, 358 Alwoody Lane, Leeds 17

● **Chrysalis Music Ltd**
(01) 408 2359, 12 Stratford Place, London W1N 9AF

● **Collins Music Company**
(01) 258 3891, 38 Kendal Street, London W2

● **Barry Collings Music Ltd**
(0702) 347343, 15 Claremont Road, Westcliffe-on-Sea Essex

● **Creole Music Ltd**
(01) 965 9223, 91-93 High Street, Harlesden, London NW10

● **Eaton Music Ltd**
(01) 235 9046, 8 West Eaton Place, London SW1X 8LS

● **John Edward Music Ltd**
(01) 806 0071, 38-40 Upper Clapton Road, London E5 8BQ

● **Edwardson Music Ltd**
(01) 935 7615, 106 Bickenhall Mansions, London W1H 3LB

● **EG Music Ltd**
(01) 730 2162, 63a King's Road, London SW3 4NT

● **EMI Music Publishing**
(01) 836 6699, 138-140 Charing Cross Road, London WC2H 0LD

● **E&S Music Ltd**
(01) 995 5432, 20-24 Beaumont Road, London W4 5AP

● **TRO Essex Music Ltd**
(01) 430 1691, 7 Bury Place, London WC1

● **Faber Music Ltd**
(01) 278 6881, 3 Queen Square, London WC1N 3AU

● **Fast Western Ltd**
(01) 723 9559/402 4024, 2 York House, Upper Montagu Street, London W1

● **Fentone Music Ltd**
(05366) 60981, Fleming Road, Earlstrees, Corby, Northants

● **Noel Gay Music Co. Ltd**
(01) 836 3941, 24 Denmark Street, London WC2H 8NJ

● **Graduate Music Ltd**
(0905) 620731, P.O. Box 1, Holt Street, Worcester

● **Handle Music Ltd**
(01) 493 9637, 1 Derby Street, London W1

● **Happy Face Music**
(0905) 820569, The Old Smithy Recording Studio, Post Office Lane, Kempsey, Worcs.

● **Heath Levy Music Co. Ltd**
(01) 439 7731, 184-186 Regent Street, London W1R 5DF

● **Hedley Music**
(0246) 79976, 71 Rutland Road, Chesterfield, Derby S40 1ND

● **Heisenberg Ltd**
(01) 703 7677, 18 Crofton Road, London SE5 8NB

● **Hensley Music Publishing Co. Ltd**
(01) 727 5118, 4 Rushton Mews, London W11 4JB

● **Hollywood Music**
(01) 806 0071, 38-40 Upper Clapton Road, London E5

● **Hub Music Ltd**
(01) 891 3146, 4-10 Queens Road, Twickenham TW1 4ES

● **Hush Music Ltd**
(01) 589 6293, 117c Fulham Road, London SW3

● **Intersong Music Ltd**
(01) 129 Park Street, London W1Y 3FA

● **Island Music Ltd**
(01) 741 1511, 22 St Peter's Square, Hammersmith, London W6 9NW

● **Ivory Coast Music Ltd**
(01) 740 0680, The Metrostore, 321 The Vale, London W3

● **Kamela Music Ltd**
(061) 652 2491, 225 Ripponden Road, Oldham, Lancs OL1 4HR

● **Kassner Associated Publishers**
(01) 839 4672, 21 Panton Street, London SW1

● **Kennick Music**
(01) 589 7711/8861, Flat 3, 50 Cadogan Square, London SW1X 0JW

● **Lantern Music Publishing Co. Ltd**
(01) 828 4595, 66 Roebuck House, Palace Street, London SW1

● **Logorhythm Music Ltd**
(01) 734 7443/4, 6-10 Lexington Street, London W1

● **Louvigny Music Co. Ltd**
(01) 493 5961, 38 Hertford Street, London W1Y 8BA

● **Magnet Music Ltd**
(01) 486 8151, 22 York Street, London W1H 1FD

● **MAM (Music Publishing) Ltd**
(01) 629 9255, 24-25 New Bond Street, London W1Y 9HD

● **Sue Manning Music Publishing Ltd**
(01) 379 5920, 31 Betterton Street, Covent Garden, London WC2

● **Martin-Coulter Music Ltd**
(01) 582 7622, 11th Floor, Alembic House, 93 Albert Embankment, London SE1 7TY

● **MCA Music Ltd**
(01) 629 7211, 139 Piccadilly, London W1V 9FH

● **Midnight Music Ltd**
(01) 950 9507, P.O. Box 333, Bushey, Watford

● **Morrison Leahy Music Ltd**
(01) 402 9238, Flat 3, 1 Hyde Park Place, London W2 2LH

● MPL Communications Ltd
(01) 439 6621, 1 Soho Square, London W1V 6BQ

● Neptune Music Ltd
(01) 437 2066/7, 31 Old Burlington Street, London W1X 1LB

● Orange Publishing Ltd
(01) 581 5982, 39 Petersham Place, London SW7

● Oval Music
(01) 622 0111, 11 Liston Road London SW4

● Page One Music Ltd
(01) 221 7179/7381, 29 Rushton Mews, London W11 1RB

● Palace Music Co. Ltd
(01) 499 0067, 129 Park Street, London W1Y 3FA

● Paragon Music Co. Ltd
(01) 681 6663, Park House, 22 Park Street, Croydon, Surrey

● Pattern Music Ltd
(01) 836 5996, 22 Denmark Street, London WC2

● Pink Floyd Muisc Publishers Ltd
(01) 734 6892, 27 Noel Street, London W1V 3RD

● Plangent Visions Music Ltd
(01) 734 6892, 27 Noel Street, London W1V 3RD

● Point Music Ltd
(01) 730 9777, The Point, 9 Eccleston Street, Belgravia, London SW1W 9LX

● RAK Publishing Ltd
(01) 586 2012, 42-48 Charlbert Street, London NW8 7BU

● The Really Useful Company Ltd
(01) 734 2114, 20 Greek Street, London W1V 5LF

● Red Bus Music (International) Ltd
(01) 258 0324/5/6/7/8, Red Bus House, 48 Broadley Terrace, London NW1

● RCA Music Ltd
(01) 437 2468, 155-157 Oxford Street, London W1

● Riva Music Ltd
(01) 731 4131, 2 New King's Road, London SW6

● Rock Music Co. Ltd
(01) 734 6892, 27 Noel Street, London W1V 3RD

● Rock City Music Ltd
(09328) 66531/2, Shepperton Studio Centre, Shepperton. Middlesex

● Rocket Publishing
(01) 937 3815, 125 Kensington High Street, London W8 5SN

● Rondor Music (London) Ltd
(01) 731 4161/5, Rondor House, 10a Parsons Green, London SW6 4TW

● Sarm Songs Ltd
(01) 229 1229, 8-10 Basing Street, London W11 1ET

● Satri Music Ltd
(01) 435 8063/4/5, 444 Finchley Road, London NW2 2HT

● Scorpio Music
(01) 455 4556, 9 Ravenscroft Avenue, London NW11 0SA

● Shapiro Bernstein And Co. Ltd
(01) 636 7777, 78 Newman Street, London W1

● Sonet Records & Publishing Ltd
(01) 229 7267, 121 Ledbury Road, London W11 2AQ

● Sound Diagrams Ltd
(031) 229 8946, 21 Atholl Crescent, Edinburgh, Scotland EH3 8HQ

● Southern Music Publishing Co. Ltd
(01) 836 4524, 8 Denmark Street, London WC2H 8LT

● St Annes Music Ltd
(061) 941 5151, Kennedy House, 31 Stanford Street, Altrincham, Cheshire WA14 1ES

● Storm Music
(0253) 864598, 25 Rossall Road, Cleveleys, Blackpool FY5 1DX

● Street Music Ltd
(01) 459 8899, Zomba House, 165-167 Willesden High Road, London NW10

● Summit Music Ltd
(01) 491 3175/409 0287, 38 North Row, London W1R 1DH

● Sunbury Music Ltd
(01) 437 2468, 155-157 Oxford Street, London W1R 1TB

● Tabitha Music Ltd
(0392) 79914, 39 Cordery Road, St Thomas, Exeter, Devon EX2 9DJ

● Tembo Music Ltd
(01) 586 5591/2, 50 Regent's Park Road, London NW1 7SX

● 10 Music
(01) 221 8585, Virgin Mansions, 101-109 Ladbroke Grove, London W11 1PG

● Thames Music Ltd
(01) 741 2406, 117 Church Road, Barnes, London SW13 9HL

● Tristan Music Ltd
(01) 836 5996, 22 Denmark Street, London WC2

● United Music Publishers Ltd
(01) 729 4700, 42 Rivington Street, London EC2A 3BN

● Valentine Music Group
(01) 240 1628/9, 7 Garrick Street, London WC2E 9AR

● Virgin Music Publishers Ltd
(01) 229 1282, Virgin Mansions, 101-109 Ladbroke Grove, London W11 1PG

● Warner Brothers Music Ltd
(01) 637 3771, 17 Berners Street, London W1P 3DD

● Bruce Welch Music Ltd
(01) 434 1839, 64 Stirling Court, Marshall Street, London W1V 1LG

● Westminster Music Ltd
(01) 734 8121, 19-20 Poland Street, London W1V 3DD

● Zebra Publishing Songs Ltd
(01) 408 1611, 3rd Floor, 243 Regent Street, London W1R 8PN

● INDEPENDENT RECORD DISTRIBUTORS

● Arabesque Ltd
(01) 995 3023/994 7889, Swan Works, Fishers Lane, London W4 1RX

● Backs Records Ltd
(0603) 26221, St Mary's Works, St Mary's Plain, Norwich

● Cadillac Music
(01) 838 3048/340 3933, 180 Shaftesbury Avenue, London WC2H 8SJ

● Caroline Exports Ltd
(01) 961 2919, 56 Standard Road, London NW10

● The Cartel
(See: Backs, Fast Forward, 9-Mile, Red Rhino, Revolver, Rough Trade)

● Conifer Records
(0895) 447707, Horton Road, West Drayton, Middlesex UB7 8JL

● Discovery Records
(067285) 406, 107 Broad Street, Beechingstoke, Pewsey, Wilts
and
24 Drury Lane, Solihull, West Midlands

● ESSP (Electronic Synthesizer Sound Projects)
(01) 979 9997, The Sound House, P.O. Box 37b, East Molesey, Surrey

● Fast Forward
(031) 226 4616, 2la Alva Road, Edinburgh EH2 4PS

● Greensleeves Records Ltd
(01) 749 3277/8, Unit 7, Goldhawk Industrial Estate, 2a Brackenbury Road, London W6

● IDS (Independent Distribution Services Ltd)
(01) 476 1476, 7 Deanston Wharf, Badfield Road, London E16 2BJ

● Jazz Horizon (Importers/Distributors)
(0279) 724572, 103 London Road, Sawbridgeworth, Herts CM1 9JJ

● Jazz Music (Manchester)
(061) 794 3525, 7 Kildare Road, Swinton, Manchester M27 3AB

● JSU Distribution
(0422) 64773, 21 Bull Green, Halifax, West Yorkshire HX1 2RZ

● Jungle Records (Bravour Ltd)
(01) 359 8444/9161, 24 Gaskin Street, Islington, London N1 2RY

● Lasgo Exports Ltd
(01) 961 1333, Unit M, New Crescent Works, Nicholl Road, London NW10

● Lightning Records And Video Ltd
(01) 969 5255, 841 Harrow Road, London NW10 5NH

● Making Waves Ltd
(01) 481 9917, 6-8 Alie Street, London E1

● Mirage
(0272) 691867, 614 Southmead Road, Filton, Bristol BS12 7RF

● 9-Mile Distribution
(0926) 881211, Lower Avenue, Leamington Spa, Warwickshire

● Oldies Unlimited
(0952) 612244, Dukes Way, St Georges, Telford, Shropshire

● Pickwick International Inc. Ltd
(01) 200 7000, The Hyde Industrial Estate, The Hyde, London NW9 6JU

● Pinnacle Records
(0689) 27000, Pinnacle House, 1 Oasthouse Way, Orpington, Kent

● Pizza Express Music Distribution
(01) 734 6112, 29 Romilly Street, London W1

● Probe Records
(051) 236 6591, 8-12 Rainford Gardens, Liverpool 2

● Projection Records Distribution
(0702) 72281/714025, 74 High Street, Old Town/ Leigh-On-Sea Essex

● PRT Distribution
(01) 648 7000, 105 Bond Road, Mitcham, Surrey CR4 3UT

● Recommended Distribution
(01) 622 8834, 387 Wandsworth Road, London SW8

● Red Lightnin' Records
(0379) 88693, The White House, North Lopham, Diss, Norfolk

● Red Rhino Distribution Ltd
(0904) 641415/27828, The Coach House, Fetter Lane, York YO1 1EM

● Revolver Records
(0272) 541291/541293, The Old Malt House, Little Ann Street, Bristol 2

● Rose Records
(01) 609 8288, 3 Ellington Street, Islington, London N7 8PP

● Ross Record Distribution
(0888) 62403, 29 Main Street, Turriff, Aberdeenshire

● Rough Trade Distribution
(01) 833 2133, 61/71 Collier Street, London N1

● Stage One Records Ltd
(0428) 4001, Parshire House, 2 Kings Road, Haslemere, Surrey

● Wynd-Up Records
(061) 872 0170, Turntable House, Guinness Road Trading Estate, Trafford Park, Manchester

● RECORDING STUDIOS

● Abbey Road Studios
(01) 286 1161, 3 Abbey Road, London NW8 9AY

● Angel Recording Studios Ltd
(01) 354 2525, 311 Upper Street, London N1

● Aosis
(01) 267 4680/485 4810, 10a Belmont Street, London NW10

● Arny's Shack
7c Bank Chambers, Penhill Avenue, Parkstone, Dorset

● The Barge
(01) 289 6204, Opposite No. 60 Bloomfield Road, Little Venice, London W9

● Basement Studio
(01) 734 5784, 145 Wardour Street, London W1V 3YB

● Berwick Street Recording Studios
(01) 734 5750, 8 Berwick Street, Soho, London W1V 3RG

● Britannia Row Recording Studios Ltd
(01) 226 3377/2290, 35 Britannia Row, Islington, London N1 8QH

● Ca Va Sound Workshop
(041) 334 5099/6330, 49 Derby Street, Kelvingrove, Glasgow G3 7TU

● Cargo Studios
(0706) 524420, Kenion Street, Rochdale, Lancashire

● Castle recording Studio
(0942) 58777, The Castle, Castle Hill Road, Hindley, Wigan, Lancashire WN2 4BH

● CBS Recording Studios
(01) 636 3434, 31-37 Whitfield Street, London W1P 5RE

● Chipping Norton Recording Studios
(0608) 3636, 28-30 New Street, Chipping Norton, Oxfordshire OX7 5JL

● Craighall Studio
(031) 552 3685, 68 Craighall Road, Edinburgh EH6 4RL

● De Wolfe Ltd
(01) 437 4933, 439 8481, 80-88 Wardour Street, London W1V 3LF

● Denmark Street Studios
(01) 836 6061, 9 Denmark Street, London WC2

● DJM Recording Studios
(01) 242 6886, 5-11 Theobalds Road, London WC1X 8SE

● Duffy's Studio
(01) 737 0817, 703 9608, 1-2 The Parade, Dog Kennel Hill, East Dulwich, London SE22

● Easy Street Studios
(01) 739 1451/8887, 45 Blythe Street, London E2

● Eden Studios Ltd
(0) 995 5432, 20-24 Beaumont Road, London W4 5AP

● Eel Pie Studios
(01) 891 1266/7/8/9, The Boathouse, Ranleagh Drive, Twickenham TW1 1QZ

● The Elephant Recording Studio
(01) 481 8615, Basement N, Metropolitan Wharf, Wapping Hill, London E1

● The Factory Sound (Woldingham) Ltd
(01) 905 2386, Toftrees Church Road, Woldingham, Surrey

● Fallout Shelter (Island Studios London)
(01) 741 1511, 47 British Grove, London W4 2NL

● Farmyard Recording Studios
(02404) 2912, Bendrose House East, White Lion Road, Little Chalfont, Buckinghamshire

● Foel Recording Studio Ltd
(0938) 810758, Llanfair Caereinion, Powys, Wales

● Good Earth Productions Ltd
(01) 734 0864/434 1490, 59 Dean Street, London W1

● Gooseberry Gerrard Street Studios
(01) 437 6255, 19 Gerrard Street, London W1

● Gooseberry Hillside Road Studios
(01) 674 0548, 2 Hillside Road, Tulse Hill, London SW2

● Grosvenor Recording Studios
(021) 356 9636, 16 Grosvenor Road, Handsworth Wood, Birmingham B20 3NP

● Herne Place Studios
(0990) 26639, Herne Place, London Road, Sunningdale, Ascot, Berksire

● Hollywood Studios
(01) 806 0071/4, 38-40 Upper Clapton Road, London E5 8BQ

● Horizon Recording Studios
(0203) 21000, Horizon House, Warwick Road, Coventry

● Jacobs Studio
(0252) 723518/726228, Ridgway House, Runwick, Nr. Farnham, Surrey

● JAM Recording Ltd
(01) 272 7545, 106 Tollington Park, London N4

● Jamm Studios
(0202) 286040/493126, Flash Mills, Great Moor Street, Bolton

● R.G. Jones Recording Studio
(01) 540 9881, Beulah Road, London SW19 3SB

● Kirkland Park Studios
(0236) 821081, Lethame Road, Strathaven M40 6EE

● Konk 'Kinks' Productions Ltd
(01) 340 7873/4757, 84-86 Tottenham Lane, London N8 7EE

● Lansdowne Recording Studios Ltd
(01) 727 0041/2/3, Lansdowne House, Lansdowne Road, London W11 3LP

● Livingston Studios Ltd
(01) 869 6558, Brook Road, Wood Green, London N22

● Maison Rouge
(01) 381 2001, 2 Wansdown Park, Fulham Broadway, London SW6

● The Manor Studios
(08675) 77551, Shipton-On-Cherwell, Nr. Kidlington, Oxfordshire

● Marquee Studios
(01) 437 6731, 10 Richmond Mews, Dean Street, London W1

● Mayfair Recording Studios
(01) 586 7746, 11a Sharpleshall Street, London NW1

● Misty Recording Studios
(0202) 295961, 24 Norwich Road, Bournemouth

● Mushroom Studios
(0272) 735994/735867, 18 West Mall, Clifton, Bristol BS8 4BQ

● Music Works
(01) 609 0808/607 9495/6/7, 23 Benwell Road, London N7

● The Nova Suite
(01) 493 7403/4/5, 21-27 Bryanston Street, Marble Arch, London W1H 7AB

● Odyssey Recording Studios
(01) 402 2191, 26-27 Castlereagh Street, London W1

● Old Barn Recorders
(01) 680 9222/4831, 39 Croham Road, South Croydon CR2 7HD

● One Two Three Music Studios
(0222) 222826, 48 Smithfield Square, Belfast, Northern Ireland

● Pathway
(01) 359 0970, 2a Grosvenor Avenue, London N5

● Pennine Studios
(061) 665 2278, 225 Ripponden Road, Littlemore, Oldham OL1 4HR

● Pluto Recording Studios
(061) 228 2022, 36 Granby Row, Manchester 1

● Polygram PRO Recording Studio
(01) 499 8686, 54 Maddox Street, London W1

● Portland Recording Studios Ltd
(01) 637 2111, 35 Portland Place, London W1N 3AG

● Producers Workshop
(01) 589 8341/6293, 117c Fulham Road, London SW3

● PRT Studios
(01) 402 8114, 40 Bryanston Street, London W1

● PWL
(01) 403 0007/0020, Vineyard off Sanctuary Lane, London SE1

● Q Studios
(0533) 608813, 1487 Melton Road, Queniborough Industrial Estate, Queniborough, Leicester

● RAK Studios
(01) 586 2012, 42-48 Charlbert Street, London NW8 7BU

● Redan Recorders Ltd
(01) 229 9054/5/6, 23 Redan Place, Queensway, London W2

● REL Studios
(031) 229 9651, 7a Athol Place, Edinburgh EH3 8HP

● Ridge Farm Studios
(0306) 711202, Ridge Farm, Capel, Surrey RH5 5HG

● Riverside Recordings Ltd
(01) 994 3142, 78 Church Path, London W4 5BJ

● Rockfield Studios
(0600) 2449/3625, Amberley Court, Rockfield Road, Monmouth, Gwent

● Roundhouse Recording Studio
(01) 845 0131, 100 Chalk Farm Road, London NW1 8EH

● Sain Recordiau (Cyf)
(0286) 851111, Llandwrog, Caernarfon, Gwynedd, Cymru, Wales

● Sarm Recording Studios (East)
(01) 247 1311, Osborn House, 9-13 Osborn Street, London E1 6TD

● Sarm Recording Studios (West)
(01) 229 1229, 8-10 Basing Street, London W11 1ET

● Satril Studio
(01) 435 8063, 444 Finchley Road, London NW2

● SAV Studios Ltd
(01) 278 7893/4/5, 26 Harrison Street, London WC1H 8JG

● Scorpio Sound
(01) 388 0263/4, 19-20 Euston Centre, London NW1 3JH

● September Sound Studios
(0484) 643211, 38 Knowl Road, Golcar, Huddersfield DH7 4AN

● Sin City Studios
(0602) 784714/708622, 22a Forest Road West, Nottingham NG7 4EQ

● Sirocco Recording Studio
(0563) 36377, 1 Glencairn Square, Kilmarnock, Ayrshire, Scotland

● Solid Bond
(01) 402 6121, Garden Entrance, Stanhope House, Stanhope Place, London W2 2HH

● Sound Suite Recording Suite
(01) 485 4881, 92 Camden Mews, London NW1

● Southern Studios
(01) 888 8949, 10 Myddleton Road, London N22 4NS

● Spaceward Recording Studios
(035 389) 600/776, The Old School, High Street, Stretham, Cambridge CB6 3LD

● Surrey Sound Studio Ltd
(0372) 379444, 70 Kingston Road, Leatherhead, Surrey

● Tapestry Studio
(01) 878 3353, 67 First Avenue, Mortlake, London SW14 8SP

● Town House Studios
(01) 743 9313, 159 Goldhawk Road, London W12

● Trident Studios
(01) 734 9901/5, 17 St Anne's Court, Wardour Street, London W1

● Utopia Studios
(01) 586 3434, Utopia Village, 7 Chalcot Road, London NW1 8LH

● Wessex Studios
(01) 359 0051, 106 Highbury New Park, London N5 2DW

● The Workhouse
(01) 237 1736/7/8, 488 Old Kent Road, London SE1

● The Yard
(01) 571 4591, Abbotsbury House, Priory Way, Southall, Middlesex

● ROCK PUBLICATIONS

● Blitz/The Beat
(01) 734-8311/3, 1 Lower James Street, London W1
Monthly

● Blues And Rhythm
(01) 906 0986, 18 Maxwelton Close, Mill Hill, London NW7 3NA
Ten times a year

● Blues And Soul
(01) 402-6869, 153 Praed Street, London W2
Fortnightly

● Blues Unlimited
38 Belmon Park, London SE13
Quarterly

● Bucketfull Of Brains
70 Prince George's Avenue, London W20
Quarterly

● Chartbeat
(01) 748 5323, 81 Rothschild Road, Acton Green, London W4
Monthly

● Country Music Round-Up
(0522) 23593/4, Belgrave House, 32 Shaftesbury Avenue, Forest Park, Lincoln
Monthly

● Country Music People
(01) 309 1606, 78 Grovelands Road, St Paul's Cray, Orpington, Kent
Monthly

● Disco And Club Trade International
(01) 278-3591/6, 410 St John Street, London EC1
Monthly

● Echoes
(01) 253-6662/4, Rococo House, 283 City Road, London EC1 1LA
Weekly

● Electronics & Music Maker
(0223) 313722, Alexander House, 1 Milton Road, Cambridge CB4 1UY
Monthly

● The Face
(01) 580-6756, 5-11 Mortimer Street, London W1
Monthly

● Folk Roots
(0252) 724638, 2 Eastdale, East Street, Farnham, Surrey GU9 7TB
Monthly

● Guitarist
(0223) 313722, Alexander House, 1 Milton Road, Cambridge CB4 1UY
Monthly

● History Of Rock
(01) 379 6711, Orbis House, 20-22 Bedfordbury, London WC2
Weekly

● The HiT
(01) 404 0700, Holborn Publishing Group, Commonwealth House, 1-19 New Oxford Street, London WC1
Weekly

● Home Studio Recording
(0223) 313722, Alexander House, 1 Milton Road, Cambridge CB4 1UY
Monthly

● i-D
(01) 430 0871, 27-29 Macklin Street, London WC2
Monthly

● In The City
(01) 267 1525, c/o Compendium Books, 234 Camden High Street, London NW1
Irregular

● International Country Music News
(05097) 3224, 18 Burley Rise, Kegworth, Derby DE8 2DZ
Monthly

● International Musician And Recording World
(01) 987-5090, P.O. Box 381, Mill Harbour, London E14
Monthly

● Jamming
(01) 602 6351, 21 Parkway, London NW1
Monthly

● Jazz Journal International
(01) 580-7244/6970, 35 Great Russell Street, London WC1B 3PP
Monthly

● Kerrang!
(01) 387 6611, Spotlight, Greater London House, Hampstead Road, NW1
Fortnightly

● Melody Maker
(01) 379 3581, Berkshire House, 168-73 High Holborn, London WC1
Weekly

● Music UK
(01) 460-4474, 26-28 Addison Road, Bromley, Kent BR2 9RR
Monthly

● Music Week
(01) 387 6611, Spotlight, Greater London House, Hampstead Road, London NW1
Weekly

● New Kommotion
(01) 902-6417, 3 Bowrons Avenue, Wembley, Middlesex
Monthly

● NME (The New Musical Express)
(01) 439-8761, 5-7 Carnaby Street, London W1
Weekly

● No. 1
(01) 404 0700, Holborn Publishing Group, Commonwealth House, 1-19 New Oxford Street, London WC1
Weekly

● Now Dig This
(01) 954-4518 (Distribution), 50 Drummond Crescent 69 Quarry Lane, Simonside, South Shields, Tyne and Wear
Monthly

● Omaha Rainbow
(01) 647-5491, 10 Lesley Court, Harcourt Road, Wallington, Surrey
Quarterly

● One Two Testing
(01) 379 3581, Berkshire House, 168-73 High Holborn, London WC1
Monthly

● Outlet
(01) 551-3346, Trev Faull, 33 Aintree Crescent, Barkingside, Ilford, Essex
Monthly

● Record Collector
(01) 579 1082, 45 St Mary's Road, London W5
Monthly

● Record Mirror
(01) 387 6611, Spotlight, Greater London House, Hampstead Road, London NW1
Weekly

● Smash Hits
(01) 437-8050, Lisa House, 52-55 Carnaby Street, London W1
Fortnightly

● Soul On Sound
(01) 240-7632, 2nd Floor, 5 Garrick Street, London WC2E 9AZ
Fortnightly

● Sounds
(01) 387 6611, Spotlight, Greater London House, Hampstead Road, London NW1

● Stick It In Your Ear
(0703) 448617, Geoff Wall, 5 Sunvale Close, Sholing, Southampton SO2 8GU
Bi-monthly

● Swing 51
(01) 641 1308, 41 Bushey Road, Sutton, Surrey SM1 1QR
Semi-annual

● What Keyboard
(01) 898 5090, P.O. Box 381, Mill Harbour, London E14
Monthly

● The Wire
(01) 437 0882, 51 Beak St, London W1
Monthly

● ZigZag
(01) 278 6615, 24 Ray Street, London EC1R 3DJ
Monthly

● MUSIC RELATED ASSOCIATIONS

● American Society Of Composers, Authors And Publishers
(01) 930 1121, Suite 9, 4th Floor, 52 Haymarket, London SW1Y 4RP

● Association Of Professional Recording Studios
(0923) 772 907, 23 Chestnut Avenue, Chorleywood, Herts WD3 4HA

● British Academy Of Songwriters, Composers And Authors
(01) 240 2823/4, 148 Charing Cross Road, London WC2

● The British Library (National Sound Archive)
(01) 589 6603/6604, 29 Exhibition Road, London SW7

● British Music Information Centre
(01) 499 8567, 10 Stratford Place, London W1N 9AE

● British Phonographic Industry Ltd
(01) 629 8642, 4th Floor, Roxburghe House, 273/287 Regent Street, London W1R 8BD

● British Tape Industry Association
(01) 688 4422, 7-18 Lansdowne Road, Croydon CR9 2PL

● Community Radio Association
(01) 263 6692, 92 Huddleston Road, London N7

● Composers Guild Of Great Britain
(01) 499 4795, 10 Stratford Place, London W1N 9AE

● Country Music Association Inc.
(01) 930 2445/6, Suite 3, 52 Haymarket, London SW1Y 4RP

● English Folk Dance And Song Society
(01) 485 2206, 2 Regents Park Road, London W1

● Independent Record Labels Association
(01) 935 2303, 56-60 Wigmore Street, London W1

● Jazz Centre Society
(01) 580 8532, 35 Great Russell Street, London WC1

● London Musicians Collective
(01) 722 0456, 42 Gloucester Avenue, London NW1

● Mechanical Copyright Protection Society
(01) 769 4400, Elgar House, 41 Streatham High Road, London SW16 1ER

● Music Publishers Association
(01) 831 7591, 7th Floor, Kingsway House, 103 Kingsway, London WC2B 6QX

● Musicians Union
(01) 582 5566, 60-62 Clapham Road, London SW9

● Performing Rights Society Ltd
(01) 580 5544, 29-33 Berners Street, London W1P 4AA

● Royal Society Of Musicians Of Great Britain
(01) 629 6137, 10 Stratford Place, London W1

● Society For The Promotion Of New Music
(01) 491 8111, 10 Stratford Place, London W1N 9AE

● Variety Club Of Great Britain
(01) 935 4466, 32 Welbeck Street, London W1M 7PG

ROCK REFERENCE US

• RECORD COMPANIES

• A&M Records
(213) 469-2411, 1416 North La Brea., Hollywood, CA 90028.
New York office:
(212) 826-0477, 595 Madison Avenue, New York, NY 10022.
Labels: I.R.S., Gold Mountain, Windham Hill

• Arista Records
(212) 489-7400, 6 West 57 Street, New York, NY 10019.
Labels: Jive, Africa, Electro, Zomba

• Atlantic Recording Corp.
(212) 484-6000, 75 Rockefeller Plaza, New York, NY 10019.
LA. office:
(213) 205-7450, 9229 West Sunset Boulevard, Los Angeles, CA 90069.
Labels: Atco, Cotillion, Finnadar, Mirage, Modern, Swansong, Duke, Island, Philly World, Little David, Bronze

• Bearsville Records
(914) 679-7303, PO Box 135, Bearsville, NY 12409.

• Bomp Records
(213) 227-4141, 2702 San Fernando Road, Los Angeles, CA 99065.
Labels: Voxx.

• Buddah Records Inc.
(212) 582-6900, 1790 Broadway, New York, NY 10019.
Labels: Sutra, Beckett, Sunnyview, Streetwise.

• Cachalot Records
(212) 254-1979, Suite 7725, 611 Broadway, New York, NY 10012.

• Capitol Records
(213) 462-6252, 1750 Vine Street, Hollywood, CA 90028.
New York office:
(212) 757-7470, 1370 Avenue of the Americas, New York, NY 10019.
Labels: Angel, Blue Note, EMI America, Harvest, Seraphim, Manhattan.

• CBS Records
(212) 975-4321, 51 West 52 Street, New York, NY 10019.
LA. office:
(213) 556-4700, 1801 Century Park West, Los Angeles, CA 90067.
Labels: Epic, Columbia, Portrait, CBS, Masterworks, Odyssey CBS, BID, Bang, Blue Sky, Caribou, Coast to Coast, Chrysalis, Curb, Johnston, Kirshner, Lynx, Nemperor, Pasha, Pavilion, Philadelphia Int'l, Precision, Rock'n' Roll, Scotti Brothers, T-Neck, TSOP, Uncle Jam, Unlimited Gold, John Hammond.

• Chrysalis Records
(212) 758-3555, 645 Madison Avenue, New York, NY 10022.

• Columbia Records
Same as CBS Records.
Labels: ARC, Stiff-Columbia, 415.

• Compendium Inc.
(404) 873-3918, 450 14th St. NW, Atlanta, GA 30318
Labels: DB, Press.

• Cream Records
(818) 905-6344, 13103 Ventura Blvd., Studio City, CA 91604.
Labels: Hi.

• EMI America/Liberty Records
(213) 462-6252, 1750 Vine Street, Hollywood, CA 90028.
New York office:
(212) 757-7470, 1370 Avenue of Americas, New York, NY 10019.
Labels: United Artists, Blue Note, Manhattan.

• Enigma Records
(213) 640 6869, PO Box 2896, 20445 Gramercy Place, Torrance, CA 90509.

• Epic/Portrait/Associated Labels
Same as CBS.
Labels: City Lights, Cleveland Int'l, Full Moon, Park Lane, Lorimar, Stiff-Epic, Virgin, Carrere.

• Fantasy/Prestige/Milestone/Stax
(415) 549-2500, 2600 10th St., Berkeley, CA 94710.
Labels: Galaxy.

• Fever Records
621 South 4th Street, Philadelphia, PA 19147.
Labels: Original Jazz Classics.

• Folkways Records and Service Corp.
(212) 777-6606, 632 Broadway, New York, NY 10012.
Labels: Asch, Broadside, RBF.

● 415 Records
(415) 621-3415, P.O. Box 14563, San Francisco, CA 94114

● Frontier Records
(213) 766-3374, PO Box 22, Sun Valley, CA 91352.

● Geffen Records
(213) 278-9010, 9130 West Sunset Blvd., Los Angeles, CA 90069.
New York office:
(212) 484-7170, 75 Rockefeller Plaza, New York, NY 10019.

● Gold Mountain
(212) 840-6011, Suite 1102, 2 West 45th St, New York, NY 10036.

● Hannibal Records
(212) 420-1780, 61 Broadway, New York, NY 10012.

● Island Records
(212) 477-8000, 14 East 4th St., New York, NY 10012.
Labels: Mango, Antilles.

● Jem Records Inc.
(201) 753-6100, 3619 Kennedy Road, South Plainfield, NJ 07080.
West Coast office:
(213) 996-6754, 18629 Topham Street, Reseda, CA 91335.
Labels: Passport, PVC, Visa, Editions EG.

● Landslide Records Inc.
(404) 873-3918, 450 14 Street NW, Atlanta, GA 30318.

● MCA Records Inc.
(818) 508-4000, 100 Universal City Plaza, Universal City, CA 916078.
New York office:
(212) 684-3377, 51 Madison Ave., New York, NY 10010.
Labels: Coral, Impulse, Motown, Permain, Solid Gold, Churchill, Rockshire, Sparrow, AVI, Nashborough, Excello, Kenwood, Creed, Booman, Out Of Town, Chess, Checker.

● Mobile Fidelity Sound Lab.
(707) 778-0134, 1260 Holm Road, Petaluma, CA 94952.

● Motown Record Corp.
(213) 468-3500, 6255 Sunset Boulevard, Los Angeles, CA 90028.
Labels: Gordy, Natural Resources, Prodigal, Rare Earth, Soul, Tamla.

● 99 Records
(212) 777-4610, 99 MacDougal Street, New York, NY 10012.

● Oak Records
c/o Tabb Rex Enterprises, 6201 Santa Monica Boulevard, Hollywood, CA 90038.

● PolyGram Records Inc.
(212) 399-7100, 810 Seventh Avenue, New York, NY 10019.
LA office:
(213) 656-3003, 8335 West Sunset Blvd., Los Angeles, CA 90069.
Labels: Casablanca, Mercury, London, Verve, Chocolate City, DeLite, RSO, Riva, Polydor, Atlanta Artists, Compleat, Deram, Emarcy, Enja Gramavision, Lection, Millenium, MPS, Oasis, Parachute, Phillips, Treshold, Total Experience, 21, Vertigo.

● Propellor Records
Box 658, Aliston Station, Boston, MA 02134.

● Ralph Records
(415) 543-4085, 109 Minna Street, San Francisco, CA 94105.

● RCA Records
(212) 930-4000, 1133 Avenue of the Americas, New York, NY 10036.
LA office:
(213) 468-4000, 6363 Sunset Boulevard, Hollywood, CA 90028.
Labels: Grunt, Millenium, Gold Seal, Bluebird, Salsoul, Pablo, Planet, Total Experience.

● Reachout International Records (ROIR)
(212) 477-0563, Suite 725 611 Broadway, New York, NY 10012.

● Rhino Records
(213) 450-6323, 1201 Olympic Boulevard, Santa Monica, CA 90404.

● Rollin' Rock Records
(213) 781-4805, 6918 Peach Avenue, Van Nuys, CA 91406.
Labels: American Rhythm Music, Boppin' Belle, California Rockabilly, Ray Campi, Ollie, Ragin' Rockabilly, Rockabilly Rebellion, Rockin' Ronny, Rockin' Weiser.

● Rough Trade Inc.
(415) 621-4045, 326 Sixth Street, San Francisco, CA 94103.
Labels: Factory US

● Rounder Records
(617) 354-0700, 1 Camp Street, Cambridge, MA 02142

● Shanachie Records Corp.
(201) 445-5561, 1 Hollywood Ave, HoHoKus, NJ 07423.

● Slash Records
(213) 937-4660, 7381 Beverly Boulevard, Los Angeles, CA 90036.

● Sounds Interesting Records
PO Box 54, Stone Harbor, NJ 08247.

● Subterranean Records
(415) 864-1649, 577 Valencia, San Francisco, CA 94110.

● Sugar Hill Records Inc.
(201) 569-5170, 96 West Street, Englewood, NJ 07631.

● Tommy Boy Records
(212) 722-2211, 1747 First Ave, New York, NY 10128.

● Twin Tone Records
(612) 872-0646, 2541 Nicolette Ave South, Minneapolis, MN 55404.

● Vanguard Recording Society, Inc.
(212) 255-7732, 71 West 23rd Street, New York, NY 10010.
Labels: 0, Flip.

● Warner Bros Records Inc.
(213) 846-9090, 3300 Warner Boulevard, Burbank, CA 91510.
New York office:
(212) 702-0318, 3 East 54th Street, New York, NY 10022.
Labels: Sire, Bearsville, Slash, ECM, Geffen, Reprise, Dark Horse.

● Windham Hill Records
(415) 329-0647, PO Box 9388, Stanford, CA 94305.

● ZE Records and Tapes
(212) 245-7233, 850 7th Ave., New York, NY 10019.

● MUSIC PUBLISHERS

● ATV Music Corp.
(213) 462-6933, 6255 Sunset Boulevard, Hollywood, CA 90028.

● Abkco Music Inc.
(212) 399-0300, 1700 Broadway, 41st Floor, New York, NY 10019.

● Acuff-Rose Publications Inc.
(615) 385-3031, 2510 Franklin Road, Nashville, TN 37204.

● Allied Artists Music Co. Inc.
(212) 541-9200, 15 Columbus Circle, New York, NY 10023.

● April/Blackwood Music Inc.
(212) 975-4886, 1350 Avenue of the Americas, New York, NY 10019.

● Augsburg Publishing House
(612) 330-3300, 426 South Fifth Street, Minneapolis, MN 55410.

● Beechwood Music Corp.
(213) 469-8371, 6920 Sunset Boulevard, Hollywood, CA 90028.

● Beserkley
(415) 848-6701, 2054 University Avenue, Berkeley, CA 94704.

● Big Music/Rohm Music/ QVQ Music
(203) 269-4465, 10 George Street, Wallingford, CT 06492.

● Big Seven Music Corp.
(212) 582-4267, 1790 Broadway, 18th Floor, New York, NY 10019.

● Buddah Music Inc.
(212) 582-6900, 1790 Broadway, New York, NY 10019.

● Bug Music
(213) 466-4352, 6777 Hollywood Boulevard, 9th Floor, Hollywood, CA 90028.

● Cameron Organization Inc.
(312) 246-8222, 822 Hillgrove Avenue, Western Springs, IL 60558.

● Chappell/Intersong Music Co.
(212) 399-7373, 810 Seventh Avenue, New York, NY 10019.

● Chrysalis Music Group
(212) 758-3555, 645 Madison Avenue, New York, NY 10022.

● Cotillion Music Inc.
(212) 484-8132, 75 Rockefeller Plaza, New York, NY 10019.

● Crazy Cajun Music
(713) 926-4431, 5626 Brock Street, Houston, TX 77023.

● Cream Publishing Group
(818) 905-6344, 13107 Ventura Blvd, Suite 102, Studio City, CA 91606.

● Duane Music Inc.
(408) 739-6133, 382 Clarence Avenue, Sunnyvale, CA 94086.

● Elm Publishing Co.
(714) 898-7317, 14621 Allen Street, Westminster, CA 92683.

● Elvis Music Inc.
(212) 489-8170, 1619 Broadway, New York, NY 10019.

● Entertainment Company Music Group
(212) 265-2600, 1700 Broadway, New York, NY 10019.

● Evansongs Ltd.
(212) 765-8450, 1790 Broadway, New York, NY 10019.

● Famous Music Corp.
(213) 333-3433, 1 Gulf and Western Plaza, New York, NY 10023.

● Carl Fischer Inc.
(212) 777-0900, 62 Cooper Square, New York, NY 10003.

● Flying Fish Music
(312) 528-5455, 1304 West Schubert, Chicago, IL 60614.

● Fort Knox Music Co.
(212) 489-8170, 1619 Broadway, 11th Floor, New York, NY 10019.

● Al Gallico Music Corp.
(212) 355-5980, 344 East 49th Street, New York, NY 10017.

● Garrett Music Enterprises
(818) 506-8964, 412½ Radford Ave., Studio City, CA 91604.

● Al Green
(901) 794-6220, P.O. Box 456, Millington, TN 38053.

● Hallnote Music Co.
(615) 790-1726, PO Box 40209, Nashville, TN 37204.

● Hilaria Music Inc.
(608) 251-2644, 315 West Gorham Street, Madison, WI 53703.

● Home Grown Music Inc.
(213) 763-6323, 4412 Whitsett, Studio City, CA 91606.

● House Of Cash Inc.
(615) 824-5110, 700 Johnny Cash Parkway, Hendersonville, TN 370770508.

● Intersong Music Inc.
(213) 469-5141
6255 Sunset Boulevard, Hollywood, CA 90028.

● Island Music
(213) 469-1285, 6525 Sunset Boulevard, 2nd floor, Hollywood, CA 90028.

● Jobete Music Co. Inc.
(213) 468-3500, 6255 Sunset Boulevard, Hollywood, CA 90028.

● Laurie Publishing Group
(914) 425-7000, 20F Robert Pitt Drive, Monsey, NY 10952.

● Largo Music Inc.
(212) 371-9400, 425 Park Avenue, New York, NY 10022.

● Hal Leonard Publishing Corp.
(414) 774-3630, 8112 West Bluemound Road, PO Box 13819, Milwaukee, WI 53213.

● MCA Music
(818) 508-4550, 70 Universal City Plaza, Room 425, Universal City, CA 91608.

● MPL Communications Inc.
39 West 54th Street, New York, NY 10019.

● Marsaint Music Inc.
(504) 949-8386, 3809 Clematis Avenue, New Orleans, LA 70122.

● Ivan Mogull Music Corp,
(212) 355-5636, 625 Madison Avenue, New York, NY 10022.

● Neil Music Inc.
(213) 656-2614, 8400 Sunset Boulevard, Suite 4a, Los Angeles, CA 90069.

● Pale Pachyderm Publishing
(415) 543-4085, 109 Minna Street, San Francisco, CA 94105.

● Phenetones
(617) 744-7678, 400 Essex Street, Salem, MA 01970.

● Rough Trade Inc.
(415) 621-4045, 326 Sixth Street, San Francisco, CA 94103.

● Screen Gems-EMI Music Inc.
(213) 469-8371, 6920 Sunset Boulevard, Hollywood, CA 90028.

● Paul Simon
(212) 541-7571, 1619 Broadway, New York, NY 10019.

● Skyhill Publishing Co. Inc.
(213) 469-1285, 6525 Sunset Boulevard, Hollywood, CA 90028.

● Special Rider Music
(212) 473-5900, PO Box 879, Cooper Station, New York, NY 10276.

● The Richmond Organization (TRO)
(212) 765-9889, 10 Columbus Circle, New York, NY 10019.

● 20th Century Fox Music Corp.
(213) 203-1487, Box 900, Music Building 222, Beverly Hills, CA 90213.

● WPN Music Co. Inc.
(516) 796-3698, 10 Swirl Lane, Levittown, NY 11756.

● Warner Bros Music
(213) 273-3323, 9000 Sunset Boulevard, The Penthouse, Los Angeles, CA 90069.

● Word Music
(817) 772-7650, PO Box 1790, Waco, TX 76796.

● DISTRIBUTORS/IMPORTERS

● Dutch East India Trading
(516) 764 6200, 81 Northforest Ave, Rockville Centre, NY 11570

● Greenworld Distribution
(213) 533-8075, 20445 Gramercy Place, Torrance, CA 90509.

● Important Records
(718) 995-9200, 149-03 Guy R. Brewer Boulevard, Jamaica, NY 11434.

● Jem Records
(201) 753-6100, 3619 Kennedy Road, South Plainfield, NJ 07080
West Coast office:
(213) 996-6754, 18629 Topham, Reseda, CA 91335

● Rough Trade
(415) 621-4307, 326 Sixth Street, San Francisco, CA 93103.

● Rounder Records
(611) 354-0700, 1 Camp Street, Cambridge, MA 02140.

● Sounds Good Import Co.
(213) 452-5949, 1201 Olympic Boulevard, Santa Monica, CA 90404.

● Systematic Record Distributors
(415) 431-9377, 1331 Fulsom Street, San Francisco, CA 94103.

RECORDING STUDIOS

Alpha Audio
(804) 358-3852, 2049 West Broad Street, Richmond, VA 23220

A&M Recording Studios
(213) 469-2411, 1416 North La Brea, Hollywood, CA 90028.

A&R Recording
(212) 397-0300, 322 West 48th Street, New York, NY 10036

Audio Innovators
(412) 471-6220, 216 Boulevard of the Allies, Pittsburgh, PA 15222.

Bee Jay Recording Studios
(305) 293-1781, 5000 Eggleston Avenue, Orlando, FL 32810.

Bullet Recording
(615) 327-4621, 49 Music Square West, Nashville, TN 37203.

Caribou Ranch
(303) 258-3215, PO Box 310, Nederland, CO 80466.

Capitol Studios
(213) 462-6252, 1750 North Vine Street, Hollywood, CA 90028.

Cherokee Recording Studios
(213) 653-3412, 751 North Fairfax, Hollywood, CA 90046.

Clover Recorders
(213) 463-2371, 6232 Santa Monica Boulevard, Hollywood, CA 90038.

Criteria Recording Studios
(305) 947-5611, 1755 NE 149th Street, Miami, FL 33181.

Different Fur Recording
(415) 864-1967, 3470 19th Street, San Francisco, CA 94110.

El Dorado Studios
(213) 467-6151, 1717 North Vine Street, Los Angeles, CA 90028.

Electric Lady Studios
(212) 677-4700, 52 West 8th Street, New York, NY 10011

Fantasy Studios
(415) 549-2500, 10th and Parker, Berkeley, CA 94710

Hit Factory
(212) 664-1000, 237 West 54th Street, New York, NY 10019

House Of Music
(201) 736-3062, 1400 Pleasant Valley Way, West Orange, NJ 07052

Image Studios
(213) 850-1030, 1020 North Sycamore, Hollywood, CA 90038.

Kendun Recorders
(213) 843-8096, 619 South Glenwood Place, Burbank, CA 91506.

Larrabee Sound
(213) 657-6750, 8811 Santa Monica Boulevard, West Hollywood, CA 90069.

Lion Share
(213) 658-5990, 8255 Beverly Boulevard, Los Angeles, CA 90048.

MCA/Whitney Recording Studios
(818) 507-1041, 1516 West Glen Oaks Boulevard, Glendale, CA 91201.

Media Sound
(212) 765-4700, 311 West 57th Street, New York, NY 10019

Motown/Hitsville USA
(213) 850-1510, 7317 Romaine Street, Los Angeles, CA 90046.

Muscle Shoals Sound Studios
(205) 381-2060, 1000 Alabama Avenue, Muscle Shoals, AL 35660.

Music Mill
(615) 254-5925, 1710 Roy Acuff Place, Nashville, TN 37203.

National Recording Studios
(718) 279-2000, 460 West 42nd Street, New York, NY 10036.

Ocean Way Recording
(213) 467-9375, 6050 Sunset Boulevard, Los Angeles, CA 90028.

Park South Studio
(212) 977-9800 231 West 58th Street, New York, NY 10019.

Pierce Arrow Recorders
(312) 328-8950, 1911 Ridge Avenue, Evanston, IL 60202

Power Station
(212) 246-2900, 441 West 53rd Street, New York, NY 10019

RCA Studios
(212) 930-4062, 110 West 44th Street, New York, NY 10036.

Record Plant
(213) 653-0240, 8456 West Third Street, Los Angeles, CA 90048.
New York office:
(212) 582-6505, 321 West 44th Street, New York, NY 10036.

Reflection Sound
(704) 377-4596, 1018 Central Avenue, Charlotte, NC 28204.

Sheffield Recording
(301) 628-7260, 13816 Sunnybrook Road, Phoenix, MD 21131

Sigma Sound Studios
(215) 561-3660, 212 North 12th Street, Philadelphia, PA 19107

Sigma Sound Studios
(212) 582-5055, 1697 Broadway, New York, NY 10019.

Sound City
(213) 873-2842, 15456 Cabrito Road, Van Nuys, CA 91406.

Sound Emporium
(615) 383-1982, 3102 Belmont Boulevard, Nashville, TN 37212

Sound 80
(612) 339-9313, 4027 Ideas Tower, Minneapolis, MN 55402.

Sound Labs
(213) 466-3463, 1800 North Argyle Street, Los Angeles, CA 90028

Suma Recording Studio
(216) 951-3955, 5706 Vrooman Road, Cleveland, OH 44077

Syncro Sound
(617) 424-1062, 331 Newbury Street, Boston, MA 02115

Technisonic Studios
(314) 727-1055, 1201 South Brentwood Boulevard, St Louis, MO 63117.

Universal Recording
(312) 642-6465, 46 East Walton, Chicago, IL 60611.

Village Recorder
(213) 478-8227, 1616 Butler Avenue, West Los Angeles, CA 90025

Warner Bros Recording Studios
(213) 980-5605, 1114 Cumpston Avenue, North Hollywood, CA 91601

Westlake Studios
(213) 654-2155, 8447 Beverly Boulevard, Los Angeles, CA 90048.

● ROCK PUBLICATIONS

● Austin Chronicle
(512) 473-8995, P.O. Box 49066, Austin, TX 78765
Bi-weekly.

● BAM
(415) 652-3810, 5951 Canning Street, Oakland, CA 94609
(213) 467-7878, 1800 North Highland, Suite 220, Hollywood, CA 90028
Bi-monthly (local)
Monthly (national)

● Billboard
(212) 764-7300, 1515 Broadway, New York, NY 10036
Weekly

● Blitz
P.O. Box 48124, Los Angeles, CA 90048
Bi-monthly

● Bomp
(213) 227-4141, P.O. Box 7112, Burbank, CA 91510

● Buddy
(214) 826-8742
501n Good-Latimer Expwy. Dallas, TX 75204
Monthly

● Cash Box
(212) 586-2640, 330 West 58th Street, New York, NY 10019
Weekly

● Circus
(212) 685-5050, 419 Park Avenue South, New York, NY 10016
Monthly

● CMJ New Music Report
(516) 248-9600 834 Willis Ave., Albertson, NY 11507
Bi-weekly

● Country Rhythms
(212) 689-2830, 475 Park Avenue South, New York NY 10016
Monthly

● Creem
(313) 642-8833, 210 South Woodward Avenue, Suite 209, Birmingham, MI 48011
Monthly

● Down Beat
(312) 941-2030, 180 West Park Ave., Elmhurst, IL 60126
Monthly

● Flipside
P.O. Box 363, Whittier, CA 90608
Bi-monthly

● Goldmine
(715) 445-2214, 700 East State Street, Iola, WI 54990
Bi-weekly

● Guitar Player Frets
(408) 446-1105, 20605 Lazaneo, Cupertino, CA 95014
Monthly

● Guitar World
(212) 807-7100, 1115 Broadway, 8th Floor, New York, NY 10010
Bi-monthly

● High Fidelity
(212) 887-8337, 825 Seventh Avenue, New York, NY 10019
Monthly

● Hit Parader
(203) 735-3381, Charlton Building, Division Street, Derby, CT 06418
Monthly

● Illinois Entertainer
(312) 298-9333, P.O. Box 356, Mt. Prospect, IL 60056
Monthly

● International Musician and Recording World
(212) 947-6740, 242 West 38th Street, 14th Floor, New York, NY 10018
Monthly

● Jazz Times
(301) 588-4114, 8055 13th Street, Silver Springs, MD 20910
Monthly

● Keyboard
(408) 446-1105, 20605 Lazaneo, Cupertino, CA 95014
Monthly

● Living Blues
(312) 281-3385, 2615 North Wilton Avenue, Chicago, IL 60614
Quarterly

● Master
(312) 491-9112, 624 Davis Street, Evanston, IL 60201
Monthly fanzine

● Musician
(617) 281-3110, 31 Commercial Street, Gloucester, MA 01930
New York office:
(212) 764-7300, 1515 Broadway, New York, NY 10036
Monthly

● Music City News
(615) 244-5187, P.O. Box 22975, Nashville, TN 37202
Monthly

● OP
(206) 352-9735, P.O. Box 2391, Olympia, WA 98507
Bi-monthly

● Progressive Media
(516) 248-9600, 834 Willis Avenue, Albertson, NY 11507
Monthly

● Radio and Records
(213) 553-4330, 1930 Century Park West, Los Angeles, CA 90067
Weekly

● Record
(212) 758 3800, 745 Fifth Avenue, New York, NY 10151
Monthly

● Relix
(212) 645-0818, P.O. Box 94, Brooklyn, NY 11229

● Rock
1112 North La Cienega Blvd., Los Angeles, CA 90069
Bi-monthly

● Rock'n'Roll Confidential
P.O. Box 1073, Maywood, NJ 07607
Monthly, subscription only

● The Rocket
(206) 587-4001, 2322 Second Avenue, Seattle, WA 98121
Monthly

● Rockpool Newsletter
(212) 686-7410, 50 West 29th Street, New York, NY 10001
Fortnightly

● Rock Scene
(203) 266-7224, 358 Fairwood Road, Bethany, CT 06525
Monthly.

● Rock Video
(212) 689-2830, 475 Park Ave. South, New York, NY 10016

● Rolling Stone
(212) 758-3800, 745 Fifth Avenue, New York, NY 10151
Weekly

● Song Hits
(203) 735-3381, Charlton Building, Division Street, Derby, CT 06418
Monthly

● Spin
(212) 496 6100, 1965 Broadway, New York, NY 10023
Monthly

● Star Hits
150 E.58th Street, New York NY 10022
Monthly

● Stereo Review
(212) 725-3000, 1 Park Avenue, New York, NY 10016

● Surburban Relapse
P.O. Box 610906, North Miami, FL 33261

● US Rock
(617) 734 7043, Suite 7, 1318 Beacon Street, Brooklyme MA 02146
Monthly

● Vox Pop
(203) 576 8767, P.O. Box 8161, Brewster Station, Bridgeport, CT 06605
Monthly

● Wavelength
(504) 895-2342, 118th Street, New Orleans, LA 70115
Monthly

● MUSIC RELATED ASSOCIATIONS

● Academy Of Country Music
(213) 462-2351, 6255 Sunset Boulevard, Hollywood, CA 90028

● American Federation of Musicians
(212) 869-1330, 1500 Broadway, New York, NY 10036

● American Musicians Union
(201) 384-5378, 8 Tobin Court, Dumont, NJ 07628

● ASCAP
(212) 595-3050, 1 Lincoln Plaza, New York, NY 10023

● Association Of Independent Music Publishers/Harrison Music
(213) 466-3834, 6253 Hollywood Boulevard, Hollywood, CA 90028

● Black Music Association
(215) 545-8600, 1500 Locust Street, Philadelphia, PA 19102

● BMI
(212) 586-2000, 320 West 57th Street, New York, NY 10019

● Country Music Association
(615) 244-2840, 7 Music Circle North, Nashville, TN 37203

● Jazz Composers' Orchestra Association
(212) 925-2121, 500 Broadway, New York, NY 10012

● National Academy Of Recording Arts And Sciences
(818) 843-8233, 4444 Riverside Drive, Burbank, CA 91505

● National Association Of Independent Record Distributors
c/o Richman Brothers Records, (att. Jerry Richman), (609) 665-8085, 6935 Airport Highway Lane, Pennsauken, NJ 08109

● National Association Of Music Merchants
(619) 438-8001, 5140 Avenida Encinas, Carlsbad, CA 92008

● Recording Industry Association Of America
(212) 765-4330, 888 Seventh Avenue, New York, NY 10106

● SESAC Inc.
(212) 586-3450, 10 Columbus Circle, New York, NY 10019